THE SECOND CRUS

Jonathan Phillips is Professor of Crusading History, Royal Holloway, University of London. He has published extensively including *The Crusades, 1095–1197* and *The Fourth Crusade and the Sack of Constantinople*, and is a frequent contributor to *BBC History Magazine* and *History Today*.

THE
SECOND
CRUSADE

EXTENDING THE FRONTIERS OF CHRISTENDOM

JONATHAN PHILLIPS

YALE UNIVERSITY PRESS

NEW HAVEN AND LONDON

For information about this and other Yale University Press publications, please contact:

U.S. Office:	sales.press@yale.edu	yalebooks.com
Europe Office:	sales@yaleup.co.uk	www.yaleup.co.uk

Set in Minion and Meridien by J&L Composition, Filey, North Yorkshire
Printed in Great Britain by Hobbs the Printers Ltd, Totton, Hampshire

Library of Congress Cataloging-in-Publication Data

Phillips, Jonathan.
    The Second Crusade: extending the frontiers of Christendom/Jonathan Phillips.
        p. cm.
    Includes bibliographical references and index.
    ISBN 978-0-300-11274-0 (alk. paper)
    1. Crusades—Second, 1147–1149. I. Title.
    D162.2.P55 2007
    956 .014—dc22
2007005980

A catalogue record for this book is available from the British Library.

ISBN 978-0-300-16475-6 (pbk)

FSC
Mixed Sources
Product group from well-managed
forests and other controlled sources
Cert no. SA-COC-001530
www.fsc.org
© 1996 Forest Stewardship Council

The paper used for the text pages of this book is FSC certified. FSC (The Forest
Stewardship Council) is an international network to promote responsible management of
the world's forests.

10 9 8 7 6 5 4 3 2 1

To Niki, Tom and Marcus
WITH ALL MY LOVE

CONTENTS

ACKNOWLEDGEMENTS

The research and writing of this book have, with a few interruptions, been in progress since 1994; it has, in the main, been a genuine pleasure to write. I have been fortunate to receive the good advice and help of a great many people on matters of history, translation and publishing. I would like to thank Marcus Bull, Alan Murray, John France, Jonathan Harris, David Bates, Rudolf Hiestand, Nikolas Jaspert, Susan Edgington, Linda Paterson, Benjamin Arnold, Peter Edbury, Matthew Bennett, Jason Roche, Colin Morris, Marco Meschini, Kurt Villads Jensen, Carole Hillenbrand, Thérèse de Hemptinne, Penny Cole, Natasha Hodgson, Mari Williams, Pedro Teixeira-Dias, Iben Fonnesberg-Schmidt, Merav Mack, Tony Luttrell, Bernard Hamilton, Osman Latiff, Emmett Sullivan, Maria João V. Branco, Zsolt Hunyadi and Francis Robinson. The enthusiastic encouragement of Jonathan Riley-Smith has been particularly motivating. I am greatly indebted to William Purkis and Martin Hoch for their views on drafts of chapters, and especially so to Malcolm Barber, who read the manuscript for Yale and made many cogent and valuable comments. I would also like to thank the Arts and Humanities Research Council for their generous 'matching leave' award in 2001–2, which gave me the time to make several major advances on this project. Similarly, my thanks to the staff and five successive heads of the History Department at Royal Holloway for backing this work over the years. Seminars at the Institute of Historical Research, the Wessex Medieval Centre, the Hebrew University of Jerusalem, York University, Cardiff University, the Portuguese Studies Centre, Oxford, and the Society for the Study of the Crusades and the Latin East Conference in Istanbul gave me valuable opportunities to try out my ideas.

I am extremely grateful to Robert Baldock of Yale University Press for his good faith in commissioning this book and his patience in waiting for its arrival. My thanks also to his cheerful and supportive staff including Candida Brazil, Hannah Godfrey, Stephen Kent and Sarah Faulkner; the index was compiled by Meg Davies. I appreciate the kindness of Jonathan and Louise

Riley-Smith and Mike Routledge in allowing me to use their translations of (respectively) *Quantum praedcessores* and *Chevalier, mult estes guariz* as appendices here.

I have had the pleasure of running a 'Special Subject' on the Second Crusade at Royal Holloway for over ten years. My sincere thanks to the many students who have taken this course and, as the book has evolved, have proven valuable and rigorous interrogators of my ideas, as well as making teaching hugely enjoyable. The friendship of Alex and Ruth Windscheffel, Austen Rose, Ed Fuller, Ian Jenkins and Lisa Barry has been essential. I would also like to thank Sophie Phillips, John Wallace and my parents for their continued kind support throughout this period. I am proud to dedicate this book, with all my love, to my son Tom, whose quick humour and sharp questions always keep me on my toes; to Marcus, our happy new arrival; and to Niki, whose constant, gentle and generous love has brought so much to my life.

ABBREVIATIONS

AA	Albert of Aachen, *Historia Ierosolimitana: History of the Journey to Jerusalem*, ed. and tr. S. B. Edgington (Oxford, 2007).
ASC	*Anonymi auctoris Chronicon ad* A.C. *1234 pertinens*, ed. I. B. Chabot, tr. A. Abouna, introduction J. M. Fiey, 2 vols (Louvain, 1952–74); tr. A. S. Tritton and H. A. R. Gibb, 'The First and Second Crusades from an Anonymous Syriac Chronicle', *Journal of the Royal Asiatic Society* (1933), pp. 69–101; 273–305.
BCE, BSJ	Bernard of Clairvaux, 'Epistolae', in *Sancti Bernardi Opera*, eds J. Leclercq and H. Rochais, 8 vols (Rome, 1955–77), pp. 7–8; many translated in: *The Letters of Saint Bernard of Clairvaux*, new edn, tr. B. S. James, introduction B. M. Kienzle (Stroud, 1998).
BF, *World*	*The World of El Cid: Chronicles of the Spanish Reconquest*, tr. S. Barton and R. A. Fletcher (Manchester, 2000).
Caffaro, *CAT*	Caffaro, 'Cafari ystoria captionis Almarie et Turtuose ann. 1147 et 1148', ed. L. T. Belgrano, in *Fonti per la Storia d'Italia* 11 (Genoa, 1890), pp. 77–91; tr. J. B. Williams, 'The Making of a Crusade: The Genoese anti-Muslim Attacks in Spain, 1146–1148', *Journal of Medieval History* 23 (1997), pp. 48–53.
CAI	*Chronica Adefonsi Imperatoris*, in *Chronica Hispania Saeculi XII*, ed. A. Maya Sánchez, *CCCM* 71/1 (Turnhout, 1990); tr. S. Barton and R. A. Fletcher in BF, *World*, pp. 148–249.
CCCM	*Corpus Christianorum, continuatio Medievalis.*

CDDRG	*Codice diplomatico della Republica di Genova*, ed. C. Imperiale de Sant'Angelo, Vol. 1 (Rome, 1936).
Conrad, *Urkunden*	*Die Urkunden Konrads III. und seines Sohnes Heinrich*, ed. F. Hausmann, *MGH, DD* 9 (Vienna, 1969).
Constable, SC	G. Constable, 'The Second Crusade as seen by Contemporaries', *Traditio* 9 (1953), pp. 213–79.
DeL	*De expugnatione Lyxbonensi*, ed. and tr. C. W. David, with a new foreword and bibliography by J. P. Phillips (New York, 2001).
EE	Eugenius III, 'Epistolae et privilegia', *PL*, Vol. 180.
FC	Fulcher of Chartres, *Historia Hierosolymitana (1095–1127)*, ed. H. Hagenmeyer (Heidelberg, 1913); tr. F. R. Ryan, introduction H. S. Fink, *A History of the Expedition to Jerusalem, 1095–1127* (Knoxville, TN, 1969).
GN	Guibert of Nogent, *Dei gesta per Francos*, ed. R. B. C. Huygens, *CCCM* 127A (Turnhout, 1996); tr. R. Levine, *The Deeds of God through the Franks* (Woodbridge, 1997).
Hagenmeyer, *Epistolae*	*Epistolae et chartae ad primi belli sacri spectantes: Die Kreuzzugsbriefe aus den Jahren 1088–1100*, ed. H. Hagenmeyer (Innsbruck, 1901).
HGRL	'Historia gloriosi regis Ludovici VII, filii Ludovici grossi', *RHGF* 12.124–33.
Horn, *Studien*	M. Horn, *Studien zur Geschichte Papst Eugens III. (1145–1153)* (Frankfurt, 1992).
IQ	Ibn al-Qalanisi, *The Damascus Chronicles of the Crusades*, ed. and tr. H. A. R. Gibb (London, 1932).
JK	John Kinnamos, *The Deeds of John and Manuel Comnenus*, tr. C. M. Brand (New York, 1976).
Logistics of Warfare	*Logistics of Warfare in the Age of the Crusades*, ed. J. H. Pryor (Aldershot, 2006).
Louis VII, *Études*	Louis VII, *Études sur les Actes de Louis VII*, ed. A. Luchaire (Paris, 1885).
MGH	*Monumenta Germaniae Historica, Scriptores*, ed. G. H. Pertz et al., 32 vols (Hannover, Weimar, Stuttgart and Cologne, 1826–1934)
MGH DD	*Monumenta Germaniae Historica, Diplomata.*
OD	Odo of Deuil, *De profectione Ludovici VII in Orientem*, ed. and tr. V. G. Berry (New York, 1948).

OV	Orderic Vitalis *The Ecclesiastical History*, ed. and tr. M. Chibnall, 6 vols (Oxford, 1969–80).
Otto of Freising, *Ddc*	*Chronica sive historia de duabus civitatibus*, ed. A. Hofmeister and W. Lammers, tr. A. Schmidt (Darmstadt, 1961); tr. C. C. Mierow, *The Two Cities* (New York, 1928).
Otto of Freising, *GF*	*Gesta Frederici seu rectius Chronica*, ed. G. Waitz, B. Simson and F.-J. Schmale, tr. A. Schmidt (Darmstadt, 1965); tr. C. C. Mierow, *The Deeds of Frederick Barbarossa* (New York, 1953).
PA	*Prefatio de Almaria*, in *Chronica Hispana Saeculi XII*, ed. J. Gil, *CCCM* 71/1 (Turnhout, 1990), pp. 253–67; tr. BF, *World*, pp. 250–63.
Phillips, *Defenders*	J. P. Phillips, *Defenders of the Holy Land: Relations between the Latin East and the West, 1119–1187* (Oxford, 1996).
PL	*Patrologia cursus completes. Series Latina*, publ. J. P. Migne, 217 vols and 4 vols of indices (Paris, 1844–64).
QP	R. Grosse, 'Überlegungen zum kreuzzugsaufruf Eugens III. von 1145/46. Mit einer Neuedition von JL 8876', *Francia* 18 (1991), pp. 85–92.
RHC Arm.	*Recueil des historiens des croisades: Documents arméniens*, 2 vols (Paris, 1869–1906).
RHC Oc.	*Recueil des historiens des croisades: Historiens occidentaux*, 5 vols (Paris, 1844–95).
RHC Or.	*Recueil des historiens des croisades: Historiens orientaux*, 5 vols (Paris, 1872–1906).
Reilly, *Alfonso VII*	B. F. Reilly, *The Kingdom of León-Castilla under King Alfonso VII, 1126–1157* (Philadelphia, 1998).
RHGF	*Recueil des historiens des Gaules et de la France*, ed. M. Bouquet et al., 24 vols (Paris, 1737–1904).
Riley-Smith, *FC*	J. S .C. Riley-Smith, *The First Crusaders, 1095–1131* (Cambridge, 1997).
R.Reg.	*Regesta regni Hierosolymitani, 1097–1291*, ed. R. Röhricht (Innsbruck, 1893).
SCC	*The Second Crusade and the Cistercians*, ed. M. Gervers (New York, 1992).
SCSC	*The Second Crusade: Scope and Consequences*, ed. J. P. Phillips and M. Hoch (Manchester, 2001).

Suger, *VLG*   *Vie de Louis VI le Gros*, ed. and tr. H. Waquet (Paris, 1964); tr. R. C. Cusimano and J. Moorhead, *The Deeds of Louis the Fat* (Washington DC, 1992).

WM   William of Malmesbury, *Gesta Regum Anglorum*, ed. and tr. R. A. B. Mynors, R. M. Thomson and M. Winterbottom, 2 vols (Oxford, 1998–99). All references to Volume 1 unless stated.

WT   William of Tyre, *Chronicon*, ed. R. B. C. Huygens, 2 vols, [continuous pagination] *CCCM* 63, 63A (Turnhout, 1986); tr. E. A. Babcock and A. C. Krey, *A History of Deeds done beyond the Sea*, 2 vols (New York, 1948).

MAPS

ILLUSTRATIONS

PROLOGUE

THE FALL OF EDESSA, DECEMBER 1144

In July 1099 the armies of the First Crusade fought their way into the holy city of Jerusalem to achieve one of the most improbable victories of the medieval age. The Muslims of the Near East took time to come to terms with this religious colonisation, and it was not until the 1140s that their counter-attack started to gather momentum. In the late autumn of 1144, Emir Imad ad-Din Zengi, the Muslim ruler of Aleppo and Mosul, targeted Edessa, a place of great spiritual importance to the Franks: it had been the first city to convert to Christianity and was the burial place of the Apostles Thomas and Thaddeus. In more recent times the First Crusaders had seized it from its Armenian rulers; it was also the eponymous capital of the county of Edessa, one of the four Frankish States in the Levant.

Alongside his determination to promote *jihad*, Zengi intended to take revenge on Count Joscelin II of Edessa for his recent alliance with the Ortuqids of Diyr Bakr.[1] Zengi convinced Joscelin that he was engaged in a distant campaign against the Ortuqids, a ploy that induced the count to leave Edessa and cross the Euphrates to his favourite castle of Turbessel. The emir's spies informed him of this; the Muslim forces quickly mobilised and, in late November, laid siege to Edessa.[2] Over the next four weeks, Zengi and his allies tried hard to breach the city's formidable defences. The absence of regular soldiers required the citizens to man the walls themselves, and the senior Armenian, Syriac and Catholic churchmen worked together to direct the resistance. Muslim sappers dug an elaborate system of mines to the north while siege machines pounded at the walls elsewhere; slowly and inexorably Zengi's men closed their grip on the city. Yet in spite of heavy losses and serious damage to the fortifications, the defenders rejected overtures of peace.[3] They probably anticipated help from Count Joscelin, who tried to organise a relief force – although William of Tyre claimed that he was hampered in this by the hostility of Raymond of Antioch, his Frankish neighbour in northern Syria. Queen Melisende of Jerusalem, whose mother was an

Armenian–Edessan noblewoman, sent troops north, but they would be too late to help.[4]

On 23 December Zengi's troops set fire to the beams that supported the mine and a long section of wall collapsed. The Christians fought hard to hold the gap, but the following day the Turks forced their way in. The panic-stricken populace fled to the citadel for safety; in the confusion, Archbishop Hugh was killed and dozens more were crushed to death as they attempted to squeeze through the gates. In the meantime, Zengi's men started to put the city to the sack and his troops slaughtered many of the inhabitants. In early January, low on water and supplies, those in the citadel surrendered. Most of the men were killed or tortured and the women and children enslaved. The Armenian 'Lament on Edessa', written within two years of the siege, provides a lurid and dramatic picture of the barbarism of Zengi and his men:

> Like wolves among a flock of lambs [they] fell upon them in their midst.
> They slaughtered indiscriminately, the martyrs let out streams of blood,
> They massacred without compassion the young and the children.
> They had no mercy on the grey hairs of the elderly or with the tender age
> of a child.[5]

The fabric of Edessa also suffered severely – seven of its towers were destroyed, as was the Church of the Confessors. An even greater calamity was the destruction of the silver coffin that held the bones of Thaddeus and King Abgar.[6] News of the disaster spread rapidly; Antioch lay 160 miles south-west, and from there messengers set out for Tripoli and Jerusalem.

Zengi had struck a powerful blow for the forces of Islam, and soon the Frankish settlers sent appeals for help to their co-religionists in Europe. These envoys provided the trigger for the Second Crusade: initially the expedition planned simply to recover Edessa, but within eighteen months a combination of inspirational preaching and political opportunism transformed it: simulta-neous campaigns in the Levant, the Iberian Peninsula and the Baltic region constituted an attack of unprecedented magnitude on the enemies of Christendom; the confidence and ambition of the Latin West were immense. Truly, as one contemporary wrote, they aspired to 'extend Christianity'.[7]

Map of Western Europe and the Mediterranean showing the campaigns of the Second Crusade

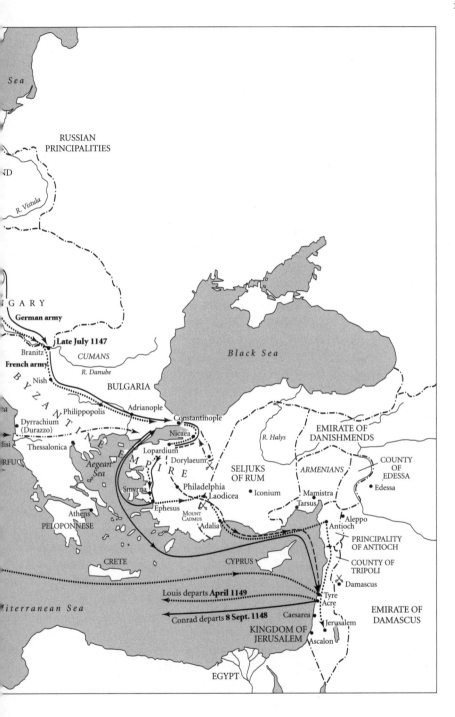

Sea

RUSSIAN
PRINCIPALITIES

ND

R. Vistula

GARY

German army

Late July 1147

Branitz   *CUMANS*

French army   *R. Danube*

Nish   BULGARIA

B Y Z A N T I N E

Philippopolis   Adrianople   Constantinople

Dyrrachium
(Durazzo)   Nicaea   *R. Halys*   EMIRATE OF
DANISHMENDS

lisi   Thessalonica   Lopardium
E M P I R E   Dorylaeum   COUNTY
OF
EDESSA

RFU   *Aegean
Sea*   SELJUKS
OF RUM   *ARMENIANS*

Smyrna   Philadelphia   Iconium   Mamistra   Edessa
Laodicea   Tarsus

Ephesus   MOUNT
CADMUS   Aleppo
Athens   Adalia   Antioch
PELOPONNESE   PRINCIPALITY
OF ANTIOCH

CRETE   CYPRUS   COUNTY OF
TRIPOLI

Damascus
Louis departs April 1149

iterranean Sea   Tyre   EMIRATE OF
Acre   DAMASCUS

Conrad departs **8 Sept. 1148**   Caesarea
Jerusalem
KINGDOM OF
JERUSALEM   Ascalon

EGYPT

Black Sea

INTRODUCTION

In the early twenty-first century the study of the crusades and their history appears to be in vigorous condition; numerous works, both academic and popular, are published each year and there is an ongoing and energetic debate concerning the extent and the definition of crusading. The so-called 'pluralist' view has emerged to the fore in recent decades; in essence, it argues that papally sanctioned expeditions engaged in penitential wars went not only to the Holy Land, but also to Spain, North Africa and Eastern Europe, and that campaigns against heretics, Mongols and political opponents of the papacy were comparable to the better-known, 'numbered' crusades to the Levant.[1] Furthermore, the movement did not end with the fall of Acre in 1291, but continued down to the sixteenth and seventeenth centuries. As Housley indicates, there are drawbacks to this conceptual framework with regard to matters such as terminology and the role of the Military Orders; nonetheless, it represents a good starting point. The Second Crusade itself, with its campaigns in Iberia, the Baltic and the Holy Land, has a pluralist aspect and, as we will see, contributed much towards the evolution of the idea of the crusade. Regardless of definition, it is remarkable that the last major monograph on the Second Crusade was published in 1866: Bernhard Kugler's *Studien zur Geschichte des zweiten Kreuzzugs.*[2] The crusade of 1145–9 has fared poorly by comparison to its triumphant and near-legendary predecessor of 1095–99 and the more glamorous Third Crusade (1188–92), dominated by the heroic Richard the Lionheart and Saladin. In one sense, however, historians have only mirrored their twelfth-century counterparts; the fact that the First Crusade conquered Jerusalem and that the Third Crusade made progress in the recovery of the Holy Land, encouraged many contemporaries to record these events. By contrast, because the Second Crusade was largely unsuccessful, it was ill served by narrative writers; few people, it seems, were interested in describing a failure. As Otto of Freising, a hugely accomplished scholar and a participant in the expedition, wrote: 'But since the outcome of that expedition, because of our sins, is known to all, we, who have purposed this time to write not a tragedy but a joyous history, leave this to be related by others elsewhere.'[3] In spite of such sentiments, a substantial body of evidence from charters, contemporary letters, songs and smaller narratives does, in fact, survive and enable this study to be made.

Simply because the Second Crusade failed does not mean that it offers little of interest to the modern historian. It witnessed several significant developments in crusading history; for example, it was the first time that major European monarchs risked leaving their kingdoms to make the dangerous journey to the Holy Land. The crusade also saw the launch of the most organised preaching tour to date and, in the issue of the bull *Quantum praedecessores* (December 1145), a consolidation, clarification and, in some ways, an extension of crusading privileges, which became the basis for papal appeals for decades to come. Above all else, the Second Crusade was remarkable for its scale. It saw campaigns to the Baltic, both coasts of Iberia and the Holy Land; Christian holy war of this magnitude was unprecedented and, in the case of the Baltic, the deployment of the formal apparatus of crusading to the region marked the emergence of another important innovation in the history of religious conflict.

A lack of monographs has not led historians to ignore the Second Crusade entirely. Shortly before Kugler wrote his book, Bernhardi published a biography of Conrad III which contained a substantial discussion of the expedition, albeit from the perspective of the German crown.[4] The campaign has also been covered in general histories of the crusades. By reason of the narrative of Odo of Deuil, the emphasis has tended to focus heavily on Louis VII's campaign to the Holy Land, although writers such as Berry (1969), in the six-volume 'Wisconsin' *History of the Crusades*, and Runciman (1952) made some effort to discuss the Baltic and Iberian campaigns too.[5] By far the most important work on the subject is Constable's brilliant article 'The Second Crusade as Seen by Contemporaries', published in 1953.[6] This seminal study offers a close analysis of the official preaching messages and considers the reaction to the dismal outcome of the campaign in the Levant. More important, however, is the conceptual framework in which Constable placed the crusade, his prime argument being that many in the mid-twelfth century saw the three theatres of war as part of one co-ordinated movement of Christian expansionism. This has tended to become the conventional interpretation of the crusade, although it is a view recently challenged with some vigour by Forey, as will be seen below.[7]

Bernard of Clairvaux is the pre-eminent figure associated with the expedition and, as one of the most important churchmen of the twelfth century, he has attracted enormous interest. At times this attention bears upon the crusade, although for the most part it concerns his career and theological beliefs.[8] Relevant textual analyses and studies of the man and his inner circle can be of considerable use; Meschini's monograph on Bernard and the crusade is particularly valuable.[9]

Over the last two decades there has been a perceptible increase in work on, or closely connected to, the crusade of 1145–9. Much of this has emerged from Germany, with the studies by Horn on Eugenius III, by Hoch on Jerusalem, Damascus and the crusade, and with a series of important articles by Hiestand.[10] Hehl's study on 'Church and War in the Twelfth Century' has covered the attitudes of ecclesiastical authorities towards Christians waging war, and Kahl's numerous articles about the Wendish Crusade and Crusade Eschatology are also of note.[11] Two essay collections in English, centred on the Second Crusade, were published in 1992 and 2001, and these brought further impetus to the study of the subject.[12]

The aims of the present work are varied. First, it proposes to relate the story of the crusade in an accessible fashion. Secondly, it will give a more detailed and accurate analysis of the successes and failures of the various campaigns than has hitherto been attempted. At the heart of the project, however, lies this thought: if the outcome was not entirely what its progenitors wished, in terms of recruitment, at least, the Second Crusade was a genuine triumph. Why did so many people take part in it? Conrad and Louis led large armies to the Levant; a fleet of almost 200 ships sailed from northern Europe via Lisbon; formidable armies besieged Almería and Tortosa, and the rulers of Denmark and the senior ecclesiastical and secular hierarchy of northern Germany campaigned in the Baltic region. It means, therefore, that those who directed the preaching of the crusade had chosen an extremely effective set of messages and/or were approaching an audience highly receptive to their appeal; it is the exploration of these points that is of particular interest. Two of the strongest themes in the papal bull *Quantum praedecessores* are the idea that the expedition was following in the footsteps of the First Crusade and the desire that the new crusaders should not let their fathers' achievements be wasted.[13] To explain the Church's choice of these themes and to understand the reasons why they proved so attractive requires one to place the Second Crusade within the context of the first fifty years of the crusading movement. In effect, this means a study of the 'post-history' of the First Crusade with particular reference to the impact that the earlier expedition made on historical writing, songs, art, politics and knightly culture.

This analysis of *Quantum praedecessores* also led me to consider the role of Pope Eugenius more closely than previous historians of the crusade have done, and I will suggest that the contribution and influence of the pope and his circle have been obscured by the charisma and energy of Bernard of Clairvaux. Madden's recent *Concise History of the Crusades* commented: 'In a very real sense it was his [Bernard's] crusade.'[14] In similar spirit, Williams' epic biography of the abbot argued: 'We may not be very far wrong in concluding not only that he was the mainspring of the movement when it had begun, but that its initiation was really due to him.'[15] Undoubtedly Bernard's seductive tongue, his persuasive quill and the fact that he spent at least nine months urging the people of western Europe to take the cross played a central part in this movement. We even have Bernard's own words to back this up: '"I have declared and I have spoken, and they are multiplied above number", towns and castles are emptied, one may scarcely find one man among seven women, so many women are widowed while their husbands are still alive.'[16] The last book of his *Vita* cited the numerous miracles that accompanied the preaching tour; hardly anyone was left blind or lame in his wake. But this is not the whole story. While one cannot dismiss Bernard's oratorical skills, the response to the call for a new crusade was not simply a question of personal influence. In a more practical vein, the dispatch of many other crusade preachers and the promulgation of a clear and comprehensive crusading bull must have been very important as well, and it is the process of uncovering Eugenius's part in the campaign that has helped to cast new light on the crusade as a whole.

This book will also investigate the recruitment and motivation of Louis VII and Conrad III; the latter's participation will be shown to have been integral and essential to the wishes of the crusade's ecclesiastical leaders. Linked to an exploration of the crusaders' motives and the question of the legacy of the First Crusade, I have followed the lead taken by Riley-Smith's prosopographical studies of the 1095–9 expedition and, largely using charter evidence, I have identified as many individuals who took part in the Second Crusade as was possible.[17] This yields proof of family traditions of crusading, which in turn can help to explain why people took the cross, while also permitting a closer look at the financial and logistical planning of the expedition. The requisite diplomatic preparations are also of note, especially concerning relations with the Byzantine Empire. The expansion of the crusade into Iberia and the Baltic region is another prominent theme of this book; such episodes will also be considered in the context of previous holy war activity. Finally, there will be a brief discussion of the aftermath of the crusade, the attempt to organise a new campaign in 1150 and the legacy of the Second Crusade for the Latin settlers in the East.

With regard to the Second Crusade as a whole, the picture to emerge is that of a dynamic and broad-ranging expedition which evolved through circumstance and the opportunism of certain lay (and in one instance, ecclesiastical) leaders, and was, in all theatres of war, fired by the vigour and spiritual enthusiasm of the papacy and its representatives. Constable suggested that the

Second Crusade 'incorporated into a plan practically every major military expedition against non-Christians of these years' and that it was 'a grandiose scheme of Christian defence'.[18] Helmold of Bosau, who wrote in the early 1170s, was the only author to make such a claim directly: 'The initiators of the expedition, however, deemed it advisable to design one part of the army for the eastern regions, another for Spain, and a third against the Slavs who live close by us.'[19] But, attractive as Helmold's words are, other evidence does not support his claim. The present work will argue that Constable's interpretation needs to be nuanced.[20] It is true that the papacy exerted a measure of control over the whole enterprise through the offer of remission of sins, but Constable's sense of formal overall direction ('a plan') is too precise. In fact, as we will see, Eugenius and Bernard were much more *reactive* than proactive. Nonetheless, the magnitude of the crusade reflected the spiritual confidence and the crusading experiences of the churchmen at its heart; they were men predisposed to be receptive to invitations to widen the range of the campaign. Their call for the expedition to the Holy Land generated a situation whereby it became appropriate for leading figures in Italy, Iberia and northern Europe to try to incorporate their ongoing aspirations, both secular and spiritual, into the apparatus of crusading. As the prime focus of the Christian faith, the Holy Land was the most important of these objectives. The expeditions to the Baltic region and eastern Iberia may well have taken place anyway but, when their leaders asked for papal endorsement it allowed Eugenius to cast them as part of a wider undertaking, if not to fit them into a preconceived plan. The circumstances of the time also created an opportunity for the Catholic and Armenian Churches to move closer, although in the event this was not fully realised.

This work will follow Constable's lead in relation to the idea that many contemporaries regarded some, or all, of these campaigns as linked in a wider, collective Christian endeavour, rather than representing a strict papal plan or scheme. Eugenius himself mentioned three theatres of war in his papal bull of April 1147, *Divina dispensatione II* – where he discussed the ongoing conflicts in Spain and officially granted to those wishing to fight the Wends the same privileges as he gave to the Jerusalem crusaders.[21] Forey, however, has argued strongly against the perception that contemporaries made links between the campaigns. He claims that 'most ... of the chroniclers and annalists commenting on conflicts with the infidel in the later 1140s ... mention only one area of combat'.[22] This is hardly surprising; most medieval writers were naturally more occupied with regional affairs because these reflected the priorities of their audience; even when writing of international affairs, chroniclers of the First Crusade inevitably emphasised the deeds of their particular local hero. In fact, numerous chronicles and charters made reference to two or more of the Second Crusade arenas of war. This reflects a combination of regional interests, the wish to record major events and the availability of information, be it from other writers and participants, or material such as the so-called 'Lisbon Letter', a document that circulated widely in northern Europe from early 1148 onwards and appeared in several works.[23] If one accepts that there was no grand plan, there is less need to insist that contemporaries had to make reference to all three areas of the conflict to demonstrate some understanding of a broader purpose; in other words, we can allow a less prescriptive recognition of what was perceived to constitute this shared Christian endeavour. Several German annalists made the point, some more explicitly than others. The author of the *Annales Rodenses* suggested: '*Expeditio haec in tria est divisa, ubique contra ethnicos pugnatura*'.[24] The *Annales Magdeburgenses* gave its readers an account of the campaigns at Lisbon, in the Baltic region and in the Holy Land – as did, with differing degrees of detail, the *Annales Colonienses maximi* and the *Annales Palidenses*.[25] Writers from a further variety of backgrounds – such as the Anglo-Norman Robert of Torigny, and the Praemonstratensian continuator of Sigebert of Gembloux (from the dioceses of Laon or Rheims) – chose to outline the fighting in the Levant and at Lisbon, Almería and Tortosa.[26] Another Anglo-Norman, Henry of Huntingdon, discussed the reasons why the crusade to the Holy Land had failed and the conquest of Lisbon succeeded; he mentioned Almería too.[27] The Vaucelles continuator of Sigebert of Gembloux noted that the Lisbon crusaders were en route to Jerusalem.[28] In 1146, an anonymous Old French troubadour writer linked the fighting in the Holy Land with the struggle on the eastern coast of Spain.[29] Otto of Freising connected the war against the Wends with that against the Muslims of the Holy Land through the idea of fighting the 'enemies of the cross', although he made no mention of the conflict in Iberia.[30]

In this assortment of sources there is relatively little consistency about what constituted the Second Crusade, but Helmold of Bosau and the *Annales Rodenses* apart, consistency was not the writers' purpose. The key point remains: they saw one or more of the campaigns to Iberia or the Baltic as part of the same enterprise. To the minds of many contemporaries, crusading had clearly developed in scope beyond an expedition to the Holy Land; they were comfortable in accommodating one or more additional theatres of war within the idea. Linked with this was the realisation that Christianity could expand further. This in itself was not a new thought, but the scale of the Second Crusade gave it unprecedented impetus. As we saw in the prologue, a charter of Countess Sibylla of Flanders stated that the crusaders were 'extending Christianity'; Otto of Freising wrote of 'extending the observance of the Christian faith'; and the *Annales Coloniensis* mentioned 'extending the borders of the Christian Empire in the East'.[31] This concept of expansion was shared by many contemporaries but, as with so many societies on the verge of war, ambition far outstripped accomplishments. The Second Crusaders proved unable to emulate the feats of their heroes in the Holy Land and made progress only in Iberia. Yet by 1145–9 the world in which the First Crusade had operated was changed in a number of ways: politically, economically, spiritually and culturally. Insofar as they impacted upon the Second Crusade this study will identify such changes in passing. In essence, however, this book is an attempt to understand the origins, the development and the outcome of the Second Crusade – a subject which has much to offer historians of the crusading age.

CHAPTER 1

Ongoing Contact between the Latin East and the West and the Development of Crusading, 1099–1145

The early decades of the twelfth century saw the formation of numerous personal and institutional connections between the nascent Latin States and the West. Many European families had relatives who settled in the Holy Land, and in some cases extensive kindred groups, such as the Montlhéry, became closely involved in the Levant while continuing to retain considerable importance in their homelands.[1] One reason why the settlers looked to the West was to find husbands or wives for eligible rulers, heirs and heiresses; they tried to identify individuals of an appropriate rank to develop further links with powerful families in Europe. Baldwin I's marriage to Adelaide of Sicily proved a controversial and unhappy union, clouded largely by the king's overwhelming desire to secure as much money as possible.[2] The need to provide a husband for Melisende of Jerusalem was considerably more serious because she was the eldest child of Baldwin II and her partner would become king. The leading men of the land unanimously selected Fulk V of Anjou and, as we will see below, the count came to the Levant with a crusade in 1129.[3] In the early 1130s political turmoil in Antioch prompted an embassy to Raymond of Poitiers to offer him the hand in marriage of Constance, the child-heiress to the principality. Raymond was a member of one of the most prestigious families in Europe and the son of the 1101 crusader, Duke William IX of Aquitaine. He duly accepted and took power in 1136.[4]

A myriad of other reasons existed for individuals to go to the East; some wanted to seek out new careers, to take on new lands, or to join a Military Order. Hugh II of Le Puiset, for example, came to the Holy Land with his wife c.1108, and was given the county of Jaffa by King Baldwin I.[5] In the case of Robert of Montfort, there was a more coercive aspect to his actions; he had been found guilty of breaking his oath of fealty to King Henry I of England

and in 1107 he left northern Europe to take part in Bohemond of Antioch's crusade. In the previous century political exile had motivated many Normans to seek their fortune in southern Italy and Sicily, and a comparable process seems evident here. Yet Robert broke faith with Bohemond too; his acceptance of bribes from Emperor Alexius was alleged to have weakened the crusading army. After the expedition collapsed he eventually reached the Levant where he soon died.[6] The life of the Hosto of St Omer, a Templar knight who travelled between northern Europe and the Levant on several occasions in the 1130s and 1140s, shows how a member of the Military Orders might be involved in both the East and West.[7]

There also emerged a practice whereby individuals came to the East to serve in the defence of the holy places. These men did not join a large expedition or respond to a specific crisis, and it is not clear what spiritual rewards they might expect. It seems, however, that they were more than simple pilgrims; they expected to fight and at the same time enhance their own noble credentials. Bishop Otto of Freising, who completed his work *De duabus civitatibus* just as the Second Crusade was being launched in early 1146, described this practice: 'some, for Christ's sake, despising their own interests and considering that it was not for naught that they were wearing the girdle of knighthood, set out for Jerusalem and there, undertaking a new kind of warfare, so conducted themselves against the enemies of the Cross of Christ that, continually bearing about their bodies the death of the cross, they appeared by their life and conversation to be not soldiers, but monks'.[8] The journey of Charles – later Count Charles the Good of Flanders – *c.*1108 is a case in point. Galbert of Bruges related that the young knight undertook 'a holy pilgrimage to Jerusalem . . . [where] he also fought strenuously against the enemies of the Christian faith'.[9] Another Flemish writer, Walter of Thérouanne, noted that once Charles reached manhood and was belted as a knight, 'about to visit the sepulchre of the Lord, he undertook from devotion there the bearing of arms against the pagan enemies of our faith, he fought vigorously on behalf of Christ the Lord for a considerable time and . . . consecrated to him the first fruits of his labours and his deeds'.[10] Likewise, Conrad of Staufen, subsequently King Conrad III of Germany, went to the Holy Land in 1124 to serve God and to help defend Christ's patrimony.[11] Fulk V of Anjou made a pilgrimage to Jerusalem in 1120 and attached himself to the newly formed Templars, presumably joining them in their work protecting pilgrims. He also paid the expenses of 100 knights for a year and gave the Order an annual endowment on his return to the West.[12] Others joined the Templars for a limited period, as detailed in the Order's rule.[13] It is also possible that the visit of Count Thierry of Flanders in 1138–9 was conceived to provide military assistance for the settlers. Considering the number of Thierry's companions, this visit was more akin to Fulk of Anjou's support of 100 knights, just noted above.[14] These small expeditions, and the participation of westerners for a short period of service in the Levant, all helped to secure a recognition in the West of the effort required to sustain the Christian position in the Holy Land. This was explicitly acknowledged by Pope Eugenius III in *Quantum praedecessores* when he wrote that the holy places had been defended by western Europeans 'over the years', after the First Crusade.[15]

Probably the most high-profile way in which the defence of Jerusalem became visible in the West was through the foundation of the Military Orders – warrior-monks dedicated to the welfare of pilgrims and to the defence of the Holy Land. The Hospital of St John was based on an earlier Amalfitan hospice, founded in the mid-eleventh century to care for sick pilgrims. After the conquest of Jerusalem it developed rapidly through strong support from the rulers of the kingdom. Many grateful pilgrims gave donations of property and money and the Hospitallers began to have a presence in Europe: the acquisition of holdings in Southern France (1100), Sicily (1101), Spain (1108), Italy (before 1113) and England (1128) give an impression of their rate of advance. In some cases, such as that of the group of forty villages held in the county of Commignes *c.*1099–1120, these properties were quite extensive. In 1113 Pope Paschal II issued the bull *Pie postulatio voluntatis* which brought the brethren under papal protection and thereby enabled them to expand further. In 1136, the Hospitallers were given the castle of Beth Gibelin by King Fulk of Jerusalem, although unambiguous evidence for Hospitaller knights (rather than for mercenaries employed by the Order) is not apparent until 1144.[16] Very quickly, however, the dual function of the Hospitallers as a military and a medical institution became well established. By reason of a letter from Bernard of Clairvaux to the Hospitaller knights in Paris in 1146–7 and a letter of Pope Eugenius from the same period, we can see that the Order was also involved in the Second Crusade.[17]

The origins and growth of the Order of the Temple were an obvious signal of the need for westerners to take responsibility for the defence of the holy sites and their pilgrim visitors. Hugh of Payns founded the organisation in 1119; it was soon endorsed by King Baldwin II, who gave the brethren property in the Temple area of Jerusalem. In January 1129 the Council of Troyes approved the foundation of a religious order to follow a Rule which combined the monastic precepts of poverty, chastity and obedience with a commitment to defend the Holy Land. Hugh of Payns came to the West during 1128–9 and secured many recruits and donations of land and rights across Europe. Most remarkably, in 1134, King Alfonso I of Aragon bequeathed his entire kingdom to the Templars, the Hospitallers and the Canons of the Church of the Holy Sepulchre. The terms were never fully implemented, but from 1143 onwards the Templars fought in the Iberian Peninsula too.[18] Overall, in the case of Templars and Hospitallers alike, their western landholdings provided income and recruits to help fight the infidel. The presence of Military Order property must have become quite familiar in some areas of the West and this, in conjunction with the help that both of these institutions rendered to pilgrims in the Levant, played a part in keeping the struggle against Islam in focus throughout the decades after the First Crusade.

Another obvious channel for relations between Europe and the Holy Land was church business. A number of controversies dogged the Latin Church in the Levant during its early years: for example the disputed election to the patriarchate of Jerusalem; arguments over the ecclesiastical province of Tyre; or the problems involving the deposition of the patriarch of Antioch, Ralph of Domfront. The First and Second Lateran Councils (1123 and 1139) provided opportunities for delegations from the East to meet their colleagues in Europe; papal legations were frequently sent to the Orient as well. Apart from these high-profile instances, there was a high volume of contact through regular confirmations of lands, offices and rights. This means that the *curia* was likely to be well informed about the military and strategic situation in the Holy Land, as well as developing personal relations with senior figures.[19]

In the aftermath of the First Crusade the idea of crusading was taken up and adopted in several other areas of Europe. The development of holy war in Iberia and in the Baltic will be examined in detail later in the book. In essence, however, these episodes help to demonstrate the profound impact that the capture of Jerusalem had upon the conduct of conflict with the enemies of the Latin Church; furthermore, the advance of holy war into such areas had a significant effect on the scope of the Second Crusade. Certain aspects of crusading and holy war in Iberia and the Baltic also generated close ties with Jerusalem; furthermore they helped to produce additional traditions of crusading and, in the case of Spain, to encourage participation by kings.

In the years after 1099 there was considerable crusading activity to the Holy Land, although, as Riley-Smith and Housley have indicated, given that crusading ideology was in its formative stages, it is sometimes difficult or artificial to separate these episodes from large-scale armed pilgrimages.[20] The biggest of these campaigns is regarded as a continuation of the First Crusade and took place in 1101–2. The expedition, led by William IX of Aquitaine and Duke Welf IV of Bavaria, had a troubled relationship with the Greeks and was routed by the Seljuks in Asia Minor. It did, however, mean that more families had traditions of crusading and that more westerners settled in the Holy Land.[21] But the expedition of Prince Bohemond of Antioch in 1107–8 was perhaps of greater interest to the development of the idea of crusading.

In the early twelfth century, the nascent principality of Antioch faced intense pressure from the Muslims of northern Syria. Bohemond himself had been captured and imprisoned by the Danishmendids from August 1100 to May 1103, and the situation in the region required action. The Latin East was still in its formative stages and the need for men to fight for a season or two, or to settle, was evident. In 1105 Bohemond set out for Europe to secure himself a bride from King Philip I of France and to raise men for a new crusade. The target of this campaign is a highly controversial subject because some sources suggest that, as well as taking on the infidel, the prince made plain his intention to attack parts of the Byzantine Empire en route to the Latin East.[22] More significantly still, there is evidence to indicate that he may have had the endorsement of Pope Paschal II for this assault on the Greeks, although – crucially – no papal bull confirms it.

It was clear that Bohemond's campaign was seen in a continuum with those of 1097–99 and 1101–2; Orderic Vitalis called it 'the third expedition from the West to set out for Jerusalem'.[23] Some writers reported sentiments that reflected a seamless link with the preaching of the First Crusade. Abbot Suger of St Denis, who, as a young man, witnessed Bohemond's speech at the Council of Poitiers in 1106, viewed the undertaking as a 'journey to Jerusalem' and an 'expedition to the Holy Sepulchre'.[24] Another French writer outlined that the famous Bohemond came to the West and, 'with papal permission, urged all to hurry to go to Jerusalem and to liberate those who were captives and to help those who were being distressed by the multitudes of the Turkish army and the daily attacks of the enemy'.[25] Bohemond himself described the campaign as an 'iter Ierosolimitanum' and his force as 'Dei exercitus' in a letter of 1106 or early 1108.[26] All of this material places the expedition firmly in line with the heritage of the First Crusade.

William of Tyre wrote that Bohemond wanted money and reinforcements.[27] It must have been a considerable strain to sustain intensive military activity from his limited territorial base; hence the explanation advanced by William seems entirely reasonable. Yet alongside this, and in an obvious departure from the links with the First Crusade, several sources point to a focus on the Byzantine Empire as well as on the Muslim lands. The long-standing antipathy between the Greeks and the Norman Sicilians was apparent to all – Bohemond's father had invaded the Empire in 1081 – and events during the First Crusade (when Bohemond took control of Antioch, in apparent contradiction of his promises to Emperor Alexius), coupled with the prince's expulsion of the Orthodox patriarch of Antioch in 1100, created quite serious tensions.[28] Alexius's hostility to the 1101 crusaders bore witness to his anger towards the Latin West. He obviously planned to bring Antioch to heel as soon as was feasibly possible; from Bohemond's perspective, therefore, this threat needed to be confronted. The troubles of the 1101 crusade fanned the anti-Greek feelings evident in some reports of the First Crusade even further, particularly in France; contemporary writers such as Ekkehard of Aura and Richard of Poitiers displayed just such attitudes.[29]

In the early winter of 1105 Bohemond met Paschal II, although the content of their discussions poses problems for the historian. Ekkehard of Aura and Albert of Aachen wrote that Bohemond came to the West to get troops to fight Alexius and the infidel.[30] Likewise, the *Historia belli sacri*, written in the early 1130s in Monte Cassino, southern Italy, indicated that Bohemond wanted to attack the Muslims and the Greeks and that a papal legate was assigned to him for assistance.[31] A contemporary Levantine source, Bartolf of Nangis, who wrote *c.*1108–9, claimed that the prince convinced Pope Paschal of the need to attack Alexius and that he was given a papal banner as a token of support.[32] When Bohemond prepared to move into northern Europe in early 1106 Paschal provided him with a legate, Bruno of Segni, to help in his recruitment and to authorise the crusaders' spiritual privileges. Bruno was a highly experienced churchman who had toured France with Pope Urban II in 1095–6 and can be assumed to have had a sound grasp of crusading theory as it stood at the time.

Bohemond and his associates had carefully prepared the ground for his visit to the north and envoys informed people of his impending arrival months beforehand. The advance mission was led by his cousin, Richard of Salerno, a man of considerable standing and a veteran of the First Crusade.[33] He would have been pleased to learn that the *Gesta Francorum* and its derivatives were in circulation because this emphasised Bohemond's role in the First Crusade. It also made much of Greek perfidy and seeded the ground for a new crusade to be directed against Alexius.[34] By the time Bohemond reached northern Europe several leaders of the First Crusade had died, such as Raymond of St Gilles and Godfrey of Bouillon; some others had been disgraced by their desertion (although redeemed as martyrs) – namely, Stephen of Blois and Hugh of Vermandois – or, in the case of Robert of Normandy, they were about to be removed from the political stage altogether. Alternatively, a few had simply remained in the Levant (Godfrey, Raymond and Baldwin of Boulogne). Bohemond was, therefore, a rare survivor from the ranks of the crusade's leadership to be seen in the West; he was certainly its most famous warrior. The prince was astute in his public appearances; he made a pilgrimage to the patron saint of prisoners, the tomb of St Leonard at Noblat, where he gave thanks for his release from captivity.[35] He also presented relics and fine gifts to the religious houses that he passed en route north.[36] In the late spring of 1106 Bohemond married Princess Constance of France at Chartres. Orderic Vitalis claimed that he used this glittering occasion, which was attended by leading

French churchmen, nobles and Bruno of Segni, to make a speech in which 'he urged all who bore arms to attack the emperor with him, and promised his chosen adjutants wealthy towns and castles. Many were kindled by his words and, taking the Lord's cross, left all their belongings and set out on the road for Jerusalem like men hastening to a feast.'[37] The author here made an explicit link between the campaign against Alexius and the subsequent journey to the holy city of Jerusalem. Pope Paschal and Bruno of Segni must have been aware of these twin aims and, as Suger recorded, the legate held a council at Poitiers on 26 May 1106, 'to make sure that zeal for the journey to Jerusalem' did not grow lukewarm.[38] The *Chronicon Malleacense* wrote that Bohemond and Bruno called an assembly to preach 'the road to the Holy Sepulchre'.[39] The prince was also accompanied by a figure alleged to be a son of the deposed Emperor Romanus IV Diogenes; if this was correct, the association, again, made his agenda plain. It was also presumably intended to give the attack on Byzantium greater legitimacy – a just cause, in fact – and, if the youth was restored, to help confirm possession of the territorial inducements offered to the crusaders.[40] Bohemond's reputation as a crusading hero, his offer of money and lands, and the allure of the Holy Sepulchre formed a potent combination; in fact, King Henry I of England refused to allow the prince to cross over to England because he feared that many of his best warriors would be lured away, although he did agree to meet the Antiochene ruler in Normandy.[41] The prince sent appeals for help to other leading figures in the Anglo-Norman realm: there survives a letter from Archbishop Gerard of York which expressed his interest in the campaign and commended the prince's chaplain, Hugh, the bearer of the missive.[42]

It seems that the spiritual rewards offered by Bruno's preaching, coupled with Bohemond's more earthly incentives, proved highly attractive and many joined the expedition. Pope Paschal himself spent much of 1107 in France and one source reported that he passed legislation 'for the journey to Jerusalem and the work of God' at the Council of Troyes in May 1107.[43] Orderic Vitalis also informs us that Bohemond paid some of these men for two years' service and this too must have increased the size of his force.[44] William of Tyre suggested that 5,000 knights were with him; while this figure is probably too high, we do know the identity of some of the nobles who took part in the crusade, both from France and other countries.[45] Rowe has argued that, while it is clear Paschal supported a new crusade and that he appointed Bruno of Segni as the legate, once in France, Bohemond struck out on his own and modified the plan so as to include the Greeks. This initiative was enthusiastically endorsed by the French nobility and Bruno was neither bold nor strong enough to oppose him; thus Bohemond cynically extended the papal blessing to encompass an attack on Alexius. Rowe also suggested that, by dating a letter from Bohemond to Paschal to 1108 instead of 1106, where it has been placed so far, we can see the prince in a new light as asking, belatedly, for the previously absent papal support and presence on the campaign.[46] This is an attractive argument, but it requires Bruno to have been extremely passive and compliant. At the very least he had gone along with the modified plan and made no attempt to block it. One alternative is to follow McQueen in the conviction that the efforts of Bohemond and Patriarch Daimbert had 'undoubtedly received papal backing', thereby removing the need for this special pleading.[47] As we will see below, other ideas are also feasible.

The details of the campaign are not of concern here; suffice to note that Bohemond spent almost a year gathering his forces in Apulia, where his own ill-health may have also contributed to the delay.[48] In October 1107 he invaded Byzantine lands and soon laid siege to Durazzo. Alexius managed to restrict Bohemond's supply lines and to buy off some of his supporters; the crusaders also suffered badly from malaria and dysentery.[49] By September they were on the point of collapse and the prince had little option but to open negotiations with Alexius. Anna Comnena, another source for this episode, was adamant that the pope gave Bohemond permission to attack the Greeks.[50] The prince was to formalise his humiliation in the Treaty of Devol in which he recognised Byzantine overlordship; by any measure, the expedition had failed. Some of the crusaders travelled on to settle in the Holy Land, but Bohemond himself went to Apulia where he died in 1111.

In military terms, the target of his campaign was probably too ambitious; but, with regard to the development of the idea of crusading, this was an important episode. The presence of an authorised papal legate in France indicated that Paschal, possibly through Bruno, if not from his own meetings with Bohemond, knew of the twofold aim to invade Byzantium and proceed to the Levant. The appearance of a pretender to the Greek throne would have made the first part of the agenda particularly clear. Rowe has plainly cast the prince as 'the villain of the piece', his use of the letter to Paschal to show papal compliance relies on a questionable dating. Nonetheless, it appears that the weight of narrative evidence leans – although not conclusively so – towards some form of papal acquiescence in the venture at the very least. There was a reasonably widespread perception that the pope supported the plan. The endorsement of an attack on Byzantium represented a combination of Paschal and Bohemond's interests, both of whom had reasons to wish the Greeks weakened (be it from an ecclesiastical or a military perspective) and wanted to enhance the security of the Frankish East from all quarters. This overlap of secular and ecclesiastical advantage was a pattern that would be followed in future crusading campaigns. Yet the lack of a papal bull, or of any subsequent reference to one, is problematic. It should not be underestimated what a radical move the declaration of a crusade against Byzantium would be. Urban II had launched the First Crusade with co-operation with the Greeks in mind; just over a decade later, to place them alongside the Muslims as sworn enemies of the Church was perhaps a step too far. When, during the Second Crusade, tensions between Byzantines and crusaders ran high, it seems strange that those who called for an attack on Constantinople did not make reference to an earlier papal blessing if one existed. Perhaps the most awkward piece of evidence on this matter is a statement by Orderic Vitalis, ignored by Rowe. The writer attributed the outcome of the campaign to the fact that 'no prophet sent from God roused us with a message from heaven' – a comment which could reflect the lack of formal papal approval.[51] Paschal surely knew of Bohemond's aim and did not attempt to deflect him – also thinking that the crusading hero would go to the Levant eventually and, in theory, give a boost to the fortunes of the Holy Land – yet it seems he stopped short of the outright promotion of a crusade against the Greeks through a papal bull.

Several other large-scale expeditions came to the Levant in the years after Bohemond's crusade. It is difficult to ascertain the crusading status of those who took part in these episodes because the source material is limited, but some tentative conclusions may be advanced. The first one involved Bertrand of Toulouse, the bastard son of Raymond of St Gilles, who had died in February 1105. Raymond's lands in the East were taken over by his relative, William Jordan, and, according to Caffaro, William sent to the Genoese and asked them to help in the capture of Tripoli 'for the service of God and the Holy Sepulchre'.[52] In the meantime, Bertrand had decided to assume control of the Toulousain lands in the Levant and, perhaps already aware of Genoa's forthcoming relationship with William Jordan, sailed to Italy himself. There, Caffaro related, Bertrand also asked the Genoese for support in the capture of Tripoli 'for the service of God overseas. Then, the Genoese, on hearing his [Bertrand's] entreaties and promises, and on account of the embassy of William Jordan, equipped 40 galleys and carried Bertrand and his knights to Tripoli.'[53] After Tripoli was taken, the Genoese were rewarded with one third of the city and also the entire port of Gibelet – a remarkably generous concession that indicated the perceived value of their help and the political tensions within the county itself. Yet the Genoese did not settle down and start to exploit their new gains; their leaders went to pray at the Holy Sepulchre – thereby acting as devoted pilgrims – before returning home to Italy in triumph.[54] While there was no papal direction in this campaign (in the way that Bruno of Segni worked on behalf of Prince Bohemond), and no mention of church councils or ceremonies for taking the cross, it is plain that the Genoese saw themselves as performing God's work in fighting to capture the Holy Land and that they behaved as pilgrims through their devotional journey to Jerusalem. In these latter senses, therefore, they resemble crusaders. Self-evidently, the Genoese were also concerned to secure a commercial advantage for themselves; the outfitting of a fleet of 40 galleys would not have been undertaken without concrete expectation of payment or future benefits, and the scale of the subsequent grants of land demonstrates that some agreement had been in place.[55] When the leaders returned to Genoa they had accomplished good works for all the Christian faithful and for their home city – a mixture that their fellow-citizens did not view as mutually exclusive and, in fact, was worthy of real admiration. As we will see, the Genoese would repeat this policy in several campaigns in the Levant and Iberia in future decades.

The expedition of King Sigurd of Norway (1103–30) is another episode difficult to pin down in terms of a definable crusading format. Sigurd was one of two brothers who ruled over Norway, and c.1107 he decided to go to Jerusalem. The main source for this is the early thirteenth-century *Heimskringla* of Snorri Sturlusson, although much of his text was based on earlier writers whose work is now lost.[56] Snorri stated that other Norwegians had already gained fame from an earlier journey to the East (presumably on the First Crusade), that the Byzantine emperor was known to require mercenaries and that he paid handsome wages.[57] William of Tyre, who wrote well after the event described, indicated how Sigurd heard the Holy Land was in Christian hands and that he desired to go to the Levant 'for the sake of devotion'.[58] Fulcher of Chartres, who was present in the Latin East at the time (1110), correctly described him as very young (Sigurd was only nineteen) and believed that he was 'inspired by God to make the pilgrimage'.[59] Sigurd and his companions (fifty-five ships according to Fulcher, sixty by the testimony of Ibn al-Athir and Snorri Sturlusson) had made a leisurely journey to the East. They set out in 1107 and stopped in England for the winter; they spent the next year in northern Spain and they fought Muslims both there and further south at Lisbon. Snorri noted that King Sigurd triumphed in no less than eight battles against the heathen and also managed to secure much booty. The winter of 1109 was passed in Apulia and the fleet arrived in the Levant in the summer of 1110. Sigurd immediately went to Jerusalem to perform his devotions and then he met King Baldwin I. The ruler of Jerusalem wished to use the Norwegian fleet to help capture Muslim-held ports on the coast and he approached Sigurd for help. The young king replied that 'they had come for the purpose of devoting themselves to the service of Christ'; as long as Baldwin provided food, they would assist him.[60] The operation resulted in the capture of Sidon (December 1110), a very positive development for the Franks. By way of thanks, Baldwin and the patriarch of Jerusalem gave Sigurd a relic of the True Cross that was also designed to help promote Christianity in Scandinavia. Sigurd and his men then travelled to Constantinople where they were received in lavish style with games in the Hippodrome. Some of his men followed a long-established practice and remained in the service of the emperor. Sigurd gave Alexius his dragon-headed ships and then started his journey northwards through Bulgaria, Hungary, Germany and Denmark before he reached home in 1111.[61]

Sigurd's expedition was not prompted by an appeal from the Latin East, nor by any papal bull. On that basis he might be seen as a pilgrim, albeit one of very high-standing who, like others at this time, was prepared to do God's work in the settlers' armies. Snorri Sturlusson's comment that some were inspired by the fame of those returning from the Levant also reveals the attraction and importance of reputation. There is little doubt that the Norsemen were looking for any opportunity to gather profit and the decision of some to work for Alexius after visiting the Holy Land shows this was plainly a powerful incentive. We see here again, therefore, another variant on the overlapping mix of secular and spiritual motives found earlier.

In June 1119 the nobility of Antioch were slaughtered at the Battle of the Field of Blood, to trigger the most serious emergency yet experienced by the Latin settlers. In January 1120 the Council of Nablus debated the issue and decided to send envoys to Pope Calixtus II and to Doge Domenico Michiel of Venice to request military support.[62] The pope – who, as a member of the Montlhéry clan, was related to the ruling house of Jerusalem – reacted quickly and launched a crusade, the first papal involvement with such a venture to the Holy Land since Bohemond's ill-starred expedition of 1108, although no actual text of an appeal survives.[63] Calixtus probably contacted the Venetians in the autumn of 1120; the following year he wrote to the leading men of Jerusalem and reassured them that he was working on their behalf both in Italy and north of the Alps.[64] The First Lateran Council in March 1123 considered the crusade and granted indulgences and the protection of the Church to those who wished to 'go to Jerusalem and offer effective help towards the defence of the Christian people and overcoming the tyranny of the infidels'.[65] The decree then commanded those who had taken the cross for Jerusalem or Spain but had removed their crosses to put them back on their clothes and depart before Easter 1124 or face excommunication or interdict.[66] Such a statement reinforces the suggestion that there had been a papal crusading encyclical with a reasonably wide circulation.[67] It appears that a number of French and German knights took the cross around this time, although it was the Venetians who provided by far the greatest level of support.[68] The patriarch and prior of the Holy Sepulchre also wrote to Archbishop Diego of Compostela and pleaded with him to send men, money and supplies to the Levant as a matter of urgency; the settlers' position was depicted as desperate. As we will see later, crusading in Spain had, by this time, been formally encouraged by the papacy and the shared cause of the struggle against Islam was a reason to look to Iberia for help. Such appeals to Spain were rare; however, Archbishop Diego was known as an enthusiastic proponent of holy war and the Holy Sepulchre had financial and property ties to the peninsula too. Unfortunately, we do not know of any response to this particular cry for help, and a papal letter of 1123 implicitly countered the call to the East by reminding those who had taken the cross in Spain to fulfil their vows in Iberia, where they would get the same rewards as if they fought in the Holy Land.[69]

It seems that some Venetians become crusaders and Calixtus sent the citizens a papal banner to signify his approval. The settlers had approached the Venetians because they wanted to strike back at the Muslims through an attack on Tyre, a venture for which naval expertise was required. In return for substantial commercial privileges, the Venetians agreed to participate. In 1123 a fleet reached the eastern Mediterranean and overcame an Egyptian naval squadron off Ascalon; Tyre was blockaded and fell in July 1124 to mark a major advance for the Christian cause. Overall, this episode was important in the development of crusading history because it saw preaching on two fronts: Iberia and the Holy Land. It also reinforced the links between Italian trading cities and the crusades, while the letter from the churchmen of Jerusalem to Archbishop Diego showed an affinity between the Frankish settlers and the Christians of Iberia in their conflict with Islam.

In 1127 the kingdom of Jerusalem sent a trio of missions to the West, each of which hoped to resolve issues that affected the long-term security of Christians in the Levant. First, as we saw above, there was the offer to Fulk of Anjou to marry Melisende; secondly, Hugh of Payns set out to secure ecclesiastical approval for the Knights Templar; thirdly, Hugh also led an attempt to organise a new crusade aimed at the important Muslim city of Damascus. This had been the subject of raids in 1125 and 1126 and King Baldwin II now wanted outside help to complete the task. The overlap between these ventures was obvious: Fulk, as the next king of Jerusalem, would be the ideal candidate to lead a new crusade; the impetus provided by the Templars could assist in this and support the broader issue of the defence of the Holy Land as well. Churchmen from the Latin East went to Pope Honorius and discussed these plans. In May 1128 the count took the cross and in January 1129 the Council of Troyes recognised the Order of the Temple. Hugh meanwhile had been busy; the *Anglo-Saxon Chronicle* stated that he had recruited the largest number of people to travel to Jerusalem since the days of Pope Urban II and that their purpose was to attack Damascus.[70] It is interesting that at least one commentator viewed the new expedition as a descendant of the First Crusade. There is, however, no clear evidence of papal preaching or of the issue of a bull, although the legate, Gerard of Angoulême, was present when Fulk took the cross and presumably some ecclesiastical sanction had been given for this ceremony to happen.[71] One other feature of this episode was that it was purely expansionist in nature. Earlier crusades were justified from their outset as defensive wars, aiming at the recovery of formerly Christian lands. Damascus had never been Christian, and an attack on the city was a rare example of a crusade designed to increase the Latin lands in the East. Charter evidence indicates that Hugh recruited nobles such as Hugh III of Le Puiset and Hugh of Amboise.[72] Ultimately, the campaign to Damascus failed because, on its approach to the city, the Christian army became divided and a Muslim ambush killed many of the knights and forced them to retreat.[73]

The next chapter will emphasise the positive legacy of the First Crusade, but it is important to note that the aftermath of the campaign and its immediate successors was not entirely attractive: while many returned as heroes, we must remember that large numbers of families had lost loved ones and that some who returned came home sick and penniless.[74] Those who remained in the West faced hardship too; notwithstanding arrangements to rule the land of absent crusaders and the fact that the property and families of such individuals were meant to be under church protection, there were times when these arrangements broke down. In Flanders, for example, in the absence of Count Robert, serious unrest had broken out in Bruges; similarly, parts of the royal domain around Paris suffered grave disorder without Count Guy II of Rochefort.[75] In the case of Count Helias of Maine, so great was his fear of the ambitions of King William II of England that he decided to stay in the West rather than fulfil his crusade vow.[76] Hugh II of Le Puiset wanted to go on crusade with Prince Bohemond in 1107, but he mistrusted the behaviour of Count Rotrou of Perche, who had built a castle in his lordship. The legislation raised new and unprecedented difficulties of interpretation and jurisdiction, as we will see below.

While many glorified the achievements of the First Crusade, the failure and casualties of the 1101 and 1108 expeditions brought some harsh words from chroniclers and showed the moral pitfalls of such campaigns. Writers regarded its collapse as a divine punishment for their perceived arrogance and other sins.[77] The motives of the 1108 crusaders provoked some forthright criticism from Orderic Vitalis.[78] He blamed the outcome of the crusade on the treachery of certain nobles, reported to have accepted bribes from Alexius in order to change sides, and he argued that the twin sins of greed for money and the lust to rule lands caused the campaign to collapse. Orderic explained that God had been merciful in putting the crusaders in a position where the threat of starvation had caused them to come to terms with the emperor, rather than allowing them to be killed in battle. One of Bohemond's companions was said to have argued that the expedition was presumptuous in attacking the emperor and that 'no hereditary right drew us to this bold enterprise'.[79] This criticism obviously reflected the disappointment engendered by the defeat, but it also marked some questioning of the motivation, or right intention, of the crusaders. Right intention was, of course, what attracted God's favour, and the fact that there was no 'hereditary right' to the Byzantine Empire, as Orderic put it, may have functioned as one explanation, in the eyes of contemporaries, as to why the crusade did not succeed. William of Malmesbury provided a brief outline of Bohemond's expedition which suggested that the participants hoped to gain land for themselves and that they attacked Alexius, 'the pretext being the ill-treatment of pilgrims, for which he was notorious'. Tellingly, William made no mention of Jerusalem or of a spiritual motivation for the campaign.[80]

Reverses in crusading expeditions might also cause the Frankish settlers to be regarded unfavourably. According to Henry of Huntingdon (writing before 1138), the 1129 crusade to Damascus failed because 'the settlers in the Holy Land had given grave offence to God by their debauchery, rapine, and various crimes, as it is written in the books of Moses and Kings, wickedness in those places shall not long go unpunished'.[81] Such views did not seem widespread at this time, but were precursors to later reactions to the defeat of western armies in the Levant. The Knights Templar were also subject to some discussion in the 1130s. As noted above, they had been involved in recruitment for the Damascus campaign and it is noticeable that, in its aftermath, there were doubts over the Templars' rationale and 'right intention'; while this was more probably connected with the emergence of so radical a concept, these doubts may also have been provoked, if in a small way, by the 1129 expedition.[82]

One final subject of importance in the background to the Second Crusade was the difficult relationship with Byzantium – although the origins of the problem lay decades back in the Schism of 1054 and in the First Crusade. To follow the contradictory twists and turns of contact between the Greeks and the different elements of the Catholic West and the Latin States is beyond the scope of this book. Only four years after Bohemond's attack on Byzantium, for example, Alexius wrote to Paschal II to put himself forward as a protector of the pope against Emperor Henry V of Germany and to suggest that he, Alexius, should receive the imperial crown and subsequently there should be a reunion of the Churches. Many political considerations and calculations lay behind this move, but it is a sign of the complex and multifaceted nature of the political and religious issues of the age that this took place so soon after Bohemond's invasion. Perhaps one might suggest that had Paschal formally endorsed a crusade against the Greeks in 1107, Alexius may have been less willing to negotiate with him so shortly afterwards; but this, of course, is to argue from silence.

Lilie has analysed the relationship between the Greeks and the Latin East very closely. In essence, after a quiet period during the 1120s, active Byzantine interest in northern Syria was rekindled.[83] In 1137–8 Emperor John Comnenus mounted a substantial expedition designed to impose Byzantine control upon the region. Prince Raymond of Antioch and the Catholic hierarchy tried hard to resist this because they did not wish to lose their political independence or to have an Orthodox patriarch imposed upon them. When John surrounded Antioch in 1137 fighting broke out for a short time. Unsurprisingly, this provoked a reaction in the West and Pope Innocent II issued an edict against Latin mercenaries who fought on behalf of the heretical emperor in the Levant.[84] John soon stepped back from a major conflict, unwilling to alienate the Latin West and perhaps fearful of provoking a crusade against himself. Yet given that Raymond was the uncle of the new queen of France, Eleanor of Aquitaine, this was a situation which might have stirred the old anti-Greek feelings in northern Europe. Having made that observation, not everyone saw John's actions as unjust. The contemporary Anglo-Norman writer Orderic Vitalis claimed that King Fulk of Jerusalem argued that 'as we have learned in the past from our elders, Antioch is part of the empire of Constantinople . . . the emperor's claims about the treaties of our ancestors are true as well. Ought we deny the truth . . . ?'[85] In spite of swearing fealty to John, Raymond's tenacious and evasive policies made plain his unwillingness to submit. When distractions elsewhere in the Empire compelled John to leave in 1138 his work was far from complete; four years later he returned to northern Syria and only his death after a freak hunting accident prevented further trouble. As will be shown later, however, Manuel Comnenus was not prepared to let the Antiochenes off the hook and the dispatch of a land and sea force in 1144–5 caused Raymond to travel to Constantinople in person and humble himself at the emperor's feet. Thus there had been considerable friction between the Latin settlers and Byzantium in the decade prior to the Second Crusade, although, as we will see, this did not prevent the papacy, for example, from perceiving relations with the Greeks in a more positive light in 1146–7.

The years between the capture of Jerusalem and the eve of the Second Crusade saw developments in the scope and form of crusading and witnessed the creation and evolution of numerous types of contact between the Latin East and Europe. Taken together, these factors create a context both for the shape and for the events of the Second Crusade; they also contribute towards our understanding of the themes and the targets of the expedition's preachers, as well as helping to explain some of the decisions made by individuals during its course. While the ideas and episodes outlined here were undoubtedly important, it was the memory of the First Crusade that loomed large over the new campaign, and it is the construction of this extraordinarily powerful legacy that forms the subject of the next chapter.

CHAPTER 2

THE LEGACY OF THE FIRST CRUSADE IN WRITING, REPUTATIONS AND ARCHITECTURE

By the late summer of 1147 the progenitors of the Second Crusade could look with confidence upon the formidable series of armies gathered in preparation for holy war; the combination of *Quantum praedecessores* and the emotive preaching of Bernard of Clairvaux and his associates had constituted a highly effective appeal to the sensibilities of Latin Christendom's noble classes. Naturally, the impact of local political and economic circumstances could also affect recruitment, but the papal bull, in particular, lay at the heart of the matter. The content of this document will be considered later on, but this chapter will try to understand why certain themes suggested themselves to Eugenius and Bernard, and to argue that this in turn helps to explain many of the motives for those who took the cross.

In an immediate sense, it was the capture of Edessa by Zengi of Mosul in December 1144 that sparked the embassies to the West and provoked the Second Crusade; in other words, the need to regain Christian territory and to defend the Holy Land from the infidel. Thus, part of the rationale was comparable to that of the First Crusade; namely, a wish to protect Christ's patrimony and to secure the spiritual rewards promised to a crusader – the remission of all sins. By the time Edessa fell it was, after all, almost fifty years since such an offer had been made to so wide an audience. In their analyses of the origins of the First Crusade, historians such as Jonathan Riley-Smith, John Cowdrey and Marcus Bull have laid great emphasis on the centrality of Jerusalem in the religious consciousness of the Latin West.[1] This manifested itself in devotional behaviour such as pilgrimage; in the choice and form of liturgy recited in religious houses; and, as the charter evidence consistently demonstrates, in a wish to free the Holy City from the Muslims. If Jerusalem was prominent in the mindset of the knights and nobles of the West prior to the seizure of the Holy City in 1099, then, after the victory of the First Crusade, one might expect it to be of similar, or greater, allure to their successors; as we will see later, Bernard of Clairvaux emphasised this theme to good effect. This chapter, however, will argue for the prominence of another factor; namely the ongoing recording of how, and by whom, the holy city had been captured. This discussion will endeavour to identify the ways in which memories of the First Crusaders' success were sustained over subsequent decades; it will also demonstrate the various means by which this incredible event came to be so deeply ingrained in the collective memory of the West as to form a literary, cultural and political landmark. A study of these ideas will, therefore, establish a broader context for many of the preaching messages employed by the church authorities between 1145 and 1149. In between the immediacy of the events at Edessa and the overarching spirituality of the time stands the legacy of the First Crusade; the prime contention here is that this 'post-history' of the 1099 expedition holds the key to understanding why so many people took the cross almost fifty years later.

The capture of Jerusalem in July 1099 was greeted with delight, thanks and considerable amazement by the crusaders and their co-religionists in the West. From 1096 onwards the arrival in Europe of a steady stream of deserters suggested that the campaign was doomed but, in spite of incredible hardship, the knights of Christ had managed to triumph in the end. Chroniclers described this divine blessing: Fulcher of Chartres, a participant in the crusade who wrote this section of his *Historia* before March 1106, related: 'It was a time truly memorable . . . because the work the Lord chose to accomplish through His people, His dearly beloved children and family, chosen, I believe, for this task, shall resound and continue memorable in the tongues of all nations until the end of time'.[2] Raymond of Aguilers, another who took part in the First Crusade, described how the crusaders clapped their hands with joy, singing and praying and giving thanks to God, because 'on this day the children of the apostles re-won their city and fatherland for God and their ancestors'.[3] The news of the conquest of Jerusalem provoked similar rapture in the West. Archbishop Manasses of Rheims wrote to Bishop Lambert of Arras in November 1099 thus: 'Be it known to you, dearest brother, that a true and joyful rumour has recently come to our ears, which we believe to have come down not from human knowledge, but from the Divine Majesty – to wit: Jerusalem stands on high with joy and gladness which it has so gloriously received from God in our times. Jerusalem, the city of our redemption and glory, delights with inconceivable joy, because through the effort and incomparable might of the sons of God it has been liberated from most cruel pagan servitude.'[4] In April 1100, Pope Paschal II stated that '[T]he Lord has certainly renewed His miracles of old'.[5]

The victorious crusaders urged their co-religionists to come to the East and help to consolidate the new conquests. In the autumn of 1099 survivors of the campaign began to voyage home and to tell of their adventures, a few enriched in material ways, or with relics, but most endowed with huge prestige and status.[6] The process of retelling and recording the history of the crusade began to memorialise and to enhance their achievement even further. Tales of the campaign quickly started to circulate by word of mouth. In the preface to his *Dei Gesta per Francos*, Guibert of Nogent noted that 'it was not fitting to talk about things other than those already being sung in public'.[7] Even during the expedition, stories about individuals had been broadcast freely – although in some cases at the rather lower level of camp gossip.[8]

Because it is almost impossible to track the oral transmission of the history of the First Crusade, the most effective way to assess the expedition's legacy is through written sources. The rapid circulation of accounts of the crusade bears testimony to the extraordinary interest generated by the events of 1095–9. In many analyses of the crusade's impact on western Europe or of the growth of historical writing in this period, the sheer scale of its literary legacy is often ignored.[9] In fact, it is difficult to think of another event in the medieval period that stimulated such an efflorescence of historical output across Latin Christendom; in turn, the creation of so many accounts of the campaign helped to spread, develop and reinforce the crusaders' achievement further.[10] Of course, the detailed assessment of the size of a medieval author's audience would be far beyond the subject of the present book – an enormously complex matter, to be investigated through the interplay of language, patronage, political circumstances and the copying and survival of manuscripts – but with regard to the history of the Second Crusade, the basic point to recognise is this: a broad sweep of writers took the trouble to cover its predecessor.[11] This overview will not attempt to establish the precise motives of every single writer, nor to understand each particular emphasis or theological refinement within these texts. It is looking to do something more prosaic: to chart the continued recording of the crusade and to follow its permeation into the heart of Christian society as a symbol of piety and honour.

The anonymous southern Italian eye-witness account known as the *Gesta Francorum* was the first narrative to appear. Rubenstein has argued that the *Gesta Francorum*, as we see it today, is 'not a first draft, nor a complete draft of an original text. Rather it is a development of an earlier text, a 'Jerusalem history' which has cut from its source and added to it.'[12] He suggests that this 'Jerusalem history' was probably a compilation of short stories, letters and sermons drawn together in the aftermath of the capture of the holy city. In the form we have at present, the *Gesta Francorum* may actually post-date the work of Peter Tudebode (see below), although, as Rubenstein indicates, in its earlier form the 'Jerusalem history' was the core text.[13] In the very early years of the twelfth century, in conjunction with the reports of returning crusaders, it was copied, adapted and plundered by northern French writers such as Guibert of Nogent, Baldric of Bourgeuil, Robert of Rheims and Gilo of Paris.[14] Guibert wrote his *Dei Gesta per Francos* around 1108–9 for Bishop Lisiard of Soissons. His narrative was not widely copied and has been traced to a few Benedictine and Cistercian houses in north-eastern France, although it also reached the more distant and prestigious abbeys of Clairvaux, Citeaux and Pontigny.[15] Baldric of Bourgeuil became abbot of Dol in Brittany in 1107 and the following year he composed his *Historia*, which achieved moderate popularity.[16] Robert of Rheims probably wrote *c*.1106–7 and his chronicle enjoyed very wide circulation indeed.[17] In the prologue he related: 'Since the creation of the world what more miraculous undertaking has there been (other than the mystery of the redeeming Cross) than what was achieved in our own time by this journey of our own people to Jerusalem? . . . And so it deserves to be publicised through a faithful account as much as to those living, as to now, as for future generations, so that through it Christians' hope in God may be strengthened and more praise inspired in their minds'.[18] Authors of non-crusading texts often included a justification for their writing and tried to demonstrate the value of their subject's actions. For example, William of Malmesbury stated in Book II of his *Gesta Regum Anglorum* that 'an agreeable recapitulation of past events excites its readers, by example, to frame their lives to the pursuit of good or the aversion from evil'.[19] In the case of an ongoing phenomenon such as the crusades, and in light of the potential to secure enormous spiritual rewards, this didactic message was particularly pertinent.

Other early accounts of the crusade include that compiled by Peter Tudebode, a priest from Civray in Poitou whose narrative was, in considerable part, a copy of an early version of the *Gesta Francorum*, augmented by his own eye-witness experiences.[20] Raymond of Aguilers was a participant in the crusade who, with his rarely mentioned co-author, Pons of Baladun, wrote the *Historia Francorum qui ceperunt Iherusalem* by 1101, to provide us with a southern-French perspective on the campaign.[21] The lost work of Gregory Bechada was also southern French, although because he was a knight who wrote in verse and in the vernacular, it offered a rare, non-clerical, viewpoint. As the later Limousin writer, Geoffrey of Vigeois commented: 'Gregory, surnamed Bechada, from the castle of Lastours and a soldier by profession, being a man of considerable refinement and with some grounding in Latin, composed a fittingly massive volume recounting the deeds of these wars in – as I might say – his mother tongue and in popular metre so that the populace might fully comprehend it.'[22] It has been argued that the narrative was commissioned around 1105 to coincide with Bohemond of Antioch's crusading recruitment campaign of the time, although in the event it took too many years to complete to have been used for this purpose. It formed part of a tradition that was reworked in the late twelfth century and is today known as the *Canso d'Antioca*.[23]

One of the most influential accounts of the expedition was that of Fulcher of Chartres who took part in the crusade and was chaplain to Count Baldwin of Boulogne. He settled in Jerusalem in late 1100 and from then until late 1105/March 1106 he wrote the first section of his *Historia Hierosolymitana*.[24] This piece made some use of the *Gesta Francorum* and of Raymond of Aguilers' text, but had much original material to offer. Around the same time as Fulcher worked, two other writers copied and, in some ways, added details to his compositions and polished the style. One of these copies is ascribed to Bartolf of Nangis, the other is known simply as Codex L.[25] Guibert of Nogent made several detailed references to Fulcher's chronicle (or to one of the copyists), albeit in a highly critical tone.[26]

It was not just Anglo-Norman and French writers who chose to recount the events of the capture of the Holy Land; Albert of Aachen presented a Lotharingian perspective in the first section of his *Historia*, composed soon after 1102. This substantial work (120,000 words) is particularly important because it did not rely on the *Gesta Francorum* or its derivatives, but was generated from a combination of the reports of returning crusaders and an early version of the Old French *Chanson d'Antioche*.[27] The Bavarian Ekkehard of Aura wrote his '*Chronicon universale*' and took part in the 1101 crusade; within this text he inserted a section entitled '*Hierosolymita*', probably written in 1102, that combined his own experiences with the brief account of Frutolf of Michelsberg.[28]

The northern Italian city–states of Genoa, Pisa and Venice were all, to different degrees, involved in the crusade and in the first years of Latin settlement. Caffaro of Genoa participated in the conquest of Arsuf and Caesarea in 1101, events that inspired him to begin to write the *Annales* of his native city. This work included details of those episodes and gave a secular northern Italian viewpoint of the crusade.[29] Large numbers of the monastic annals of Europe also mentioned the subject in varying degrees of detail; for example, the chronicle of the abbey of Monte Cassino incorporated sections of the *Gesta Francorum* into its text.[30] Taken together, all of these writers form what we might broadly call a first generation of crusade historians. Their enthusiasm to record this episode bears testament to the unprecedented impact of the First Crusade on the writing and recording of history in the medieval West – and, of course, it reflects the interest shown in the crusade by the people of Europe too.

Quite naturally, in retelling the crusade the deeds of the holy warriors came to the fore and, as a group, they were characterised as Christian super-heroes. Robert of Rheims wrote that 'no matter how much the terrible glint of [enemy] arms glittered from innumerable columns, the splendour of their courage would still outdo it if it were visible. They march out to fight with one mind – not to flee but to die, or win. They do not see death as loss of life, winning is the evidence of divine help.'[31] Certain individuals' bravery was emphasised, sometimes according to the origins of the source and the exigencies of patronage: Raymond of Aguilers focused on the efforts of Count Raymond of Toulouse; the northern French sources highlighted the standing of Godfrey of Bouillon, Robert of Flanders and Hugh of Vermandois; Gregory Bechada told of the bravery of his patron, Gouffier of Lastours. Apart from simply retelling the story of the expedition, some writers took the subject further. As Riley-Smith has shown, in the decade after the fall of Jerusalem, the theology of the First Crusade was given a thorough reworking by Guibert, Robert and Baldric. They told 'of a miraculous demonstration of divine power in a war fought for Christian brothers and for Christ's inheritance by a chosen people, the French lay knights' and, although these accounts of the crusade were obviously idealised, they were 'still recognisably the crusade'.[32] As Riley-Smith concluded, this work gave the crusade a basis for theological as well as popular development, and it enabled the idea of the crusade to become more coherent and theologically sophisticated.[33]

The history of the expedition and of the nascent Latin States continued to receive attention from literary sources in subsequent decades – a second generation of texts. There is no sense, therefore, that the crusade began to fade in collective memory. The verse account of Gilo of Paris, the *Historia vie Hierosolimitane*, was composed in the first two decades of the twelfth century and could, along with that of Robert of Rheims, have employed another, now lost, narrative version of the crusade.[34] A further text, known as the 'Charleville Poet', was a continuation of Gilo's work with extra verse sections that gave greater prominence to the local hero, Godfrey of Bouillon.[35] An important reason why the continuator wrote was to record the deeds of the crusaders – such worthy men who were an example for all to come. He stated: 'My mind moves me to describe the celebrated actions of the great-hearted leaders who strove not only to equal the brave deeds of their fathers by their grand achievement, but to outdo them in deeper faith. I am fired, I say, and my mind is firmly set, to pass on to posterity in verse how, by the impulse and auspicious favour of God, in a memorable fashion, the noble journey was undertaken.'[36]

Ralph of Caen was a Norman who travelled to the East *c*.1107 in the entourage of Bohemond and when the prince died, the author joined the household of his successor, Tancred. Ralph began the *Gesta Tancredi* after Tancred's death in late 1112 and completed it before 1118.[37] In the early 1120s

Albert of Aachen produced the remainder of his *Historia* and continued the story of the crusade into the early decades of the Frankish East; Fulcher of Chartres added two further books to his *Historia*, and Walter the Chancellor composed his *History of the Antiochene Wars* which was in circulation in the West by the 1130s.[38] Accounts of the Latin settlement, therefore, became part of this literary legacy, although in terms of importance it was a subject that ranked a poor second to the capture of Jerusalem. The First Crusade itself remained a golden episode in recent history and, if anything, its reputation became burnished even brighter. William of Malmesbury wrote his extremely popular *Gesta Regum Anglorum* in the 1120s.[39] His lengthy description of the crusade amounted to 46 out of 449 chapters and he acknowledged using the narrative of Fulcher of Chartres, as well as eye-witness accounts. Of course, in the telling of the story the deeds of particular men came to the fore; he described Godfrey and Tancred thus:

> leaders of high renown, to whose praises posterity, if it judge aright, will assign no limits; heroes who from the cold of uttermost Europe plunged into the intolerable heat of the East, careless of their own lives, if only they could bring help to Christendom in its hour of trial . . . Let poets with their eulogies now give place, and fabled history no longer laud the heroes of Antiquity. Nothing to be compared with their glory has ever been begotten by any age. Such valour as the Ancients had vanished after their death into dust and ashes in the grave, for it was spent on the mirage of worldly splendour rather than on the solid aim of some good purpose; while of these brave heroes of ours, men will enjoy the benefit and tell the proud story, as long as the round world endures and the holy Church of Christ flourishes.[40]

Anglo-Norman writers pursued this theme into the next decade. Henry of Huntingdon, who wrote the relevant part of his *Historia Anglorum* before 1138, included a lengthy section on the First Crusade, in part based on the *Gesta Francorum*, but in other respects with no obvious literary source.[41] He too compared the crusaders to classical heroes and also marvelled at their achievement:

> This is the Lord's great miracle, unheard of in all ages, that came about in our own times, that such diverse nations and such courageous noblemen, leaving behind their splendid possessions, wives and sons, all with one mind sought totally unknown places, spurning death! On account of the magnitude of this event, I beg the reader's indulgence for a digression, for it would be impossible to keep silent about the wonderful and mighty works of God, even if I should wish or be compelled to do so. . .[42]

Orderic Vitalis wrote Book IX of his *Ecclesiastical History* in 1135 and revised it in 1139. He relied heavily on Baldric of Bourgeuil's *Historia Ierosolimitana* for much of the relevant detail, but before embarking on the story of the crusade he set out his reasons for including what came to take up an entire Book of his *opus*:

> A tremendous movement is taking place in our own day, and a noble and marvellous theme for exposition is unfolded for writers to study . . . Holy Sion is delivered by her sons . . . Never, I believe, has a more glorious subject been given to historians of warfare than the Lord offered in our own time to poets and writers when he triumphed over the pagans in the East through the efforts of a few Christians, whom he had stirred up to leave their homes through an ardent longing to be pilgrims.[43]

Orderic then mentioned that his friend Baldric had written of the campaign, as had Fulcher of Chartres. 'Many other Latin and Greek writers have treated this memorable subject, and have preserved the great deeds of the heroes for posterity in their vivid writings'.[44] Orderic's work seems not to have been copied, but was well known to other writers such as Robert of Torigny, a monk at nearby Bec.[45] Orderic evidently regarded the crusade as an event of monumental importance.

Flanders was another region to contribute strongly to the First Crusade. Walter of Thérouanne composed a life of Count Charles the Good in late 1127 and this included chapters on earlier counts of Flanders, most particularly the First Crusader, Count Robert, who wore 'the sign of His cross on his upper arm', and whose 'conspicuous virtue and bravery we might commemorate'. Walter related of Robert: 'In that expedition and at the cities of that land, especially at the conquest of Antioch and holy Jerusalem, he gave innumerable very clear examples of his bravery and trustworthiness and much of this is included in the history that is written of the deeds of the Franks who conquered Jerusalem for Christ.'[46] This shows Walter powerfully sustaining the reputation of a First Crusader in the late 1120s and citing literary material to support his claims. He was also using Robert's actions as a way to emphasise the standing of the main subject of his text, Count Charles. In 1133, a monk from the abbey of St Andrew at Cambrai included a concise account of the First Crusade in the annals of his monastery. In a telling aside, he explained why he had not written more about that famous episode. There was, he argued, no point in doing so because the story was better preserved in books and various songs and hymns. Thus the writer shows the ways in which the crusade was remembered and clearly suggests that such records were numerous.[47]

It was not just in northern Europe that the crusade continued to attract attention. Around 1130–40, a monk from the powerful southern Italian monastery of Monte Cassino built upon personal reports and the works of several authors to write a history of the First Crusade and the early years of the principality of Antioch. He utilised Peter Tudebode, the early version of the *Gesta Francorum*, Ralph of Caen and Raymond of Aguilers to create the *Historia Belli Sacri*.[48]

The accomplishments of the First Crusaders, and indeed those of the settlers in the Levant, were seemingly regarded as appropriate reading (or listening) matter for Louis VII of France at the time of his coronation in 1137.[49] William Grassegals, a First Crusade veteran from the Le Puy region, presented the king with a volume that contained copies of the histories of Walter the Chancellor, Fulcher of Chartres and Raymond of Aguilers. William's preface spelt out very plainly his reasons for making the gift and his view of the legacy of the First Crusade. He described the importance of memorialising this great event in writing and he reminded Louis of the behaviour of his ancestors. 'In this way you might look in this book with the eye of reason as if in a mirror at the images of your ancestors – Hugh the Great, Robert, count of Flanders, and others – and you might follow in their footsteps on the path of virtue.' He urged Louis never to fall short of these men in physical exertion and in the use of the temporal sword; William also beseeched the king never to have the volume removed from his or his successors' presence, such was the wisdom contained therein. Given the inclusion of Walter and Fulcher's works, both of which were written in the Levant, Rubenstein has argued that the manuscript originally came from the Holy Land to Velay. William Grassegals then added the introduction and gave the collection to Louis VII as a book of instruction to a young man about to begin his reign; for this old knight, therefore, the deeds of the First Crusaders formed the best possible exemplar for the new king. Assuming that Louis heard these texts (or at least the preface), this is direct evidence of him being exposed to the ideas of the First Crusade, learning of the actions of his predecessors and being encouraged to emulate them.

This flood of literary recordings of the First Crusade and its apparent role as a prompt for future generations meant that it was important for an individual's achievements on the crusade to be recognised; families were concerned to sustain a good reputation acquired in the East. Duke William IX of Aquitaine was a sufficiently skilled and confident orator to spread word of his own adventures on the 1101 crusade. Orderic Vitalis mentioned that the duke 'often recited the trials of his captivity in the company of kings and magnates and throngs of Christians, using rhythmic verses with skilful modulations'.[50] Although he worked in the late twelfth century, the evidence of

Lambert of Ardres, who composed a *History of the Counts of Guines and the Lords of Ardres*, is worth citing here. Lambert related that Lord Arnold the Old of Ardres came back to the West as a great hero, in fact as 'the best of the best among the many nobles of many nations and peoples, because of the strength of his spirit as much as the skill in knighthood of his outstanding body. He fought so that in his strength he might please God's gaze'.[51] Lambert made great play of Arnold's bravery at Antioch, as well as of his subsequent modesty; he also expressed outrage that the singer of the *Chanson d'Antioche* had not included an account of his deeds because, Lambert claimed, Arnold had refused to pay the man what he asked for. In consequence, his role in the crusade was omitted.[52] Clearly there was a strong element of local pride in Lambert's writing, but the importance of stressing Arnold's moral and physical attributes indicated the virtues of a First Crusader. Furthermore, by referring to the singer of the *Chanson d'Antioche* (which was therefore in circulation well before Arnold's death in 1138) Lambert shows that at least one professional was touring northern Europe reciting this epic.[53]

Thus it was not simply the multitude of narrative accounts of the First Crusade that helped to cement the event into the consciousness of the Latin West. Given the limited levels of contemporary literacy, the appearance of *Chansons de Geste* was of huge importance. Some were concerned with events from the expedition, such as the *Chanson d'Antioche* and, from c.1135, the *Chanson de Jérusalem*; others dealt with the wider struggle between Christianity and Islam, as found in the *Chanson de Roland*. In all such instances, the *Chansons* brought the crusade to a far wider and more secular audience than many of the earlier writers could reach. As Geoffrey of Vigeois observed, it was the verse and vernacular format of Gregory Bechada's work that were particularly important in broadening the appeal of his account.[54] The knights and nobles spent evenings together listening to the deeds of their forefathers and the *Chansons* linked the behaviour of crusaders with the knightly ideal to reinforce the perceived worth of such expeditions. The first Old French text of the *Chanson d'Antioche* is from the 1170s, but this extract from the opening section may well demonstrate the tone of what had circulated in earlier decades:

> Be still my lords, leave off your chatter now,
> If you want to hear a glorious song be sung.
> No jongleur ever sang a better song;
> Hold this song in your heart and love it deep,
> It tells a story great, and of brave men.
> You ought to love this song and hold it dear;
> In it you'll find examples of brave men

And other things you'll need to keep in mind.
No better song is sung, as we all know,
About that holy city that we praise,
Where God let weak men pierce and harm His body
Strike it with lance and hang it on a cross,
Jerusalem, by right the city's named.[55]

The *Chanson* also does much to reveal the heroism of various individuals on the crusade, such as Raimbold Croton, the first man over the walls of Jerusalem in 1099.[56] The *Chanson de Roland* described Charlemagne's wars against the Muslims of Iberia and the events connected with the Battle of Roncesvalles in 778 where the Christian rearguard was attacked and defeated. The exact date of the composition of the *Chanson de Roland* is unclear; a version may well have been in circulation in the late eleventh century, but it is thought more likely that it was written fairly soon after the First Crusade because the language and imagery employed in the text are appropriate to events in Iberia and in the Holy Land.[57] Other works connected with Charlemagne and the crusades were the widely known '*Descriptio*' or 'Pilgrimage of Charlemagne to the Holy Land', written in the late eleventh century, and the popular 'Pseudo-Turpin', a Latin prose version of the Roland story which has been described as 'a pious and exemplary crusading tale'.[58]

Crusading imagery could also permeate other contemporary writings. Geoffrey of Monmouth wrote his *Historia regum Brittaniae* in 1136 and chose to employ such ideas several times in his tales of King Arthur. For example, at the Battle of Bath, Arthur hoped that divine help would allow him to take revenge on the pagan Saxons. Archbishop Dubricius urged those 'marked with the sign of the Christian faith' to be prepared to die for their faith and offered that death for anyone killed in the war would be 'as a penance and an absolution for all sins'.[59] This was obviously not a call for a crusade, but it contained many of the key elements of the idea and it shows the relevance of such values to the writer and his audience. Interestingly, one of the dedicatees of Geoffrey's work was Waleran II of Meulan, himself a crusader later on.

Further forms of written evidence to record the success of the First Crusade, or to commemorate the capture of Jerusalem, were songs, hymns and feasts. A text from the abbey of St Martial of Limoges from the early twelfth century has a song, *Jerusalem mirabilis*, which exhorted individuals to make sacrifices to free the land where Christ had lived and to destroy the Saracens. *Jerusalem laetare* is a victory song, preceded by a prose text that praises Godfrey of Bouillon. Around 1100, Archbishop Anselm of Milan encouraged his troops to sing *Ultreia, Ultreia* in preparation for battle.[60] A feast to mark the capture of Jerusalem was held on 15 July and Gerhoh of Reichersberg recorded that this was still celebrated in the West in 1146–7.[61]

It was not just the mere recording of the history of the First Crusade that was important but, as William Grassegals' introduction to the crusade texts presented to Louis VII made clear, in conjunction with accomplishing God's work, the success of the First Crusade also created a benchmark of honour, valour and nobility for knights to measure themselves against. Whether some of the deeds ascribed to individual crusaders were true or not, the principles that underlay the expedition could be used to judge the behaviour of the crusaders themselves, or indeed of any Christian knight.

Duke Robert of Normandy was soon known as 'Robert of Jerusalem', in recognition of his deeds during the crusade and his fame on the campaign was said to have contributed to the relatively comfortable captivity he was placed in by King Henry I of England from 1106 until his death in 1134.[62] In spite of Robert of Normandy's valour on the First Crusade, Robert of Torigny, for example, judged the duke's refusal of the throne of Jerusalem to be the trigger for his dismal career back in the West. He wrote: 'Although the Lord had given Robert great renown for his actions at Jerusalem, yet the duke refused the kingdom of Jerusalem when it was offered to him, preferring to be the slave of rest and idleness in Normandy, rather than to labour for the Lord of kings in His holy city. And therefore the Lord condemned him to eternal idleness in an eternal prison'.[63] Count Robert II of Flanders acquired the sobriquet 'Jerusalem', and Walter of Thérouanne proudly related that 'It is also written that because of the steadfastness of his invincible soul he is called Saint George by the Arabs and the Turks'.[64] Abbot Suger of St Denis described Count Robert as 'a remarkable man who initially won fame and renown among Christians and Saracens for his skill as a warrior during the expedition to Jerusalem'.[65] When recording Robert's death Henry of Huntingdon wrote that the count 'had been illustrious in the Jerusalem campaign. For this reason his memory shall not fade for all eternity'.[66]

On occasion a great crusading warrior could return home and act in a way entirely contrary to the positive reputation he had secured on the expedition. Thomas of Marle was recognised for his bravery at Dorylaeum, Antioch and Jerusalem. He had, however, persecuted the Jews of the Rhineland in 1096 and in the early twelfth century he became known for the atrocities he inflicted on the people and lands around Laon, Rheims and Amiens. Suger described him as 'most accursed . . . like a wolf gone mad . . . [with no] feeling of humanity to the people'.[67] In 1114, a church council anathematised him and stripped him of his knightly status. The following year, just before Louis VI led an assault on Thomas's castle at Crécy-sur-Serre, the clergy turned the idea of holy war against the former crusader. Guibert of Nogent reported that 'the archbishop and bishops . . . assembled the multitude of the faithful and gave them instructions, absolved them of their sins, and ordered them, as an act of penance in full assurance that their souls' would be saved, to go to attack the castle of Crécy'.[68] Riley-Smith has suggested that Thomas was a particularly brutal individual with a violent nature, most suited to warfare, who was involved in a bitter family feud before the crusade, to which he simply returned with greater vigour after 1099.[69]

The notion of the crusade being a reference point of honour continued to hold valid through subsequent decades. In 1142 Brian Fitz-Count, lord of Wallingford, and Bishop Henry of Winchester were in dispute because the former had allegedly confiscated goods that belonged to the bishop. Brian rejected this accusation and then attacked the moral standing of his opponent: he called attention to Henry's own recent behaviour in the ongoing civil war, namely his change of sides from Empress Mathilda to King Stephen. Brian drew a parallel between his own good faith in following the instructions of the Church by supporting Mathilda and the obedience of the First Crusaders to the command of Pope Urban. Brian said that when the pope spoke, everyone responded, including Henry's own father, Count Stephen of Blois. Brian argued that, like the First Crusaders, he had obeyed the Church and sacrificed his land for honour, not for reward. He then challenged the bishop to resolve the matter by arms or by an ordeal. It is interesting that shortly before the Second Crusade individuals were prepared to invoke in their lives the sense of honour created by the First Crusade, and, by implication, God's approval of that enterprise.[70]

It was not just in terms of exemplars of behaviour that the First Crusade exerted a continuing influence. The fame of individual crusaders undoubtedly affected their subsequent careers and this again forms part of the legacy of the expedition. Bohemond of Taranto was probably the greatest warrior on the First Crusade. He was the hero of the *Gesta Francorum*; the circulation of this text prior to his visit to France in 1106 and its intensive use by other writers must have helped to enhance the prince's image considerably. With his story further embellished by a period spent in captivity to the Muslims, Bohemond travelled to northern Europe in 1105–6 in search of a wife and of men for a new crusade.[71] William of Malmesbury wrote that people joined his expedition 'in the hope of bettering themselves, and also of seeing in action at close quarters that living image of valour, whose glorious fame made him talked of everywhere'.[72] Orderic Vitalis provided a vivid account of the prince's arrival in France. People wanted him to be the godfather of their children, the name Bohemond 'was popularised in Gaul, even though it had been virtually unknown to most people in the West'.[73] The prince embarked upon a tour and crowds gathered to hear him describe his exploits. The crusade and the conquest of Antioch had also advanced Bohemond's worth to the ruling houses of Europe. From being the son whom his father Robert Guiscard chose to ignore in the succession of southern Italy, Bohemond could now approach the king of France to marry his daughter – a sign of real standing – and a splendid wedding took place at Chartres in the late spring of 1106.[74] Bohemond's cousin, Tancred, was bethrothed to another of Philip's daughters, Princess Cecilia.[75] The details of Bohemond's efforts to secure military support have been discussed elsewhere, but Orderic Vitalis and Suger made it plain that he was highly successful in raising men for his new crusade – again, a reflection of his profile.[76]

The counts of Boulogne also took great pride in the family's achievements at the head of the crusaders. The local mint struck coins with a lion above the walls of Jerusalem as a reminder of the efforts of Godfrey and Eustace outside the holy city. This was a period of growth in the writing of family histories and several copies of the Boulonnais genealogy were made in northern France in the early twelfth century.[77]

It was not just the leading men who came back from the Holy Land with their status enhanced. In spite of the apparent failure of the 1101 crusade, Count Guy II of Rochefort 'returned from the expedition to Jerusalem renowned and rich'.[78] Guy also received a splendid welcome from the abbot and monks of Morigny, an important Cluniac house about fifty miles south of Paris. Guy had sent a messenger ahead to announce his imminent arrival and he was met by a procession of monks and laymen and received with the greatest honour (honorificentissime suscipitur). The day after this he went to the nearby church of St Arnoult-en-Iveline where even more people came to meet and hear him; these, it was claimed, had travelled from many different areas.[79] In another case, Count Rotrou of Perche 'and many others returned safely and all repossessed themselves of their lands amid the well-deserved praises of their close friends and kinfolk'.[80] The First Crusade offered to some, therefore, a legacy of fame and heroism, and to the families of these individuals it brought the prestige and status of numbering a 'Jerusalemite' amongst them.[81] When a former crusader died it is unsurprising that this aspect of his life was emphasised most. A striking example was the epitaph of Count Eustace of Boulogne, written by a Cluniac monk c.1125:

The present grave of Prince Eustace, by whom France once
prospered, is made famous by [his] arms.
The arms of this man made the Persian Empire tremble,
And Babylon, which was the fear of the world, feared him.
The darkness of Ethiopia reddened with its own blood,
Which the sacred right hand poured out to Christ.
The East was still pale, stunned by the slaughter of its men;

While it fears to be oppressed again by the enemy falling upon them.
Jerusalem the capital having been captured by this duke, he raised
To the stars the battle standards, the royal relics of Christ, deserving to be
venerated.
This man believes in you, Cluny [and] in the hope of his salvation
So that he might please God and himself, with you [Cluny] helping.
A pilgrim coming from distant shores with this hope,
And lo, this man lies dead here, and on his behalf he prays for you.
The golden cross of the twin chapels and the fish of the sea
Proclaims that you may not refuse anything to this oath,
You have prepared your chambers for the limbs of man
Now prepare with this prayer the heavenly kingdom for the Spirit.
And these bones which you bury in a fortunate Sepulchre
After this sojurn, return to his native land.[82]

The success of the First Crusade could also be important to cultural or
ethnic groups rather than just to individuals; the capture of Jerusalem and the
conquest of Antioch formed a notable part of the Normans' sense of achievement. Henry of Huntingdon reported a speech given by an Anglo-Norman
churchman before the Battle of the Standard in Yorkshire in 1138:

Noblemen of England, renowned sons of Normandy, before you go into
battle you should call to mind your reputation and origin: consider well
whom you are and against who[m] you are fighting this battle. For no one
has resisted you with impunity. Bold France, when she had put you to the
test, melted away. Fruitful England fell to your conquest. Wealthy Apulia,
gaining you, renewed herself. Jerusalem the celebrated, and famous
Antioch, both submitted to you.[83]

Ralph of Caen emphasised the importance both of the Normans and of the
French (Gauls) in the First Crusade, while Bull has shown how some chroniclers used the shorthand of *Franci* to denote the shared, northern French,
origins of many of the crusaders and to signal links to the legacy of
Charlemagne.[84]

In conjunction with the written material outlined above there survives a
quantity of visual and physical evidence connected to the success of the First
Crusade and the perpetuation of crusading ideas in the decades thereafter.
Katzenellenbogen has considered the decoration of the great abbey church of
Vézelay, created *c.*1120–32.[85] The church had ties with Cluny and the sense of
mission associated with that abbey can be discerned here too. The tympanum
depicts the mission of the Apostles, an image that can be understood in

crusading terms: Christ had sent out the Apostles and assured them of salvation, whereas now the pope had sent out clerics and laymen and promised them remission of sins. Raymond of Aguilers described the First Crusaders as children of the Apostles.[86] The sculptures also show the prophecies of Isaiah, a text mentioned several times by Robert of Rheims, with the priests and soldiers of the Romans acting in parallel to the clerics and warriors of the First Crusade.[87]

Another set of images linked to crusading is to be found at the church of S.Maria in Cosmedin, Rome.[88] These intriguing frescoes probably date to 1123, the year in which Pope Calixtus II consecrated the church, although he had earlier presented it with relics from the Holy Sepulchre. This was also a time when the pope himself was encouraging crusading activity in both Iberia and the Levant (see pp. 11–12, 246–7). Calixtus came from a crusading background: three of his brothers had died in the 1101 expedition and a fourth one fought the Muslims in Spain; he was also related to the Montlhéry clan, the ruling family in Jerusalem.[89] The interpretation of these frescoes is difficult because they are so badly damaged. Some scholars believe they tell the Old Testament story of Ezekiel (an example rarely used in manuscripts or monuments), which concentrates on the idea of pollution of holy places by false gods – a dominant theme in the preaching of the First Crusade.[90] The frescoes also show the threat from the Babylonian ruler Nebuchadnezzar but they end the story on a suitably inspiring note with the massacre of the godless and the triumph of the Three Hebrews. The depiction of such events would have symbolised the success of the First Crusaders and encouraged the fight against the infidel. Earlier views on the images, however, associated them with the life of Charlemagne and his struggle against evil.[91] As someone not qualified to judge on matters of art history, I cannot suggest which interpretation is the more plausible; however, in terms of this study the answer is actually irrelevant, since both views favour a fundamental connection with a depiction of holy war in a prominent public place.

The town of Le Puy was an important stop for Urban II as he prepared to launch the First Crusade in the late summer of 1095. It is unsurprising, therefore, that its cathedral contains images with biblical scenes, including the entry of Christ into Jerusalem and a scroll containing the lines: 'Rejoice and exult with all your heart, O daughter of Jerusalem!' (Zephaniah 3: 14). This, according to Derbes, should be seen as a memorial to Bishop Adhémar of Le Puy, who played a leading role in the First Crusade and died after the capture of Antioch in the autumn of 1098.[92] The ceiling fresco from the crypt at Auxerre cathedral has a scene from the Book of Revelation (19: 11–16) with Christ on horseback, surmounting a huge cross and with a mounted angel in each quadrant. Denny has linked this image to the triumph of the First

Crusade and to the episcopate of Humbaud (1092–1114), an individual known as a patron of the arts, a keen supporter of the crusade movement and a man who died on the return journey from a pilgrimage to Jerusalem.[93] Similarly, Seidel argues that the triumphal arch in the entrance porch of the church of Moissac, an object dated to the 1120s and modelled on the Arch of Titus, conqueror of Jerusalem in AD 70, has a strong link with the First Crusade. Moissac is in the lands of Raymond of St Gilles, count of Toulouse and founder of the county of Tripoli. It has been described as 'a haven for crusade propaganda'; it also had links with Urban II and the papal court in Rome.[94] The images at Moissac illustrated the 'belief that the recent Christian victory in Jerusalem followed a tradition of providential events regarding control of the holy sites' and again emphasised the achievement of the First Crusade.[95] Camille extends this idea further by connecting the depiction at Moissac of the fall of the idols (found in the book of Matthew) with 'then current concerns with Christian reconquest of the Holy Land'.[96] Another example from a town in the south-west of France with intimate links with the crusade movement, is the façade of the cathedral of St Gilles du Gard. This monument features the entry into Jerusalem, the casting down of the Dome of the Rock and other images derived from the cathedral's position in the heart-lands of a major crusading dynasty as well as its role as a Cluniac-controlled house.[97]

The involvement of Cluny in the crusades is much debated, but in the early twelfth century Abbot Hugh initiated a programme of mural paintings at the nearby chapel of Berzé-la-Ville. Lapina has studied these and posited that they focus on the need to evangelise non-Christians, instead of taking a more belli-cose approach. This is a further example of the First Crusade – and, in this case, of the reconquest of Spain – appearing in artistic form.[98] When Fulk V of Anjou became king of Jerusalem in 1131 his county acquired close ties to the Latin East; this may be one reason why the church of Cunault has a capital depicting a Christian knight fighting a devilish Saracen.[99] A different body of visual evidence connected with the early crusades appears in the form of St George either defeating his Saracen enemies, as revealed on a doorway at Fordington near Dorchester, or slaying the dragon, as he is shown in the fresco at Poncé-sur-le-Loir. St George was believed to have assisted the First Crusaders at the Battle of Antioch in 1098 and the early twelfth century saw a number of such images being created, for instance those at Ferrara cathedral, the mosaics at Ganagobie in Provence and the capitals at St Georges-de-Boscherville in Normandy.[100] Finally, one might note that scenes from the *Song of Roland* also began to appear in churches. The knights who adorn the lintels of Angoulême cathedral are regarded as portraying parts of the Roland story; at Verona cathe-dral, from *c.*1139, statues of Roland and Oliver were added to the portals, and in the same city the Church of St Zeno shows images of Roland fighting the pagans, again reinforcing the connection with holy war.[101]

Morris has analysed western Europe's ongoing interest in the veneration of the Church of the Holy Sepulchre.[102] The practice of constructing churches on the pattern of the Holy Sepulchre existed before the First Crusade; but the events of 1099 encouraged this further with replicas being built at Cambridge (c.1130) and at Northampton by the First Crusader Simon of Senlis on his return (before c. 1116). The church of Santo Stefano, Bologna had a special affinity with Jerusalem that dated back to the ninth century; within its octag-onal central structure there was a copy of the Holy Sepulchre itself, possibly originating from the period 1117 to 1141.[103] Morris has also noted other copies at Asti in Piemonte (dating from the return of Bishop Landulf from the Levant in 1103), at Orphir in the Orkneys (built by Earl Hakon Paulsson), at Lanleff in Brittany, and at Helmarhausen in northern Germany. These wide-spread examples indicate how the visibility of the physical goal of the First Crusade – while, admittedly, already a central part of religious life in the West – grew further in the twelfth century.

One of the most obvious consequences of the creation of the Latin States was the opening up of the Holy Land to western pilgrims. The originators of the First Crusade had laid considerable emphasis on the importance of protecting pilgrims as a reason to take the cross back in 1095, and the oppor-tunity for westerners to complete their penitential journeys was enhanced by the capture of Jerusalem. The involvement in the Levant of the Italian trading cities of Genoa, Pisa and Venice, along with the southern French ports of Marseilles and Montpellier, meant that it was much easier to reach the Holy Land and this fact, along with the Catholic control of the holy sites, encour-aged a flood of new visitors. The history of pilgrimage to the Levant is a huge topic in itself, but a number of pertinent points can be drawn out here. First, pilgrims from all over western Europe venerated the holy sites. The cartularies and narratives of the time are peppered with the grants and arrangements of individuals who went to the East. Furthermore, these people came from all areas; in other words, visiting the holy city was important to people right across the Catholic West, and the attraction of Jerusalem was sufficient to persuade large numbers to make the journey with its attendant risks and expense.[104] The stories of these pilgrims would, in turn, further augment the profile of the land in which, to the minds of the people of the West, Christ was sacrificed. Those who made the pilgrimage could be of high standing, such as King Eric of Denmark and his wife, who went c.1103; Count Henry of Portugal, who visited c.1103; Hugh, count of Champagne, who travelled to the East c.1104–8, and in 1114, and finally became a Templar in 1125; or Pons, former abbot of Cluny, who visited c.1122.[105] Others are less familiar or otherwise unknown: Viscount Bernard of Comborn gave lands to the abbey of Tulle before his journey in 1119; Robert, the mayor of Ver, near Chartres, went to Jerusalem c.1115; Stephen, from the same area, went c.1131–41.[106] Numbers of pilgrims came from imperial lands in Germany, for example Count Dudo of Wettin in 1125; others travelled from the Iberian Peninsula, such as John of Clariana in 1126. Some pilgrims were former First Crusaders; these included for instance Ralph of Montpinçon, who died en route to the Holy Land in 1110 – a fate later shared by his aunt Mathilda's lover, Matthew, and by Mathilda herself, who passed away at Jaffa.[107] The list could be amplified one hundred-fold, but the key point is this: western European enthusiasm for pilgrimage grew dramatically and the tangibility and importance of a Christian hold on the earthly Jerusalem became ever stronger.

Some pilgrims chose to write guides to their experiences and these soon circulated widely in the West. Once again, a sample list brings out the geographical diversity of those who travelled to the Levant. The English traveller Saewulf visited in 1101–3; the Russian cleric, Abbot Daniel, in 1106–8; an anonymous German author, in 1102–6; another anonymous writer left a description that found its way into the 1137 collection of Peter the Deacon, librarian of Monte Cassino; while finally, the Icelandic monk Abbot Nikulas of Pverá, made his journey c.1140.[108]

Crusaders and pilgrims might also bring back relics from their visits to the Holy Land and these acted as a permanent visual link to the East and to the spiritual events of its history. A couple of examples will serve to illustrate this widespread practice. Arnold the Old of Ardres transported relics of the True Cross, the Lord's beard, some of the stone from which the Lord ascended into Heaven, a piece of the holy lance from Antioch and relics of St George to the church of St Mary of Capella, near Ardres.[109] On behalf of his brother Godfrey of Bouillon, Eustace of Boulogne conveyed Marian relics to his mother and these were placed in the abbey of Capelle.[110] The chronicle of St Peter's at Sens related the story of Alexander, chaplain of Stephen of Blois, who presented to the abbey relics, originally given to his master in Jerusalem in 1102, of the True Cross, of the Holy Sepulchre, of a tooth of St Nicholas and of the body of St George; they were received with all due ceremony in October 1120.[111] The dispatch of other artefacts such as ampullae and coins depicting Jerusalem might also add to this picture.[112]

To summarise, in the aftermath of the capture of Jerusalem, an unprecedented burst of historical writing memorialised this remarkable event across Latin Europe. The authors in question emphasised divine approval, the bravery and honour of the crusading heroes and the importance of the holy city itself. Crucially, this interest was sustained over the subsequent decades, and the crusade became a benchmark for moral behaviour and a core element of knightly values. People began to place non-crusading events in a crusading context, for instance the 1142 dispute of Brian Fitz-Count noted above. In conjunction with this, physical reminders of the First Crusade and of the Holy Land emerged in and on buildings as well as through objects brought back by pilgrims, traders and crusaders. I am not suggesting, however, that simply because a knight had seen, for example, an image of Roland on a church doorway, that he would have taken the cross. But the numerous depictions of holy war in prominent public places do help to demonstrate a high level of importance and approval of the idea. Thus, when Eugenius and Bernard came to compose *Quantum praedecessores* and their crusade appeals, they did so against a background on which the achievements of the First Crusaders and the allure of Jerusalem were writ conspicuously and invitingly large.

CHAPTER 3

QUANTUM PRAEDECESSORES
THE CRUSADE APPEAL OF POPE EUGENIUS III –
CONTEXT AND CONTENT

On 1 December 1145, Pope Eugenius III addressed the bull *Quantum praede-cessores* to King Louis VII and the nobles of France. This marked the formal launch of what has become known as the Second Crusade. The bull was re-issued in March 1146 and it formed the bedrock of papal crusade appeals for decades to come.[1] In 1165, Pope Alexander III chose to base the bulk of his crusade call on *Quantum praedecessores*, and the following year his next entreaty to help the Holy Land also borrowed heavily from the older text.[2] We can still see the influence of *Quantum praedecessores* in Alexander's 1169 *Inter omnia*, and more distantly in his 1181 *Cor nostrum*, reissued in 1184/5 by Lucius III.[3] The content of Eugenius's bull represented, therefore, a landmark in the development of crusading. It was a drawing together and clarification of ideas and privileges, many of which had been expressed before but do not survive in a formal document and, for Eugenius's contemporaries and successors, were best combined in *Quantum praedecessores*. The fact that references are made back to his bull, rather than to some earlier text, bears testimony to this.

The later history of *Quantum praedecessores* is not of major concern here; more significant was its impact over the period 1145 to 1147 when the Second Crusade was getting underway. Probably the most outstanding feature of the crusade to the Holy Land was the huge scale of recruitment as Louis and Conrad led two substantial armies to the East. *Quantum praedecessores* must take a considerable amount of credit for inspiring this; while, as we will see later, the efforts of Bernard of Clairvaux and his Cistercian colleagues have attracted greater attention, the charisma of the 'mellifluous doctor' has dazzled some writers in their assessment of the reasons behind this huge response.[4] As an official crusade bull *Quantum praedecessores* was, after all, the centrepiece of the Church's recruitment drive and it reached at least as wide an audience as Bernard and his letters, simply because it must have accompanied every official preacher of the expedition.

The pervasive influence of *Quantum praedecessores* can also be judged by the absorption of some of its ideas into other contemporary writings. Examples include the anonymous trouvère song *Chevalier, mult estes guariz*, which was designed to encourage support for the expedition and dates from 1146–7 (see Appendix 2, below).[5] This song was originally composed in Old French; it is not known whether the author listened to *Quantum praedecessores* in Latin and understood it or whether he heard the bull translated into the vernacular during preaching sermons. Eugenius's bull is also apparent in the account of the capture of Lisbon, *De expugnatione Lyxbonensi* – a work originally written in 1147, although it survives today in a manuscript dating from the late 1160s.[6]

Quantum praedecessores was issued in response to appeals from the Latin settlers in the Levant after the fall of Edessa in December 1144. Writers record the dispatch of embassies from Antioch and Jerusalem, although the identity of these envoys and the content of their letters are unknown.[7] The time lapse between the Muslims' capture of Edessa and the issue of *Quantum praedecessores* has been much discussed. The inevitable confusion after the loss of the city and the time taken for the news to reach Jerusalem via Antioch (a distance of *c.*450 miles), in winter, would account for several weeks. Edessa to Antioch is *c.*140 miles as the crow flies, but the direct route to the principality through Aleppo was blocked; a detour northwards via Marash at *c.*170 miles was a safer – if slower – option. There must have been a period of consultation in the holy city before envoys were sent to the West. It was unlikely that a vessel departed before mid-March anyway; the voyage from the Levant to Italy – against the prevailing winds – took at least 10 weeks and there was also the possibility of delays caused by storms.[8] This means it was unrealistic for the papal court to have heard about the disaster until May at the earliest. Historians who accuse Eugenius of a casual response to the crisis are perhaps, therefore, a little unwarranted in their criticism.[9] Back in 1119, the defeat at the Battle of the Field of Blood prompted envoys to the West, a papal appeal to Venice and some further, if hard to discern, efforts to organise help.[10] As we saw earlier, in July 1121 Calixtus II wrote that the papacy was 'working on [the settlers'] behalf every day both beyond the Alps and this side of them'.[11] The response to this call to arms materialised in the form of a Venetian fleet that set sail on a successful campaign in August 1122. Thus there was little precedent for Eugenius to react rapidly to a crisis in the Levant and to initiate an immediate and fully organised international preaching tour.

Simply because *Quantum praedecessores* was not issued until 1 December does not, however, mean that the papacy was uncaring or passive; in fact, the reverse was the case and the content of the bull gives the proof of this. Eugenius and his associates laboured hard to produce a carefully structured and closely researched appeal, which would form a proper basis for a major crusading expedition – one that, with the planned participation of a king, was already breaking new ground. To compose a document of this sort was not the work of a day.[12] Before analysing the content of *Quantum praedecessores* it is important to establish the circumstances in which it was published. First, it is worth sketching Eugenius's earlier career and background, as well as looking at some of his earlier papal bulls. It is also useful to identify the circle of people around him, individuals whose experiences and advice may well have affected the content of the bull and who would become closely involved in the expedition's launch.

Bernard Paganelli was the son of the lord of Montemagno, near Lucca.[13] He embarked upon a career in the Church, at Pisa, and by 1134 had risen to the position of *vicedominus* – that is, a deputy to the bishop. Pisa was closely involved in the First Crusade, possessed relics from the Holy Land and took part in the ongoing trade with the Levant; furthermore the city had been the target of an appeal for help from the patriarch of Jerusalem in 1134.[14] Pisa had also contributed to the successful crusade against the Balearic Islands during 1113–15, an episode celebrated in an inscription on the city gate.[15] Innocent used Pisa as his principal refuge during the papal schism and in 1135 the city hosted a church council that represented a substantial gathering of his supporters, many of whom would later play a prominent role in the Second Crusade.[16] Bernard Paganelli was present at this assembly and it is likely that here he met his namesake, the abbot of Clairvaux. It seems that the Italian was profoundly moved by this experience and decided to leave his position at Pisa and become a monk at Clairvaux. Four years later Bernard of Pisa was sent to reform the monastery of Scandriglia, just north-east of Rome, but in 1140 he wrote to Abbot Bernard and to Innocent II to complain about the lack of progress.[17] He also made no secret of his admiration for Abbot Bernard and of the fact that he looked to him as a source of guidance: 'I have lost sight of the pattern on which I tried to fashion myself, the mirror of what I ought to be, the light of my eyes! No longer does that sweet voice sound in my ears, nor that kindly and pleasant face, which used to blush at my faults, appear before my eyes'.[18] The pope responded by transferring the monks to S. Anastasius-apud-Tres-Fontes, a house recently given to the Cistercians by Pope Innocent. The abbey was in a swampy district and some of the monks contracted malaria; nonetheless, Bernard of Pisa soon imposed a rigorous regime onto his flock and his mentor wrote to congratulate the brethren on their close observance of the Cistercian Rule.[19]

On 15 February 1145 Pope Lucius II died of injuries suffered while fighting the Romans, and the cardinal-bishops of Rome gathered in the monastery of Saint Caesarius to choose his successor. They feared interference from the

Roman people and settled upon Lucius's replacement within a day. To everyone's surprise, they unanimously selected Bernard of S. Anastasius-apud-Tres-Fontes.[20] On 18 February he was consecrated as pope and took the name of Eugenius III. Bernard of Clairvaux's shocked reaction to this appointment is at the root of many of the less glowing assessments of Eugenius's career. The abbot wrote to the *curia*: 'God have mercy on you; what have you done? ... What reason, what counsel, made you, as soon as the late pope had died, suddenly rush upon this rustic, lay hands upon him when hiding from the world, and, knocking away his axe, mattock or hoe, drag him to the palatine, place him upon a throne, clothe him in purple and fine linen, and gird him with a sword ... ? Had you no other wise and experienced man amongst you who would have been better suited to these things? ... Ridiculous or miraculous? Either one or the other ... I fear that he may not exercise his apostolate with sufficient firmness.'[21] This famous passage surely holds an element of hyperbole on Bernard's part, something frequently seen in his writings. In reality, in the traumatic circumstances of Lucius's death it is hard to imagine the cardinal-bishops selecting such an unworldly pope at this time of crisis. Given the speed of Eugenius's election he must have been reasonably well known to many of the cardinals in order for them to have voted him in unanimously. Notwithstanding this initially lukewarm assessment, Bernard quickly offered his full support to the new pontiff – who was, after all, the first Cistercian monk to ascend to the chair of Saint Peter. Bernard also recognised that Eugenius was a popular choice when he wrote that 'the whole Church ... has a confidence in you such as she does not seem to have had for a long time in your predecessors'.[22]

Three contemporaries offer us further insight into Eugenius's character. John of Salisbury, who was present at the papal court between 1149 and 1152, depicted a stern yet thoughtful man who was independent-minded and suspicious of others – 'unless he were convinced by his own personal experience or the highest authority'.[23] Boso, the biographer of popes of this period, praised Eugenius's eloquence, wisdom and generosity.[24] Another contemporary, Robert of Torigny, indicated that the pope had an interest in academic matters because he ordered the works of Saint John the Damascene to be translated from Greek into Latin.[25] It is, nonetheless, the pervasive words of Abbot Bernard that have tended to colour the historians' views of Eugenius and of his suitability to steer a crusade; in turn, this has caused them to assign Bernard an overwhelmingly dominant role. Barber writes that the abbot 'almost single-handedly put together a crusade which neither pope nor king [Louis VII] had been able to launch on their own, and consequently the Second Crusade bears Bernard's stamp'.[26] Likewise, Hiestand argues that 'the propaganda and the preaching of the Second Crusade [were] not the work of the pope but that of Bernard of Clairvaux, his fellow-abbots and [his chancery] ... The Second Crusade was not Eugenius III's but Bernard of Clairvaux's crusade'.[27] Tyerman, too, gives the sense that Eugenius was 'remarkably passive'. He described him as 'chronically insecure', needing a 'schoolmasterly' prompt from Bernard to focus on the expedition; the abbot, meanwhile, 'made the crusade his'.[28] But these assessments are too simplistic: they do Eugenius a considerable disservice and also fail to take into account the formidable body of churchmen present at the papal *curia*, a group whose close relationships with him – and between themselves – were of genuine relevance to the genesis of the expedition. When one examines the personnel in attendance on, or in contact with, the *curia* at this time, a different picture emerges.

Alberic, cardinal-bishop of Ostia, was one of the most important figures in Eugenius's administration.[29] He was a Cluniac who became sub-prior at the great abbey, then prior at the church of St Martin-des-Champs in Paris, before he rose to the bishopric of Vézelay by 1131. He was present at the Council of Pisa in 1135, and on 3 April 1138 Pope Innocent II appointed him cardinal-bishop of Ostia. He soon set out on his first legation – to England and Scotland where he met the chronicler Richard of Hexham. Richard was very impressed with the legate and described him as 'eminent of learning, both sacred and secular, of much experience in ecclesiastical works, of remarkable eloquence and sound advice; and, what is far beyond all this, he gave proof in behaviour and appearance, and in fact by all his conversations and actions, of great goodness and piety'.[30] He met King David of Scotland and King Stephen of England, held a synod in London, and settled upon a new appointment to the archbishopric of Canterbury.[31] Back in Rome for the Second Lateran Council in 1139 he soon headed off on his next legation, this time to the Holy Land. Abbot Peter the Venerable of Cluny wrote of his sadness and anxiety at seeing his friend depart on this dangerous journey and described him in glowing terms as 'the sole solace of our Order (*ordinis*) and heart'.[32]

Alberic witnessed a campaign at Banyas, where his exhortations were said to have inspired the troops, and he held a synod at Antioch that deposed Patriarch Ralph. The legate then called a synod at Jerusalem (1141) where the Armenian *catholicos* discussed dogma and professed a number of orthodox beliefs; Alberic also oversaw the consecration of the church on the site of the Dome of the Rock. [33] He was back in Rome in March 1144 before departing on a legation to France where he resolved various ecclesiastical disputes that included problems at Morigny and his old house at Vézelay.[34] He may have interrupted this journey to be in Italy for the consecration of Eugenius in February 1145 where his legation was reconfirmed. Alberic spent the summer in France, working with Bernard of Clairvaux and Bishop Geoffrey of

Chartres in the struggle against heresy, as will be seen below. He was in Viterbo by mid-November 1145 in the build-up to the issue of *Quantum praedecessores*, and was in almost constant attendance on the pope during 1146; Alberic also joined with Eugenius on his journey north through Italy and France to Paris in the first half of 1147.[35] He was clearly a trusted advisor and a man possessed of a wide range of diplomatic abilities, as well as considerable contemporary knowledge of the Holy Land.

Another figure close to Eugenius was his fellow-Pisan, cardinal-deacon Guido of SS. Cosmas and Damian. Guido had been the papal legate to Spain and Portugal and he went to the peninsula in 1134, 1135–7 and 1143.[36] Constable notes his presence at the Council of Burgos (1136), where remission of sins was promised to the Confraternity of Belchite, and he oversaw the Council of Gerona (1143), where Count Ramon Berenguer IV of Barcelona made a substantial grant of land to the Templars.[37] Guido was at the Council of Pisa in 1135 and later that year he went to Milan along with Bernard of Clairvaux and Bishop Geoffrey of Chartres to try to reconcile the citizenry with Pope Innocent II. Guido was appointed papal chancellor in late 1146, although he had been with Eugenius at the *curia* from June 1145. Like Alberic, he remained with the pope during 1146 and on his journey to France in early 1147, but in April he branched away from the main party, to Germany, in order to assist in preparations for the governance of the Empire during Conrad's absence.[38]

Theodwin of Santa Rufina was a long-standing papal legate with expertise in German matters. He had been to the Empire in 1135 and 1136 and was responsible for the coronation of Conrad III in 1138. He made further visits to the king in 1140 and 1142 but was present at Eugenius's court from March to June 1145.[39] It seems that he was dispatched north again in August 1145 to help settle Germany and he appeared at Corvey with another papal representative, Thomas, cardinal-priest of San Vitale.[40] By September of 1146 he had returned to the *curia*, but in the early spring of 1147 Eugenius sent him back to Germany to support Conrad's crusade preparations.[41]

Robert Pullen was Eugenius's chancellor and the first Englishman ever appointed to the ranks of the cardinals, as cardinal-priest of SS Martin and Sylvester. He was evidently admired by Bernard of Clairvaux who wrote to him in early 1145 and urged him to watch over the new pope and make sure he made prudent decisions.[42] Robert was alongside Eugenius at the time of the launch of *Quantum praedecessores* but died in September 1146.[43]

Imar of Tusculum was another Cluniac and, like Alberic, a product of the church of St Martin-des-Champs in Paris. He went to France and England on legations in 1144–5, was a correspondent of Abbot Bernard and was at the *curia* from December 1145 through most of 1146. He then accompanied the pope to Italy and France in the following year.[44]

Two other senior figures in the ecclesiastical community of Latin Christendom were in Eugenius's company when the crusade appeal was issued: Peter the Venerable and Otto of Freising. The former was, between 1122 and 1156, abbot of the internationally influential Cluniac Order, with its countless houses across the heartlands and frontiers of Christendom. Peter was a correspondent of many of the leading figures of the day, including King Louis VII of France, Alberic of Ostia, Bernard of Clairvaux and the pope himself; he attended the Council of Pisa and the Second Lateran Council of 1139. Notwithstanding the fact that Pope Urban II was a Cluniac, the Black Monks' role in the origins of the First Crusade has been widely debated.[45] One aspect of Cluny's involvement in crusading is perceived to relate to an interest in the idea of conversion, something that had been apparent in the abbey's activities in the Iberian Peninsula. Abbot Hugh (1049–1109) had urged the hermit Anastasius to preach to the Saracens of Spain in 1073–4.[46] In 1087 Hugh wrote to the Cluniac archbishop of Toledo and encouraged him to 'preach the word of God fearlessly and constantly to those who hitherto, owing to our sins, have not shown proper honour to their Creator'; further-more, he was to 'dispense faithfully the word of God through arguing, beseeching and rebuking in all patience and leaning to the learned and unlearned, to Christians and Unbelievers'.[47] As noted above, Lapina has drawn attention to the theme of conversion in the wall-paintings of Berzé-la-Ville, created soon after the First Crusade.[48] Furthermore, Katzenellenbogen hypothesises that it was Peter the Venerable who, during his spell as prior of Vézelay earlier in his career, may have conceived the design of the tympanum there with its strong message of apostolic mission.[49]

In 1142–3 Peter visited Spain, probably at the request of Alfonso VII of León-Castile (1126–57). He began an intensive study of Islam, wrote the polemical text *Liber contra sectam sive haeresim Saracenorum* and commis-sioned a translation of the Koran designed to refute Islamic belief. His book claimed that he addressed Muslims 'not, as our men often do, with arms, but with words; not with force, but with reason; not in hatred, but in love'.[50] Kedar has pointed out that there are tensions between these sentiments and Peter's support for the Second Crusade, but a broader point concerning Cluniac interest in conversion as a part of the genesis of the Second Crusade remains valid.[51] With regard to the build-up to the launch of *Quantum praedecessores*, Peter was actually with Eugenius from November 1145 until February 1146.[52]

Otto of Freising is (and was) well known as the author of *De civitatibus duabus* and the *Gesta Friderici I Imperatoris*.[53] He was a former Cistercian monk from the abbey of Morimond and had been bishop of Freising since

1137; he was also the half-brother of King Conrad III, no less. Otto knew Theodwin of Santa Rufina from the former's legations to Germany and he was at the *curia* in November and December 1145, as related in *De civitatibus duabus* and shown in papal documents.[54]

Eugenius, Alberic, Guido, Theodwin, Robert, Imar, Peter and Otto constituted a formidable network. They were men from a variety of backgrounds – Cistercian, Cluniac and Benedictine – who had led legations across the Latin world to areas that either were to be a target of the Second Crusade, such as the Holy Land, Spain, and Germany; or/and were to be major contributors to the Christian armies. From this group, as well as the continuing arrival of further envoys, Eugenius must have had a wealth of relevant advice and information on developments across the Catholic world. The political situation in Germany, for example, a region fraught with difficulties at this time, had to be resolved so as to enable any worthwhile participation from the Empire; hence the legate for Germany, Theodwin of Santa Rufina, was sent there in the autumn of 1145. [55] Several of the individuals noted above, such as Alberic, Guido and Theodwin, had recent experience of conflict with non-Christians and they could have been especially useful to the pope. It may also be relevant that most of those mentioned above were at the 1135 Council of Pisa. This assembly met at a time of huge tension in the schism between Innocent II and Anacletus and issued decrees that elevated the status of the struggle with the antipope and his supporter, Roger II of Sicily, to a holy war. All who served or traded with the Sicilian or Anacletus were anathematised, and to those who 'set out against them by land or sea to free the Church, and labour faithfully in that service, the same remission was granted which Pope Urban decreed at the Council of Clermont for all who set out for Jerusalem to free the Christians'.[56] Housley indicates that, while this equated with Urban's indulgences, it remains unknown whether it was a call to a formal crusade with a vow and cross-taking ceremony.[57] With regard to the personnel we are concerned with here, this shows a link to the development of crusading ideology and to turning the focus of a twelfth-century holy war against targets other than Iberia or the Holy Land. By the time of the crusade, far from being the rather unworldly and naïve monk depicted by Bernard of Clairvaux and fixated upon by historians, Eugenius was in a position to possess a genuine insight into crusading and the frontiers of Christendom. This range of knowledge must have had some impact on the conception and content of *Quantum praedecessores* as well as on the preaching and recruitment of the expedition. It was also, potentially, a factor that made the pope more receptive to approaches to broaden the scope of the crusade and helped him to respond to unfolding circumstances. To give two examples: first, as we will see later, cordial relations between Alberic of Ostia and the senior figures of the

Armenian church hierarchy – initiated during the former's legation to the Holy Land – must have enhanced the reception given to the Armenian embassy to the West in late 1145. Secondly, the concept of conversion emerged from time to time during the Second Crusade and, as we have seen with regard to the First Crusade, it is an idea that historians have connected to the Cluniacs. Hitherto, the strong Cluniac presence around the Second Crusade has been ignored because of a general perception of Cistercian domination, but in the case of the 1145–9 expedition it did, from time to time, appear to form part of what one might call the overall topography of the campaign.

Aside from the personnel around him, the narratives and letters pertinent to the early months of Eugenius's pontificate reveal four issues of particular currency, and these can be connected with what was to follow; in essence, it is evident that, prior to the issue of *Quantum praedecessores*, Eugenius had already engaged with a variety of challenges to the papacy and opponents of the Christian faith.

First, in May 1145, he issued a bull that granted the *pallium* to Archbishop Bernard of Tarragona in eastern Spain and encouraged the recovery of the same city.[58] In itself, this act had two points of note: first, in doing so, Eugenius was – pretty routinely – following in the footsteps of his predecessors Gelasius II and Lucius II, who in turn had looked back to a grant made by Urban II in a bull now lost.[59] The texts of the three surviving bulls that concerned the grant of the *pallium* are very similar indeed; there is a sense that such encyclicals were often derivative works. The papacy, as an institution which gained some of its authority through reference to precedent, would naturally seek to build upon that. In the case of the recapture of Tarragona, apart from the brief updating of personnel involved, the need to re-cast a new text every time seems redundant anyway. Eugenius copied Gelasius's letter almost verbatim and Lucius used large sections of it too. Secondly, with regard to the Second Crusade, this shows that Eugenius had some level of engagement with one aspect of the ongoing reconquest, although – crucially – neither his bull of May 1145 for Tarragona, nor its predecessors, made explicit promises of spiritual rewards; rather, they simply placed the action in a broader context of the Christian–Muslim struggle. At this point, therefore, Eugenius seemed neither willing nor inclined to initiate a new crusade in Iberia. For this to happen required an ongoing expedition to the Holy Land and the stimulus of lay rulers to take the lead. Urban II had, of course, made a formal call to help Tarragona in a letter sent to several Catalan nobles *c.*1096–9, in which he stressed the need 'to make a vigorous effort to restore [the Church] in every way possible for the remission of sins'.[60] It was another of Pope Gelasius's bulls, the one directed at the capture of Zaragoza, that raised the offer of spiritual rewards for fighting in the peninsula.[61]

A further connection between Spain and the crusades to date from the early period of Eugenius's pontificate was through his support for the Military Orders. In April 1145 he issued the Templars with the bull *Militia Dei* which safeguarded their independence at parish level and did much to strengthen their financial position.[62] The following month Eugenius granted the remission of one-seventh penance of sins to those who provided help for the Hospitallers in Jerusalem or to the Templars in Spain, and in November he issued a bull that stressed the Templars' work in defending the Church in the Orient and emphasised that Spanish churchmen should not appropriate or infringe upon their property or rights.[63]

The second episode of interest concerns events in France. Departures from religious orthodoxy were an obvious cause for worry to the papacy and in the late spring of 1145 – presumably before the news of the fall of Edessa had reached the West – it was decided that the activities of Henry of Le Mans (sometimes known as Henry of Lausanne) merited serious attention.[64] Henry's preaching was essentially anti-clerical – he disparaged the sins of priests and argued that the sacraments dispensed by them were worthless. He also questioned the value of baptism and marriage and suggested that churches were unnecessary and prayers for the dead were a waste of effort. By this time, he had expressed his ideas for over thirty years; he had been brought before the Council of Pisa and condemned only to continue to spread his message across western France. Alberic of Ostia, as legate to France, may have brought the matter to Eugenius's attention and the pope ordered him to deal with the problem. Alberic called in some powerful support: Bernard of Clairvaux and Bishop Geoffrey of Chartres, a former legate to France and close associate of the abbot. Bernard wrote letters that decried Henry's ideas and disparaged his morals, attacking him as a trickster, a womaniser and a heretic.[65] The *Vita prima* recorded the mission's progress through Poitiers, Bordeaux, Albi and Toulouse, and in most places Bernard's presence produced a positive reaction.[66] Henry was apparently captured by church officials and his fate is unclear. By the time Bernard's involvement ended in August, the loss of Edessa must have been widely known, although Alberic of Ostia remained in southern France to tidy matters up before his return to the *curia* around the time *Quantum praedecessores* appeared. Together with Henry's obvious challenge to papal authority and orthodoxy, a couple of other ideas emerge from Bernard's letters at this time that would be echoed later on. First, his concern that Henry was denying people the chance of salvation – obviously the opportunity of God's mercy was a central element of the call for the Second Crusade – and, second, his warning to the people of Toulouse that they should beware of unknown preachers, another matter to arise in 1146–7.[67] The abbot had terminated Henry's threat fairly quickly, but his actions showed the Catholic Church to be sharply focused on any challenge to its authority and to be prepared to crack down heavily on those who did not recognise its power.

The third important issue was connected with the German Empire. We know that Bishop Otto of Freising was present at the *curia* in the latter half of 1145, in part to oversee the ongoing canonisation process for Emperor Henry II of Germany (1002–24). The impact of this episode upon the crusading ambitions of King Conrad of Germany will be considered later; but for Eugenius too, the timing of the episode was significant. Emperor Henry had played a large part in pushing Christian lands eastwards into the pagan territories of the Slavs.[68] He had founded the church of Bamberg, described in the *Vita Heinrici* as a place through which the evil of the Slavs was defeated and many souls were saved.[69] Henry also helped to engineer the peaceful conversion of Hungary through the marriage of his sister, Gisela, to King Stephen in 1001. It seems that Bishop Egilbert of Bamburg and Conrad himself had written to Eugenius to suggest Henry's canonisation and, with Conrad's half-brother Otto at the papal court, one imagines that a powerful advocate of the proposal was present in person. On 14 March 1146 the formal document confirming canonisation was issued, thus indicating that the process of investigating the claim had taken place over the preceding months – the time of the launch of the crusade. Alongside the dramatic news emerging from Edessa and the dispatch of bulls to Spain, Eugenius had, therefore, actively endorsed the deeds of a man who had extended Christian lands against enemies of the faithful in a third area.

As the issue of *Quantum praedecessores* drew near, another incident took place that may well have influenced the papal conception of the Second Crusade.[70] Otto of Freising, an eyewitness to these events, reported that in the autumn of 1145 a delegation of Armenians arrived at Viterbo and allegedly offered the submission of their Church to Rome.[71] Otto was the only writer to recount this episode, and historians have suggested that he may have overstated the Armenians' position.[72] By asking Eugenius to arbitrate over questions such as the correct way to celebrate the Eucharist and the right date for keeping Christmas, it is possible that the envoys were recognising papal primacy of jurisdiction over such matters, rather than offering full subordination to Rome and the loss of their independence. It is interesting, however, that Otto saw the Armenians' actions in that way because such a feeling could well have been shared by those in the papal *curia* too. In any event, for the Armenians, the decision to choose to look to the papacy and the West at this time was probably connected with events in northern Syria. Recent Byzantine advances in Cilician Armenia had provoked disquiet amongst them. The Greeks viewed the Armenians as monophysite and heretical and the re-establishment of Orthodox bishoprics in Cilicia in the late 1130s raised tensions between the two groups of Eastern Christians. On top of this, of course, Zengi's spectacular capture of Edessa had compounded the pressure on the indigenous Armenian population.

Relations between the Franks and the Armenians can be generally characterised as positive.[73] At times, the latter had come to form a notable element in the government of Edessa; Prince Vasil acted as regent for Joscelin I when he was imprisoned by Balak of Aleppo in 1122–3, and Armenians led the attempt to rescue the count from captivity.[74] The two groups also shared symbols of their faith, such as the Holy Cross of Varag, a seventh-century relic from the Lake Van region which was taken into battle by the joint Frankish–Armenian force that faced the emir of Mosul in 1110.[75]

The Armenian and the Latin Churches were not in communion, but they had enjoyed good terms since the days of Pope Sylvester (314–35) and of St Gregory the Illuminator, the first *catholicos*.[76] There had been contact during the pontificate of Gregory VII (1073–85), although the Latin settlement of northern Syria created the conditions for a closer level of contact.[77] The head of the Armenian Church, *Catholicos* Gregory III, had attended a church council in Jerusalem in 1141, a meeting called by Alberic of Ostia – who, as we have seen, was a prominent figure in Eugenius's administration – and, according to William of Tyre's report, cordial relations were established between the two groups.[78] A later Armenian writer stated that the *catholicos's* 'profession of faith had made plain his perfect orthodoxy'.[79] After the synod, Pope Innocent II wrote to Gregory to express continued positive feelings.[80]

The fact that Queen Melisende of Jerusalem was half-Armenian and a strong supporter of the Armenian Church in the kingdom must also have contributed to a warm atmosphere. Another indication of the Armenians' attitude towards the Catholic West at this time – and one connected with the Second Crusade – can be seen in the content of Nersēs Šnorhali's 'Lament on Edessa'. This poem was written between May and August 1146 in reponse to Zengi's capture of Edessa and was, amongst other things, an elegy to the fall of the city.[81] It contained, however, several ideas that were highly relevant to the crusade and to close relations between the Armenians and Rome. Its author, Nersēs Šnorhali, would later become *Catholicos* himself, but he had been present at the Council of Jerusalem and at a similar meeting at Antioch. Nersēs was not writing for a western audience, but his message would certainly have been well received in the papal *curia*. There was a strong sense of ecumenicalism within his work, and also a very positive series of references to Rome. For example:

Lament, O churches,
   Brides of the upper room,

My beloved sisters and brothers,
    you, who can be found on all sides of the Earth,
Cities and villages all together,
    peoples and generations all over the world,
Believers in Christ,
    worshippers of His cross.[82]
And you, Rome, Mother of Cities,
    Brilliant above all and honourable,
You throne of the great Peter,
    first among the apostles,
You immovable church,
    built on the rock of Cephas . . .[83]

Given the dating and content of the poem, it was likely that the delegation that met Eugenius and Otto returned from Italy with the news that the West was planning a new crusade. In the final stages of the work there was clear reference to the forthcoming expedition and to the hopes that the Armenians placed in that enterprise:

And you prisoners who are locked up,
    the Lord will set you free among the free ones,
And He will exchange
    my captivity, my exile for a home again,
And He will smack my captivator,
    sword and prison for him, instead of you.
Anew the Frank is on the move,
    unfathomable numbers of horsemen and footsoldiers
Like the waves – wave upon wave – of the sea
    in anger and ferocious fury
The whole of the Muhammedan nation
    they will sack and fall on.[84]

Even if Otto of Freising misjudged the exact nature of the Armenian embassy in 1145, the formation of closer ties with Rome may well have been prompted by the feeling that the papacy, through a new crusade, could offer vital protection and a response to the threat of Zengi. Certainly the 'Lament on Edessa' left no doubt as to the brutality of his sack of the city and was a serious attempt to depict his actions as inhuman. From the papal perspective, the securing of such recognition from the Armenians – at the expense of the Greek Orthodox Church – was a great coup and must have done much to increase the confidence in the *curia* at this time. It may also have contributed towards a desire on the part of the papacy to offer support to the Armenians as a part of the appeal for the new crusade.

All of the factors above combined to form the immediate context for the launch of *Quantum praedecessores*. Some can directly be discerned in the bull itself, although we will see the influence of several of the others on the shape and form of the crusade in due course.

At heart, the purpose of *Quantum praedecessores* (see Appendix 1 below for the text itself) was to rouse the knights of France 'to oppose the multitude of infidels' and 'to save the Church of God'. Judging by the scale of the response it was a remarkably effective piece of communication – and, given the numerous preachers sent to publicise it, it may have been the most widely circulated papal document in medieval Europe to date.[85] The strengths of *Quantum praedecessores* lay in the astute selection of imagery employed in the bull and in the immense clarity of its key themes. Eugenius himself, along with his cardinals and colleagues, such as Otto of Freising and Peter the Venerable, must take credit for this.

The basic structure of the letter was, however, entirely conventional; this was not the moment to take a radical approach to such matters. The art of letter-writing was dominated by the Ciceronian tradition and an anonymous treatise written in Bologna in 1135 offers a local and contemporaneous insight into what it termed 'the approved format'.[86] A letter was defined as 'a suitable arrangement of words set forth to express the intended meaning of its sender . . . a discourse composed of coherent yet distinct parts signifying fully the sentiments of its sender. There are, in fact, five parts of a letter: the Salutation, the Securing of Good-will, the Narration, the Petition, and the Conclusion'.[87] Clearly, Eugenius and his circle adhered to a familiar template.

The content of the document was borne out of an understanding of the history of crusading, the ongoing crisis in Edessa, the recent concerns of the papal *curia* and an understanding of what was appropriate for, and attractive to, the target audience. The authors of the bull also had a very sound grasp of the art of communication. They realised that *Quantum praedecessores* was going to be at the heart of almost every crusade recruitment meeting. They were aware that it would be read out loud, sometimes to a lord and his retainers, sometimes to larger gatherings of people from a wide variety of backgrounds; such episodes are mentioned by Otto of Freising and Nicholas of Clairvaux.[88] Whilst an individual preacher might add his own sermon and do much to stimulate a reaction, the concepts and images of the papal bull needed to be accessible and to inspire. They also had to be able to survive the process of translation from Latin into the appropriate vernacular for the delivery of the speech.[89] Furthermore, given the scale of the commitment that was being asked of people, it had to be crystal clear what was required of them and what was the nature of the rewards and privileges they would receive. Clarity of message would remove the possibility of misunderstanding and could prevent the papacy from losing the tight control it desired to maintain over the campaign. The principal device employed by Eugenius to get his ideas across was that of repetition. The main themes of the bull were elucidated on several occasions, a tactic regarded as the correct approach to fulfil the purpose of the document. A detailed analysis of the text reveals the ideas, images and precedents that Eugenius sought to utilise and shows how the elements of Narration and Petition noted above interwove.[90]

The six dominant themes in *Quantum praedecessores* were as follows. First, the precedent of Pope Urban and of the First Crusade; secondly, the image of fathers and sons – in other words, a legacy handed down through generations; thirdly, the offer of remission of all sins; fourthly, the need to help the Eastern Church; fifthly, that Eugenius acted with divine authority; and sixthly, an appeal to the sense of honour of the Christian knighthood of France.

The bull started with a careful grounding of the new expedition in a continuum with the First Crusade. Eugenius wanted to show that he had taken full notice of that great event by the statement that he had 'learned from what men of old have said and we have found written in their histories'.[91] In other words he had talked to elders, some of whom may conceivably have been around at the time of the First Crusade.[92] Even more significantly for this study, the quoted claim is explicit proof – at the very start of the crusading bull – of the seminal importance of the recording of the First Crusade discussed in the previous chapter; here this fact can be seen to exert an impact at the formative stages of the new campaign. The pope also wanted to demonstrate that he had consulted documents and narratives connected with the First Crusade and subsequent events and, in a couple of instances, it is possible to suggest the sources he referred to. As noted earlier, with regard to the papal bulls to Tarragona, a strong element of recycling was evident. *Quantum praedecessores* itself began with lines that echoed a phrase used early on in the most recent of these when, in May 1145, Eugenius himself had written of the city 'for the reconquest of which our predecessors are known to have laboured greatly'.[93] In spite of the fifty-year period since the launch of the First Crusade, the present appeal seems to have been based on thorough investigations into the earlier expedition and its smaller successors.

By placing the new campaign in line with the First Crusade Eugenius linked it to the success of, and – crucially – the divine approval for, that episode. He outlined the achievement of the 1095–9 campaign in liberating the Eastern Church and praised the French and the Italians for their involvement therein. He also described the pious motivation of the crusaders and noted their sacrifice and the shedding of their blood to free 'that city in which it was our saviour's will to suffer for us and where he left us his glorious Sepulchre as a memorial of his passion . . .'.[94] We have seen above the prominence and durability of the First Crusade in the imagination and deeds of the people of the Latin West, and we also noted the continued importance of pilgrimage to the Holy Sepulchre; Eugenius plainly intended to tap into these notions very deeply.

After this history lesson and the establishment of the crusade's antecedents, Eugenius began one of his key arguments: the work of the 'fathers', that is, the First Crusaders and their successors, should not be wasted by 'the sons' who heard this present appeal. The pope indicated that the effort to conquer and hold the Latin East had taken place over many decades, and in doing so he recognised the labours of those who had gone to the Levant to fight for short periods since the First Crusade. He acknowledged the work of those who had settled there and who had shed their blood in trying to preserve the Christian hold on the holy places.[95] In other words, Eugenius registered that there was an ongoing tradition of crusading that would have resonated in the numerous families with a relative who had taken the cross in the past. He was also counting on the new crusaders' sense of honour and a feeling that they should live up to the deeds of their predecessors – which, as we have seen above, was a source of real pride and lay at the heart of the consciousness of western European nobility.

Eugenius then explained the present crisis; events caused, he argued, by the sins of those in the West as well as in the Levant. There was no attempt to assign blame in a specific direction; culpability was shared by all Christians – this was in strong contrast to the approach of Pope Gregory VIII in 1187, who made plain his view that the Frankish settlers had brought their troubles upon themselves.[96] Eugenius then announced the fall of Edessa and noted its importance to early Christianity as the first city to accept the faith. William of Tyre, who was educated in the West between 1145 and 1165, can provide some insight into this matter. He wrote of Edessa (with regard to its capture in 1098) that it was associated with Tobias, the eponymous hero of the Old Testament book. Tobias was sent to '*Rages Medorum*', identified as Edessa by William; in other words Edessa would be a name recognised by all clergy, regardless of how well or poorly they had been educated. A good example of this can be found in the Praemonstratensian continuator of the work of Sigebert of Gembloux: when he wrote of the fall of Edessa, Sigebert described it as the first city to convert to Christianity and as the burial place of Thomas and Thaddeus.[97] William of Tyre also stated that the city had received the words of Christ through the Apostle Thaddeus immediately after the Passion, and that the Letter of Christ to Abgar could be read in the first chapter of Eusebius of Caesarea's *Ecclesiastical History*.[98] William had probably read Eusebius in the Latin translation of Rufinus, which was a fairly common text in the twelfth-century West. Thus Edessa would have been known to the clergy who preached and heard the call for the Second Crusade.[99] Edessa would also have been familiar to people in Europe through its prominent position in the events of the First Crusade. Narratives such as those of Fulcher of Chartres and Albert of Aachen dwelt upon Baldwin of Boulogne's capture of the city, as did lesser works, for instance the brief anonymous chronicle of the reign of Baldwin I – a text from the first half of the twelfth century that was often appended to other contemporary writings such as Bartolf of Nangis and Fretellus.[100] Albert paid considerable attention to subsequent events in the county too.[101] Otto of Freising was another to note that the city of Edessa had been a pilgrimage destination for centuries, although it may be suggested that only a relatively small number of the Latin pilgrims who visited the Holy Land ventured so far north.[102] Edessa also had specific ties to certain institutions in the West, such as Cluny. In the early twelfth century, as Hugh (later to become archbishop of Edessa) travelled from his homeland in Flanders to Jerusalem, he passed by Cluny where the abbot invested him 'with the society of all the goods of the congregation'. In gratitude, Hugh sent back to the abbey a relic of St Stephen.[103] In 1123 he also sent relics of SS Thaddeus and Abgar to the archbishop of Rheims.[104]

In conjunction with this historical and biblical grounding, Eugenius added a more human perspective to his narrative by reference to the slaughter of the archbishop of Edessa, his clerics and many Christians, as well as the loss of numerous castles. Archbishop Hugh had indeed been killed, although the majority of the population of Edessa was likely to have been Armenian Christian rather than Catholic. As noted above, in late 1145 the Armenians appeared to acknowledge the authority of Rome; this may have had some impact on Eugenius's thoughts here, particularly with regard to the idea of assisting the Eastern Church. This theme recurs later in the text and, with the Armenian Church in closer relations with Rome, 'protection of the Eastern Church' was presumably relevant to the Armenians as well as to the Catholics of the East.

The pope also reported that 'the relics of the saints have been trampled under the infidels' feet and dispersed'.[105] The cult of relics was a central element in the devotional practices of western Christendom and after the First Crusade many more relics had been brought back from the Holy Land to Europe.[106] The image of the infidel defaming such important objects was something that Eugenius's audience could easily relate to and it would have helped to provoke a response in them. The destruction of relics and holy places was also prominent in accounts of Pope Urban's preaching of the First Crusade and creates another parallel with that campaign.[107]

After he had built up the tension by outlining the terrible events at Edessa and the injury done to Christian people and to sacred objects, Eugenius came to a further vital element of his appeal: 'We recognise how great the danger is that threatens the Church of God and all Christianity because of this . . .'. In other words, he broadened the impact of the loss of Edessa to a real threat that embraced the Church as a whole – events in the Levant were made relevant to Christians everywhere. Logically, therefore, action was needed and the pope framed this call skilfully:

> It will be seen as a great token of nobility and uprightness if those things acquired by the efforts of your fathers are vigorously defended by you, their good sons. But if, God forbid, it comes to pass differently, then the bravery of the fathers will have proved diminished in the sons.[108]

These most powerful words of the bull laid down a challenge to its audience; a challenge to prove themselves worthy of the efforts of their fathers and not to lose their own sense of honour. We have seen how the reputation of the First Crusaders as pious men of valour continued to grow during the twelfth century through works of literature and in physical forms; here Eugenius engaged with this idea directly. Of course, the notion of appealing to the deeds of fathers was not something original to Eugenius or to crusading. This was an age of growing awareness of family histories and patrimony.[109] Twelfth-century historians of Normandy looked back to the glory days of the past and to the conquests of England and Sicily.[110] In a crusading context, Gilo of Paris wrote of the heroes of the First Crusade striving to equal and outdo 'the brave deeds of their fathers'.[111] Robert of Rheims reported that Urban II employed a similar theme when he mentioned a sense of disgrace if the men of France did not respond to his appeals. Robert quoted Urban thus: 'O most valiant soldiers and descendants of victorious ancestors, do not fall short of, but be inspired by, the courage of your forefathers!'[112] The 'forefathers' referred to here were Charlemagne and Louis, whose armies had fought the pagans; it was important for men such as Robert of Flanders, Godfrey of Bouillon and Baldwin of Boulogne to trace their ancestry back to the great Carolingians. In 1145–6 Eugenius used the familiar idea of living up to the actions of one's fathers as a central plank in his arguments. He was also taking a direct hold of that sense of knightly worth, which incorporated the overlapping notions of Christian faith and a warrior ethos, to make his point even more effectively.

Immediately after this, the pope launched a direct request for help, cloaked in his divine authority and phrased in a compelling, almost coercive fashion: 'And so in the Lord we impress upon, ask and order all of you . . . to defend the Eastern Church . . . and to deliver . . . our captive brothers . . . '.[113] The 'captive brothers' were those under Muslim rule – obviously a terrible and shameful prospect for his audience. Inserted within this appeal was the prime reward the pope could offer, namely remission of sins. Constable and Hehl are amongst those who have pointed out that this represented an advance on Pope Urban's formulation of the remission of all penance, and that Eugenius included the 'absolution from temporal (i.e. divine) punishments of sin which, independent from the ecclesiastical penitential discipline, are inflicted by God for every sin'.[114] Riley-Smith has nuanced this view to indicate that Eugenius' formulation reflected a commonly held belief amongst western knights, who blurred the distinction between remission of penance and remission of sins.[115]

At this point in his appeal, Eugenius made some attempt to focus on those who were best equipped to accomplish his aims, namely 'the more powerful and the nobles'. These were the men whose sense of honour and tradition he had engaged and who were best suited to defeat the infidel in battle. We should note, however, that Eugenius did not explicitly ban others from taking part. The direct address to the nobles was bolstered by the repetition of the need to defend the Eastern Church, although this, in turn, was reinforced by the additional call to help 'deliver from their hands the many thousands of our captive brothers'. The imperative to liberate Christians is found, in the broadest sense, at the time of the First Crusade and is another echo of the themes played upon by Pope Urban.[116]

Eugenius tied together his call for action with a strong and multi-layered image. He urged the knights that the spilling of their fathers' blood might not be in vain and that 'the dignity of the name of Christ may be enhanced in our time and your reputation for strength, which is praised throughout the world, may be kept unimpaired and unsullied'.[117] This constituted a third reference to the 'fathers and sons' imagery noted above; it also harked back again to the success of the First Crusade. By implication, the name of Christ had been enhanced in 1099 and it was down to the present generation to ensure that the process continued. This particular task had a further dimension because it was the knighthood of France that were charged with this responsibility. We have seen above how the 'Franks' were rightly proud of their achievements in the past and how they perpetuated this notion; Robert of Rheims wrote of the fame of the French as First Crusaders: 'After all, are we not French? Did not our parents come from France and take this land for themselves by force of arms? For shame! Are our relations and brothers to head for martyrdom – indeed to paradise – without us?'[118] Here, therefore, Eugenius was giving the knighthood of the mid-twelfth century an opportunity to create their own glorious deeds while following in the footsteps of their fathers.

To round off his exhortation Eugenius cast the crusaders in a biblical light by comparing them to Mattathias of the Maccabees. This Apocryphal story featured a Jewish tribe which, against all odds, resisted the persecution of the Romans. A ninth-century commentary had transposed this episode of Jewish history into a Christian context with the Maccabean army becoming the army of Christ, fighting at God's command to defend His people and seeking not gold or silver, but knowledge, heavenly conversion and martyrdom.[119] The story had been used in a military context prior to the crusades – for example by William of Poitiers in connection with the Norman invasion of England: 'Thus, with their soul victorious, they fought with energy rivalling the Maccabees ... to win everlasting freedom of spirit and peace ... '.[120] However, the parallel between the struggle of the Maccabees against the Romans and the Christians against the Muslims was particularly appropriate to the crusades and the story came to be heavily used by chroniclers and preachers alike. Guibert of Nogent wrote that the Maccabees 'deserved the highest praise for their piety because they fought for the sacred rituals and the Temple', and he suggested that the knights of the First Crusade merited similar respect.[121] Fulcher of Chartres made reference to the Maccabees' labours in the prologue of his *Historia*, and later in the text he paralleled the numerical inferiority of the Maccabees to the success of a small Frankish army at Tell Danith in September 1115.[122] The inscription on King Baldwin I's tomb compared him to Judas Maccabaeus: '*Rex Balduinus, Iudas alter Machabaeus, spes patriae, vigor ecclesiae, virtus utriusque*'.[123] Geoffrey, abbot of the Templum Domini in Jerusalem (1137–60), wrote a paraphrase to the first book of the Maccabees – an interesting and possibly contemporaneous choice of subject matter which showed the prominence of the story in crusading circles.[124] In *Quantum praedecessores* Eugenius evoked Mattathias's efforts in order to show the sacrifices made to preserve what was believed to be right and to emphasise that, with divine aid, he had triumphed. He also described fathers and sons working together in this struggle – yet another reference to this core theme of his letter.

The final section of *Quantum praedecessores* was a clear statement of the privileges offered to those who took the cross.[125] Parts of the text echoed earlier legislation; some clarified concerns to potential crusaders; other sections set out new rules. Once again this whole passage was grounded in the precedents established by Pope Urban and his successors and was based on the authority granted to Eugenius by God. In measures such as the financing of the crusade, there was a clear sense of the practical experience of the First Crusade being put to good use and of an effort to prevent some of the difficulties that arose in the planning and execution of that campaign. Eugenius confirmed that those 'inspired by devotion' would receive remission of their sins. This opening phrase was reminiscent of Urban's statements at Clermont and indicated the need for the crusaders to proceed with the right intention to secure the spiritual reward they desired. Eugenius then promised that the Church would protect the crusaders' close families and their property.[126] There is evidence that such legislation dated back to the First Crusade because a letter of Paschal II urged the churchmen of France to ensure that the returning crusaders received back all their property 'as you will recall our predecessor, Urban of blessed memory, ordained in a synodal declaration'.[127] The canonist Ivo of Chartres discussed the matter in 1106–7 with regard to the complex legal case involving Hugh of Le Puiset and Count Rotrou of Perche and, while this too made reference to the status of absent crusaders, it seems that matters were not entirely clear until the Decrees of the First Lateran Council in 1123. There it was stated that 'the houses and households and all of the property' of crusaders were under papal protection and that 'whoever shall presume to appropriate or make off with these things shall be penalised with the reprisal of excommunication'.[128] Eugenius 'enlarged and clarified the temporal privileges that the crusaders enjoyed'.[129] He stated explicitly that wives and children, goods and possessions were protected and that the local ecclesiastical hierarchy, as well as the pope, were responsible for providing and reinforcing this guardianship. Eugenius also forbade the initiation of legal suits against crusaders, their immediate families and their lawfully held possessions from the taking of the cross until 'certain knowledge of their return or death' was received.[130]

Eugenius's Cistercian background is revealed in a series of admonitions against fine clothes and the use of hawks and dogs. In other words the apparel of the secular knight, so decried by Bernard in his *De laude novae militiae* (*c.*1130), was deemed inappropriate for the pursuit of God's work. The pride and lasciviousness aroused by it would undoubtedly distract the crusaders and incur God's disfavour. Such criticisms had been levelled at the 1101 crusaders and this section may be a subtle reference to their failings.[131] The second issue of *Quantum praedecessores*, in March 1146, added an extra line that included strictures against 'multi-coloured clothes or minivers or gilded and silver arms', which merely followed the general themes outlined already.[132] A practical point underlay these ideas as well, because, as Eugenius continued, the focus had to be on the arms, horses and equipment really needed to defeat the infidel, not on fripperies and display.

The pope provided immunity for crusaders, and for those acting on their behalf, from usurious contracts. He also tried to facilitate the financing of an individual's journey by permitting them to raise money on their lands or possessions from churches or churchmen, 'or any other of the faithful without any counterclaim, for otherwise they will not have the means to go' – as long as they informed their neighbours or the lord from whom they held the property. The First Crusade and subsequent expeditions had undoubtedly shown the enormous cost of crusading and the problems in securing adequate funding before setting out. Prior to the days of mercenary armies and national taxes designed to support such campaigns, the need for an individual to source money was paramount. Here Eugenius opened out the possibilities for the devoted crusader should his family or overlord be unable or unwilling to offer help.[133]

The close of *Quantum praedecessores* repeated the heart of Eugenius's offer. In the strongest term yet – 'By the authority of omnipotent God and that of Blessed Peter the Prince of the Apostles conceded to us by God . . . ' – he granted the remission and absolution of sins, as provided by Pope Urban. Eugenius made plain that this absolution was only open to those who had made full and contrite confession of all their sins and that they had to complete their journey to secure the rewards on offer, 'the fruit of everlasting recompense from the rewarder of all good people'. He also noted that those who died on the journey would be rewarded in this way, perhaps clarifying a point of concern for some crusaders, although the phrase quoted above left the survivors of the journey in no doubt as to the fact that they too would be the recipients of a special recompense.[134]

Practical difficulties surrounded the issue of the bull. In recent years cities across Italy had challenged the nobility and established communes; in 1143 the inhabitants of Rome rejected the claims of the pope to exercise secular authority over them.[135] Overlapping this situation was the long-running family feuding between the Pierleoni and Frangipani clans. Lucius II had died as a result of wounds sustained when leading his troops against the Pierleoni outside Rome in February 1145 and the cardinals had required the protection of the Frangipani to meet and elect Eugenius. As soon as the new pope was enthroned the Roman senate demanded that he confirm their authority: he could not do so and was compelled to flee, first to Farfa for his consecration, and then to a more secure base at Viterbo, just over fifty miles north of Rome. In late 1145, the situation improved through a peace agreement between the pope and the citizens in which the latter promised to abolish the office of patrician, to restore the prefect to his former authority and to retain the senators by his authorisation. With this deal in place Eugenius returned to Rome to celebrate Christmas there. The new state of affairs lasted only a matter of weeks before more problems with the citizenry compelled Eugenius to retreat to Trastevere and resume his exile. These were not ideal conditions for organising a new crusade and this situation was one of the reasons given by Eugenius for his delegation to Bernard of the main crusade preaching.[136]

Quantum praedecessores was dispatched first to Louis VII and his nobles. We are aware of its use in Brittany, Denmark, Bohemia and Germany as well.[137] In addition, Eugenius is known to have written about the crusade to the town of Tournai, to Count Thierry of Flanders and to the people of England, and it is likely that the bull formed part of this communication.[138] As will be seen later, the pope issued further bulls to other areas such as Spain and northern Germany. Given that *Quantum praedecessores* would have been read out to large gatherings on occasion, it is unrealistic to expect that every listener picked up on all the nuances outlined above. But, in light of the context of the expedition and of the bull's repetition of certain themes – the promotion of the new campaign as a successor of the First Crusade; the suffering of the Christians in the East; and the simple ideas of honour, the father–son relationship, divine authority and remission of all sins – there must be little doubt that the basics of Eugenius's message would have been understood. Plainly, other factors motivated the crusaders too, and these varied across time and space, but the ideas put forward in the bull were central and highly appropriate to the target audience. In many instances, it is likely that those who attended meetings where the bull was broadcast had already decided to take the cross, or were at least predisposed to do so. But the pope's position as the head of the crusading movement and sole figure endowed with the authority to launch such an expedition gave this document an absolute centrality to the start of the campaign. The bull had, in a sense, to live up to the expectations generated by its author's position and, judging by the response, this was a task that it met with real success.

There is, however, an inherent tension between *Quantum praedecessores* looking back to the First Crusade and the fact that much had altered in western Europe since the capture of Jerusalem in 1099. To name but a few changes: the increase in the number and power of crowned heads; dramatic advances in scholasticism and theology; the emergence of religious orders such as the Cistercians and Praemonstratensians; the growing commercial strength of the Italian city–states. Indeed, even within *Quantum praedecessores* itself, Eugenius's clarification of privileges marked a significant step forward for crusading ideology. From this angle, it was perhaps artificial to look back to the First Crusade and wish to replicate that episode completely. The First Crusade had been of such importance that it was absorbed into, and was itself influenced by, many new aspects of Latin Christian society – for example the advance of the reconquest of Spain, the advent of the Military Orders, the presence of a Christian king in Jerusalem, a more aggressive attitude towards the Jews, or the economic strength of the Italian trading cities. Similarly, while the First Crusade had not seen the participation of kings, by the time of the Second Crusade several monarchs had taken the cross to fight in Iberia, such as Alfonso I of Aragon, or had gone to the Holy Land, such as Eric the Good of Denmark. A major challenge for the historian is to explore the extent to which this desire to replicate the 1099 expedition influenced the recruitment of the new crusade and how far it actually hampered the progress and outcome of the campaign.

CHAPTER 4

THE LAUNCH OF THE SECOND CRUSADE

BOURGES, VÉZELAY AND THE PREACHING MESSAGE OF BERNARD OF CLAIRVAUX

After the fall of Edessa in December 1144 messengers from Jerusalem and Antioch came to the West to seek support and, as we have seen already, their first approach was to Pope Eugenius III. They also targeted, specifically, King Louis VII of France and King Conrad III of Germany, while making a broader appeal to the nobles and princes of the West.[1] The reaction of the Germans will be analysed later, but in any case the first response came from France.

Why was Louis chosen for particular attention? His marriage to Eleanor of Aquitaine brought a substantial area of land into the orbit of the Capetain monarchy. This, along with Louis's position as *Rex Francorum*, meant that, theoretically, he was the most high-standing figure in France – the homeland of many of the First Crusaders and early generations of settlers.[2] Louis's great-uncle, Hugh the Great, had been one of the leading men on the expedition and the king himself was related by marriage to the Poitevin, Prince Raymond of Antioch, the uncle of Louis's wife, Eleanor. The grandmother of Princess Constance of Antioch was one of Louis's aunts; besides, the king had other, more distant, connections to the ruling houses of Jerusalem and Tripoli. Crusade traditions and family ties between Louis and the leading houses of the Latin East, combined with – in a broader sense – those between many of the settlers and the people of France, were obvious stimuli to send an embassy to the young monarch.[3]

On the other hand, the early years of Louis's reign were fraught; his political judgement was poor and the period saw rival factions emerge at the royal court. Obstinacy and immaturity brought him into conflict with powerful nobles such as Theobald of Champagne, as well as with the French Church and the papacy.[4] A series of disputed elections to the bishoprics of Langres, Rheims, Poitiers, Bourges and Châlons-sur-Marne earned him the enmity of many in the ecclesiastical elite. The controversy over the marriage between

Raoul of Vermandois and Theobald's niece inflamed tensions even further; by the early 1140s, Innocent II described the king as 'a boy who must be instructed' in proper behaviour and placed his lands under interdict. The dispute escalated rapidly and Louis invaded Champagne; in January 1143, in an act of appalling savagery he burned the church at Vitry with 1,300 innocent people inside. Bernard of Clairvaux was amongst those who tried hard to resolve the situation, although he grew increasingly exasperated by the king's actions:

> But you [Louis] will not receive any peaceful overtures or keep your own truce or accept sound advice . . . we the sons of the Church cannot overlook the injuries, contempt, and ignominy to which you have subjected our Mother . . . provoked by the constant excesses you commit almost daily, I am beginning to regret having stupidly favoured your youth more than I should have done, and I am determined that in future, to the best of my limited ability, I will expose the whole truth about you . . . I tell you, you will not remain unpunished if you continue in this way.[5]

Eventually, the efforts of senior clergy brought calm and in March 1144 Pope Celestine II lifted the interdict; in October of the same year the king and Count Theobald made peace to close a particularly undistinguished start to the reign.

The precise series of events concerning the beginning of the Second Crusade is a matter of some controversy.[6] There was no clear sequence of papal initiative followed by recruitment and the preparations of secular figures, as had happened in 1095–6. Instead, there was an awkward overlap between the first issue of *Quantum praedecessores* on 1 December 1145 and Louis's attempt to launch the crusade at his Christmas court at Bourges. This bid to arouse general support failed and the matter was deferred until the great assembly at Vézelay at Easter 1146. The previous chapter discussed the origins of the Second Crusade from a papal perspective; historians have long sought to unravel the reasons behind Louis's false start and to understand whether the initiative for the crusade lay with him or Eugenius. Our two main sources, Odo of Deuil and Otto of Freising, were contemporaries to the events, but have left frustrating lacunae in their accounts.

In December 1145 Louis attempted to convince his court at Bourges of the need to journey to the Levant but, in spite of a powerful sermon by Bishop Godfrey of Langres, the assembled nobles and churchmen wished to defer a definitive commitment.[7] William of Saint-Denis's *Life of Suger* stated that the abbot was opposed to the plan, although the author gave no precise grounds for this stance.[8] Given that William was aware of the outcome of the crusade, one may suggest that he was trying to distance his subject from the fiasco; certainly other evidence – such as the creation of the crusade windows at Saint-Denis – indicated that before the expedition set out Suger was firmly behind the project.[9] It is also possible that the French nobility felt uneasy with the prospect of their young monarch embarking upon such a massive commitment. As we have seen above, the early years of Louis's reign had not been at all stable and the king's own character had, at times, led him into serious trouble. It is important to remember that, as yet, no major western ruler had taken the cross and journeyed to the Holy Land. To raise the money necessary for the crusade, to be away from one's lands for two or three years and to stand a fair chance of losing one's life constituted a serious set of calculations for any individual, let alone one with the God-given responsibilities of a crowned head. If they agreed to his proposal, Louis's nobles would be entering unknown and potentially hazardous territory. The First Crusade had also shown the problems that could arise when dissident forces sought to exploit the absence of a lord to their own advantage and, once again, Louis's patchy record to date may have given concern. Against these considerations, however, stood both the personal wishes of the king – which, as we will see shortly, covered a variety of motives – and, as noted in an earlier chapter, the involvement of other crowned heads in crusading in Iberia and the Levant.

But probably the most important reason for the false start at Bourges was connected to the absence of the papal bull *Quantum praedecessores*. Given that the bull was published at Vetrella, about fifty-five miles north of Rome, on 1 December, it is unrealistic to imagine that it could have reached Bourges in just over three weeks. This entailed a journey of at least 600 miles travelling north to Turin, crossing the Alps via the Mons Cenis Pass – in deepest winter, of course – and then heading up the main route northwards to Vienne and Chalons-sur-Saône before turning west to Nevers and Bourges.[10]

Odo of Deuil, our most detailed source for events at the Christmas court, described the arrival of a papal bull at a later point in his narrative.[11] It was the lack of this official statement of the rewards and privileges of the crusade that probably checked the actions of Louis's associates. It was unlikely that the king acted entirely independently of Eugenius; he was simply a little too enthusiastic. Perhaps he felt his Christmas court was a suitable time to air the idea – both in terms of Christian symbolism and given that many of his nobles could be present. The churchmen at Bourges must have been aware of the centrality of the papacy to the crusade movement and understood that an expedition on this scale could not be set up without Eugenius's wishes. It is certain that there had been contact between the French crown and the papal *curia* in the summer and autumn of 1145; for example, we know that Alberic of Ostia was present on a legation in France at this time.[12] The fact that the 1 December issue of *Quantum praedecessores* was addressed to Louis and his magnates bears this out: Eugenius would not have risked sending out such an appeal if he believed it might fall on deaf ears. This exchange of communications took several weeks by itself – which also helps to explain the timing of the bull. Louis may have anticipated *Quantum praedecessores*'s arrival before gathering his nobles at Bourges but when the bull failed to appear he decided to air the issue anyway since so many people were in attendance.

Louis's motives in taking the cross have been the subject of some debate.[13] Odo of Deuil famously recounted that the king had invited people to Bourges 'to reveal the secret in his heart'.[14] Otto of Freising wrote that he 'was impelled by a secret desire to go to Jerusalem because his brother Philip had bound himself by the same vow but had been prevented by death. He was unwilling further to postpone this resolve; he therefore summoned certain of his princes and revealed what he was turning over in his mind.'[15] The Praemonstratensian continuator of the chronicle of Sigebert of Gembloux suggested that the king felt terrible remorse at the burning of the church at Vitry.[16] He had also incurred the wrath of the Church in the course of his struggles over the various electoral issues noted above. By late 1144, however, the king had become reconciled with the Church and, Grabois has hypothesised, by way of making good his misdeeds, he agreed to undertake a penitential pilgrimage to Jerusalem.[17] For reasons of prestige he needed a cover, hence his brother's old vow was offered as a pretext, only for the fall of Edessa to provide an even more convenient rationale. For this project to work, however, the scheme needed a bigger preaching campaign, in the course of which Bernard 'forgot' the original plan and broadened it into the Europe-wide concept it became. It is argued that the crusade's failure to fight at Edessa, Louis's focus on Jerusalem and his rather other-worldly bearing on the expedition betrayed the fact that he was really only interested in a pilgrimage and this was one reason why the crusade did not succeed.[18]

Some elements of this interpretation are attractive, but the argument excludes the influence of the fall of Edessa on the king and, with regard to the progress of the crusade, it does not match up to reality.[19] Several other authorities, such as the *Chronicle of Morigny* and the 'Historia gloriosi regis Ludovici VII', commented on the impact of the loss of the Christian city upon the king.[20] Odo of Deuil described a monarch who, after Godfrey of Langres's oration, shone with the zeal of faith and demanded that his men should follow him to aid their brothers in the East.[21] A more sensible way forward, therefore, is to suggest that the events at Vitry, the vow of Prince Philip, a possible wish to atone for his conflict with the Church – as well as Louis's own piety – may well have predisposed him to react to the appeals from the Latin East. When the envoys arrived he was moved to relieve their plight, being pleased to know that he could visit the holy places as well.[22] This proposal also removes the awkward concept of a change of plan by Bernard of Clairvaux and the need for any cover for the king's actions. Finally, as Bull indicates, Louis took the cross and 'the rites for taking the cross, although substantially based on the rituals used for those departing on pilgrimage, distinguished between the crusader and the pilgrim.'[23]

It seems likely that Louis had made plain his wish to crusade for some time because Odo of Deuil informs us that the king had invited many more people than usual to the annual crown wearing at Bourges – to discuss, as Bernard of Clairvaux put it, 'the business of God, namely the expedition to Jerusalem.'[24] In other words, he had advertised the purpose of the meeting in order to ensure a larger than usual audience. The Christmas crown wearing was designed to restate royal authority and dignity and would have been the perfect occasion to announce such a plan.[25] Bishop Godfrey of Langres delivered what was unmistakably a sermon calling for a new camapaign to the East. Godfrey was a Cistercian, distantly related to Bernard himself.[26] He spoke of the devastation of Edessa, the suffering of the Christians and the arrogance of the heathen. Odo of Deuil reported that 'he aroused great lamentation', and that the king was burning with desire help the Christians.'[27] Yet Odo did not mention that Godfrey offered spiritual rewards for the simple reason that *Quantum praedecessores* had yet to reach the royal court. Nobody rejected Louis's plan outright, but the mixture of secular and spiritual concerns noted above ensured that a formal commitment was postponed until a meeting set for Easter 1146 at Vézelay. By then the papal bull would have arrived and, given Urban's speech at Clermont, there may have been a hope that Eugenius himself could be present to launch the expedition.

Louis was said to have sent messengers to Eugenius who asked for support, perhaps also wondering where *Quantum praedecessores* was. He then received letters 'sweeter than any honeycomb', including a document (summarised by Odo) that was plainly *Quantum praedecessores*. Political troubles in Rome prevented Eugenius from giving 'the initial blessing to such a holy undertaking', which may well show that he had had in mind to emulate Pope Urban, but he delegated the matter to Bernard of Clairvaux.[28]

It is not possible to ascertain definitively whether it was Louis or Eugenius who first raised the idea of the crusade. We know that envoys from the Levant approached both parties, and they reached the pope before the king. The most contemporaneous source is a letter of Abbot Bernard, dating from April 1146, which wrote of 'the good work that he [Louis] has begun so whole-heartedly under your [Eugenius's] encouragement.'[29] On the other hand, both Odo of Deuil and Otto of Freising placed the initiative with the king; in the former case, quite possibly out of loyalty to his master.[30] In any event there is no doubt that both men wanted a crusade to take place and that its formal launch was set for Vézelay at Easter.

Between Christmas and Easter the royal court saw an intense burst of diplomatic activity. Those present at Bourges would have been aware of the projected meeting (sadly we do not know exactly who was in attendance at Christmas), but other nobles must have been informed of developments and pondered whether or not they wanted to go to Vézelay. This must have been the time when the leading nobles took the decision to go on crusade. Events at Bourges would have made plain what was afoot and it was obvious that Vézelay was the moment when people would take the cross. Given the king's intentions and the overt trailing of the purpose of this assembly it would be very difficult for an individual to attend and then not to follow his monarch and fellow-magnates in joining the crusade. In the meantime, Bernard must have received the news that Eugenius was trapped in Rome; the pope sent him a formal commission to preach the crusade along with *Quantum praedecessores* (II); the abbot started to recruit for the expedition immediately.[31]

By all accounts the meeting at Vézelay was an emotive and stirring occasion. We must picture a carefully orchestrated event that stretched over several days – Odo reported that the assembly was to begin on Palm Sunday, although the climax of the meeting – the launch of the crusade itself – was not to happen until a week later when the largest possible audience would be gathered. The coincidence of timing this sermon to match Christ's resurrection was highly appropriate as the spirit of renewal and of the divine created a strong backdrop to the beginning of the crusade.

The week after Palm Sunday saw the convergence of many of the great nobles and churchmen of France. Some arrived by horse, others came via the nearby River Yonne. The anonymous 'Historia gloriosi regis Ludovici VII', written *c.*1165, gives a list of attendees that reveals an impressive geographical spread.[32] From the south came Count Alphonse-Jordan of Toulouse, a member of the great crusading dynasty, and the rulers of the county of Tripoli. From northern France came Count Thierry of Flanders, who had already visited the Holy Land in 1138–9 and was related by marriage to the rulers of Jerusalem. Robert, count of Dreux, was King Louis's brother and based to the west of Paris; Bishop Arnulf of Lisieux was from Normandy; Ivo of Nesle, count of Soissons, lived in Picardy, to the north-east of Paris, while Count Hugh VII of Lusignan travelled from the county of Poitou to the west. Unsurprisingly, the bulk of the audience was more local, reflecting both the heartlands of Capetian influence and the dominions of Count Theobald II of Champagne (1102–52).[33] Simple practicality dictated a greater number of nearby nobles and churchman in attendance, these included the lords of

Tonerre, Coucy, and Châtillon, and also the bishop of Langres and two abbots from Sens.

Vézelay is located in gently rolling hills in northern Burgundy and its geographical location was doubtless part of the reason why it was chosen to be the gathering point for the crusaders. It is c.70 miles from Citeaux, c.80 miles from Cluny and close to many other important religious houses; furthermore, it is only c.115 miles from Paris itself. Urban II had considered using Vézelay as the place to initiate the First Crusade, but then preferred Clermont.[34] Personal connections between the network of men around Pope Eugenius may also explain the choice. Alberic of Ostia, the papal legate to France, was a former abbot of Vézelay and the current incumbent, Pons, was none other than the brother of Peter the Venerable who had been the prior there earlier in his career.[35] It is also interesting to note that the church was part of the Cluniac empire (a situation that lasted until 1159) although not in the more closely affiliated way of most Cluniac houses that were headed by a prior rather than an abbot. There had been considerable tensions between the two abbeys, but Cluny possessed sufficient weight to force the monks of Vézelay to accept Alberic's candidacy.[36]

The town itself stands on top of a high hill and is still dominated by the beautiful church of St Mary Magdalene. In the narthex, above the main doorway to the nave, there is a lavishly sculpted tympanum decorated with scenes of the Apostolic mission that dates from the first third of the twelfth century.[37] The basic message of mission was, in any case, appropriate to an expedition that would have as one of its aims 'to extend the observance of the Christian faith'.[38] As a starting-point for the pilgrimage to Santiago de Compostela, Vézelay also had close connections with pilgrimage that contributed further to its suitability as a setting to start the crusade.

As the crowds gathered in Vézelay and the central players including the king, Queen Eleanor, Bernard of Clairvaux and nobles such as the counts of Flanders and Toulouse appeared, the sense of anticipation must have been immense. No king of France had made such a commitment before, and even the First Crusade had not seen a single assembly of such powerful men preparing to take the cross. Furthermore, the main attendees at the Council of Clermont had been churchmen, rather than laymen specifically summoned for the occasion. Odo of Deuil commented that 'at last the day long desired by the king was at hand'.[39] In one sense, there was little spontaneity because the leading nobles were aware of what they were going to do, yet this should not have detracted from the splendour or excitement of the occasion. Today people attend a religious rally, a sporting event or a rock concert having a fairly good idea of what is going to happen (in outline at least), yet they are still subject to intense emotional feelings and can behave in unpredictable ways.

So great was the multitude assembled that the main sermon had to be held outside the church. A makeshift platform was erected on the south-east slopes of the hill of Vézelay to enable the leading figures to address the crowds. It seems that Louis himself was already adorned with the cross so he must have taken it at a smaller ceremony beforehand; the king had been sent a special cross by the pope – a mark of particular favour and indicative of Eugenius's desire to nurture Louis's crusading interest.[40] For the crowds gathered below, however, there was much to hear. Bernard himself was known as one of the greatest orators of his time and he certainly rose to the occasion. He delivered an impassioned speech that used both *Quantum praedecessores* and his own words to urge the masses to help the Christians of the East. The *Chronicle of Morigny*, written in 1149–51, reported that King Louis himself addressed the assembly as well. We know that Bohemond of Antioch had incited people to crusade at meetings in 1106 and this, combined with the fact that Louis had already addressed the Christmas court at Bourges on the same subject, means it is likely that the king spoke at Vézelay too. Louis's message emphasised the disgrace of the Franks if the Muslims should succeed. 'Let us not suffer this valour to grow haughty, but by brave assistance, let it raise up the friends of God and ourselves overseas, that is the Christians, let it strike down in heavy persecution its enemies who are base and not even worthy to be called men.' He reminded his audience of the sanctity of the holy places and called upon them to help: 'Know that a great devotion to this war is come upon me; where-fore I pray earnestly that you will endeavour to give strength to my resolution by your company and assistance'.[41]

Famously, such was the desire of the audience to commit themselves to the crusade that the pre-prepared parcel of crosses Bernard had with him was soon exhausted and the abbot had to tear up his own garments to fulfil demand. Odo of Deuil wrote of (unspecified) miracles taking place; another contemporary writer mentioned that the platform upon which the main party was standing collapsed – with, miraculously, the exception of the segment bearing King Louis – although no one was hurt.[42] To commemorate the launch of the expedition Abbot Pons commissioned the construction of a chapel (which still stands today) on the site where the sermon was delivered.

After the assembly at Vézelay broke up the nobles and churchmen who had taken the cross returned to their homes and started the complex business of getting ready to crusade. Louis travelled back to Paris while Bernard began his recruitment tour in earnest.[43] Odo wrote that in spite of his physical frailty the abbot 'hastened about, preaching everywhere, and soon the number of those bearing the cross had been increased immeasurably'.[44] He was at Verdun on 12 May, but otherwise we are unsure of his movements in the late spring and early summer of 1146. One may imagine that the rest of the summer passed in practical and spiritual preparations for his lengthy tour. Some of his time must have been spent preaching in France because Bernard wrote a letter, dated by its editors to April 1146, in which he famously – and surely tongue-in-cheek – boasted of the scale of his achievement: 'As for the rest, you have ordered and I have obeyed and your authority has made my obedience fruitful. "I have declared and I have spoken, and they are multiplied above number": towns and castles are emptied, one may scarcely find one man amongst seven women, so many women are there widowed while their husbands are still alive.'[45]

At some point in this period he also organised three other essential elements in the preaching of the crusade. First, on the instructions of Pope Eugenius, he planned to move outside of France to preach in the Low Countries and the German Empire.[46] Secondly, he delegated the responsibility of recruitment for the crusade to trusted colleagues in specific areas. Some of these assemblies would have come into being as the preaching tour took place and no definitive list could have been drawn up at this early stage, but Bernard was aware of the need to spread the word as widely and as accurately as possible. Thirdly, he wrote a series of letters, intended to be sent to regions that he could not visit in person. Some of these districts were probably visited by designated preachers, but others would have relied on the local clergy to read out Bernard's letter in conjunction with *Quantum praedecessores*.

The contents of Bernard's communiqués provide insight into the energy and intensity that he brought to his preaching of the crusade. First of all, we should note where Bernard is known to have sent his letters. Understandably, for reasons of efficiency and consistency of message, he (and his secretariat) seem to have generated a core text, which was then tailored to the particular circumstances of its recipients.[47] We are aware of the contents of letters to the clergy and people of Speyer, to the clergy and people of Eastern *Francia* (meaning, as Otto of Freising informs us, an area which included the central Rhineland around Mainz and Frankfurt)[48] and Bavaria, to the people of England, to Arnold, archbishop of Cologne, to Manfred, bishop of Brescia, and to the Knights Hospitaller.[49] We also know of letters sent to Flanders, and that preachers such as Adam of Ebrach and Henry of Olmütz read out his letters at meetings at Regensburg and in Bohemia respectively. There also survives a terse epistle to the archbishop of Mainz about the preaching activities of Radulf (see below, pp.84–6); a communication 'to all the faithful' concerning the proposed Wendish Crusade; and a letter to the duke of Bohemia.[50] In addition there is a letter from Bernard's secretary, Nicholas of Clairvaux, to the count and nobles of Brittany that follows the same basic pattern as the 'standard' letter above.[51] Although a couple of other pieces of relevant correspondence also exist, a vast amount of other communication must have been lost – letters between Eugenius and the abbot, for example.[52]

The purpose of Bernard's letters was, in some ways, different from that of *Quantum praedecessores.*While both men intended to incite people to take the cross, the papal bull was also concerned to set out the spiritual rewards and legal privileges of a crusader. Bernard had to compose a message that he knew would often be read out in conjunction with *Quantum praedecessores.*[53] It could not, therefore, cover exactly the same ground, but had to carve out a distinct and complementary approach; if *Quantum praedecessores* was designed to provoke a spark, then Bernard had to fan that spark into a flame or, in certain circumstances, control a flame that already existed. Given Bernard's vast experience as a letter writer and his many years on the political stage of western Europe it is unsurprising that he was able to fulfil his brief to perfection. Even now, conviction, power and a sense of moral imperative shine through his writing and there is little doubt that his words inspired audiences across Europe. While Eugenius's bull combined practical clarity with a carefully calculated pitch at the overlapping senses of knightly and family honour and Christian duty, Bernard's was an emotive and highly personalised appeal for each individual to consider his relationship with God, coupled with an overriding sense of urgency to act to save one's own soul and Christ's patrimony.

There is also, as Meschini has observed, a reactive element to these letters.[54] In the letter to England, for example, Bernard wrote: 'They will do well who have taken up the heavenly sign'. This suggests a response to what Odo of Deuil had noted: news of the crusade had flown across the Channel – perhaps *Quantum praedecessores* had arrived, or there had been a more spontaneous outbreak of crusading enthusiasm.[55] Bernard's words probably helped to persuade more people to join the campaign, but he was also concerned to ensure that they heard the correct message and did not, for example, behave wrongly by attacking the Jews. Similarly the paragraph sent specifically to Eastern Francia and Bavaria (discussed below) shows another reactive situation that concerned leadership of the expedition. Thus, without sounding disparaging, I would say once again that Bernard should not be identified as the sole reason for everyone taking the cross; the news of the campaign had some momentum of its own.

The words '*Sermo mihi ad vos*' were a core phrase within Bernard's main crusading appeal. Leclercq and Rochais, the editors of his letters, chose the epistle to Eastern Francia and Bavaria for their volume and this text, along with some of the variations introduced for particular regional groups, merits close scrutiny in order to ascertain precisely what messages the abbot used so as to engage his audience.[56] The letter opens with the words 'I address myself to you . . . in the cause of Christ, in whom lies your salvation.'[57] Given that he was not present in person to deliver the crusade sermon this was a direct way to overcome the problem. In spite of his absence, for which he apologised, Abbot Bernard immediately introduced a highly personal note to his audience, setting himself out as Christ's representative and placing himself in their midst on the Lord's behalf. He addressed each man or woman who heard the appeal as an individual, demanding reflection and attention and bringing home the point that their hope for salvation lay in Christ.

The first full paragraph of the letter stressed the present crisis in the East and drew out brief reminders of Christ's sacrifice for man and the sanctity of the Holy Land. There was a real sense of urgency in his call to act, both for the sake of Christianity and of the audience.[58] 'Now is the acceptable time, now is the day of abundant salvation. The earth is shaken because the Lord of Heaven is losing His land, the land in which He appeared to men, in which He lived amongst men for more than thirty years; the land made glorious by His miracles, holy by His blood; the land in which the flowers of His resurrection first blossomed.'[59]

Bernard continued: 'for our sins, the enemy of the Cross has begun to lift his sacrilegious head there, to devastate with the sword that blessed land, that land of promise'.[60] We can see here the use of the imagery of the cross – a device that was of enormous resonance for those about to bear that same symbol as a mark of their commitment. Robert of Rheims and Baldric of Bourgeuil related how Pope Urban II invoked the sign of the cross at the Council of Clermont and the image was also used once by Eugenius in *Quantum praedecessores*.[61]

Bernard started his appeal for people to act when he raised the threat of the Devil: 'Alas if there should be none to withstand him, he will soon invade the very city of the living God, overturn the arsenal of our redemption and defile the holy places which have been adorned by the blood of the immaculate lamb.'[62] Once again the imagery here was both vivid and multifaceted: a call for action, combined with a reminder that the Holy Land was a storeroom of salvation and that the holy places sanctified by Christ's own blood could be defiled by the Devil. He also made a link between the Devil as the agent of this evil ('he will soon invade . . .') and the Muslims, the perpetrators of these foul deeds: 'they have cast their greedy eyes' on the holy places of Jerusalem, particularly the most important site of all, the Holy Sepulchre. We may also note an echo of *Quantum praedecessores* and, as we saw above, the use of a common theme from First Crusade preaching – the desecration of holy places – as an image to shock and to provoke a reaction.

It is interesting that Bernard chose not to mention the fall of Edessa; perhaps he felt that Eugenius had dealt with the matter sufficiently in

Quantum praedecessores. In fact, he placed emphasis on the danger to the very heart of the Christian faith, namely to Jerusalem, and, within the city, to the Holy Sepulchre itself. As we have seen, Edessa was of considerable religious significance, but it could not match that of Jerusalem. A threat to the holy city itself had a far greater emotional pull on the people of the West than danger anywhere else. Furthermore, given Bernard's stress on Christ's own sacrifices for man, it was appropriate that he should link these actions to their physical location and, in turn, connect the locations to the need for his audience to act to protect them. In an entirely practical sense, the loss of Edessa might not be seen as a particularly direct threat to Jerusalem, c.450 miles to the south. But, as the scale of their appeals (compared to earlier defeats) shows, the Franks were deeply unsettled by the fall of one of their major cities and felt vulnerable across the Latin East. While those western Europeans who had visited the Levant on pilgrimage or crusade may well have had some grasp of the layout of the region and possibly doubted a strategic threat, many others would not have had such knowledge.[63] Back in 1112, Pope Paschal II had asked for guidance on the geography of the Levant.[64] In fact, evidence from a contemporary Muslim source reveals that Zengi considered turning towards Jerusalem. This information gave Bernard's message – intentionally or not – greater relevance; Ibn Munir, a Tripolitan poet driven from his home city by the crusaders and working under the patronage of Zengi by the 1140s, wrote: 'He [Zengi] will turn tomorrow towards Jerusalem.'[65]

The next phase of Bernard's appeal consisted of a series of challenges that began thus: 'What are you doing, you mighty men of valour? What are you doing, you servants of the Cross?'[66] The first theme here is again familiar from *Quantum praedecessores*, namely a call to the military prowess of his listeners. Such an idea was commonplace and was also found, for example, in the letter of Nicholas of Clairvaux to the count and nobles of Brittany.[67] Linked to this call to martial valour we see another reference to the cross and here the phrasing applies directly to a crusader as a 'servant of the Cross'. The closest link with Eugenius's bull here was through a reminder of its dominant theme: that the efforts of the First Crusaders should not be wasted by their sons. Bernard reminded his listeners that the holy precincts had been 'cleansed of pagan filth by the swords of our fathers', but if the present audience did not react 'it would be a source of confusion and endless shame for our generation'.[68] Bernard also made the point that since the time of the First Crusade many sinners had been able to visit the Holy Land to confess their sins and receive absolution. In other words, therefore, the spiritual wellbeing of the faithful would be compromised by the loss of Jerusalem.

The heart of Bernard's message was contained in the next challenge that he issued. The abbot argued that, if God so wished, such was His power that He could easily save the Holy Land. Yet, out of kindness towards man, He did not; the reason being that God was taking pity on man and offering sinners a way to salvation through the crusade: 'I tell you that God is trying you.'[69] Bernard used the rhetorical device of a series of short statements, the last two of which were opposites, to drive this point home: 'Look, sinners, at the depths of His pity and take courage. He does not want your death, but rather that you should turn to Him and live. So he seeks not to overthrow you, but to help you'. This was followed almost immediately by a powerful exhortation to act: 'Do not hesitate, sinners.' Bernard then turned God's generosity around by saying that He pretends to be indebted to those who take up arms and must reward them with the pardon of their sins. This first reminder of the central attraction of crusading was very quickly emphasised, and to enormous effect, by a compelling passage that ranks as one of the most persuasive and powerful in crusading texts: 'I call blessed the generation that can seize an opportunity of such rich indulgence as this, blessed to be alive in this year of jubilee, this year of God's choice. The blessing is spread throughout the whole world, and all the world is flocking to receive this badge of immortality'.[70] The lure of being God's chosen people – a lucky generation selected for the chance to achieve eternal redemption – defied the listener to decline.

Bernard then repeated his piece of flattery towards the warriors amongst his audience, praising their courage and urging them to fight for a just cause.[71] In the case of his letter to England this had particular resonance because the long-running civil war between Stephen and Mathilda was the cause of huge upheaval and misery; similarly, Germany was riven by conflict. In the same way that in 1095–6 the warring castellans of France were told to stop fighting one another and to turn their energies towards a morally correct conflict, Bernard urged the protagonists to 'take vengeance on the heathen and curb the nations' rather than kill each other. To all recipients of the letter he stressed the need to look outwards and asked: 'What is this savage craving of yours? Put a stop to it now, for it is not fighting, but foolery. Thus to risk both soul and body is not brave but shocking, is not strength but folly. But now, O mighty soldiers, O men of war, you have a cause for which you can fight without danger to your souls: a cause in which to conquer is glorious and for which to die is gain'.[72] In a broader sense, Bernard's criticism of knights fighting for the wrong reasons, followed by his offering them a noble cause to turn to, has an echo of De laude novae militiae, his justification of the Knights Templar written c.1130.[73]

In the next paragraph Bernard's letter turned away from knights and towards merchants. This is the first time that the text of a direct appeal to the mercantile classes survives in crusade preaching, but, as we have seen, the history of crusading shows that their involvement in such expeditions was entirely normal. Given the prominent role of the Italian mercantile communities of Genoa, Pisa and Venice in the conquest and settlement of the Latin East, the participation of the Italians in the capture of the Balearics and, even as the Second Crusade was being launched, the Genoese making contractual arrangements to fight alongside the king of León-Castile at Almería, the link between merchants and crusading was well established. Previous appeals had tended to concentrate on the military classes (the one to Venice in 1120 was an exception), but the reality of the situation in 1146–7 was different. Here Bernard decided to extend the scope of his message to another group that could offer constructive and active support to God's cause. Unlike Urban, whose letters and sermons showed no sign of commercial interests, the abbot chose to engage more closely with the make-up of contemporary European society – a society in which the economy had grown strongly and mercantile communities were increasingly prominent, especially by comparison with 1095. Many areas in which the crusade was being preached, particularly the Low Countries and the Rhineland, contained rapidly developing urban centres and Bernard saw a chance to tap into the spiritual needs of these people while at the same time recognising openly that they could properly finance an expedition.[74] Bernard's appeal astutely keyed into the language of commerce even as he emphasised the spiritual benefits of taking the cross:

> But those of you who are merchants, men quick to seek a bargain, let me point out the advantages of this great opportunity. Do not miss them. Take the sign of the Cross and you will find indulgence for all the sins which you humbly confess. The cost is small the reward is great. Venture with devotion and the gain will be God's kingdom.[75]

In other words he linked the notion of profit to a spiritual dimension; the crusade was a good deal because in return for a relatively small investment (taking part in the expedition), the reward was eternal salvation.

After his efforts to encourage support for the crusade Bernard introduced a note of caution. The First Crusade had seen outbreaks of anti-Semitism in France and the Rhineland and, as the preaching of the new expedition got underway, there were signs that similar tensions had started to emerge again. These will be explored in greater detail below, but here Bernard issued a strong and unequivocal instruction to all his listeners not to persecute the Jews. Given the activities of Radulf and of the abbot of Lobbes, this may well have been a reaction to events that were already underway. He cloaked his message in the power of scripture and quoted from the Psalms to support this. In essence, he indicated that the presence of the Jews was a living reminder of Christ's suffering and that one day 'all Israel shall be saved', but those Jews who were killed before this would be lost to the faithful forever. This message was followed by a brief injunction against moneylenders whose usurious practices, for long a target of reform-minded churchmen of the medieval period, made them 'worse than any Jew'. Bernard then drew a parallel between Jews and pagans (the Muslims), arguing that the former were subjugated to the Christians, but the latter were attacking the faithful. He introduced therefore a technical justification for the crusade; because, according to the doctrine of holy war, violence was acceptable in defence. Clearly the capture of Edessa was an assault on Christian lands and, for that reason, the expedition had a just cause. The abbot wrote: 'But as they have now begun to attack us, it is necessary for those of us who do not carry a sword in vain to repel them with force.'[76]

Bernard's epistle to England finished at this point. However, in addition to this core text shared by other letters, some of the continental letters included extra passages worthy of discussion. First, Leclercq and Rochais draw attention to a paragraph in a manuscript from Copenhagen that was placed before the admonition against the persecution of the Jews.[77] This passage has received remarkably little consideration from historians and seems to pre-empt some ideas more fully developed by Pope Innocent III over fifty years later. In this section Bernard again extended involvement in the crusade beyond the knightly classes. He urged all people, regardless of age, to offer support for the crusade through their prayers, thus drawing the entire Christian community into the campaign:

> It may be known that those of all ages, both old and young are joined in good order in the forces of this work. Those who are young and strong in body can go to fight in the service of the army of the living God. Those who are weak in body can, through things of the mind, help those who are making the journey. Those who are poor and struggle against weaknesses of the body can support the army of God through their prayers, words and comfort.[78]

We may notice that Bernard did not offer any obvious spiritual rewards for these latter actions – as Innocent would do – but the attempt to focus the religiosity of everyone onto the crusade is an interesting idea nonetheless.

A second major addition is a paragraph in the surviving texts to Archbishop Arnold of Cologne and his clergy and people, and to the clergy and faithful of Eastern Francia and Bavaria.[79] In this section the abbot gave further practical advice, this time concerning leadership of the crusade and, once again, as a response to ongoing developments. Clearly his words about the Jews and his careful directions in the letters here were deemed necessary, otherwise two problems that had caused considerable difficulty in these regions during the First Crusade could arise again. Bernard reminded his listeners of the actions of Peter the Hermit who, according to the abbot of Clairvaux, had gained the trust of his audience, yet most of his army were killed or died of starvation. Bernard made it plain that those in charge of the new crusade had people in mind to lead the expedition ('warlike men and wise leaders') and those who wished to take part in the campaign should turn to them alone for direction. The recent problems caused by Radulf, the renegade preacher also elicited a note of caution: Bernard warned that if someone wanting to lead the crusade came forward purporting 'to have letters from us, it is not true; or if he shows letters which were sent from us, they are all false – stolen words may not be spoken'. One may deduce that people such as Radulf had claimed to have letters of authorisation from the abbot and were using them to pursue their own ambitions.[80] In sum, therefore, Bernard provided a mixture of powerful and persuasive messages designed to incite individuals to take up the challenge offered by God, to channel the enthusiasm of those already so inspired, and to secure salvation for their souls. Coupled with this was clear practical advice to ensure that the crusade remained properly focused.

Bernard almost certainly corresponded with Pope Eugenius to report on events at Vézelay and to set out or discuss his plans for the autumn. The abbot also appointed other churchmen to recruit for the crusade on his behalf. Before examining the route and the events of Bernard's tour in detail it is worth considering the identity of these preachers and the areas they covered It is likely that a number of other individuals were used to spread word of the crusade – quite probably including the papal legates – but their exact identity remains unknown.

Geoffrey of Lèves, bishop of Chartres (1118–49) was described by Bernard as a man who possessed 'fragrant virtues'.[81] He had also worked closely with King Louis VI of France and Abbot Suger of St Denis, as well as supporting Innocent II and acting as his legate in France from 1131 until the pope's death in 1143.[82] The Chronicle of Morigny regarded him as 'a famous disposer and arranger of secular business'.[83] By the time of the crusade he had been a high-profile figure in ecclesiastical and political affairs for almost thirty years and, given his standing and network of personal relationships, he was a logical choice to help recruitment. Nicholas of Clairvaux announced Geoffrey's forthcoming visit to Brittany to preach for the expedition.[84]

The abbey of Morimond was known as the intellectual centre of the Cistercian Order; it was from here, and from several of its daughter-houses, that we can see Bernard employing a network of other preachers. Morimond had also been under the abbacy of Otto of Freising in the mid 1130s. In April

1146 Bernard asked Abbot Reynald to preach at Bassigny.[85] Furthermore, he may have directed Adam of Ebrach (a daughter-house of Morimond) to give copies of his own and Eugenius's letters to Gerlach, abbot of Rein (near Salzburg and a daughter-house of Ebrach) to preach in Carinthia and Styria.[86] Bernard had certainly delegated the preaching of the crusade to the assembly at Regensburg in February 1147 to Adam, and the latter also conveyed a letter to Henry, bishop of Olmütz, to organise the crusade in Bohemia.[87] Finally, as we will see below, one other individual who gave a crusading sermon was Peter the Venerable, who spoke in Paris in the spring of 1147, although given his standing, this was hardly a surprise. In addition to these officially designated preachers, the Cistercian monk Radulf recruited many people for the expedition and his illicit activities will be discussed below.

Bernard's attempts to exert total control over recruitment for the crusade were not, therefore, entirely successful. Aside from the unauthorised preaching of Radulf there were also the efforts of troubadours. These men could never pretend to offer the spiritual benefits dispensed by a churchman but, as we will see, their message – delivered in verse in the vernacular – was a powerful encouragement to join the expedition.[88] We have noted the First Crusade work of Gregory Bechada, the composition of crusading epics such as the *Chanson d'Antioche* and the celebration of the virtues of Christian warriors in the *Chanson de Roland*. There is evidence that songs were composed during the First Crusade; later, Duke William IX of Aquitaine described his adventures of 1101 'using rhythmic verses with skilful modulations'.[89] From the time of the Second Crusade, however, there survive the first texts for songs with a specifically crusading theme; for campaigns in the Levant, Iberia, or both. One of these songs is in Old French and ten are in Occitan. Such songs would have been sung at courts and in public places, and so it is quite possible that they were heard by a large number of people. Appendix 2 below contains a translation of the Old French song, *Chevalier, mult estes guariz*, the most detailed of those concerned with the Second Crusade.[90]

The author of this song was anonymous, presumably a layman, albeit one familiar enough with the Bible to use the Book of Exodus confidently. The tone and emphases of the song reflect an interesting mixture of secular and lay elements. In some respects they are quite different from the message conveyed by Eugenius and Bernard, although in a number of other ways the songs did echo particular ideas quite closely. There is, in fact, sufficient overlap with *Quantum praedecessores* to suggest that the author had heard the papal encyclical and used it in creating his own song. The intended audience consisted of the knights and nobles of northern France who would march under the leadership of Louis VII. The king had evidently taken the cross by the time the song was written, which gives a window between April 1146 (post-Vézelay) and June 1147 (when the expedition departed) for its date of composition. The king's behaviour was held up as an exemplar to all and this may suggest that the compositor was from the royal circle. In large part, the language was slanted heavily towards the contemporary chivalric ethos and the values of the knightly class, although given the subject matter it was closely intertwined with spiritual issues as well. In view of the provenance of songs of this nature one might suggest that they provide a better insight into the concerns of the medieval knight, as perceived by someone writing directly for that audience, than the writings of churchmen.

The author immediately revealed that he viewed the crusade as an expedition against the Muslims of both Iberia and the Holy Land, which reflected a widely shared perception amongst contemporaries. The song opened with a verse describing how the Muslims had wronged God by taking his fiefs: a clear use of a conventional crusading theme – the stealing of Christian territory – clothed in imagery appropriate to a knightly audience. The listeners learned of this 'dishonour'; another notion guaranteed to connect with their values. The song also related the destruction of churches in Edessa and noted that the Christian faith was no longer practised there – a situation of particular poignancy given, as the author indicated, its well-known status as the first city to adopt the faith.

The concept of self-sacrifice was also quite prominent: there was a call to the knights to make a gift of their bodies to God by way of recognition to Christ of the sacrifice that he made for mankind on the cross. The sacrifices made by Louis were cited as worthy of emulating because, as the richest and most powerful king, he had surrendered all his fine clothes and lands to the Lord's cause. This was a familiar theme of crusade preachers; it was mentioned by Guibert of Nogent and by Robert of Rheims; also by Bishop Peter of Oporto in his sermon to the men of the northern European fleet who arrived in Iberia in June 1147.[91]

The most striking image invoked by the singer was his call to regard the crusade as a divinely organised tournament, held at Edessa and fought between Hell and Heaven, in which God asked all those who wished to support his cause not to fail him. Tournaments are believed to have started in a recognisable form in the 1120s, but they were deeply frowned upon by the Church. Several attempts were made to legislate against these events – for instance the decrees of the Councils of Clermont (1130) and Rheims (1131) and those of the Second Lateran Council of 1139 where Pope Innocent II had decreed, 'we entirely forbid, moreover, these abominable jousts and tournaments in which knights come together by agreement and rashly engage in showing off their physical prowess and daring, and which often result in human deaths and danger to souls'.[92] Just a year after the crusade, Bernard of Clairvaux himself described tournaments as 'accursed' events.[93] Nonetheless, they remained enormously popular amongst the knightly classes and, in the required co-ordination of men and horses, they were by far the most realistic preparation possible for war. The choice of this imagined scene is the clearest demonstration of the secular-minded standpoint of the songwriter. The text also indicated that, at this stage of the crusade, there was a common perception that Edessa was the target of the campaign. The author was not entirely secular in his approach, however, and he chose to employ biblical imagery when describing the Muslims, comparing the demise of Pharaoh and his men in the Book of Exodus with the hoped-for fate of Zengi and his army (Zengi is called here *Sanguin*, in a pun on 'blood' commonly used in the West at the time).[94] After every verse of the song there was a chorus, again of a spiritual theme, that constantly reminded potential crusaders of the rewards that awaited them should they die – namely a place in Paradise in the company of the angels of the Lord. In essence, the crusade was cast in terms of an opportunity to make good an outrage against the knights' ultimate lord, God. It was also represented as an act of rightful vengeance – another theme familiar from the preaching of the First Crusade as well as from that of 1146–7. Although we do not know how widely this song was circulated, its themes appear to be a carefully thought out combination of the secular and the spiritual which would have proven an effective complement to the mainstream church recruitment.

To sum up, we can perceive a range of reasons why Louis VII took part in the crusade and we can track the organisation of the magnificent event at Vézelay. Following on from this, we can see the themes and ideas used by Bernard to encourage and, where necessary, to direct existing crusade enthusiasm. Those outside his control could be of help, such as the anonymous songwriter or, as we will see next, extremely dangerous, as in the case of the monk, Radulf.

CHAPTER 5

Bernard's Preaching Tour of Flanders and Germany

THE ATTACKS ON THE JEWS
AND THE RECRUITMENT OF KING CONRAD III

Before discussing Bernard's tour in detail it is important to assess the wider agenda of the abbot and his superior, Pope Eugenius. After the successful meeting at Vézelay the launch of the crusade in France seemed to be reasonably assured. It was to the Low Countries and the German Empire, including Italy, that Bernard and Eugenius turned their attention next. Here we can see a broader conception of the scope of the crusade emerging, both in terms of the participants involved and, eventually, with regard to its targets. A charter from Flanders dated 14 August 1146 placed the initiative for the preaching tour firmly with the pope, saying that Bernard 'had come from France at the orders of Pope Eugenius to preach the Cross against the Saracens in Flanders and Brabant'.[1] Otto of Freising set out the background to the journey; he wrote that, at the outset of the crusade, Eugenius had granted to the abbot the authority 'to preach and move the hearts of all the peoples of France *and* Germany' (my italics). Furthermore, 'when countless throngs in western Gaul had been aroused for the expedition across the sea, Bernard decided to turn his attention to the eastern kingdom of the Franks, to stir it with the ploughshare of preaching, both that he might move the heart of the prince of the Romans to accept the cross and that he might silence Radulf who, in connection with the Jews, was moving the people in the cities to repeated outbreaks against their lords'.[2] Otto's first statement suggests that the Empire was seen as a part of the crusade from its inception; the second has more precision, putting a definite focus on the recruitment of Conrad himself and the need to quell the effects of Radulf's anti-Semitic preaching. Alberic of Trois-Fontaines was another, admittedly later, writer to state plainly that Eugenius dispatched Abbot Bernard to Germany to preach to the faithful.[3]

The involvement of Conrad would change the whole tenor of the crusade. Louis VII had been the first major western monarch to take the cross, but to enlist the emperor-in-waiting would bring on board the most powerful ruler in Christian Europe and, potentially, give the expedition far greater military strength. The participation of Conrad and the end of the threat from Radulf will be analysed shortly, but first of all we must look at the early stages of Bernard's tour, namely to Flanders and the Low Countries.

After his mesmerising performance at Vézelay Bernard organised the preaching of the crusade in France and oversaw the dispatch of letters across Europe; he then prepared for his long tour. The abbot took Eugenius's commission to lead the crusade appeal with the utmost seriousness and committed himself to an enormous effort; a great risk given his well-documented physical frailties.[4] To accompany him he chose Baldwin of Châtillon, a Fleming with First Crusade ancestry, and two monks from Clairvaux, Gerard and Geoffrey – the latter being a former pupil of Peter Abelard who had joined the abbey after hearing Bernard's *Sermo de conversione ad clericos* at Paris in 1140 and acted as his secretary until 1145. Geoffrey wrote Books 3, 4 and 5 of the *Vita Prima S. Bernardi* and drew the assembly of the hagiographical texts together. He is one of our principal sources for the tour of Germany, although, given that his work was a contribution towards the abbot's canonisation, it is deeply problematic because invariably (if understandably) it portrays Bernard in a consistently positive light; as Ward commented, 'a theme of absolute holiness runs throughout the biography'.[5] The sixth book of the *Vita* is the *Historia miraculorum in itinere Germanica patratorum*, a compendium in three sections of first-hand accounts of the abbot's journey, running from November 1146 to February 1147.[6] At the heart of this book was the idea that the numerous miracles from this period were understood as a sign of divine approval of the preaching of the crusade. These Bernardine writings can be supplemented with various other narratives and charter evidence in order to reconstruct the abbot's tour.

Bernard's initial destination was Flanders, a stronghold of genuine crusading enthusiasm. The counts of Flanders had an unparalleled record of journeys to the Holy Land, beginning with the pilgrimage of Count Robert I in 1087–90 and followed by the prominent role played by Robert II 'Jerusalem' on the First Crusade, by the year of service given by Count Charles the Good *c.*1108 and by Count Thierry's own expedition of 1138–9. Flemings had also formed part of the north-European fleets that sailed to the Levant in 1102, 1104 and 1110, and in the aftermath of the civil war of 1128 some of the defeated partisans of William Clito probably took part in the 1129 Damascus Crusade. All of this meant that the county seemed a perfect fit for Eugenius III's idea of the sons following in their fathers' footsteps. The fact that Count

Thierry had travelled to Vézelay to take the cross in March 1146 indicated a level of commitment from the region was already apparent.[7]

There was also ongoing contact between the Holy Land and Flanders, in part because a number of Flemings had chosen to settle there in the aftermath of the First Crusade.[8] The Saint-Omer family had a claim to the lordship of Galilee and their relative Hosto was one of several Flemish Templars active in the 1140s.[9] Most pertinently, perhaps, there were close family ties between the comital house and the rulers of Jerusalem. Thierry's second wife, Sibylla, was the daughter of King Fulk (1131–43) and, at the time of the preaching of the crusade, King Baldwin III and his mother, Queen Melisende, were Sibylla's half-brother and stepmother, respectively. One further consideration in assessing the area's crusading potential was the prosperity of Flanders; the expansion of the commercial markets had generated considerable wealth for the mercantile classes – a group already identified as amongst Bernard's target audience.[10]

It seems that the abbot chose to capitalise on these highly promising circumstances and spent a substantial amount of time in the county, probably around three months in total. The only precise dates we have are from a charter given at Ghent on 14 August 1146 and another marking his presence just outside the county at Villers in Brabant on 18 October.[11] It is generally assumed that he spent the intervening period in Flanders. Several other charters (dated only to 1146) and narratives attest to this and it is interesting to observe Bernard's name on witness lists alongside those of men whom we know to have taken part in the crusade.

In the late summer of 1146 the ecclesiastical province of Rheims held a council at Arras and here Bernard met people such as his old friend Bishop Alvisus of Arras, who would die on the journey to the East.[12] Given the number of other prominent churchmen present, such as Archbishop Samson of Rheims and Bishop Joscelin of Soissons, it is highly likely that the planning of the crusade was discussed. The charter at Ghent from mid-August was a confirmation by Count Thierry to the local abbey of Saint Pharailda and mentioned the recitation of the antiphon *Salve Regina* for Bernard, in 'the presence of many nobles'.[13] The abbot also witnessed a confirmation of privileges by Thierry for the abbey of Saint Martin's of Ypres, and another one for the church of Saint Nicholas at Furnes.[14] The latter document is especially noteworthy because of the presence of Christian of Gistel, who became one of the leaders of the expedition to Lisbon, and that of Anselm of Ypres, Thierry's steward and companion on the crusade to the Holy Land.[15] A charter of Radulf, castellan of Bruges, was witnessed by Bernard and by the crusaders Abbot Leo of Saint-Bertin and Anselm of Ypres.[16] There is a possible reference to Bernard's presence at the abbey of Loos, near Lille.[17] Finally, the chronicle of the abbey of Saint Bertin noted that when Bernard came to the region to preach the Cross of the Lord many monasteries were built and repaired. From this, Pitra has quite reasonably inferred that the abbot stayed in a variety of religious houses in Flanders, most obviously the Cistercian abbeys of Vaucelles, Clairmarais and Les-Dunes, as well as in the famous abbey of Anchin. Given the time he spent in the area it is probable that he visited the towns of Boulogne and Tournai (the town is known to have received a letter from Pope Eugenius and was the home of one of Bernard's correspondents, Ogier of St Médard).[18]

In October Bernard and his party moved into the imperial lands of Brabant and Namur. Their destination was the abbey of Afflighem, a house that had received gifts from Godfrey of Bouillon and Baldwin of Boulogne prior to their departure on the First Crusade.[19] It was here that the *Chronicon Affligemense* reported the first miracle of the journey: when Bernard approached a statue of the Virgin Mary near the church door he said '*Ave Maria*' and the image duly responded '*Ave Bernarde*'.[20] As we will see below, this was to herald many more such happenings; the abbot's miracle-working became a prominent aspect of the tour. Such was his immense charisma and the heightened sense of spiritual excitement he generated that there seems to have been a general acceptance of his powers.[21]

From Afflighem the party moved to Gembloux and then on to Liège where Philip, the local archdeacon, joined the abbot's retinue. Liège was the home of one of the earliest copies of Albert of Aachen's *Historia*, a narrative that emphasised the heroism of Godfrey of Bouillon and his brother Baldwin. The fact that the latter had been the first Frankish count of Edessa indicates that Bernard was in a place with a strong sense of crusading traditions, which thus dovetailed neatly with the core message of *Quantum praedecessores*.[22]

Once Bernard reached the edge of the Rhineland, however, he had to confront one of the most serious problems to face him in the preaching of the Second Crusade. From the start of recruitment for the expedition there had been an undercurrent of anti-Semitism that seemed to presage a repetition of the terrible events of 1096 when thousands of Jews were slaughtered or forcibly converted by bloodthirsty crusaders.[23] As Guibert of Nogent wrote, the First Crusaders attacked the 'internal enemies of Christendom' before going on to confront the 'external enemies of Christ'.[24] Or, as a Jewish writer expressed it:

It came to pass in the year one thousand twenty-eight after the destruction of the [Second] Temple [1096] that this calamity befell Israel. The barons, nobles and commonfolk in France ... decided ... to clear the way to Jerusalem the Holy City, and to reach the sepulchre of the crucified, a trampled corpse that can neither aid nor save because he is vanity. They said to one another: 'Behold we travel to a distant land to do battle with the kings of that land. [We take] our lives in our hands to kill or subjugate all the kingdoms which do not believe in the crucified. How much more [should we subjugate or kill] the Jews who killed and crucified him?'[25]

A gravestone in Mainz that commemorates the burial of a murdered Jewish woman on 19 April 1146 could well stand amongst the first stirrings of trouble with the Second Crusade.[26] The eyewitness account of Ephraim of Bonn, who was aged thirteen at the time of the crusade and wrote his *Book of Remembrance* in the 1170s, indicated that it was around August and September 1146 that the situation intensified.[27] The chief cause of this violence was the work of one of the most intriguing figures of the crusade: Radulf, a Cistercian monk, whose name, as Ephraim tells us, was uncannily close to '*radof*', the Hebrew verb meaning 'to persecute'.[28] Radulf came from an unknown Cistercian monastery in France and first appeared in the Low Countries, probably at the abbey of Lobbes in Hainault. Radulf then passed through Cologne, Mainz, Worms, Speyer, Strasbourg and other neighbouring towns – the very locations where the pogroms had taken place fifty years previously. As we will see, the church authorities abhorred the localised consequences of his preaching, yet as a recruiting agent for the crusade he seems to have been remarkably effective. Those sources closest to the Church, such as Otto of Freising, former abbot of the Cistercian house of Morimond, decried Radulf as a man only 'moderately imbued with the knowledge of letters'.[29] Yet several others wrote of him in glowing terms. The *Annales Rodenses*, composed just north of Aachen, described him as a man 'of wonderful sanctity', and mentioned that his 'great and famous preaching' was so compelling that it was as if 'one-tenth of the entire land' were marked with the cross to make the journey to Jerusalem.[30] There survives a manuscript from Trier which, as well as explicitly linking the First and Second Crusades in a continuum, depicted Radulf in the most positive terms: 'In the year of the incarnate word 1147, in the fiftieth year from the earlier expedition, that is to say, of Duke Godfrey and the other leaders . . . at the exhortation of a certain venerable priest, Bernard . . . and also of Radulf the splendid teacher and monk [the crusade took place]'.[31] Radulf could not, however, speak German, although his working methods were revealed in the *Gesta abbatum Lobbiensium*, which mentioned him using Abbot Lambert of Lobbes, 'who was competent in both languages, that is German and Roman', to speak for him.[32] Therefore three independent sources complimented Radulf; he was undoubtedly a charismatic orator who tapped into the similar combination of the crusaders' need for money and popular enthusiasm for the removal of unbelievers that drove events back in 1096. Whether this shows these chroniclers passively espousing his ideas or simply recognising his ability as a public speaker is a moot point; as far as Bernard, the Church and, indeed, the secular authorities of Germany were concerned, he was a menace.

Chazan indicates how the Christian view of the Jews had developed between the time of the First Crusade and the Second. Opposition to the Jews became more earthly and real; it moved from a perception of the Jews as the historic opponents of Christianity to more tangible signs of concern at their involvement in financial dealings, blasphemy against Christianity and its symbols, and violence towards Christian people. Some people believed that this merited a direct reaction – clearly Radulf and his followers were amongst them – but others, such as the abbot of Clairvaux, were more measured.[33] Bernard used verses from Psalm 59 to explain his ideas, although at the start of the text (not in the abbot's letter) there was a biblically grounded reference to the ancient enmity from the Jews: 'Deliver me from my enemies, O my God; defend me against my assailants. Save me from evildoers; deliver me from murderers' (Ps. 59: 1–2). Thus the traditional sense of Jewish hostility was restated, but Bernard expressly forbade violence towards the Jews because he felt that this was contrary to divine wishes. God preferred the Jews to be kept alive, to 'remind us of what our Lord suffered. They are dispersed all over the world so that by expiating their crime they may be everywhere the living witnesses of our redemption.' If they were killed now, then their souls would be lost forever: 'If the Jews are utterly wiped out, what will become of our hope for their promised salvation, their eventual conversion?'[34] Because they lived peacefully under the Christians, some restraint was required.

Bernard's words do not seem to have been sufficient because Archbishop Henry of Mainz was compelled to write to him and report Radulf's activities.[35] The abbot's reply gave a revealing insight into his feelings. His first reaction was to break down any idea that Radulf has been given permission to preach: he 'has received no authority from men or through men, nor has he been sent by God'. Furthermore, as a monk, he should have been praying inside his monastery, rather than abandoning his duty and preaching in the world. Bernard then set out the heart of his complaint: 'I find three things most reprehensible in him: unauthorised preaching, contempt for episcopal authority, and incitation to murder.' The abbot's concerns to maintain a proper hierarchy and delineation of power seem to have had a greater priority than stopping Radulf's message. We know that Bernard chose his fellow-preachers carefully and we have seen how he warned against rabble-rousers calling for the crusade; clearly he wanted God's message to be spread in a coherent, consistent and properly controlled manner. After venting his anger at this improper state of affairs, the abbot set out again the biblical arguments against killing the Jews: 'Is it not a far better triumph for the Church to convince and convert the Jews than to put them all to the sword?' He then rounded upon Radulf and dismissed his hellish learning and arrogance.[36]

Yet once more, in spite of these words of advice, the local hierarchy could not bring the renegade to heel. The situation was beginning to generate civil unrest as the masses tried to attack or to extort money from the Jews who, in turn, sought protection from the local secular and ecclesiastical lords. Any breakdown in law and order was hardly a positive environment to recruit for a crusade and, as Otto of Freising suggested, along with Bernard's wish to enlist the support of King Conrad III, it was the need to silence Radulf that prompted the abbot to go to Germany and track down the troublemaker in person.[37]

In early November Bernard travelled south from Worms to Mainz for a face-to-face encounter with Radulf. According to Otto of Freising he summoned the renegade and, presumably in the strongest possible terms, told him 'not to arrogate to himself on his own authority the word of preaching, roving about over the land in defiance of the rule of monks'. Once again, the issue of proper authority appeared paramount to Bernard. Radulf eventually backed down and agreed to return to his monastery, although the news was ill-received by the local population who threatened to riot and were only prevented from doing so by respect for Bernard's piety.[38] However unpalatable Radulf's message is to the present-day reader, this evidence, along with the three independent sources cited above, shows that he was a persuasive individual with a message of considerable popular appeal.

Ephraim of Bonn described a number of assaults on Jews, led by 'the priest of idolatry [who] rose against the nation of God to destroy, slay and annihilate them'. Radulf sought 'to contaminate the Christians with the horizontal–vertical sign. He went along barking and was named "barker", summoning all in the name of Christ to go to Jerusalem to war against Ishmael. Whenever he went, he spoke evil of the Jews of the land and incited the snake and the dogs against us, saying: "Avenge the crucified one upon his enemies who stand before you; then go to war against the Ishmaelites." '[39] This demonstrates that Radulf recruited for the expedition to the Holy Land, but urged the crusaders to kill the Jews as a precursor to fighting the Muslims.

Ephraim perceived the arrival of Bernard as the reason for the Jews' deliverance. The abbot countered Radulf's arguments and, by the efforts of 'this decent priest', the tension began to abate. The Jews survived through more practical methods too: at the time of the First Crusade they had given protection money to local lords and churchmen and this practice proved effective again.[40] In 1146, the community of Cologne paid the archbishop to let them use the fortress of Wolkenburg (south-east of the city) as a refuge and pledged their lives, homes and wealth in the city as collateral. Ephraim himself went to Wolkenburg and this stronghold seemed to act as a magnet for many Jews in the region. There is also an implication that King Conrad protected the Jews because Ephraim worried (wrongly, as it transpired) about his absence.[41]

The episodes of persecution Ephraim described were largely isolated incidents; no less tragic for those involved, of course, but not a systematic slaughter. Simon of Trier was murdered in Cologne; Mistress Mina of Speyer was mutilated; Isaac and Judah of Mainz were killed as they worked in their vineyards and Samuel of Worms was slain in a roadside ambush. Christians tried forcibly to baptise Gutalda of Aschaffenburg but she refused to be profaned and drowned herself in the river. Interestingly, some Jews fought back against their attackers and in one case, when the killer of two young boys was identified, on the payment of a bribe to the local bishop, the man was seized by the authorities, blinded, and soon died.[42] Where Ephraim reported troubles on a bigger scale it was at a distance: in Ham 150 were killed, in Sully 'a great many were slain', and in Carentan too. It seems, therefore, that there was some violence towards Jews in France, although in England King Stephen acted to bring them under royal protection.[43] The *Annales Herbipolenses* related an outbreak of violence in February 1147 against the Jews of Würzburg and showed the civil disorder that might result. The troubles were caused by the mysterious death of a Christian; the Jews were held responsible and they were attacked by the locals who killed many of them and stole their property. When the townspeople began to see miracles at the tomb of the murdered Christian they tried to get the man canonised, but Bishop Siegfried resisted. Such was the crowd's fury at his decision that he had to take refuge in a tower. Only the departure of the agitators on crusade brought the matter to a close.[44] By July 1147 – after the crusaders had set out for the East – Ephraim stated that the Jews had returned to their native cities and homes; the danger had passed. The author continued his chronicle by noting, with some satisfaction, that the crusade failed and that 'only a small number of the murderers ever returned to their homeland'. Ephraim ended his work by recalling the sacrifice made by the martyrs of the faith and recorded it in his Book of Remembrance.[45]

From Mainz Bernard moved on to Frankfurt where, around the second week of November, he met Conrad III. The king's involvement in the Second Crusade has been a matter of some historical debate.[46] The traditional view, recently supported by Loud, is that an unwilling monarch was pressured into taking the cross by the overambitious Bernard who had not consulted Pope Eugenius on the matter; furthermore, this foolish act of bravado made the crusade to the East far too large and unwieldy and sowed the seeds for its inevitable defeat.[47] Following on from this, historians have often treated the

German crusaders as a support act to the French army.[48] This is largely because the Germans lack a detailed eyewitness account of their expedition, whereas the narrative of Odo of Deuil provides just such a text for King Louis's campaign. Yet this is misleading; every contemporary regarded Conrad as the senior figure on the crusade and saw that he set out with a larger army.[49] For these reasons it is important to explore the background to the German involvement in the Second Crusade and to explain why it was logical for the king to take part in it.

Conrad probably learned of the fall of Edessa in the summer of 1145. The *Annales Reicherspergenses* recorded that messengers from Jerusalem came to the kings and princes of the West.[50] The king must also have received a report on the causes of the crusade – and probably on its early planning – from a very well-placed source indeed. Conrad's half-brother, Otto of Freising, was at the papal court at Viterbo when Bishop Hugh of Jabala brought an appeal for help to the *curia*. Otto was also present at Vetrella when Eugenius first issued *Quantum praedecessores* on 1 December 1145.[51] As we have seen above, the crusade appeal was initially directed towards King Louis VII rather than towards Conrad. Several factors may have lain behind this, including the position of the French as the main contributors to the crusade movement to date and the family ties between Prince Raymond of Antioch and his niece, Queen Eleanor. Equally, however, Otto would have updated the pope on the series of ongoing problems in the Empire which meant that conditions were not remotely conducive to crusading. Otto himself tells us that – in contrast to the situation in France – the imperial lands were in turmoil. He had passed through Italy en route to the papal court and witnessed the grim aftermath of a bitter struggle between the Florentines and the Pisans against the people of Lucca and Siena. Other conflicts involved the cities of Venice and Ravenna, as well as Verona and Vicenza against Padua and Treviso. In part, Otto blamed this violence on the absence of Conrad from the region.[52] The position in Germany was equally bad: 'all over the world the whirlwind of war filled the earth and involved practically the whole of the Empire in seditious uprisings'. Otto mentioned troubles in Swabia, between the duke and Conrad of Zahringen; in Bavaria, between Henry of Austria (Otto's brother) and Bishop Henry of Regensburg; and in Namur, where Archbishop Adalbert of Trier fought Count Henry. Furthermore, tensions between Germany and neighbouring Hungary had reached a point where he wrote in 1146 that 'a great conflict is expected'. Poland too was in a state of chaos, with three of the sons of Boleslaw III in conflict with their fourth sibling.[53]

Given these dismal conditions it was logical to begin recruitment in France until the political climate in the Empire improved. Nevertheless, it must have been inevitable that the people in Conrad's lands would want to take part in the crusade. As had been seen in 1095–6, if the inhabitants of one particular land were offered the chance of salvation, quite naturally their neighbours would want to share in this opportunity too. Furthermore, through the heroic deeds of Godfrey of Bouillon, duke of Lower Lorraine, there was an obvious tie to the First Crusade and the 'deeds of the fathers' so emphasised by Pope Eugenius; other traditions of crusading and holy war existed as well. Robert of Rheims suggested that some German bishops may have been present at the Council of Clermont.[54] The Investiture Controversy had prevented Emperor Henry IV from joining the crusade, but Count Hartmann of Dillingen and Kyburg from southern Germany linked up with Godfrey's forces.[55] Few other nobles took the cross, although Peter the Hermit's persuasive preaching in the Rhineland generated a rush of popular enthusiasm known as the 'People's Crusade' which amounted to an army estimated at 20,000 under the leadership of Emicho of Leiningen, count of Vlanheim, near Mainz.[56]

In 1100 the patriarch of Jerusalem asked all Germans to come and assist in the defence of Jerusalem.[57] This, in part, may have prompted Duke Welf IV of Bavaria to lead a substantial contingent of men on the crusade of 1101. Welf had been sympathetic to papal reform and in any case, he was on good terms with Henry IV as well. There is little evidence for papal preaching in the region apart from the general appeals of Paschal II from 1100.[58] Close ties existed between Welf and other crusading families; his wife Judith was the sister of Count Robert II of Flanders, one of the leaders of the First Crusade. Welf was also distantly related to the Capetian royal house; this meant a connection to Hugh of Vermandois, another prominent figure from the earlier expedition. Mullinder estimates that 10,000 Germans participated in the 1101 crusade and indicated that the army included several important nobles such as the counts of Regensburg, Passau and Scheyern, the bishop of Bamberg and many *ministeriales*.[59] In the period after 1101 there is less evidence for German involvement in crusading, although Emperor Henry IV expressed an interest in visiting Jerusalem as a penitent.[60] Hadewerk of Westphalia was a leading figure in the northern European fleet that assisted King Baldwin I of Jerusalem in his attack on Jaffa in 1102.[61] It is also likely that Pope Calixtus II directed a crusade appeal to Germany in *c*.1121–2 and it seems that there was some reaction.[62]

There was, however, a further theatre of holy war developing – the campaigns against the pagan Wends of the Baltic and Eastern Europe. This may have encouraged the popularity of crusading in the Empire and, ultimately, it would exert a profound impact on the shape and form of the Second Crusade itself. This struggle had been going on for several decades prior to the time of the Second Crusade and its evolution will be discussed in more detail below, but a couple of examples illustrate the situation briefly. In *c*.1107–8 a clerk of the archbishop of Magdeburg sent a letter on behalf of a long list of senior churchmen from eastern Saxony to the provinces of Mainz and Cologne, the county of Flanders and the duchy of Lorraine. The author drew a parallel between the wars with the pagans in the Baltic and the liberation of Jerusalem by the First Crusade:

> Declare a holy war, rouse up the strong. Arise ye princes against the enemies of Christ, take up the shield, gird yourselves valiant men, and let all men of war come . . . Break forth and come all ye lovers of Christ and the Church, and prepare yourselves like the Franks for the liberation of Jerusalem. Our Jerusalem, which from the beginning was free, is made a slave by the cruelty of the heathens.[63]

His appeal fell on deaf ears and failed to persuade the church hierarchy to extend the concept of the crusade to northern Europe at that time, but it does show how the capture of Jerusalem had impacted upon the ideas of those fighting the pagans. Secondly, during the 1120s the *Millstäter Exodus*, a vernacular epic that equated the Book of Exodus to the crusades, was composed for a knightly audience; again, this shows such ideas were current in the Empire.[64] If one combines this history with the opportunity of salvation put forward in *Quantum praedecessores* – bearing in mind that nothing like that opportunity had been offered in such widespread and compelling terms for fifty years – it is self-evident that it was both impractical and impossible to exclude the Empire from the Second Crusade. If, therefore, crusaders were to come from imperial lands then who, other than Conrad III, should head them?

Bernard of Clairvaux's letters to the people of Eastern Francia and Bavaria, Cologne, and Brixen included a warning against setting out for the Levant without proper leadership. As he reminded them, Peter the Hermit had been a disastrous commander on the First Crusade – and while Conrad was not named (he had yet to take the cross at that time), the king was probably the 'proper' leader whom the abbot had in mind.[65] There were many other reasons why Conrad should be approached. He was aged about fifty and was an experienced ruler and a brave warrior. He had also vowed to visit the Holy Land in 1124, a promise he almost certainly fulfilled, or else it would probably have been mentioned as part of his motivation for crusading in 1146–7.[66] As the ruler of the largest political entity in the West his presence would help to attract a substantial army and to enhance the military capability of the crusade. Conrad's enmity to the Sicilians also dovetailed with the pope's political agenda, and the likelihood that this would prompt a land-crossing of Asia Minor, rather than a sea-passage involving the Sicilians, was another positive point as far as the papacy was concerned.

Eugenius and Bernard's conception of the relationship between the papacy and Empire is also of relevance here. Compared to the situation at the time of the First Crusade and the Investiture Controversy, matters were vastly improved by the 1140s; indeed, in the previous decade, support from Lothar III had been essential for Innocent II's success in the papal schism. Another reason why the papacy looked to Germany was the long-standing threat from the Sicilians to the Patrimony of St Peter. This positive tenor, although not entirely free from tension, prevailed over the next decade. In 1144 Bernard wrote of the Church and Empire: 'God did not unite them for their mutual destruction, but for their mutual support.' He argued that it was the duty of the Christian prince to protect the Church when it was under attack: 'It is clearly the concern of Caesar to both succour his own crown and to defend the Church.'[67] Eugenius himself has left little sense of his views prior to the start of the crusade, although, as Newman observed, the Cistercian attitude to relations between the secular and ecclesiastical authorities generally favoured partnership.[68] In other words, the idea of the 'two swords' working together to advance the cause of Christianity was quite natural in the ideological climate of the time. Interestingly, the same principle can be ascertained at the German court through the work of Conrad's half-brother, Otto of Freising, whose *De duabus civitatibus* dated from early 1146 and was written, according to Southern, 'to emphasise the co-operation of secular and ecclesiastical rulers in the triumphant rise of western Christendom under the joint guidance of popes, emperors and scholars, culminating in those of the present day'.[69]

Historians such as Cosack have suggested that Eugenius's wish for Conrad to protect him from the Roman citizenry and his fear of Roger of Sicily meant that he was opposed to the king's participation in the crusade.[70] It is true that Eugenius had previously asked the German for help in the former matter, and that Roger could have posed a greater threat if Conrad was absent on crusade; however, this is to ignore that in 1144 Lucius II had signed a seven-year truce with Roger – which, with the benefit of hindsight, we know that he kept to.[71] Furthermore, the most recent of Conrad's letters to the pope made no mention of such fears on Eugenius's part.[72] The dispatch of the legate Theodwin of Santa Rufina, accompanied by cardinal-priest Thomas of San Vitale, to try to bring peace to Germany in the autumn of 1145, may have reflected a desire by the pope to calm a troubled situation, although it must also be noted that their presence would have helped to create the necessary conditions for the expedition.[73] Ongoing communication between the *curia* and the imperial court can be observed further through the visit of Abbot Wibald of Stavelot, another very senior figure in the German Church and government, who was with the pope at Sutri on 7 May 1146.[74]

From Conrad's perspective there was a matter of his demonstrable personal piety and, with Louis VII having taken the cross already, a measure of prestige involved too. Conrad was, as noted, the senior ruler in the Latin West and the emperor-in-waiting. His need to be seen as worthy of this role may have motivated him to take part in the crusade. He would have been well aware – as were all the potential crusaders – of the potential for fame and glory. While Conrad faced challenges from within his lands and from the emerging new Sicilian monarchy, as well as the vexed question of the 'other' emperor in Byzantium, his behaviour during and immediately after the crusade showed that he was deeply self-conscious in his use of titles (see below, p. 213); it is worth suggesting that the issue of status was on his mind back in 1146 as well.

At the time that *Quantum praedecessores* was issued the king was involved in a project that connected royal honour and holy war. In 1145, Bishop Egilbert of Bamburg proposed the canonisation of Emperor Henry II (1002–24), an idea embraced by Conrad who wrote letters to Eugenius in support of the plan.[75] The papal document that authorised the canonisation was dated 14 March 1146, and it is almost certain that Otto of Freising made representations to Eugenius on the matter. The grounds for Henry's canonisation bear scrutiny; the bull claimed the following reasons: Henry's chastity (he was married but childless); miracles took place at his tomb; he had founded the church of Bamburg (amongst others); and had a primary role in the conversion of King Stephen and all of Hungary.[76] The third of these points can be amplified. The foundation charter for the see of Bamburg, dated to 1007, stated that it was established 'so that the paganism of the Slavs should be destroyed and the name of Christ remembered there for always'.[77] Pope Benedict VIII had visited Bamburg in 1016 and the town became a centre for the extension of Christianity eastwards.[78] Henry's involvement in the conversion of Hungary was based on promoting peaceful means rather than conquest, and the baptism of King Stephen seems to have coincided with his marriage to the emperor's sister, Gisela, in 1001.[79] Henry made attacks on the pagans in 1003–4 and 1017, although his image was somewhat tarnished by the fact that in his struggle against the Christian ruler, Boleslaw of Poland, he was assisted by pagan allies – a point that provoked an outcry at the time.[80] Naturally, the canonisation documents omitted this difficulty, as well as passing over Henry's domineering hand in the selection and appointment of the majority of figures in the German Church – hardly an attraction to twelfth-century reformers.[81] The relevance of this episode to the Second Crusade is that just as recruitment for the expedition began, Conrad had looked to the papacy for the highest possible recognition of the actions of one of his predecessors in a struggle against non-Christians. Presumably this sent a positive message to Eugenius as to Conrad's interest in crusading. As an aside, it is worth noting that Conrad was buried next to Henry II in Bamburg; further evidence of the affinity and perceived connections between the two men.[82]

Just as Bernard entered imperial territory in Germany in October 1146, the pope issued another papal bull, *Divini dispensatione I*, directed to the people and churchmen of northern Italy.[83] Eugenius related that Louis and his nobles were going to 'conquer the enemies of the cross of Christ', exposing themselves to danger and to death. He urged the powerful warriors of Italy to take part in 'such a holy labour'. He mentioned that he had dispatched apostolic letters with rules for the peace and utility of those wishing to set out on the journey; this may be a reference to copies of *Quantum praedecessores*. Eugenius also made the offer of spiritual privileges, the remission of sins instituted by Pope Urban. He then outlined, in very similar terms to those of his earlier bull, the protection offered to the crusaders' families, various financial provisions, and he threatened excommunication upon those who broke such rules. The emphases in this document were on practicalities; it lacked the narrative sections of *Quantum praedecessores*, an omission that suggests it would be presented in conjunction with an exhortatory sermon to incite people to act. It would be perplexing if recruitment for the crusade was given a boost in Conrad's lands if the papacy had no plans to involve the king in the campaign. In a similar vein, in December 1146, Eugenius issued a letter to the Genoese that encouraged them to join the crusade.[84]

There is, therefore, ample evidence to show the logic of involving Conrad in the campaign and to suggest that he was likely to be receptive to a crusade appeal. As noted above, however, the Empire was in a state of considerable disorder. It would, therefore, be both irresponsible and dangerous for him to leave his lands in such a condition, and this was something that Bernard knew too. As the *Vita prima* indicated, 'on entering Germany it was Bernard's *first* task to talk to the emperor about the peaceful settlement of various troubles before he was able to begin preaching the crusade' (my italics).[85] In other words, the abbot needed to use his considerable powers of persuasion, coupled with raising a general sense of Christian duty, to bring some calm to the situation. For these practical reasons, it was understandable that the king rejected Bernard's request to take the cross at Frankfurt in mid-November.[86]

The next time the two men met, however, it was at Conrad's Christmas court at Speyer. In the interim, Bernard had been hard at work. The *Vita prima* noted that the abbot had briefly faltered in his commitment to the preaching; he worried that he should return to his fellow-monks at Clairvaux until the Holy Spirit gave him the resolve to continue. Bishop Herman of Constance urged him to visit his diocese, and Conrad himself added his support, to demonstrate once more royal backing for the principle of the crusade.[87] In December 1146 the abbot delivered crusade sermons as he passed through Freiburg, Krotzingen, Heitersheim, Schliengen, Basel, Rheinfelden, Schaffhausen, Constance, Winterthur and Zürich; he turned northwards again and passed through Rheinfelden, Basel and Strasbourg before he sailed up the Rhine and reached Speyer on 24 December.[88]

The descriptions of Bernard's journey are filled with stories of excited crowds and extraordinary healings. Ward has extracted the remarkable statistics that 235 cripples were healed, 172 blind people recovered their sight, and there were cures for the deaf and dumb, demoniacs and others; there was also one alleged raising of a person from the dead.[89] News of Bernard's progress must have spread rapidly, which encouraged even more people to flock to his sermons. Bernard could not speak German, yet Gerald of Wales, writing several decades later, recalled – with a touch of exaggeration, perhaps – 'that the blessed Bernard, who speaking to the Germans in the French tongue of which they were wholly ignorant, filled them with such devotion and compunction, that he called forth floods of tears from their eyes and with the greatest ease softened the hardness of their hearts so that they did and believed all that he told them; and yet when an interpreter faithfully set forth to them in their own tongue everything that he said, they were not moved at all'.[90] Sometimes the atmosphere became so fevered that Bernard could not venture out; like a modern celebrity he was forced to remain in hiding for his own safety.[91] At Freiburg only the poor responded to his message; the abbot was not to be confounded and cannily he called for prayers to be said for the wealthy so that they might see their mistake; inevitably many responded and took the cross.[92] Because the sources for the journey are Bernard's admiring companions writing for his *Vita* there was an emphasis on the miraculous and, to the modern historian, a frustrating omission of most political developments. Yet some effects can be discerned: interestingly, the area that Bernard toured was under the influence of Welf of Bavaria, Conrad's main rival; the abbot also met Conrad of Zähringen, one of Welf's main supporters. Most importantly, Welf himself had accepted the cross from Bernard's hands.[93] Bearing this vital news, the abbot made arrangements to join Conrad at Speyer for his Christmas court.

Like Louis VII's gathering at Bourges the previous year, Conrad used the festive court with its annual crowning ceremony – an occasion where large numbers of his most important nobles would assemble anyway – to try to launch his crusade. Even the *Vita prima* wrote that Bernard came to Speyer because he had heard reports that some of the princes were trying to dissuade Conrad from joining the crusade, information which indicates that the king was already in favour of the idea anyway.[94] It would need no dramatic sermon from the abbot to convince Conrad to do something he was already predisposed to do; if anything, the spectacle would be for the benefit of those who worried whether the king should take the cross; such a display might help to convince them of the importance of the cause. As noted above, no major European monarch had yet been on crusade and the risks were obviously huge; the chaotic situation in the Empire outlined earlier merely compounded this problem. Yet since Bernard's preaching tour started, progress had been made. Early on the abbot resolved the vicious dispute between the abbey of Liessies and advocate Walter of Avesnes.[95] It seems that the idea of the crusade had indeed made an impact on the people of Germany and Italy and some of the troubles had ended. Otto of Freising noted 'the serenity of peace that suddenly shone forth again, contrary to the expectation of many, after this world conflict'.[96] For Conrad in particular, the news of Welf's decision would have answered many of his critics and cleared the way for him to take the cross.

At Speyer, Bernard preached the crusade in public and then met Conrad in private on the Feast of St John (27 December). The abbot is said to have 'approached him with his customary gentleness' and suggested that it would be unwise of the king to turn away from such a light, brief, honourable and efficacious penance.[97] Conrad promised to talk further with his counsellors and to give a decision the following day. Perhaps this was the king's chance to convince the doubters in his entourage that all would be well; he seems to have succeeded. The *Vita prima* portrayed the events of 28 December with a particular – and understandable – slant. In the course of Mass in the splendid cathedral at Speyer, Bernard was seized with the Holy Spirit and he turned to Conrad and personalised the call to crusade onto the person of the emperor-in-waiting. He reminded the king of the Last Judgement and asked him how he would respond to the question of Christ: 'O man, what have I not done for you that I ought to have?' The abbot described Conrad's exalted standing, his physical strength and his vigorous soul; in other words, he had a Christian duty to act in the Lord's cause. The impression given is that a previously recalcitrant Conrad was finally shamed into a response (a view followed by several historians); yet, as we have seen, this was hardly the case. The king burst into tears and cried out: 'Now I recognise clearly that this is a gift of divine grace, nor now shall I be found to be ungrateful . . . I am ready to serve Him!' A swell of noise filled the cathedral as the audience voiced their acclaim. Bernard turned to the altar and picked up a cloth cross, approached the king and pinned it on him; the most powerful secular ruler in Europe had become a crusader.[98]

Adding to the sense that the king had already made up his mind is the point that Conrad would never have allowed himself to be cornered in such a way had he not resolved to take the cross already. He must have been aware that Bernard would preach a crusade sermon and that he would be the obvious focus: to reject the abbot brandishing a cross at him in front of his senior nobles would have been incredibly difficult. By the evening of 27 December, confirmation that Welf had indeed taken the cross could have reached Speyer and Conrad and Bernard's conversation must have included an agreement that the king would assume the cross the following day. He could not have made a decision of such enormous consequence without being certain it was a sensible course of action; in the weeks since his first meeting with Bernard at Frankfurt in mid-November, the gap between Conrad's readiness to crusade and the practical difficulties of implementing such a wish had closed. In the emotional atmosphere at Speyer, many other nobles came forward to take the cross, including Conrad's nephew Frederick of Swabia, the future emperor.[99] Again, these actions must have been the result of careful thought; while for some senior nobles the need to uphold their honour and accompany the king was a factor, the same balance of religious motivation, personal feelings and political reality had to be assessed before making such a life-changing commitment.

At an assembly on the day after, Conrad and Bernard continued to generate enthusiasm for the crusade and they urged the inhabitants of Speyer to join the expedition. The king and his nobles had to form a bodyguard around the abbot as they left the assembly. As they squeezed along, a lame boy was held out for Bernard to cure. The abbot turned to Conrad and said 'This is for you, so that you know that God is truly with you and that he has accepted the work that you have begun.'[100] Such was the optimism and excitement in the atmosphere of the German court in late 1146; God approved of the crusade; how could Bernard's 'blessed generation' fail? We might also note a letter of Eugenius dated 31 December 1146 in which he referred to Conrad as 'a special knight of St Peter', which seems an appropriate, almost prescient, turn of phrase.[101]

Bernard's associates sent a report of his activities back to Clairvaux addressed to the monk Henry, the brother of Louis VII and a man who later became the archbishop of Rheims. The abbot's preaching tour continued, doubtless given new impetus by the news that Conrad had taken the cross. He left Speyer on 3 January 1147 and went through Worms, Kreuznach, Pichenbach, Coblenz, Remagen, Cologne, the abbey of Brauweiler, and then on to Aachen by 15 January. Thence he went to Maastricht, Liège, Huy, Gembloux and then Villers, a recently founded daughter-house of Clairvaux, Fontaine-l'Evêque, Binche, Mons, Valenciennes and Cambrai. At the last of these places, again, a dangerous crush developed, and the abbot had to take shelter in a house of the local canons regular. After this came another daughter-house of Clairvaux at Vaucelles, and then on to Gomme, the abbey of Hombleux, the abbey of St-John of Laon, Rheims and, on 1 February, Châlons-sur-Marne.[102]

Bernard's actions at the last of these places were of a different character to the recruitment and preaching aspects of his journey. Turning the idea of the crusade into a reality was now the priority; waiting for him was King Louis himself, along with messengers from Welf and Conrad.[103] Bishop Godfrey of Langres, who was to take a prominent role in the French contingent on the crusade, was also present. We know little of what was discussed in this two-day gathering; presumably the date of departure, the choice of route to the Holy Land, the decision as to who should march ahead, as well as the myriad of other practical and diplomatic issues that had to be resolved. The French set another meeting for 16 February at Etampes and Conrad convened assemblies at Frankfurt for March (see below, pp. 116–18 and pp. 129–33 respectively).

Bernard was now on the return leg of his journey back to Clairvaux. He passed though Rosnay, Brienne and Bar-sur-Aube, finally entering the gates of his beloved monastery on 6 February.[104] The abbot had been away for seven months; he had travelled hundreds of miles and given dozens of sermons in the cause of the crusade. Truly he must have been exhausted by his labours, yet also satisfied. His inspirational preaching, combined with his rigid grip on the dissemination of the crusading message, had brought many thousands under the armies of the Lord. For a few days Bernard relaxed, resisting calls to cure the dozens of invalids who now came to Clairvaux in the hope of his healing touch. Within a few days, however, he would be back in the public eye at Etampes as the planning for the crusade gathered momentum.

While Bernard completed his epic tour, Pope Eugenius set out from Viterbo to join the final preparations. In a journey largely ignored by historians, he moved northwards along the main road systems via Lucca, Potremole, probably through the Cisa Pass, then to Vercelli and Susa, to cross the Alps via the Mount Cenis Pass and into Burgundy.[105] Perhaps he was trying to help bring some calm to the warring north Italian cities listed by Otto of Freising. There are no explicit reports of crusade preaching, although it is not unreasonable to suggest that he would have tried to reinforce the message of *Divina dispensatione*, issued a few months previously. A charter given at Susa on 8 March 1147 recorded that Eugenius 'advised and instructed' Amadeus of Savoy to go to Jerusalem, which indicates that the pope did engage in some recruitment work.[106] The proximity of his route to the seat of Marquis William III of Montferrat, near Turin, may have brought him into contact with this powerful noble – a man who was not at Vézelay but whom we know took part in the expedition.[107] The presence in the papal entourage of Alberic of Ostia (former legate to the Holy Land) and Theodwin of Santa Rufina (soon to be legate on the crusade) further emphasises the likelihood that Eugenius would have attempted to gather support for the campaign.

One important region of Europe has hardly figured in the discussion thus far, namely England. As Bernard himself wrote, he could not visit in person, and we do not know of any specific individual preaching the cross. Given this letter, the significant numbers involved in the attack on Lisbon (see Chapter 8 below) and the known participation of several Anglo-Norman nobles in the crusade to the Holy Land, there must, however, have been some effort to raise recruits and offer spiritual rewards. The main barrier to large-scale English involvement was the civil war between Stephen and Mathilda. Such conditions meant that many prominent figures were either unwilling or unable to leave their lands for any length of time. Notwithstanding this, a group of crusaders from the south of the country (in pro-Mathildine lands) went to Lisbon, while several nobles joined the army of Louis VII. William of Warenne was at Vézelay, and others who took the cross included his half-brother, Waleran II of Meulan. It seems that the crusade appealed across party lines, and both Stephen's supporters (such as Philip of Gloucester) and Mathilda's supporters (such as Baldwin of Redvers, Stephen of Mandeville and his nephew, Arnulf) took the cross.[108] William of Aumale was another royalist to commit himself to the cause – and he was a man whose father had been on the First Crusade – but he was too old and fat to actually depart for the East.[109] In general, however, the seriousness of the conflict, which obviously impacted upon Normandy and Anjou as well, was unhelpful to the recruitment.

With the bulk of the crusade preaching complete it is now appropriate to examine the identity of those – other than the central figures already identified – who took their vows. Tied in with this are the questions of finance, arrangements for travel, provisioning and regency; these form the subject of the next chapters.

CHAPTER 6

PEOPLE, PRACTICALITIES AND
MOTIVATION

Bernard, Eugenius and the other preachers motivated many thousands of people to join the crusade (suggested figures below, pp. 168–9). We have seen that there were particular occasions when large numbers of nobles were recruited, such as at Vézelay in March 1146 and Speyer in December of the same year; a writer listed thirty-one barons and senior churchmen taking the cross at the former assembly.[1] Other sources described smaller events that included the sermon delivered by Abbot Reynald of Morimond at Bassigny, where a lord and fourteen of his (unnamed) men joined the crusade on Ascension Day 1146.[2] Often chroniclers simply stated that large numbers of people took the cross without naming any individuals.[3] Through a study of narrative and charter evidence we can establish the identity of some of the crusaders; we can also gain an insight into particular crusaders' motives as well as getting an idea of the practical arrangements they needed to make. This requires the painstaking examination of a great many narratives and cartularies; Constable and Riley-Smith pioneered this approach, with the latter undertaking a monumental survey of the First Crusaders.[4] The present study has identified over 350 individuals who are known to have taken part in one or more theatres of war during the Second Crusade.[5]

The idea of crusading traditions formed the centrepiece of Pope Eugenius III's appeal. For this reason one would expect to be able to demonstrate connections between the two campaigns – although, given the extension of the Second Crusade's preaching into areas that the 1095–9 expedition had a more limited impact upon, such as Bavaria, it is mainly in France that one would look for a sense of continuity. The crusading ancestries of King Louis VII and, by default, of his brother, Count Robert of Dreux, as well as those of Queen Eleanor and Count Thierry of Flanders, have been discussed above. Of the twenty-seven others listed by the 'Historia gloriosi regis Ludovici VII' as taking the cross at Vézelay, it is possible to identify close relatives with crusading experience, or who had visited the Holy Land, for the majority of them. Close relatives are defined as parents, aunts and uncles, grandparents, or parents-in-law. Alphonse-Jordan, count of Toulouse, was the son of Raymond of St Gilles, the great First Crusader who had established the county of Tripoli.[6] Henry of Champagne was the grandson of the First Crusader Count Stephen of Blois, who died on campaign in Egypt during his second visit to the Levant in 1101.[7] William III, count of Nevers, and Count Reynald of Tonnerre, were the sons of another 1101 crusader, William II of Nevers, who was related by marriage to a further participant in that expedition, Hugh of Vermandois.[8] Simon of Vermandois, bishop of Noyen-Tournai, was Hugh's son, and his nephews Waleran II of Meulan (who had been on pilgrimage to Spain in 1144) and William III of Warenne (both of them at Vézelay), also took part in the 1146–8 campaign.[9] Count Guy II of Ponthieu was the grandson of a First Crusader;[10] Archibald VII of Bourbon was married to Agnes of Savoy, the daughter of the crusader Humbert II of Savoy;[11] Enguerran II of Coucy was the son of the infamous First Crusader Thomas of Marle.[12] Hugh VII of Lusignan's father, Hugh VI, had fought the Muslims in Spain in 1087 and took part in the First Crusade.[13] Everard III of Breteuil's uncle, Everard III of Le Puiset, had participated in the First Crusade,[14] and William of Courtenay's uncle was a member of the Montlhéry clan, which provided over twenty First Crusaders.[15] The lords of Toucy, represented here by Itier II, had a fine crusading pedigree, with Itier I and his brothers Hugh and Norgaud going to the Holy Land between 1097 and 1110, although all three perished in the course of their travels.[16] Drogo II of Mouchy-le-Châtel was the son of Drogo I, who had taken part in the First Crusade.[17] The latter was also the stepfather of Hugh II of Gournay, another Second Crusader; and Hugh's natural father, Gerard, was on the First Crusade too.[18] William Aguillon II of Trie's father, Drogo of Chaumont, was on the same campaign as well; he, too, was a member of the Le Puiset crusading clan.[19] Ivo of Nesle, count of Soissons, was more distantly related to crusading ancestors, being a descendant of the First Crusader Drogo of Nesle.[20] Finally, there was Abbot Theobald of St Columba's at Sens, a man who has one of the most interesting (and overlooked) crusading lineages of all: his father was no less a figure than Hugh of Payns, the first master of the Knights Templar.[21] It has not been possible to discover the crusading antecedents for Geoffrey III of Rancon, Gautier of Montjay, Anselm of Traînel and his brother, Guerin, William 'the Butler', and three churchmen: Arnulf of Lisieux, Godfrey of Langres, and Herbert, abbot of St Peter's, Sens. In Arnulf's case, little is known about his father, Hardouin, although his family was well established in the northern French Church, and his uncle John was bishop of Lisieux from 1107 to 1141 and his brother (also named John) the bishop of Séez from 1124. Arnulf himself was a protégé of Bishop Geoffrey of Chartres – a leading figure in the circle of Innocent II, papal legate to France and one of the preachers of the Second Crusade (see above, pp. 46, 76).[22] The failure to trace a crusading lineage for some of these men may also reflect the state of the evidence rather than the facts.

This substantial proportion of individuals with crusading forefathers is a conclusive demonstration that Eugenius and Bernard had chosen a message with a powerful resonance for the bulk of their audience. Of course, such traditions did not apply simply to those at Vézelay. We have seen that Welf VI of Bavaria had crusading ties, and that both Conrad III and Frederick of Swabia had uncles who were on the First Crusade. Many French nobles not recorded as being at Vézelay had crusading antecedents too: Guy IV of Turenne,[23] Bertrand of St John[24] and Count William IV of Mâcon,[25] to name just a few.

In one area of known First Crusade activity, however, traditions are harder to find. Robert II of Flanders led a large contingent of men to Jerusalem in 1097–9; almost fifty years later, Bernard of Clairvaux toured the county and Pope Eugenius sent letters to various towns. The region contributed substantially both to the army of Louis VII and to the northern European fleet that conquered Lisbon; one might therefore expect to find strong evidence of crusading antecedents. We can indeed see such links for Count Thierry and the nobles Baldwin of Ardres, Goswin of Avesnes and Robert II of Lille.[26] It is possible to identify ten other participants in the expedition from the region – not a large body of information, but one that offers a fair cross-section of society with nobles, members of the comital household, castellans, an advocate, lesser men, as well as a bishop, an abbot, a monk and a priest. Yet none of these individuals has an apparent family history of crusading; in light of the Flemish involvement in both the First and the Second Crusades, and of the connections shown for those at Vézelay, this needs some consideration. Of course, lack of evidence might be the simple answer, but the county has a level of charter materials comparable to that of France. Another explanation may lie in the turbulent history of the area, most particularly the civil war that followed the murder of Count Charles the Good on 2 March 1127.[27]

This bitter struggle divided Flemish society and saw conspiracies, coups and open warfare. At one point, William Clito, the dispossessed son of the First Crusader, Count Robert of Normandy, held the comital title, but he died of battle wounds and was replaced by Thierry of Alsace. Once the new count established himself in power, quite naturally, he set about purging the nobility of those he regarded as untrustworthy and reorganising the court officials; thus, he appointed many new castellans and redistributed several lordships.[28] On close analysis we can see that a number of Flemish families with First Crusade pedigrees were affected by death or displacement caused by the civil war. For example, the lords of Loker had a tradition of crusading but Walter I was murdered with Count Charles in 1127 and the family remained away from the court until the late 1150s.[29] The peerdom of Eine-Oudenburg had contributed to the First Crusade through Cono I and had ties with other crusading families, but his successor changed sides several times in the course of the war and the family was disinherited and lost standing.[30] The lords of Aalst took part in the 1097–9 campaign through Baldwin II and his brother Gilbert, but Iwan, a close ally of Count Thierry, was murdered in August 1145, as the resentments about the civil war festered on.[31] Thus, the destruction and dislocation engendered by the murder of Count Charles continued to echo for decades after his death. The consequences of this struggle provide a unique set of circumstances to explain an apparent reduction in one of the primary motives to take the cross. In light of this, other reasons may have come to the fore during recruitment in Flanders, particularly the sustained presence of Abbot Bernard – who, as we saw, spent almost three months there – and his close links with Count Thierry.

A study of the charter evidence reveals several other interesting features in the make-up of the crusade armies of 1147–9. In his work on the First Crusade, Riley-Smith noted that many families contributed more than one member to the expedition.[32] Fifty years later the same pattern of behaviour held true. In a few cases we can see fathers and sons taking the cross together: Peter and Fulcher of Bré;[33] Guy II of Ponthieu and his son, John;[34] Walter and Erard II of Brienne;[35] Bernard and Hugh of Brancion;[36] Adalbert and Adalbert junior of Berge.[37] More common was the case of brothers going on crusade; numerous examples can be cited. From France these included: Louis VII and Robert of Dreux; Odo and Hugh of Guyencourt;[38] Reynald of Tonerre and William III of Nevers;[39] Robert of Boves and Enguerran II of Coucy;[40] Manasses of Bulles and his brother Reynald;[41] Guy II and William of Ponthieu;[42] Waleran II of Meulan and William III of Warenne;[43] Anselm and Guerin of Traînel;[44] Bernard V le Gros of Brancion and Hugh of Brancion;[45] Raymond and William of La Baume.[46] From England, William and Ralph Viel took part in the Lisbon campaign.[47] From the German Empire, Poppo of Gieche-Plassenburg and Berthold of Andechs;[48] Otto and Walcher of Machland;[49] Renier and Gerlach of Sleiden;[50] Gerold and Bernhard of Gremertshausen – all went to the Holy Land.[51]

Charters and narratives can also give us snapshots of men of lesser standing gathering together to prepare for the crusade; here we are looking at what France has labelled, with respect to the First Crusade, patronage.[52] This meant that if a lord took the cross, then some of his knights (health and age permitting) and members of his household were probably obliged to follow suit. A charter for the abbey of Vauluisant mentioned Milo of Ervy and his knights taking an oath to join King Louis on the crusade.[53] Adalramus was noted as taking the cross with his master, Walcher of Machland, in a charter for the abbey of Admont.[54] Likewise, Radebert accompanied his master Alram of Perge.[55] The chronicle of Lambert of Ardres neatly shows how one small part of the French army came together: Baldwin of Ardres was accompanied by his knights – Baldwin Wallameth, Marsilius of Bredenarde and some others – and this group, in turn, combined with the men of Count Thierry of Flanders, who then joined the force of King Louis VII.[56] We can see a trio of Normans who set out together and, in this instance, we can also glimpse the effect of a judicial ruling on an individual's reasons for crusading. Waleran II of Meulan took the cross at Vézelay out of piety and a wish to associate himself with Louis VII. In the settlement of a court case he managed to get the sentence on one of his knights mitigated on the promise that the man, Richard fitz Humphrey of Etreville, took part in the crusade. One of Waleran's tenants, Reynald of Gerponville, also worked closely with the count.[57] A less coercive example of the effect of patronage is from the *Vézelay Chronicle*, which stated that many followed Louis VII in taking the cross because they were motivated by the 'fame and example' of his actions.[58] In other words, the very fact that the monarch himself had taken this step seemed enough to convince others to follow.

Aside from reasons of family tradition, kin-association and patronage, the primary motives for many of the crusaders were, as Bernard and Eugenius so powerfully reminded them, to receive remission of their sins and to free or protect the holy places. While the narratives can give us a broad flavour of such ideas, charters offer a more personal insight into the actions of particular individuals. As Bull has indicated, there are always caveats in using this form of evidence but, when employed judiciously, the material can be highly illuminating. The growing propensity for record-keeping that emerged in the twelfth century should, in theory, have caused more charters to survive for the Second Crusade period as compared to the First; however, the increasing standardisation of documents meant that fewer charters for the later period contained the elaborate and informative stories that showed why particular individuals took the cross in 1095–7.[59]

Nonetheless, the material for the period of the Second Crusade does reveal a range of motives and understandings as to why the expedition was happening. Many expressed conventional religious sentiments: Hartnid of Riegersberg and Hartmann of Uberach took the cross for the salvation of their souls.[60] Other charters expressed a tie with the importance of the holy sites; to 'worship in the place that Christ walked' was crucial to Goswin of Randerath,[61] while Adalbert of Starkhaushofen wanted 'to sustain those on military service for God in the place of the martyr';[62] Arnold of Morith wished to visit the sepulchre of the Lord,[63] and Walter of Malentin 'had set out to go' ('*se ire preposuisset*') '*ad limina sancti sepulchre . . . pro remedio anime sue*'.[64]

Udalschalk and Ulrich of Sandau wished 'to go on pilgrimage overseas',[65] and Raymond and William of La Baume wanted to go to Jerusalem 'for the remittance of our sins and desiring to renounce all our wicked ways'.[66]

Some charters put forward a more aggressive view of the crusade; they reflected a sense of anger towards the Muslims, echoing the inflammatory tone of parts of Bernard and Eugenius's preaching. A charter of Walter of Brienne stated: '*inimicos nominis Xprsti agressa est expugnare*'.[67] Bertrand Falco's gift to the Templars of 11 September 1146 was made 'when Louis, glorious king of the Franks, with an innumerable crowd, set out on the journey to Jerusalem to repress the enemies of the cross of Christ'.[68] Hugh of Berzé went on crusade 'when King Louis of France went with a very great army to crush the ferocity of the Gentiles and to exalt the Eastern Church'.[69] Charters can also reflect a wider context for the crusade. A confirmation issued by Sibylla of Flanders is particularly revealing in its agenda of Christian ambition. The countess stated that the gift was made by her, rather than the count, because her 'lord and husband Count Thierry had gone overseas for the purpose of extending Christianity with the host of the army of the true Christ'.[70] We know that Sibylla was a very pious woman (she became a nun at the convent of Bethany in Jerusalem in 1157); she had met Bernard during his tour of Flanders in 1146 and was a strong supporter of Cistercian monasticism. It is interesting to see a contemporary expressing such a confident and expansionist concept of the crusade.[71] A charter for Adalbert of Moosburg stated that 1147 was the year when the kingdom of the Christians was roused against the insolence of the pagans.[72] Likewise, a charter from the Regensburg region described the army of the Christians moving against the pagans.[73] A sense of the crusade as a widening of Christendom – in this case, through military means – appears to have been present in the minds of some of its senior figures, both secular and ecclesiastical. This also dovetails with the increasingly close ties with the Armenian Church noted above and, as we will see below, with the broadening of the crusade into Iberia and the Baltic.

A charter from Strasbourg revealed the continuity with the First Crusade so strongly emphasised by Eugenius in *Quantum praedecessores* when it described the expedition as '*secunda Iherosolimorum profectione exorta*'.[74] Some twelfth-century writers made the same connection, for instance the brief narrative of the reign of King Baldwin I and his successors, which was written in the Low Countries and referred to the '*viam Iherosolimitanam secondo*'.[75] Other texts that make a similar point include the *Annales Mosomagenses*, which in the entry for 1147 simply stated: '*Motio secunda christianorum*'.[76]

Another factor contributory to the willingness of individuals to take the cross, as well as a demonstration of their commitment to the Holy Land, was a track record of pilgrimage. There is evidence that many knights and nobles either went to the Levant as pilgrims *per se* or combined this with a year's service in the defence of Christ's patrimony.[77] As seen above, Conrad of Germany had been to the Holy Land in 1124 and Count Thierry of Flanders in 1138–9. There is charter material that shows Thierry planned to make a second visit as early as 1142, when a document outlined a hand-over of power to Countess Sibylla and their son, Baldwin.[78] For unknown reasons, however, the count never made this journey and, as Sibylla herself noted in a charter of 1147/9, her husband was then on his second trip to Jerusalem.[79] Several other Second Crusaders are known to have been to the Holy Sepulchre before, including Count Adalbert II of Berge (*Adelbertus Iherosolimitanus de Werde*),[80] Bernard V *le Gros* of Brancion in 1116,[81] Enguerrand II of Coucy in 1138–9,[82] Walter II of Brienne in the second decade of the twelfth century,[83] and Rainald of Bar-le-Duc in 1128.[84]

There is some evidence that financial motives played a part in the Second Crusade. A charter from the abbey of Fleury mentioned that men sought their fortunes abroad after experiencing hard times at home.[85] The *Annales Herbipolenses* – admittedly written in the aftermath of the failure of the campaign to the East – suggested that, as well as the religious ideals expressed by 'powerful men', the 'intentions of the various men were different. Some lusted after novelties and went in order to learn about new lands. But others, who were in dire straits at home, were impelled by poverty and went to fight – not only against the enemies of the cross of Christ, but even against the friends of the Christian name – wherever the chance appeared so as to relieve their poverty.'[86] Others were said to be evading debts or service owed to their lords, or even punishments. Many individuals had pretended to be moved by zeal but had acted out of diabolical intent; only a few of the crusaders were genuinely motivated by a holy purpose. There may be an element of hindsight here: such base motives would have incurred divine disfavour, and that must help to explain the outcome of the crusade. The wish for outright profit from the expedition was, however, something that could easily overlap with the need to secure booty. The requirement for the latter was an essential element of crusading and can be seen most clearly in the behaviour of a part of the English contingent at the siege of Lisbon in 1147.[87] The desire for loot was obviously premeditated and had been a primary reason why some of these men took part in earlier voyages to Lisbon. While the English were plain in their intention to carry on to Jerusalem as crusaders, money was an overt part of their motivation too.

The financing of the Second Crusade was a complicated and wide-ranging issue. Basic considerations included the substantial expense of crusading, the absence of systematised national or regional tax systems to generate income for the crusade leaders, and the prevailing economic conditions of the day.

The experience of the First Crusade had demonstrated the huge, and potentially destructive, costs of crusading to an individual and a family. It has been estimated that it required four times a knight's annual income to finance such an undertaking and, as Riley-Smith has shown, the need to sell lands or allow others to take the revenue from property until loans were repaid was a burden on whole families because it alienated their patrimony and had a permanent effect on their resources.[88]

To mount a campaign required a variety of materials; the *Annales Reicherspergenses* outlined the necessity for 'swords and coats of mail and other objects of war', as well as tents, wagons and innumerable horses.[89] To this one might add saddle-bags, horseshoes, tools, cooking equipment, as well as (for the leading men) a supply of gifts for diplomatic purposes. Practicalities dictated that food could only be carried in limited quantities and would, therefore, have to be purchased or sourced en route. Prior contacts could help set up markets, but again the crusaders would need funding to buy the goods in the first instance. Murray has pointed out that medieval coinage was of such low denomination that it would have been almost impossible to gather enough together anyway; furthermore, to transport such huge volumes of cash would have been extremely difficult.[90] On this basis it was a more logical proposition to take precious objects, such as vases, bowls, or plates, to trade with or to exchange into the local currency at the appropriate time.

A crucial element in the financing of the crusade was the contemporary economic climate. The years leading up to the First Crusade, including 1095, saw droughts in France with poor harvests, famine and outbreaks of ergotism – a disease caused by eating mouldy rye that can induce insanity. Ekkehard of Aura described this situation in detail and suggested that such conditions did much to encourage people to seek their fortunes abroad on the crusade.[91] The harvest of 1096, however – the year in which the expedition actually set out – was excellent. Fulcher of Chartres wrote: 'in that year peace and a very great abundance of grain and wine existed in all countries by the grace of God, so that there was no lack of bread on the trip for those who had chosen to follow Him with their crosses ... '.[92] By contrast, the background to the Second Crusade was not so propitious. The *Annales Herbipolenses* related that 1146 was marked by 'a mighty famine'; the *Annales Rodenses* called it 'the most strong famine', of a level 'unheard of in a generation', whereby prices rose so that a *modius* (a measure of wheat) was sold at twenty *solidi* and six *denari* in Cologne and at three livres and six *solidi* in Trier.[93] A charter given at the abbey of Fleury early in 1147 mentioned that 'at the time a great famine afflicted all of Gaul so greatly that many nobles and others who were once rich went to foreign parts and distant lands owing to the unbearable necessity of hunger, since they were ashamed to beg after all their possessions were sold and divided'. The abbot of Fleury also claimed that his abbey's vineyards had failed for the previous seven years.[94] The chances of raising money for the crusade were, therefore, compromised by this situation. The lack of food probably meant that there was an even greater need to take money if supplies were not present in the first instance. Some of the First Crusade's leaders managed to raise substantial amounts of money in advance and they augmented their wealth by gathering booty en route; after the siege of Antioch Raymond of St Gilles was able to offer to pay several of the other senior nobles if they would march south under his leadership.[95]

As one of the most important individuals on the crusade it is possible to examine how King Louis VII of France financed his expedition. Compared to later crusaders he was hugely handicapped by the vestigial condition of the Capetian fiscal system and he was almost certainly unable to call for a national levy in the way Henry II of England, Richard the Lionheart or Philip Augustus did in the 1180s.[96] There is some evidence that Louis VII made such a demand, but it is questionable: Robert of Torigny, who composed his chronicle after 1153, argued that the crusade was financed out of 'plunder from the poor and the despoiling of churches', while Ralph of Diss, who wrote in the 1190s, described 'a general census' made across France.[97] The Fleury charter related that the king 'extracted many things from the treasures of the churches in his realm', but this was not the same thing as the systematic taxation of the late twelfth century and it was quite logical that the king should turn to the Church anyway. Similarly, a charter for the church of Le Puy from August 1146 or February 1147 mentioned him asking the bishop of Le Puy for support 'out of the money of the city' for his journey to Jerusalem.[98] Again, urban centres were another obvious source of income. The highly detailed records available for the crusade of Louis IX around 100 years later show that the king looked to towns and cities for considerable levels of funding.[99]

The Fleury charter is informative because it reveals a process of negotiation. Louis's first demand for 1,000 marks of silver was rejected by Abbot Macharius, who offered the following reasons why he felt this was excessive: first, the recent failures of the vineyards; secondly, a history of disputes during the previous abbacy that had involved papal legates; thirdly, the intolerable exactions of the king and his men. Louis slashed his request to 500 marks, but Macharius still refused to pay. After several days of stalemate the king settled for 300 silver marks and 500 gold bezants (worth about 92 silver marks). The charter shows Louis's inability to drive a bargain on his terms and the harsh economic conditions of the time.[100] In light of the surviving material it is safest to suggest that the king made a series of piecemeal requests to religious institutions and towns to finance his crusade.

The other obvious source of money was the Jews. We have seen that crusaders from the Rhineland had plundered the Jews' wealth in 1096 and 1146–7, and there are clear indications that the French Jewry was identified as an appropriate target by some involved with the Second Crusade; an infamous letter from Peter the Venerable is the principal evidence for this.[101] The abbot set out the historical reasons for his objections to the Jews and excoriated them for rejecting an understanding of the Christian faith and for spilling Christ's blood. In spite of his remarkably inflammatory language, in which he described the Jews as 'vile blasphemers and far worse than the Saracens', Peter stated that they should not be slain: 'I must emphasise that I am not asking that they should be killed, but to encourage strongly that they should be punished for their evil in accordance with His set limits.'[102] He advocated that they should finance the crusade: 'Let their lives be saved but their money be taken away in order that [their] money can help the Christians fight the Saracens.' As Chazan has shown, unlike Bernard of Clairvaux, who saw the Jews as existing peacefully under the Christian yoke, Peter regarded them as an active force, agitating against the faithful.[103] He accused them of amassing grain, wine, money, gold and silver by fraud, and of stealing into churches at night to plunder holy vessels and relics, a practice that he complained was condoned by the Christian princes. He concluded that 'it would be foolish, if not actually insulting to divinity, I think, if this holy expedition should be properly financed by Christian property unless the moneys of the profane were not used to a greater degree'.[104] Historians have explained this tough stance by reference to Cluny's own financial troubles at this time. This meant that the abbey could not offer an appropriate level of support to the crusade, although Peter's basic attitude towards the Jews must have been his primary motive.[105] In spite of Peter's prominent position there is no sign that the king implemented such a plan, at least to any noticeable extent. Ephraim of Bonn claimed that Louis exempted all crusaders from any debts to the Jews and that many lost a large part of their wealth as a consequence.[106] In reality, Pope Eugenius, rather than King Louis, had released crusaders from interest on loans to Jews.[107] Whatever measures Louis employed to raise funds, judging by the chronic condition of the king's resources from an early stage of the crusade – he wrote to the regent of France, Abbot Suger, from Hungary and asked for more money only a matter of weeks after he had set out – these measures were largely unsuccessful.[108] The financial dealings of Conrad III of Germany are even more difficult to discern and no records of attempts to make such impositions on Jews, on towns or on the German Church survive. The king seemed to suffer less hardship than Louis VII, from which we might tentatively infer that he managed to raise a substantial amount of money from the extensive royal domain.

It is from charters and a few narratives that most of the evidence for fundraising remains, and it is possible to demonstrate a broad range of methods by which crusaders made the necessary arrangements to finance their journeys and to try to safeguard their lands and families while they were absent, or in the case of their death. A charter concerning the Fleming Nicholas of Thines described an individual's struggle to organise his affairs and to raise the large sum of money required to go on crusade.[109] Nicholas experienced serious difficulties in gathering money for the expedition because, after he had mortgaged his lands at Fretin to Anselm of Lambres, he fell upon hard times. He could no longer afford to make the journey and implored Anselm for help, yet it was not until the intervention of Thierry and Sibylla of Flanders that Anselm was persuaded to co-operate and Nicholas could fulfil his vow.

The simplest way to get money was to sell land outright. Beringer of Löchgau was a free man who was said to have needed a large amount of money on account of the great cost of the journey. For this reason he made a decisive move and sold his entire patrimony in Löchgau to the monastery of Maulbronn – namely a church and its farms, meadows, pastures, vines, woods, rights, rents and crossings of water – except for one courtyard in the village sufficient for his family to live in. In return, Beringer received 26 livres of the purest silver.[110] Beringer's brothers and sister witnessed the agreement and consented that no one could dispute Maulbronn's claim to the lands in future; presumably they all had properties elsewhere to live on, or were content with the one specified in this deed. To give a couple of other examples: Bertrand of St Jean sold lands to the cathedral of Auch for 30 *solidi*;[111] Hauvinus of Creuttes sold the right to an annual measure of grain that the abbey of Saint-Martin of Laon had given to him for 10 livres.[112]

Some individuals mortgaged lands and rights. Again, the Fleury charter is good illustrative material. Four men – Mayor Joscerand, Godfrey, the abbot's butler, Guido Belini and Adelard de Porta – asked the abbot to mortgage the possessions they held from the abbey for five years. Macharius agreed, as long as 'the revenues deriving from these gages, both for their support and for the service owing to us, will for five years be considered ours for whatever we wish to do in this house and that if they have not returned after five years, or if they die, all the revenues ... will be ours so long as they or their successors are unable to redeem them, as is contained in the charters written about this'.[113] Another mortgage was that of the fief of the crusader Hugh Tirel, for three years, to the bishop of Beauvais for 100 livres of Provins.[114]

A technical problem for those wishing to raise money was, of course, the ban on usury. One of the most common forms of arrangement was for a crusader to 'gift' (rather than mortgage) an area of land, or rights, to a religious house and, in return, to receive a 'gift' back, although there were often clauses in the charter to guard against future claimants. William Gorram was given 7 *solidi* and 4 *denarii* 'in caritate', assessed against various lands by the priory of La Charité-sur-Loire.[115] Duke Welf VI himself received 10 talents for land from the monastery of Wesobrunn.[116] Other charters can be cited, although the case of the aptly named Walter Sineterra, who gave a church a *rusticus* (peasant) instead of land, is worth noting.[117] Odo of Troyes made a detailed arrangement with the priory of St Sepulchre near Payns in Champagne. He gave a mill to the priory in perpetuity, in return for 40 livres of coin and the promise of twenty more on his return. The monks, however, could use the oven in his absence, and his wife and son would get 20 livres and the oven if Odo did not return.[118] Adam of Villeron made an agreement with the abbey of Chaalis which included a clause that, if he died without heirs on the expedition (he was married, perhaps his wife was pregnant and would give birth after he set out), then his land at Louvres would go to the monks, with the provision that his father could hold it for the remainder of his lifetime and that four (named) men could have a carucate each.[119]

There are many examples of complicated agreements that concerned a crusader's possible failure to survive the expedition. In Bavaria, Henry of Hohenbrunnen gave his allods and serfs to the abbey of St Stephen's; in return, he was presented with 30 talents and, should he come home, he was offered relief of the debt and the use of almost all of the property for life. One small farm was stipulated as being outside these conditions; it was a direct gift to the monastery.[120] Starfrit of Ismaning (near Munich) transferred his farm to the same abbey with the proviso that if he did not return from Jerusalem it would be held for life by his brother.[121]

Some crusaders simply made a gift to religious houses with no record of anything being sought in exchange. Such acts of piety are frequently attested in the charters. Richard of Perche presented woods and fields to the abbey of Lèves;[122] Sebrand Chabot gave lands to the abbey of Absie;[123] Odo and Hugh of Guyencourt both granted fields and taxes to the monks of St Acheul;[124] Josbert of La Ferté-sur-Aube (a relative of Bernard of Clairvaux) donated his possessions in the village of Perrecin to the abbey of Clairvaux in perpetuity, although if he survived the crusade he could, if he chose, enjoy his rights of lordship and justice over the villagers and after his death this would revert to the abbey.[125] In August 1146 or April 1147, Louis VII made a gift of lands at Andilly-les-Marais for the souls of himself and his wife Eleanor, and of their predecessors as kings of France and counts of Poitou; presumably this formed part of his spiritual preparations for the crusade.[126]

Often gifts were accompanied by requests for church protection of a family and loved ones, and especially for the saying of prayers. Gosbert of Loos gave lands to the Abbey of Afflighem; in return he wanted a candle lit for a year for him and his family.[127] Aimery of Daver made an agreement with the monks of Noyers in which a false claim was settled before the knight went on crusade and, if he died, his name would be put in the abbey's martyrology and the monks would sing a mass for him; Abbot Bernard also gave him 7 livres 'in caritate'.[128] This latter example looks more like the 'exchange' form of agreement noted above. Hugh of Trignach agreed with Abbess Agnes of Saintes that she would protect his wife during her lifetime and would pray for her and for him after they died.[129] More dramatically, some gifts were made at the moment of departure. Roger of Carcasonne gave a substantial donation to the Templars of Douzens on the quayside at the port of La Tourette at Agde in southern France.[130] Similarly, Walter of Brienne made over property to the church of St Mary Ramerupt (a house with which his family had longstanding links) on the Day of Pentecost (7 July 1147) the day before he set out for Jerusalem.[131]

As well as money, the crusaders required practical objects for their journey and on occasion these were given in exchange for lands or rights, or else were presented as outright gifts. Lambert of Ardres provides an example of the latter: 'The abbot Thierry [of Saint Mary of Capella] generously offered my father an excellent packhorse in helpful support of the holy journey and he presented it as a free, or rather a completely gratuitous gift.'[132] Hartmann of Uberach was given a palfry by the church of St Peter at Freising in return for some lands,[133] and the crusader Adolph received money and a measure of oats for lands sold to the abbey of Rolduc.[134] Poppo of Biber sold his property at Getzendorf to the abbey of Admont for a horse and 32 pounds cash.[135] The abbot of Noyers made the generous gift of two silver cups to the crusader Thomas of Furniolis.[136]

Because religious institutions needed to generate large sums of cash in a short space of time there are indications that they resorted to quite desperate measures to provide departing crusaders with the requisite funding. The abbot of St Mary's of Capella – in records of a sale described as highly useful and necessary to the church – purchased a mill, adjacent lands, a marsh and fishery for 'a goodly sum of money' from Baldwin of Ardres, but he could not afford to pay the crusader and so he 'denuded and despoiled the bier of St Mary and certain crosses of both their gold and silver'.[137] Bishop Godfrey of Langres appropriated many gold and silver vessels from his church and promised to restore them at a later date. He also took gold and precious stones from the arm reliquary of Saint Mamas, although when the bare arm was exposed blood began to flow copiously and had to be caught in an alabaster vase, becoming then an object of veneration.[138] Abbot Macharius of Fleury struggled to find the means to pay Louis VII and so his monks provided two silver candelabra 'mirifici operis' that weighed the equivalent of 30 marks of silver, as well as a censer, or thurible, of 8 marks of gold and 3 ounces. The censer was mortgaged on condition that it would be returned or replaced within three years of the Easter of the agreement, although a later document stipulated that the value could be used to build a new dormitory instead; setting the cost of (presumably) a reasonably large building project against this item gives a glimpse of the sums of money needed to crusade.[139] While such actions seem rather radical – sacrilegious even, to the modern reader – similar measures had been used before the crusades when religious institutions urgently required funds. In the mid-1060s Archbishop Adalbert of Bremen bought the county of Emsgau in Frisia from Henry IV for 1,000 lb of silver. He did not have the money and so ordered crosses, altars and candelabra to be melted down. Two gold and jewelled crosses were worth 20 marks of gold alone, although the blacksmith who broke them up told people that in the clanging of his hammer he was sure that he heard the sound of the voice of the craftsman moaning. 'In one miserable hour', lamented Adam of Bremen, the treasures of the church of Bremen were reduced to nothing.[140] Clearly, if the cause for which such drastic actions were required was not a good one, then a controversial reaction was inevitable.

Churchmen who wished to take part in the crusade could also use objects from their own institutions. Abbot Theobald of St Columba's at Sens took on his journey a golden crown, adorned with sparkling gems, presented to the church by King Radulf, and a beautifully made reliquary cross of Saint Eloi which was secretly taken to the Jews of Troyes and mortgaged there, although the abbey's history sadly related that neither object was seen again. The latter episode, in particular, again neatly illustrates the need for cash and the Jews as a source of money.[141] If a church could not generate funding at all, it had to think of alternatives. An agreement between the abbey of Klosterrad (at Rolduc, near Aachen) and the crusader Renier of Sleiden involved moneylenders paying him and being allowed a supply of victuals for their lifetimes, after which full ownership of the land specified in the charter passed to the church.[142]

Charters and narratives can reveal further facets of the practical policies set in place by crusaders and their families prior to departure. Sometimes the crusade was an opportunity to resolve long-running disputes between kin-groups and religious houses. A charter given by Bishop Thierry of Amiens illustrates this. It ended a struggle between Robert of Boves, count of Amiens, and the abbey of St Acheul that dated back to a grant of 1085 given by Robert's grandfather, Enguerrand I. 'Voices of malcontents' had caused his son Thomas and then Robert himself to withhold payment. The count had been moved by the counsel of religious men and, in the presence of his mother and several holy men, he acknowledged his fault, sought absolution and reconfirmed the original gift before he set out to Jerusalem.[143]

The arrangements made by Louis and Conrad will be examined in the next chapter; while the provisions made by lesser men have generally left slimmer evidence, a few instances can give some picture of the measures put in place. On occasion these caused ill-feeling: Baldwin, lord of Ardres, entrusted the safety of his lands, including the formal positions of baliff and provost, to Arnold Gohel, lord of Surques because he was 'known to be wise and trustworthy to him', but Baldwin's brother-in-law, Arnold, viscount of Merkes, grumbled and complained about the decision. He felt that he should have been given this responsibility, particularly because he was apparently Baldwin's heir; when the count died, Viscount Arnold succeeded him and became count of Guines himself.[144]

The survival of five charters given by Sibylla of Flanders, along with the existence of numerous documents from Thierry before and after the crusade (at a rate of around seven a year), allows some insight into the organisation of the county.[145] She was given full control over the region – a role she accomplished in style, fighting off an invasion by Count Baldwin IV of Hainault who evidently hoped to exploit Thierry's absence and annex some of his lands. Thierry's eldest son, Baldwin (d.1150), had remained behind to secure the succession if his father died and he witnessed several charters too.[146] This material also allows us to see that a core of valued advisors – senior churchmen, nobles and members of the household – remained in Flanders to assist the countess.[147] Thierry of Beveren-Waas, the *camerarius*, Razo of Gavere, the butler, Ogier, the *notarius*, were all present, as was Michael I, the constable of Flanders (also the castellan of Cassel); Alold, a notary from the church of St Walburga, Furnes; Roger III of Wavrin, steward of Flanders; and Roger, the chancellor and also a priest of Saint-Donatian's, Bruges. Thierry, Ogier and Michael all died in 1147; this may have been a coincidence – or the same illness – but their age and general health might have caused them to remain in the West. Several key castellans stayed in Flanders as well, most notably Walter of Douai and Roger of Kortrijk, who were near to the southern border with Hainault. Three churchmen were also in close attendance to the countess: Milo, bishop of Thérouanne (a very frequent witness to Count Thierry's charters); Lucas, archdeacon of Arras; and Weric, abbot of Saint-Vaast. As an aside, we can see that Thierry took two men in the position of dapifer with him. Obviously he needed a household too; Anselm of Ypres was one of these men and Gislebert of Bergues was probably the other.[148]

Hugh of Poitiers' *Historia Vizeliacensia* gives some information on the arrangements made in Nevers. The decisions of the senior men in the comital family created a set of circumstances that required some help. William III and Reynald had taken the cross at Vézelay, but because their ageing father, William II, had resolved to join the Carthusians there was no other immediate family member to look after the land and the rest of the clan. Hugh wrote that Abbot Pons of Vézelay 'took care of the territory and the family . . . protecting them from attacks on all sides'. It seems that Pons oversaw the comital house-hold and all their possessions too – and, as events turned out, he did indeed preserve everything unharmed. His actions were not entirely altruistic, however, because Hugh also wrote that the abbot believed this course of action would best serve the interests of the abbey as well.[149]

Lastly, and appropriately, there is evidence for crusaders making a will. Many of the charters above dealt with the possibility of a crusader failing to return from the expedition, but such depositions only pertained to the piece of land or rights in that particular deed. In the case of William VI of Montpellier, however, his full testament exists, given on 11 December 1146 on account of his forthcoming participation in the crusade in Iberia. He made spiritual provisions by mandating that a fragment of the True Cross and other relics he had brought back from a pilgrimage to the Holy Land were to be transferred to the church of Sainte-Croix, near his palace in Montpellier. He also made numerous other arrangements that concerned his relations with monasteries and the local church. We may also note provisions made for reli-gious houses that included offering his third son, Raymond, to the abbey of Cluny. Plans for his mother, his sons and daughters and his sister took into account the possibility that the children might die before the age of majority, and he set out the monies and rights to be awarded to them should they live. His son William was given the theoretical right to Tortosa in Spain, the city that became the actual target of one element of the crusade just two years later. William's mother, Ermesende, had a very prominent role in the testa-ment and was appointed regent.[150] Another example of a will is that of Stephen, chaplain of St Peter's of Mèze (near Agde, southern France). Stephen designated his nephew Pons to hold the usufruct of his lands, except one house that was reserved to a specified individual. When Pons died, Stephen set out a more complex division of lands with the churches of St Peter's and St Stephen's at Agde as the beneficiaries.[151]

To conclude, we can ascertain the expression of a range of motives that covered secular and religious ideas; we can also see that family histories of crusading can be significant. Furthermore, it can be observed how hard it was to raise money for this crusade, particularly in the difficult economic condi-tions of the time (the comparison with the good harvest of 1096 is worth re-emphasising), and we can note the attempts some nobles made to regulate their lands and family on their departure.

CHAPTER 7

THE FINAL PREPARATIONS OF LOUIS AND CONRAD

DIPLOMACY, REGENCY AND CEREMONIAL

By the end of January 1147 the work of the crusade preachers was nearing completion; the majority of those who wished to go to Jerusalem had taken the cross and were engaged in the appropriate preparations. We have seen how individuals made the necessary financial provisions and how some set in place arrangements for the control of lands in their absence. Given the scale of their territories and the political issues at stake, Louis and Conrad – in consultation with their leading advisors and nobles – faced particularly sensitive decisions about matters such as regency; in addition, they had to make a number of vital strategic and logistical choices.

On 2 February 1147 Louis, Bernard and a group of French nobles met ambassadors of Conrad and Welf of Bavaria at Châlons-sur-Marne.[1] The presence of Welf's men shows his importance and the intrinsic link between his presence on the crusade and Conrad's decision to join the expedition. The duke had received the cross from Bernard himself and may have struck up a close bond with the abbot.[2] Also in attendance was Bishop Godfrey of Langres who had been such an enthusiastic proponent of the crusade at Louis's original attempt to launch the expedition back in December 1145.[3] This was the first time that representatives of the two main armies had encountered one another and it must have been an opportunity to discuss the modes of transport they proposed to use, the precise target of the crusade, the interaction of their forces and the diplomacy necessary to follow their chosen route. Because the sources do not provide a detailed report of this gathering historians have tended to pass over the episode but it was plainly of seminal importance. From Odo of Deuil's account of the major assembly held at Étampes two weeks later we can suggest the likely thrust of some of the discussions at Châlons.

The question of how to reach the Levant was closely bound up with the wider international situation. Judging by the presence of Sicilian envoys at Étampes, Louis had been in touch with King Roger II about working together on the crusade and the possibility of sailing to the eastern Mediterranean. It may be recalled that Hugh of Vermandois had travelled via Sicily during the First Crusade, thereby providing a precedent for Capetian–Sicilian co-operation on such campaigns.[4] The contacts between Louis and Roger were initiated in the summer or autumn of 1146, before Conrad committed himself to the expedition. The Germans and the Sicilians were, at this time, arch-enemies and Conrad's embassy at Châlons must have made it explicit that Roger's involvement would be deeply unwelcome. Louis's dealings with the Norman king were also politically insensitive given the considerable animosity between the papacy and the Sicilians. In spite of the warm relations between the French and the Sicilians (Odo described Roger as 'one who orig-inally came from our part of the world and cherished the Franks', a reference to the Norman origins of the Sicilian rulers), Louis could not afford to alienate the two most powerful men in Europe.[5] To be fair, it should be emphasised that Louis had not formalised an alliance with Sicily; it might be noted that the French king had opened a dialogue with Manuel Comnenus too. Given the existing close relationship between Byzantium and the German crown, the gathering at Châlons almost certainly steered Louis towards his subsequent rejection of the offer made by Roger's envoys.

The German nobles would have indicated their intention to take the land route east. Given the geography, the likely size of their army and the contem-porary state of naval technology, it was not realistic to suggest that the entire imperial force should sail down the English Channel, around Iberia and across the Mediterranean, although we know that one contingent from the Rhineland did make the journey via Lisbon. If the French decided to go along with the land choice, then geography dictated that it would be logical for them to follow the Germans; in any case Conrad, as the senior political figure, may have wanted to lead the march. When the Châlons meeting broke up, a skeleton plan of the crusade had probably been settled upon, although both groups needed to ratify it with their respective colleagues. The two main armies would head overland, via Constantinople, and then move towards northern Syria. It was the fall of Edessa that had prompted the crusade and there is no reason to think that its recovery was not the main aim of the expedition at this stage.[6]

Two weeks later, the French nobility and senior churchmen gathered at Étampes, about thirty miles south of Paris, for a three-day council to debate these matters and to settle upon the regency.[7] On 16 February the assembly began with a speech from Bernard in which he formally announced that Conrad and the men of Germany had taken the cross. Interestingly, given the subsequent tensions between the French and the Germans, this piece of news was greeted with great acclaim.[8] Then various of the overseas messengers, including those from Sicily and Byzantium, made presentations to the meeting although a formal debate concerning any final decisions was held over until the following day.

Our source for these events is King Louis's chaplain, Odo of Deuil. Odo, of course, had the benefit of hindsight and it is clear that one of his primary reasons for writing *De profectione Ludovici VII in Orientem* was to highlight the duplicity of the Greeks as a reason for the failure of the crusade.[9] In Odo's mind, the root of these problems lay in the decision at Étampes when the council chose to reject the prospect of joining with King Roger of Sicily and instead – fatefully, as the chaplain saw it – elected to trust the Greeks.[10] Odo related that 'men in the assembly' – whom he was strangely reluctant to identify – said that the Greeks 'as they had learned either by reading or by experience, were deceitful'.[11] We can suggest that the king was not one of those who put forward this argument. The reference to written texts is an interesting corroboration of the presence of First Crusade narratives at the royal court, many of which, as we saw, were very hostile to the Greeks. The latter part of Odo's statement was probably an allusion to the recent Byzantine invasions of Antioch in 1137–8, 1142–3 and 1144; not an encouraging background to the crusade. While Odo lamented the resolution to decline the Sicilian offer it was the only realistic option, both in terms of practicalities and of the bigger political picture. Roger's recent claim to Antioch was another potential cause of trouble; given that Queen Eleanor's uncle Raymond ruled the principality he would hardly welcome the arrival of the Sicilian.[12] Furthermore, from a modern perspective, one can observe that had Roger been a truly selfless supporter of the holy war he would not have attacked the Byzantine Empire when the expedition was underway – a course of action that undoubtedly compromised the crusaders' relations with the Greeks. Finally, as Odo himself noted on two occasions, the French were keen to follow (literally) in the footsteps of the First Crusaders.[13] Given the emphasis on the deeds of these heroes in *Quantum praedecessores*, as well as the success of the earlier armies, this was another powerful reason to take the land route.

On 18 February, the Étampes assembly gathered to debate the regency. Louis turned the matter over to his churchmen and nobles; a slightly strange move perhaps, although a strategy probably dictated by the king's recent political difficulties and by the need for consensus amongst the most powerful men in the land. A separate conclave gathered before Abbot Bernard led the group back into the main meeting room to announce its decision. Citing the famous image of the two swords, one representing the sacred, the other secular, he pointed out Abbot Suger and Count William II of Nevers as the men chosen to govern.[14] These were entirely logical choices because both were individuals of huge experience and high standing. As abbot of St Denis, Suger was the head of a religious house intimately tied to the Capetian dynasty and he had been tutor to the young king. He was also a wise political and diplomatic operator, although his relationship with Louis had, at times, been turbulent.[15] Suger's biographer, William of St Denis, reported that the abbot was initially unwilling to accept the regency, 'judging the dignity that he was offered to be a burden rather than an honour', but after the intervention of Eugenius he agreed.[16] Given that the pope was travelling northwards at the time, presumably the matter was not actually resolved either until his first meeting with Louis at Dijon on 30 March (Suger may have been present), or Eugenius's arrival in Paris on 19 April.

William of Nevers had held his comital title since 1089 and was a veteran of the First Crusade. Unfortunately for the council, he had already sworn to become a Carthusian monk and could not be swayed from this vow. The count may well have known that he was physically failing, for he died before the year was out; had this happened when the crusade was underway, choosing his replacement could have proven especially contentious. We might note that the later Capetian crusading practice of using the monarch's mother or wife as regent was not employed here, although the presence of Eleanor on the expedition obviously rendered one element of this impossible.[17]

Louis took the opportunity of this gathering to make grants to the church of St Mary of Grâce Dieu and, at the request of Bernard of Clairvaux, to the abbey of Prémontré.[18] In the eleven months since Vézelay the king had issued numerous charters; as Odo of Deuil noted, 'the king set the condition of his realm in order by examining everything, while he ensured future peace for his subjects'.[19] Prior to Châlons he had visited Orléans, Sens, Poitiers, Le Puy, Saintes, Melun, Nevers and Senlis.[20] The journeys to Poitiers, Le Puy and Saintes were, respectively, about 210, 325 and 285 miles from Paris and demonstrate the effort that Louis put in to be seen across France. While his travels were undoubtedly designed to raise funds for the crusade, he had also tried to prepare the ground for his absence by resolving disputes, making gifts and confirming privileges. Notwithstanding the vagaries of survival, the number of extant charters gives some sense of the burst of diplomatic activity occasioned by – and let us remember this crucial fact – the unprecedented prospect of the king of France leaving his lands for at least two years and quite possibly not coming back. Prior to the crusade, there remains an average of about eighteen charters per annum. For 1146, this number jumps to around thirty and, most dramatically, in 1147, no less than twenty-four for the shorter period prior to Louis's departure in mid-June.[21] The subject matter of these documents shows the concerns of the king: some gifts, for example to the Templars; to leper-houses in Paris and Étampes; to the bishop of Chalons-sur-Marne; to churches in Laon; and to the abbeys of St Peter at Chartres,

Coeur-Dieu at Orléans and St Victor. Charters reveal that he took religious houses under his protection, including the priory of Lignan, the abbey of Barbeaux and the abbey of Fleury; he also renounced the right of *mainmorte* in the bishopric of Orléans. Another category of charter was the confirmation of the rights of an individual or institution, sometimes with regard to people connected with crusaders, such as the one bearing upon Hugh Tirel.[22]

After the council at Étampes, Louis headed southwards, via Autun, to welcome Pope Eugenius to his lands. The pontiff had crossed the Alps via the Mount Cenis Pass and then passed through Oulx and Lyons to the great abbey of Cluny where he encountered Peter the Venerable for the first time since the abbot's stay at the papal court between late 1145 and the spring of 1146. For the Cluniacs Alberic of Ostia and Imar, cardinal-bishop of Tusculum, this was a return to their mother-house. The party then proceeded up the River Saône towards Dijon.[23] There, on 30 March 1147, pope and monarch met each other, certainly for the first such occasion in their respective roles; the following day, Eugenius consecrated the church at Dijon.[24] They must have discussed progress in the crusade's preparations and considered how the pope could become involved in the final stages of this process. Peter the Venerable, who had attended the meeting of the German princes at Frankfurt on 13 March (see below), was also present. More importantly, a trio of envoys from King Conrad carried the news that Bernard had permitted a group of German nobles to fulfil their crusading vows against the pagan Wends. This embassy also invited the pope to a meeting at Strasbourg on Good Friday, 18 April, but Eugenius declined. The reasons for this are unclear – perhaps he had already committed himself to staying with Louis, or, as Acht suggested, he was more concerned with the ongoing issue of an imperial coronation.[25]

Eugenius then passed through Magny-Lambert to his own spiritual home of Clairvaux on 6 April. It is possible that Bernard was at Dijon, but there is no record of it. Assuming this to be the case, Eugenius's arrival at Clairvaux was the first face-to-face meeting of the Cistercian pope with his mentor since the former had been elected to the chair of St Peter. From Troyes, Eugenius went to Provins, Meaux, Lagny-sur-Marne and reached St Denis just north of Paris by 19 April, shortly before Easter.[26] It is not clear how far, if at all, Louis accompanied him on this leg of the journey.

The pope was to be present in and around Paris from this time until the crusade set out in early June. This was a substantial gesture of support for the campaign and perhaps a demonstration that, although he had been compelled to delegate the preaching to Bernard, Eugenius was fully committed to the expedition. The appearance of a pope north of the Alps was still a relatively rare event, notwithstanding the need for Paschal II in 1107, Calixtus II in 1119–20 and Innocent II in 1131–2 to seek sanctuary in France during their various troubles.[27] Eugenius attracted large numbers of visitors, eager to secure a papal judgement in their favour. As in the case of Louis's chancery, the period prior to the crusade saw a considerable diplomatic output by the papal scribes and administrators with over seventy surviving documents issued at Paris.[28]

Other diplomatic preparations gathered pace. A letter from Welf of Bavaria to Louis – in which the duke described himself as a knight of Christ and a servant of the cross – was a response to a lost message from the French king.[29] This most cordial communiqué talked of their shared bond as crusaders; the duke apologised for being unable to attend a meeting (probably that at Étampes in February) and discussed the practical concerns of the expedition, especially supplies. Welf was on good terms with King Geisa II of Hungary and this may have allowed him to assure Louis of his help in crossing this region. Dozens of other communications must have passed back and forth between the crusaders, churchmen and the rulers of the lands the expedition planned to go through. Duke Wladislaus of Bohemia was another noble to have taken the cross and the existence of a fragmentary letter addressed by him to Louis is also suggestive of this complex web of diplomacy.[30]

Relations with the Greeks began to develop too.[31] Manuel had already written to Louis, probably in the autumn of 1146, in response to a request from the king for markets and passage. The emperor responded positively; 'Our majesty's welcome here will be warm . . . our majesty is ready to co-operate in those things which you sought in your letter' – although there was a significant caveat: Manuel recalled the agreements made between the First Crusaders and Alexius I and asked that such arrangements should be renewed. He closed the letter by mentioning that he was fighting the Seljuks when the French envoys arrived, thereby advertising his own credentials as a Christian warrior.[32] Louis's envoys had also brought a letter from Pope Eugenius, to which the emperor responded in similar terms, expressing his readiness to support the expedition and provide supplies. In return, he mentioned again his wish for a repetition of the homage paid by the First Crusaders to his grandfather and he urged the pope to secure this. Manuel expressed surprise that Eugenius had not contacted him earlier about the crusade, which he said was a matter so close to his heart, and he asked the pope for a benediction.[33]

In March 1147 Manuel once more wrote to Eugenius concerning the French crusaders – presumably he was not yet aware of Conrad's decision to take the cross and, in any case, his positive relations with the Germans ensured that he was less troubled by the prospect of their appearance. The emperor wondered why he had not heard from the pope, but he continued to profess a willingness to assist the crusaders' crossing of his Empire. More pointedly this time, he asked them to promise not to cause damage to his lands and, should the crusaders conquer any territories listed on a document carried by his envoys, they should be restored to him. He also urged the pope to send a cardinal with the crusaders to guarantee that they kept good order. Manuel's letter ended with a highly positive expression of concord and unity for the Christians.[34]

The emperor's position was plain: the French were viewed as a potential threat, he wanted oaths of good behaviour from the crusaders and hoped to see the recovery of former Greek lands. The recent conflicts in Antioch and the ongoing Byzantine–Sicilian tensions made this entire situation highly fraught. We can see, however, that the emperor's second letter to the pope did not ask for homage. Presumably Eugenius had contacted Louis and the French king had rejected the idea; at this stage Manuel could not press such a demand. The emperor tried to get Eugenius's help in extracting such undertakings by stating his enthusiasm for the campaign and expressing strong sentiments of Christian brotherhood, as well as by asking that a papal legate should ensure that the French army behaved. The presence of papal representatives in the army was always likely anyway, but it seems that the pope, for a while at least, responded strongly to the possibility of forming closer ties with the Orthodox Church. Pope Urban II had hoped that the First Crusade would bring better relations with his fellow-Christians, but events during the campaign prevented this. It was a subject that his successors returned to: embassies had gone between Rome and Constantinople in 1111–12 and 1117;[35] Calixtus II had sent a delegation under Archbishop Roffridus of Benevento to John Comnenus in 1123–4. The emperor's reply survives and shows John's approval of the reasons Calixtus gave to reunify the Churches, although no further progress was made in connection with this exchange.[36] In 1136, Anselm of Havelberg visited Constantinople on behalf of Emperor Lothar and engaged in a series of extremely cordial debates over the differences between the Catholic and the Orthodox.[37] On the other hand, the following year, a Greek embassy to Lothar attacked the papal position on the *filioque* clause and, in a debate with Peter the Deacon, described the papacy as a worldly, warmongering and militaristic institution.[38] In the summer of 1147, with the Second Crusade poised to set out in an environment flushed with optimism and a sense of Catholic expansionism, Eugenius delegated Bishop Henry of Moravia to engage with the issue again. Otto of Freising stated that the pope knew his famous predecessor had 'won back into the unity of the church' the patriarchates of Antioch and Jerusalem; perhaps Eugenius – again in the spirit of re-living the First Crusade – hoped to add Constantinople.[39] In a letter of early 1147 the pontiff wrote to Bishop Henry:

> Since we have the greatest confidence regarding your love and we know that the king's good counsel lies in the highest degree in your wisdom and dispensation, we commend to your concern, in the matter of urging the king, that you concentrate your efforts by all means on advising him that he strive for the honour and exaltation of his holy mother the Roman Church and that he may work faithfully to join to her the Church of Constantinople in the way it was known once to have been, in accordance with the power granted to himself by God.[40]

Eugenius may briefly, therefore, have aspired to use the crusade to generate some form of grand Christian alliance against the infidel and to crown the campaign with the reunification of two of the great denominations of Christendom. In the end, Henry was distracted by the emergence of the Wendish Crusade and never went to the Holy Land.

In the course of Eugenius's stay in Paris a number of grand occasions took place in connection with the crusade. All contributed to what must have been a growing mood of anticipation in the city; feelings of adventure, purpose and fear; as well as the bustle of trying to make the myriad of practical arrangements necessary to set out for the Holy Land. In a public sense, the crusading preparations culminated in the remarkable ceremony at St Denis in early June, just prior to the expedition's departure; but other formal events were staged too. The first of these was on 20 April, Easter Day. King Louis and the pope celebrated the festival at St Denis where, as Odo of Deuil reported, 'many people from many places flocked together because of the double marvel, that is, the king and the apostolic father as pilgrims'.[41] This was also a great moment for Suger, because the pope consecrated a magnificent Golden Cross, titled 'The True Cross of the Lord Surpassing All and Every Pearl', crafted for the abbot from 80 marks of refined gold. It had taken two years and five goldsmiths to make it, and it was covered in a marvellous array of precious stones and images from the Old Testament and Christ's life.[42] The following day, Eugenius dedicated an altar at the church of Montmartre with Bernard and Peter the Venerable in attendance.[43]

Less easy to pinpoint in terms of chronology is another matter connected to St Denis, namely the creation of the so-called 'Crusading Windows'. The timing of the commission and completion of this work is subject to some scholarly debate. Brown and Cothren connected them with the abbacy of Odo of Deuil and with the proposed expedition of Louis and Henry II of England to Spain in 1158.[44] This seems rather odd: given the outcome of the Second Crusade – and the outpouring of discontent afterwards – surely it would have been incongruous to highlight the successful First Crusade and thus to emphasise the failure of Louis's campaign even more starkly. Odo, of all people, would have been aware of this and it is far more probable that the windows dated from the time of the Second Crusade; indeed, the presence of Eugenius and Louis would have been a particularly auspicious moment to show them off.

Suger's biographer, William of St Denis, wrote of the abbot's reluctance to support the launch of the crusade in 1146 and for this reason it might appear strange that he commissioned the windows.[45] But in view of the fact that the abbot's *Vita* was written after the crusade, it may be rather that William was trying to remove Suger from association with the expedition. There is contrary evidence to show that Suger was actually supportive of crusading: for example, he participated fully in the build-up to Louis's departure and he must have influenced Odo of Deuil's decision to write an account of the journey to the East. This was intended to form part of Suger's biography of the king; it was expected that the crusade would provide a central chapter of the planned *Vita*. In the same anticipatory vein, the windows in St Denis could be seen to herald the triumphant moment when the king of France took his place alongside the heroes of the First Crusade. Suger was also a key mover in the (ultimately unsuccessful) attempt to organise a new crusade in 1150.[46]

The window consists of fourteen panels, all but two of which were destroyed in the French Revolution, although engravings published in 1729 provide a record of their content. Brown and Cothren have skilfully reconstructed the likely plan of the window, formed of seven pairs of roundels placed in one of the westernmost radiating chapels of the abbey. This location on the ambulatory meant that the images could be seen by the many pilgrims who processed around the church.

The lowest pair depicts: first, a king on horseback in the midst of a group of mounted knights; secondly, nine figures in groups of three (see Illustration 6). A heavenly hand crowns the central trio, the others are already crowned and are gesturing their approval. Several of the figures hold palms, probably signifying martyrdom. In other words, they represented crusaders leaving for the earthly Jerusalem – shown here as a generic royal campaign against unbelievers – who would gain the reward of crowned martyrs in the heavenly Jerusalem.[47]

The second pair is concerned with Charlemagne's legendary pilgrimage and the Holy Land. To the left, as the caption tells us, Charlemagne is asked to help Emperor Constantine, and, to the right, he arrives at the gates of Constantinople. Clearly the historical plausibility of this encounter is somewhat stretched by the near 500-year gap between the two men's lives, but the point was to show Charlemagne helping the Eastern Empire against the infidel – just as the First Crusade had responded to Alexius's call, and in anticipation of co-operation between Manuel and Louis. Charlemagne was widely, if wrongly, believed to have made a pilgrimage to Jerusalem and his name was frequently invoked in this context.[48] Numerous writers, such as Robert of Rheims, mentioned him as a proto-crusader and noted that the First Crusaders travelled on the road that Charlemagne had constructed for his army. Robert also reported that Urban II had cited the emperor's battles against pagans in Spain and Saxony in his speech at Clermont and Ralph of Caen wrote that Oliver and Roland were reborn at the battle of Dorylaeum.[49] In a similar vein, the Song of Roland emerged in its present form soon after the First Crusade.[50] The text produced at St Denis in the 1140s known as the 'Pseudo-Turpin' also featured Charlemagne prominently.[51] The emperor had many further connections with the abbey – his banner was kept there, for example, and the Capetians worked hard to emphasise their links with him. As Brown and Cothren indicate, the depiction of a historical, non-saintly figure, in such a panel in a major ecclesiastical building, was 'without parallel in the twelfth century' and shows what an extraordinarily potent figure Charlemagne was in the context of the French crown, crusading and St Denis.[52]

The remaining five pairs of roundels have two possible arrangements but, whichever is correct, their content was entirely concerned with the First Crusade. The panels illustrated battles between the crusaders and the Muslims, including the struggle with Kerbogha outside Antioch and the battle of Ascalon. The images show Christian successes; hence the capture of Nicaea, the taking of Antioch, the siege and fall of Jerusalem and the final retreat of the enemy after their defeat at Ascalon. The other roundels reveal Robert of Flanders and Robert of Normandy, two of the heroes of the First Crusade, each one being described later as 'Ierosolimitanus'.[53] The material to compose the stories was close at hand: it is known that the Gesta Francorum and the history of Raymond of Aguilers were familiar to the St Denis library, as was the narrative of Walter the Chancellor – a work that shared the use of the rare word 'parti', employed in one of the captions.[54] Whether the windows were completed for the Easter celebrations of 1147 or for the events held before the crusade departed in June, they formed a compelling set of images. Yet again the knights of the mid-1140s were being reminded of the deeds of their forefathers. Furthermore, the pursuit of the heavenly and earthly Jerusalem was being connected to the actions of the greatest Christian monarch of the West, Charlemagne – surely a source of even greater inspiration.

A moment of particular spiritual power in the build-up to the crusade was a sermon delivered by Peter the Venerable.[55] The abbot was present on a number of occasions during the conception and planning of the expedition. His extensive and careful advice to Abbot Theobald of St Columba of Sens on how he should conduct himself on the campaign also indicated his positive attitude.[56] Berry has demonstrated that Peter's earlier involvement with the Holy Land included contact with the Cluniac monks at Mount Tabor and letters to the king and patriarch of Jerusalem.[57] Peter wrote to Sigurd of Norway, praising him for his crusade of 1107–10 and wishing him good fortune in an expedition planned for 1130.[58] The abbot was also a strong advocate of the Knights Templar. Unlike some of the French clergy connected with the 1147–8 crusade Peter had, in the recent past at least, been more positive in his attitude towards the Greeks. A letter from the reign of John Comnenus, probably written around 1138–9, complimented the emperor on his labours as a barrier against the infidel. It also reminded him of the sacrifices of the First Crusaders and argued that the Latin States merited good treatment from John because they defended the holy places.[59] In 1144 Peter downplayed divergences in Eucharistic practices with the Greeks and wrote of 'faith and mutual charity' bringing the Catholic and Orthodox together.[60] Perhaps this idea had resurfaced in Eugenius's planned use of Henry of Moravia as an envoy to the Orthodox. Peter had stated earlier during the preparations for crusade that he perceived his role as being that of one who should offer King Louis prayer and advice about the campaign; and we have seen how he pointed to the Jews as a source of funding for the expedition.[61] In the lead-in to its departure he gave a stirring peroration on the nature of the crusade: *De laude Dominici Sepulchri* is the first surviving sermon on such a subject in this context.

The actual date of its delivery is not known, but it is generally believed to have happened in the course of Pope Eugenius's stay in Paris in the spring of 1147. This long and complex work – at over 900 lines of modern text – was a powerful composition which placed crusading in the context of the redemptive act of Christ's sacrifice and focused closely on the Holy Sepulchre as the place to be revered above all others – the source of 'incorruption and life'.[62]

Peter dramatically emphasised the sacred nature of Christ's tomb: 'it is the greatest reason, O man, why you should worship with special affection the tomb in which he lay dead that you might live, and why you should venerate it with singular reverence above all other places in the entire world'.[63] He reminded his audience of Christ's sacrifice and advocated a Christomimetic act in which a crusader placed complete hope in Him and would be prepared to love, worship, obey and die for Christ. He preached that Christ's sacrifice had closed Hell and opened up a way to Heaven for all men and given them the opportunity of immortality. As Bernard of Clairvaux had done, he pointed out that the material costs of the crusade were far less than the spiritual benefits. He also argued that the Holy Land had previously been populated by pious men and that the Holy Sepulchre would be a place of glory for all people; even those who had strayed, such as the Jews and the Muslims, could still be saved. Inevitably, the First Crusaders were mentioned and praised: 'in fierce battle they seized that holy place from the yoke of the Persians and Arabs'.[64] Their warriors had gone 'not as enemies, but as His Creations, servants and as redeemed men, with pious swords' to cleanse the holy places and to allow the favoured sons to come to their father's tomb.[65] Cole has noted similarities here to accounts of Urban II's speech at Clermont in the explanation of why the glory of the Sepulchre required that it should be cleansed from pollution.[66] Peter described the miracle of the Easter Fire as proof of divine favour bestowed on the age of the crusaders. The sermon climaxed with a prayer that God should favour the expedition and protect those who went with such true faith and were marked with His sign of the cross. He concluded with a restatement of the link between crusading as an act of salvation and Christ's redemption of man.[67]

The final, and most spectacular, of the crusading ceremonies took place at St Denis on the occasion of the Lendit Fair, 11 June 1147. The recently redeveloped church, probably boasting its fine crusading windows and splendid relic of the True Cross, was a perfect setting for such a display.[68] The abbey-church of St Denis was intimately linked with the French crown; the fact that the fair attracted big crowds anyway added further to the logic of the occasion. The annual Fair was associated with the Holy Land through the abbey's relics of the Passion (a thorn and a nail), and it opened with a procession and a benediction of the Chapter of Notre-Dame of Paris's fragment of the True Cross, an object sent over by the patriarch of Jerusalem in 1120.[69] As the last big gathering prior to the departure of the expedition it was a great opportunity to exhibit, in front of as many people as possible, the power and purpose of those involved. No ceremony of a similar scale is known from the First Crusade and its staging must be a consequence of royal involvement in crusading. The choreography of the event was carefully arranged so as to emphasise the piety of the king – and hence the likelihood of divine favour – and his ties to the person of St Denis. All the major figures at the heart of the French crusade were present: Louis, Eleanor, the king's mother, Adelaide of Maurienne (sister to Pope Calixtus II), Abbot Bernard, Abbot Suger and Pope Eugenius.

St Denis lies a few miles north of Paris and even Louis's journey there formed a part of the day's spiritual activities. First, the king paused at an unnamed monastery and then, presumably just outside the city boundaries, he stopped at a leper colony. Odo himself vouched that he saw Louis enter with only two companions, leaving the rest of his retinue outside. The symbolism here was plain: leprosy is a terrifying disease, more so in the medieval period before the advent of modern medicine.[70] Lepers were shunned by society and segregated for fear of contagion. Their position was paradoxical; to some they were being punished for their sins (often sexual in nature), to others they were a select group, paying for misdeeds in this life and therefore achieving redemption earlier in the next. It became a common practice to imitate Christ and to wash lepers' feet. In June 1147 the public nature and the timing of Louis's visit drew attention to parallels between the earthly king and the King of Heaven.[71] Louis himself seems to have had some affinity for lepers because he made a gift to the house of St Lazarus when he was in the Holy Land in 1149.[72]

On his arrival at St Denis the king was greeted by 'great crowds'. Clearly the sense of anticipation had been building and on a day of intense heat the atmosphere became quite fevered; Odo reported that Eleanor and her mother-in-law nearly fainted. Pope Eugenius, Suger and the monks of St Denis waited to receive the king at the church. Then, in full view of everyone, Louis requested the *vexillum* and asked the permission of the patron saint to depart. The crowd lamented the prospect of his leaving, perhaps expressing a ritual rather than a realistic sentiment. The *vexillum* was a vermillion banner on a golden lance that the abbot of St Denis gave to the count of the Vexin (one of the king's titles) when he went to war. It was equated with the *oriflamme*, the banner of Charlemagne himself, and it had been used successfully in 1124 by Louis VI in his campaign against Emperor Henry V of Germany.[73]

Louis prostrated himself on the ground in front of the tomb of St Denis and venerated it with the utmost humility – a moment that Odo, as a member of the abbey, reported in appropriate detail. Here the monk's skill as a writer is well shown; from the huge outdoor settings the action closed in to focus on a small, intimate scene that featured just the king, the pope and Bernard. These three most pious and powerful of men crowded around the altar. The abbot himself opened the golden doors of the shrine and took out the silver reliquary of St Denis 'so that the king might be rendered more eager for his task by seeing and kissing the relic of him whom his soul venerated'.[74] For Odo, here was St Denis himself inspiring the king to great deeds. Suger took the banner from its place above the altar and presented it to Louis; the pope then confirmed the king's status as a crusader by giving him the traditional pilgrim's wallet and a blessing. Again the crowd lamented their monarch's imminent departure, but the highpoint of the day was over. Louis and a few of his retinue withdrew and dined in the calm of the monks' refectory; then, after embracing them all and receiving the kiss of peace, he asked for their prayers and goodwill before setting out.

Conrad III's preparations are more difficult to follow because there is no detailed narrative comparable to Odo of Deuil's account of events in France. Some comments by Otto of Freising, however, along with a number of contemporary letters, permit a reasonably useful picture to be constructed.

Probably the most striking aspect of the king's actions – and those of most of his senior nobles and churchmen – was the sheer speed with which they were made. It was less than six months from the time that Conrad took the cross in late December 1146 to his departure from Regensburg in early June 1147; this was an incredibly short period in which to prepare for such a major undertaking. Louis VII took fifteen months and most of the senior figures in the First Crusade spent at least nine months making ready. Given the outcome of the Second Crusade, perhaps even more telling is the contrast with the Third Crusade: Richard I took the cross in the autumn of 1187 and set out in July 1190; Philip Augustus took the cross in January 1188 and also departed in July 1190; while Frederick Barbarossa, who had participated in the expedition of 1147–8, became a crusader in early June 1188 and left in May 1189.[75] As noted above, it is likely that Conrad had already decided to go to the Holy Land before he made his formal commitment at Speyer in December. If this was the case, he could have made some tentative preparations and at least thought out some of the measures he would need to take. Nonetheless, he had to be ready to go in the summer of 1147 and, as he mentioned in a letter of late March to Pope Eugenius, he had 'not any time to get ready for [his] journey'.[76]

Conrad summoned a major assembly of the German nobility to Frankfurt in March to set the affairs of the kingdom in order. In the meantime he began to settle any outstanding disputes. Otto of Freising described a quarrel in 1138 between Henry of Namur and Archbishop Adalbert of Trier that concerned the abbey of St Maxim. This struggle had led to years of warfare in the Moselle region, but finally, at Speyer, on 4 January 1147 and in the presence of Abbot Bernard and other crusaders, including the bishop of Basel, the trouble was resolved.[77] Conrad moved from Speyer to Fulda, where he can be located in late January and where we know that he called to him Wibald, abbot of Stavelot and Corvey. Wibald would be chosen as regent of Germany; presumably this was a preliminary meeting designed to raise the issue.[78] Wibald had only been invested with the abbacy of Corvey in December and was said to be in poor health at the time, although he did not rebuff Conrad. The king then went some 100 miles south-east towards Nuremburg, on 8 February, and then some 55 miles further to be in Regensburg from mid to late February.

The meeting in Regensburg was a particularly notable one, described as a 'general council' by Otto of Freising. With Bernard of Clairvaux back in France it was the learned Cistercian, Abbot Adam of Ebrach, who gave a sermon. Otto, who was an eyewitness, described what was probably the standard preaching process, whereby Adam celebrated Mass, then read the letters of Pope Eugenius and Bernard followed by a brief speech of his own.

According to Otto, almost all of the audience came forward to take the cross, although they were said to have been favourably disposed to do so 'by previous report'. It seems the news that Conrad had taken the cross, combined with his personal presence, opened the floodgates to recruitment in Bavaria. The bishops of Freising, Regensburg and Passau, Margrave Henry of Austria, many other nobles and even highwaymen and robbers committed themselves to the campaign.[79]

After this Conrad headed north-west, via Bischofsheim on the River Tauber, to reach Frankfurt by 11 March, where the most significant gathering in his kingdom took place. In the period since Christmas Eugenius had learned of Conrad's decision to join the crusade and, in a letter now lost, had urged him to make careful provision for the rule of his lands. To this end, he sent his legate to assist; this was the German Theodwin, cardinal-bishop of Santa Rufina, a man hugely experienced in the affairs of the Empire and the person who had crowned Conrad in March 1138.[80] Also in attendance at Frankfurt were Bernard of Clairvaux and Abbot Peter the Venerable of Cluny; their presence was a clear sign of the importance of the assembly, of Bernard's support for Conrad, and of the continual flow of information between the French and German courts.

The Frankfurt gathering made or confirmed several weighty decisions. Most crucial of all, the princes unanimously agreed that Conrad's ten-year-old son, Henry, should be chosen as his successor. This was a real triumph for the king because, in spite of the Empire's political troubles, it indicated that he had used the crusade to advance the cause of his own dynasty ahead of the elective principle which had operated in recent successions. The obvious concern created by the imminent and unprecedented departure of the crowned monarch, combined with the distinct possibility that he might not return, had brought about this situation. Conrad moved swiftly to confirm this arrangement by informing Pope Eugenius and setting the date of 30 March for his son's coronation at Aachen.[81] A charter issued at Frankfurt on 23 March proudly announced that the document was issued 'at the curia in which Henry, son of King Conrad, was elected'.[82]

In the course of his letter to Eugenius the king made several statements which have provoked some controversy amongst historians.[83] In 1914 Cosack inferred from a lost letter of the pope that Eugenius was berating the German monarch for going to the Levant; this view has been followed by numerous writers since.[84] Cosack argued that the pope wanted Conrad to protect him both from the citizens of Rome and from Roger of Sicily. Eugenius had certainly asked for the king's help in the former matter in the past, although his presence in northern Europe meant that this was now, perhaps, less urgent. Roger could have been a problem too, but there was an ongoing truce between the two parties, and it appeared to be holding well at this time. More significantly, there was no reference in Conrad's letter to any papal worry over the Romans or the Sicilians:

> Assuredly, that which has disturbed your pleasure – namely, that we have taken up such a great enterprise, as a result of a sign of the life-giving cross, and the proposal for a great and long expedition without your knowledge – has proceded from a great disposition for true devotion. But 'the holy spirit, which breathes where it wishes' (John, iii.8), and which has become accustomed 'to come suddenly' (Mark, xiii.36), has permitted us to have no delays in taking up your, or anyone's, advice; but straight away, when it touched our heart with its wondrous finger, drove the whole direction of our thought to follow it without any time for an intervening delay.[85]

The main caveat that can be found here is the words 'without your knowledge', although in this context it hardly seems a critical comment; more a simple statement of fact.[86] In all seriousness, given that Bernard had been in the Empire since October, the pope can hardly have been surprised at the news. If Eugenius had really wanted to stop the abbot from recruiting Conrad he would surely have needed to make this plain at some point; yet there was no suggestion of this beforehand, nor any sense of subsequent anger towards Bernard or the king. As discussed earlier, there were numerous logical and positive reasons why the pope should hope and expect the king to go to crusade. Later in the expedition, Conrad wrote that he had set out 'at the advice and urging of the most holy Pope Eugenius and the lord Bernard'; the king himself, therefore, placed at least some of the initiative with the pope and implied that he had received letters from the *curia*.[87] On the part of Eugenius, there was lavish praise for Conrad. A letter from the latter half of 1147 to the young King Henry VI lauded his father's crusading zeal and noted that Conrad had entrusted his son's wellbeing to the churchmen of Rome; the pope also stated that he was keen to offer advice and encouragement when required.[88]

Eugenius's primary worry seems to have been one of timing and setting the kingdom's affairs in proper order – hence the dispatch of legate Theodwin. In the course of 1147, at least four other papal legates were active in Germany trying to keep the land at peace, which again shows the pope's commitment to this issue.[89] Cosack's emphasis on the king's unwillingness to delay – something used to bolster the pope's alleged hostility to the whole enterprise – has hardened over time into a complete negative. Given the wide-ranging troubles that had afflicted the Empire in recent years this was a fully understandable concern but, as we have seen, much had been set right. Conrad indicated, however, that the Holy Spirit would not let him pause – and, in any case, he needed to co-ordinate his march with the French.

The king knew that Eugenius was travelling northwards and he sent a delegation of senior German churchmen, namely the bishops of Worms and Havelburg, and Abbot Wibald, to meet the pope and try to organise a face-to-face meeting at Strasbourg on 18 April. Conrad wished to discuss several matters, including the crusade, peace in his lands and 'the enhancement of our honour'. This last point must have been a reference to his imperial coronation, an issue of huge importance to him, especially given that he was going to meet the Eastern Emperor, Manuel Comnenus. The relative status of these men was a delicate matter and Conrad's position as emperor-in-waiting was not ideal. The rush to prepare for the crusade meant that he could not be crowned before the expedition, but trying to settle upon some future arrangements must have been on the king's mind.[90]

Against this background the Council of Frankfurt also confirmed a 'genuine peace' throughout the land, another point of huge importance to the king. The details are unknown, although as Hiestand has noted, when Emperor Henry IV proposed to set out for Jerusalem in 1103 a similar four-year edict was promulgated, designed to create political calm and to bring the Jews under royal protection. We saw earlier how Radulf's preaching had caused problems in the Rhineland in 1146 and the need for Bernard himself to quell the situation. At the start of the First Crusade, Henry IV had been in Italy and his absence was one reason why the pogroms of that time were so severe. Conrad clearly wished to avoid such a breakdown of civil authority when he was away and it is almost certain that similar measures to the 1103 edict formed part of the 1147 legislation.[91] An interpolation of the chronicle of Alberic of Trois-Fontaines noted Conrad's successful efforts to make peace before his departure.[92]

The outcome of the earlier discussions with Louis VII at Châlons-sur-Marne on 2 February was probably relayed to the Council of Frankfurt. Out of sheer practicality, the bulk of the German army would travel by the land route, although a group sailed via Lisbon with other northern Europeans. The decision raised a number of practical and diplomatic issues. How could a large army move reasonably quickly and cross natural obstacles? The use of river transport was a logical answer to the first of these points; it means that the senior figures in Germany sent instructions for the gathering of boats on the Rhine and on the Danube. They also ordered the construction of fine bridges, most famously across the Danube at Regensburg, to allow the crusaders to make good progress in German lands. Conrad gave his permission for the French crusaders to use these routes, and this is the sort of information that would have formed part of the continual flow of news that passed from envoys and ambassadors between the two kings' courts.[93] It is apparent that Peter the Venerable was present at Frankfurt – again, it was entirely appropriate for a man of his standing to attend such an important event.[94]

A combination of geography and logistics meant that some groups from imperial lands would march with Louis – namely the bishops of Metz and Toul and the counts of Monzon and Vaudemont. Two northern Italian nobles from the Empire, the powerful Marquis William of Montferrat and his half-brother, Amadeus of Maurienne, also travelled separately, probably via Brindisi.[95] The use of the land route required diplomatic contact with the rulers of Hungary and Byzantium. In the case of the former, this was rather delicate because of the recent warfare between the two lands. Otto of Freising was scathing about the Hungarians, describing them as 'of disgusting aspect, with deep-set eyes and short stature. They are barbarous and ferocious in their habits and language.'[96] Conrad's support of Boris, a claimant to the Hungarian throne, and an attack on the frontier fortress of Pressburg by troops of Henry of Austria (Conrad's half-brother), had provoked a fierce response. In September 1146 Geisa had crushed Henry's army near the River Leitha (Virvelt) and caused the duke to flee for his life to Vienna.[97] From this unpromising situation, peace was brought about and the likely influence of Bernard and Louis, who had written to Geisa, helped to facilitate an agreement for the Germans to cross Hungary.

The relationship between the Germans and the Greeks was considerably better, although it operated on many levels and contained elements of friction. The two ruling houses were united by their dislike of Roger of Sicily. The Greeks saw him as the false claimant to their former lands in southern Italy; the Germans opposed him because they had supported Pope Innocent II in the papal schism and Roger backed the anti-pope, Anacletus. Emperor John Comnenus had made an alliance with Lothar against Roger, and this was renewed under Conrad. Otto of Freising preserved letters from Conrad, both to John and to Manuel Comnenus, which spoke of a united front against the Sicilians: 'both should have the same friend and the same foe, whether on land or sea . . . whether Norman or Sicilian or whoever else, anywhere'.[98] The cordial relationship was to be sealed by the betrothal of Manuel, John's fourth son, to Bertha of Sulzbach, Conrad's sister-in-law. When, in 1143, John died unexpectedly and Manuel acceded to the imperial throne the status of this union rose dramatically as Bertha became the senior empress. The Greeks took a tough line in another round of negotiations and Lilie suggests that before the marriage was celebrated they extracted a dowry consisting of the Italian territories that Conrad was expected to conquer from Roger II.[99] Manuel married Bertha in January

1146 when she took the imperial name Eirene. The *Annales Herbipolenses* recorded that in the same year Conrad sent the bishop of Würzburg to Greece to conduct 'secret' negotiations, although we can only speculate whether these were connected with the crusade or with wider political issues.[100] There was further contact between the two rulers in early 1147, although the details of this have been lost. Conrad must have informed the emperor that he planned to travel ahead of the French and that he would need provisions and guides. Manuel's response to this will be discussed below.

The final major issue under discussion at Frankfurt was the extension of the crusade to include a campaign against the Wends, a matter of vital importance to the scope of the crusade and also to the development of the German Empire. A letter written by Bernard described how he, by virtue of his authority as the preacher of the crusade, promised to many in the audience the same spiritual privileges for fighting the pagan tribes across the River Alba in Bohemia as the ones promised to those who were going to Jerusalem.[101] The theological aspect of Bernard's message will be examined in a later chapter, but Otto of Freising succinctly stated that the Saxons 'refused to set out' for the Holy Land because they had pagan neighbours.[102] There is also evidence that a papal legate had preached the crusade in Denmark, and the reaction to this may have influenced the approach of the northern Germans.[103]

On 30 March, within days of the end of the Council of Frankfurt, Eugenius met a delegation from Conrad at Dijon where the pope must have been informed of this new development.[104] It is unclear whether Eugenius and Bernard had communicated on this issue at all, or if the abbot, presented with a strong representation from the northern German nobles and churchmen, saw this as further opportunity for the Catholic Church to extend its influence. King Conrad presumably favoured the plan because these nobles could cause trouble in his absence; he probably approved of the spiritual aspect of the campaign as well. By this time it might have been too late to make realistic preparations for a journey to the Latin East and the closer holy war offered a more practical option. The German envoys at Dijon included Anselm of Havelberg, whose diocese bordered on the pagan lands, and it is almost certain that this was when the pope appointed the bishop as legate for the northern crusade. Wibald of Stavelot wrote about the Dijon conference and indicated that Eugenius gave a positive reception to the news from Frankfurt: 'immediately he enjoined to us . . . in remission of our sins, to war to the end (*debellandos*) the enemies of the Christian name . . . and to fight the pagans across the River Alba [Elbe]'.[105] This suggests prompt encouragement to the legates to begin directing the holy war. No sources hint at any controversy or equivocation on the matter.

Shortly after the meeting at Dijon, and after a visit to Clairvaux – where he could have sounded out Bernard on events at Frankfurt even further – the pope issued *Divina dispensatione II* at Troyes on 11 April. This gave papal authorisation for the crusade against the Slavs and officially announced Anselm's legatine status. Constable has suggested that in light of Bernard's customary deference to papal authority and of his insistence on the proper order of things, the abbot's letter cited above was issued after the papal bull; it seems, however, to read more as a continuous narrative in which Bernard gave his formal encouragement to the venture at Frankfurt.[106] He wrote of the council that 'the might of the Christians was armed against the [pagans] . . . ; they have put on the cross and we, by virtue of our authority, promised them the same spiritual privileges as those who set out for Jerusalem . . . all Christians who have not yet taken the cross for Jerusalem may know that they will obtain the same spiritual privileges by undertaking this expedition . . . It has pleased all those who were gathered at Frankfurt to decree that a copy of this letter should be carried everywhere and that the bishops and priests should proclaim it to the people of God.'[107]

In any event, the crusade was now to be fought simultaneously on three fronts: the Holy Land, the Baltic and Iberia. The spiritual privileges for all three elements of the holy war were identical; such an unprecedented offer shows the huge confidence and ambition of the church authorities and of the secular rulers of the time. The sense of enthusiasm, divine blessing and the chance to repeat the near-mythical deeds of their forefathers combined with political opportunism and the secular rulers' territorial aspirations to link this series of campaigns. *Divina dispensatione II* stated: 'we believe that it has come about through the providence of divine counsel that so great a multitude of the faithful from diverse regions is preparing to fight the infidel, and that almost the whole of Christendom is being summoned for so praiseworthy a task'.[108]

While his envoys went to Dijon, Conrad and the German court had moved northwards to Aachen. There, on 30 March, in Charlemagne's city, in the traditional heart of the German monarchy, the king's ten-year-old son was crowned as Henry VI and the Empire was bestowed upon him for the duration of Conrad's absence. In turn, the young king was entrusted to the care of Archbishop Henry of Mainz and the regency to Abbot Wibald.[109]

Wibald and Anselm's delegation left Dijon and went to Nuremburg, the location of Conrad's court from at least 24 April to 16 May. This was the city earmarked for the first big gathering of the German army and Otto of Freising reported that the troops set out from there in late May in full battle array.[110]

Wibald and Anselm would have made their way north, from Nuremburg to Magdeburg, where the forces for the Wendish crusade were to assemble for 29 June.[111] Thus, in the early summer of 1147, armies from France and Germany began the long march to the Holy Land, and men from the north of the Empire and from Denmark prepared to campaign in the Baltic region. Already, however, the fleets from Cologne, Flanders, Normandy and England were fighting the Muslims in Portugal: the first battle of the crusade had commenced.

CHAPTER 8

THE CONQUEST OF LISBON

The quickest military response to the preaching of the Second Crusade came from northern Europe. In late May 1147 a fleet of between 164 and 200 ships sailed from Dartmouth in southern England to take part in the siege of Lisbon; five months later, on the 24 October, the city fell to the combined forces of the crusaders and King Afonso Henriques of Portugal (1128–85). In the longer run this would mark one of the major achievements of the Second Crusade and a fundamental episode in the development of Portugal, but the primary concerns here are to consider how this expedition fitted into the broader scope of the crusade and to examine the reasons behind the campaign's success.

The main source for these events is *De expugnatione Lyxbonensi* ('The Conquest of Lisbon'), a narrative written in the form of a letter by a participant in the crusade: a Norman–French priest, identified by Livermore as Raol.[1] The letter was addressed to Osbert of Bawdsey, a cleric associated with the Glanvill family of East Anglia who were represented on the crusade by Hervey, the leader of the Anglo-Norman contingent. It seems likely that some form of communication was dispatched to East Anglia in the early winter of 1147 (when the events described in the letter end) or in the spring of 1148 before the crusaders carried on to the Holy Land. The sole surviving manuscript dates from the period between the late 1160s and the early 1170s and may represent a reworking of the original diary/report with some of the key themes enhanced. Contrary to the rather dismissive views of Constable, who described him as a 'a simple parish priest', and of David (the editor of *De expugnatione*), Raol was a well-educated man who constructed a sophisticated and largely homogeneous work.[2] The author appeared to be familiar with the writings of Bernard of Clairvaux, Guibert of Nogent, Saint Augustine, and the canon law collections of Ivo of Chartres and Gratian. Raol was quite a belligerent churchman; in a charter given after the capture of Lisbon he stated that he had 'expelled the infidels with my own bow'. He also had access to considerable funds since he built a chapel for the dead English crusaders from his own money and later gave 200 silver marks to the monastery of Santa Cruz in Coimbra.[3] The basic accuracy of Raol's narrative seems high: corroborative evidence confirms the strategic and chronological developments related by him. The extant version of the text, written in the aftermath of the failure of the campaign to the East and of the weak response to the 1157 and 1159 crusade appeals (to the Levant and Spain respectively), may have acted as a blueprint for a successful crusade.[4] In the event, the Glanvill clan responded positively to the call for the Third Crusade: three members of the family took part in the expedition.[5] Raol's text also provides a vivid insight into the ideas and motives of the crusaders at Lisbon, as well as detailing the challenges that faced them in the course of the siege.

The narrative links together what is represented as four major speeches by different figures during the campaign; on closer inspection, it is apparent that these 'orations' are a combination of genuine reporting interspersed with a series of interpolated themes that the author wished to emphasise.[6] Most prominent amongst them were the need for the crusaders to have right intention for their actions and the notion that the Christian armies should act with unity of thought as well as of deed.

In addition to *De expugnatione*, there is a series of contemporary letters based around a common core, sometimes known as 'The Teutonic Source' or (in a recent translation) as the 'Lisbon Letter'.[7] Several participants in the campaign wrote back to northern Europe and these communications were preserved in monastic annals. The details found in this source, which runs to just under 100 lines in its modern edition, are a valuable complement to *De expugnatione*. Further useful information is contained in contemporary charters given in Portugal, in the comments of other writers, particularly Anglo-Norman authors such as Henry of Huntingdon, and also in the foundation document of the monastery of Saint Vincent, written in 1188, some forty years after the house itself was built in the immediate aftermath of the conquest.[8]

The sources reveal that a broad-ranging group of crusaders from across northern Europe fought at Lisbon. *De expugnatione* tells us that the three main contingents were the Anglo-Normans, the Flemings and the Rhinelanders. These rather broad categories can be augmented by noting reports of Scots, Bretons, Aquitanians and crusaders from around the River Weser, east of the Rhine. Several reasons can be suggested as to why such a substantial force assembled. As we saw above, Bernard of Clairvaux spent a considerable period of time in Flanders and the northern Rhineland. There was also the preaching of the renegade Cistercian monk Radulf and, although it was eventually suppressed by Abbot Bernard, it was reported to be highly persuasive. There is evidence that Pope Eugenius wrote to Count Thierry and to the town of

Tournai. For the areas not visited by Bernard, we know of his letter sent to the people of England and that by Eugenius to the bishop of Salisbury; in the case of Brittany, we know of a letter written by the abbot's secretary, Nicholas of Clairvaux, and of a sermon delivered by Bishop Geoffrey of Chartres in which Nicholas's and Eugenius's letters were read out.[9] The deeply engrained religiosity of the time and the powerful message of crusade preaching – to save Christ's patrimony and to secure the remission of sins – must have been strong motives for many of the recruits.

Across this diverse group of people it is possible to identify some areas with strong histories of crusading and others with a record of involvement in warfare in the Iberian Peninsula. As discussed earlier, Flanders had a particularly rich tradition of crusading. The Anglo-Norman region also had crusading antecedents, most obviously through Duke Robert's leading role in the First Crusade, and several contingents sailed from England to the Holy Land between 1097–1102.[10] Furthermore, as seen above, the work of writers such as William of Malmesbury and Orderic Vitalis helped to keep the memory of the First Crusade very much alive. The northern Rhineland had a much more limited history of crusading, although the First Crusade clearly exerted some influence in the area, as will be seen below. Rhineland contingents had also sailed via Iberia to the Holy Land in 1102 and 1110, showing some involvement in warfare in the peninsula.[11]

Apart from the effect of preaching and crusading traditions, other motives may have prompted this diverse group of people to fight. It is generally accepted that the Rhineland and the Low Countries were amongst the most commercially advanced regions of the time and Bernard's carefully pitched message to the merchant classes to seek a bargain may well have proven particularly attractive; such people could have had the financial resources to undertake a crusade close to hand.[12] William of Malmesbury described Cologne as being 'as crowded with merchants as it is packed with the shrines of the saints'.[13] If these people were minded to take the cross, for whatever reason or combination of reasons, then it was quite natural to sail to the Holy Land – as they had done in decades past – because of the ready availability of shipping. Of course, not all the Flemings sailed; Count Thierry led a large contingent overland, and reasons of limited space on the ships may have, in part, dictated this. He probably wished to travel with the main armies of King Louis out of political expediency and also in order to follow in the footsteps of his First Crusader predecessor, Count Robert II.

Taken as a whole, the north European and English Channel region had a tightly bound political, cultural and economic history that added to the logic of a co-ordinated naval expedition. England and Flanders certainly enjoyed close ties; physical proximity was important and it took only two days for the news of the murder of Count Charles the Good to travel from Bruges to London in 1127. Commercial links were influential, especially concerning the important wool trade, and Flemish merchants are known to have settled in London.[14] Furthermore, Flemings had formed a significant element in the armies of Duke William of Normandy in 1066 and some of their number had remained in England. Others came over and rose to high rank – such as Gilbert of Ghent, who became a nobleman in Lincolnshire, and his uncle Robert of Ghent, who became King Stephen's chancellor c.1140 and, seven years later, dean of York.[15] There was a tradition of military alliances between the English crown and Flanders, although this relationship could have been complicated by the struggle for the English crown. Stephen was, through his marriage to Mathilda, the count of Boulogne – a traditional vassal of the Flemings. He had been sent to Flanders in 1127 by Henry I to support the king's favoured candidate, Count Thierry, and when the latter triumphed the earlier treaties between Flanders and England were renewed. Furthermore, William of Ypres, a frequent witness to Thierry's charters, became earl of Kent and led the English king's notorious Flemish mercenaries. On this basis, Count Thierry could be viewed as a partisan of Stephen. Yet he also possessed close ties to the Angevins because his wife, Sibylla, was Count Geoffrey's sister and in 1144 the Fleming provided troops to help him in Normandy. In spite of the apparent contradictions in this story, Thierry managed to remain on cordial terms with both parties, thereby helping to facilitate co-operation for the crusade.[16] Religious institutions shared links too; on 28 October 1146 Thierry's nephew, William of Ypres, founded the Cistercian abbey of Boxley in Kent.[17] With regard to Flanders and Cologne, an old Roman road ran from the latter to Boulogne and Flemings lived in the city at the time. Politically, the eastern part of Flanders, between the Scheldt and Dender rivers, was an imperial fief.[18]

The fleet set sail from Dartmouth on 23 May 1147 and the timing of the attack on Lisbon offers one further motive for those taking part in this episode. Historians have conventionally argued that the crusaders' involvement in the campaign was an accident; they state that the fleet sailing to the Levant was simply flagged down by the Portuguese and persuaded to participate in King Afonso's ongoing siege. Forey and Tyerman, for example, write of the coincidental arrival of the crusaders and of a lack of premeditation to go to Lisbon.[19] In recent years, this view has been questioned and counter-questioned by historians. I am of the opinion that various issues of chronology and other references in De expugnatione Lyxbonensi indicate some level of contact between the Portuguese and the crusaders prior to the fleet setting out; in other words there was an element of premeditation in the northern Europeans' actions, although not, as we will see, a formal agreement.[20]

First, there is the question of timing: if the fleet had sailed directly from Dartmouth to the Holy Land it would have reached the eastern Mediterranean by the late summer of 1147. Given that the main armies under Louis and Conrad had barely set out at this point, the northern Europeans would have faced a lengthy and highly expensive period of waiting before the arrival of their fellow-crusaders. At the very least a late-summer departure would have narrowed the gap before the other armies joined them, but the fleet's move in May 1147 is strongly indicative that other plans were afoot – namely the siege of Lisbon. If it succeeded, then the crusaders would have helped the Christians in Iberia and gained vital booty for themselves; if, however, the campaign was still going on by the autumn, or even by the spring of 1148, the crusaders could simply have left and carried on to the Levant. The presence of a Pisan siege engineer in Iberia rather than in the Levant may also indicate that a decision to invest a major urban site had already been made. Bennett has noted the lack of experience in siege warfare in the peninsula at this time and, given the failure of an attack on Lisbon in 1142, the employment of a professional demonstrated a desire to be as well prepared as possible.[21]

Afonso Henriques of Portugal certainly seems to have anticipated the crusade's arrival: on 15 March 1147 he captured the town of Santarém, about forty-six miles north of Lisbon. This reveals a determination to prepare the ground for a campaign against Lisbon; being aware of the forthcoming crusade, he could see that it was essential to complete this important ground-work for an assault on Lisbon.[22] Afonso's desire to besiege Lisbon can be appraised from a number of perspectives, both secular and ecclesiastical. First was the matter of the king's piety; he was generous to the Cistercians who made their first appearance in his lands 1138/40.[23] The foundation document of the monastery of Saint Vincent – admittedly written soon after the king's death in 1185 – described him as 'wanting to exterminate the enemies of the cross of Christ'.[24] Afonso had a strong crusading pedigree: his uncle, Duke Odo I of Burgundy, had taken part in the 1101 crusade and his father, Count Henry of Portugal, set out on pilgrimage for Jerusalem in 1103.[25] He was also closely connected to the Templars, whom he rewarded in 1129, very soon after their foundation – and early on in his own reign – with a gift in which he described himself as 'a brother in your fraternity'.[26] In 1145 Afonso and his brother-in-law gave the Templars the castle of Longrovia and a house in Braga. The king's relations with the order continued to be close: a charter stated that he made anticipatory grants to the brethren before the attack on Lisbon in April 1147 and that he had given them possession of all the churches in Santarém. This also suggested that the Templars were present in sufficiently large numbers to justify such gifts by contributing a worthwhile contingent to his forces.[27] Afonso had already defeated the Muslims at the battle of Ourique in 1139, an important step in the reconquest. Just at the time of the Second Crusade, the king furthered his links with crusading through his marriage to Mathilda, the daughter of Duke Amadeus of Savoy, himself a Second Crusader.

There were also more secular aspects to his actions. Afonso became ruler of Portugal in 1128 after a difficult struggle with his mother, Countess Teresa. Later years saw conflict with the Muslims in the Tagus valley and tensions with Alfonso VII of León-Castile (1126–57). In 1139 Afonso started to take the title of king and four years later his lands came under papal protection. Lucius II commended him for his intention 'to oppose the pagans' but would not recognise his royal title and continued to refer to him as a duke.[28] Afonso's involvement in the crusade would clearly benefit his political and religious aspirations.

Yet beyond this, from a purely strategic point of view, the Second Crusade arrived at a most opportune moment. The power of the Almoravid dynasty, the Muslim rulers of Iberia, was in sharp decline (more detail on pp. 249–50 below). In 1143 'Ali ibn Yusuf died, followed two years later by his successor Yusuf ibn Tashufin, the ruler of al-Andalus. This left a minor as the heir, and the dynasty was exposed to attack from the fierce Berber tribesmen, the Almohads of North Africa. Afonso must have gauged that 1147 was a good time to make advances because of the turmoil amongst the Muslims; this wish to exploit the weaknesses of the Islamic world proved a great benefit to the king in much the same way that the First Crusade seemed (unwittingly) to arrive in northern Syria at a time of crisis for the Muslims of the Middle East. In fact, Ibn al-Athir, who wrote his 'Complete Work of History' in northern Syria in the early thirteenth century, commented on the Frankish conquest of Santarém and Lisbon and judged this event to be the result of Christian exploitation of Muslim disunity.[29]

In the autumn of 1146 the aims of Afonso and of the crusaders would be served by an attack on Lisbon. The former could extend his territory and drive back the infidel; the latter would advance Christianity and at the same time might secure considerable financial rewards on their journey to the East. There is little doubt that Afonso would have learned of the launch of the crusade at Vézelay in March 1146 through family contacts such as the Savoyard marriage, or through the visits of Iberian churchmen to the papal *curia*. Archbishop John of Braga (1138–75), for example, was present in mid-1145 and the archbishop of Toledo was with the pope around the time when *Quantum praedecessores* was issued.[30] It was likely that once the king heard of the plans for crusading, he made contact with the church authorities and with the northern Europeans familiar to him. The choreography of Afonso's move on Santarém and the departure of the crusaders is strongly suggestive of some form of communication between Portugal and northern Europe. It is also pertinent that Bernard of Clairvaux met Christian of Gistel, the leader of the Flemish contingent, during his tour of Flanders.[31] There is, however, no extant bull specifically for the Lisbon campaign. This may be a matter of survival, although we might suppose that Raol would have made some mention of it. Given the issue of *Quantum praedecessores* – a document obviously known to Raol – and the fact that the crusaders were headed towards Jerusalem, perhaps a bull may have been deemed unnecessary. There is little to substantiate the view that Eugenius would have actively disapproved of the campaign and the likelihood that Raol was a legate of some sort (see below, p. 162) gives a form of official gloss to the affair. It is plain, however, that the initiative for this campaign, in common with the attacks on Almería and Tortosa, lay with a secular ruler rather than with the papacy. Afonso was a monarch whose interest in, and need for, reconquest coincided with the heightened climate of religious warfare across Latin Christendom in 1147–8.

In spite of the slightly hazy origins of the expedition, its positive outcome demonstrated divine approval to participants and contemporaries alike. For this reason, as well as the pride of regional commentators, several contemporary and near-contemporary writers across Europe comfortably assimilated this episode with the expedition to the Holy Land.[32] Robert of Torigny, for example, placed it between references to the siege of Damascus, the capture of Almería, and the victory at Tortosa.[33] The Valcellensis continuator of the chronicle of Sigebert of Gembloux wrote: '*Pars christiani exercitus, Hierusalem navigio petens, Olisiponem urbem Hispaniae, virtute Dei Saracenis pulsis, cepit et christianis reddidit*'.[34] The *Annales Palidenses*, Helmold of Bosau and the *Annales Brunwilarenses* all followed descriptions of the Damascus crusade with the success at Lisbon.[35] In other words, there was a reasonably widespread acceptance of the idea that the work of the northern Europeans in Iberia was recognisably part of the Second Crusade.

In mid-May 1147, the crusader fleet gathered at Dartmouth in southern England. A mass of letters and messages must have moved around northern Europe to plan this rendezvous. The news of each region's interest in the crusade would have become apparent and someone made an executive decision, probably based on the practicalities of sailing routes, to muster at Dartmouth.[36] The more important nobles involved would have been aware of this and they (or contacts, such as William of Ypres, earl of Kent, and the Dover contingent) may have communicated amongst themselves and, given the chronology outlined above, possibly discussed a stop at Lisbon. The local Flemish and Rhineland contingents must also have set a calendar for their meetings.

The bulk of the Rhineland force assembled at Cologne in late April and moved downriver before sailing down the coast, then out to sea and across to

England. The sources are in reasonable agreement on the size of the total fleet at Dartmouth: *De expugnatione* told of 'about 164' ships, the 'Lisbon Letter' of 'about 200', and the foundation document of Saint Vincent of 190 ships.[37] Given the difficulty in counting such a force and the possibility that some ships became separated from others these figures present a tolerable degree of consistency. From other information in the text, it seems that the Anglo-Norman force probably numbered *c.*4,500 and the Flemings and Germans a few more. Bennett suggests a total force of *c.*10,000 at an average of around fifty men per ship, although obviously some vessels must have been larger than others.[38] The *Sigeberti continuatio Praemonstratensis* noted a total Christian army of 13,000 at Lisbon. Again, if this included some troops from King Afonso, a figure of just over 10,000 northern-European crusaders seems justifiable.[39]

The crusaders' first act was to make provisions for discipline and good order. The Rhinelanders were headed by Count Arnold of Aerschot, a nephew of Godfrey of Bouillon and a nobleman with a proud crusading tradition and distant family ties to the ruling house of Jerusalem.[40] Christian of Gistel led the Flemish and Boulogne force and the Anglo-Normans were commanded by four constables: those of Norfolk and Suffolk under Hervey of Glanvill; those of Kent under Simon of Dover; those of London under Andrew; and all the others under the northern Frenchman Saher of Archelle.[41] *De expugnatione* provides us with the details of the regulations agreed upon amongst the crusaders, a series of rules that did much to establish the tenor of the expedition and contributed substantially to its success:

> Amongst those people of so many different tongues the firmest guarantees of peace and friendship were taken; and, furthermore, they sanctioned very strict laws, as for example, a life for a life and a tooth for a tooth. They forbade all display of costly garments. Also they ordained that women should not go out in public; that the peace must be kept by all, unless they should suffer injuries recognised by the proclamation; that weekly chapters be held by the laity and the clergy separately, unless perchance some great emergency should require their meeting together; that each ship have its own priest and keep the same observances as are prescribed for parishes; that no one retain the seaman of another in his employ; that everyone make weekly confession and communicate on Sunday; and so on through the rest of the obligatory articles with separate sanctions for each. Furthermore, they constituted for every thousand of the forces two elected members who were to be called judges or *coniurati*, through whom the cases of the constables were to be settled in accordance with the proclamation and by whom the distribution of moneys was to be carried out.[42]

It is evident that experience of earlier campaigns, probably including the First Crusade, had demonstrated the need for groups from different regions (and speaking different languages) to create a strict framework in which to operate. During the 1096–9 crusade there had been episodes of tension between various parties and such instances obviously hampered the overall efficiency of the force.[43] Strict discipline and strong moral fortitude were the hallmarks of this agreement. In line with the doctrine of right intention in holy war, violence was to be a response to injuries suffered, rather than an actively sought aim.[44] The measure against displaying costly garments shows a clear link to *Quantum praedecessores*. The reference to women remaining out of public sight was the only mention of females in the entire text of *De expugnatione*. The influence of the Reform Papacy was apparent with its strictures concerning separate weekly chapters for clergy and laity, and there was an emphasis on the importance of weekly confession and communion – again, to ensure good moral standards. As Eugenius's bull stated and *De expugnatione* repeated, the need to confess all of one's sins was a vital part of the crusade vow. The final arbiters of justice were two elected judges for each 1,000 men (a council of twenty in total, if the estimates of the size of the army are correct); this group was also responsible for the distribution of money, which indicated some form of common purse. The editor of *De expugnatione* mentioned that the first part of the regulations echoed contemporary edicts promulgated in Flanders and northern France and he indicated that, by contrast, there was little evidence of similar measures in England at this time.[45]

The fleet set sail on Friday 23 May and three days later the crusaders sighted Brittany; soon afterwards, however, they struck trouble. As they crossed the Bay of Biscay the ships were hit by a terrible storm that scattered vessels in all directions. The threat of imminent death caused many to despair and they began to pray for forgiveness. Raol noted that some believed the storm was God's punishment for 'the perversion of their pilgrimage', which, given that the army had yet to land at Lisbon, may be a further indication that they planned to fight there and that some of the crusaders were worried that the campaign in Iberia would not meet with divine approval.[46] In any case, their prayers were answered and the storm abated. The fleet had been badly scattered and some boats put in at the northern Spanish port of Gozzim, modern day Luanco. Raol noted the presence there of a church that had recently been damaged by the Muslims, thus providing fuel to sustain an argument that the fighting in Spain was justifiable as a response to attacks on the Christian faithful.[47] The vessels then moved along the northern Spanish coast towards Tambre, the closest port to the great pilgrim centre of Santiago de Compostela. Just before arriving at Tambre on 7 June, the crusaders passed a stone bridge that had risen up from the sea, an event that was said to prophesy the destruction of the heathen and an end to idolatry in Spain.[48] The 'Lisbon Letter' recounted that a visit to 'Saint James's venerable sepulchre', brought 'great joy'.[49] The chance to visit one of the greatest shrines of the age must have been very welcome for the crusaders and provided an opportunity for devotional acts and attempts to secure God's support.

On 16 June the fleet reached the town of Oporto; there it was greeted by Bishop Peter Pitões, who had evidently expected the crusaders. *De expugnatione* recorded that the bishop 'knew in advance of our coming' and the 'Lisbon Letter' was aware that King Afonso had bidden him to greet them.[50] Afonso himself continued his campaign against the Muslims, presumably in preparation for an assault on Lisbon. Because he was unable to receive the crusaders in person, the king had instructed Bishop Peter to make them welcome (the dispatch of his mandate was, again, an indication that Afonso clearly expected them) and gave him licence to offer whatever was needed as security in order to conclude an agreement so that they would come 'to me at Lisbon'.[51]

The following morning many of the crusaders gathered outside the cathedral to hear the bishop address them. Peter spoke in Latin to allow each part of his audience to understand his speech through translators.[52] This was the first of the set-piece speeches included by Raol in *De expugnatione* and its content and ideas bear close scrutiny for their reflection of themes used in campaigns to the Holy Land. Parts of the text have clear echoes of the crusade preaching and indicate either that Raol exerted influence over the words attributed to Bishop Peter or that the bishop – as a senior churchman – had read or heard *Quantum praedecessores*. The speech began with a reminder to the crusaders of their good fortune in being chosen by God for this task: 'They are blessed on whom God has by some inestimable privilege conferred both understanding and riches'; an echo of Bernard of Clairvaux's reference to a 'lucky generation'.[53] Similarly, the bishop's phrase 'truly fortunate is your country which rears such sons and . . . unites them in such a unanimous association in the bosom of the Mother Church' has resonances with the letters of Bernard and his secretary, Nicholas of Clairvaux.[54] Peter argued that the crusaders were helped by having the understanding to 'know the ways of discipline' and would be blessed with the riches of divine reward. Here we see an early reference to the maintenance of unity that would prove so important during the campaign. The bishop also acknowledged the faith of the crusaders by citing the Book of John: 'Blessed are they that have not seen me and yet have believed.'[55]

Peter paraphrased the biblical story of the rich man giving away all his possessions and praised the crusaders for their financial and personal sacrifices in undertaking God's work. 'They have exchanged all their honours and dignities for a blessed pilgrimage in order to obtain from God an eternal reward.'[56] He recognised the pain of separation from wives, children and loved ones; these were familiar motifs from First Crusade preaching, and also echoed themes in the contemporary anonymous troubadour song.[57] In addition, Peter acknowledged the dangers of the sea voyage and the expense of the campaign and he emphasised his own delight in the crusaders' coming to Iberia:

> The alluring affection of wives, the tender kisses of sucking infants at the breast, the even more delightful pledges of grown-up children, the much desired consolation of relatives and friends – all these they have left behind to follow Christ, retaining only the sweet but torturing memory of their native land. Oh, marvellous are the works of the Saviour! ... led by the impulse of the [Holy] Spirit they have left all and come hither to us, the sons of the primitive church, through so many perils of lands and seas and bearing the expenses of a long journey.[58]

These events were, he believed, 'the most recent proof of the mysterious power of the cross', thereby echoing another image employed by Bernard.[59] Peter urged the crusaders to look after the gift that had been divinely bestowed upon them just as a good farmer should look after his seeds and he counselled them to take care and produce a fruitful crop; in other words, he was concerned that the crusaders should preserve their right intention or else their opportunity would be wasted. Peter spoke of the crusaders having undergone a rebirth; he warned them not to spoil their newfound purity and to guard against the sins of lust and envy. The latter was a particular worry because it would break down the unity of the army and nourish discord and faction. The bishop also urged caution against the sins of gluttony and sexual excess. Orderic Vitalis had blamed the failure of the 1107–8 expedition of Bohemond of Antioch on the greed, pride, ambition and vanity of the crusaders.[60]

The next passage was a history lesson that outlined the devastation wrought by the Muslims against the Christian peoples and their property. Peter brought a personal touch to the tale by mentioning that only seven years previously the insignia, vessels and ornaments from his own church had been taken 'after they [the Muslims] had slain the clergy and made them captive'.[61] Here one sees a parallel to the stories of violence and bloodshed that circulated in the preaching of the First Crusade and, with regard to contemporary events, in connection with the fall of Edessa. The *Chronica Adefonsi imperatoris*, written around this time on the eastern side of the Iberian peninsula, also reflected a similar feeling.[62]

The bishop then came to the heart of his appeal. He employed extremely emotive language to outline exactly why the crusaders should fight at Lisbon:

To you the Mother Church, as it were with her arms cut off and her face disfigured, appeals for help; she seeks vengeance at your hands for the blood of her sons. She calls to you, truly, she cries out loud. 'Execute vengeance upon the heathen and punishments upon the people' [Ps 149: 7]. Therefore, be not seduced by the desire to press on with the journey that you have begun; for the praiseworthy thing is not to have been to Jerusalem, but to have lived a good life along the way; for you cannot arrive there except through the performance of His works . . . Therefore, re-clothe her soiled and disfigured form with the garments of joy and gladness. As worthy sons look not on the shame of a father . . . Weigh not lightly your duty to your fellow men; for, as Saint Ambrose says, 'He who does not ward off an injury from his comrades and brothers, if he can, is as much at fault as he who does the injury'.[63]

The depiction of the Mother Church as such a hideously brutalised woman remains extraordinarily powerful and must have struck deeply at the crusaders' sense of religious and moral outrage. The notion of vengeance for this seems both natural and just; besides, it echoed a theme widely used in the reporting of the First Crusade and also found in the Psalms.[64] The phrases which tried to draw the crusaders into action at Lisbon rather than letting them press on to Jerusalem are intriguing. This section was based upon a letter of St Jerome to Paulinus, a reasonably familiar text, employed by writers from St Augustine to Peter the Venerable.[65] In this context, Raol suggested that there was a need to perform good works on the way to heaven, and fighting at Lisbon would fall into this category. The monastic writers of the First Crusade argued that the liberation of the earthly city of Jerusalem was a preliminary to securing entry to the heavenly one.[66] Raol made the diversion to Lisbon fit into 'crusading theory' by presenting it as a meritorious aspect of a penitential journey which could popularly be described as going to the spiritual as well as to the earthly Jerusalem.

As we have seen above in relation to the storm in the Bay of Biscay, there may have been some debate as to the spiritual value of fighting the Muslims (for booty) in Iberia instead of going directly to the Holy Land. Bishop Peter had to address this issue and Raol himself probably felt some need to explain to his readers the moral worth of the campaign too. He tried to explain the terrible damage wrought to the Christian Church in Spain and claimed that this constituted a valid reason to fight the Muslims there. By the end of the section cited above, the speech has taken the argument a step further: it suggested that a failure to act was, in itself, sinful. The use of the image of fathers and sons was, of course, another echo of *Quantum praedecessores*.

Once he had established a just cause for the attack on Lisbon, Bishop Peter set out to provide a detailed and highly scholarly exposition on the legal and biblical justification for the campaign.[67] He argued that the conflict benefited from God's inspiration – in other words it had proper authority – which was either a way of deflecting attention from, or compensating for, the absence of a bull issued for this campaign or, on the contrary, an oblique reference to the existence of such a document. The bishop then cited a series of cases from Gratian's *Causa* 23, in which violence was justified in the following circum-stances: to secure the patrimony against barbarians; to resist enemies at home; to defend comrades from robbers. Doing such work was a duty incumbent upon Christians and to abandon it was a crime answerable to God.[68] Peter claimed: 'such works of vengeance are duties which righteous men perform with a good conscience. Brothers, be not afraid.' He then advanced the authority of Isidore of Seville: 'A war is just . . . which is waged after a declara-tion, to recover property or to repulse enemies.'[69] Plainly the crusade fell under this definition and, as we will see, the Christians were careful to declare war on their enemy formally, once the siege of Lisbon started. To buttress his case, Peter cited several other authorities, such as Jerome, Saint Augustine, John Chrysostom, and the Book of Deuteronomy, all found in the collections of Ivo of Chartres and Gratian. He then placed the focus back onto the crusaders themselves, again with a strong echo of the basic message put forward by Abbot Bernard about knights ceasing to fight one another and turning their weapons towards a true enemy of the faithful: 'Behold how pious, how just, how merciful is God! God has taken nothing from you: he has permitted the same enterprises on behalf of your country, only your purpose has been changed . . . You were committing acts of pillage and other misdeeds . . . You are still bearing arms and the insignia of war, but with a different object . . .' .[70] He closed the exhortatory part of his speech with a reminder that war should not be fought for the sake of plunder (again, preserving right intention), and in battle their righteousness would earn the palm of victory from God. He concluded assertively: 'For when a war has been entered upon by God's will, it is not permitted to doubt that it has been rightly undertaken.'[71]

A few practicalities formed a coda to the speech: Afonso had already left to attack Lisbon and 'knowing in advance of your [the crusaders'] coming, he commanded us to remain here to await you'. If the crusaders would go to assist the king in the capture of the city he promised money 'as far as the resources of the royal treasury will permit', and put himself forward as a hostage as a mark of good faith.[72] In response to this offer the crusaders decided to await the appearance of Christian of Gistel and Arnold of Aerschot who had still not rejoined the main fleet after the earlier storm. The 'Lisbon Letter' indicated that the crusaders were well provided for and 'enjoyed the fair sale of both wine and other delights by goodwill of the king'.[73] Once they arrived, it was resolved to take Bishop Peter and Archbishop John of Braga on board with them and to go on to Lisbon to hear the king himself make his proposals.[74] The full fleet sailed southwards and when they arrived at the mouth of the River Tagus at Lisbon a miraculous sign appeared: a squall created a huge collision between white clouds coming from the direction of the fleet and black clouds over the land. They appeared to lock horns and to do battle until eventually the white cloud triumphed. The crusaders were hugely encouraged: 'Behold, our cloud has conquered! Behold, God is with us! The power of our enemies is destroyed! They are confounded, for the Lord has put them to flight!'[75] Such portents were few and far between in reports of the Second Crusade, a reflection of the generally negative outcome of the campaign.

Raol described the environs of Lisbon in glowing terms, delighting in the abundant fish and shellfish of the River Tagus, in the vines, pomegranates and figs grown in the province of Almada to the south and in the fame of its hunting grounds and honey production. Olives, citrus fruits and salt were also found in the vicinity. Such a fertile setting could only be of benefit to the crusaders if they had to settle in for a long siege because, unless the Muslims chose to adopt a scorched-earth policy, it was a ready source of foodstuffs; in fact, Raol was forced to admit that the number of figs was so enormous that 'we could hardly eat a fraction of them'.[76] Lisbon itself is eight miles from the sea down the estuary of the Tagus and positioned on the top of several hills. In 1147 a citadel girdled one hilltop and strong walls ran down to the river-bank to the right and the left. Outside of these walls were densely packed suburbs, some cut into the rock of the mountain, which formed an obstacle in themselves. Raol reported that the population was 145,000, a figure which seems extremely high, notwithstanding the added numbers of refugees from Santarém, Sintra and the local people who had fled to the city for protection. He estimated the fighting force at 15,000 men – roughly the same as that of the combined Christian forces.[77]

In late June or early July the attack started. As the Christians landed they engaged with a group of Muslims who were soon driven back to one of the gates of the suburb. Saher showed good military leadership by recalling his troops before they followed the enemy into the city in case they might be shut in and massacred. Raol himself was part of a force of thirty-nine men, which included Saher of Archelle and Hervey of Glanvill: these bravely pitched their tents on a hill just outside the walls. This small group passed a nervous night before their co-religionists joined them on the following morning to establish a proper camp.

The next important step was to meet with Afonso and clarify terms of the agreement between the two parties. The king enquired as to the identity of the crusaders' chief representative and received the intriguing, if politically sensitive, answer that no one had yet been given such authority; but he was told that if he spoke, someone would be chosen to reply.[78] Such a response reveals an awareness of the risks involved in putting forward a single leader from such a diverse group of crusaders, none of whom seems to have been of an especially prestigious or powerful stock.

Afonso's appeal to the crusaders played upon their religious duty to fight the infidel and laid weight on their supposed right intention; it also made plain that he would offer them financial rewards – but he argued that these could only be of a limited scale according to his means. It is likely that part of this emphasis on moderation was provided by Raol who was determined to stress right intention throughout his work. Afonso cleverly set the crusaders' desire for worldly gain against their spiritual motivation: 'we feel certain that your piety will invite you to the labour and exertion of so great an enterprise more than the promise of our money will incite you to the recompense of booty'.[79] From his perspective, of course, the less he paid the crusaders the better. The crusaders' discussion of their response to the king was described as prolix, but in the course of the day the first cracks in the expedition's unity appeared. They were created by the need to fix the agreement with the king, or, in more theologically vexing terms, by the desire for monetary gain. It appears that the Flemish contingent had made a separate deal with Afonso – something that Raol disapproved of, although not in particularly strong terms. Interestingly, he raised the issue that some of the crusaders were short of money, even at this stage of the campaign. As we will see later, chronic lack of funding was a major problem for the expedition to the Holy Land, and 'those who were feeling the pinch of want' had evidently acted to secure their position.[80]

A further and, for the Anglo-Normans, more dramatic dispute also erupted at this time. As we have seen above, five years earlier some of the crusaders had joined Afonso in an unsuccessful attack on Lisbon. This failure had caused bad feelings on both sides, and a group from Southampton and Hastings, who had taken part in the previous episode, argued that Afonso was a man of bad faith. Raol indicated that these people were fools whose weak arguments showed only their own stupidity; he also saw that they were unwilling to bear the expense of a potentially long siege. William Viel led the protestors and claimed that easier pickings could be had from merchant vessels further south – a plain instigation to piracy. Yet, alongside such a worldly motive, he argued that this was the best season for favourable winds to Jerusalem; this revealed that, ultimately, he wished to reach the Holy Land too.[81] This is a particularly striking example of the assimilation of secular and spiritual motives. It seems that all the other contingents, such as the

Boulogners, the Rhinelanders, the Bretons and the Scots fell into line with the Flemings and were prepared to work with Afonso. William Viel and the crews of eight ships, however, held out. The Anglo-Normans debated their colleagues' reaction and met with the objectors, either to persuade them to remain or else to cast them aside. Raol described the latter prospect in particularly strong terms, indicating that the group would be 'cut off from all communion with ourselves and with the holy Mother Church as violators of sworn faith and our oath-bound association'.[82] We see here a heavy emphasis laid upon the value of the Dartmouth oath as a fundamental bond between all the crusaders; the maintenance of their unity was deemed essential for success. Furthermore, the ecclesiastical penalties for breaking such a vow were made clear: excommunication from the Church. To make such a threat suggests the presence of a senior churchman; in this case, probably Raol himself.

The Anglo-Normans were determined to try to hold their force together because, apart from the fear of reducing the crusade's strength (although eight ships out of 200 hardly constituted a massive blow), there was a desire to preserve the integrity of the vow, and also perhaps a wish that theirs would not be the contingent to fracture the expedition's unity. Hervey of Glanvill made an impassioned speech to the renegades. Hervey was, as we saw above, closely connected to Raol's addressee, Osbert of Bawdsey. Raol probably expected that Hervey would hear his text read aloud and for this reason he may have felt it important to include this appeal, but he also provided a small caveat: a marginal note, in the same hand as the main manuscript, explaining that the speech did not reproduce Hervey's exact words.[83] Raol thus admitted to manipulating his text and we can see that some parts, inevitably, seem to support his central agenda of establishing right intention; others, however, fit more closely with Hervey's immediate purpose.

Hervey began with a reminder of the importance of the oath of unity. He continued with an echo of the message in *Quantum praedecessores* concerning the need to cherish the deeds of one's forefathers: 'recalling the virtues of our ancestors, we ought to strive to increase the honour and glory of our race rather than cover tarnished glory with the rags of malice. For the glorious deeds of the ancients kept in memory by posterity are the marks of both affection and honour. If you show yourselves worthy emulators of the ancients, honour and glory will be yours, but if unworthy, then disgraceful reproaches.'[84] He also appealed in a very secular manner to the Normans' sense of honour at their own achievements. This echoed a theme found in many Norman writers in the mid-twelfth century and reflected pride in their successes over previous generations.[85] Hervey, perhaps with Raol providing a guiding hand here, castigated the men for the sins of sloth, idleness and envy at the achievements of others. He drew parallels with the other contingents on the crusade and reminded William and his associates that the Flemings, the men of Cologne or (even) the Scots had no quarrels amongst themselves. Hervey claimed that they would do God's power no injury through their departure, but, aside from having broken an oath, their names would be forever shamed. The greed of these men and their fear of a glorious death would bring dishonour to the other Normans on the crusade, in fact to all Normans – a dishonour which was undeserved. Hervey questioned the motives of the men: 'Your pilgrimage certainly appears not to be founded on charity, for love is not in you.'[86] *Quantum praedecessores* stated that the crusaders were 'fired by the ardour of charity'.[87] He urged them to lay aside their grievances against Afonso; reminded them that their hopes for future gains might not be realised; told them that their chances of success were far greater at Lisbon and they should not 'exchange certainties for uncertainties'.[88] In conclusion, he called upon William to 'spare shame to your race. Yield to the counsels of honour.' Such was Hervey's determination to preserve the unity of the force that he broke into tears and offered to humble himself before the renegades.

This carefully pitched and emotional appeal made a strong impact on its audience. William and his men would not allow Hervey to kneel and they finally consented to remain at Lisbon as long as Afonso took them on as paid soldiers for the duration of the siege and ensured sufficient foodstuffs for them. There was relief all round that a solution had been reached and Raol reported that everyone wept for joy. The king agreed to the proposal; William had secured a particularly profitable deal for his men.[89]

The entire crusader army came to terms with Afonso, and Raol included a copy of this charter within his letter. The crusaders were allowed to sack the city of all its possessions and to capture and ransom the populace; Afonso and his men would take none of these things. But, once the city had been thoroughly despoiled, it would be handed over to the king. If any of the Franks wished to stay then he would apportion them lands according to their rank, retaining the position of overlord. All those present at the siege and their heirs were released from merchant tolls throughout his lands. The tenor of this agreement was extraordinarily generous towards the crusaders and it reveals how much Afonso valued and wanted their help. He appreciated that 1147 was the optimum moment to make a strategic advance against the Muslims and he saw that the crusade presented him with a highly motivated force of a size and expertise that he might never see again. While giving up any rights to the sack of the city might seem a large burden to bear, the taking over of such an important metropolis on a permanent basis would more than compensate for the initial loss. Furthermore, of course, as a successful Christian ruler, his prestige would be hugely enhanced. This was of enormous consequence: as

Hervey's speech to his fellow Anglo-Normans showed, honour was a key aspect of the status-conscious medieval world. In his recently claimed position of king, rather than as a duke, such an achievement would be even more important. In fact, Afonso did not have his title recognised by the pope until 1179, although he himself started to use the appellation *rex* from 1140 onwards. The privileges offered by Afonso also indicated his willingness to sustain and, in commercial terms, to enhance the links established at the siege, which emphasised existing trade between the English Channel and Iberia.

Hostages were given on both sides and Afonso swore not to leave Lisbon unless compelled to do so by illness or by enemy attacks elsewhere in his lands. Before the siege began the Christian forces sought to parley with the defenders – as Raol noted, 'so that we may not appear to be attacking them except unwillingly'.[90] One reason for this was a simple issue of practicality. If, faced by such a large enemy force, the Muslims felt their position to be hopeless, then an offer of surrender would obviously save bloodshed on both sides.

Archbishop John of Braga led the Christian envoys; he was an experienced churchman who had acted as papal legate in Spain for Innocent II.[91] His speech combined conciliation with menace to try to prevent conflict from breaking out. He appealed to the common humanity of both Christians and Muslims as a reason why they should not fight – a rare and tolerant assessment of his enemies, given the stereotypical depiction of Muslims in First Crusade texts such as the *Gesta Francorum*, as inhuman.[92] Ironically, this emphasis on the common humanity of both warring sides echoes closely one of the teachings of the Koran: *Surah* 49:13 makes just such a point.[93] The archbishop also made the case for the crusaders' right intention. He argued that their actions were defensive in nature and that the Christians were not seizing the property of another, but merely reclaiming what was rightfully theirs – in other words, he put the crusade in the context of recapture of territory as well as holy war.[94] John accused the Muslims of stealing Lisbon and the surrounding lands and he suggested that their deeds had broken fealty to their own lord and to the Christians. Presumably previous agreements had been violated and this enabled the archbishop to make such a claim. John outlined the history of the area and pointed out that 358 years ago it had been unjustly taken from the first converts to Christianity; he named several august figures amongst the early Iberian Christians, such as Isidore of Seville. He also noted the existence of ruined Christian churches in the city – again, a sign that the crusaders were reclaiming land that was rightfully their own.[95]

With regard to the present, the archbishop encouraged the inhabitants to leave with their goods and property. This was a common enough offer at this stage in a siege and an entirely plausible report of the archbishop's words. He even suggested that a simple handing over of the castle was acceptable and that those who wished to remain could do so and they might 'live according to [their] own customs'.[96] This indicates that the Muslims would continue to practise their faith. In reality, the Christians needed the bulk of the populace to remain *in situ* because there was not enough of them to fill the city. As the Norman conquerors of Sicily and the Franks in the Levant had found out, locals were needed as a labour force and as a fiscal base, without which newly won conquests would be very hard to maintain.[97] The speech closed on a much darker note: John observed the greed of the attacking crusaders and (inevitably) mentioned the strength that derived from their oath-bound association. He urged the defenders to save their crops, their property and their lives, or else they faced grave danger.[98]

A Muslim elder responded to this oration with his own analysis of the crusaders' motives. One presumes that in reality Raol could not understand the man and relied on a summary provided by the Christian envoys who went into the city to parley. The version included in *De expugnatione* appears to be a mixture of ideas appropriate to the context, as well as carrying echoes of Raol's customary themes. The elder's first criticism of the crusaders concerned their rationale. He wondered at their greed in wanting even more land to control: 'it is not the want of possessions, but ambition of the mind which drives you on'. He accused them of upsetting the natural order through this greed. Interestingly, however, the wording used was practically the same as that attributed to the bishop of Oporto in his speech: 'Labelling your ambition zeal for righteousness, you misrepresent vices as virtues. For your greed has already grown to such proportions that base deeds not only please you, but even delight you . . .'.[99] The Muslim elder also claimed that the crusaders were driven by pride and he wondered at the series of efforts to take Lisbon – by both barbarians and pilgrims, as he put it – an obvious reference to the previous attacks on the city. He even argued that such frequent comings and goings were an indication of mental instability! Another echo of an earlier phrase is his comment that the defenders would not surrender because they did not wish 'to give up certainties for uncertainties'.[100] He admitted that the city had once been in Christian hands; but now, by God's will, the Muslims continued to hold it and would do so for as long as He wished. Thus he dismissed the Christians and subjected the whole matter to divine judgement.

The bishop of Oporto chided his opponent for adopting this viewpoint; he conceded that previous crusader attacks on Lisbon had failed, but he chose to view this as a challenge and suggested that a repeated test was taking place. This interpretation of earlier setbacks was consistent with crusading ideology, which regarded such episodes as a divine test of willpower and motivation. Even Bernard of Clairvaux's analysis of the failure of the Second Crusade made reference to the persistence of the Israelites as a reason not to give up.[101]

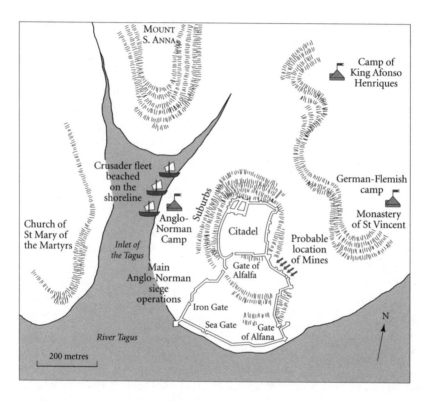

The Siege of Lisbon, 1 July to 23 October 1147

On 1 July the attacks began. They were led by slingers, followed by archers and men carrying portable ballistae. The defenders were pushed back into the suburbs on the west of the city and, by sunset, the enemy had fled from one district, although the rest remained strongly defended. At this point, Raol revealed some aspects of the command structure established in the army. It appears that Saher of Archelle and the other constables were liaising closely with King Afonso and that Saher, in particular, had a leading role. He seems to have been the most experienced military man present and an individual who made quick and incisive decisions. The command group wanted to withdraw from the suburbs before the entire army, including the royal troops, made a concerted assault the following day. By this stage, however, too many men were committed to the fighting. Saher saw that retreat was no longer possible and he issued orders for all the other men to join in the attack. The bishop of Oporto quickly blessed and absolved these troops and Saher and men from Raol's own tent hurried into the fray. Saher gathered the soldiers together at a cemetery and then repulsed Muslim attacks and inflicted heavy casualties on them. While some of the crusaders gave themselves over to seeking booty, the knights and archers pushed the enemy back to the city gates, to complete the capture of the suburb. Raol saw this as a miracle on account of the large number of inhabitants in the area and of the relatively small size of the crusader force. Some houses had been set ablaze and Saher and a small group of knights spent an anxious night camped in the cemetery prepared to face a Muslim counter-attack the following morning. A brief attempt was made to drive the crusaders away, but help from the royal guard ensured that this was beaten off.[102] Raol noted with pride that the Flemings and Cologners on the other side of the city envied the Anglo-Normans' success, but they too made progress when the Muslims, dispirited by these events, withdrew from the suburbs to the east of the city as well, leaving the Christians to press the siege up to the walls of Lisbon itself.

The Anglo-Normans set up a rota of night watches that numbered 500 men per night and, with Raol's report that the cycle was completed every nine days, we can calculate that a force of 4,500 made up this contingent of the army. A number of boats were posted on the River Tagus to guard against waterborne assaults. At this point the attackers had a real stroke of good fortune: because the walled part of the city was constructed on very hard rock and, given the premium on space in this area, the bulk of Lisbon's storehouses were located in the suburbs, on the side of another hill. The crusaders discovered cellars filled with vast amounts of wheat, barley, millet and pulses; in short, more than enough to conduct the siege with, particularly in conjunction with the fertility of the soil observed by Raol earlier. Proper provision of supplies was a basic necessity for any besieging army; one only has to think of the events at

Antioch in 1097–8 to realise the sufferings that a crusading army could endure if it faced such difficulties.[103] Much to the contrary, the Lisbon crusaders' discovery brought increased hardship to the defenders, whose numbers were already swollen by refugees from Santarém, Sintra, and now the suburbs too.

The siege began to settle down; the defenders made frequent sorties from the three gates of their city and the crusaders engaged and repulsed them. The 'Lisbon Letter' recorded the construction of siege engines and an attempt to prepare for a waterborne assault when four bridges were lashed onto seven ships (presumably tethered together) to sail up to the sea walls.[104] Raol also provides a fascinating insight into some of the psychological aspects of a long siege as he reports how the Muslims baited their attackers. They accused the Christians of greed and covetousness and they taunted the crusaders with the thought that their wives were being unfaithful in their absence and that numerous bastards would await them on their return home. If, however, they died, their wives would not mourn them because they would have enough progeny to replace them. The Muslims also claimed that the crusaders would leave Lisbon in 'poverty and misery', after their defeat. While such abuse may correspond to the Muslims' views to a certain extent, it probably also mirrors (through Raol) the crusaders' own anxieties concerning their loved ones; on the whole, it acts as a reminder of the sacrifices mentioned in the preaching of the crusade and in the speech given by the bishop of Oporto. The point concerning poverty and misery may also echo the experiences of many earlier crusaders. The triumph of the First Crusade was not accompanied by huge hauls of booty and other expeditions, for instance the crusades of 1101, 1107–8 and 1128–9, were, by and large, failures that must have resulted in most of the participants returning home impoverished.

Raol also records that the Muslims attacked the Christian faith by questioning the value of venerating the child of a poor woman – that is, the Virgin Mary. They wondered why God would appear in a human form if He was so powerful and they argued that a man should not usurp the name of God. Kedar has observed that these comments reflect key theological questions which Islam poses to Christianity; on this basis we must acknowledge the accuracy of Raol's reporting.[105] Some Muslims spat upon crosses, urinated on them and wiped their backsides with them to show their disrespect for Christianity. The cleric himself simply observed that the Muslims' behaviour made the crusaders more bitter against 'the enemies of the cross'. He lamented that the Christians offered a peaceful resolution to the siege on several occasions, but concluded that the Muslims' rejection of it meant that they merited divine punishment. 'For God had ordained, especially in these times, that vengeance should be wrought upon the enemies of the cross through the most insignificant of men.'[106] Raol again touched upon the familiar themes of vengeance and the cross, but his reference to the humble origins of the crusaders is interesting; it was something evidently perceived by him as part of the reason for their success. There is no explicit parallel to the fate of the main crusading armies in the East, led by King Conrad and King Louis, although near-contemporary writers, such as Henry of Huntingdon, saw fit to make the comparison:

> In the same year, the armies of the emperor of Germany and the French king, which marched out with great pride under illustrious commanders, came to nothing because God despised them . . . Meanwhile, a naval force that was made up of ordinary, rather than powerful men, and was not supported by any great leader, except Almighty God, prospered a great deal better because they set out in humility. Truly 'God resists the proud, but gives grace to the humble'. For the armies of the French king and the emperor had been more splendid and larger than that which earlier had conquered Jerusalem, and yet were crushed by very much smaller forces and were destroyed like a spider's web. But no host had been able to withstand the poor men of whom I spoke above, and the large forces who attacked them were reduced to weakness.[107]

As the siege dragged on through the summer other practicalities needed to be attended to. The foundation charter for the monastery of St Vincent described how Afonso was moved by the sacrifices of the crusaders and wanted to make proper provision for their dead. He called a council and addressed Archbishop John of Braga thus, his words giving a perfect spiritual rationale for the crusaders' actions:

> I look at these most brave barons who have left their homelands to fight and who came here so as to give up their lives for Christ, to fight their battles and to struggle strongly against the enemies of the faith. Caring not about this present life, they try above all else to eliminate with their swords the repulsive pagans – that great is their ardent zeal for the house of the Lord. It matters then, that we also demonstrate care and consideration towards them, with regard to the burying of the bodies of those that fall in their midst, thus let us carry out their funerals with the dignities accorded to the martyrs of Christ. I have no doubts that, by the grace of God, they will be put in the company of the martyr–saints in Heaven, as their enormous commitment proved that they have followed in their footsteps on earth. For that reason, my lord churchman, I ask you not to postpone for long the finding of an adequate cemetery for them not far from their encampments.[108]

Two cemeteries were created, one to the west (Saint Mary of the Martyrs), for the Anglo-Normans, and one to the east, for the Rhinelanders and the Flemings.[109] The latter became the monastery of Saint Vincent, memorialised in the foundation document noted above – a building that still remains today (though modified).

When it became obvious that the Muslims were not going to surrender quickly, the crusaders settled down to construct siege engines. The Anglo-Normans created a tower ninety-five feet high and the Flemings and Rhinelanders made a sow, a ram, a movable tower and a projectile described as a Balearic mangonel. This all indicates a fairly high level of poliorcetic skill; the specialist knowledge of the Pisan siege engineer was evidently being put to good use. The mangonels and the ram were brought up to the wall, but the enemy responded swiftly and burned them all. The defenders also had mangonels of their own. The Anglo-Norman tower was moved up to the wall only to become stuck in the sand, and after four days bombardment with stones was burned by the enemy (around 6 August 1147). Six weeks into the siege little progress had been made and the crusaders' spirits seem to have sagged a little: 'our men were discouraged for a while' as the 'Lisbon Letter' noted.[110] During a communion ceremony, a Flemish priest found the bread soaked in blood. Some interpreted this as expressing the crusaders' greed for slaughter and saw it as a sign that their motives were not proper.[111]

As the siege drew on, however, the Muslims' limited foodstocks began to weaken and, as Raol stated, the ever more obvious contrast with 'the untold abundance' of the crusaders' supplies began to boost the latter's morale. The 'Lisbon Letter' reported the deprivation in the city and accused those who controlled the food of starving their fellow-citizens and reducing them to eating cats and dogs.[112] Some of the population deserted and came to convert to Christianity. A few of the crusaders, in contrast to the sentiments expressed by Raol later (see below), gave these would-be recruits a harsh welcome and sent them back to the city with their hands cut off.[113] The Christians drew their ships up onto the shore as a sign that they would be staying for the winter, while the Rhinelanders made five attempts to dig mines under the city walls; all failed. The crusaders were using the full range of siege techniques against their opponents, but the lack of results caused some dissenters to raise questions again about their presence at Lisbon; easier pickings might be had elsewhere.[114]

The Christians then had two more strokes of good fortune. First, their naval patrol captured a Muslim boat trying to break the blockade. It carried a number of letters which, when translated, were revealed to be addressed to the ruler of Evora based 94 miles to the east: the Lisboners pleaded for help; they argued that the Franks were 'not so very numerous or warlike' and emphasised their own successes in burning the towers and siege engines. They also dwelt upon their own lack of supplies and fears for their fate. While this news greatly fortified the crusaders, their morale was improved further when the body of a Muslim swimmer was found drowned. The man bore a message from the king of Evora to the effect that the king would not join the fight because he had made a truce with Afonso Henriques. Perhaps he was afraid of the Christian armies, or else he felt that his co-religionists' position was hopeless. In any case, as Raol triumphantly wrote: 'So, finally, the Moors' last hope of relief was destroyed.'[115]

The crusaders kept themselves occupied by undertaking raids on local sites, such as the nearby castle of Sintra. This is located on top of a particularly steep rocky outcrop, about twenty miles north-west of Lisbon. The strength of the castle rendered it almost impregnable, although the town at its foot was a likely source of plunder and the crusaders acquired a great quantity of booty there. Another raid took place as a reprisal for the capture of five Bretons near the town of Almada on the Tagus. Saher of Archelle led a party of Anglo-Norman knights and 100 footsoldiers (strangely enough, the Flemings and Rhinelanders withdrew from the mission) and achieved a great success. They captured 200 men, slew many others and brought back over eighty heads on spears, all for the loss of one man. The parading of the heads was a traditional tactic used to demoralise defenders and the people of Lisbon pleaded for their return; their entreaties were answered and the heads were received with terrible grief and wailing. For Raol, of course, this was another demonstration of Anglo-Norman valour and, he claimed, it brought great respect from all the other attacking forces. By this time, Afonso's forces were reduced in number because he had sent many of them to hold his earlier conquest of Santarém, although a few of his knights, his household, the bishop of Oporto and, presumably, the local Templars remained.[116]

In early September the Pisan engineer oversaw the construction of another siege tower, built at the expense of Afonso Henriques. The Anglo-Normans tried to dig a new mine, but its entrance was visible to the Lisboners and they endlessly bombarded it, much to Raol's exasperation. Two large mangonels pounded the walls, operated in shifts of 100 men, with the result – so Raol claimed – that 500 stones an hour could be hurled by the two machines. Meanwhile, over to the east, the other part of the army was digging yet a further mine; this time they had constructed a masterpiece. It had five entrances and, in spite of Muslim harassment, it was completed within a month.[117] At dawn on 16 October the shaft was filled with flammable material and lighted. The mine worked: at least 200 feet of wall collapsed. The Muslims cried out in horror as they feared the end; they quickly attempted to improvise a barrier amongst the ruins using heavy beams as walls. The crusaders tried to enter, but were repulsed, in part by stout defence, in part because the steep hill that led up to the breach rendered an assault difficult.[118] This latter detail may suggest that the walls here were closer to the citadel than on the west. The Anglo-Normans rushed around to the east, trying to force home the attack, only for the Flemings and Rhinelanders to bar their way. The sense of pride and honour in military achievement, so apparent in reports of the First Crusade (as we saw above in chapter 2) and so happily recorded by Raol when the Anglo-Normans accomplished a great deed of their own, was now turned against the cleric's people. The Flemings and the Rhinelanders said that they had prepared the breach for themselves, 'not for us'.[119]

Raol's men readied the Pisan-directed siege tower, taking care to cover it with heavy matting to absorb enemy bombardment, as well as with ox-hides, presumably soaked in an anti-inflammable liquid, to prevent the construction from being burned. Everyone was ordered to make shields and protective screens in anticipation of the final assault. At this crucial moment, spiritual preparations were also required and Archbishop John of Braga was asked to bless the tower with prayers and holy water. With the army gathered together Raol himself gave a sermon to encourage and inspire the troops before the battle started. He began with a theological passage based upon Romans 13 in which he stressed the link between truth and righteousness and he urged the crusaders to confess all their sins and be reconciled with the Lord through penance. Such a process was essential before a crusading battle in order to fulfil the criterion for the reward of martyrdom, as stated in *Quantum praedecessores*.[120] Raol drew attention to Christ's life on Earth and voluntary sacrifice on behalf of mankind. Perhaps stung by the Muslims' taunts earlier, Raol argued that God had not needed to become a man born of woman but had chosen to do so in order to endure human suffering. This humility was a medicine to cure man's sins; 'what fear can be cured if it may not be cured by his resurrection?'[121]

Raol urged the crusaders to have courage and called them voluntary exiles who followed Christ. Once again, he spoke about the need to confess previous sins and to proceed into the attack with right intention, 'lest your affections cling to those very things which you have given up'. This was a warning against greed, envy and vain ambition – potential traps for the crusaders as they conquered the city and all themes touched upon earlier in the text. He compared their condition to that of the newly baptised – cleansed and immaculate. He reminded them of God's kindness in bringing them unharmed across the sea: they were poised for victory having lost relatively limited numbers of men. The priest became bullish: 'I confidently promise you that you will shatter the power of your enemies.'[122] Again, he suggested to the crusaders that the duration of the siege and the hardships they had endured (expenses included), had been planned to strengthen their resolve and to test their endurance. As he stated 'for the prize is promised to those who start, but is given to those who persevere.'[123] Times of failure or limited progress can be explained as God challenging the true motives of a man. Now, however, the time for victory was ripe. Raol was, by implication, telling his audience that they had passed God's test; they were ready and deserving of reward.

The priest seems to have carried with him a piece of the True Cross.[124] Livermore argues, sensibly and logically, that this – in conjunction with his apparent wealth – probably meant that Raol was a legate, because why else would he be the one to carry such a valuable and venerated relic?[125] He was able to remind the men of Christ's sacrifice on the very wood they saw before them and he said that the sign of the cross would bring them victory. He assured the crusaders that if any of them died he was certain of eternal reward: 'To live is glory and to die is gain' – another Bernardine statement that echoed the abbot's description of the crusade as 'a cause in which to conquer is glorious and for which to die is gain'.[126] Raol also told his audience that he would share their trials and labours in the final attack and that they would all partake in the rewards of victory. He closed his sermon with an appeal for divine assistance and for courage. After such an emotive oration the crusaders wept and fell to their knees. Raol commanded them to stand and they were again signed with the cross and began the assault.[127]

The Anglo-Norman siege engine was pushed up to the west wall. The following day, 20 October, it was moved towards a tower at the south-west corner of the city. As the enemy massed to confront it, the crusaders performed an exceptional manoeuvre. The advance was a feint, since they swung their machine towards an adjacent doorway which overlooked the original point of attack. This was a remarkable feat, considering that the machine was eighty-three feet tall. It was a tactic that bore some comparison to Godfrey of Bouillon's decision to shift his siege tower along the northern walls of Jerusalem in July 1099, a move acknowledged to have played a significant role in the crusaders' success.[128] Crucially, the tower in the walls of Lisbon was open at the back and the crusaders' archers and crossbowmen drove the Muslims from the building. Night was about to fall and a guard was set up, but, unforeseen by the crusaders, the tide came in and cut the tower off. The Muslims saw this and emerged from the nearby gate to attack the machine. They also gathered a huge range of projectiles and inflammable material and began an intense bombardment of the tower. The small contingent of crusaders was in a terrible plight. They tried to stem the fires, they dug trenches and bravely resisted the enemy onslaught. The siege engine seems to have been trapped: on the following morning it was isolated again and in the subsequent engagement the commander of Afonso's galley was killed by a missile. Far worse for the crusaders was a serious injury to their engineer who

1 The tympanum of the abbey church of Vézelay, located in the narthex. The sculpture shows Christ and the apostles and represents a parallel between their apostolic mission and the hoped-for success of the crusaders in the Holy Land.

2 Bernard of Clairvaux preaching the Second Crusade, from an Old French manuscript of William of Tyre's *History of Outremer*, late thirteenth century.

3 Caffaro of Genoa dictating the 'Annals' of Genoa to the scribe Macrobius, image from the twelfth-century manuscript of the text.

4 A statue of Bishop Otto of Freising in the courtyard of the monastery of Freising.

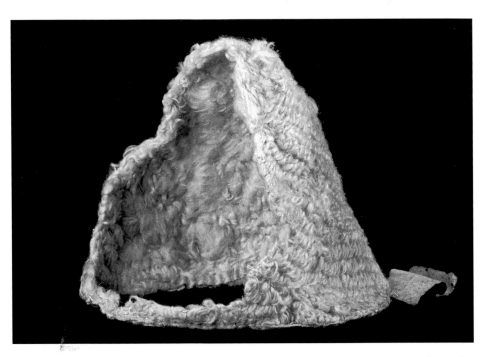

5 The woollen hat worn by St Bernard of Clairvaux and given to the German knight William of Helfenstein and his wife Benigne in 1152 by the abbot. Its sanctity was believed to have helped the couple have a son who then took part in, and survived, the Third Crusade, helped by the intervention of a heavenly host of horsemen.

6 Roundels from the 'Crusading Window' of the abbey of St Denis, probably installed in 1147 in preparation for the departure of King Louis VII to the Holy Land. The roundels survive in the Glencairn Museum in Bryn Athyn, Pennsylvania.

Left: A king leading his army of mounted warriors; a generic image of a royal expedition upholding the Christian faith against the infidel with a possible emphasis on Charlemagne.

Right: In contrast to the temporal activity of the other image this shows a scene of heavenly reward: the glory of martyred heroes. The three figures in the centre are being given the crown of martyrdom to the acclaim of their comrades.

7 Romanesque façade of the Sé, Lisbon's cathedral, constructed by King Afonso Henriques in the aftermath of his capture of the city in October 1147.

8 A fragment of a fresco from the south wall of the nave of St Lawrence's cathedral, Genoa, depicting and celebrating the capture of Tortosa in December 1148. Lost sections of the fresco showed the attacks on Minorca (1146) and Almería (1147).

9 Silver penny of Bishop Bucco of Worms (1120–49), a participant in the Wendish Crusade of 1147.

10 Gold hyperpyron of Manuel Comnenus (1143–80) of Byzantium wearing the imperial-robes and carrying a sceptre and chlamys.

11 View of the city of Damascus and surrounding orchards. This picture was taken in 1894 by an American party and published in J. H. Vincent and J. W. Lee, *Earthly Footsteps of the Man of Galilee*, New York, 1894. The previous decade a visitor wrote: 'The beauty of Damascus is all the more striking for the contrast to the barren desert which surrounds this oasis. The white city looks like a diamond set in the dark green of fruitful gardens. These gardens and orchards extend several miles around the city to the borders of the desert, and are a marvel of fertility. The fields of wheat and barley and beans are shaded by fruit and forest trees – the poplar, the cypress, the palm, the walnut, the citron, the pomegranate, the orange, the apricot, the fig-tree, arrayed in a rich variety of colours, laden with golden fruit, and filling the air with sweet fragrance' (*Picturesque Palestine, Sinai and Egypt*, ed. C. Wilson, 4 vols, London, 1881, 2.144).

was so badly hurt that he could no longer advise them. Many fled the siege tower, leaving only a small group who resisted manfully for over two days: a much admired feat.[129] The 'Lisbon Letter' added that a group of Lotharingians played a major role in defending the machine and that it was the departure of a contingent of royal troops that created heavy pressure on those in the defensive tower.[130] The crusaders fought off the Muslim counter-attack and finally the Christians were able to move their siege engine up to the wall. Even though the Muslims gathered to resist the lowering of the tower's drawbridge they realised that their fate was sealed. They asked for a truce and a night to consider their position: the crusaders agreed.

Hostages were given over and placed in the custody of Hervey of Glanvill and Fernando Captivo, a royal representative. They were delivered to the king rather than to the Anglo-Norman crusaders, an act that provoked huge resentment from the latter group. Once again, we see matters of pride, standing and prerogative causing friction; there was considerable anger towards Fernando and Hervey. The following morning, 22 October, the Anglo-Norman constables and the leaders of the Flemings and of the Rhinelanders assembled to hear what the Muslim hostages had to offer. They proposed to hand over the city to the king and to deliver all gold and silver and other property into his hands. Such a suggestion outraged the crusaders who saw in it great harm to their chances of taking booty. Raol described a tumultuous debate in which many of the leaders lost their temper. The precious oath of unity was deeply challenged and, as the priest described it, the Devil spread his malice everywhere until the Holy Spirit brought calm and 're-established the grateful bond of returning concord'.[131]

Yet while the debate settled down, the seamen and other lesser men were also in conference, this time down by the shoreline. There a 'certain renegade priest from Bristol' began to incite rebellion. He considered their successes a result of divine inspiration rather than something achieved through any positive actions on the part of their leaders. Raol felt that this bad character 'disfigured the innocence of the many', and he resorted to a familiar juxtaposition of vices and virtues to ask: 'Who would not become indignant at seeing the sincerity of virtue soiled by the accusation of vice, when those who criticise know not what they want or do not want, or what is satisfactory in good things, or unsatisfactory in evil?'[132]

The crowd's fury was directed towards Hervey for failing to deliver the hostages to the king rather than to themselves and, perhaps more revealingly, because he had (presumably in his role as constable) judged some of the crusaders guilty of certain offences and decided that they would forfeit their share of the booty. Raol reported that a mob of 400 men sought out the constable. The Muslim hostages learned of this situation and tried to exploit it to their own ends. They declared that they would make an agreement with the king but could not trust the crusaders – who, after all, were even prepared to turn on their own lords. More meetings ensued and it was resolved that the *alcayde* (chief man of the city) and his son-in-law should keep their property, the citizens would receive food, but otherwise Lisbon was to be surrendered. If the inhabitants of Lisbon rejected this, the outcome would be left to the vicissitudes of war.

Once again, the crusaders' fragile unity came under threat. The Anglo-Normans were happy to accept the deal, but the Flemings and Rhinelanders wanted to take everything. Raol contrasted the honourable motives of his own group who, notwithstanding the heavy costs already incurred, were prepared to agree. The others, however, driven by greed and, on a more practical note, worried by the heavy expenses that lay ahead of them, wished to secure maximum profit. Eventually it was agreed that the *alcayde* alone should be allowed to take food and property (except his mare; for Arnulf of Aerschot insisted that the animal should be his). The day ended in stalemate and the options of war or peace remained open.

Possession of the hostages continued to excite huge passions and on the morning of 23 October a mob of Flemings and Rhinelanders went to the royal camp to seize them by force of arms. Christian of Gistel and Count Arnulf learned of this and managed to quell their men, although they had to conciliate King Afonso and to convince him that they had played no part in the dissension. The king was understandably furious and felt his honour greatly challenged. To placate him the crusade leaders agreed to swear fealty to Afonso and to be his subjects for as long as they remained in Portugal. Once this had been settled it was decided to follow the terms of surrender outlined earlier by the Muslims.[133]

A body of 140 Anglo-Normans and 160 Flemings and Rhinelanders was to enter the city and peacefully occupy the upper castle; the inhabitants were to bring all their money and possessions to the same place. This central treasury was obviously a way to ensure equal distribution of booty and was a reflection of the original oath of association. The crusaders were also at liberty to search the city and, if anything of value was found, they could kill the owner. Once it had been verified that all the valuables were in the castle the population was to be released. As the crusaders entered the city at river level, the Flemings and Rhinelanders introduced an extra 200 men beyond those already designated. The archbishop of Braga and his bishops led a procession into Lisbon; they were accompanied by a banner bearing the sign of the cross and followed by the king, the leaders of the Anglo-Normans and the others chosen to make up the party. The flag was taken up to the highest tower and the king symbolically circled the walls of the castle to take possession of, and survey, his new property. At these moments of victory there was an outpouring of emotion from the crusaders; Raol wrote of tears of joy and piety, of the singing of *Te Deum laudamus* and *Asperges me*, and of the recital of prayers. He also mentioned the (justifiable) pride of all.

The crusaders' success was soon to be tainted, however. The unity that had been so delicately nurtured was broken by the Flemings and Rhinelanders who ignored their oaths and started to ransack the place. People were abused, driven from their homes and maltreated; property that should have gone to the common purse was stolen and the Mozarab bishop of Lisbon had his throat cut. All of this, Raol felt, was 'against all right and decency'. The *alcayde* and his property were also seized. In contrast to this, the Anglo-Normans held true to their promises and stayed calm in order to preserve their oaths and the ordinances of their association. Once again, Raol positioned his men on the moral high ground. Finally, however, by prayers and entreaties, order was established and the booty could be shared out equally.[134]

From 25 October on a steady stream of inhabitants started to leave Lisbon, departing from the squalor of a city that had endured seventeen weeks of siege; 200 corpses and 800 sick were discovered by the crusaders in the central mosque. The Muslim collapse continued with the surrender of Sintra to the north and the abandonment of the castle of Palmela to the south-west. The crusaders settled down to pass the winter in Iberia before planning to carry on to the Holy Land in the spring. One prominent crusader to stay in Portugal was a churchman, Gilbert of Hastings, who was accorded the honour of being elected the first bishop of Lisbon. This was an interesting choice which must bear some reflection of Afonso's gratitude towards the crusaders, particularly the Anglo-Normans, for securing the capture of the city. Gilbert held the position until his death in 1166; intriguingly, he is known to have visited England in 1150 to recruit men for new campaigns against the local Muslims.[135] Afonso was evidently trying to build upon his recent successes and could probably offer tempting financial and territorial inducements to those who followed Gilbert.[136] On 1 November 1147 the Christian churchmen purified the central mosque and restored the bishopric of Lisbon, enthroning Gilbert at its head. Afonso ordered the construction of a new cathedral, a building that still stands today (see Illustration 7).

In the aftermath of victory divine portents were noted at the tombs of those martyred on the crusade. Two dumb men were cured, and lamps were reported to glow at night. As Duodechin of Lahnstein's version of the 'Lisbon Letter' reported: 'We do not mention this from our own inspiration, but on the contrary we have the assent of many and truthful witnesses, we saw it with our own eyes and felt it with our own hands.'[137]

Raol claimed that the Muslims of the area suffered a great pestilence and began to turn towards God. How much this was a portrayal of divine punishment for the sinful is hard to tell. Raol acknowledged that the Christians had erred too, but now they knew the light and were blessed. His tone then took an unexpectedly gentle turn. He saw that God had delivered the enemy into their hands and that they had suffered divine vengeance, but now he felt pity for their misery and infirmities.[138] Such a sympathetic approach is very rare in crusade writings of this period.[139] He argued that even Christians continued to be punished, by way of being instructed and corrected. He called for the crusaders to have modesty in their victory and not to boast of God's power and of the rewards He had accorded them. They should not delight in the suffering of the enemy. He then formulated the hope that 'affliction will draw [them] to glory', indicating a wish that the Muslims might see the light.[140] After a passage ruminating on the impenetrable mysteries of divine decision-making, Raol drew attention one last time to the crusaders' own state of mind. He asked them to think not of their enemies' sins, but of their own consciences and impurities. Most remarkably of all, he ended with a plea to God to end the suffering of the Muslims and he expressed the hope that they might one day turn to Christianity: 'if it be possible, let their sorrow be turned into joy, "in order that they may know thee, the only living and true God, and Jesus Christ, whom thou hast sent".'[141] Riley-Smith has indicated how the powerful rhetoric of the First Crusade stressed the inhumanity of the Muslims and encouraged vengeance and war, rather than conversion.[142] As we have seen, however, there was some interest in the concept of their conversion amongst the Cluniacs. Perhaps Raol's thoughts here were another hint of the presence of this idea in the ever-broadening spectrum of crusading thought. It is not usually until the thirteenth century and the advent of the Mendicant Orders that serious efforts at conversion are recognised, although Odo of Deuil mentioned this phenomenon, if in passing, in his *De profectione Ludovici*.[143] Conversion had, of course, also been seen in the Baltic and, to a lesser extent, elsewhere in Iberia.[144] This notion corresponds more closely to Raol's sentiments and his attitude may have been born out of an appreciation of the local circumstances in the peninsula, as well as of his own feelings. The archbishop of Braga had hoped that some Muslims 'should voluntarily be added to the Church of God'.[145]

As the crusaders settled down for the winter the correspondents of the 'Lisbon Letter' began to write their messages for their friends and colleagues at home. On 1 February the fleet set sail, 'as they had vowed', for Jerusalem.[146]

The conquest of Lisbon was one of the prime achievements of the Second Crusade. The city would become an integral part of King Afonso's burgeoning kingdom (Coimbra remained the capital) and marked a major advance for

Christianity in Iberia. The success of the expedition showed contemporaries that God approved of their work and, as we have seen, Raol's *De expugnatione* did much to demonstrate the reasons why the crusaders merited such rewards; their humility and right intention had prevailed. Even allowing for his careful management of the narrative, this text, in conjunction with the other sources, reveals how and why the crusaders captured the city. There is little doubt that the sworn association promoted discipline and rigour amongst the northern European forces. This unity of military effort and spiritual motivation did much to help their cause. The desire for booty was obviously an important motive behind the crusaders agreeing to sail to Lisbon in the first instance and, notwithstanding the tensions towards the end of the siege, it blended with their spiritual aspirations in reasonably good order. The regional contingents engaged in some level of rivalry and Raol did much to emphasise the integrity and heroism of his own people; the 'Lisbon Letter' indicates the importance of the other groups. The crusaders were able to conduct the siege largely on their terms; they were a strong and well-equipped force, with good leaders, particularly Count Arnulf of Aerschot. They were more than adequately supplied, while their opponents struggled for food; furthermore, the crusaders also faced no enemy relief force; the Muslims had to cope with the knowledge that no one was coming to help them. In these circumstances, as long as crusader morale and unity held up, their ultimate victory was always likely; once achieved, the majority could then continue their journey to Jerusalem.

CHAPTER 9

CONRAD'S MARCH TO CONSTANTINOPLE AND INTO ASIA MINOR

A combination of basic geography and the intense diplomacy of early 1147 ensured that Conrad's army was set to march ahead of the French. The original plan required the two monarchs to meet at Constantinople, in much the same way that the First Crusaders had assembled there in 1096 before heading on towards Edessa. Odo of Deuil wrote that when Louis heard Conrad was likely to press on into Asia Minor, he sent messengers who urged that 'he should wait for him on this side of the Arm [the Bosphorus] and that those whose common will had undertaken a common task should also use a common plan of action'.[1] The ultimate target of the crusade was Edessa; Conrad himself made this plain in a letter of late February 1148, where he wrote that he was going to Jerusalem at Easter to 'assemble a new army and proceed to Edessa'.[2] Other sources, such as John of Salisbury and the Würzburg Annalist, also stated this.[3] This basic idea can be refined further; Odo of Deuil described the way across Asia Minor: 'From [Constantinople] three routes, unequal in length and unlike in character, lead to Antioch.'[4] In other words, the expedition was to travel to Edessa via Antioch, a logical choice given the close relationship between Prince Raymond and the French royal house; there is also evidence that communication had taken place between these parties that anticipated just such a strategy.[5]

Conrad's army set out from Nuremburg in the latter half of May and then went to Regensburg where it is likely that he was joined by the large Bavarian contingent. The size of his force is difficult to gauge. Various sources speak of its immense numbers. The largest figure – and a strangely precise one – is the 900,566 cited by Odo of Deuil as the total counted by the Greeks when the Germans crossed the Bosphorus.[6] Intriguingly, the Byzantine official John Kinnamos gave a figure of 900,000 and Niketas Choniates and Helmold of Bosau also noted that the Greeks stationed scribes to try to record the number of crusaders.[7] While it seems that some attempt was made to count the Germans, modern scholars are understandably wary of the results.[8] Another source for the Second Crusade, the *Annales Palidenses*, put Conrad's force at 70,000, the Vaucelles continuation of Sigebert of Gembloux gave 50,000, while the Peterhausen Annalist claimed that Otto of Freising led 30,000 people when the larger group of non-combatants was separated off from the main fighting force in Asia Minor; the *Annales Palidenses* suggested a figure of 15,000 for this same contingent;[9] finally, the *Annales Egmundani* wrote that the combined French and German crusading army was 100,000.[10] Given the substantial number of senior nobles, churchmen and members of the royal family present in Conrad's force, coupled with the consistent references to a large army, an upper estimate of 30,000–35,000, plus non-combatants is probably a reasonable number. By way of comparison, the assembled armies of the First Crusade have been estimated at 50,000–60,000, plus non-combatants, and Henry of Huntingdon reckoned the combined French and German armies of 1147–8 to be larger.[11]

The Danube runs through Regensburg and from there Conrad took a ship downriver, via Passau, to reach Ardagger by 29 May where he paused to let those travelling behind catch up.[12] The king had arranged for a large fleet to carry the nobles while the foot-soldiers and horses walked alongside on the riverbank.[13] Given the Danube's long-standing role as a major transport route this was an eminently sensible way to proceed. The limits of the Empire were around the River Fischa, just past Vienna, where men such as Ottokar of Styria joined the expedition. Then, on 8 June, Conrad moved all of his troops across the River Leitha and into the kingdom of Hungary. The German king needed to be careful here because of the recent history of conflict with Geisa II (1141–62). As we saw above, there had been open war between Germany and Hungary in 1146, in which the latter had emerged victorious.[14] Nonetheless, the arrival of a substantial army, coupled with the lurking presence of Boris, a rival claimant to the Hungarian throne, meant that Geisa probably had to be prudent to ensure that the crusaders passed by as smoothly as possible. He gave Conrad and his men gold to prevent the king allowing Boris to travel with his army and by late July the Germans had moved across his lands and continued down the Danube to Branitz on the Bulgarian border. There the Germans abandoned their boats and took the road southwards towards Constantinople itself.[15]

This point marked the edge of Byzantine territory and it was here that Manuel's representatives waited. Niketas Choniates implied that the Germans had already requested permission to pass through Byzantine lands and asked for the provision of roadside markets. The emperor had agreed and sent out decrees to make the necessary arrangements.[16] Kinnamos and Choniates also reported that when the Germans reached the Bulgarian border the emperor dispatched envoys to discover the crusaders' aims and to confirm, by oath, their proper intentions. The messengers supposedly challenged the westerners' motives and asked why they wished to wage war; they indicated that should the crusaders consent to make the requisite promises they could travel in peace through the emperor's lands. There is a suggestion that the provision of supplies was conditional upon this agreement. An assembly of the king and the nobles averred their good faith and the march continued.[17]

The appearance of a large crusading army was a cause for grave concern in Constantinople. Unlike in the background to the First Crusade, when Alexius I had requested a western force to come to his aid, there was no such invitation in 1146–7. The current tensions with Roger of Sicily were a particular worry, since it was possible that the crusaders would join him and attack the Greeks. The situation with Roger formed a constant backdrop to the progress of both the German and the French crusaders; hence it is worth setting out his activities in some detail. In the autumn of 1147, obviously aware of the imminent arrival of the crusade at Constantinople, Roger sent a fleet under Admiral George of Antioch to raid and seize Byzantine lands. From Brindisi the Sicilians quickly took Corfu, depriving the Byzantines of their natural bridgehead to southern Italy. Next they moved down to Methone on the western tip of the Peloponnese peninsula and then went eastwards to Monemvasia. They raided along the coastline of the peninsula to the Gulf of Corinth where they stormed the lower town and took enormous quantities of gold, cloth and precious metals, as well as the revered icon of Theodorus Stratelates. The Sicilians soon captured the supposedly impregnable fortress of Acrocorinth and seized the most desirable noblewomen as slaves. Athens and Thebes were raided, and from the latter they captured highly valued silk-workers who were soon put to work in Palermo.[18] By the end of the expedition, such was the Sicilians' wealth that Niketas Choniates, perhaps betraying a lack of maritime expertise, wrote that 'so overladen were they with fine merchandise that they were submerged very nearly to the level of the upper rowers' bench'.[19] The Sicilian fleet was obviously a dangerous and flexible force which could strike swiftly towards the heart of the Byzantine Empire if required. Aside from the loss of honour and income, the simultaneous presence of three western armies posed a serious strategic threat. Manuel's need to bolster the defences of Constantinople may also have left the Peloponnese more vulnerable to the Sicilians. Although Conrad was an avowed enemy of King Roger, as we will see below, some of the Greeks feared the German army anyway; western reaction to the recent Byzantine attacks on Antioch was another reason to fret about a broader counter-assault from the Catholic West. John Kinnamos, who wrote over thirty years later as an imperial court official, suggested that the crusade was set in motion not 'on the handy excuse that they were going to cross from Europe to Asia to fight the Turks en route and recover the Church in Palestine and seek the holy places, but truly to gain possession of the Romans' land by assault and trample down everything in front of them'.[20] While Choniates wrote in the early thirteenth century he still expressed a similar viewpoint. In spite of the oaths the crusaders took, the Greeks still regarded them as 'wolves coming in sheep's clothing or lions concealed in the disguise of an ass to reverse the fable'.[21] In another instance, however, Choniates's view was tempered by hindsight: 'The pretext for this expedition was provided by the Lord's empty tomb . . . they declared and affirmed by oath that Jerusalem was the motive for their expedition. Later events proved their declarations were not false.'[22] The benefits of reflection aside, the ongoing Sicilian presence exerted a substantial influence on the Byzantines and coloured their attitude towards both of the major crusading armies.

From Branitz, the German army marched south via Nish and then into the Balkan mountains towards Sofia. At Nish they met more Byzantine officials, including Michael Branas, the governor of the region; at Sofia they encountered a senior treasury officer, Basil Tzintziloukes, and Michael Palaeologus, a cousin of the emperor. Branas had been ordered to supply the army with provisions and this he duly did; at this stage all seemed well. Once the crusaders moved into the plains of Thrace, however, matters began to deteriorate. Kinnamos wrote that 'they applied unjust force on those who were offering them goods for sale in the market. If one resisted their seizure, they made him a victim of their sword.'[23] Manuel was sufficiently troubled to send a senior commander, Prosuch (the man who had led the invasion of Antioch in 1144–5), to shadow them.[24]

A couple of incidents were particularly serious: at Philippopolis, a drunken dispute involving a snake charmer turned into a major riot, although this seems to have concerned stragglers from the army rather than the main body of troops. Conrad himself prepared to intervene in the matter but was placated by the local bishop.[25] At Adrianople, a German noble who lay ill in a monastery was attacked, robbed and killed by Greek footsoldiers. Unsurprisingly, the crusaders were furious and Frederick of Swabia turned around and marched back to burn down the monastery. Prosuch responded with force and, according to Kinnamos, he drove the Germans away with 'great slaughter', although Choniates described the same individual as brokering a more peaceful outcome.[26]

Clearly the Byzantines were getting increasingly anxious: another senior Greek envoy reminded the crusaders of their oaths and tried to convince them to take the route down to Abydos and the Dardanelles, thereby steering well away from Constantinople. By now, however, in late August, the Sicilian fleet was at work. Conrad and his council rejected the Greek suggestion, probably because they wished to follow in the footsteps of the First Crusaders and also because it would compromise their planned link-up with Louis at

Constantinople.[27] Further skirmishing marked the Germans' progress and more troops were dispatched to shadow the crusaders; in addition, Manuel deployed extra Byzantine soldiers to protect Constantinople. It seems that the Greeks remained dubious as to the crusaders' motives, but Manuel was prepared to wait until they showed overt aggression before he embarked on a major confrontation. It must be remembered that, for the Greek emperor, the crusade was but one element in a much wider series of diplomatic, strategic and religious calculations he had to make.[28] While Conrad potentially posed an immediate threat, the crusaders were likely to be only a temporary problem. Manuel had also to deal with the danger from the Sicilians and, on a much more local basis, that of the Seljuk Turks. Furthermore, there was the Byzantine interest in northern Syria, especially Antioch and Armenia; the threat from the Zengids of Aleppo; relations with other Balkan and Black Sea powers, such as the Georgians and the Bulgarians; as well as dealings with the Italian trading cities and the papacy. Any commitment to war against one group would affect the emperor's ability to fight another and, as Harris cogently argues, because the protection of the 'queen of cities' was always Manuel's highest priority, it was essential that any decisions he made did not compromise that principle.[29]

On 7 September, as the Germans camped on the plains of Choirobacchoi (west of Constantinople), near the River Melas, they were struck by a terrible flood. It was an episode widely reported in both Latin and Greek sources and it dealt a notable blow to Conrad's military strength. In the early morning of 8 September a freak storm brought destruction to the camp; winds tore away the tents and the river, hugely swollen by the downfall, poured out over the plain. Otto of Freising was present and he wrote that men tried to ride across the torrent; as it grew, some clung to their steeds or were hauled along by ropes, but many could not swim or were overpowered by the water and swept away. Duke Frederick of Swabia and Welf of Bavaria had pitched camp on higher ground and people tried to reach safety there. Otto sadly observed: 'How great a loss our army sustained in both men and goods and in the utensils necessary for so long a journey I need not relate.'[30] Kinnamos suggested that the waters 'swept away a large portion of the Germans' army with the horses, weapons, and the very tents'.[31] The Würzburg Annalist claimed that only one-third of the horses escaped the waters.[32] Unfortunately, we lack a letter from Conrad himself that makes detailed reference to the incident. Both Kinnamos and Otto ascribed the calamity to divine judgement; justly deserved according to the former, by reason of the crusaders' broken oaths; more a simple matter of deep dismay to the latter.[33] Even with the benefit of hindsight, this does seem an accident that could have been foreseen. Choniates provided a description of the plain and details what was obviously an annual flood; in other words, as well as being unlucky, the Germans had been badly advised or else failed to take the proper precautions in a potentially unstable area.[34]

It is impossible to make an accurate assessment of the scale of this disaster. All the descriptions indicate a serious blow to the Germans' fighting ability, yet there is no list of high-ranking casualties and, in a letter of early 1148, Conrad remarked that his army had reached Nicaea 'numerous and untouched'.[35] Perhaps the losses were largely in terms of baggage and materials and the deaths were mainly amongst the pilgrims. The fact, however, that Manuel sent envoys to Conrad sounding a more conciliatory note could suggest basic humanity and courtesy, but also a sense that the Germans were no longer quite the threat they had been. The king, however, remained defiant and demanded that Manuel should meet him outside Constantinople – something that the emperor angrily declined to do.

Conrad arrived at Constantinople and surveyed the mighty Theodosian walls, over three and a half miles long and formed of an inner wall of ninety-six towers, a broad terrace, an outer wall and a moat (possibly a dry moat); undoubtedly these constituted the most formidable defences the Germans had ever seen.[36] Choniates noted that as the crusade approached, Manuel had ordered the walls to be repaired and he issued armour and weapons.[37] Troops were stationed in front of the moat and on the inner wall as well. The crusaders moved across the Golden Horn and camped in the Pera district opposite. With a bridge as the only way back to the main city there was a measure of security for the Greeks. Kinnamos described an exchange of letters between Conrad and Manuel, the tone of which appears to be a literary device designed to show the inherent superiority of the Byzantine, although the underlying content is plausible. In essence, Conrad was required to pass peacefully through Greek lands; given his status as a king there could be no question of him having to swear homage to the emperor. According to Kinnamos, the German ruler tried to distance himself from blame for the disruptive behaviour of his men during the march and suggested that problems of this nature were inevitable with such a large army. Manuel's response was to thank the king sarcastically for this information and to suggest that he, too, would be unable to rein in the impulses of his people in future; in other words, he made a thinly veiled threat that the Germans could expect trouble.[38] There were indeed outbreaks of disorder on the German march – both Latin and Greek sources testified to it. These might have been over-exaggerated by the Byzantines so as to show the inferiority of the 'barbarian' crusaders; however, as we saw in the incident at the monastery, the Greeks were not always blameless in these matters. Furthermore, as Choniates described, there were more positive episodes, such as Conrad's meeting with

Michael Italikos, the bishop of Philoppolis, which, on the surface at least, was a cordial affair.[39] The intervention of Empress Eirene (Conrad's sister-in-law) also helped to facilitate supplies at one point.[40]

Diplomatic posturing persisted and one long-standing element of Byzantine policy emerged when Manuel told Conrad 'that previous subjection owes us whatever lands will presently be regained from the neighbouring Turks' – a reminder of the Greeks' persistent wish to re-establish their former empire in Asia Minor.[41] Around this time Prosuch defeated a German force outside the city walls and soon Conrad prudently decided to move his men across to the Scutari district on the Asia Minor side of the Bosphorus. Niketas gave an indication of the size of the king's army when he wrote that 'every rowboat, ferryboat, fishing boat and horse transport was commandeered'; thus Constantinople was freed from one danger.[42]

With the waterway as a genuine security barrier the Greeks must have felt more comfortable. Some measure of the seriousness with which Manuel viewed the German crusaders transpires from two verse *encomia* addressed to the emperor by a writer named 'Manganeios Prodromos' by modern scholars and discussed by Jeffreys and Jeffreys.[43] The author was an eyewitness to the crusade and probably composed his work under imperial patronage; the intention was for it to be performed within days or weeks of the passing of the western armies. Even with a section missing, one poem is over 600 lines long and relates the crusaders' passage through Thrace; the other is only 284 lines and congratulates the emperor in seeing off the crusader threat. Notwithstanding the conventions of a genre undoubtedly designed to laud the emperor, the poems were a potential indicator of attitudes towards the crusade. As the later writers Kinnamos and Choniates suggested, the view-point of the Greeks was one of fear and suspicion, mixed with distaste for the perceived arrogance of King Conrad and contempt at the 'barbarian' crusaders' failings. The first poem ascribed hostile intent to the westerners; argued that they wanted to steal Constantinople's wealth and even to impose a Latin patriarch on the city. Jeffreys and Jeffreys indicate that 'press releases' were issued to such writers, designed to prompt them to provoke the greatest public hostility towards outside threats.

Thomas and Stephenson argue that the probable date of composition for the First Crusade section of Anna Comena's *Alexiad* was around the time of the Second Crusade. Aside from Anna's determination to cast a positive light upon the reign of her father, Alexius I (1081–1118), her treatment of the earlier expedition bears close parallels to themes in the work of Prodromos. The crusaders were greedy and fickle barbarians, they wanted to capture Constantinople, and the Catholics were heretical because of their use of unleavened bread. The ideas within her text can be seen, therefore, as a further signal of the concern generated in the 'queen of cities' by the presence of the 1147 crusaders.[44]

There is no German evidence that Conrad ever contemplated besieging Constantinople; while it may seem an unlikely prospect to a modern historian, it was apparently viewed as a real possibility by the Greeks. Conrad himself was particularly disparaged by Prodromos and he was variously described as a fox in disguise, a chameleon, a secret wolf and a savage beast.[45] This depiction was probably fuelled by the Byzantines' wish to assert Manuel's superiority over the western emperor-in-waiting. The German's false pride was one reason why his army received the divine punishment of the flood of Choirobacchoi, an event the poet gloated over. The crusaders' struggles for food outside the walls of Constantinople and on the Asian side of the Bosphorus were also sources of satisfaction to him. Almost in contradiction, however, was a recognition that the Germans' Christian faith meant they should not be killed. Eventually, the German army crossed the Bosphorus and the sense of relief felt in Constantinople is neatly summed up by Choniates: 'The passage of the king . . . was viewed with satisfaction by the [Greeks], like the passing of some dire portent from Heaven.'[46]

It is difficult to judge how the Germans saw these events. There survives one brief letter from Conrad to Abbot Wibald in which the king stated that after going through Hungary he had been attended with honour by the ruler of the Greeks.[47] Whether this was to avoid telling the regent about the calamity of Choirobacchoi or to smooth over the series of problems at Constantinople is hard to guess. Once across the Bosphorus, Conrad asked Manuel for guides to help him traverse Asia Minor. He was sent Stephen, the commander of the Varangian guard, who, according to Kinnamos, offered an alliance against the Seljuks. This Conrad declined, but he did make some decisions about his route.[48] From Nicaea, as Odo described, there were three ways across Asia Minor. The first was that taken by the First Crusade and the Aquitanians in 1101; it led directly across Anatolia via Dorylaeum and Iconium, towards Cilician Armenia and Antioch. The second was to go along the coast, a march that offered greater safety and supplies, but was slow and arduous because of the numerous rivers and streams that had to be traversed. A third route lay in between the two, following some of the coastline and then striking inland at Ephesus and along the Maeander valley.[49]

Once over the Bosphorus, as several sources attest, Conrad was determined to press on. John of Salisbury, who met the French contingent in Rome in 1149, explained that 'the Germans declined to have anything to do with the Franks in shipping their baggage across the Hellespont, and went to the length of refusing a request to wait for [Louis] who was a few days behind, saying that . . . they would wait for no one whatsoever until Edessa, which they came to

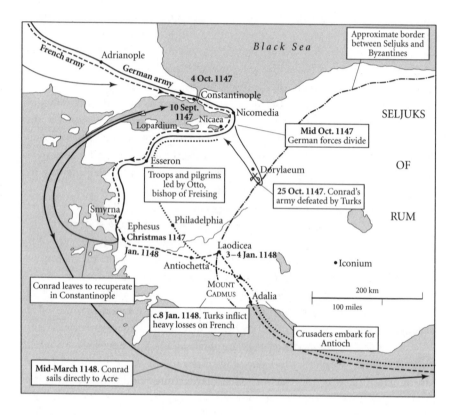

Routes taken by the French and German armies across Asia Minor, 1147–8

liberate, had been captured'.[50] Most telling of all, Conrad himself wrote that he 'wanted to complete the expedition in good time'.[51] He chose the first road: the most direct and the most confrontational. According to the king, Iconium could be reached in twenty days and there, as William of Tyre wrote, the crusaders 'would find themselves in a most fertile country full of all kinds of provisions'.[52] This information was discovered by the First Crusaders because the *Gesta Francorum* wrote of Iconium as a 'fertile country, full of good and delicious things to eat and all sorts of provisions'.[53] Odo stated that if all went well it was three weeks from Nicaea to Antioch, with twelve days to Iconium and then five to the edge of Frankish lands.[54] Aside from this, one wonders what other knowledge Conrad based his decision upon. He was presumably confident in the military capabilities of his men. Odo of Deuil met the king after he was forced to retreat in late 1147 and quoted a speech in which Conrad blamed his defeat on his own sins and suggested that, 'when reckoning on victories over the Turks, [he should not] have been puffed up on account of my large army, but placed my hope humbly in the God of hosts'.[55] To permit his men to move rapidly he had divided the German crusaders into two contingents. He was to command the better-armed fighting force into Asia Minor while his half-brother, Otto of Freising, was ordered to lead the large number of non-combatant pilgrims along the supposedly safer coastal route. The *Annales Palidenses* commented that a disagreement between the wealthy and the impoverished caused this split, but in strict military terms this was probably a positive development and must have made Conrad more sure of success.[56]

The route from Nicaea to Dorylaeum is about 60 miles long and follows an old Roman road. Even though it was mid-October, this was a fertile region in which the crusaders had a reasonable expectation of finding water and fodder for their horses.[57] Given that it was late autumn, Conrad was evidently trying to beat the oncoming winter. The scale of his ambition – or the level of misinformation that he was presented with – is revealed by reference to the First Crusade. The earlier expedition took ten days to move from Nicaea to Dorylaeum althought the crusaders were severely harassed by the Turks, most obviously at the Battle of Dorylaeum (1 July 1097). The armies then took a further 108 days (including rest days) to march the *c.*730 miles from Dorylaeum to Antioch, an average of *c.*6.8 miles per day.[58] Given the level of knowledge of the First Crusade, this timescale must have been a reasonably familiar fact. Of course, much of the fighting in the latter stages of that campaign, such as that in Cilicia, would be unnecessary because the Second Crusade was not interested in the conquest of land en route. Modern studies of medieval rates of march suggest an absolute maximum of *c.*17.5 miles a day, which gave Conrad's crusaders an upper range of 350 miles in his own estimated 20 day journey, with Iconium being c.260 miles from Nicaea.[59] With reference to the speed of the First Crusaders, however, he could only expect to cover c.135 miles, which would leave him well short of his target – clearly he required a trouble-free march to increase his rate of progress. It may be worth noting that Conrad had made good time from Regensburg to Constantinople, (c.1200 miles), with a journey of around 112 days at an average of c.11 miles a day. Given that he had now removed the non-combatants from his force, perhaps this, too, gave him a false sense of his potential speed.[60]

The area of Dorylaeum was, in some senses, a frontier. It lies at the north-western edge of the Anatolian plateau, and the land soon rises from 800 m above sea level to over 1,000 m, with a corresponding change in vegetation: the plateau is steppe-like and semi-arid, with much thorn-scrub.[61] Thus the crusaders would need to have as many provisions as possible to traverse this region. Dorylaeum also lay towards the limits of Byzantine political authority. The border between the Greeks and the Seljuk Turks was porous and, in many respects, difficult to define. Odo of Deuil described areas 'where the Greeks still hold castles [but] the two peoples [meaning the Turks also] divide the revenues.'[62] In some areas, local tribes were allies of the Greeks, in others, the Turks acted independently and could range freely into Byzantine lands.[63] Only the previous year a powerful Byzantine raid had re-established a garrison at Melangeia (between Nicaea and Dorylaeum), and another thrust had pushed along the Maeander valley to Philomelion and threatened Iconium itself.[64] The former success provided a further possible supply station for the expedition.

The crusaders set out from Nicaea around 25 October accompanied by their Byzantine guides. Conrad claimed that they carried as many supplies as possible, but after ten days, and with another ten to go to Iconium, they began to run short.[65] Odo, who met the survivors, wrote that the Germans were provisioned for eight days only.[66] Pryor argues that each man needed 800 g of grain per day to survive; his horse could graze, or would need, 5–6 kilos of food per day, although the environment in this case was not conducive.[67] Whether Conrad could gather these supplies is uncertain. Foraging was a possibility, but it was a dangerous business and in itself consumed valuable time and energy, detracting from the advance. Almost every German writer emphasised the harsh, sterile landscape that the crusaders found themselves in. The Würzburg annalist described it as a desert lacking in water, the *Annales Palidenses* wrote in similar terms and stated that the crusaders saw only shepherds' tents and flocks of sheep and then, followed by circling birds, they entered a horrible wilderness, a barren, empty place.[68] Meanwhile, the Turks constantly harried the army. They inflicted the greatest losses on the footsoldiers, who were least able to resist the lightning raids of the mounted archers and, as the poorest group, carried less food and were the weakest. The *Annales Palidenses* also mentioned a particularly heavy Turkish raid on the German camp; this attack was occasioned by a division of the army when it found a water supply. The heavy cavalry was absent and the Turks charged and killed many of the crusaders. It was only when Conrad heard of the situation and rushed back that the enemy were driven from the field.[69] Roche has carefully established that the crusaders probably got three days beyond Dorylaeum before the princes and nobles demanded a council.[70] Conrad himself explained the situation: everyone was hungry and the crowds of those on foot, who were struggling to keep up anyway, were being regularly picked off by the Turkish archers. The king wrote that it was at the request of the nobility that a decision was made to turn back and regroup, 'preferring to keep [the army] intact for greater events than to triumph in a bloody victory over the archers'.[71] Odo of Deuil offered a more chivalric version of this, presenting the Germans as being torn between a pointless death if they continued and fearing the shame of a retreat. The writer appreciated their dilemma and sympathised when they chose the latter, because it was more useful to the Lord's service to live to fight another day.[72] Thus the crusaders turned around and began the painful return to Nicaea.

In the course of the march one notable casualty was Bernard of Plötzkau, a Saxon noble, who was helping to escort the stragglers. In an eerie precursor of the disaster that was to afflict the French crusaders, he became separated from the other troops by a mountain range. Then, pinned down by the Turkish archers and with his horses lost, or so fatigued that they could no longer charge, he was killed, much to the consternation of the main force.[73] The retreat became evermore desperate and, as the starving crusaders struggled on, the Turks relentlessly harassed the vanguard and even the centre of the army. William of Tyre, familiar as he was with Turkish tactics, gave a detailed account of the crusaders' difficulties that noted the speed and good condition of the local horses compared with the undernourished and weak western mounts. Once the Turks had let loose their hail of arrows, they turned their horses and sped out of reach of the fatigued Christians' swords.[74] Any counterattack was foiled by the common Turkish stratagem of breaking ranks and scattering, a practice which gave the crusaders' heavy cavalry no fixed target and left them with two choices: to pursue the enemy so far that they lost cohesion and risked being separated from the main force, or else reining in their horses and watching the Turks disappear. Gerhoh of Reichersburg gave a neat sense of the remorseless pressure faced by the crusaders when he wrote of archers firing from the left and the right, day and night.[75] John Kinnamos described the Germans as being repeatedly duped by the Turks' feigned retreats and suffering heavy casualties.[76]

Conrad himself was wounded quite seriously by arrow-fire, and increasing numbers of the weak fell behind and were slaughtered. By early November, however, the Germans had struggled back to Nicaea where the Greeks exploited their desperation by charging exorbitant prices for food. Odo of Deuil wrote that many of the army were broken by this experience and sought to return home, although whether this referred to pilgrims or warriors is unclear; Conrad wrote that the sick and poor left the army around this time too, which suggests that it was the pilgrims rather than the soldiers who were affected.[77] Some of the crusaders went to Constantinople, where Manuel, possibly at the bidding of his German wife, helped them to continue their journey west.[78] Conrad was not of such a mind, however, and he sent messengers, headed by Duke Frederick of Swabia, to see the French crusaders who had just entered Asia Minor.[79] Louis went to the king's camp where the two men met for the first time during the campaign, they exchanged warm greetings and lamented the losses that had taken place. Conrad wrote of Louis that 'he and all his princes faithfully and devotedly offered us their service. They supplied us with money and whatever else they had that we wanted.'[80] The Germans were to regroup and then rendezvous with the French at the nearby castle of Lopardium before the two armies moved on together.

The causes of the Germans' defeat were numerous. As noted above, Conrad seems to have been overconfident and unwilling to wait for the French crusaders. Clearly lack of food was a major issue: the march to and beyond Dorylaeum must have proven harder and slower, and consumed more victuals, than had been expected. A comparison with the First Crusade – an expedition that hardly enjoyed plentiful supplies – is instructive. Bachrach has concluded that the reason why the 1097 crusaders survived was that 'the intelligence and good will of the Byzantines and the emperor's edict permitting markets to be made available were the operational essentials that made the march of the crusaders both possible and successful'.[81] In spite of the division of the German army, the large number of poorly equipped foot-soldiers hampered the pace of the advance and compromised the supply calculations. It may be no coincidence that Odo chose this point in his narrative to include his salutary warning to future crusaders and, indeed, even a criticism of Pope Eugenius:

When the Holy Father forbade dogs and falcons and restricted the nature of knights' arms and clothing, men who did not concur with this command acted with a lack of wisdom and utility which equalled the presence of wisdom and utility in his command. But, would that he had instructed the infantry in the same way and, keeping the weak at home, had equipped all the strong with the sword instead of the wallet and the bow instead of the staff; for the weak and helpless are always a burden to their comrades and a source of prey to their enemies.[82]

Over 40 years later, Emperor Frederick Barbarossa instigated strict rules to try to ensure that his crusaders were properly equipped, thereby showing that he had learned from bitter personal experience. In 1196–7 Henry VI went a step further and mandated that the entire army should travel by sea to prevent such burdensome individuals from taking part in the crusade.[83]

Another contributory factor that some writers, such as Odo, William of Tyre and the Anonymous Syriac Chronicler, put forward to explain Conrad's demise was the treachery (at Manuel's direction) of the Greek guides, although it is interesting that the king himself, who was in the most obvious position to make such an accusation, chose not to. In Odo's case, the duplicity of the Greeks was one of the themes of his work anyway. William placed Byzantine antipathy in the context of their view of the Germans as particular rivals, especially on account of Conrad's use of the title 'emperor of the Romans' – an honour they felt was Manuel's prerogative alone.[84] By compromising Conrad's campaign, Manuel had prevented the Germans from increasing their prestige; had the king defeated the Seljuks, for example, he would have accomplished something that the Greek emperor had failed to do only the previous year. With regard to the guides, William added that the men were either instructed by Manuel to betray the crusaders or bribed by the Turks.[85] The fact that the guides fled was seen as proof of their bad faith, although such accusations are hard to prove. William indicated that Conrad confronted these men and asked why the march had made so little progress. They managed to convince him that they were only three days from their destination but disappeared overnight; moreover, they compounded their crime by going to Louis's army and reporting that the Germans had taken Iconium to deter the French from helping their co-religionists.[86] One might argue that the guides, having seen that the Turks had gathered and realising that the crusade was doomed, chose to flee anyway; it would hardly have been sensible for them to wait around and be blamed for leading the Germans into a trap. The presence of the Turks was inevitable, rather than a direct result of betrayal by the guides.

The reasons why Manuel might wish ill towards the Germans have been reasonably easy to identify, but it seems improbable that he aimed to destroy them. In light of such conflicting evidence, this is impossible to prove; the failure of Conrad's contemporary letter to charge the Greeks with treachery is of considerable weight. The emperor's care for the king and the provision of a fleet to allow his return to Constantinople do not suggest complete antipathy. Lilie also emphasises subsequent good relations – for instance the 1148 Treaty of Thessalonica, a pact against the Sicilians – which gives an indication that no deep-seated animosity reigned between the two powers.[87]

It is much harder to assess the number of casualties suffered. William of Tyre wrote of the collapse of the crusader army – 'merely a remnant of their vast forces' remained; perhaps one tenth survived, a statement accepted at face-value by Runciman.[88] Odo stated: 'I cannot describe the losses on that journey.'[89] On the outward leg of the march, Conrad's letter described the level of mortality amongst the crowd on foot. During the retreat and its aftermath there was a strong emphasis on the ill-health of the crusaders; clearly their efforts had left them weakened and prey to sickness; in some cases they had also suffered wounds, like Conrad himself. As Loud has noted, however, except for Bernard of Plötzkau, no senior noble was mentioned as having been killed.[90] While this is an *ex silentio* argument, the lists of French casualties after the disaster at Mount Cadmus included many figures of high standing (see below, p. 201). An analysis of Germans identified as taking part in the crusade might offer some guidance.[91] Of the 113 recorded as having set out with Conrad, 22 are known to have died on the crusade, 42 are known to have returned and the fate of the remaining 49 has proven impossible to ascertain. This leaves a definite mortality rate of *c.*19 per cent. Only Bernard is known to have died at this point in the campaign, although the accounts make it clear that the march into Asia Minor was the one where the Germans incurred their highest casualties. There is also the fact that the Turks took large numbers of prisoners and these men effectively counted as 'losses', since they were no longer fighting in the army.[92] Leaving some margin for deaths known elsewhere, casualties of *c.*17 per cent can be suggested.[93] There is a further caveat, of course: individuals mentioned in the charters tend to be of the princely and knightly class, who were likely to have been better armoured and provisioned than the masses; both Odo and Conrad were explicit that it was amongst the foot-soldiers that the most serious losses occurred. Thus, a figure of *c.*17 per cent for the nobility, even allowing for the further 49 per cent whose fate is unknown, represents one crude effort to quantify the impact of this defeat in numerical terms. At the very least, it seems that the overwhelming level of loss represented by Runciman should be moderated. Interestingly, and by way of comparison, it is worth noting that these figures seem rather lower than those for the First and Fifth Crusades. In the case of the former, Riley-Smith calculated a casualty rate of 37.3 per cent; and for the latter, Powell gives 34.1 per cent.[94] Almost as important as the losses, however, was the damage to crusader morale. In the case of the Germans, as we saw earlier, some may have decided to abandon the expedition; but the shocking news of Conrad's rout must have shaken the French troops as well, particularly as they had already heard rumours of their colleagues' success.[95]

The strength of the crusaders' opposition was also important. Sultan Mas'ud would have known about the approach of the expedition since the latter months of 1146; indeed, this was probably a contributory factor behind contemporary Turkish peace offers to the Greeks, and it was an important reason why they were accepted.[96] The latter stages of the 1146 war with Byzantium saw Mas'ud reconciled with one of his rivals, Yagibasan, the governor of Sivas, and as the crusade drew near the sultan called for help from all possible quarters, arguing that it was essential to gather as large a force as possible to confront the Christians because they might take control of much of the East. He also refortified cities and repaired castles. As William of Tyre commented, rumours of the size of the crusader army were hugely exaggerated, but they still struck fear into the Turks' hearts.[97] Similarly, Ibn al-Qalanisi, a contemporary Damascene writer, stated that the crusaders had more than a million horse and foot and claimed that they had allegedly seized 'the dependencies of Constantinople and its king was obliged to bow to their will'.[98] The memory of the triumph of the First Crusade was a significant factor in the Seljuks' assessment of the new expedition and, naturally, the defeat of the Germans was a source of huge satisfaction. Ibn al-Qalanisi stated that 'men were restored to some degree of tranquillity of mind and began to gain some confidence in the failure of their [the crusaders'] enterprise'.[99] Because Conrad's force was larger than the French army they felt sure that they could vanquish the next cohort of westerners; as events turned out, their belief was well placed. The Turkish tactics of using quick, mounted archers who fired and then retreated were perfectly suited to the terrain. By contrast, the crusaders' heavy cavalry was unable to deliver a charge to any effect and, as Gerhoh of Reichersberg noted, they lacked the archers to respond in kind to the Turks.[100]

In December, the combined German and French force moved to Ephesus – a city important to the crusaders as the shrine of St John – and there they celebrated Christmas. Again, Conrad wrote that he and many of his men remained ill and soon it became apparent they could not carry on in such a weakened condition. Louis wanted to continue and so the two monarchs parted company. William of Tyre indicated that this was because of the scale of the losses Conrad had suffered, but also the fact that he found the arrogance of the French unbearable – although John of Salisbury and Conrad himself suggest that personal relations between the German ruler and Louis were good.[101] Emperor Manuel heard of Conrad's troubles and he generously sent boats to Ephesus that picked up the king and brought him back to Constantinople where he was looked after by imperial doctors and brought back to full health. The good offices of his daughter-in-law, Empress Eirene, and the fact that Manuel was now undoubtedly in the superior position, made this a most convivial visit with many fine receptions, outings to the hippodrome and other lavish entertainments.[102] Conrad was able to write to Wibald of Stavelot that the emperor had shown him greater honour than had been offered to any of his predecessors. He also stated that he planned to resume the campaign in the spring and set the date of 7 March for his departure before gathering a new army to march on Edessa.[103]

The progress of the other section of the German crusade is harder to follow. Otto led his pilgrim army along the shore route which, although safe from the Turks, was tough going: they needed to cross the countless streams and rivers swollen by the winter rains. Otto went down the coast, probably to the valley of Hermes or the valley of Ephesus, before he turned inland along the Maeander valley towards Laodicea. Like their compatriots, these westerners struggled for food and were reduced to slaughtering their pack animals. Then, probably in mid-December, they were attacked by the Turks and lost many men, including Count Bernard of Carinthia, while the younger members of the group were taken prisoner and sold into slavery. In a pitiable condition – Otto of Freising had even lost his boots – the survivors struggled on to the southern coast of Asia Minor where they were finally able to take ship to the Holy Land.[104] Intriguingly, the passage of this army has left traces in the numismatic record: several contemporary German coins have been discovered. A hoard from Side on the southern coast has currency of Archbishop Arnold of Cologne (1138–51), Archbishop Adalbert II (1138–41) or Henry I of Mainz (1142–53), Bishop Bucco of Worms (1120–49), Bishop Burchard of Strasbourg (1141–62), Archbishop Conrad of Salzburg (1125–47), Margrave Leopold IV of Austria (1136–41). The dating and location of these coins almost certainly links them to Otto's expedition. They neatly illustrate the range of the crusaders' origins in Germany, as well as the need to carry cash on the march.[105]

CHAPTER 10

The March of Louis VII to Constantinople and into Asia Minor

The army of King Louis had, initially at least, a smoother journey. The principal source for this is the epistolary narrative of Odo of Deuil, a monk of St Denis and chaplain to the king during the expedition. This text is fundamental to our understanding of the Second Crusade because it is the only lengthy account concerning (part of) the campaign to the Holy Land. Its 35,000 words cover the crusade from its first launch at Bourges in December 1145 to the arrival of the army at Antioch in March 1148. Odo's writing has attracted considerable attention but, as I have argued elsewhere, it is a work that should not be viewed as narrow-minded – or even consistent.[1] Odo offered his text to Suger to enable him to write a history of Louis VII in a similar vein to the abbot's earlier *Deeds of Louis the Fat*. While there is, as Mayr-Harting suggests, 'a hagiographical streak' to this narrative, Odo's account is not entirely uncritical of the king.[2] The date of composition is problematic; there is certainly a sense that the account was based upon a diary, but it is not clear whether it was sent back from Antioch in the spring of 1148, as its structure suggests, or, as Mayr-Harting argues, it was composed as part of an attempt to rouse a crusade against the Greeks in 1150.[3] Odo had studied histories of the First Crusade and he even took a copy of one narrative with him on campaign. This reading must have had some impact upon his understanding of the crusade. In particular, it may have helped to shape his attitudes; for while he provides pithy descriptions of geography, battles and local customs, certain prejudices shine through. Most famously, his anti-Greek rhetoric is responsible for clouding many analyses of his narrative and several views of the Second Crusade as a whole.[4] Yet the picture was not so simple; while Odo did regard the Greeks as largely responsible for the defeat in Asia Minor, he was prepared to praise certain individuals and could show insight into, and appreciation of, various aspects of Byzantine culture and Orthodox religious practice. He also viewed the Germans in a largely negative light, although he was able to see that the French themselves were, at times, at fault.[5] The narrative also served as an instruction manual for future crusaders and warned them against some of the mistakes made by the French and the Germans; the survival of only a single manuscript suggests that Odo's work was not widely circulated.

The French army assembled at Metz where, as Odo reported, everyone voluntarily subjected themselves to Louis's authority. Given the problems the king had experienced in the early years of his reign, it appears that the crusade had, as a side-effect, given him a hitherto unseen (albeit temporary) level of recognition. As the crusaders gathered, the king tried to pre-empt one of the more obvious difficulties for any large army: that of indiscipline. There were times when the First Crusaders had fought amongst themselves, and problems over supplies and distribution of food and booty were inevitable. As we saw earlier, the participants in the expedition to Lisbon had set out a series of rules to try to govern their behaviour and these were generally successful. Louis evidently enacted something similar but, as Odo wearily commented, because the crusaders 'did not observe them well, I have not preserved them either'.[6] Thus, from the outset of the journey an underlying flaw in the expedition was signposted to Odo's audience.

The French force moved to Worms on 29 June and almost immediately the lack of discipline became apparent. The diplomatic skills of Bishop Alvisus of Arras and Abbot Leo of St Bertin had ensured that sufficient ships were available to move the army across the Rhine where they awaited the arrival of an Anglo-Norman contingent under Bishop Arnulf of Lisieux. But a quarrel broke out between the citizens and the crusaders, and a Frenchman was killed. The flow of commerce ceased and it took several negotiations to restart the trade. Yet here – already – 'a foreboding about the people' was felt and this, added to the early discovery of the high cost of food, caused a contingent of men to leave the main group and march south across the Alps to take ship from Brindisi.[7]

Alvisus and Leo, along with Bartholomew, the royal chancellor, were dispatched to Regensburg. The crusaders were very well received and found an ample fleet waiting to take them down the Danube as far as Bulgaria. This was surely an example of the earlier diplomacy between the French and Germans bearing fruit and facilitating the smooth passage of the second wave of crusaders. Odo also noted a meeting with envoys from Manuel Comnenus. He gave a lengthy description of the Greek envoys' fine silken garments and of their concern for etiquette before launching into a scathing dismissal of the Byzantines' ornate and fulsome diplomatic practices; they tried so hard to flatter the king that an exasperated Bishop Godfrey of Langres had to cut them short. The ambassadors conveyed two conditions which repeated the requests made in Manuel's letter to Eugenius in March 1147. First, that the French should not capture any settlements in the emperor's lands; secondly, if the Turks were driven away from territories which formerly belonged to the Byzantine Empire, the places in question should be restored to the Greeks. These conditions were very similar to ones laid out by Alexius Comnenus in 1097, except that they did not include a call for homage – at this stage, Manuel felt unable to insist on this.[8]

The French nobles debated the demands; the first seemed reasonable, but the second was more contentious. Some felt that the Greeks should compensate them if they took lands from the Turks but handed them over; others, sensing the potential for different interpretations of the expression 'former Byzantine lands', asked for clarification, although the Byzantines' previous embassy had included a list of the places covered in the deal. The discussions dragged on and the Greeks tried to force the issue by threatening to destroy the waiting supplies if the matter was not resolved quickly. In the end, however, certain nobles swore to observe the first clause on Louis's behalf, while a decision on the second was put off until the two monarchs met face to face. Alvisus, Bartholomew and Count Archibald of Bourbon were sent ahead to Constantinople to continue the diplomatic process, while Louis remained with the slow-moving main army.[9]

The French crusaders went down the Danube from Regensburg to Passau and thence to Klosterneuburg, one day from the Hungarian border. Their progress was generally easy and they used the same bridges constructed for Conrad's army. It took fifteen days to cross Hungary where they 'had such marketing privileges as were wished'. As the Germans had found, the turbulent political situation in Hungary could not be ignored; Boris, King Geisa's rival for the throne, secretly joined the French army as a way of trying to pass unnoticed through the land. Boris had already attempted to win Louis to his cause by sending letters to him at the meeting at Étampes, back in February 1147, and hoped to convince him that his case was just, although he received no apparent response. As etiquette required, Louis had to meet King Geisa. Odo used this encounter as an opportunity to eulogise his own monarch's kingly, Christian qualities and to depict him as a man of charity and humility. The two rulers confirmed that the crusaders could pass through Hungary in peace and exchanged gifts. Then Geisa learned that Boris was in the French camp and his messengers requested that he should be surrendered. Odo described a farcical scene in which a terrified and naked Boris tried to escape but was captured and brought before Louis. Geisa, of course, was frantic in his attempts to secure the capture of his enemy, but perhaps Boris's earlier diplomacy had made some impression on the king; at any rate, the French crusaders refused to hand him over to his death and escorted him out of Hungary.[10] Geisa simply departed, possibly fearing that Louis might turn against him, although he caused no problems for the king and did not withdraw the promised supplies.

Louis wrote to Suger with the positive message that he had received a warm welcome in all the places he had passed through, but at the same time he conveyed a sense of alarm at the expense of the expedition. It is startling that as early (or as late, in the sense of failing to foresee it) as the friendly lands of Hungary the king realised the huge costs of running the crusade. He asked Suger to send him extra funds as soon as possible.[11] From Hungary the French moved into Bulgaria which Odo described as a well-watered place; with his experience of running monastic estates in France, he judged the land to be most suitable for farming and crop-raising.[12] The route matched that of the Germans in passing through Belgrade, Nish, Sofia, Philippopolis and Adrianople. Once again, the French crusaders' journey was reasonably easy, although Odo did mention a couple of difficulties. The first was in connection with his aim of providing information for future expeditions; namely, the problem of using four-horse carts. These seemed to break with irritating frequency and then, rather like a modern caravan on a country lane, caused all those behind to come to a halt or get into more trouble trying to avoid the obstacle. Many horses died in these accidents and large amounts of time were lost; essentially, Odo urged that such vehicles should not be used.[13]

As they marched into Byzantine lands the issue of monetary exchange arose and Odo suggested that the Greeks, contrary to their earlier promises, had perjured themselves by giving highly disadvantageous rates. Tensions started to emerge over provision of food; the Greeks were unwilling to let the crusaders enter their cities – possibly on account of the unruly behaviour of the Germans – and would only let down food on ropes. When this proved insufficient, the French began to ravage the countryside. It would be under-standable if the activities of the Germans had induced caution on the part of the Greeks; Odo himself reported several stories about the trouble caused by Conrad's men which shows that such tales circulated freely. When some French crusaders caught up with a party of German stragglers there was even conflict between the two groups; similar brawls between regional contingents had broken out during the First Crusade fifty years earlier.[14] As Odo dismissively remarked: 'The Germans were unbearable even to us.'[15]

Yet overall the march was a success, in part because the French seemed to have been better disciplined than the Germans, and also thanks to the work of Michael Branas who 'honourably' – a rare note of praise for a Greek official from Odo – facilitated peace and provisions for the French. Louis himself was said to have distributed most of his food evenly amongst his people, both rich and poor, and gained the respect of all.[16] From a Byzantine perspective, John Kinnamos also reported a positive atmosphere at this point; he contrasted the

French with the Germans, and lauded Louis in particular.[17] The crusaders' rapid progress was another sign of good relations with the locals. Louis journeyed from Metz to Constantinople in 110 days, just faster than Conrad's 112 days (over a shorter distance) and, as a further point of comparison, than Godfrey of Bouillon's 130 days.[18]

A notable blow to morale occurred on 6 September at Philippopolis, when Alvisus of Arras died after a long illness.[19] As we have seen, the bishop was an important diplomat who seems to have been held in extremely high regard by the army, acting as a spiritual confessor to all. Odo chose to include a detailed description of his passing, and Louis and the bishops sang the entire service for the Festival of the Virgin in his memory. Odo also mentioned that he had seen the sick cured by sleeping on Alvisus's grave. The First Crusade witnessed many examples of the miraculous, but, given the gloomy outcome of the second major expedition to Jerusalem, this was a rare example of such a phenomenon.[20]

As the main French army drew closer to Constantinople several incidents began to generate suspicion towards the Greeks. A contingent of French crusaders had travelled with the Germans but chose to wait for Louis at Constantinople. The Greeks wished them to proceed with Conrad's men, but the presence of the French ambassadors caused, in theory, an exception to be made. In spite of this, a group of Patzinak and Cuman tribesmen cornered the French crusaders and forced them to make a defensive barricade of their carts. Chancellor Bartholomew and Everard of Barres, the master of the Templars, rushed to the emperor and urged him to intervene. Manuel swore that he knew nothing of the incident and had the men rescued and given a market.[21]

At this point in his account Odo assembled several pieces of evidence that, to him at least, proved the duplicity of the Greeks and explained the traumas experienced by the French army. The reader has to be cautious, however; Odo was always concerned to divert the blame for the outcome of the campaign away from King Louis. While it is plain that there was a vehement anti-Greek group in the French army, it did not command a majority and, more importantly, it did not have the backing of the king. Most notably, Louis's own letters make no reference to these troubles.[22] Nonetheless, there was cause for suspicion in the French ranks because the envoys learned of a new twelve-year truce between Manuel and the Turks.[23] This must have come as a severe shock to the crusaders. The emperor's letter to Louis in the autumn of 1146 had spoken of fighting the Seljuks and of his joy at the advent of the crusade. His references to the First Crusade must also have put the French in mind of a Christian-versus-Muslim scenario, yet Manuel seemed to have overturned this.[24] In the period between the Byzantine–Seljuk conflict of 1146 and the arrival of the crusaders in Constantinople much had changed. Most significantly, the Sicilian invasion of Corfu and of the Peloponnese had caused huge alarm to the Greeks. With the possibility of Sicilian–crusader co-operation coming to life and, coupled with his inability to secure satisfactory agreements as to the westerners' behaviour, Manuel had been receptive to Seljuk peace offers because they removed one major source of danger to his lands. The Turks, as we have seen, were fearful of the crusaders and similarly keen to neutralise a potential threat: the power of a joint Byzantine–crusader army was clear – indeed such an army had defeated their predecessors at Nicaea back in 1097.

Other episodes stirred the antipathy of the French towards their hosts. Godfrey of Langres, one of the fiercest opponents of the Byzantines, had lost men and possessions sent on ahead to Constantinople. Odo added a religious dimension to the friction through his allegation that after the French bishops celebrated mass the Greeks purified the altars as if they had been defiled; a clear source of offence.[25] Similarly, Odo had heard that if Catholics married into Orthodox families, they were re-baptised; he made reference to 'other heresies of theirs', such as the long-standing controversy over the *filioque* clause. He then suggested that 'it was for these reasons that the Greeks incurred the hatred of our men . . . because of this they were judged not to be Christians, and the Franks considered killing them [to be] of no importance and hence could with the more difficulty be restrained from pillage and plundering'.[26] Quite how convincing this line of argument was remains debatable; one wonders whether the average footsoldier was more concerned with the *filioque* clause than about food supplies, or whether Odo sought grounds to justify the crusaders' actions. Furthermore, issues regarding the Eucharist and the *filioque* were not new and the papacy was far from seeing in them a reason for open warfare. On the contrary, as already noted, the atmosphere between the Orthodox and the papacy was positive; only four months earlier Eugenius instructed Henry of Moravia to seek a reconciliation between the two Churches.[27]

On a more pragmatic level, the Greeks and the French needed to engage in diplomatic contact; even Empress Eirene wrote to Eleanor. Odo dismissed much of the Byzantine displays as empty flattery designed to do nothing more than please the crusaders. In spite of his tendency to view the imperial diplomats as vapid and insincere, he did make one particularly penetrating observation: 'In general [the Greeks] really have the opinion that anything which is done for the holy empire cannot be considered perjury.'[28] As Harris has convincingly shown, this was a neat summary of the guiding principle of Byzantine diplomacy – namely to ensure the safety of the Empire, and partic-ularly Constantinople, at any cost.[29] As they had done with the Germans, the Greeks tried hard to divert the French away from Constantinople. Given the ongoing Sicilian attacks to the west, coupled with the history of good relations between Roger II and the French, this was a matter of critical importance to Manuel. The decision of one contingent of French crusaders to march via Apulia would have caused even greater concern.[30] Yet the crusaders disregarded the emperor's wish; Odo suggested that they were guided in this by their desire to follow in the footsteps of the First Crusaders: 'the king did not wish to undertake something which he had never heard that the Franks had done'.[31] News of the Sicilian invasion circulated freely in Constantinople and Odo wrote that some in the army – almost certainly including himself and Godfrey of Langres – urged Louis to contact Roger and to mount a joint attack on the Byzantine capital. The king appears to have given this idea short shrift and the French duly arrived outside the walls of the city on 4 October.

The senior churchmen and nobles of the Empire came out to greet the king and requested him to have an audience with Manuel. Louis agreed and the two men met at the imperial palace. They embraced, kissed and then sat down, to talk through an interpreter. There is an amusing discrepancy between the descriptions of this meeting in the accounts of John Kinnamos and Odo. The former stated that 'when Louis came inside the palace the emperor was seated on high, and a lowly seat, which people who speak Latin call a chair, was offered to him'.[32] Such arrangements were standard practice and left no doubt as to who was the superior ruler. Odo, presumably to avoid any sense of inferiority on the part of Louis, chose to omit this detail and simply commented that the two men sat down. The exchange was seemingly cordial and the emperor promised support; the two rulers parted on good terms.[33] The king himself wrote to Suger that he had been received with great honour and rejoicing.[34]

During Louis's stay in Constantinople Manuel showed him due respect and escorted him around the magnificent palaces, churches and shrines of the city, including the wondrous Sancta Sophia.[35] It is a neat irony that one of most important relics associated with Edessa, the letter sent by Christ to Abgar, was kept in the Church of the Holy Virgin of Pharos, inside the Bucoleon palace. Given its location, it is almost certain that Louis was shown this sacred object.[36] The two men celebrated a splendid banquet and all seemed well. Sensibly, the Greeks barred the city gates to the mass of crusaders who, as Odo himself admitted, were causing trouble, burning houses and olive trees, be it in their need for firewood or out of drunken stupidity. Given the slow growth of olive trees and their centrality to Byzantine life, this was particularly antagonistic behaviour. Louis meted out a variety of punishments and ordered the cutting off of ears, feet or hands, but so many offences had taken place that he could not exert control over the entire army. Prudently, Manuel ensured good provision of food and a fair rate of exchange outside Constantinople to help keep the majority of the French happy.[37]

While the crusaders waited for the arrival of those contingents who had travelled via Brindisi there remained a tension between those who wished to attack the Greeks and those who did not. At this time, however, the Byzantine attitude appeared to be generally positive and did much to calm the more aggressive amongst the French. Notwithstanding his dislike of the Greeks, Odo's own writings give some flavour of these conflicting feelings. The 9 October marked the feast of St Denis – naturally, a matter close to Odo's heart and an event he was keen to record. But St Denis was also venerated by the Greeks, and Manuel, with his customary diplomatic acuity, sent a group of splendidly attired Orthodox clergy to take part in the ceremony. Odo's antipathy towards Orthodox religious practices seemed to vanish on this occasion, and he lavishly praised their 'sweet chanting and ... graceful bearing'. (As a monk of St Denis, Odo would have been familiar with parts of this liturgy being performed in Greek because such had been the practice in his abbey long before the crusade.[38]) Predictably, however, Odo then chose to contrast this display of friendship with the Byzantines' subsequent treachery. Louis himself was evidently impressed with these ceremonies, as he chose to mention them in a letter to Suger.[39]

Yet in the middle of these displays of friendliness Godfrey of Langres persisted in his efforts to convince the other crusaders that they should besiege and take Constantinople. He tried to argue that the walls of the city were weak and its water supply vulnerable; he drew attention to Emperor John's recent attacks on the principality of Antioch and to the expulsion of Catholic churchmen from Tarsus and Mamistra and their replacement with Orthodox clergy. He claimed that John had allied himself with local Muslims in his siege of Antioch, and hence his death by a self-inflicted wound from a poisoned arrow was a result of divine judgement. Godfrey stated that Manuel continued his father's crimes and had compelled Prince Raymond to swear homage to him. He also claimed – erroneously – that the Latin patriarch of Antioch had been displaced by an Orthodox one, although such a rumour would have helped to increase the crusaders' antipathy towards the Greeks.[40]

Odo indicated that Godfrey's remarks were well received by some of his audience, although he was honest enough to relate that even more disagreed. The counter-argument was strong: there was a recognition that the emperor could have had good reasons to march on Antioch. This analysis has an interesting parallel in a remark made by Orderic Vitalis who wrote less than ten years previously. The Anglo-Norman monk described the 1137–8 Byzantine invasion and included a speech in which King Fulk of Jerusalem was quoted as explicitly acknowledging that the Greeks' actions were justified: 'We are all well aware ... [that] Antioch is part of the empire of Constantinople, and that it was wrested from the emperor by the Turks ... the emperor's claims about the treaties of our ancestors [referring to the promises of Bohemond I to Alexius] are true as well'.[41] The fact that such knowledge was current in northern Europe at this time suggests there was an understanding that the Byzantine cause was not without some foundation. The issue of Greek intervention in the principality had been discussed between Louis and Eugenius although the pope gave no specific guidance on the point, which perhaps indicated that he felt unable to condemn the Byzantines outright. The opponents of a siege of Constantinople made an ironic contrast between the crusaders' true purpose of going to Jerusalem to defeat the infidel and an assault on the Greeks: 'If slaughtering Christians wipes out our sins let us fight. Again, if harbouring ambition does not sully our death, if . . . it is as important to die for the sake of money as to maintain our vow . . . then wealth is welcome; let us expose ourselves to danger without fear of death.'[42] As noted above, Louis must have favoured the latter argument because Godfrey's case failed and no major hostilities broke out. It is also worth observing that Louis continued to experience financial difficulties. In October he wrote again to Suger to encourage him to send without delay the funds he had requested earlier. There was no indication as to the exact reasons why the extra money was required: it is not clear whether he was spending more on food than anticipated, or the needs of the host were greater than predicted.[43]

The French army became impatient to move onwards into Asia Minor. News of huge German victories began to circulate, probably a device used by the Byzantines to encourage their guests to leave. Louis's men wanted their share of fame and booty and complained to the king, but he was still waiting for the seaborne troops to arrive. Manuel quickly assembled a fleet to transport the French across the Bosphorus; supply ships and money-changers followed. Odo mentioned that the money-changers' tables 'gleamed with gold and were groaning from the silver valuables which they had bought from us'.[44] This ties in with the charter evidence that we saw earlier; the transportation and exchange of precious objects was the most convenient way to generate funding en route.[45] Unfortunately, a Flemish crusader was overcome with greed at the sight of so many riches laid out in front of him and he triggered a riot; gold was seized and the money-changers and the supply ships fled back across the Bosphorus. Louis was furious; he had the main culprit hanged in front of the city and made full reparation to the money-changers. Inevitably, the incident caused a cooling of relations with the Greeks and it was necessary to send an embassy to Manuel to try to restore the markets. Chancellor Bartholomew and Bishop Arnulf of Lisieux met the emperor but allegedly found him far more hostile than before – unsurprisingly perhaps, given recent events. A market appeared, although Odo claimed it was of insufficient size;

one wonders how many local merchants trusted the crusaders not to attack them again.[46]

Louis and Manuel still had to settle upon terms for the provision of supplies and the return of territory. The emperor sent his terms: in return for guides and fair markets he wanted marriage to one of Louis's kinswomen for one of his nephews and the homage of the French nobles for himself. Back in 1097 Alexius had extracted oaths of fealty from the leaders of the expedition; now he wanted the same from the French barons, although he did not require it of the king. With the crusaders now over the Bosphorus, Manuel felt able to increase his demands; the question of homage returned to the fore for the first time since his letters of August 1146. Where markets were unavailable it was suggested that the crusaders could take plunder and if a town or castle refused food, it could be seized, as long as it was returned to the Greeks afterwards.[47] This presumably reflected the limited nature of Manuel's authority in the borderlands between his own empire and that of the Seljuks.

In the meantime, the counts of Maurienne and Auvergne and the marquis of Montferrat reached Constantinople, although Manuel cannily refused to help them cross the Bosphorus; this was a gentle way of increasing the pressure on Louis to agree to his terms. As the French considered the offer, the king's brother, Robert of Dreux, abducted the lady identified as the bride-to-be and moved on ahead of the army, also avoiding the possibility of paying homage to the emperor himself. This seems a particularly odd episode; either Robert acted without the king's knowledge, which shows the weakness of Louis's authority (the count's subsequent rebellion against his absent brother in 1149 is another sign of this), or else he did it with royal approval – a dangerously inflammatory move against the Greeks.

There was a debate over Manuel's demands. Inevitably, Godfrey of Langres was against accepting them; he recommended, again, the use of force and claimed that it would be a disgrace 'to do homage to an infidel', language of a remarkably extreme nature.[48] The majority countered that they were accustomed to hold fiefs from many lords and yet maintain loyalty to the king above all; hence, if 'our customary usage neither injures the king nor disgraces us, let us observe our custom'. Crucially, there was an appreciation that Manuel's insistence was driven by fear of 'our people, of whom he had already had experience in his realm'. But this is an ambiguous phrase. It could refer to the French crusaders, whose poor behaviour had been demonstrated on several occasions; it could include the Germans as well, whose discipline had been even worse; or given Odo's own sense of fraternity with the Sicilians, revealed during the meeting at Étampes, and their continued attacks on the Empire, it may well have been a generic reference to all the westerners, even encompassing the invasions of Bohemond I.[49] Those in favour of swearing homage to Manuel made the same calculation as their predecessors fifty years earlier; they could not do without supplies and guides and, most logically of all, 'we are marching against pagans; with Christians let us be at peace'.[50]

Louis himself put pressure on Manuel by ordering the crusaders to break camp. The king appeared to want to gain repute as the Germans had – a clear sign that he was not entirely blind to securing his reputation and defeating the infidel; he was reported at the time to be 'excited about speeding against the pagans'.[51] He realised, however, that a conference was necessary and the two rulers met, probably at Nicaea.[52] By this stage, it was in the interests of both men to finalise an agreement. Manuel wanted some reassurances and it was quite plain that, if he did not get them, he would withdraw all co-operation. It was confirmed that the French would not take any Byzantine castle or town and in return the Greeks would send senior nobles to accompany the army, to act as guides and to facilitate markets. Pillage was permitted if a market was not forthcoming. It seems that with the French safely away from Constantinople, Manuel did try – opportunistically – to persuade the king to form an alliance against Roger of Sicily. He offered huge financial inducements but was rebuffed and the treaty was settled in the terms described above. The French nobles swore homage, as required, and after they had received fine gifts they set out to catch up with the main army. Further ahead, the troops had seen a semi-eclipse of the sun and feared that their monarch had been lost; later, however, they learned of the defeat of the Germans and interpreted the portent by identifying Louis with the shining half of the sun and the vanquished Conrad with the hidden half. In any event, it was an inauspicious and widely recorded sign.[53]

Like the Germans before them, the French had to select which route to follow from Nicaea across Asia Minor. Out of three roads to Antioch, they decided on the one in the middle, ignoring the direct route to Iconium taken by Conrad, perhaps in the belief that his reported successes rendered their presence there worthless; they also shunned the slow coastal route employed by Otto of Freising. In choosing the one road yet to be used, the French may also have hoped to find more supplies of food. Almost immediately, however, they suffered a grievous setback: the first messengers from Conrad's army brought the shocking news of the Germans' rout. The French were said to be 'stupefied with grief' that such a strong army had failed.[54] While natural disasters such as the flood at Choirobacchoi could be accepted, a defeat by the Turks ran counter to the crusaders' expectations, both in terms of the information they had received and with regard to the colossal self-belief engendered by the preachers of the expedition and the victories of the First Crusade. The French asked how the calamity had happened and were told of the Germans' over-confidence, of the treachery of their guides, of the lack of food and of the effective tactics of the Turks. Each of these factors must have given the French leadership pause for thought because all could apply to them as well; surely greater caution would be needed.

Louis and Conrad soon met and arranged to assemble their forces at the castle of Lopardium. The provision of markets began to decrease which caused the French to scavenge and pillage. While Odo's complaints about Greek duplicity in this respect might have had some foundation, it should also be borne in mind that three crusading armies were now in fairly close proximity and in early November it would have been harder to gather supplies from the land anyway. It seems that the main German army could barely reach Lopardium because they appealed to Louis for an escort to fight off continued Seljuk harassment. Count Ivo of Soissons was sent to assist. He duly drove the enemy away and Conrad's army reached safety.[55]

Louis and Conrad talked further and Odo quoted a long speech in which the German monarch lamented his overconfidence again, although he also stated that he had managed to preserve some of his wealth. He asked to remain with Louis's forces but wished to march at the centre of the troops rather than the more dangerous vanguard or rearguard. Louis agreed and suggested that Conrad should proceed with his own uncles, the count of Maurienne and the marquis of Montferrat, and with his other relatives – the bishop of Metz and Count Reynald of Bar.[56]

The crusaders reached the castle of Esseron in mid-November 1147. Their next planned destination was Philadelphia and, once again, two roads were available: one on the coast; the other, a more direct route that lacked supplies. Conrad was, naturally, highly attuned to the dangers of the latter option and made an impassioned speech that argued whatever the army's military strength, a lack of food would conquer it. Louis took heed of this and struggled along the coastal road, although it seems that some of his men took the faster route and arrived at their destination quickly and safely, an outcome that may have caused those who urged caution to lose credibility. From mid-November until late December the army made slow and painful progress, tiresomely fording rivers and streams and traversing mountains and valleys. Many pack animals died and supplies were hard to come by. The locals prudently hid their animals and stayed behind their town walls. As Odo conceded, this was partly on account of the 'insolence of our mob', although any food that was available was inevitably sold at inflated prices. Some of the crusaders took ships whenever they could find them, while a few of the most destitute deserted and stayed behind in the service of the Greeks.[57]

The crusaders passed through the classical cities of Smyrna and Pergamon and reached Ephesus, where Count Guy of Ponthieu died and was buried in the vestibule of the church of St John.[58] Messengers from Manuel arrived to warn that the Turks were gathering in huge numbers and to advise Louis to halt and seek safety in nearby Byzantine castles. While this appeared to be friendly and useful information, Manuel also complained about the losses inflicted by the crusaders on imperial lands and cautioned that he was unable to restrain his men from vengeance. The crusaders' behaviour had not, however, seemed to breach the terms of the treaty; perhaps this was a way for Manuel to suggest that his control over the people of Asia Minor was weak. In any case, Louis chose not to reply to his letters and prepared to move out of Ephesus along the nearby valley.[59] As we have seen earlier, it was at this point that Conrad was forced to remain behind because of his illness.

On Christmas Eve the first – brief – Turkish raids took place, but they were fought off. Heavy rains and snow fell over the holy days and around 28 December, worried about being trapped by floods, Louis gathered supplies and set out east along the Maeander valley – a wide plain with (mainly) gentle slopes leading down to the river that runs along its centre. The Turks were waiting; clearly they had prepared a strategy. Some held the mountain crags, some blocked the far side of the river (the crusaders needed to cross it sooner or later), and others still were down on the plain to harass the French directly. The customary tactics of quick feints, arrow-fire and swift retreat were used to prevent the crusaders bringing their enemy to battle. To counter this, Louis set up a careful order of march with well-armed knights at the front, rear and sides of his force and with the baggage-train and the wounded safely contained in the centre. In this simple yet effective formation the crusaders made slow, steady progress. On the second day of the march, however, the Turks made a serious mistake.

As the French searched for a place to ford the river, the Turks tried to catch them in a pincer movement. One group began to press from the rear while another, at a crossing point where the entrance to the water was easy but the exit steep – and therefore in principle hard for the Frankish horses to ascend – started to attack the vanguard. A small body of archers fired at the crusaders approaching by the river and then retreated. On this occasion the Turks seem to have been slow to retire because a rapid counter-charge led by Henry of Champagne, Thierry of Flanders and William of Maçon hammered after them and used their momentum to scale the side of the river. Plainly the Muslims had not expected such a fierce riposte and had misjudged the strength of a Frankish horse-charge. At the same time, Louis rode 'at top speed' into the enemy troops at the rear and again the Turks were caught out as the impact of the Frankish cavalry drove them from the field with notable casualties. William of Tyre recorded that much booty was secured as well.[60] The whole episode was given a lengthy treatment by Choniates: a somewhat strange choice on his part, given that he related little else about Louis's crusade.[61] Choniates offered a more romanticised and florid account of the battle, complete with a lengthy pre-engagement exhortation attributed to the king.While the strict accuracy of this speech is highly suspect it did demonstrate a clear understanding of the motives and ideas of the crusaders. The oration reminded the French of their sacrifices, of leaving their homes and their loved ones; it described the Turks as the enemies of Christ and talked of vengeance against them; it also held out the prospect of martyrdom and reminded the men of Christ's sacrifice for man. The speech closed with a rallying cry for 'this deed . . . [to] be eternally commemorated by our descendants', a sentiment that fitted well into the knightly culture of the crusaders. Niketas elaborated considerably on the Christians' success and wrote that the Turks were crushed 'like grapes pressed in wine vats', although his closing assertion that the French met with no further resistance was considerably wide of the mark.[62]

This battle is worth analysis because, given the failure of the German army and the subsequent defeats of the French, it is easy to imagine that the warriors of the Second Crusade were entirely ineffectual. The close formation established on the march along the Maeander valley and the rapid reactions of the Frankish cavalry showed that the crusaders could preserve their discipline and that – in the right conditions – they were perfectly capable of defeating the Turks. To emphasise the French victory there were even reports of the miraculous appearance of a white-clad knight, never seen before or since, who had struck the first blows in battle. Such a vision naturally recalled the presence of similar divine helpers so widely reported at the siege of Antioch in 1098. In spite of the heavy Turkish arrow-fire, the only French casualty of note was Milo of Nogent, who drowned while crossing the river.[63]

After the battle the crusaders passed by the small town of Antiochetta, another classical site that the locals had adapted to form a walled defensive outpost.[64] A day or so later, around 3 January 1148, the army reached Laodicea. This was the region where Byzantine authority was at its most tenuous; as Odo reported, 'the Turks and the Greeks together held the boundaries'. [65] The commander of the city was supposed to help guide Otto of Freising's contingent but he was alleged to have betrayed them and shared the spoils with the Turks. The Muslims summoned reinforcements and prepared to take revenge for their recent defeat while the crusaders hoped to march onwards. Aside from his now wholeheartedly anti-Greek rhetoric, Odo sounded a cautionary and reflective note when he commented that the French were 'careless because of our stubborn self-confidence'.[66] At Laodicea they faced a dilemma, however, because the southern coast lay within fifteen days' march away and the town had been closed, largely emptied of foodstuffs and evacuated. The king called a council to debate the next move and to consult with the nobles and bishops. Odo praised Louis for this humility, although it was perhaps a reflection of the monarch's inexperience and of the serious state of affairs that he needed to do this.

As the senior figures began to consider their situation a disturbing truth dawned on them; they could not devise a proper plan to see their way out of the predicament.[67] Because the locals had disappeared there was no food to seize or buy and the march ahead was barren. In light of the breakdown of their relationship with Manuel (and hence of any Byzantine provision of materials), the crusaders' complete reliance on being able to purchase or plunder supplies for their journey turned out to be very short-sighted. It seems that a combination of French indiscipline, which had alienated the indigenous population, and the mutual ill-feeling between the Greeks and the crusaders, plus the latter's arrogance – remember the sweeping dismissal of the emperor's messengers at Ephesus – had reduced their options to pillaging. The leadership had failed to anticipate such an eventuality and was now in a real quandary. The fact that the army was caught in deep winter in a mountainous, hostile region with only a few major settlements nearby was another factor that seems to have been ignored, although Odo recorded that apart from a few storms around Christmas the weather was unusually mild.[68]

The crusaders spent a day trying to find the locals and to persuade them to return and sell their wares, but even when these people were discovered they could not be induced to come back. Realising that nothing was going to change the French set out; they must have found some supplies, unless they still carried a little stock from earlier on. The Turks and, according to Odo, the Greeks shadowed them ahead and behind. This was now plainly Seljuk territory; the army passed by the site where Otto of Freising's men had been slaughtered – their blood was still visible on the stones and corpses lay unburied. Odo signalled a note of doom to his reader when he commented that, 'forewarned in vain', the king set out – probably on 5 or 6 January.[69] The crusaders were in battle order with the cavalry at the front, the baggage train and footsoldiers in the middle and Louis and the royal guard at the rear. It seems that on each day particular individuals were given responsibility for heading the various parts of the army; a system designed to share out the honour rather than to promote consistency or quality of leadership. A Poitevin, Geoffrey of Rancon, was in charge of the vanguard on the second day and he, together with Count Amadeus II of Maurienne, Louis's uncle, led the troops.

They faced Mount Cadmus, an obstacle of such size that it was decided, in consultation with the king and the nobles, to take an entire day to traverse it.[70] When, however, the vanguard began to ascend, they found the climb much easier than anticipated and also unopposed by the Turks. In consequence, they ignored their orders and kept going past the summit and down the other side where they pitched camp. According to William of Tyre the guides suggested that the far side offered a better place to rest.[71] But, crucially, they did not send anyone back to explain this to their colleagues, when in fact they had become completely separated from the baggage train in the middle of the army. Because the baggage-train believed the vanguard was going to stop on, or before, the summit, they chose to lag behind, thinking – not unreasonably – it would be possible to catch up by nightfall.[72] The rearguard had not actually set out at all; it was still camped a long way behind the pack-horses and did not intend to cross the mountain until the following day. To all intents and purposes, the most vulnerable section of the force was now unprotected – a terrible mistake and one that the Turks quickly capitalised upon. Their troops closed in on the baggage train; some of the attackers seized the peak of the mountain and others came in from the sides. To a modern reader, the idea that an army could become so separated seems faintly ludicrous; it should be remembered, however, that the crusaders needed hundreds of carts to transport food and equipment along (probably) single-track roads, and these, added to the thousands of troops, would have taken up at least six miles.[73] With this in mind, the notion of being out of sight of one's comrades makes more sense.

Odo himself was in the central part of the army and he transmits a feeling of the gathering panic to his audience.[74] It seems that the higher reaches of the path were quite narrow, with a severe drop to the valley below. There must have been thousands of people in this section, fearful of the sheer cliff edges and trying to manage frightened pack animals. A crowd leaving a modern sporting event or a concert through a narrow opening can easily start pushing and shoving as it gets congested and tense. This is what happened there. As people became agitated the march ground to a halt – which increased the distance to the vanguard even further. The rocks and stones of the path were slippery and pack-horses began to topple from the cliffs; in the rising panic some began to climb away from the path to seek their own routes, only to stumble to their doom. The Turks, of course, had watched the crusaders slow down and, with both the enemy vanguard and rearguard out of sight, they closed in, killing the defenceless westerners or causing them to plummet to their deaths. Odo was sent back to the royal camp to alert the king to the situation; presumably the rearguard was camped too far away to witness the massacre on the mountain.

The king was horrified and he gathered the royal escort as quickly as possible to rush to the aid of his colleagues. Odo described a valiant leader, careless of his own safety and even though outnumbered, fighting with all his heart – and God's protection – to free his people.[75] Perhaps less impressive is

Odo's description of Louis's escape. At one point he was forced to use a (divinely provided) tree root to climb a rock and then fend off the enemy; fortunately they did not recognise him as anyone important and soon left him alone.[76] William of Tyre, however, was distinctly uncomplimentary and suggested that the king survived by chance rather than by his own efforts.[77] On this occasion the topography neutralised most of the crusaders' military strengths. They were unable to charge their enemies to any great effect and many of their horses were killed; in contrast the Turks could simply hide behind rocks and trees and pick the Christians off with their arrows. The sheer numbers of Turks threatened to sweep away the mail-clad knights, but Louis's efforts managed to create a breathing space for most of the baggage train to struggle towards the peak of the mountain. Many of the royal guard, however, were cornered and, in spite of killing numerous Turks, were slain and, as Odo recorded, won the martyr's crown.[78]

Finally, nightfall brought some relief. Louis found a horse to ride and caught up with the baggage-train. Men from the vanguard had learned of the disaster and came to meet him, relieved that he had appeared yet sorrowful at the absence of so many of their comrades. Throughout the night, individuals straggled into the camp, joyful recognition of survivors mingled with stories of the loss of others. Relatives, friends and wives waited and hoped for good news, but many senior nobles had perished, including Count William of Warenne, Everard of Breteuil, Manasses of Bulles, Gautier of Montjay, Reynald of Tours and Itiers of Meingnac.[79] Louis himself wrote to Suger and told him of the defeat, stating that he would send a more complete casualty list at a later date.[80] Several sources claimed that Geoffrey of Rancon was responsible for the calamity because he had disobeyed Louis's orders and carried on over the mountain. There were calls for summary justice: a hanging. Amadeus of Maurienne was also identified as responsible, but because he was Louis's uncle he could not be executed; nor therefore, by association, could Geoffrey.[81]

To the Turks, coming so soon after their defeat of the two German armies, this victory was another massive boost to their morale. William of Tyre commented wearily: 'That day the glorious reputation of the Franks was lost through a misfortune most fatal and disastrous for the Christians; their valour, up to this time formidable to the nations, was crushed to the earth. Henceforth, it was as a mockery in the eyes of those unclean races to whom it had formerly been a terror'.[82]

The French had been far too casual in their order of march and now, belatedly, they addressed the issue and tightened their formation. With twelve days to go to the coast, food was in ever shorter supply, particularly the grain and the grass for the horses. The Turks could see the crusaders' weakness and harassed them ever more intensely; now, however, the French held firm. Most effective of all in resisting were the Knights Templar who had originally contributed a contingent of perhaps 130 men at Paris in April 1147.[83] Louis made a remarkable decision for a king and commander: he could see the need for discipline and so, with the agreement of all, he encouraged everyone to establish common fraternity with the Templars. This was unprecedented; thousands of laymen – albeit already travelling under a vow – temporarily associated themselves with a religious order. They swore to obey the officers appointed to them by the Templars and promised not to flee the field of battle. The knights were divided into groups of fifty and given a Templar commander. Some basic rules were set out which showed the Templars' experience of fighting the Turks in the East, as well as some fundamental tenets of military practice. The crusaders were instructed not to fall for the Turks' feigned retreat, to wait until ordered to counter-charge and then to withdraw when told. They were also taught how to preserve strict formation on the march, while those nobles who had lost their horses were stationed at the rear to oppose the enemy with bows. Louis was theoretically subject to these ordinances too, but Odo wrote that no one dared to issue all but the most basic commands concerning good order.[84] It was astonishing that a king should hand over leadership of an army. This incredible gesture demonstrated several things. First, the crusaders had been hugely shaken by their defeat; perhaps some had muttered about the lack of discipline instilled by the hierarchy. Secondly, Louis himself was plainly unable to impose proper order on his senior nobles. Using the Templars might have been a way to surmount this, albeit with considerable cost to his personal standing. John of Salisbury wrote, rather caustically, that the French army had 'neither military discipline, nor a strong hand to dispense justice and correct faults'. This is a contemporary view of the king's weak leadership.[85] One cannot imagine other crusading monarchs, such as Richard the Lionheart, allowing their men to lose formation in such a way, let alone contemplating surrendering their authority. Louis's great-grandson, Louis IX, led an expedition to Egypt which was largely undone by the reckless charge of Robert of Artois at Mansourah (1250) but the king's overall command was never in question.[86] Thirdly, the incident shows just how soon after their foundation the Templars had become a highly respected fighting unit.

The next stage of the march saw several difficult moments, such as the crossing of two rivers with very muddy banks and the heavy defeat of a Turkish force that held a strategic position. Throughout these engagements the crusaders worked closely together and followed the commands of their leaders. With their new discipline they achieved a total of four victories; evidently the Turks were not invincible and the crusaders were not entirely powerless. Food remained a serious problem, however. The indigenous population and the Seljuk commanders had agreed to execute an 'environmentally friendly' form of scorched-earth policy. They gathered all the cattle and sheep from the surrounding area to graze the land that lay ahead of the Christians. Thus they denied the crusaders' horses grass, although the French rescued something from the situation by using dead horses as a food supply. The loss of so many horses meant that fewer provisions, clothing, tents and arms could be carried and these objects had to be abandoned or destroyed en route; the military capability of the surviving troops was therefore curtailed, albeit in ways that could be replaced once more friendly lands were reached.

Around 20 January 1148 the crusaders struggled into Adalia on the southern coast of Asia Minor. This was a Byzantine port, although it was surrounded by Turkish-controlled lands and reported to pay tribute to them too.[87] It had taken the French over three months to march there from Constantinople, a slow rate of progress. As the army settled down, the imperial representative required the nobles to reconfirm their oaths to Manuel in order to secure market privileges; the Greeks still seemed highly distrustful of the crusaders' continued good faith. Markets did duly appear, although the prices were said to be grossly inflated; for the horses, however, there was little grain from the barren local soil and the grasslands further afield were guarded by the enemy. Louis tried to persuade his nobles to fight, but they pointed out that some of them had no money to buy horses, or those who still had the funds could find no steed to purchase. A more practical solution was put forward – to make the three-day voyage from Adalia to Antioch rather than the forty-day march along a difficult coastline, harassed by Turks. The Greeks were pleased to collect a fleet to facilitate this – probably happy at the prospect of getting rid of the crusaders as fast as possible.[88]

Louis then made a most magnanimous speech in which he tried to propose that the weakest of the French should take the fleet and that he and his knights should – as they had been so urged by Pope Eugenius – follow in the footsteps of their fathers and gain honour on earth and glory in heaven. The nobles' answer to his fine words revealed a sharp insight into the crusaders' understanding of their predicament. The strict parallel to the First Crusade was politely broken down and it was pointed out that their predecessors had started fighting the Turks almost immediately, and kept themselves rich by capturing fortresses and cities en route. By contrast, it was suggested that because the army of the Second Crusade had encountered the Greeks (whom they had mistakenly spared) and spent all their money, they had become sluggish and idle. As France has demonstrated, the armies of the First Crusade became a well-honed fighting force through the series of battles, skirmishes and sieges they had experienced.[89] Except for the small group that had rescued some of the retreating German crusaders, Louis's men had marched for months without combat and only encountered the Turks for the first time at Ephesus in late December. Of course, engaging in warfare carried the obvious risk of casualties; yet the point made in Odo's text does parallel France's idea neatly enough. The slack discipline shown on Mount Cadmus was a result of complacency. The point about money is also interesting. From Nicaea onwards the First Crusaders had gathered booty; while this source of income might have dried up from time to time, as long as it was acquired periodically it could provide funding and supplies. This is not to say that the First Crusaders were well fed throughout their campaign – the *Gesta Francorum* provides graphic testimony that they were not – but they did forage to good effect. By contrast, their successors were simply spending money and relying on the Greeks. Once their relationship with Byzantium began to falter, they faced severe difficulties, given the inflated prices they had to pay and the seemingly limited resources with which they had set out (remember Louis's letter to Suger from Hungary, bemoaning a lack of funds).

Out of respect for the king, his nobles indicated that they would march along the coast if sufficient horses could be found. These were not available and so the barons urged the king to take ship.[90] Bad weather delayed the arrival of the vessels and curtailed the possibility of setting out for several weeks. In the interim, food became increasingly scarce – a situation exacerbated by the snowy conditions – and the price of goods rocketed. The crusaders fought off a Turkish attack, again with the help of the Templars, a contingent who had managed to keep their horses alive, perhaps because their knights were among the better financed crusaders. When the Greeks finally provided shipping it was, inevitably, at a high cost, but the French had little choice. Odo reflected: 'I believe we paid more dearly for our respite in this town than we did for all the hardships on the journey'.[91] He also justified the crusaders' failure to capture Adalia by citing its formidable defences, the ongoing hostilities of the local Turks and Louis's distaste for seizing the city by treachery. He might also have added that that would have broken the oath to Manuel, although many of his colleagues could have regarded the breach as redundant by this point. As Odo lamented, 'how will a just judge, either God or man, spare the Greek emperor, who by cunning cruelty killed so many Christians in both the German and French armies?'[92]

As he prepared to depart Louis tried to make provision for the poor who were to march along the coast. He gave 500 marks to the local commander to guide and protect them on their journey as far as Tarsus and to bring the weak and invalided into Adalia to recover. He also handed over as many horses as could be found and, to give a modicum of reassurance to his people, he left behind Count Thierry of Flanders and Archibald of Bourbon, to try to ensure that these measures were enacted. Louis then embarked for Antioch, seemingly the first of the French to leave, and he arrived there after a three-day voyage on 19 March. The remainder of the army continued to face attacks from the Turks whom Odo believed were acting in collusion with the Greeks. The Adalians also reneged on their agreement to provide an escort for the crusaders, although they were allowed to remain behind the fortress wall and have a market. It seems that the plight of these men was acute: some were killed by Turkish arrow-fire, many more starved to death or died of disease from the nearby corpses. One group set out eastwards but was routed.

Odo provided one final story to complete his account of the crusade. It was a strange episode and may well have been intended to cast a last slur on the Greeks, but is interesting nonetheless. He claimed that after this latest defeat of the footsoldiers, the Turks took pity on the survivors and gave them money; yet the Byzantines beat the French and put the strongest of them into forced labour. So compassionate were the Turks, and so loathsome were the Greeks that 'we have heard more than three thousand young men went with [them]'. Odo added that these men were not even compelled to deny their faith! By contrast, God visited divine punishment on the citizenry because they too succumbed to the illnesses that had afflicted the crusaders.[93]

Odo ended his epistolary narrative here, assuring Abbot Suger that the king had arrived safely in Antioch in spite of some of his vessels suffering shipwreck in storms. Odo himself had taken three weeks to make a voyage that the king accomplished in three days. Historians have discussed why the text finished there; perhaps it was an appropriate moment to pause and write an account of the crusade thus far. The autograph manuscript does not survive and the only extant version is a twelfth-century copy made by the monks of Clairvaux.[94] One is tempted to suggest that Odo made notes en route and then collated them, either at Antioch in the spring of 1148 or in the kingdom of Jerusalem in the early summer. Given the controversial events that involved Queen Eleanor at Antioch it is understandable that he chose to end his text before he needed to discuss this incident. There is no sense of foreboding about the siege of Damascus, except for the perplexing line 'the flowers of France withered before they could bear fruit in Damascus'; but Berry has interpreted this line as revealing knowledge of the forthcoming attack on the city rather than as a cryptic comment on the outcome of that campaign. This again puts the date of composition in the late spring or early summer of 1148.[95]

At this point, setting aside the persuasive tone of Odo of Deuil, it is worth reviewing the Greeks' responsibility for the French defeat.[96] We have seen that the French posed a serious threat to Constantinople and that Manuel was deeply troubled at the possibility of their joining forces with the Sicilians.

Once over the Bosphorus, the emperor had to consider the wider strategic picture. The French supplied themselves with food by foraging the land, but during their march through Byzantine territory they were subject to hostility from the inhabitants and attacks from the Seljuks. In some senses this was inevitable. On the one hand, as Odo noted, the crusaders marched along the boundary between Christian and Muslim territory; the Seljuks were bound to harass their enemies as much as possible.[97] On the other hand, the indigenous Greek population may have felt an obligation to join in so as to conciliate the Seljuks: the crusaders would pass by but the Turks would remain and they could not afford to alienate them. The fact that this was a highly porous frontier meant the Byzantines could not guarantee the crusaders' safety. The likelihood that the imperial army was distracted by the activities of the Sicilians to the west cannot have helped the crusaders' hopes of support from Constantinople either. Manuel was therefore both disinclined and less able to send an escort with the French; in any case, to do so would bring him into conflict with the Seljuks and contravene his recent treaty with them. There is even evidence that the Turks were encouraged to attack the crusaders. This suggestion is particularly compelling because the source of the information is the Byzantine writer Niketas Choniates: 'The emperor's purpose was neither in doubt nor was it cast in the shadow of the curtain of falsehood . . . he commanded others to inflict such harm that these things should be indelible memorials for posterity, deterrents against attacking the Romans [i.e. the crusaders].'[98] A further reason why Manuel behaved in this way was offered by Michael the Syrian, the Jacobite patriarch who wrote in the late twelfth century: 'The emperor of the Greeks knew that after having crossed the sea and established their influence, they [the crusaders] would not give it up to the empire of the Greeks and therefore he worked in concert with the Turks. He hindered them over a period of two years by a variety of schemes.'[99] As we will see shortly, Raymond of Antioch aimed to use the Second Crusade to augment his power in northern Syria. If he managed to do this, Manuel would lose his recently imposed overlordship on the principality. While the emperor had less reason to be troubled by the approach of the Germans, if he could compromise the French army it would prevent them from offering assistance to Raymond and help the Greeks to preserve their authority over Antioch. A desire to control the patriarchal city had done much to steer Byzantine relations with crusaders and settlers since the time of the First Crusade. As Kinnamos wrote when Manuel received a hostile Antiochene embassy in 1144: 'why did you not earlier yield Antioch to the Romans . . . depart from what does not belong to you. I would increase, not diminish what came into my hands from my father.'[100] Manuel's priority – regardless of shared faith – was always to protect the interests of Byzantium.

CHAPTER 11

THE CRUSADE AT ANTIOCH AND THE SIEGE OF DAMASCUS

Louis and the surviving French nobles arrived at Antioch in March 1148. They had finally reached friendly territory and were close to the nominal goal of the crusade; first it was necessary to recover from their ordeal in Asia Minor, to take stock of their situation and to form a working relationship with the Franks of the Latin East. It was during the three-month period of the French stay in northern Syria that the most infamous episode of the Second Crusade did – or did not – occur: the alleged affair between Prince Raymond and Queen Eleanor. Before discussing this, it is more important to set out how the presence of the Second Crusade might have impacted upon the strategic situation in northern Syria, particularly from the perspective of the Antiochenes.

William of Tyre gave a valuable insight into Raymond's thinking when he related how eagerly the prince waited for the crusade's arrival. It seems that as soon as he heard of the expedition Raymond saw a real opportunity to increase the power of his principality. He sent fine presents and treasures to France to draw the crusaders towards him; furthermore, the fact that he was Queen Eleanor's uncle meant that he had an especially close tie to the royal house and he hoped that this would also count in his favour. After the exhausted crusaders landed at the port of St. Simeon the prince and all his nobles gathered together to give them a splendid welcome to Antioch itself. Notwithstanding their losses, the appearance of a Western army was a moment of huge importance to the Antiochenes. Raymond and his officials escorted the procession into the city where the clergy and people greeted the crusaders with all honour. Once such formalities were over, the prince continued to show the king and his nobles the greatest generosity; it is even possible that the *Chansons des Chétifs*, an epic poem in Old French based on events on the People's Crusade, was composed for this occasion.[1] Leaving aside the sense of shared kinship, there was a definite agenda behind Raymond's actions. William outlined his aims: 'he felt a lively hope that with the assistance of the king and his troops he would be able to subjugate the neighbouring cities, namely Aleppo, Shaizar and several others. Nor would this hope have been futile could he have induced the king and his chief men to undertake the work.'[2] In spite of the Seljuk victories in Asia Minor, the Syrian Muslims were still concerned by the advent of the crusade.[3]

The details of Raymond's plan are intriguing, not least because of their remarkable reflection of the terms of his 1137 submission to John Comnenus. The emperor had besieged Antioch and compelled the prince to swear fealty to him and grant him free access to the city. If, however, John peacefully restored 'Aleppo, Shaizar, Hama and Homs to the prince . . . Raymond was to rest content with these cities and without contest give back to the emperor the city of Antioch to be held by right of ownership'.[4] If John took these cities and their lands, Raymond and his successors would hold them in perpetuity as a Byzantine fief. Antioch had, of course, been part of the Greek Empire from 1032 until 1084 and Emperor Alexius felt that the principality should have been returned to him after the conquest of the First Crusade.

Raymond's attitude towards Byzantium was a combination of resentment and hostility, borne out of a determination to preserve the independence of his land and the dominance of the Catholic Church. He did not wish to become part of the Byzantine Empire and he did not want an Orthodox patriarch in his city. Raymond had only agreed to the 1137 terms when faced with a siege of Antioch; his serial attempts to frustrate Greek plans to conquer his principality, or at least to bring him to heel and to install an Orthodox patriarch, were clear evidence of his attitude. As we have seen earlier, it was only the dispatch of a combined land and sea force in 1145 that cowed him and forced him to travel to Constantinople in person and humble himself in front of Emperor Manuel. The arrival of the Second Crusade, however, changed the situation dramatically. If, as William of Tyre indicated, the prince could take Aleppo and Shaizar with the help of the crusaders, then the treaty with the Greeks would be obviated. The Byzantines could no longer give him these cities and exchange Antioch in return. Raymond's relative power in the region would be dramatically increased and he could contemplate another attempt to resist or throw off Manuel's overlordship; at the very least, his tenure of Antioch would be far more secure. We might also note that Shaizar had almost surrendered to the combined Byzantine and Antiochene forces in May 1138 (the town fell, but the citadel held out), which is a further indication that its capture was a realistic proposition.[5]

This, surely, was the reasoning that underlay his desperate attempts to gain the favour of the French. It must also be remembered that the original aim of the crusade was to recapture Edessa – something that would be more likely to happen with the seizure of Aleppo beforehand. Bearing in mind the antipathy between Raymond and Count Joscelin II prior to the fall of Edessa, it is also possible that the prince was unenthusiastic about an effort to recover the city on behalf of someone whom he disliked anyway.[6]

Raymond discussed his ideas with Louis in private, then brought them before a full assembly of the French and Antiochene nobles. He set out how the campaign would work and how it would bring fame and renown to the crusaders; this council probably took place in mid-May 1148.[7] To Raymond's horror, however, the plan was rejected. The only explanation given by William of Tyre was that Louis 'ardently desired to go to Jerusalem to fulfil his vows'.[8] It was almost certainly true that the king's intense personal piety drew him towards Jerusalem; his later resolution to spend a year in the Holy Land after the siege of Damascus was to reveal his devotion to the sacred sites. Yet this seems an unsatisfactory answer when set against the wider spectrum of a large military campaign and the strategic needs of his fellow-Christians in the Levant. Did he need to rush southwards to Jerusalem immediately and create the need for a 600-mile round-trip back to Antioch? His decision has been much debated by historians; a number of ideas have been put forward to try to understand this controversial move which seemed so completely counter to the Antiochene prince's expectations.[9]

The combined effect of the losses suffered by the French in Asia Minor and of the presence, or imminent landing, of Conrad at Acre may have drawn Louis southwards. If the German monarch, as the senior western ruler, was in the kingdom of Jerusalem, Louis may have felt it necessary to join him. There is also the possibility that Conrad's own evolving agenda for the crusade could have influenced his decision (see below, pp. 213–14). Besides, the French ruler was suffering continued financial woes. Two letters from his stay in Antioch survive and both make reference to this problem; the first repeated his earlier requests for Suger to send him money; the second was addressed to the abbot, to Raoul of Vermandois, and to Archbishop Samson of Rheims, and stated that he had sent the master of the Templars, Everard of Barres, to Acre to arrange a loan for him. Later in the year, Louis ordered his regents to repay the Templars and noted that it was only thanks to the Order that he had been able to continue on the expedition, but the Templars were now close to bankruptcy. He asked Suger to find 2,000 silver marks and Raoul of Vermandois 30,000 livres of Paris to give back to the Order.[10] Barber has noted that by 1170 the likely demesne revenues for the Capetians amounted to 60,000 livres per annum which gives some sense of the sums borrowed by the king.[11] Hence, Louis may have been struggling to afford a campaign at this moment in time. Yet the anger which Raymond showed towards him suggests that the king indicated he had no intention of returning to fight in the north. The rupture between the two men was deep; if Louis had simply wanted to go south, meet Conrad, return to Antioch in a couple of months and then to campaign, it seems unlikely that the prince would have broken with him so completely.

Part of the explanation may lie with the condition of Edessa. In between the original call for the crusade and the expedition's arrival in the Latin East the local population had attempted to recapture the city. In October 1146 the Armenians rose in revolt to restore Count Joscelin, but the rebellion was crushed, the ringleaders executed and the walls of the citadel damaged beyond repair; many other Christians were slaughtered or sold into slavery.[12] Michael the Syrian wrote: 'Edessa was deserted of life: an appalling vision, enveloped in a black cloud, drunk with blood, infected by the cadavers of its sons and daughters! Vampires and other savage beasts were running and coming into the city at night to feed themselves on the flesh of the massacred people.'[13]

It has been argued, logically enough, that Louis learned of this and realised there was no point in such a campaign because the original target of the crusade was no longer viable.[14] Such a turn of events would not, however, prevent an assault on Aleppo, for example. In September 1146 Zengi had been murdered. His successor in Aleppo, Nur ad-Din, posed probably the greatest threat to the Latin hold on the Levant, and for this reason it would have made strategic sense for the crusaders to take him on. Yet this option appears to have been ignored. One other line of reasoning may, however, cast some light on Louis's decision. Notwithstanding Raymond's evident wish to escape Byzantine overlordship, he was, as the French crusaders were well aware, a vassal of the emperor.[15] Given that the king explicitly cast blame on Manuel for his recent troubles, the idea of increasing the lands of a man subject to the Greeks – and thereby, indirectly, benefiting the Byzantines themselves – must have been unpalatable to Louis.[16] The Greeks' wish to recover as much of their Empire as possible – even through the hands of the crusaders – was made clear in Manuel's letter to the pope in March 1147.[17] While Raymond could have hoped to downplay this situation and, as suggested earlier, possibly to cast it aside, there were no guarantees that he would succeed. Thus the French refused to fight in the north and the prince's plans were shattered. William of Tyre could have omitted this from his description of the Second Crusade because, at the time he was writing, in the 1170s, Jerusalem was subject to Greek overlordship and he may not have wished to denigrate such a position.

With Louis having made up his mind, Raymond became hostile to the king. Herein lies the root of the legendary *cause célèbre* of the crusade – the alleged relationship between Queen Eleanor and her uncle.[18] The principal evidence for this was provided by William of Tyre and John of Salisbury. William, as we saw, wrote several decades later; he was in France at the time of the crusade and knew of the royal divorce of 1152. He had, however, by his own statements, researched the events of the Second Crusade quite closely.[19] John was present at the papal court in Tusculum in mid-1149 when Louis and Eleanor visited Eugenius on their way home, although his description of these events in his *Historia Pontificalis* probably dated from 1164.[20] William wrote that once Prince Raymond learned of the king's decision to march south he sought revenge and decided to steal Eleanor from him; the queen, 'a foolish woman', agreed to the plan and 'contrary to her royal dignity she disregarded her marriage vows and was unfaithful to her husband'. The author coloured his comments by the phrase 'her conduct before and after this time showed her to be far from circumspect', which may reflect hindsight.[21] John indicated that 'the attentions paid by the prince to the queen, and his constant, indeed almost continuous, conversation with her aroused the king's suspicions'.[22] Close conversation between Raymond and Eleanor was quite likely given their family ties and the fact that, as fellow-Poitevins – and perhaps unlike the king – they could communicate in Occitan. Speaking the tongue of their shared homeland may well have been a pleasant experience, although to outsiders a 'secret' language might arouse suspicion.

John of Salisbury wrote that Eleanor expressed a desire to remain in Antioch when the king went southwards and Raymond was keen to support her wish. When Louis declined, the queen allegedly tried to lay the grounds for a separation and raised the known fact that they were related in the fourth and fifth degrees, that is, within the banned range of consanguinity.[23] Louis was said to have been prepared to agree to a divorce had his advisors concurred. John then mentioned the testimonial of a knight-eunuch in the royal service whom the queen strongly disliked. This man told the king that 'guilt under kinship's guise could lie concealed' and it would be of great shame if, on top of the military disasters, Louis lost his wife too. John qualified the eunuch's evidence thus: 'so he argued, either because he hated the queen or because he really believed it, moved perchance by widespread rumour'.[24] The king there-fore, forced Eleanor to come with him and they left for Jerusalem. William of Tyre related that once Louis discovered these intrigues he secretly left Antioch; 'his coming had been attended with glory . . . and his departure was ignominious'.[25]

The later comment ascribed to Eleanor that Louis was 'more monk than man' added a whiff of sexual innuendo to the situation, with its suggestion that the king was an unsatisfactory lover, although the royal couple were evidently capable of producing children because they already had a daughter. More pragmatically, it could be suggested that so important was the preserva-tion of the royal bloodline that neither Eleanor nor Raymond would have risked an affair. The nature of medieval courts, with the presence of countless servants, would have made such liaisons difficult – although not, of course, impossible.

The problem with this entire episode is one of separating fact from rumour. Both William and John are regarded as fairly sober historians, not especially given to groundless gossip but, as we have seen, some questions about their statements do arise. The most contemporaneous piece of information – and one often ignored by historians – is a letter of Abbot Suger from 1149 in which he wrote: 'Concerning the queen your wife, we venture to congratulate you, if we may, upon the extent to which you suppress your anger, if there be anger, until with God's will you return to your own kingdom and see to these matters and others.'[26] This certainly ties in with the reference to rumours made by John of Salisbury. In short, while the truth is unlikely to emerge, the letter from Suger is compelling evidence that speculation about Eleanor's behaviour undoubtedly enjoyed wide circulation at the time of the crusade; that Suger had heard something of this in France and had written back to the king mentioning it confirms the point. Such innuendo obviously did much to poison the atmosphere among the crusaders and the Antiochenes and destroyed the possibility of any campaigning in northern Syria. William of Tyre offered a Levantine analysis of the episode when he pointedly stated that some believed Louis got what he deserved when he declined to help Raymond after receiving such (initial) kindness from him. William also restated the opinion that, 'if the king would have devoted himself to that work, one or more of the above-named cities might easily have been taken'.[27] From the settlers' perspective, therefore, the crusade had blundered and missed a golden opportunity to enhance the strength of the Christians in the East.

King Conrad spent the early months of 1148 in Constantinople where he recovered his health after the trauma of the march into Asia Minor. At one point he seemed to be on the verge of death but a few weeks at the imperial court refreshed the king before he resumed his holy endeavours.[28] With the crusade no longer representing a threat to Constantinople and out of a desire to secure the German ruler's support for a counter-attack on the Sicilians, Manuel's treatment of Conrad was far more cordial than that offered during the latter's previous visit to Constantinople. It is likely that the monarchs agreed, in principle at least, to an alliance against Roger of Sicily, while good relations were cemented further by the marriage of the emperor's niece, Theodora, to Conrad's brother, Henry of Austria.[29] In February 1148 the king wrote to Wibald of Stavelot to praise the emperor's kindness towards him and to say that he intended to leave for Jerusalem on 7 March, to gather a new army there over Easter and then proceed to Edessa, as originally planned.[30] John Kinnamos and William of Tyre recorded that Manuel gave Conrad money, fine gifts and a fleet of triremes to transport him to the Holy Land.[31] The *Annales Herbipolenses* added that the emperor provided 2,000 finely equipped horses.[32]

It was a rough voyage and Otto of Freising claimed that some men suffered shipwreck; in early April the scattered fleet arrived in several ports, including Acre, Tyre and Sidon. The first groups to land entered Jerusalem on Palm Sunday, celebrated the Passion and the Resurrection and then, as all pilgrims did, went around the holy sites. The king arrived slightly later; he reached Acre in early April 1148 (Easter fell on 11 April), and celebrated the festival there before he journeyed on to Jerusalem in the company of many of his senior nobles and churchmen. From the perspective of the Latin settlers, the presence of the most powerful monarch in the Latin West was a cause for great delight. King Baldwin III, Patriarch Fulcher of Jerusalem and the entire populace greeted him outside the city and escorted him inside to the sound of chants and hymns.[33]

The king lodged in the palace of the Templars – formerly the royal palace – a sign that the other western monarch on the crusade was also forming close ties with the nascent Order.[34] The king then went on a pilgrimage through Samaria and Galilee. As Hiestand has indicated, Conrad was the only major western monarch to visit the Holy Land twice, although his first pilgrimage in 1124 took place many years prior to his coronation. It may have been during his journey northwards, in the early summer of 1148 that Conrad made a gift of privileges to the monastery of St Martin at Mount Tabor. Furthermore, Hiestand demonstrates that around this time the king began to augment his title of *rex Romanorum* with the additional qualification *Augustus*, which assumed strong imperial connotations. This step could have been designed to reinforce his position as the most important Catholic monarch present in the region, ahead of Louis and Baldwin, and to pre-empt his (theoretically) forth-coming imperial coronation.[35] It may also have represented an attempt to enhance Conrad's status in relation to Manuel Comnenus – a sensitive issue, alluded to by William of Tyre.[36]

Of particular interest at this stage is a comment from the eyewitness source Otto of Freising. Otto wrote that around this time (May 1148) Conrad made an agreement with Baldwin, Fulcher and the Templars to lead an army against Damascus in July. Clearly this pre-dated the crusaders' major strategic council at Palmarea in late June (the event crusade historians tend to focus on) but it must have influenced that discussion. Conrad's incli-nation towards an attack on Damascus was a radical change from his February statement that he wished to go to Edessa. As noted in the analysis of King Louis's decision not to campaign in northern Syria, the news of the massive damage to the fabric of Edessa and the slaughter of the Christian inhabitants may have contributed towards this new approach. One might also speculate that Conrad's stay in Constantinople had exerted an effect too. Otto of Freising wrote that once he reached the Levant the king spent substantial sums of money to retain knights in his service and to gather 'what troops he could by a lavish expenditure'.[37] Given that a significant proportion of the money involved was given to him by Manuel before he left, the king may have felt uneasy about spending it on an expedition in the north. We have seen that this would probably have benefited Raymond of Antioch and – given his track record – might have encouraged the prince to challenge Byzantine overlordship. With his newfound Greek 'sponsorship', marriage ties and shared enmity towards King Roger, Conrad was perhaps inclined – or before he left Constantinople, maybe he was persuaded or advised – to ignore Edessa and fight in the Holy Land. Furthermore, the German must have discussed the possibility of co-operation against the Sicilians, something that would be formalised with the Treaty of Thessalonika on his journey home. Again, involvement with Antioch might have compromised this. With regard to hiring troops, it seems that after the disasters in Asia Minor, the German army was reduced in strength. Most of the losses were, however, amongst the footsoldiers; it also appears that a few crusaders had departed for home in the immediate aftermath of these events.[38] The core of the German nobility survived, although Conrad felt that his force needed to be bolstered to make a contribution commensurate with his status as the senior western monarch. Once he had made the pact with Baldwin, Fulcher and the Templars, the Germans then based themselves at Acre, to await the arrival of the French.

The crusaders suffered another serious setback around this time with the death of Count Alphonse-Jordan of Toulouse. This important nobleman had, for practical reasons, sailed from southern France to the Levant and he landed at Acre in April. He was a member of one of the great crusading dynasties. His father, Count Raymond, was a leader of the First Crusade and the founder of the county of Tripoli; Alphonse himself had been born at the siege of Mount Pilgrim in 1104. The count had been present at Vézelay in March 1146, which was a sign of his wholehearted commitment to the Second Crusade, and he is likely to have brought a respectable contingent of knights with him from Toulouse. When he described the arrival of the Franks the contemporary Damascene writer, Ibn al-Qalanisi, mentioned only King Conrad and Count Alphonse by name, which suggests that the latter's presence was perceived as significant by the local Muslims.[39] Unfortunately, at Caesarea he became acutely ill and died. Throughout the crusading period numerous western nobles fell sick soon after they reached the Holy Land, but the fact that Alphonse had a stronger claim to the county of Tripoli than the present ruler, Raymond II – grandson to the old count's bastard son, Bertrand – led many to suspect poison, a plot which possibly involved Queen Melisende, too. In addition to the fact that this event deprived the crusade of an important figure, the subsequent controversy seems to have caused Count Raymond II to opt out of any involvement in the campaign as well.[40]

The news of the rift between Louis and Prince Raymond of Antioch quickly reached Jerusalem. The nobility saw a golden opportunity before them; earlier on they had genuinely expected the king to fight in northern Syria. While the recovery of Edessa or, more seriously, the capture of Aleppo could benefit all the Christians in the East, a foray against either Damascus or Ascalon would be of greater immediate advantage to Jerusalem. By 1148, the situation in the Levant had changed. When the crusade was first launched, relations between Jerusalem and Damascus had been good. Since then, as we will see in detail below, the atmosphere had become hostile, and Edessa no longer seemed worth retaking. For these reasons it was now far more important to the nobles of Jerusalem that the crusade should be pursued in the south. The fact that Conrad's own agenda also inclined him towards a campaign against Damascus rather than Aleppo or Edessa was a neat coincidence of interests, which led to the agreement recorded by Otto of Freising above. William of Tyre's comments on the attempt to lure Louis southwards offer a revealing insight into the rivalry between the four Latin States of Edessa, Antioch, Tripoli and Jerusalem:

> the great and powerful lords of these lands had cherished the hope that through the assistance of [the crusaders] they might be able to enlarge their own territories and extend their boundaries immensely. All had powerful enemies whose hated cities, so near their own territories, they longed to add to their own domains . . . Accordingly, each one, intent on anticipating the others, sent messengers with gifts and invitations to the two monarchs.[41]

Any sense of the greater overall security of a Christian presence in the Levant was evidently lost behind the more immediate demands of regional priorities. As chancellor of the kingdom, William – naturally – argued that 'the hopes of the king and people of Jerusalem seemed most likely to be realised', contradicting his earlier insistence that Aleppo and Shaizar could have been captured by the crusade. On hearing of the breach with Raymond, the leading men of Jerusalem feared that the close family ties between the prince and Queen Eleanor might still keep him in the north. Patriarch Fulcher was sent to capitalise on the situation and he duly convinced the king to continue on from Tripoli to Jerusalem. If Fulcher carried news of Conrad's arrangement concerning an attack on Damascus, the French king could have been even more inclined to join forces in the south. Louis was then greeted with great honour and delight and, to the accompaniment of hymns, he and his fellow French crusaders were escorted into the holy city, probably in early June.[42]

With the two main crusading armies together in the Levant for the first time, a discussion on their next move was needed. A general assembly was called to the town of Palmarea near Acre for the feast of St John the Baptist, on 24 June 1148.[43] This was a magnificent occasion – it was a meeting of the most important individuals yet to gather in the history of the Latin East. The presence of the two senior crowned heads of the West, accompanied by many close members of their families, along with senior churchmen and nobles, was unprecedented. One may imagine that the feeling of anticipation, for settlers and crusaders alike, was enormous. William of Tyre felt that it was important to record who took part and it is worth repeating his list in order to give a sense of the surviving strength and standing of the crusaders who had reached the Holy Land.

Conrad was given top billing, followed by his brother, Otto of Freising and by the bishops of Metz, Toul (brother of Count Thierry of Flanders) and Theodwin, bishop of Santa Rufina, the papal legate. The secular nobles included Henry of Austria, Duke Welf of Bavaria, Duke Frederick of Swabia, as well as the marquises of Verona, Montferrat, and the counts of Blandras and Andechs.

The French counted King Louis; Bishop Godfrey of Langres; Bishop Arnulf of Lisieux; Guido of S. Grisogono, the papal legate; Robert of Dreux, Louis's brother; Henry of Champagne; the count of Flanders, brother-in-law to King Baldwin III of Jerusalem; and Ivo, the count of Soissons. The leading families of the kingdom were also present, headed by the co-rulers of Jerusalem, King Baldwin III and Queen Melisende. The king was only eighteen years old and, while technically above the age of majority (he had also led his first military campaign the previous year), his mother was still very much the senior partner in the royal house. Melisende's presence was rarely noted in accounts of the Second Crusade, but she had been co-ruler of the kingdom, with King Fulk, after the end of the civil war of 1134 and queen regnant since his death in 1143. The queen was, of course, unlikely to take part in warfare, but her strong political ambitions and years of experience must have ensured that she exerted some influence over the proceedings.[44] The church hierarchy of the kingdom was in attendance, too: the patriarch, the archbishops of Caesarea and Nazareth, the bishops of Sidon, Beirut, Banyas and Bethlehem. The masters of the two military orders were there along with the royal constable and the lay lords of Nablus, Tiberias, Sidon, Caesarea, Transjordan, Toron and Beirut.[45]

The assembly had to consider where to attack, although in light of the deal noted above, this was something of a foregone conclusion; perhaps there was a need to give King Louis the chance to register his opinion in a formal settlement. William described a debate in which various options were discussed, although, sadly, he did not elaborate. He then stated that by unanimous agreement it would be best to besiege Damascus. This decision was described by Mayer as 'a plan as ridiculous in execution as in conception' and by Runciman as 'utter folly'.[46] In recent years, however, the work of Hoch has done much to overturn this view and to present the choice as entirely sensible in the circumstances.[47] The Christian force had three options: to open a campaign against Aleppo, possibly leading on to Edessa; to attack the city of Damascus to the east; or move to the south-west and invest the Fatimid-held port of Ascalon. As we have already observed, the first of these was no longer a viable choice, leaving only Ascalon or Damascus. In the case of Ascalon, the construction between 1136 and 1142 of castles at Bethgibelin, Ibelin and Blanchegarde had done much to neutralise it.[48] As Hoch has argued, there were many reasons why the council chose Damascus. It was, of course, the largest Muslim city close to the kingdom of Jerusalem and, as the Prophet Isaiah stated, it was the *caput Syriae*. For many years it had posed a serious threat to the settlers: Tughtegin had fought the Franks in 1105, 1112 and 1113. In the 1120s Melisende's father, King Baldwin II, had mounted a series of raids on Damascus but he realised that the city was too strong for the forces of the Latin East and summoned help from the West – a call that culminated in the failed crusade of 1129.[49] Smail observed that Melisende may have endorsed a new campaign for Damascus because she had witnessed these events.[50] The objection to this line of approach, raised by Mayer, is that from 1140, the Damascenes were allies of the kingdom of Jerusalem; it was therefore a grave error for the crusaders to confront a friendly Muslim force. The alliance had been prompted by the increased danger from Zengi who, between 1135 and 1138, took control of Hama, Banyas and Homs. The following year he invaded Damascene territory, captured Baalbek and laid siege to Damascus itself. It was in these difficult circumstances that a delegation approached King Fulk and Queen Melisende and offered a large financial inducement to come to the relief of the city and to hand over Banyas if it was recaptured. Both of these conditions were fulfilled. It was in the interests of Damascus and of the Christians to resist the expansion of Zengid influence; the former needed to preserve their independence, the latter, to prevent the city from being used as a springboard to assault Jerusalem. After Zengi was murdered in 1146, however, there was a realignment of Muslim powers. Unur of Damascus seized Baalbek and made a truce with Hama and Homs. Zengi's lands were divided between his sons Saif ad-Din, who held Mosul, and Nur ad-Din, who took Aleppo. From a Damascene perspective, the northern Syrian Muslims no longer appeared to be a serious problem. This new situation encouraged Unur and Nur ad-Din to come to terms with each other; in the spring of 1147 they made a treaty, sealed by the marriage of Unur's daughter to the Aleppan ruler. For Jerusalem, the potential consequences of this union were plain, and the treaty with Damascus was rendered obsolete.[51] As Hoch points out, in 1113 a combined army from Mosul and Damascus had invaded Jerusalem and nearly broken the Christian hold on the city; a similar prospect could be envisaged again. It seemed unlikely that Unur and Nur ad-Din would come into conflict soon after the departure of the Second Crusade, as in fact they did. In light of these conditions, around May–June 1147, the governor of the semi-independent Hauran region south of Damascus offered to surrender Bosra and Sarkhad to the Franks in return for financial payments. The council of the kingdom agreed to this and Baldwin III led the army east to take possession of these fortresses. After failed negotiations with Unur, the Christians invaded his lands, but he appealed to Nur ad-Din, who brought down a force to block the Franks' progress. A settlement was arranged whereby Damascus took over Bosra and Sarkhad and the Christians retreated. This episode showed that the danger of Aleppan–Damascene co-operation was real. As Hoch concludes: 'Thus the Latin kingdom's strategic situation vis-à-vis its Muslim neighbours in Syria had deteriorated dramatically in the year immediately preceding the arrival of the Second Crusade'.[52]

With a campaign against Damascus the unanimous choice of the Palmarea assembly, a call was put out to muster the entire military strength of the kingdom, 'cavalry, infantry and natives'. Once the settlers' forces had mobilised, they joined the armies of Conrad and Louis and marched through Tiberias, along the Sea of Galilee to Banyas, on the north-eastern edge of the kingdom of Jerusalem. From there they crossed Mount Lebanon and descended towards Damascus. At the village of Daria, a few miles from Damascus, the army settled into battle formation, headed by King Baldwin, followed by King Louis with King Conrad at the rear. The city of Damascus is on a flat plain overlooked to the north by Mount Kaisoun. The Barada river runs west–east around the northern edge of the walls, and this precious waterway supplied a network of irrigation channels that allowed the locality to support a huge number of orchards. According to William of Tyre, these extended up to five miles northwards and westwards – the direction from which the Christians approached.[53] Ibn Jubayr, who visited the city in 1184, wrote that 'gardens encircle it like the halo around the moon . . . wherever you look on its four sides its ripe fruits hold the gaze'.[54] Eighteenth- and nineteenth-century prints and engravings (see Illustration 11 for an example) clearly show the city being circled by a dense tree crown; even today, if one stands on Mount Kaisoun looking down southwards over the modern sprawl of Damascus, one will see see a similar feature.

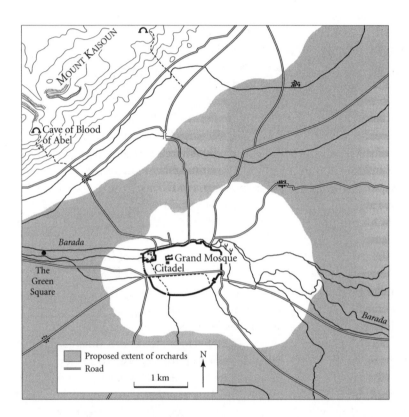

The Siege of Damascus, July 1148

The orchards provided a fine defensive barrier. Each plot was surrounded by a dry mud wall to demarcate ownership and some had towers to allow the proprietor to see over his land and to defend it. The only way through these densely planted trees was along narrow pathways, which were wide enough to permit pack-animals and small carts to transport the fruit back to the city, but in no way conducive to the passage of a large army. Yet the Franks had made a conscious choice to approach from this direction. The decision was under-pinned by the belief that, if they succeeded in breaking through the city's strongest defences, then on the one hand the morale of the inhabitants would collapse and, on the other, the fruit trees and irrigation channels would provide essential supplies of food and water.[55]

On Saturday 24 July Baldwin's troops started to work their way through the miles of orchards. The narrow paths, low walls and dense tree-cover were ideal conditions for small-unit warfare and the locals used all their knowledge to hinder the Franks. Arrows and lances emerged from special peepholes and the watchtowers were a perfect place from which to fire arrows down onto the Christians; a series of barricades contrived to block the way even more. The crusaders incurred some casualties, but as the day wore on they made good headway, pushing down the barriers and capturing the towers and their defenders. The Muslims began to despair and fled back out of the orchards across a plain and over the river to regroup in front of the city itself.

The Damascenes realised that the orchards were lost and that the city walls would soon be under attack. They deployed mounted archers and small mobile ballistae to try to stem the crusaders' advance before the river. For obvious reasons, the Christians needed to reach the water and, after a pause to regroup, King Baldwin's men began to close ranks with the enemy. It seems that they made little progress until the arrival of Conrad's troops. The king had heard of the loss of momentum and he gathered his knights and charged towards the fray. According to William of Tyre, the German knights leapt down from their horses, as was their custom in a desperate situation, and engaged the enemy with swords and shields. The impact of this new onslaught drove the Damascenes back and the river was won. Interestingly, this descrip-tion of the Germans' tactics tallied with that of John Kinnamos who empha-sised their preference for fighting on foot rather than on horseback and their skill in using the great sword rather than the spear.[56] Several sources stated that Conrad himself was at the forefront of the battle; and he was reported to have severed the head, neck and shoulder of one bold opponent with a single mighty blow, a deed that caused many of the Muslims to lose heart and flee.[57] The Damascenes had also lost one of their senior men, the aged North African *imam* and jurisconsult, Yusuf al-Findalawi. Unur had tried to persuade him not to take part in the battle because of his advanced years, but Yusuf insisted upon his duty and was killed later on that day in an exchange near the village of al-Rabwa, c. 2 miles due west of Damascus by the Barada river.[58]

By this time the Christians were in an excellent position; they were able to camp on the plain in front of the city walls and could get food and water from the orchards and the river. The Damascenes barricaded the streets with tall beams in a bid to block the enemy advance, but there appeared to be little chance of holding out. With victory seemingly in their grasp, however, the crusader armies made a highly controversial decision – one that provoked much discussion at the time and has attracted considerable attention from modern historians too.[59] Perplexingly, the armies chose to abandon their strong, well-supplied base to move to the opposite (south-eastern) side of the city, where it was claimed that they could achieve a quick victory because there were no orchards, river or moat – only a low, weak wall that could be easily forced. Ibn Jubayr indirectly confirmed this vulnerability when he observed there were no suburbs to the east and south-east.[60] William of Tyre painstakingly explained that the Damascenes promised large sums of money to certain nobles of Jerusalem to convince the Christians to lift the siege from the west and move to the other side of the city, where the attack would be doomed to failure. Kings Conrad and Louis relied on the advice of the local nobility and consented to the plan, leaving their hard won gains for the dry side of Damascus. Once in the new location, they quickly began to run out of food but could not return to their original camp because the locals had barred the roads with beams, rocks and squadrons of archers. The defences to the south-east were not as feeble as had been claimed and, faced with the prospect of starvation – something that the Germans and French had already endured once on the expedition – the Christians, reluctantly and with great ill-feeling, began to leave. It is worth emphasising that the crusaders had not even been seen off in battle; arguably, therefore, their retreat was an even greater humiliation than defeat in some epic military encounter.

William of Tyre was a student in western Europe at the time of the crusade and he wrote his account of the campaign more than twenty-five years after it took place.[61] He was aware of the importance of the event, however, and, in his own words, 'interviewed wise men and those whose memory of those times is still fresh . . . I endeavoured to learn the reason for this great wrong; who were the instigators of such treachery; and how so detestable a crime could have been carried through. I found that the reports vary greatly in regard to this matter.'[62] In other words, the writer had made exhaustive efforts to uncover the truth but came up with no definitive answer; he was clear, however, that treachery on the part of someone was to blame. The moral weakness of certain Christians, who let themselves be tempted by greed, was at the root of the defeat. This analysis excluded the unpalatable possibility that the Muslims may have been too strong for the Christians and caused their retreat. In view of the crusaders' huge confidence in their divinely sanctioned cause the human failings of the settlers in the Levant was a relatively tolerable interpretation of the calamity.

William reported that some blamed Count Thierry of Flanders who had allegedly asked the two western kings to be given Damascus when it fell.[63] They had agreed – certainly Thierry was a strong and wealthy lord who could have provided the influx of men required to have a chance of holding the city; he was also related to the ruling house of Jerusalem. Some of the local nobility resented an outsider seizing land for himself while the men who had fought in the Levant for decades would go unrewarded. On the one hand, it is possible that a faction that represented Baldwin III did not wish such a senior figure as the count to take a position of power in the East while Baldwin was so young. Conversely, Hoch has argued that nobles favourable to Melisende caused the campaign to fail, not wanting her youthful son to augment his strength at the expense of the queen.[64] Some of William's other sources blamed the simmering ill-feeling of Prince Raymond of Antioch for encouraging nobles in the army of Jerusalem to ensure that Louis's crusade failed, but this seems impractical and unlikely.[65]

Conrad III of Germany was certain as to who was responsible. He wrote:

> With general consensus we reached Damascus and set up our camp in front of the city gate. Although our men faced considerable danger, there can be no doubt at all that the city was close to being captured, and surrendering. But then, those whom we had no reason to distrust behaved in this way: they claimed that the side of the city we were on was impregnable and intentionally led us to another district where there was neither water for the army, nor was it possible to gain entry. Everyone was angered by this and turned around and retreated in grief with the siege a failure.[66]

In this case, betrayal by the local nobility had the benefit of removing any stigma for the defeat from the royal personage. Conrad's letter was probably the source for several German annalists who repeated a broadly similar story.[67] Given that the leadership of Jerusalem had been so keen to encourage Conrad towards an assault on Damascus when he first arrived in the kingdom, such behaviour must have seemed even more frustrating.

John of Salisbury suggested that the Templars were to blame for the treachery in some unspecified way, although Conrad himself would hear nothing of this rumour.[68] The Würzburg annalist also accused the Templars of accepting bribes.[69] John hinted at the desire of 'others', including perhaps Count Thierry of Flanders, to return home and who thus wished the campaign to end as soon as possible. Again, to do this for the sake of a few days out of the many months that the expedition took, and when it was not even near the end of the sailing season, does not sound particularly plausible.[70] Eastern Christian writers, including Michael the Syrian and the 'Anonymous Syriac Chronicle', mentioned the offer of substantial bribes to the king and local nobility. The latter source also put forward a variation on the theme of the settlers' fear of westerners taking control of Damascus, although this time Conrad was identified as the source of suspicion.[71] By way of a parallel it is worth observing that the siege of Shaizar in 1138 had ended with the Christian attackers accepting payments from the defenders as a Muslim relief force approached.[72]

But, while these various authors advance explanations of a supposed treachery, as Forey astutely observed, 'if the city was about to fall [on the west], Conrad and Louis would hardly have accepted any arguments for a change in the point of attack'.[73] Therefore, it is necessary to consider why the need to move – or to consider moving – arose. The evidence of an eyewitness Muslim writer, Ibn al-Qalanisi, is of prime importance here. He wrote that the Franks did indeed make substantial progress on the first day of the siege and they took the orchards and suburbs and killed two important holy men. All the people 'were discouraged and straitened in spirit through fear because of the horror of what they had witnessed'.[74] What Ibn al-Qalanisi adds to the Christian accounts of the siege is that on the following day, Sunday 25 July, the Damascenes launched sorties against the Christians and there was fierce fighting. Both sides charged against one another from dawn to dusk, with Unur taking a leading role in the defence of his city. The inhabitants gathered in the Great Umayyad Mosque and the revered Koran of Caliph 'Uthman (644–56) was displayed, while the people sprinkled their heads with ashes and prayed for divine aid.[75] In previous analyses of the siege of Damsascus, crusade historians – in their concern to focus on the military reasons for the Christians' failure – have tended to ignore a further important factor in the struggle for the city: namely its spiritual value to the Muslims. Aside from broader political strategy and the wish for self-preservation, the Damascenes were defending a place of considerable significance to the people of Islam. Traditions describe it as the stage for the coming of the Messiah before the Day of Judgement; some claimed that this would take place at the Great Umayyad Mosque, one of the holiest sites in Sunni Islam. While it is true that Damascus was not mentioned in the Koran by name, many writers of *fadā'il* (merits) associated the city with verses from the holy text. The city's beauty – it was frequently extolled as God's Paradise on Earth – helped to increase its sanctity.[76] The Muslim pilgrim Ibn Jubayr visited the city in 1184 and emphasised that it was the place where God gave asylum to Jesus and his mother.[77] Mount

Kaisoun was especially important; he noted that Abraham was born on its slopes and that a cave containing traces of the blood of Abel (now known as the Grotto of Blood) was on the same hillside. Ibn 'Asakir, a twelfth-century Damascene writer, included this poem in his work on the city:

> Oh my companion, how many a shrine at Mount Kaisoun and its foot is there worthy of exaltation
> The Upper Hill – whoever masters the exegesis on the Book extols its praises
> The renowned Nayrab – whoever visits it or experiences there a blessing knows its virtue
> The Grotto of Blood – its virtue is widely reported. I still hear it [said]: may you be given aid, a great miracle
> The cave of Jibril the Guardian – possesses a miraculous virtue which I experienced a long time ago
> The noble Grotto of Hunger – how many a pious servant beneath it does reside
> The Oratory at Barza – its merit is not to be denied; I mean the Oratory of your father Abraham
> How many a place there not possessing a mosque became noble for the devout
> The Prophet was seen praying at its foot; Bless him and grant him eternal peace and salvation
> It contains the tombs of the prophets; whoever sets out to visit them, desires a miracle
> Tarry not in visiting it [i.e. Mount Kaisoun] and do so regularly so that you may attain great recompense in Paradise.[78]

Damascus and its environs was also the burial place of companions of the Prophet, such as Bilal ibn Rabah, his *muezzin*, and other martyrs and members of the Prophet's family, such as Ruqayya, the daughter of 'Ali.[79] Religious zeal is ascribed to the Christians as a primary motivation for seeking to regain their holy places; although Damascus undoubtedly ranked behind Mecca, Medina and Jerusalem, in the circumstances of a *jihad*, the determination of the Muslims to defend a vital spiritual centre of their own should not be ignored.

Ibn al-Qalanisi suggests that Damascene appeals for help began to produce a response with the arrival of a steady stream of reinforcements – particularly bowmen – from the Beqa Valley. The Monday saw further fierce fighting with neither side giving ground. By the following day, however, the Muslims seemed to be gaining the upper hand; parts of the crusader camp were surrounded. At the same time the Christians heard of the advance of further Muslim relief forces, all eager to engage in the *jihad*; for this reason the attackers' nerve failed and with no prospect of victory they broke camp and set out for their own lands. Ibn al-Qalanisi wrote that his people pursued the crusaders and killed large numbers of their men and many of their fine war-horses.[80] While there may be a sense of exaggeration and natural pride in the achievements of the Muslims (the losses on the retreat, for example, are not mentioned by any Christian source), the kernel of the account can be accepted.

Thus, by reason of their loss of momentum to the west of the city, coupled with the imminent appearance of Muslim reinforcements, the Christians' need to gamble on a quick victory can be understood. This interpretation can be nuanced further if we add a statement from John of Salisbury. He wrote that the best authorities believed that Damascus would fall if an attack from the western side persisted for fifteen days.[81] The local Franks evidently counted on the river and orchards for supplies, because they had brought little in the way of foodstuffs with them. It is also worth considering what the Latin sources omit. To invest a major city, one would expect to require siege machinery, yet no accounts mention the Christians bringing along, or using, such equipment. Either they did not get close enough to the walls to employ it or they believed that a victory in battle would cause their enemy to capitulate. There is little sense that Damascus had particularly formidable walls, and, although the later citadel survives today, neither it nor the old walls are particularly impressive; instead, the Muslims relied on the orchards and the suburbs as defences.

Evidence from another Arabic source casts further light on the story. Ibn al-Athir, who wrote in northern Syria in the early thirteenth century, indicated that Unur had appealed to Saif-ad-Din of Mosul, who joined Nur ad-Din at Homs and was poised to march south when the Christians gave up. Unur had threatened to hand over Damascus to the Zengids if the crusaders did not retreat ('and then, by God, you will repent'). He wrote to the nobles of Jerusalem and claimed that if he surrendered the city to Saif ad-Din then the Christian lands would not survive. He offered Banyas as a bribe and this convinced the local Franks to persuade the crusaders that they should retreat.[82] The distance from Damascus to Mosul is over 400 miles, and Forey has expressed concern that the time between the crusaders' decision to target Damascus at Acre on 24 June and the siege one month later might not have been long enough to allow them to get organised and bring a relief force.[83] Yet the presence of the crusaders in the Holy Land was widely known and Saif ad-Din would surely have moved westwards as a precaution in case they attacked his brother in Aleppo. The sense of Ibn al-Athir's writing is that an appeal was made well before the siege began; furthermore, the Franks' understanding that it would take fifteen days for Damascus to fall from the west gave a bigger window for the Zengids to arrive. There is a tension between William of Tyre's claim that the crusaders had been persuaded by the settlers that 'Damascus would be easily taken at the first attack' and the fifteen-day period recognised as necessary to complete the siege.[84] In the case of the former, Muslim reinforcements would be irrelevant, but with regard to the latter, the approach of Saif ad-Din meant that a quick success was vital. After four days of engagement, news that the Zengids would appear within the eleven remaining days needed to succeed to the west could have spurred the Christians to change their plans. In light of the Muslim resistance being stiffer than expected, the nobles of Jerusalem may well have suggested switching the attack to the southeast. Although Ibn al-Qalanisi failed to mention the crusaders shifting their camp, not all of the Christian writers include this either. John of Salisbury recorded a reconnaissance mission made by the bishop of Langres while the crusaders discussed their options and prepared to move, but the decision to depart had already been taken. Perhaps Godfrey's survey confirmed the lack of water, and this, combined with the Muslim advance, suggested that a retreat was prudent. At this point, it is possible that the Damascenes made a payment to the Franks (rather than the crusaders) to ensure their departure and this was the basis for the allegations of duplicity. In fact, John indicates that Conrad wanted to go back to Jerusalem and prepare more thoroughly – perhaps a reference to the need for siege materials, or for more supplies – and then return.[85]

In the event, the Christians did not make another attack on Damascus, although as Conrad informs us (and William of Tyre also records), they discussed the prospect of a campaign against Ascalon at a gathering with Baldwin III and Louis. It was argued that the city was close by and could be taken easily and quickly. As noted earlier, Ascalon was a long-standing target of the Christians and its capture would have been a considerable achievement. Conrad wrote that he prepared to set out on this enterprise, but hardly anyone joined him and after eight days of waiting around, having 'been deceived by these people a second time', he gave up.[86] Perhaps the local nobles felt that a fleet was needed to make a proper blockade of Ascalon and they were reluctant to attempt another quick storming of a city, similar to the failed assault on Damascus. As Hoch observes, however, even after the retreat from Damascus there must have been some trustworthy nobles among the men of Jerusalem for the crusaders to contemplate such a plan. That the locals were divided over the Ascalon project is evidenced by the fact that too few showed up for the muster of the armies at Jaffa – perhaps this sense of division is an echo of some of the troubles that caused the problems at Damascus.[87] Gravely disappointed, Conrad prepared to set sail for home on 8 September 1148. He travelled via Thessalonica and as the Byzantines prepared to respond to the recent Sicilian invasions of their lands, he made an alliance with Manuel against King Roger.[88] Conrad finally returned to Germany in the spring of 1149.

Louis stayed in the Holy Land for many months after the debacle at Damascus. Most of his nobles went home in the autumn of 1148, but the king and queen remained in the Levant over the winter. Little is known about this stay; apparently Louis engaged in no military action and he visited as many holy sites as possible. Charter evidence indicates support for the community of St Lazarus.[89] The king celebrated Easter 1149 in Jerusalem before finally setting out for France in late April.

Louis and Eleanor endured a difficult journey back, in part because of their decision to sail in a Sicilian ship, thus revealing a belated affinity with Roger and taking a position that was certain to antagonise the Greeks. Predictably, when they encountered a Byzantine fleet, the Sicilian convoy was attacked and the vessel that carried the queen was temporarily detained. Once freed, the royal couple went to Sicily where (in late July 1149) Roger greeted them with all honour, no doubt delighted to have such a high-profile visitor, particularly given the imminent outbreak of war with the Greeks. Eleanor was ill after the voyage and needed to recover. After he had lavished the warmest hospitality on his guests, Roger personally escorted them northwards. On 4 October Louis and Eleanor reached the famous monastery of Monte Cassino where they remained for three days before heading onwards.[90] At Ceprano they met Eugenius, who must have wanted to hear their account of the crusade and also tried to offer some marriage guidance to the couple. After this brief visit they carried on northwards and reached Capetian France in November.[91] Thus, in the Holy Land at least, the Second Crusade ended in failure; as the home-coming crusaders brought news of the fiasco back to the West, the emotional and political consequences started to play themselves out.

CHAPTER 12

THE WENDISH CRUSADE

'The initiators of the expedition deemed it advisable to design one part of the army for the eastern regions, another for Spain and a third against the Slavs who live close by us.' Thus Helmold of Bosau, writing c.1167–8, related his own understanding of the scope and format of the Second Crusade.[1] The Slavs to whom he referred are generically known as the Wends, a group that lived to the east of the River Elbe and adjacent to the Baltic Sea in what is now north-eastern Germany and Poland.[2] They consisted of five main tribes: the Abotrites, the Rugians, the Liutizians, the Wagrians and the Pomeranians. In the aftermath of the fall of the Roman Empire these pagan peoples had spread slowly eastwards; from the eighth century onwards German churchmen and nobles tried to pull them into the Christian sphere of influence. The Wends were polytheists who worshipped in great wooden temples that contained carved effigies of their gods; they also reverenced sacred groves and springs. Helmold described their practices – which included human sacrifice – in lurid detail.[3] In economic terms, the Wends relied upon fishing, cattle raising and hunting, and were traders in fur, wax, honey, fish and slaves. From the mid-tenth century in particular, waves of German expansion encroached upon their lands. Otto I (936–73) subdued the western Slavs, set up six new bishoprics and established a degree of imperial overlordship. Adam, archbishop of Bremen, wrote a *Historia* of the archbishops of Hamburg-Bremen in the mid 1070s which offers a churchman's perspective on the ebb and flow of mission and war over the previous centuries.[4] Emperor Otto II (973–1002) had advanced Christian power considerably but in the decades after his death the Slavs rose in revolt, setting fire to churches, murdering priests and leaving 'not a vestige of Christianity beyond the Elbe'.[5] There were periods of more peaceful relations too; Hamburg had been burned to the ground in 1011/13 but it was later restored and Archbishop Alebrand (1035–43) constructed a stone church and a palace to provide protection for the clerics. According to Adam, 'across the Elbe and throughout the realm there was a firm peace at this

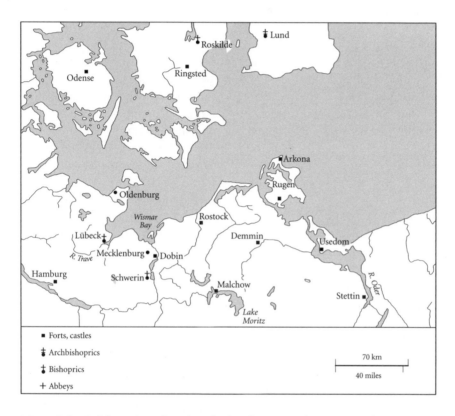

Map of the Baltic region showing the key locations for the Wendish Crusade
of 1147

time. The princes of the Slavs . . . came peacefully to Hamburg and rendered military service to the duke and prelate.'[6] This positive state of affairs was soon to be compromised, however. In a summary which anticipated the problems that would bedevil the Second Crusade, he wrote: 'but then as now [the 1070s] the duke and the bishop worked at cross-purposes amongst the Winuli people; the duke, indeed, striving to increase the tribute; the archbishop, to spread Christianity. It is clear to me that on account of the efforts of the priests the Christian religion would long ago have become strong if the avarice of the princes had not hindered the conversion of the folk'.[7] Adam obviously had his own clerical viewpoint as to why the advance of Christianity periodically faltered, but the balance between the wishes of the secular and ecclesiastical powers – between conquest and conversion – was potentially a fine one. Of course, if the former body imposed their authority on a region, it could create a better environment for missionary work, but at times there were tensions between the two groups. In 1066, another revolt saw the murder of Prince Gottschalk 'by the pagans whom he was trying to convert to Christianity', and Bishop John of Mecklenburg was captured and brutally killed, with his severed head being offered to the pagan god Redigast as a token of victory. Hamburg was devastated again; as Adam lamented, 'O God, the heathen are come into thy inheritance; they have defiled thy holy temple.'[8]

The gradual pushing back of paganism continued in the late eleventh and early twelfth centuries, but in parallel to this the crusading movement emerged to add a powerful new dimension to relations between Christians and the outside world. What contemporaries saw as the divinely blessed success of the First Crusade in 1099 inevitably influenced other theatres of Christian–pagan conflict. An early manifestation of this phenomenon in northern Europe was the so-called 'Magdeburg charter' of 1107/8, probably written by a Flemish cleric who lived in eastern Saxony and was in the retinue of the archbishop of Magdeburg.[9] There is some controversy as to whether the document was ever circulated, but in any case it represents evidence of the arrival of the crusading idea alongside ongoing events in the Baltic. Given the profound impact that the capture of Jerusalem exerted across western Europe, it was not surprising that people engaged in other holy wars would look to the First Crusade and see their own struggle represented therein.

The document was a call from the churchmen and nobles of north-eastern Germany to their counterparts in north-western Germany and Flanders, including the archbishop of Cologne, the duke of Lorraine and the count of Flanders (Count Robert II, 1093–1111, a veteran of the expedition to the Holy Land) and 'all greater and lesser men' to come and fight the heathen. The language and the imagery employed here were startling; the writer drew a direct parallel between the capture of the holy city in 1099 and the liberation of 'our Jerusalem'. The conflict in northern Europe was depicted in terms remarkably similar to those of the call for the First Crusade: 'Let the voice sound in the ears of the faithful of Christ, so that all may hasten to the war of Christ and come to help the soldiers of Christ.'[10] It was an appeal structured in the fashion of a papal bull with a *narratio, exhortatio*, a discussion of the planning of the campaign and a brief statement of the rewards on offer. It was also riddled with biblical imagery to a quite remarkable extent, even by the standards of the age. The writer lamented the years of oppression by the pagans and the damage done to the Mother Church. The heathens 'have profaned the churches of Christ with idolatry; they have destroyed the altars; and they do not hesitate to perpetrate upon us things that the human mind shrinks from hearing.'[11] The pagans captured and tortured Christians (something related in similar terms by Adam of Bremen, as we have seen above); this was described in spine-chilling detail, so as to leave the audience in no doubt as to the absolute inhumanity of their enemy. The pagans made offerings of Christian heads and bowls of blood to Pripegala, their principal God, while the faithful lived in constant fear of attack. The author appealed to the people of Saxony, Franconia, Lorraine and Flanders – the last three areas all closely associated with the First Crusade – to follow the example of the 'Franks' (presumably a shorthand for all the crusaders) and to declare a holy war against the enemies of Christ. He drew a direct link between the crusade in the Levant and the proposed expedition in northern Europe: 'prepare yourselves like the Franks for the liberation of Jerusalem. Our Jerusalem, which from the beginning was free, is made a slave by the cruelty of the heathens.' He also employed the familiar argument that this state of affairs had come about because of 'our sins'.[12]

The phrase 'our king himself, the authority who has declared this war' seems to indicate that the originator of the idea for this campaign was Henry V of Germany (1106–25). As noted above (see p. 89), his father's struggle with the papacy had ruled out imperial involvement in the First Crusade, but in April 1100 a letter from the patriarch of Jerusalem told of the miraculous capture of the city and appealed to the churchmen, princes and the faithful of Germany to achieve salvation and assist the holy places against pagan oppression.[13] Emperor Henry IV had also raised the idea of going to Jerusalem in 1103.[14] It appears, therefore, that his son wished to harness the wave of enthusiasm for holy war generated by the conquest of Jerusalem to extend the battle against unbelievers in the north. Presumably on account of his poor relations with the *curia*, Henry V had not involved Paschal II in the scheme and this lack of papal endorsement for the campaign has rightly led historians to disregard it as a proper crusade.[15] The absence of ecclesiastical approval – as well as continued troubles with the German nobility – may have contributed to the failure of Henry's plan; certainly the regions that had already taken part in crusading would have appreciated the need for a valid offer of the remission of sins, something that this proposal seemed to lack.[16] Indeed, to join the campaign as it stood could have brought men such as Robert of Flanders into conflict with the papacy, a situation they presumably wished to avoid. Henry's plan had, however, gathered some support because King Niels of Denmark (1104–34) and his people had apparently agreed to the idea. The participants were to meet at Merseberg in the month of May.

The cleric called upon the churchmen to help and he used the image of the contemplative Mary being joined by the more vigorous Martha as a way to encourage them to pray for success. To the secular people, 'the soldiers of Christ', as he described them, he held out a double incentive to take part in the expedition. First, the prospect that the heathens' land 'is very good for meat, honey, grain, birds' and cultivation; secondly, the chance to save their souls, although he did not expound further on this point. The mixture of secular and spiritual motives can be seen in Robert of Rheims' account of the First Crusade and Knoch has pointed out a number of parallels between these texts, which indicate that the author probably knew Robert's work.[17] The attraction of these earthly rewards was particularly apposite in an age when the colonisation of land by Flemish or Frisian settlers was gathering considerable momentum.[18] The text closed with another parallel to the capture of Jerusalem: 'He who with the arm of his strength gave victory to the Franks who went from the farthest west against his enemies in the most remote east, let Him give to you the will and the power to subdue these nearby and utterly inhuman heathens and in all things have good success'.[19] As Lotter notes, however, nothing was said about conversion, which seemed to be one of the aims of the tenth-century Ottonian wars.[20]

In the end, little came of this effort; whether the document itself was issued or not, the matter was evidently in the public domain. The decades prior to the Second Crusade saw the continuation of conquest and mission across northern Germany and Denmark. Lothar of Supplinberg became duke of Saxony and he commanded a trio of raids to the east between 1110 and 1124 (this was the later Lothar III, ruler of Germany, 1125–37). Duke Boleslaw III (1102–38) of Poland led forays into Pomerania and against the Liutzi; in 1143, Count Adolph II of Holsatia moved into Wagria, and his foundation of the new city of Lübeck marked a further advance. Yet alongside these military episodes there was a strong sense of mission with an emphasis placed on peaceful conversion, albeit in conjunction with submission to increased secular authority as well. In 1114, the foundation of the church at Lentzkau, south-east of Magdeburg, provided a base for Praemonstratensian preachers and, in the aftermath of Duke Boleslaw's invasions, Bishop Otto of Bamberg undertook missions to Pomerania in 1124–5 and again in 1128, this time under the protection of Lothar. There was a climate of zealous monastic reform in which Cistercians, Augustinian canons, Praemonstratensians and reformed Benedictines all set to work.[21] Guth cites the cleric Honorius Augustodunensis, who wrote c.1136/40: 'How are they [the heathens] to believe something of which they have heard nothing? But how should they believe without preachers? How can there be sermons if no preachers are sent to them?'[22] Bishop Otto himself was a great preacher and his range of linguistic skills helped his cause further.[23] Other churchmen, such as Bishop Anselm of Havelberg, also spent part of their careers trying to missionise the Slavs.[24] The Praemonstratensian abbey of Jericho was established on the River Elbe with the purpose of correcting 'a vicious and perverse generation'.[25] There had indeed been numerous Wendish attacks on Christian territories and Niclot, prince of the Abodrites, was characterised by Helmold of Bosau as 'a truculent beast, intensely hostile to Christians, under whom paganism grew throughout Slavia'.[26] Helmold also reported that many Christians had been killed and crucified by the pagans as a sign of contempt.[27]

In the 1120s, the Dane, Prince Canute, became duke of Schleswig. Around 1128 he purchased the title to the kingdom of the pagan Abodrites from Emperor Lothar III and proceeded to wage war against the Slavs to further the Christian cause.[28] Canute was killed by a rival in 1131, but within a few years he was regarded as a holy warrior and a missionary. The monastery of Ringsted was founded in his memory in 1135 and a *Vita*, written under two years later by Robert of Ely, explained that he was 'called no less a canon than a knight' and referred to him as a '*Cristi miles*'.[29] Around the same time Canute's brother, Eric Emune (1134–7) conquered the island of Rugen, which had been designated by the papacy as a place to be missionised; indeed, it was rumoured that it had been converted to Christianity back in the time of Louis the Pious (d. 840) by monks from the abbey of Corvey only for the Rugians to 'go astray from the light of truth' and worship as God an image of the martyr, St Vitus.[30] In the mid-1130s the Wends of Rugen were baptised, but the Danes soon lost control of the island and its inhabitants apostasised. In 1137, the dispute between the Welf and Hohenstaufen families allowed the Wagrians to invade Holsatia and to burn down the church and settlement of Sigeburg.[31] Henry the Lion responded with a mighty raid into the area between the River Schwale and the River Trave. The following year, the Holsatians made a similar attack; as Helmold wrote, 'they did to the Slavs what the Slavs had set themselves to do to them: their land was reduced to a wilderness'.[32]

Yet an image of constant, brutal warfare would be misleading. Just as the frontiers between Christians and Muslims in Spain and the Holy Land often saw a state of *convivencia*, so too did the situation in northern Europe. Jensen has demonstrated the existence of dynastic links between the Danish and the Wendish princely houses; large amounts of Wendish pottery have been found in Denmark; added to them, the remains of Wendish ships indicate that a considerable volume of trade took place; and the high number of Slavic place-names suggest Wendish migration into southern Denmark.[33] As Lotter writes of the early twelfth-century, 'in Havelberg and Brandenburg there were Slav counts or governors who were Christian but ruled over a pagan population'.[34] Even Niclot himself was said to have been an ally of Count Adolph of Holsatia at the time of the Second Crusade.[35] In many respects, therefore, the situation was quite fluid and the presence of a number of religious, political and economic variables could influence the progress and outcome of a large-scale campaign in the region.

In 1145–6, Pope Eugenius launched his appeal for a new crusade to the Holy Land. In connection with this, Ohnsorge and Jensen have shown that the statement of a sixteenth-century historian (quoting a lost source), published in the *Diplomatarium Danicum* is probably trustworthy. According to this, a papal legate named Hubaldus was sent to Denmark to invite King Eric the Lamb (1137–46) to join the enterprise preached by Bernard of Clairvaux to the princes in Germany. This claim is corroborated by the absence of Hubaldus of Sancti Crucis from the *curia* between 6 June and December 1146.[36] Thus it seems that the pope anticipated Danish interest in the expedition to the Holy Land soon after the preaching campaign started.[37] In sending Hubaldus to the Danes, Eugenius was approaching a people who already had a history of involvement in crusading to the east.

In 1098 Bishop Adhémar of Le Puy wrote to the people of the North to come and assist the First Crusaders. This may have induced a response in Denmark because in 1101 King Eric the Good (1095–1103), his wife Bodil and an armed contingent left for the Levant, although the king died on Cyprus. The queen reached the Holy Land; she died on the Mount of Olives and was buried in the Valley of Jehosophat.[38] Markus Skeggjason, a Dane who wrote *c*.1107, stated that Eric the Good had undertaken the journey to seek remission for his sins.[39]

In 1146, however, Eric the Lamb was ill and in the summer he abdicated and went to the monastery at Odense where he died on 27 August. He was succeeded by Sven Grathe, who, together with Prince Valdemar, Canute's son, transferred the late duke's bones to the high altar at Ringsted. The archbishop of Lund protested on the grounds that papal approval for the elevation was missing, but this had no effect on the budding cult. Given the context of preaching for the crusade and of the resignation of Eric the Lamb, Jensen suggests that this episode 'is best understood as an attempt by Sven to strengthen his own position and to present himself as a sincere crusader'.[40] The parallel with the recent canonisation of Henry II of Germany (see above, pp. 47, 92–3) is worth noting; the emperor had been a leading figure in the struggle with the pagans, and Canute's admirers could certainly claim that he too had been a worthy holy warrior. In the short term, however, the emergence of a rival king would stifle the prospect of Danish involvement in crusading; the people of Jutland decided to elect Canute V, the son of the man who had killed Duke Canute in 1131, which precipitated a civil war.[41]

While these events absorbed the Danes, to the south King Conrad of Germany had committed himself to the crusade to the Levant, and in the spring of 1147 he set his lands in order. As we have seen above, the meeting held at Frankfurt between 11 and 23 March was the most important of these assemblies, and Bernard of Clairvaux was in attendance. At some point in the proceedings, a group of Saxon noblemen declined to go to the Holy Land 'because they had as neighbours certain tribes that were given over to the filthiness of idolatry' and wanted to fight them instead.[42] Thus, in the same way that the secular rulers had approached the papacy to extend the crusade to the Iberian Peninsula, local nobles sought to harness the privileges of the crusade to the Holy Land to their own long-running war against unbelievers and to secure spiritual rewards.

We lack details of the decision-making process at Frankfurt, but a letter from Bernard, seemingly written very soon afterwards, claimed that

at the council at . . . Frankfurt, the might of the Christians was armed against them [the pagans] and . . . for the complete wiping out or, at any rate, the conversion of these peoples, they [the Germans] have put on the Cross, the sign of our salvation; and we, by virtue of our authority, promised them the same spiritual privileges as those enjoy who set out for Jerusalem.[43]

The meaning of this will be analysed below, but the impression that Bernard himself, without apparent reference to Pope Eugenius, agreed to the idea of extending the crusade, is remarkable in itself. Presumably King Conrad consented because the plan could extend German power to the east and occupy numbers of potentially restive nobles in a worthy cause. This had been an understandable preoccupation of his during the autumn of 1146, and on this basis alone Bernard would have appreciated the value of such a move. Equally, the Saxon nobles may have feared leaving their lands open to pagan incursions, particularly given recent attacks. Bernard also believed that it was the prerogative of the secular princes to declare and wage wars; it was for the pope (or, presumably, his representative) to authorise them.[44] In concept, however, ecclesiastical approval for the proposal was a highly significant development and represented the most innovative aspect of the Second Crusade. This was the first time that the full and formal apparatus of crusading had been extended to the Baltic. As noted above, the 1107–8 attempt to link the two theatres of war had failed to secure ecclesiastical endorsement, although the notion of holy war was certainly present in the region, then and subsequently. Here though, Bernard placed the participants in the conflict with the Wends on a par with those who headed to the East, and he offered identical indulgences to both. Taken at face-value, this means that Bernard had interpreted his divine mandate – which he was careful to remind his audience that he possessed – as allowing him to take such a step. This is, however, problematic – the abbot was a man obsessed with hierarchy, and it seems natural that he should have at least consulted with Eugenius over such a drastic step. Yet there is no evidence for this, and Bernard seemingly used his authority to the full. One may assume, therefore, that he felt in accord with the idea of extending the crusade so as to include the Baltic. Given that Iberia was already involved in the crusades, and because of the long history of conquest and conversion in the north, it was not, perhaps, a wholly startling move. Also, as noted above, if the political consider-ations of the plan were also favourable (especially as far as Conrad was concerned), the abbot may have been further inclined to agree. A reference to the canonisation of Henry II is relevant as well, because it showed Eugenius to be supportive of a holy warrior in eastern Europe, and Bernard could have felt in this some indication of potential papal approval.

The meaning and justification of Bernard's phrases: 'for the complete wiping out or at least conversion of these peoples', and 'we utterly forbid that for any reason whatsoever a truce shall be made with these peoples, either for the sake of money, or for the sake of tribute until such a time as, by God's help, either their ritual or their people are wiped out' – are perplexing.[45] The appar-ently uncompromising options of 'death or conversion' have puzzled histo-rians because of the direct clash between this and the biblical principle that faith should not be imposed by force.[46] Ivo of Chartres and Gratian's *Decretum* stated this idea and Bernard himself made the same point in one of his sermons.[47]

Nonetheless, there are a number of possible ways to explain this; not one of them is conclusive, but they are worth outlining. First, the point that the inhabitants of Rugia – one of the targets of the crusade – could have been seen as apostates. If so, it was legitimate to use force to bring them back into the Christian fold. As Burchard of Worms wrote in the eleventh century, 'it is in the order of things that even those who were brought over to the faith by means of violence or compulsion have to be forced to remain faithful'.[48] If one follows this line of reasoning then Bernard's statements merely reflected a convention and the need for convoluted explanations is removed. There is, however, no evidence that he referred to the Rugians in such terms. In a similar vein, the recapture of land upon which the blood of missionaries had been spilt allowed ideas of recovering former Christian territory and vengeance to emerge too – as we saw in the 1107–8 letter.[49]

Two other views are important. Lotter has emphasised Bernard's use of the verb *delere* (to destroy) solely in connection with the collective *natio(nes)*, rather than with (unnamed) Slav individuals, whom he mentioned several other times. This, he argues, was no accident. A 'nation' was a community identified by origin, law and custom. Such a community could be destroyed by the breaking of their traditions and ties, and through their subjugation. Thus, if the Wends converted, they would be permitted to exist in their national units under their own leaders, as the Poles, Bohemians and Pomeranians had done. If they declined, they were to be broken, as had recently happened to the Wagrians. Lotter also draws a link with the Old Testament Book of Deuteronomy where the Israelites followed a divine command and destroyed the people of Canaan; those who resisted were to be killed, those who complied were not.[50] Conversion did feature earlier in Bernard's letter as well; the abbot stated that 'abandoned men are now being converted', which put the present campaign into a broader context of history and mission.

Eschatological concerns were also important, to Bernard at least. With the abbot's recruitment of Conrad, a key condition of the so-called 'Sibylline Prophecies', which heralded the End of the World, had been fulfilled. The Last Emperor (*Endkaisertum*) was to be a 'king of the Romans' and his name would begin with the letter 'C'; Conrad was clearly that man. Kahl interprets the tone of Bernard's letter concerning the Wendish crusade in this light.[51] The abbot's desire was to extirpate the enemies of Christ from the earth; given the gathering pace of the crusade and Conrad's decision to participate, Bernard suggested that the End of Days seemed imminent to the devil. Kahl argues that, in the context of this prophecy, it was not so monstrous for Bernard to push for the 'death or conversion' options. Other writers such as Otto of Freising, Gerhoh of Reichersberg, the Chronicle of St Peter at Erfurt and Helmold of Bosau referred to this idea too.[52] Bernard's uncompromising resolve to defeat the devil so wholly might have stemmed from his eschatological beliefs, already visible in his career in the 1130s. Nevertheless, other historians have argued that Bernard only saw the Last Days as a more distant idea. When, for example, he stated that the Jews should not to be persecuted and would eventually be converted, there was no hint that this had to be in the near future to head off disaster.[53] It is noticeable that Pope Eugenius did not take up the eschatological theme in his papal bulls and there is no sense of the theme emerging at a more popular level in the Baltic crusade or in the Holy Land; Conrad himself has left no record of being influenced by the concept.

Bernard was plain that he did not want the crusade in the Baltic to end in any way other than the terms he envisaged, that is, with the conversion or destruction of the Wendish faith. He was evidently aware that many previous wars against the pagans had resulted in truces for money or tribute, and he urged the churchmen of the region to exert maximum vigour in maintaining what he regarded as superior objectives. The abbot anticipated increasing numbers of people being drawn to this campaign and he tried to prevent those who had already indicated that they would go to Jerusalem from changing their minds. Some contemporary writers were rather sceptical about the parity between the campaign in the north and the crusade to the Holy Land and doubted the motives of those involved in the former enterprise. The author of the Peterhausen annals suggested that Duke Conrad of Zähringen felt the journey to the Levant was too demanding and so he decided to fight the pagans closer by; going to the Baltic was seen in some quarters, therefore, as an easier option.[54]

Towards the close of his letter, however, Bernard stated again that the 'uniform of this army, in clothes, arms and in all else, will be the same as the uniform of the other as it is fortified with the same privileges'. He wrote that the entire Frankfurt assembly encouraged the appeal to be sent out, thus demonstrating Conrad's approval – and he ended with a call for all the crusaders to meet at Magdeburg on 29 June.

Within a week of the end of the Council of Frankfurt, Conrad sent a legation that included Bishop Anselm of Havelberg, Bishop Bucco of Worms, Wibald of Stavelot and Odo of Frankfurt to Dijon to meet the pope.[55] There is no record of Eugenius's reaction to the news. In reality it seems that he had little choice in the matter, although the prospect of further extending the frontiers of Christianity was seemingly agreeable to him. A week later Bernard himself met the pope at Clairvaux and, within five days, on 11 April, *Divina dispensatione II* was issued to provide papal endorsement for the campaign to the Baltic.

Eugenius expressed the belief that it was through divine counsel that so many of the faithful from diverse regions were preparing to fight the infidel.[56] He mentioned the crusaders going to Edessa and to Spain and then addressed himself to those who, 'wishing to share in this sacred work and in the ensuing reward, intend with God's help to go against the Slavs and the other pagans living in the North and subject them to the Christian religion'. In other words, he now saw the crusade as a wider confrontation with non-believers on three fronts. Trying to prevent a haemorrhage of men from the main expedition to the Baltic, he decreed, for those who had not yet taken the cross to the Holy Land, the same remission of sins as for those going to the Levant.[57] He continued: 'By the authority of Almighty God and St Peter, prince of the apostles, which has been granted to us, and using the same authority to forbid the contrary on pain of excommunication, we grant that nobody is to accept from the pagans whom it is possible to subjugate to the Christian faith, either money or any other form of bribe to allow them to remain in their state of faithlessness'.[58]

The last of these statements appears to be a slight moderation of Bernard's more uncompromising approach. The starkness of 'destruction' is replaced by 'subjugation', although this could require the use of force – again, in contradiction to canon law. There was the insistence that the pagans could not remain in their faithlessness. The move towards giving a more missionary feel to the enterprise was perhaps underscored by the selection of Anselm of Havelberg as a legate – a man who had a history of conversion work. Because Anselm was part of Conrad's embassy to Eugenius at Clairvaux, it is almost certain that his appointment to the legation was made at this meeting. Anselm and his colleagues – who were all from northern Germany and hence entirely familiar with the region – must have discussed the situation with the pope in detail and perhaps their input helped to shape the tone of his bull. Furthermore, it was probably their advice that influenced the prohibition of a financial deal with the Slavs of the kind that had often happened in the past.

Within three months the warriors and churchmen of northern Germany, Denmark and Poland had responded to Bernard and Eugenius's calls and were ready to set out. The *Annales Magdeburgenses* reflected a Bernadine message in the statement that a huge number of Christian knights had taken the sign of the life-giving cross to subjugate or destroy the pagans.[59] On the other hand, Vincent of Prague emphasised the missionary aspect when he wrote that 'many of the bishops of Saxony with many of the Saxon knights went to Pomerania to convert the Pomeranians to the Christian faith'.[60] Helmold of Bosau described the crusaders as wanting 'to avenge the death and destruction which [the Slavs] had inflicted upon the worshippers of Christ, especially upon the Danes'.[61] The last words presumably covered the general acts of piracy conducted by the pagans against the Danes and were also, possibly, a reference to the loss of Rugen. The combination of ideas here may suggest some lack of clarity or unified sense of purpose to the expedition.

The Baltic Crusade was to have two distinct parts. The first attacked the town of Dobin near the coast in the bay of Wismar, the second fought further east, around Demmin and Stettin. Before the expedition got underway, Niclot, the leader of the Abodrites, tried to forestall it by diplomatic and military means. He sent messengers to Adolph of Holsatia to remind him of their earlier pact, but the count declined to meet him and indicated that such a move would deeply upset the other Christian princes. Niclot was angered; he wrote a letter, reported by Helmold of Bosau, in which he explained how he had undertaken to keep the Slavs calm in spite of their claim to have been unjustly deprived of their fathers' lands, and now he could no longer do this since the count had abandoned him in his hour of need. When he saw the crusaders gathering their men, Niclot resolved to strike first and he assembled his fleet and sailed to the mouth of the River Trave.

On 26 June he attacked the city of Lübeck, killed 300 men and laid siege to the citadel for two days. Niclot also sent two troops of horsemen to ravage the countryside; settlements of Frisians and Hollanders took the brunt of the damage. Men were killed and women and children led into captivity; most urban sites were sufficiently well fortified not to attract attention, however. The fortress of Süssel resisted, inspired by a local priest, Gerlav, who warned the defenders against surrender. He argued that the Slavs hated the Frisians more than anyone; hence the inhabitants should expect no mercy and believe no promises of safe-conduct. Count Adolph heard of the siege and marched to the rescue, but on his approach Niclot's men disappeared.[62] Clearly Niclot was a formidable and quick-thinking opponent, although his pre-emptive strike had the effect of galvanising Christian opposition to the pagans.

Niclot fell back to his base at Dobin, 'a famous piratical town' as Saxo characterised it.[63] It was located in a marshy area about eight miles in from the sea; larger vessels anchored in a harbour on the coast while the shallow rivers allowed only smaller boats down to the settlement – a perfect base for raiding activities. On learning of the crusade, Niclot had fortified Dobin. A nineteenth-century survey of the site revealed a long, oblong-shaped earth wall on a narrow isthmus that separated the land between the seawards and southern sides and, if cut across the neck of the land, it could isolate the site fully.[64]

The crusaders who attacked Niclot were a combined Danish-Saxon force that consisted of the fleets of Canute V and Sweyn III and the armies of Duke Henry the Lion of Saxony, Archbishop Albert of Bremen, Duke Conrad of Burgundy and Bishop Thietmar of Verden.[65] As noted in connection with the planned 1108 campaign, such German–Danish co-operation in this arena was not, in theory at least, unprecedented. According to Saxo Grammaticus, who wrote c.1200, it was on receipt of letters from the pope – presumably *Divina dispensatione II* – that Sweyn and Canute put aside their differences in order to invade the neighbouring barbarians: 'Rather than neglect the duties of public religion in the pursuit of private warfare, the Danes therefore assume the emblems of holy pilgrimage and obey the command'.[66] The two men exchanged hostages and 'turned their weapons to the vindication of the faith'. The thirteenth-century *Knytlinge Saga* described how the two kings took the cross because of papal promises of plenary indulgences and martyrdom if they died.[67]

The Saxons and Danes tried to pincer Dobin, the former coming by land and the latter by sea. Canute's fleet arrived first, followed by that of Sweyn. The Saxons, 'burning to vindicate their faith', moved up to the town, but the pagans took the initiative again. Saxo noted that the Rugians saw how few men guarded the Danish vessels and sent out a raiding party. They descended upon Sweyn's ships and killed or captured many of the crews; the remaining defenders had little appetite for the fight and some tried to desert. Sweyn rallied his troops and drove the Rugians out to sea. Helmold suggested that the Danes had acted too casually, 'for they are pugnacious at home and unwarlike abroad', and were caught unawares by a sally from the town. The topography prevented the Saxons from coming to their relief and many men were lost.[68] Angered by this, the crusaders pressed the siege harder, but soon the mutual distrust between Sweyn and Canute began to reappear, detracting from the Danes' focus on the campaign.[69] More damagingly, an insidious questioning as to the purpose of the attack began to surface. Troops from the contingents of Count Adolph and Albert the Bear, margrave of Saxony (who was with the other crusading army) asked: 'Is not the land we are devastating our land, and the people we are fighting our people? Why are we, then, found to be our own enemies and the destroyers of our own incomes? Does not this loss fall back on our lords?'[70] Bernard's rigid principles of conversion or destruction seemed far out of step with the aspirations and sensibilities of many of the crusaders themselves. In their view, if the Slavs were destroyed, it would remove their source of taxation and they would lose out. Eugenius's calls for subjugation and conversion seemed closer to the prevailing mood of the northern crusaders; perhaps his discussions with the German churchmen at Clairvaux, away from the intense atmosphere at the court of Frankfurt, gave him a better insight into what was appropriate for this theatre of holy war.

The fighting at Dobin became less fierce, truces were arranged and, even when the crusaders gained the upper hand in the numerous small engagements, the nobles held them back from a full assault on the fortress. Blomqvist argues that the Saxons worried the crusaders might bring other entrepreneurs into the area who could usurp their position.[71] Eventually, the Slavs agreed to convert to Christianity and to release the Danes. Helmold observed sourly that this was only a false baptism and that the able-bodied among the captives were kept: 'Thus that grand expedition broke up with slight gain. The Slavs immediately became worse: they neither respected their baptism nor kept their hands from ravaging the Danes'.[72] In one sense, this was not strictly accurate because, as Helmold himself wrote, Count Adolf and Niclot soon became friends again.[73]

The second crusading army set out from Magdeburg towards Demmin, around 130 miles to the north-east. It was led by Albert the Bear and Conrad of

Meissen and included many churchmen such as Archbishop Anselm of Havelberg, Abbot Wibald of Stavelot, the Bohemian Bishop Henry of Moravia, Archbishop Frederick of Magdeburg, Bishop Rolf of Halberstadt, Reinhold of Merseburg, Werner of Munster, Wichman of Brandenburg. Miesko Stary, brother of the duke of Poland, also led a contingent.[74] The crusaders first crossed the Elbe and captured Havelberg, they then went on to the town of Malchow near Lake Moritz, where they burned a pagan temple. The *Annales Magdeburgenses* reported that the army moved around and laid waste to a vast area, burning towns and fortresses over a period of three months.[75]

The crusaders then arrived at Demmin where the army split. Albert the Bear led one group to Stettin at the mouth of the River Oder where they duly laid siege to the city – only for the inhabitants to confound the crusaders by displaying crosses above their citadel! The defenders sent out a legation led by Bishop Albert who had been appointed by Bishop Otto of Bamburg during his mission a couple of decades earlier. Bishop Albert asked why the Saxons were attacking them – surely it made no sense. The approach on Stettin seems a very strange move indeed, either explained by a complete ignorance of the work of Bishop Otto or motivated by Margrave Albert's desire to take an important strategic location. In the second case, the presence of numerous clergy in the crusader army, including Anselm of Havelberg, prevented him from using force against a Christian target. Vincent of Prague stated that the Saxon nobles were more interested in conquering territory than in extending the Christian faith, but a council between the Saxon bishops, Bishop Albert and Prince Ratibor of Pomerania led to a peace agreement and the crusaders withdrew.[76] The bishop pondered why the crusaders had appeared: 'if they had come to confirm the Pomeranians in the Christian faith, then they ought to have done this through the preaching of bishops, not by arms'.[77] The military aspect of the campaign had become redundant. Ratibor was required to come to Havelberg and swear before the princes to defend the Christian faith in Pomerania. The *Annales Magdeburgenses* wrote that Ratibor 'confessed the same Catholic faith that he had recently received through the preaching of Bishop Otto of Bamberg . . . and he recognised, praised and swore that he would always labour with all his might to defend and propagate the Christian faith'.[78] As Taylor argues, this indicated that the prince was now the religious leader of his people; in other words Anselm had combined political submission with conversion.[79] The crusaders who remained at Demmin – including Wibald of Stavelot – achieved little of any note. Wibald blamed the failure of the campaign on tensions amongst the invaders. He had returned home by early September.[80]

The Wendish Crusade did not live up to the expectations of the papacy; to the churchmen and nobles in the region, however, it was less of a disaster. It seems that the harsher side of Bernard's crusading ideals was too out of step with the experiences and aspirations of the northern Europeans. The idea of conversion, in conjunction with political rule, was more familiar. We can see from the cases of Ratibor and Niclot how the crusaders came to terms with pagan rulers. While the crusade may have created a larger than usual military threat, and this could have helped to convince the pagans to submit, Bernard and Eugenius's initiative did not produce a distinctive outcome to the campaigns in the north. The harder, more religious edge to holy war, apparent in parts of Iberia, was, for the moment at least, lacking in the Baltic region. Elements of crusading – such as the offer of spiritual rewards – were attractive, but the extreme form of crusading stipulated by Bernard in 1147 did not take seed immediately. Conversion was the priority for men like Anselm of Havelberg, and this helped to shape the direction of the crusade. Eschatology was another element in the thinking of those who launched the crusade which did not really dovetail with the ideas and aims of those on the ground in the north.[81]

The importance of secular motives was especially relevant and had been a theme of note for decades. Adam of Bremen related an episode in the mid-eleventh century when the king of Denmark complained that the Slavs could have been converted to Christianity but for the avarice of the Saxons: 'They are more intent on the payment of tribute than on the conversion of the heathen'.[82] Helmold of Bosau described events in the late 1130s and complained that 'the princes were accustomed to watch over the Slavs for the purposes of increasing their incomes'.[83] In other words, eradication was unlikely to fulfil the needs of the nobles because there would be no one to take tribute or tax from. Submission was a familiar outcome and benefited everyone; on this basis killing all the Slavs was simply not a viable option and the prohibition on coming to terms was equally unwelcome and unfamiliar. The involvement of outside forces, such as the Danes, could have entailed a reduction in the spoils for the local German nobility – another potential problem. In this sense, Lotter's argument that Bernard really meant the destruction of a culture, rather than of a people, could fit in quite well. True it could be seen as a line of argument too subtle for the majority of the crusader army; on the other hand it would match the *modus operandi* of both Church and state in the region and avoid accusations that Abbot Bernard flouted biblical injunctions.[84] In terms of outcome, at least, there was a parallel to events of fifty years ago, when popular opinion and military reality swept aside Pope Urban II's hopes of using the First Crusade to form closer ties with the Greeks. It seems that the Wendish crusaders also deflected the aspirations of a senior churchman, in this case Bernard of Clairvaux.

CHAPTER 13

CRUSADING IN IBERIA
ALMERÍA, JAEN, TORTOSA AND LÉRIDA

In 711 the Arabs of North Africa invaded Iberia and soon defeated the Visigothic king. As they swept northwards to bring most of the peninsula under their control the ruler of Asturias was the only Christian monarch to offer any effective resistance. Muslim power remained considerable over the next few centuries, and while the ninth-century 'Chronicle of Alfonso III' expressed the idea of reconquest, it was not until the eleventh century that the Christians were able to make real progress when the Ummayad caliphate of Cordoba began to weaken.[1] This situation resulted in the emergence of numerous *taifa* states, none with sufficient authority to reunite Muslim Spain, yet at the same time strong enough to prevent the nascent Christian kingdoms of the north from picking them off. There was by no means a strict inter-faith division to these conflicts; Muslims and Christians formed alliances and rulers of both sides fought amongst themselves, but by the latter half of the eleventh century it is possible to ascertain a growing religious edge to the struggle.[2] In a document from 1092, King Sancho Ramírez I of Aragon and Navarre (1063–94) outlined his wish to liberate lands previously taken from the Christians and to drive the infidel out:

> I took care to settle inhabitants in [Montemayor] . . . for the recovery and extension of the Church of Christ, for the destruction of the pagans, the enemies of Christ, and the building up and benefit of the Christians, so that the kingdom, invaded and captured by the Ishmaelites, might be liberated to the honour and service of Christ; and that once all the people of that unbelieving rite were expelled and the filthiness of their wicked error was eliminated therefrom, the venerable Church of Jesus Christ our Lord may be fostered there forever.[3]

Outside parties began to influence the situation in the peninsula. To name but three: the monastery of Cluny; intermarriage with French nobles; and the

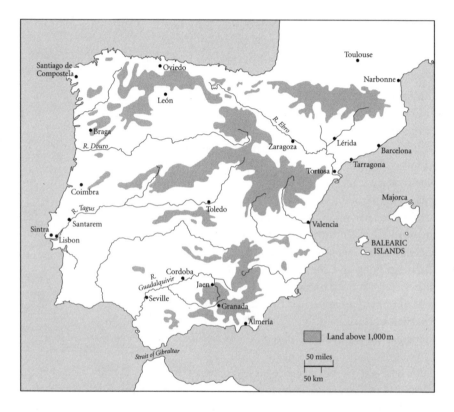

Map of the Iberian Peninsula showing key locations for the events of the Second Crusade

interest of the Reform Papacy. These are seen by some historians as factors in the genesis of the crusading movement as a whole. O'Callaghan is adamant that the offer of indulgences by Alexander II (1062–73) and the approval of the Barbastro campaign in 1064 were clear examples of crusading in all but name.[4] The relationship between such early instances of papally directed warfare and the emergence of crusading has been the subject of much historical debate and its details fall outside the scope of this book.[5] Historians such as Cowdrey, Fletcher, Bull and Jaspert are less convinced; they prefer a more tempered approach, emphasising the offer of limited indulgences, but rejecting the absolute overlap between holy war in Spain and the Levant asserted by O'Callaghan. For Bull, in particular, events in the peninsula were important only as a background to the First Crusade – they did not give it a special momentum.[6]

Nonetheless, the ideological and political background to the events of 1147–9 is important in explaining the planning and outcome of these campaigns. Back in the eleventh century, the Iberian Muslims responded to the Christian advance, most obviously after the capture of Toledo in 1085 by Alfonso VI (1065–1109), with a summons for support to the Almoravids of North Africa. In the following year the newcomers defeated the king and took control of the majority of the *taifas*. Three years later, another wave of Almoravids arrived and prompted Pope Urban II to call for resistance to this threat to Christendom. In a letter of 1089 he urged the secular and religious leaders near Tarragona to rebuild the town as 'a wall and bulwark of Christianity against the Muslims' and he offered them the same indulgence as if they were to fulfil a pilgrimage to Jerusalem.[7]

In 1095, Urban launched the First Crusade. The lure of the Holy Sepulchre was such that some in Iberia were drawn to the Levant – an unwelcome development for the pope who urged people to remain in the peninsula. He wrote:

> We beseech most carefully your lordships on behalf of the city, or rather the church, of Tarragona, and we order you to make a vigorous effort to restore it in every possible way for the remission of sins. For you know what a great defence it would be for Christ's people and what a terrible blow it would be to the Saracens if, by the goodness of God, the position of that famous city were restored. If the knights of other provinces have decided with one mind to go to the aid of the Asian Church and to liberate their brothers from the tyranny of the Saracens, so ought you with one mind and with our encouragement to work with greater endurance to help a church so near you resist the invasions of the Saracens. No one must doubt that if he dies on this expedition for the love of God and his brothers, his sins will surely be forgiven and he will gain a share of eternal life through the most

compassionate mercy of our God. So if any of you has made up his mind to go to Asia, it is here instead that he should try to fulfil his vow, because it is no virtue to rescue Christians from the Saracens in one place, only to expose them to the tyranny and oppression of the Saracens in another.[8]

A letter of 1098 to the bishop of Huesca expressed a similar idea and tried to deter Spaniards from crusading in the East.[9] Likewise, in 1100 and 1101, Pope Paschal II reiterated the principle, although a number of Spanish knights did make their way to the Holy Land.[10] We can see some elements of the crusade to the Levant present in the peninsula; for example, at Zaragoza in 1101, Pedro I of Aragon (who had originally taken the cross for Jerusalem) bore a banner of the Cross of Christ.[11] Yet O'Callaghan has overstated the case in suggesting that the apparatus and process of crusading was 'precisely the same' as that for the Holy Land at this time.[12] The offer of remission of all confessed sins to those who took part in the expedition is not apparent. Given the lack of unambiguous evidence to support O'Callaghan's view, it is probably safer, as Housley argues, to regard the period between 1095 and c.1113–14 as an evolutionary period.[13] From the latter dates onwards, however, there are clearer signs of closer parallels between crusading to the East and Iberia and the existence of ties between the two theatres of war.[14]

An attack on the Balearics from 1113–15 by Count Ramon Berenguer III of Barcelona, William VI of Montpellier and a Pisan fleet is moving towards something more obviously identifiable as a crusade. Ramon 'received on his shoulder the sign of the cross', and the expedition succeeded in taking Ibiza and Mallorca.[15] A year later there was a plan to attack Tortosa; Pope Paschal II praised the ruler of Barcelona for his plans and a legate was appointed but the campaign never took place. More significantly, in 1118 Pope Gelasius II acknowledged the virtuous work of those who fought the Muslims and offered substantial spiritual rewards for Alfonso I of Aragon's assault on Zaragoza, although full remission of sins was only granted to those who lost their lives.[16]

The pontificate of Calixtus II (1119–24) marked an important point in the development of crusading and laid down a vital cornerstone for the overall shape of the Second Crusade – complete parity between Iberia and the Holy Land; over time, links between the two theatres of war would grow ever stronger. Calixtus had been the papal legate for Spain and was well aware of the potential role of the crusade in the reconquest. At the First Lateran Council in March 1123, the most important gathering of churchmen for many years, he placed holy warfare in Iberia and the Levant in the same category with the elements of vow, cross and indulgence all evident.[17] Within a month Calixtus had issued a bull for a Catalan crusade in which he explicitly promised the same remission of sins as for those who fought in the Holy Land. He stated: 'With apostolic authority and the power divinely bestowed upon us we graciously grant to all those fighting firmly on this expedition the same remission of sins that we conceded to the defenders of the Eastern Church.'[18] The participants wore a cross on their clothes and Bishop Oleguer of Tarragona was appointed as the official legate to preach what ended up as an unsuccessful foray to Corbins near Lérida in 1124.[19]

The growing ties between crusading in the Holy Land and Iberia were to be reflected in a speech of Archbishop Diego Gelmírez of Santiago to a Church council at Compostela in 1125. In this famous oration he broached the idea of opening a new way to the Holy Land, via Spain and North Africa: 'Just as the soldiers of Christ . . . have opened up the road to Jerusalem by much toil and bloodshed, so let us become soldiers of Christ too and by defeating his enemies . . . let us open . . . a shorter and much less difficult road towards the same Holy Sepulchre by way of Spain.'[20] The archbishop also spoke in terms of the crusaders making proper confession and serving in God's army for the remission of their sins.

A generation of rulers began to advance the reconquest further. The reign of Alfonso I 'the Battler' of Aragon (1104–34) saw several notable changes.[21] In 1122, for example, he established the *militia Christi* of Belchite (near Zaragoza), an organisation that bore some similarities to the Knights Templar, with spiritual rewards offered to those who dedicated their lives to the defence of Christians.[22] Within a few years he had also created the *militia Christi* of Monréal. Its foundation charter reflected the thinking of Archbishop Diego in expressing a wish to defeat the Muslims of Spain and then to open up a new route to Jerusalem.[23] Alfonso led numerous campaigns against the Muslims, particularly down the Ebro river valley, and he also carried a casket containing a relic of the True Cross on campaign with him.[24] The Anglo-Norman writer Orderic Vitalis described the king and his men as '*Christi cruce signatos*', an indication that a northern European writer was aware of, and comfortable with, recording participation in the conflict in Iberia in those terms.[25] Alfonso finally met his end in 1134 when he died of wounds incurred at the Battle of Fraga. Famously, he left his kingdom to the Knights Hospitaller, Knights Templar and the Canons of the Holy Sepulchre.[26] The consequences of his will have been widely discussed, but the most pertinent point here is that the growing presence of three institutions intrinsically associated with the Levant further emphasised the ties between the Holy Land and Iberia.

To the west, King Alfonso VII became the ruler of León-Castile in 1126 and once properly established in power he began to extend his lands. In 1133 he led a large raid southwards towards Cordoba, Seville and Jerez that even reached the shores of the Mediterranean. His coronation as emperor two years later showed his growing confidence and by the 1140s he was making regular campaigns to the south.[27] The occasional visits of Spanish nobles to the Holy Land represented a further element in the broader struggle against Islam. In the 1130s, the pilgrimage to Jerusalem of Count Rodrigo González de Lara saw him build the castle of Toron, near Ascalon, and before his return to Iberia he entrusted the fortress to the Templars.[28]

In tandem with the emergence of strong rulers to lead the fight against Islam, the political situation in Muslim Spain and North Africa played into the hands of the Christians as well. In much the same way that during the 1090s the death and disorder in the ruling classes of Asia Minor and Syria were key factors behind the success of the First Crusade, the steep decline of the Almoravids in the 1140s was of great help in the build up to, and the progress of, the Second Crusade.[29] From the 1120s onwards, stirrings against the authority of Almoravid rule in North Africa had began to appear. The Almohads, a group with a particularly rigorous and puritanical interpretation of Islam, started to move out from their tribal bases in the Atlas Mountains and to threaten the Almoravid capital of Marrakesh. The latter had originally advocated austerity, but had apparently slipped towards a more indulgent lifestyle.[30] The troubles in North Africa meant that the Almoravids in Iberia were without support from their homelands.[31] Alfonso I of Aragon raided southwards in 1125–6 and 1129 to test this growing vulnerability, although the effective command of Yusuf ibn Tashufin brought the Muslims some victories, most notably with the death of Alfonso of Aragon noted above. Tashufin's recall to North Africa in 1138 weakened the Almoravid position and there was widespread disaffection with them in Iberia. By the early 1140s their power in North Africa started to disintegrate too. In 1143 and 1144 Alfonso VII mounted substantial forays deep into al-Andalus. He gathered considerable booty and sparked further discontent amongst a Muslim population frustrated by their leaders' lack of response; rebellions against the Almoravids broke out across the peninsula. Some of the rebels based their opposition on spiritual grounds as well and the emergence of Sufi groups provided a notable focus. Almoravid rule in North Africa crumbled further with the death of Tashufin in March 1145. A later Muslim writer neatly summed up the situation:

What with the Christians of every denomination who assailed his frontiers, and what with the Muslims of Andalus themselves, who showed everywhere symptoms of disaffection and wished to rid themselves of the Almoravids, [it was not possible] to stem the torrent of calamity and misfortune which broke out more furiously than ever in the fair domains of Islam. At last, when the peoples of Andalus saw that the empire of the

Almoravids was falling to pieces ... they waited no longer and casting away the mask of dissimulation, broke out into open rebellion against their African rulers.[32]

Tensions between García Ramírez IV of Navarre and Ramon Berenguer IV of Barcelona and Aragon meant that the Christian side could not focus its full attention on the situation in the south, although Alfonso VII worked hard to try to mediate.[33] It was at this time that the fall of Edessa prompted appeals to the West for a new crusade. From a Spanish perspective, therefore, the background to the call for a crusade to the Holy Land was an intensification of their own efforts to drive the Muslims of Iberia southwards. Given the connections between the two theatres of war in terms of ideas, institutions and personnel, it is unsurprising that the rulers of Iberia and the papacy started to work together to link this element of the conflict with Islam to the struggle in the Levant – after all, as we have seen in 1123, Calixtus II had, in theory at least, drawn such a parallel.

Those in Iberia would have heard about the loss of Edessa and the proposal to launch a new expedition to the East in the course of normal ecclesiastical and diplomatic business; for example, the archbishops of Braga and Toledo were at the papal *curia* in May 1145.[34] In fact, as Eugenius planned the release of *Quantum praedecessores*, he was already involved in promoting crusading of a limited nature in Spain. On 27 May he granted the new archbishop of Tarragona the *pallium* and re-issued an earlier bull for a campaign to Tarragona (rather than a wider agenda), for the 'reconquest of which our predecessors are known to have laboured greatly'.[35] This bull had already been sent out by Lucius II in 1144, Gelasius II in 1118 and even Urban II, although the earliest surviving text is that of Gelasius.[36] Thus, only a few months before he sent out a document resonant with the history of crusading to the Holy Land, Eugenius had recalled the work of his predecessors in another theatre of war and encouraged the continuation of crusading in Iberia. At this point, of course, the Spanish campaign was an enterprise distinct from the one planned to the Eastern Mediterranean. As Reilly indicates, Alfonso VII's cousin, Count Alphonse-Jordan of Toulouse, was at Vézelay in March 1146 and this formed a further channel for news to reach the south. The Toulousain's decision to go to the Holy Land would have removed another problem within the Christian camp because Ramon Berenguer IV was regent of Provence and there had been some difficulties between the two men.[37]

In the summer of 1146 Alfonso VII led his (by now) annual expedition southwards. He besieged Cordoba and took the town, but not the citadel, in May. Its ruler, Ibn Ghaniya, swore homage to the emperor and the great mosque became a church. While Alfonso was at Cordoba representatives arrived from Genoa to suggest a joint attack on the port of Almería on the south-east coast of the peninsula. This episode, and the Tortosan campaign of the following year, would involve a broad group of forces from across southern Europe and ultimately secured papal recognition; the annual *razzias* became part of a wider movement of Christian expansionism that dovetailed neatly with the territorial and commercial ambitions both of the *curia* and of the secular powers; as we saw above, contemporaries often viewed the 1147–8 crusades in the Levant and Iberia as part of the same enterprise.

Two important sources allow us to follow the Iberian element of the Second Crusade. The *Chronica Adefonsi imperatoris* is a contemporary, or near-contemporary, account of part of the life of Alfonso VII. It is formed of two books and a poem. In the first book, the hero was mainly concerned with fighting other Christians and bringing them to heel. In the second, however, Alfonso VII and his nobles waged bloody campaigns against the Muslims of Spain. At the end of this section the author announced that he did not wish to bore his audience and launched into a verse account of the Almería campaign, although the text breaks off just before the siege began in earnest. The author was probably Bishop Arnaldo of Astorga, a man educated at the great Catalan monastery of Ripoll (a celebrated centre of poetry), who had spent many years in Toledo before taking the position at Astorga.[38] Emperor Alfonso himself was compared to Charlemagne; they were 'equal in courage and the power of their weapons, equal was the glory of the campaigns which they waged'.[39] Charlemagne's involvement in Iberia was of particular concern to contemporary authors in the peninsula – such as the composer of the 'Pseudo-Turpin', written in Santiago *c*.1140 – and it is no surprise to see the parallels drawn here as well.[40] The *Chronica* and the *Poem* are suffused with a sense of holy war and a concern for vengeance against the Muslims of Almería which probably indicates that these were strong motives for those who took part in the expedition: Alfonso's destiny was said to be to make war on 'the evil pestilence of the Moors'.[41]

Alongside Bishop Arnaldo's work is the briefer *De Captione Almerie et Tortuose*, written by Caffaro of Genoa, a layman.[42] Caffaro was a truly remarkable individual. He was born *c*.1080 and had a career that stretched from participation in the First Crusade, through to the eve of the Second, and down into the 1160s.[43] He was a high-level diplomat, consul, crusader, judicial administrator, historian and military leader; he also wrote the *Annales Ianuenses*, adopted as the official history of the city in 1152, and the brief *De liberatione civitatum orientis* (written in 1155) about Genoese involvement in the First Crusade.[44] He probably visited the Holy Land again *c*.1140. The narrative concerning Almería and Tortosa is a fascinating text, which displays the author's enormous pride in the achievements of Genoa and is laced with the interweaving ideals of crusading ideology and commercial gain.

The Genoese had long, close links with crusading to the Holy Land and with campaigns in the Iberian Peninsula. A brief outline will emphasise the series of connections that existed between the Genoese and these theatres of war.[45] The First Crusade was preached at Genoa in 1097 and a fleet from the city helped in the siege of Antioch. It returned home with important relics of the bones of John the Baptist, as well as commercial concessions in the city. Caffaro himself went to the Levant in 1100 and visited Jerusalem before he took part in the capture of Arsuf and Caesarea in 1101. On the latter occasion, the Genoese secured the stunning emerald green coloured glass bowl that still survives in the treasury of the cathedral of St Lawrence and was, at one time, identified as the Holy Grail.[46] Participants in this campaign were richly rewarded, getting 45 Poitevin *sous* and 2 lb of pepper each. In the next few years, the Genoese were present at the sieges of Tortosa (in Syria), Tripoli, Gibelet, Jaffa, Arsuf and Acre, and in most cases they gained healthy privileges and promises of generous shares in future conquests. King Baldwin I of Jerusalem saw their maritime skills as essential for the capture of the coastal cities and believed they were well worth cultivating.[47] The Italian city-states' role as providers of transport for the thousands of pilgrims who went to the Holy Land and their ongoing importance in commerce were highly significant as well. The Genoese did not, however, trade exclusively with the Latin East but were involved with Armenia, Egypt and Byzantium too. The Genoese also fought the Muslims in the western Mediterranean. There had been campaigns against Tortosa (in Spain) in 1092 and 1097 (see below) and they had attacked Muslim ports in North Africa, most notably in a joint expedition with the Pisans to Mahadia in 1087, while they raided the port of Bougie in 1136.[48] As noted above, when Alfonso was at Cordoba in the summer of 1146 he was approached by 'eloquent envoys of the Genoese' who urged him to join in a large-scale attack on Almería. The port was said to be a base for pirates who were raiding Christian lands throughout the Mediterranean and it was a flourishing commercial centre; located in the far south of the peninsula, it would offer Alfonso a foothold deep into Muslim territory. [49] For similar reasons it had attracted the attention of the Genoese and in the spring and summer of 1146 Caffaro himself led a raid against Minorca and Almería. The Genoese fleet of twenty-two galleys and six smaller ships, which contained 100 horses and cavalry, spent several days looting the island. They then crossed to the mainland where they stole the cargo from vessels in the harbour and besieged the city. They were promised 113,000 gold *morabetinos*, 25,000 of which were paid immediately, but when the remainder did not arrive within the stipulated eight days the siege was renewed. At the onset of winter the Genoese departed 'in triumph and with a large amount of money'.[50] Against a background of ongoing problems for Muslim Spain, the Genoese had evidently gauged Almería's strength. This assessment must have convinced them that it was worth trying to persuade Alfonso – who was plainly interested in fighting the forces of Islam in the region as well – to take part in a full-scale attempt to capture the city.

In late September 1146 the Genoese undertook to bring an army and siege engines to besiege Almería. In return, Alfonso promised to pay 10,000 gold *morabetinos* within a month and a further 10,000 by the following Easter, all towards the cost of siege equipment; the defences of Almería had been judged formidable enough to require this kind of preparation and expenditure.[51] As Rogers noted, Alfonso had accumulated a fair amount of experience in siege warfare against both Christian and Muslim opponents, although to tackle Almería would apparently require several strong allies.[52] The Genoese were also to have one third of all the lands and goods taken in 1147 and, within the former, they could maintain their own factories, markets, churches, baths and ovens. Their subjects were also granted exemption from all tolls in León-Castile and promised safe conduct. The whole agreement was contingent upon a similar deal being struck with the count of Barcelona; again, this is an indication of the scale of the task and of the intention to co-ordinate these projects.[53] A substantial list of nobles forms the witness list to Alfonso's document: 'A roster of the secular magnates of [Alfonso's] kingdom', as Reilly observed; the emperor was making the commitment of his people plain to all.[54]

The *Chronica Adefonsi* tells us that Alfonso sent Bishop Arnaldo to the count of Barcelona and William of Montpellier 'so that, for the redemption of their souls', they would join the campaign.[55] While the exact timing of Arnaldo's mission is unclear, his phrase is some indication of the presence of crusading ideology, even at this preparatory stage. Although no papal bull survives for the Almería campaign there is a strong suggestion that one was issued because Caffaro reported that the Genoese, 'prompted and called by God through the Apostolic See, swore to lead a army against the Saracens of Almería'.[56] In October, Eugenius had addressed *Divina dispensatione I* to the churchmen of Italy to crusade in the Levant.[57] It is possible that the pope had heard of the planned campaign in Iberia – or he may have been approached by the Genoese directly – and was willing to support this venture as part of a wider war of Christian expansion. As we saw above, in mid-1145 the pope had issued a bull concerned with crusading in the Iberian Peninsula and he encouraged Bernard Tort to fight at Tarragona; with this background, the likelihood of Eugenius approving a campaign in Spain was surely high. In a broader sense his action would line up with the earlier parity between crusading in Iberia and the Holy Land expressed by Calixtus II. Some formal expression of papal enthusiasm helps to explain Arnaldo's offer of spiritual rewards, as mentioned in the *Chronica Adefonsi*. Presumably this helped to prompt a positive response to the bishop's embassy; the fact that Ramon Berenguer's participation was stated to be essential for the execution of the Genoese–Leónese pact added another reason for Eugenius to back the expedition. It may also be no coincidence that in January 1147 the *infanta* Sancha gave a grant to the monastery of Clairvaux.[58] This suggests cordial relations between the Leónese court and the abbot while the latter preached the crusade – again, an interesting connection. Bishop Arnaldo's mission succeeded: both Ramon Berenguer IV and Count William promised to join the campaign in the following autumn, as requested.

Ramon also came to an agreement with the Genoese. This stipulated that after the Almería campaign the Genoese would assist him in an attack on Tortosa (and would go nowhere else without the permission of the count). If victorious, they were to receive the same privileges as awarded by Alfonso at Almería; in other words, one third of the city to the Genoese, two thirds to the count, and the usual exemptions in his ports and lands. Both parties put forward substantial numbers of witnesses to these deeds.[59] As Jaspert has demonstrated, Tortosa had been a target of the reconquest for many years; it was an attractive prize because it controlled the coast down towards the riches of al-Andalus and the river valley of the Ebro inland; it was also known for its shipyards and supplies of excellent, hard wood.[60] The 1148 campaign against Tortosa is particularly interesting because the planned division of the city even featured a church dedicated to the Holy Sepulchre, which emphasises the emerging ties between warfare in Iberia and the Eastern Mediterranean.[61] The Genoese had generally maintained cordial relations with the Catalans and in 1127, for example, they signed a commercial deal with Count Ramon Berenguer III.[62] Back in 1092 the Genoese and Pisans had combined to attack the city. Ramon Berenguer II fought there in 1095 and two years later, his successor, Ramon Berenguer III, besieged it in conjunction with a Genoese fleet. Land and revenues were (theoretically) divided, although the campaign ultimately failed. In 1113–14, 1116 and 1121 the counts of Barcelona made further plans to take the city, each time securing active papal support; on the second of these occasions, Ramon Berenguer III travelled to Italy in person. He sought Genoese and Pisan assistance to compensate for the weakness of the Catalan navy and to work 'for the liberation of the Spanish Church'.[63] Ramon IV was also a patron of the Knights Templar and he showed his continued support for them in a grant of 1143. As part of the settlement of Alfonso 'the Battler's' will he gave them six castles and promised various other privileges, as well as one fifth of his future conquests. It was stated that the purpose of the grant was 'for the crushing, conquest and expulsion of the Moors, for the exaltation of the faith and religion of sacred Christianity ... for the exercise of the office of a military order in the region of Spain against the Saracens, for the remission of my sins'.[64] Barcelona itself had just seen, in 1145, the foundation of the Augustinian community of Santa Anna, a priory of the Order of the Holy Sepulchre of Jerusalem. Individuals buried there received the same spiritual benefits as if interred near the Holy Sepulchre itself, thus providing another spiritual channel for crusading ideas into the peninsula.[65]

The involvement of William VI of Montpellier (1121–49) was also vital. The count had a family history of warfare against the Muslims: his father had fought in the First Crusade and his son had been to Jerusalem, brought back a relic of the True Cross and also participated in the capture of Zaragoza. In 1136 Ramon Berenguer had granted the entire city and diocese of Tortosa to William VI, who bequeathed it to his son in his will.[66] William VI worked closely with the Genoese as well and the Italians and the pope had helped him to retain control of Montpellier in his struggles with the citizenry there between 1141 and 1143.[67]

Ramon and William's actions here combined religious zeal with the achievement of a long-held strategic goal. The gathering of so many forces and the prospect of spiritual rewards meant that it made sense to try to capture Tortosa again, in much the same way that Afonso Henriques of Portugal took the opportunity afforded by the prospect of Anglo-Norman crusaders sailing to the Levant to fulfil his ambition of taking Lisbon. In sum, therefore, by the end of 1146, Alfonso VII, Ramon Berenguer IV of Barcelona, William VI of Montpellier and the Genoese had committed themselves to a series of co-ordinated campaigns in southern and western Spain over a two-year period; this plan was then, in turn, given papal support and the status of a crusade.

Alfonso worked to bring about peace in Christian Iberia and to settle discord between the count of Barcelona and King García Ramírez of Navarre. The king also made an important strategic move preparatory to a campaign in al-Andalus through the capture of the fortress of Calatrava.[68] In the meantime, the situation in Muslim Spain was changing: in early 1147 the first wave of Almohad invasions swept across to the peninsula and began to take over land near Algiciras and towards the Algarve. Back in North Africa, Almohad troops closed around Marrakesh and on 24 March 1147 they entered the city and slaughtered the population to establish their ascendancy.[69]

Papal enthusiasm for the expedition against Almería was expressed on 11 April 1147 in the issue of *Divina dispensatione II*. Eugenius was writing about the planned crusade in the Baltic region and, in doing so, he placed it in the broader context of a struggle on behalf of Christianity in both the Levant and Iberia. He wrote that 'the king of Spain is strongly armed against the Saracens of those regions, over whom he has already frequently triumphed through God's grace'. Eugenius anticipated the forthcoming campaign: 'we believe that it has been brought about through the providence of divine counsel that so great a multitude of the faithful from diverse regions is preparing to fight the infidel and that almost the whole of Christendom is being summoned for so great a task'.[70] He could not have given a clearer expression, in his statement, to the sense of shared endeavour between the three theatres of war.

The crusading aspect of the expedition to Almería was also made apparent in the descriptions of the Genoese and Leónese preparations. Caffaro related that the newly elected consuls called for everyone to make peace and, 'guided by the Holy Spirit', they agreed to do so.[71] These elections always took place in late January.[72] The populace urged the consuls to raise funds for the fleet and 'after hearing the admonition of God' – perhaps a reference to crusade preaching – they began to make ready for the campaign.[73] It may be worth observing that this burst of crusading enthusiasm took place just after Pope Eugenius had passed through northern Italy on his journey to France. There is no record that he visited Genoa, although we know of his presence at Lucca to the south and at Vercelli to the north in January 1147.[74]

Thus, in early 1147 the citizens gathered food, tents, arms and siege machinery (as promised in the pact with Alfonso). According to Caffaro, it took five months to assemble the necessities of war and around late June a fleet of 63 galleys and 163 other ships set sail.[75] This was a large fleet even for the Genoese, and it included ships from nearby ports such as Ventimigilia. Apparently it could muster 12,000 armed men, although this probably included many of the sailors; the commune had even needed to issue an order to prevent men from leaving the city so as to avoid service in the campaign.[76] This fleet was bigger than the northern European one which had sailed towards Lisbon a couple of months earlier; in total, the number of ships is comparable to that of the Venetians in the Fourth Crusade, although the latter included large numbers of specialised horse transport vessels (c.100) not mentioned here.[77]

The fleet sailed from Genoa to Port Maó on Minorca where they paused; an advance party of fifteen galleys was sent to reconnoitre the district around Almería. They went to the Cabo de Gata where they expected to meet Alfonso and there, c.17 miles east of Almería, they waited for him for a month. When the emperor failed to appear the Genoese grew increasingly anxious and sent out envoys who found him at Baeza (c.130 miles away) at the start of August.[78] By this stage, much of Alfonso's army had returned home which left him with 400 knights and 1,000 footsoldiers; a matter of further irritation to the Genoese.

Before discussing the progress of the expedition it is worth making a few more observations on the ideological background to the campaign and to emphasise the crusading context of the confrontation. As noted above, papal support must have been given for the clergy to offer the remission of sins. Unlike at Lisbon, there was no question of going on to Jerusalem and hence of having taken the cross already. The *Poem of Almería* said: 'All the bishops of Toledo and León, unsheathing the divine and material sword, exhort the adults and urge the young so that all may go bravely and surely to battle. They pardon sins and raise their voices to heaven, pledging to all the reward of life and the next. They promise prizes of silver and with victory they assure them once more that they will have all the gold which the Moors possess'.[79]

It seems that the senior clergy in Alfonso's lands had been mobilised to preach the crusade. Intriguingly, the offer of spiritual rewards was overtly coupled with an assurance of financial gain. The enterprise was regarded as a partnership between the divine and the secular. The writer perceived no apparent clash between the two kinds of reward; a message like this was unlikely to have been expressed by Bernard of Clairvaux. There was, of course, an element of hindsight here – the campaign did succeed and booty was secured, but there was also a recognition of what was required to motivate the Iberian crusaders, namely something broadly similar to what attracted the Wendish crusaders.

As the *Poem* eulogised the determination of the Spanish people to do battle with the Muslims, one further comment placed the struggle in a broader context: 'The trumpet of salvation rings out throughout all the regions of the world.'[80] The metaphor of the trumpet was used prominently in crusade preaching, most pertinently in *Quantum praedecessores*: 'Our predecessor of happy memory, Pope Urban, sounding forth like a heavenly trumpet, took care to induce sons of the Holy Roman Church from several parts of the world to free it.'[81] What is most interesting about the phrase in the *Poem* is the awareness that the crusade in Spain was part of a wider Christian enterprise. Although there were no explicit references to the campaigns in the Holy Land or in the Baltic, it is implicit in the words, 'the trumpet of salvation rings out throughout the world' that the author recognised such a situation. This, of course, echoed the overt statements made by Eugenius in *Divina dispensatione II*, and constitutes further evidence of contemporaries' acknowledgement of the scale of the crusade. In a similar vein, the anonymous *Trouvère* song of 1146–7 also drew a parallel between the expeditions to the Holy Land and Iberia and to the reasons behind them:

Knights, you are in very good hands now that God has called for your help against the Turks and Almoravids who have done Him such dishonour. They have wrongfully snatched his fiefs; our sorrow at this should indeed be great since it was there that God was first offered service and acknowledged as Lord.[82]

Given the nature of the text, each one of the nobles listed in the *Poem of Almería* had a suitably heroic character-portrait, the details of which are not especially relevant here but the general tenor is worth a comment, because it reflected a strong crusading zeal. The nobles included Count Fernando Pérez and Count Ramiro Froilaz of León 'concerned for the salvation of León'; the Asturian Pedro Alfonso, a Castilian contingent, Count Ponç of Cabrera, 'the ruin of the Moors'; Fernando Yáñez and his sons from Limia; Alvaro Rodríguez from Galicia who 'truly . . . hates the Moors'; Martín, lord of Hita; Count Ermengol VI of Urgel; Gutierre Fernández, the tutor of Sancho, Alfonso VII's son, and Count Manrique of Lara.[83] The author summarised the mentality of the crusaders: 'Conflict is peace for the Franks, but for the Moors it is a most famous scourge.'[84]

Notwithstanding the obvious wish to glorify the deeds of Christian warriors defeating the pagan tribes, the *Poem* did offer justification for the attack and described the vengeance wrought by the crusaders: 'The evil that had been wrought earlier was not allowed to go unpunished. The divine sword destroyed young and old alike in wars, not sparing the children in turn. The rest of the people are put to the sword like sheep . . . The terrible divine wrath falls on them.'[85] As we have seen earlier, the theme of vengeance was common in some accounts of the First Crusade (those of Guibert of Nogent, Robert of Rheims and Baldric of Bourgeuil); it was expressed in the letters of Bernard of Clairvaux and, more briefly, in the writings of Odo of Deuil and in Raol's *De expugnatione Lyxbonensi*.[86] Yet the level of ferocity here is considerably in excess by comparison with those authors; to Bishop Arnaldo, the imperative to couch the holy war in such terms was a strong one. In contrast to Raol, however, there was no sense of a desire for conversion of the infidel, but only for their destruction.[87]

Alfonso probably set out with an army of 5,000 men, and in May 1147 he reached Toledo, ready to move into al-Andalus. In June he passed through his recent acquisition of Calatrava and in July he attempted to capture Andújar. This siege failed, but he took Baeza, Ubeda and several other castles by mid-August. He was joined there by the forces of García Ramírez IV, king of Navarre.[88] The *Poem of Almería* recorded that around this time the emperor allowed many of his men to depart for home 'when the time of the campaign had expired'.[89] This suggests that, alongside the crusaders proudly listed above, much of the army was formed of municipal militias who were only obliged to serve for a fixed term, perhaps three months. This left, as Caffaro noted, 400 knights and 1,000 footsoldiers.[90] Reilly makes a virtue of this slimming down of the imperial force, arguing that the practicalities of the c.130-mile march from Baeza to Almería meant that a smaller army was an advantage. Fewer supplies would be needed in hostile territory and the final stages of the journey were across particularly arid land.[91]

By this stage, the battle for Almería had begun. The Genoese were encouraged by the arrival of Count Ramon Berenguer IV of Barcelona, his fleet and fifty-three knights, as well as Count William of Montpellier and his men. There had been preliminary skirmishing between the Almeríans and the Genoese advance party; with the Catalan fleet in attendance, the first real assault on the city could take place, probably in late August. A Genoese contingent of fifteen galleys moved towards the mosque area of the port to try and lure the Muslims out, but meanwhile the Catalans and another group of twenty-five Genoese galleys hid near the mouth of the Andarax river and the promontory of the Punta del Rio to await the signal from a solitary lookout ship. The defenders sensed a trap and sent men to reconnoitre the situation, but they failed to spot the lurking crusaders and indicated to their comrades to come out of the city and fight.[92] A force of 1,400 Muslims poured out and attacked the men from the fifteen galleys, killing eight Genoese and causing them to retreat back onto their ships. With the defenders committed, the lookout gave the sign and the twenty-five galleys and Catalan soldiers moved in. The remainder of the fleet, waiting close by at the Cabo da Gata, also joined the assault, led by a further twelve galleys. This latter group sailed to the front of the Christian force and pushed into the arsenal at the heart of the port. Meanwhile the Catalans engaged with those defenders who had come out of the city and 'with divine help' began hand-to-hand fighting. The Muslims were soon in retreat. Caffaro reported the heroism of William Pellis, who single-handedly killed a number of Saracens. With the initiative running their way, the troops on the twelve leading Genoese galleys, as well as those on the fifteen galleys near the mosque, began to land and, according to Caffaro, killed 5,000 Muslims on the shore.[93] Some of the Almeríans tried to escape by sea but the remaining Genoese shipping intercepted them. A change in the wind caused the Genoese consuls to call a halt to the battle; they ordered the fleet to the port at Punta del Rio, where they made camp and held a parliament. After thanking God for their great victory, they decided to bring the galleys onto the beach and to assemble the siege machinery. The Christian forces had dealt a strong opening blow to the enemy and were in a position to start to apply real pressure to the city's defences.[94]

While the artillery and towers were under construction the presence of Alfonso VII and his men added further impetus to the assault, but determined defence meant the engagement dragged on for six or seven weeks. The Muslims attempted to disrupt the preparation of the machinery, but to no avail. The Christians tried to move their towers up to the walls, but the Muslims used fire and their own siege engines to repel them. Eventually, the Genoese managed to get their machines close to the fortifications and seized two of the city's towers and broke down an eighteen-yard length of wall. In fear of imminent defeat the Almerians sent envoys to the imperial camp and offered payment in case the Spanish would abandon the Genoese and leave.[95] Caffaro is our only source for this suggestion, although the idea of the Muslims buying off the local Christians has an eerie echo of the rumoured events at Damascus the following year; given the situation it was presumably a worthwhile ploy. Likewise, according to Raol in *De expugnatione Lyxbonensi,* there was a rumour amongst the lesser troops of bribery at Lisbon, although this appears to have been groundless.[96] In any case, the Genoese learned of the scheme and decided to forestall it by trying a rapid assault.

Early the next morning, 17 October, they drew up their men in twelve companies of 1,000 each. The consuls made emotional appeals to the emperor and to the count of Barcelona to help them; finally they agreed to join their co-religionists. The consuls told their men to enter the city at the signal of a trumpet but to proceed in silence, presumably counting on an element of surprise. The crusaders used the gap in the wall to make their way into the city and within three hours, 'with the help and favour of God', they had taken the whole place except the citadel.[97] The slaughter was immense: Caffaro claimed that 10,000 died in the ruined part of the city and 20,000 around the citadel. These numbers are suspiciously round, but the general sense is of a massacre. This certainly matches the bloodthirsty sentiments of the *Poem of Almería,* although it is in striking contrast to the relative restraint shown at Lisbon (only a week later) and to the subsequent peaceful surrender of Tortosa.[98] A further 10,000 women and children were taken as slaves to Genoa. Within four days the citadel surrendered on the payment of 30,000 *morabetinos*. The booty taken was enormous. The sum of 60,000 *morabetinos* was kept for the commune, a debt of 17,000 Genoese pounds was paid off and the rest of the money was divided up amongst the remaining ships. Consul Otto of Bonovillano and 1,000 men were left to guard the city. Otto evidently had long-term plans for the port: on 5 November the consuls granted him the Genoese share of the city for thirty years in exchange for a nominal annual tribute for fifteen years and a half-share of revenue for the other fifteen. He, in turn, promised to provide a garrison of 300 soldiers.[99]

The bulk of the Genoese force then sailed back to Barcelona and hauled their galleys up onto land for the winter. Two of the consuls returned to Italy to report their deeds and to pay off the city's debts, but most of the fleet stayed away from home. Caffaro chose to depict this episode in his customary unblinking combination of standard crusading terms – references to the participants' sacrifice in remaining apart from their wives, children and homes for a year – and praise for the advancement of his city: 'they spent the winter there for the honour of God and the city of Genoa'.[100] The Genoese passed the winter of 1147 and the spring of 1148 getting ready for their next campaign. The collection of timber to construct the parts for the siege towers and machines was important; they also sent requests to their home city for reinforcements of men and ships.

Before the attack on Tortosa began, Alfonso VII led another thrust against Islamic Spain. Barton has rescued this little-known episode from obscurity – a fate largely dictated by its failure and subsequent omission from most Spanish narratives.[101] In April 1148 Alfonso met with Ramon Berenguer at Almazán, possibly to discuss their respective strategies for the year ahead.[102] The emperor then disappeared from contemporary charters and chroniclers until the autumn, although the writing of later Toledan and Arab authors fills the gap. It seems that he advanced towards Jaen, an important castle in central al-Andalus. Ibn Ghaniya, the Almoravid governor, promised to hand it over to Alfonso, but, under pressure from his co-religionists in the south, he reneged on his word and treacherously seized a number of Christian magnates including Count Manrique of Lara. In truth, Ibn Ghaniya was trapped between the advancing Almohads and the Christians; before Alfonso's arrival he had already made a deal with the Almoravids to hand over Cordoba and Carmona but to keep Jaen. Then, when Alfonso appeared, he had to resort to trickery to get the Christians to break the siege. The prisoners were released early in 1149, soon after Ibn Ghaniya's death.

A letter from Pope Eugenius dated 27 April 1148 could tie this campaign to the crusade. Iberian bishops attended the Council of Rheims in March 1148 and they may have discussed the matter with the pope and requested his blessing; similarly, the presence in the peninsula of Nicholas Brakespear as an unofficial legate might also indicate papal interest.[103] On 27 April, Eugenius wrote to Alfonso in highly complimentary terms concerning his involvement in the crusade. The pope stated that he 'had willingly granted your requests to make an expedition against the tyranny of the infidels'.[104] Barton argues that this refers to the Jaen campaign, although it could be the Almería expedition; in either case, Eugenius was re-affirming his support for crusading in Iberia.[105] The letter continued by urging good relations between the Leónese and Portugal and between the churchmen of Braga and Toledo (there had been a long-running dispute over primatial rights between the two), so that, with divine help, the barbarian nations might be subjugated in future.[106] The bishop of Segovia was given the task of conveying a golden rose, a sign of special papal favour, to the king.[107] This was usually carried by the pope on a *Laetare* Sunday and it was intended to remind Alfonso of the singing of *Laetare, Jerusalem* and of the glory of Christ's resurrection; the reference to Jerusalem in this crusading context was surely no coincidence.[108] In spite of its unsuccessful outcome, the Jaen foray should be included as another element in the concerted effort by Christian Spain to extend its frontiers.

In late June the crusaders assembled to attack Tortosa.[109] The forces of Genoa and Barcelona set sail on 29 June and reached the mouth of the River Ebro on 1 July.[110] There they were joined by the counts of Montpellier, Urgel and Toulouse, the viscount of Béarn, contingents of Templars and Hospitallers, and a group of Anglo-Normans and Flemings who had taken part in the capture of Lisbon.[111] Another notable presence was Ermengard, the viscountess of Narbonne (the Narbonnese were long-term allies of the counts of Barcelona); to find a woman leading a contingent of crusaders was a genuine rarity.[112] A number of important churchmen were also present, including Bernard Tort, archbishop of Tarragona, the bishops of Barcelona, Girona and Vic, as well as Nicholas Brakespear, abbot of Saint Rufus, near Avignon, and Berenguer, abbot of La Grasse.[113] A council decided to make a general reconnaissance, although the city's substantial defences were familiar from earlier efforts to capture it. Half of the Genoese contingent and some of Ramon Berenguer's men were to be stationed on the riverside by the lower part of the city; the others would join William of Montpellier on top of Mount Magnara to the west of the citadel, while the remainder of the army, including the Templars and the Lisbon crusaders, set up camp by the river to the north of the city.[114]

One group of Genoese was quickly into the fray. Without the permission of their leaders they engaged the defenders, supposedly 'to determine their valour in battle'; casualties on both sides were heavy, although no significant advances were made. The lack of discipline shown by these men was, however, troubling. Numerous crusader armies had been defeated by such recklessness and Caffaro recorded that the consuls called the men together and made them all swear not to go into battle before receiving orders from their leaders.[115] As we have seen earlier, the need for a strict regulation of crusader armies was a vital aspect of success – for instance at Lisbon – and the failure to observe such measures might well contribute to a disaster, as in the French crossing of Asia Minor.

The siege towers were brought up to the walls and soon broke through. One tower was moved into the city towards the mosque, another one in the direction of the citadel. The defenders soon realised that the town was lost and retreated to the citadel. This was defended by a broad, deep ditch – about 140 feet wide and 105 feet deep – that constituted a formidable defensive barrier. It was decided that the only way to take it was by trying to fill in the ditch to permit the siege towers to move up to the walls. This was a monumental task; the entire force set to bringing timber, rocks and earth to pack the trench. When it was two-thirds full, the Genoese sent forwards 300 men, a new siege tower and a siege machine (probably a covered cat). On the approach of the tower the Muslims began to hurl down huge stones, one of which broke off a corner of the device, but the Genoese quickly repaired it. Meanwhile, a group of Catalan knights abandoned the siege because they had not been paid; evidently they had expected an easy victory. Hence Count Ramon was left with only twenty knights. The Genoese were not deterred; they intensified their bombardment of the citadel and the palace. The defenders started to despair and sent out messages offering a deal: they would surrender the city if, after a forty-day ceasefire, the Muslims of Valencia had not come to the rescue. Should the relief force defeat the Christians, the defenders could keep the city, but if the reinforcements failed to arrive in forty days, they would capitulate. One hundred Muslims of noble birth were given over as hostages. The fact that the crusaders accepted such a proposal suggested that the defences of Tortosa were proving a serious obstacle; the dimensions of the ditch alone were testimony to that. They risked a possible battle in order to hold on to the city, but they must have judged it unlikely that the Muslims were in a position to act; in just the same way, no help had reached Lisbon in the previous year. The potential loss of life in forcing a way into the citadel was evidently deemed to be a greater deterrent than the likelihood of an appearance by the Valencians. The Christian capture of the castle of Ascó helped to block any Muslim counter-attack and, on 30 December 1148, with no sign of help arriving, the city surrendered.[116] The flags of Genoa and Barcelona were raised above the citadel and the Christians assumed control; the Italians took one third and the Catalans two thirds, as agreed in 1146.

Caffaro proudly summarised the achievement of his fellow citizens: 'after this triumph over the two cities of Almería and Tortosa, giving thanks to God, they returned with the entire army to Genoa'.[117] It is worth reviewing Caffaro's account of the crusade to see the way in which he and his colleagues interpreted the event; given the failure of most of the Second Crusade, it is rare to be looking at a positive memory of the episode. We have seen how the First Crusade was memorialised and the Genoese, too, showed great pride in their successes of 1147–8. Caffaro's opening remarks concerned the campaigns to Almería and Tortosa and set out a fairly familiar justification for taking up the fight against the Muslims, namely the killing, imprisonment and torture of Christians, and the divine vengeance to be exacted for these atrocities:

It is known throughout the world that for a long time in the past Christians were captured by the Saracens of Almería in many regions, on both land and sea. Some were killed by them, while many were put in prisons and suffered a variety of tortures and punishments. Wracked by fear of such a fate, many Christians abandoned the law of God and invoked the diabolical name of Mohammed. God did not fail to exact vengeance for such a great shedding of blood; for the Genoese, reminded and called by God through the Apostolic See, swore to lead an army against the Saracens of Almería.[118]

Such ideas were used with regard to the Holy Land in the accounts of First Crusade historians such as Guibert of Nogent.[119] Caffaro did add the extra dimension that many Christians had apostasised out of fear, a reflection perhaps of the assimilation of indigenous populations under Muslim rule.[120]

A Genoese charter from November 1147 dovetailed with Caffaro's tone. It explained that 'the consuls have made this grant because they have captured the city of Almería for the honour of God and all of Christianity and they have determined to remain in control of the city out of the greatest necessity of Christians, and most of all because they know that it is honourable and useful to the city of Genoa'.[121] Crusading ideology had, in this instance, become entwined with the burgeoning sense of civic pride that came from the rising strength of urban and communal areas during the twelfth century.[122] After the First Crusade, authors wrote of advancing both the honour of God and that of an ethnic group such as the Franks. Here, a specific city was highlighted and, with public knowledge of the commercial treaties in place beforehand, the expedition's success was connected overtly to financial as well as religious advantage. As the *Poem of Almería* shows too, some contemporary churchmen had little problem in making such a link. While the likes of Pope Eugenius and Pope Urban before him had tried to uncouple these issues and insist on the purity of spiritual motives as a prerequisite for God's favour, to those recording the Almerían and Tortosan expeditions, this was not necessary. For the *Poem* and Caffaro there was no clash of interests when the Christian cause was served alongside their own secular needs. This was, in part, simply a question of practicality – without the participation of the Genoese the campaign could not take place. There was also, of course, no reason why the Italians were less pious than the rest of contemporary Europe – their cities were filled with churches too – and they had every reason to defeat the infidel. In spite of the overt statements which urged exclusively spiritual motives, the fact that Eugenius must have been aware of the deal between the Spanish and the Genoese, yet still chose to encourage the crusade, showed a recognition of the reality of the situation and of the prospect of benefits to all. The caveat that could get around the overt association of holy war and profit – a link which, to modern eyes, is maybe too coloured by accusations of Venetian rapacity at the time of the Fourth Crusade – is this: as long as the crusaders did not become greedy, they could still gain God's favour and succeed. This was a matter covered *c.*1140 by the canon lawyer Gratian who indicated that the spoils of war went to the victorious leader who would then distribute them to his soldiers according to their efforts. Based on the sermon of John the Baptist to the Herodian soldiers, Gratian argued that it was acceptable for troops to receive legitimate and necessary wages for their services, but he condemned seeking booty for private gain. Thus it was permissible, as well as practical, to make payment from a centrally gathered fund – just as the crusaders did.[123]

The most powerful demonstration of this assimilation of religious and secular motivation in Genoa can still be seen in the remains of the frescoes painted on the south wall of the nave of the cathedral of St Lawrence. The surviving section depicts the capture of Tortosa by the Genoese and, in parts now lost, events at Minorca and Almería as well. Thus, in the spiritual heart of the city, these images formed a public commemoration and celebration of this achievement (see Illustration 8).[124] Other examples can be noted too; Williams cites the comments of a sixteenth-century Genoese who recorded that a priest named Vassallus had a pair of bronze doors from Almería mounted in the cloister of the parish church of St George in the centre of the city. Similarly, another part of the loot was a large candelabrum with Arabic inscriptions that was hung in the cathedral, although it was stolen in the late seventeenth century.[125] Williams also draws attention to the words engraved on the Porta Soprana, one of the principal entrances to the city which was part of a proud statement of Genoa's strength and self-identity as the portal ('*janua*', 'door') of Italy. The inscriptions, which can still be seen today, read as follows. On one side:

> In the name of almighty God, Father, Son and Holy Spirit
> I am defended by wonderful men and wonderful walls,
> By my virtue I keep enemy weapons away.
> If you bring peace, then you can approach these doors,
> If you are looking for war, go away sad and defeated,
> The south, west and north winds know
> How many wars I, Genoa, have won.

On the opposite side:

> By the war of my people, Africa was moved.
> Then parts of Asia and all of Spain.
> I took Almería and subjected Tortosa.

In the seventh year from one and the eighth from the other
I Genoa built this wall.[126]

Aside from the fact that Almería fell back into Muslim hands within a year of
the creation of the inscriptions, these public references to the city's long
heritage of campaigns against the Muslims, from the sack of al-Mahdiyya in
Tunisia in 1087 to the First and Second Crusades, show the importance of
these activities to the Genoese.

In the Iberian sphere of the Second Crusade there was no conflict between
the performance and execution of the crusading and the commercial aims
of the campaigns. There were no grounds for outside criticism; unlike, for
example, in more controversial episodes in the future, such as the Italian
trade with Muslims in materials of war or the Venetian involvement in
the Sack of Constantinople in 1204. Much to the contrary, the Genoese
used their achievements in reducing the menace from Muslim raiders in the
Mediterranean as one plank in their (ultimately successful) argument against
paying tribute to Emperor Frederick I of Germany in 1158.[127]

In the immediate aftermath of the conquest of Tortosa Ramon Berenguer
made several grants. One of them, of September 1148, gave the Narbonnais
contingent a trading-station and exemptions from taxes by land and sea, 'in
gratitude for what the people of Narbonne have expended of their goods
and of their lives in the defence of the faith against the infidels'.[128] Other
grants included those made to the Genoese, to the Templars, and also to the
canons of the Holy Sepulchre, presumably as part of the settlement of
Alfonso I's will.[129] Hiestand notes that an English contingent chose to settle
in the city permanently; so did Frenchmen, Aragonese, Flemings, Germans
and men of the Templars and Hospitallers, and, as Jaspert has argued, 'a
multi ethnic and [multi] confessional world' grew in the city'.[130] Within
months, the distinguished crusader William VI of Montpellier had retired
from the world and joined the Cistercian abbey of Grandeselve near
Toulouse.[131]

The final element of the Iberian campaigns to be linked with the Second
Crusade – albeit in a lukewarm fashion by some historians – was the conquest
of Lérida, about 56 miles north-west and inland of Tortosa, in October
1149.[132] One piece of evidence connected with the build-up to this campaign
is of particular note: the Occitan song *Vers del lavador* written by the troubadour Marcabru, a man described by Paterson as 'a fervent supporter' of the
reconquest.[133] This song was probably composed in early 1149, just after the
seizure of Tortosa; it was designed to encourage disheartened Poitevin and
Aquitanian crusaders recently returned from the Levant to look to Iberia as a
place where they might achieve heavenly and earthly success. The song

referred to the general disquiet that followed the defeat at Damascus and to the need to make good ('we [must] avenge God of the wrongs that they do to Him both here and over there towards Damascus'). It also mourned the death of Count Baldwin of Marash in Syria and praised the work of the Templars and of Ramon Berenguer in Spain; it ended with a call to join in further labours to help defeat the pagans.[134]

The capture of Tortosa had opened up the territories inland and contributed to the isolation of Lérida. In June 1149, Count Ramon took advantage of this and, with his allies, blockaded the outlying castles of Fraga and Mequinenza and laid siege to the city itself. On this occasion Ramon was accompanied by the count of Urgel, the lord of Huesca, the viscount of Béarn, the abbot of St Rufus and the Catalan Templars. The Muslims were unable to secure outside help and eventually, on 24 October, all three places surrendered.[135] As with the capture of Tortosa, there was no massacre and the indigenous population was allowed freedom of property, law and religion on payment of an annual tribute.[136] Ramon presumably made this agreement in order to secure a peaceful hand-over of the city and because he wanted to incorporate an economically viable and relatively stable settlement into his lands; on this basis, a massacre would have been entirely counter-productive. No crusade bull exists for this episode, although a charter given by the count fits in with the general tenor of the time in thanking God – 'who, in His love, after the space of so many years, has deigned to restore in our times the church of Lérida, which was subjected to the perfidy of the pagans, to its former state of the Christian religion'.[137] In July 1150, Eugenius wrote to the count to congratulate him on his achievements and in anticipation of a continued advance against the Muslims.[138] In reality, however, political and dynastic distractions in Christian Iberia occupied the main protagonists by this time and the reconquest lost momentum.[139]

In conclusion, we can see that the Second Crusade marked a significant development in the ongoing tradition of crusading in the Iberian Peninsula. The initiative for this lay with the secular leaders of Spain rather than with the papacy, although the desire to push the forces of Islam southwards would be eagerly endorsed by Pope Eugenius. The close links between crusading in Iberia and the Holy Land were emphasised by papal bulls that explicitly offered the same spiritual rewards, and also through the involvement of crusaders en route to, and from, the Holy Land in the peninsula wars. Political circumstances in the Muslim world were also of considerable assistance to the crusaders and this factor, in tandem with the spiritual and secular rewards available in 1146–9, induced several groups of people from the western Mediterranean to take the cross and, in most cases, to defeat their enemies.

The general policy was one of conquest and assimilation – rather similar to the approach used in the extension of Christian power in the Baltic region. The exception was the massacre at Almería. The reasons for this can only be suggested, although given the events at Jerusalem in 1099 and at Edessa in 1146, the slaughter of a city's defenders was hardly an unheard of outcome. Perhaps the location of Almería, deep within Muslim territory, meant that the usual process of absorbing Muslim lands into Christian territory was not operative. If Almería was simply to be a lone bastion of the faith, then a message of force might have been deemed necessary. Furthermore, the *Poem of Almería* conveyed a strong sense of religious fervour and a zeal for taking vengeance on the Muslims. This attitude, in combination with the specific strategic circumstances, meant that no mercy was shown to the defenders. Tortosa and Lisbon, by contrast, were immediately adjacent to Christian lands and perhaps necessitated a more conciliatory style on account of that. In any event, the Second Crusade marked a large stride forwards in the Christian reconquest of Iberia.

CHAPTER 14

THE AFTERMATH OF THE SECOND
CRUSADE IN THE HOLY LAND
AND THE WEST

The departure of Louis VII marked the end of the Second Crusade in the Levant; over two decades later, as Saladin gathered the forces of the Islamic Near East and the Latin settlers struggled to deal with the unprecedented challenge of a leper-king, William of Tyre concluded his coverage of the 1147–9 expedition with this gloomy comment: 'from that time onwards the condition of the Latins in the East became visibly worse'.[1] Sharpened by the benefit of hindsight, William's words revealed the grim legacy of the crusade to the Holy Land and showed the profound and long-lasting consequences of its failure. The impact of these events was felt well beyond the Levant, however; so great had been the hopes for the crusade, and such were the political and strategic shifts generated by its existence, that its outcome would have repercussions across western Europe and the Mediterranean as well.

In the short term, the military situation in the Latin East declined considerably. Nur ad-Din increased the pressure on northern Syria and, on 29 June 1149, at the Battle of Inab, he defeated and killed the Franks' most formidable ruler, Prince Raymond of Antioch. The Muslim leader devastated the principality and blockaded its capital. One result of the crusade was immediately apparent: while the Muslims had previously feared the western armies, now they did not. William of Tyre felt that 'they mocked at the shattered strength and broken glory of those who had represented the substantial foundations of the Christians'.[2] As the crusaders suffered their various reverses in the course of the expedition, Ibn al-Qalanisi observed that his people had grown in confidence.[3] To add to the Franks' problems, the sultan of Iconium and the Persians of Khurusan also attacked their lands.[4] The defeat of the crusade, coupled with the death of Prince Raymond, caused the balance of power in the Levant to swing quite dramatically in favour of the Muslims and, under the energetic leadership of Nur ad-Din, the *jihad* gathered further momentum; Tabaa has shown how the emir began to memorialise his successes on buildings.[5] In the autumn of 1149, young King Baldwin III of

Jerusalem headed north and forced Nur ad-Din to retreat, but the king soon needed to return home to continue his ongoing struggle for power with his mother, Queen Melisende.[6] Without doubt, the situation in Antioch had become sufficiently serious to require another appeal to the West. The patriarch of Antioch and King Baldwin wrote to the French court stating that the city was close to surrender; the loss of a patriarchal seat would constitute a catastrophic blow to Christianity. Their pleas are reported in the 'Life of Suger', and the text of a letter from the Templar Andrew of Montbard to the master of the Order, Everard of Barres (who was in France at the time), also survives. Andrew appealed for help for 'the oppressed Mother Church of the East' and urged King Louis to send men and money 'so that we are able to survive'. Andrew, or his scribe, cited the Book of Job: 'Have pity upon me', and reminded his audience that Christ had shed his blood to save the holy places. He stressed the role of the Templars in the defence of the Holy Land. This was a natural emphasis given his position, but also a reminder to the king of the military and financial help provided to him during the crusade.[7] It is apparent that the Latin settlers focused on Louis for their latest appeal. The overt rift between King Conrad and the Franks was evidently too deep for an approach to be made to the German monarch. The fact that Louis had stayed in the Levant for almost a year after the siege of Damascus had probably fostered cordial relations and showed his interest in the sacred sites – an emotional commitment worth trying to pursue.

The Frankish envoys reached the West in the late autumn of 1149 and a series of letters which discussed a possible response circulated between Abbots Suger, Bernard and Peter the Venerable, and Pope Eugenius.[8] In early 1150 Bernard wrote to Suger and stated that he had heard from Everard of Barres of the misery of the Eastern Church. Suger had tried to organise an emergency meeting to consider the issue, but Bernard was unable to attend at short notice. The Cistercian did, however, express a wish to debate the matter in future and offered to bring along the bishop of Langres, whose advice he felt would be useful.[9] In March 1150, King Louis and the principal secular and ecclesiastical figures of France gathered at Laon, but made little progress. The plight of the Frankish settlers was not entirely ignored, however. Abbot Suger, prompted by Pope Eugenius himself, took the lead in trying to inject some impetus into the proceedings when he called for a major assembly to be held at Chartres on 7 May.[10] He wrote to Peter the Venerable of the 'calamity of the Eastern Church' and pressured him to come to Chartres. Peter excused himself from attending in person because of Cluniac business, but responded to the troubles of the Holy Land in stirring fashion:

For isn't it the greatest of all matters to provide and to see that the Holy Land should not be given to dogs? Lest the places where stood the feet of Him who brought salvation into the midst of the Earth should again be trampled by the feet of the wicked? Lest royal Jerusalem, consecrated by the prophets, the apostles, the saviour of all, lest Antioch, that noble metropolis of all Syria, should be subjected again to blasphemous and wicked men? Lest the very cross of salvation, now besieged by the wicked . . . should be seized? Lest the very Sepulchre of the Lord, which up to now . . . was the glory of the entire world, should perchance, be destroyed completely.[11]

Bernard of Clairvaux also chided Peter, as a senior churchman, to attend. He argued that the Cluniac should be 'consumed with zeal' for the welfare of the Church and claimed that his eminent presence would benefit the discussion.[12]

In the meantime, Pope Eugenius had begun to issue papal bulls. The 'Life of Suger' records that he wrote letters that described the suffering of the Christians and explained the need to assist the Eastern Church.[13] On 25 April 1150, however, he issued a curiously ambiguous text; in part encouraging the enterprise, yet at the same time revealing great caution – a contrast to the apparent overconfidence of the *curia* four years earlier. The pope praised the piety of King Louis but worried that the new campaign could lead to another 'outpouring of blood'; he also expressed concern at the recent damage to the name of Christianity. The failure of the crusade had troubled him profoundly. He instructed Suger to consider whether the whole scheme was practical or not and to look into the hearts of the king, nobles and other potential recruits, to see if they were ready to fight again. In spite of these reservations, in another letter, now lost, he promised to offer the crusaders remission of their sins; in other words, this was quite probably a re-issue of *Quantum praedecessores.*[14]

The gathering at Chartres chose Bernard to lead the new crusade in person, a role that he professed to have no aptitude for at all. Perhaps the meeting hoped that the participation of such a holy man would inspire the crusader armies and encourage God's favour – in any case, Eugenius apparently approved of the appointment.[15] Other senior churchmen besides Peter the Venerable had been absent from the assembly, and it seems that the enterprise did not attract the wholehearted support a crusade required. Bernard tried to arrange yet another gathering for 15 July at Compiègne and, again, he exhorted Peter the Venerable to come, but to no avail. Nothing else is known of this meeting and it seems that the effort to launch a new crusade ended.[16] The 'Life of Suger' wrote of the apathy and cowardice of the French bishops; Bernard of Clairvaux expressed the view that the secular princes were lacking in enthusiasm: 'The hearts of the princes are untouched. In vain they carry the sword. It is sheathed in the skins of dead animals and consecrated to rust. They will not draw it when Christ suffers, where he is suffering again, unless his grievous suffering in one corner is seen to affect the whole world.'[17]

The Christians' defeat on Mount Cadmus and the retreat from the walls of Damascus had evidently dealt an enormous blow to the cause of crusading in the West. Before they set out, the organisers and the leaders of the expedition had generated huge confidence in their recruits. Peter the Venerable felt that the crusade was a renewal of ancient times and miracles: God directed Louis against the Saracens just as he sent Moses against the Amorrhites and Joshua against the Canaanites.[18] Odo of Deuil expressed the opinion that 'it appeared that the undertaking had pleased God'; most famously of all, Bernard had told the recipients of his letters that they were 'a blessed generation . . . blessed to be alive in this year of jubilee'.[19] It is probably fair to observe that the cumulative effect of fifty years of literary and architectural recording and commemoration of the First Crusade had contributed to a widespread belief that God approved of the new crusade and that it would be victorious. Hence, when the campaign collapsed so dismally, morale plummeted too. Furthermore, some fairly obvious practical and psychological issues discouraged people from organising a new crusade so soon after such traumatic events; many must have shrunk from engaging in such a dangerous undertaking again, while their families were probably less than enthusiastic about a second period of absence and a repetition of the risk. The campaign had also been ruinously expensive; to raise the money for another expedition would have been very hard. The 'Life of Suger' showed some recognition of this factor when it noted the extremely brief time period available to the king and his men to recover.[20] In the case of Louis, he was being asked to turn around and prepare to set out again within six months of reaching home.

Writers and critics dismissed the crusade entirely, presumably reflecting the widespread displeasure with its outcome; and again causing a lack of enthusiasm for the new campaign. John of Salisbury stated that the crusade had done irreparable harm to the Christian faith.[21] The 'Chronicle of Morigny' derided it as having achieved 'nothing useful or worth repeating'; the 'Life of Suger' suggested that there were 'no traces of virtue apparent from that illustrious pilgrimage'.[22] The poet Marcabru wrote: 'the public outcry relating to [the Holy Land] pours down on the highest-ranking leaders: broken failures, weary of valour, who love neither joy or delight'.[23] Thus, the Second Crusade is significant because it prompted the first major questioning of crusading – a process that seemed to deter some people from taking the cross.[24]

Certain churchmen were targeted for their behaviour on the crusade. There appears to have been tension in the French army amongst the senior clergy and also a lack of direction from the papal legates. Guido of S. Grisogono was the official legate to Louis's forces; but this shy, bookish man, who spoke little French, was wholly unsuited to the task. This allowed the forceful personalities of Bishop Arnulf of Lisieux and Bishop Godfrey of Langres to vie for status; the wealth and standing of both men led to the creation of factions and, as the contemporary writer John of Salisbury wrote, this meant that 'few, if any, brought more harm on the Christian army' – had they worked together, he noted, then they could have contributed much to the crusading cause.[25] The responsibility for this failing must, therefore, rest with the individuals concerned and with Pope Eugenius for appointing them in the first instance.

Bernard himself was not immune from criticism for the fiasco of 1148 and he was obliged to try to explain the outcome of the crusade.[26] The *Vita Sancti Bernardi* recorded such attacks: 'certain men raised great scandal against him because of his preaching of the journey to Jerusalem', and the *Annales Brunwilarenses* even questioned the divine inspiration of his preaching.[27] Bernard gave a sermon – possibly at the meeting at Chartres – in which he explained the disaster as a combined result of the sins of man and the judgement of the Lord, rather than identifying particular individuals, or groups, as responsible.[28] He also wrote a treatise, *De consideratione*, a book of advice to the pope that emphasised God's mysterious ways and His merciful judgements, in part concerning the crusade.[29]

As people absorbed the outcome of the campaign the papacy began to feel the consequences too. Hiestand has shown that the annual output of letters from the papal chancery reduced sharply: 152 from March to December 1145, 193 in 1146, 260 in 1147, 223 in 1148, yet just 62 in 1149, 81 in 1150, 104 in 1151, 157 in 1152. From around 250 between the spring of 1147 to the spring of 1148, the number fell to one quarter of that total.[30] One might add two caveats to these results; first, that departure on a crusade would inevitably provoke a temporary increase in the number of people and institutions who wished to have their rights confirmed; secondly, the rare presence of a pope north of the Alps would have compounded such a situation. Nonetheless, these figures do signal a decline in papal authority after the crusade. This sense of a backlash was recalled by Pope Adrian IV in a letter to King Louis, written in 1159, where he described 'the damage inflicted upon the Church of God' and how the holy Roman Church 'was not a little injured by it; and everyone cried out against her with much indignation, saying that she was the author of so great a peril'.[31]

Such feelings may have influenced the pope's caution over a new expedition. Yet this was not what Bernard wanted from the pontiff; he was irritated by Eugenius's hesitancy and issued a coruscating call for leadership:

I believe that the time has come for both swords to be drawn in the defence of the Eastern Church. You hold the position of Peter, and you ought also to have his zeal. What could we think of one who held the primacy but neglected the responsibility? We hear the voice crying: 'I go to Jerusalem to be crucified a second time.' Although some may be indifferent to this voice and others may be deaf to it, the successor of St Peter cannot ignore it . . . Do you then, the friend of the Bridegroom, prove yourself a friend in need. If you love Christ as you should, with all your heart, with all your soul, and with all your strength; if you love him with that threefold love about which your predecessor was questioned, then you will have no reservations, you will leave nothing undone while his bride is in such great danger, but rather you will devote to her all your strength, all your zeal, all your care and all your power. An extraordinary danger demands an extraordinary effort.[32]

Yet this appeal, as well as the trio of unsuccessful meetings in France, achieved almost nothing; there was simply insufficient will to make the massive commitment demanded by another crusade.[33] Notwithstanding Bernard's own desire to act, some sources suggested that his fellow-monks were partially responsible for the enterprise collapsing. Apparently the Cistercians were unwilling to let their frail abbot attempt so arduous an undertaking; besides, the white monks also experienced difficulties in raising recruits and funds in the aftermath of 1147–8.[34]

Wider political circumstances, too, conspired against the launch of a new crusade. The English civil war was in full swing; Henry of Anjou had spent time in England during 1149 and he took control of the duchy of Normandy the following year. These events precluded the Angevins, as well as King Stephen and his son, Eustace of Boulogne, from involvement in the crusade; moreover, they demanded the attention of King Louis and his barons.[35] As for the south, when Eugenius returned to Italy in the summer of 1148, he soon faced further challenges from the citizens of Rome and from the radical anti-clericalism of Arnold of Brescia; such were the tensions that the pope found himself again unable to live in the city.[36]

There remains one other – highly controversial – issue connected with the failure of the Second Crusade and the plan for the new campaign. Some contemporary writers indicated that the latter should turn against the Greeks; Runciman, Berry and Lilie are amongst the historians to have followed this view.[37] In fact, as others have demonstrated, there was little overlap between the French attempts to respond to the pleas from the Holy Land and rumblings about a possible attack on Byzantium.[38] As we have seen above, Roger II's actions during the crusade had caused great alarm to the Greeks. In the autumn of 1148, Manuel Comnenus persuaded Conrad of Germany to reaffirm the proposal made earlier in the year, to attack Sicily (see above, pp. 212, 227). It was probably agreed that Manuel should revive Byzantium's traditional claims to Sicily and hold the land after it was taken. Such developments were hugely unwelcome to Pope Eugenius because he did not want the Greeks to possess teritory so close to the *curia*. He did, however, need military help against the Roman commune – ideally, this would come from Conrad, and in letters of the mid-1140s Bernard had expressed this hope.[39] If the German king backed a Byzantine occupation of the south, then Eugenius would have to look elsewhere. As noted earlier, Lucius II had made a truce with Roger in 1144; five years later, the Sicilian agreed to provide Eugenius with protection.[40]

As the Second Crusade ended Roger continued to antagonise both Conrad and the Byzantines. The fragile détente forged between the king of Germany and Welf of Bavaria did not outlast the expedition. The duke had visited Roger on his way home and agreed to foment trouble against Conrad; an armed conflict broke out, although the king's forces (led by his son Henry) triumphed at the Battle of Flochberg in February 1150; meanwhile the Sicilian navy continued to raid the Byzantine Empire and even made a foray against Constantinople itself.

Conrad's increasingly close relationship with the Byzantines, coupled with his persistent antipathy towards Roger, aroused great concern in the West, in part because a rift between the pope and the emperor-in-waiting was to be avoided, in part to try to preserve papal independence from the Greeks and the Sicilians. Chancellor Guido wrote to Wibald of Stavelot in October 1149 to register his fear that Conrad and Manuel's alliance was not to the benefit of the Roman Church.[41] People tried to bring about a rapprochement between Roger and Conrad; in early 1150, Bernard used Conrad's half-brother and fellow-Cistercian, Otto of Freising, to tell the German monarch that Roger was potentially useful to the Church and that the abbot was prepared to act as a mediator with the Sicilian. Wibald recorded that the papal legate, Theodwin of Santa Rufina, put himself forward as middle-man.[42] Similarly, in late 1149 or early 1150, Peter the Venerable tried to engage with Roger in a similar way, urging '*pax et concordia*' between the Sicilian and the German for the good of the Church and the spread of Christianity.[43] As Reuter indicated, all of this correspondence pre-dated the effort to get a new crusade underway and was, therefore, distinct in terms of focus and message. Peter the Venerable's letter had a strong anti-Greek tone; as we have seen, some of the French blamed the Greeks for the failure of the campaign and the abbot was explicit in such statements. He wrote of 'the unheard of and lamentable treachery of the Greeks and their wicked king [that was] enacted against our pilgrims'. He appealed to Roger to 'avenge the many insults, the many injuries, the many deaths, and the great amount of the blood of the army of God which was spilled by so much wickedness', although he mentioned that both the French and the Germans had suffered in this way.[44] On account of the antipathy between the Sicilians and the Greeks, an assault on the latter would have struck a chord with Roger, but in reality the abbot had little chance of inducing Conrad and Roger to make peace, or of prising Manuel and Conrad apart. Peter's appeal had no effect; it was, in any case, a personal call and not an attempt to direct any emerging crusade towards Byzantium. It is noticeable that no account of the meetings in France mentioned such a plan for the new crusade.

The other evidence for a possible attack on the Greeks was in a letter of April 1150 from Conrad to his sister-in-law, Empress Eirene (Bertha of Salzburg). In spite of continued health problems and the rebellion of Welf, the king asserted his willingness to fulfil his agreements with Manuel. He also noted that 'it is reported to us that the whole nation of the Franks [French], with its king, has conspired to make war against the power of our most excellent relative, I mean your most glorious husband, at the behest and instigation of the tyrant of Sicily', although he assured Eirene that 'we have decided to pledge ourselves and our power on behalf of our brother'.[45] From his own experience he could see that Welf of Bavaria's visit to the Sicilian had led to an uprising in the German Empire; by the same token, Louis's recent stay with Roger may have caused him to fear more plotting. The possibility that the French and the Sicilians could have worked together during the crusade was widely known and it now appeared that Roger was trying to exploit Louis's recent maltreatment at the hands of the Greeks to bring himself an advantage. Again, the timing of this letter and the lack of corroborative material indicate that it should not be linked directly to the new crusade.

Given Eugenius's caution over a new expedition to the Holy Land he was unlikely to take as radical a step as endorsing a crusade against Byzantium. To do so would inevitably bring him into conflict with Conrad and also remove a crucial check on the Roman citizenry. Notwithstanding Eugenius's agreement with Roger in 1149, a successful crusade for the Sicilian could encourage him to be more ambitious in future, something the pope may have wished to avoid. In sum, there is little substance to the notion of the proposed crusade being turned against the Greeks. The main concern was the situation in the Levant, not in Byzantium. The two issues should be seen as separate, and in the case of the latter, a crusade would be an unrealistic proposition anyway.

For the settlers in the Holy Land, however, the collapse of the crusading plans of 1150 must have been a serious blow; the capture of Count Joscelin III of Edessa in May was yet another calamity for the Franks of northern Syria. As Gregory the Priest recorded: 'All the Muslims far and wide were in ecstatic joy. Gravely imperilled by this capture, the Christian territories were ruined for they no longer had a leader on whom the remnants of their forces could lean for support.'[46] The final break-up of the county of Edessa took place later in 1150 when King Baldwin III agreed that Joscelin's wife, Beatrice, could sell the few settlements that remained in Christian hands; the buyer was none other than Manuel Comnenus. Given the controversy between Manuel and the crusaders it was deeply ironic that the Greeks acquired lands in Edessa. As has been discussed elsewhere, this marked the beginnings of a policy whereby the Franks, especially the ruling house of Jerusalem, began to form closer ties with Byzantium through marriage agreements and plans for military co-operation.[47] The most dramatic expression of this came in 1171 when King Amalric went to Constantinople in order to pay homage to Emperor Manuel. Along with the developing power of Nur ad-Din and his successor Saladin, the prime reason for such a radical move was a lack of large-scale crusading help from the West.

It seems certain that the failure of the Second Crusade had an impact upon the interest and enthusiasm for such ventures; notwithstanding repeated professions of support for the Christian Holy Land, there was never quite enough political will to bring such plans to fruition. External reasons can also be advanced for this, notably the political tensions between England and France, the Thomas Becket affair, and the trouble between Germany and the papacy. While the settlers made numerous appeals for help in the decades after the Second Crusade and the papacy issued bulls that called for new campaigns in 1157, 1165, 1166, 1169, 1173, 1181, 1184 and 1187, it was only after the Battle of Hattin and the fall of Jerusalem that people finally responded on the desired scale. It would be grossly misleading, however, to conclude that crusading itself was in decline or that the affairs of the Holy Land were completely ignored; several medium-sized expeditions took place, most notably those of the count of Flanders in 1157–8, 1164 and 1177–8. Numerous west-erners went on pilgrimages and served in the defence of the holy places and, on occasion, the papal appeals induced nobles of the standing of the count of Nevers to take the cross. Financial support to the defenders of the Holy Land was also forthcoming and, after a brief fallow period, donations to the great Military Orders grew as well.[48] Events at Damascus in 1148 had, however, shattered the illusion that the crusaders were divinely blessed and could achieve victory almost by right. The expectation that they would follow in the triumphant footsteps of the First Crusaders had not been realised. The inevitable accusations of blame had damaged the settlers' reputation (in Germany, Conrad was succeeded by Frederick of Swabia, who had also been on the crusade), and, by the 1180s, suspicion of the morals of the Franks of the East became an underlying theme in contacts between the Levant and the West. Even as enthusiastic a supporter of crusading as Pope Alexander III equated Baldwin IV's leprosy with God's judgement on sin, a view that hardly constituted a ringing endorsement of the rulers of Jerusalem.[49] A desire to counter this negative mood was one stimulus for William of Tyre to compose his *Historia*.[50] A rare, but more profound, question was raised by Peter, a cleric from Troyes. At some point after the Second Crusade he wrote to the patriarch of Jerusalem and asked if it was acceptable for Christians to fight and kill pagans. This can be seen as an extreme reaction to the failure of the 1147–9 campaign – a questioning of whether God still approved of the concept of crusading. In response, the patriarch used arguments from Gratian's *Causa* 23 and Ivo of Chartres's *Panormia* to conclude that it was licit to spill the blood of the enemies of Christ.[51]

The Second Crusade had, however, achieved some advances in the Iberian Peninsula through the capture of Lisbon, Almería and Tortosa. Lisbon and Tortosa remained in Christian hands, but Almería, located in the far south, was lost in 1157. The emergence of Almohad power, first in North Africa and then in Iberia, brought some unity to the Muslim lands. This, combined with the death of Alfonso VII in 1157 – which in itself provoked a dynastic crisis – caused the reconquest to lose momentum. Although the Almohads checked the Christians' expansion they lacked the resources to reverse it.[52]

The Wendish crusade had made minor progress in line with the usual nature of warfare in the region; after the Second Crusade, relations between the Christians and the Slavs continued to be a mix of co-operation, raid and counter-raid, with the Cistercians also involved in the effort to bring the pagans to heel in a war of conversion. In 1168 the fortress of Arkana, near Rugen, was taken. A year later Pope Alexander recognised the conquest and almost simultaneously he canonised Duke Canute who had helped to Christianise the Wends several decades earlier. There was not, however, another formal crusade in the region until Alexander III's bull of 1171 which targeted Estonia in the eastern Baltic.[53]

It took the shock of the fall of Jerusalem to provoke the next major crusade to the Holy Land and there would be no repetition of the aggressive and wide-ranging agenda of the Second Crusade until the time of Pope Innocent III in the early thirteenth century. In spite of its limited achievements, however, the Second Crusade does stand as an important point in the development of holy war. The content and wide circulation of *Quantum praedecessores* marked a significant moment in papal crusade appeals, and the eventual engagement in three theatres of war showed just how popular and flexible the concept of crusading had become. In outcome, the crusade's failure was a missed opportunity to inflict serious damage on the nascent power of Nur ad-Din in northern Syria; the aftermath created the conditions for him to take control of Damascus too. The expedition to the Holy Land was fatally hamstrung by poor funding (exacerbated by bad economic conditions), overconfident leadership and military errors. None of these factors applied to the successful campaigns in Iberia. Most importantly for this study, the Second Crusade showed the profound and pervasive impact that the events of 1099 exerted on Latin Christian society. In terms of its size and the sense of expectation it generated, this crusade was a brief manifestation of quite extraordinary ambition on the part of the papacy and the people of the Latin West.

TRANSLATION OF *QUANTUM*
PRAEDECESSORES
POPE EUGENIUS III TO KING LOUIS VII AND
HIS SUBJECTS, 1 MARCH 1146

We have learned from what men of old have said and we have found written in their histories how greatly our predecessors the Roman pontiffs have worked for the liberation of the eastern Church. Indeed, our predecessor of happy memory, Pope Urban, sounding forth like a heavenly trumpet, took care to induce sons of the Holy Roman Church from several parts of the world to free it. In answer to his call men from beyond the Alps, especially the most strong and vigorous warriors of the kingdom of the French, and also those from Italy, fired with the ardour of love, assembled and once a great army had been collected together, not without much shedding of their own blood but attended by divine aid, freed from the filth of the pagans that city in which it was Our Saviour's will to suffer for us and where he left us his glorious Sepulchre as a memorial of his passion, together with many other places of which, to avoid being lengthy, we have refrained from reminding you. By the grace of God and the zeal of your fathers, who strove to defend them over the years and to spread the Christian name among the peoples in the area, these places have been held by Christians until now and other cities have coura-geously been taken from the infidels. But now, because our sins and those of its people demanded it, there has occurred what we cannot make known without great sadness and lamentation. The city of Edessa, in our tongue known as Rohais, which also, it is said, alone under Christian rule had respect for the power of God at that time when all the land in the East was held by the pagans, has been taken by the enemies of the cross of Christ, who have also occupied many Christian castles. And the archbishop of that city and his clerics and many other Christians have been killed there, while the relics of the saints have been trampled under the infidels' feet and dispersed. We recognise how great the danger is that threatens the Church of God and all Christianity because of this and we do not believe that it is hidden from your understanding. It will be seen as a great token of nobility and uprightness if those things acquired by the efforts of your fathers are vigorously defended by you, their good sons. But if, God forbid, it comes to pass differently, then the bravery of the fathers will have proved to be diminished in the sons.

And so in the Lord, we impress upon, ask and order all of you, and we enjoin it for the remission of sins, that those who are on God's side, and especially the more powerful and the nobles, should vigorously gird themselves to oppose the multitude of the infidels who are now rejoicing in the victory they have gained over us, to defend in this way the eastern Church, which was freed from their tyranny, as we have said before, by so much spilling of your fathers' blood, and to strive to deliver from their hands the many thousands of our captive brothers, so that the dignity of the name of Christ may be enhanced in our time and your reputation for strength, which is praised throughout the world, may be kept unimpaired and unsullied. And let the good Mattathias be an example to you. He did not hesitate for a moment to expose himself with his sons and relatives to death and to leave all he had in the world to preserve his ancestral laws; and at length with the help of divine aid and with much labour he and his offspring triumphed powerfully over their enemies.

We, providing with a father's concern for your peace of mind and the abandonment of the eastern Church, by the authority given us by God concede and confirm to those who, inspired by devotion, decide to take up and complete so holy and very necessary a work and labour that remission of sins which our aforesaid predecessor Pope Urban instituted. And we decree that their wives and children, goods and possessions should remain under our protection and that of the archbishops, bishops and other prelates of the Church of God. And by apostolic authority we forbid any legal suit to be brought thereafter concerning all the possessions they hold peacefully when they take the cross until there is absolutely certain knowledge of their return or death. Since, moreover, those who fight for the Lord ought not to care for precious clothes or elegant appearance or dogs or hawks or other things that are signs of lasciviousness, we, in the Lord, impress upon your understanding that those who decide to begin so holy a work ought to pay no attention to multi-coloured clothes or minivers or gilded or silvered arms, but should with all their strength employ care and diligence in taking such arms, horses and the rest with which they may the more ardently overcome the infidels. All those who are encumbered with debts and undertake so holy a journey with pure hearts need not pay usury on past loans; and if they or others on their behalf are bound by oath or faith to usurious contracts we absolve them by apostolic authority. And they may raise money on their lands or other possessions, having informed relatives or the lords to whose fiefs they belong, and they may freely pledge them to churches or churchmen or to others of the faithful without any counterclaim, for otherwise they will not want or have the means to go. By the authority of omnipotent God and that of Blessed Peter the Prince of the Apostles conceded to us by God, we grant remission of and absolution from sins, as instituted by our aforesaid predecessor, in such a way that whosoever devoutly begins and completes so holy a journey or dies on it will obtain absolution from all his sins of which he has made confession with a contrite and humble heart; and he will receive the fruit of everlasting recompense from the rewarder of all good people.

Translated by L. and J. S. C. Riley-Smith, *The Crusades: Idea and Reality, 1095–1274* (London, 1981), pp. 57–9.

TRANSLATION OF *CHEVALIER,*
MULT ESTES GUARIZ

Knights, you are in very good hands now that God has called for your help against the Turks and the Almoravids who have done Him such dishonour. They have wrongfully snatched his fiefs; our sorrow at this should indeed be great since it was there that God was first offered service and acknowledged as Lord.

[Repeat after each verse]
Anyone who now goes with Louis need have no fear of Hell, for his soul will be in Paradise with the angels of Our Lord.

Edessa is taken, as you know, and the Christians are sorely afflicted because of it; the churches are burnt and abandoned, God is no longer sacrificed there. Knights, make your decisions, you who are esteemed for your skill in arms; make a gift of your bodies to Him who was placed on the cross for you.

Take your example from Louis, who has more to lose than you; he is rich and powerful above all other crowned kings; yet he has given up miniver and ermine, castles, towns and citadels and turned to Him who was crucified for us.

God gave up his body to the Jews that he might free us from bondage. They wounded Him in five places so that he suffered passion and death. Now He is calling upon you because the Canaanites and the troops of the cruel Sanguin [Zengi] have played many a wicked trick upon Him; the time has come to pay them back for it!

God has organised a tourney between Heaven and Hell, and so He is asking all His friends who are willing to support His cause not to fail Him. . .

For the son of God the Creator has fixed a day for being at Edessa; there shall the sinners be saved . . . who will fight fiercely and, for love of Him, will go and help Him in this hour of need . . . to wreak the vengeance of God.

Let us go and take possession of Moses in his tomb on Mount Sinai. Let us snatch it from the hands of the Saracens as also the rod with which, at a single stroke, he opened the Red Sea and all his people came after; Pharaoh followed in pursuit and was killed with all his men.

Les chansons de croisade avec leurs mélodies, ed. J. Bédier and P. Aubry (Paris, 1909), pp. 8–11; translated from the Old French by M. Routledge.

NOTES

Notes to Prologue

1. ASC, pp. 88–9; tr. p. 280; C. Hillenbrand, '"Abominable Acts": The Career of Zengi', in SCSC, pp. 111–32.
2. Ibn al-Athir, *The Chronicle of Ibn al-Athir for the Crusading Period from al-Kamil fi'l-Ta'rikh. Part 1 : 491–541/1097–1146,* tr. D. S. Richards (Aldershot, 2006), p. 373. The Anonymous Syriac Chronicle suggested that Joscelin was raiding Zengi's lands towards al-Raqqa to the south. See ASC, p. 89; tr. pp. 280–1.
3. ASC, pp. 89–91; tr. pp. 281–3.
4. WT, pp. 718–21; tr. pp. 140–4; Phillips, *Defenders,* pp. 73–4.
5. Nersēs Šnorhali, 'Lament on Edessa', tr. T. M. Van Lint, in *East and West in the Crusader States II: Context, Contacts, Confrontations,* ed. K. Ciggaar and H. Teule, Orientalia Lovaniensia Analecta 92 (Leuven, 1999), pp. 49–105, text here at p. 75.
6. Ibn al-Athir, p. 373; ASC, pp, 92–4, 98–9; tr. pp. 283–6, 289–90; Gregory the Priest, *Armenia and the Crusades, 10th to 12th Centuries,* ed. and tr. A. E. Dostaurian (Lanham ML, 1993), pp. 243–4; WT, pp. 719–21; tr. pp. 140–4.
7. *De oorkonden der graven van Vlaanderen (Juli 1128–17 Januari 1168) II. Uitgave Band I,* ed. T. de Hemptinne and A. Verhulst with L. De Mey (Brussels, 1988), no. 112, pp. 182–3.

Notes to Introduction

1. N. Housley, *Contesting the Crusades* (Oxford, 2006), pp. 2–23 summarises the arguments about the definition of a crusade and steers towards a nuanced form of pluralism at pp. 20–3.
2. B. Kugler, *Studien zur Geschichte des zweiten Kreuzzugs* (Stuttgart, 1866).
3. Otto of Freising, *GF,* pp. 218–19; tr. p. 79.
4. W. Bernhardi, *Konrad III* (Leipzig, 1883).
5. V. G. Berry, 'The Second Crusade', in: *A History of the Crusades,* 6 vols, ed. K. M. Setton (Wisconsin, 1969–89), 1.463–511; S. Runciman, *A History of the Crusades,* 3 vols (Cambridge, 1951–4), 2.247–88.
6. Constable, SC.
7. A. J. Forey, 'The Second Crusade: Scope and Objectives', *Durham University Journal* 86 (1994), pp. 165–75.
8. The principal biographies remain: E. Vacandard, *Vie de Saint Bernard, abbé de Clairvaux,* 2 vols (Paris, 1927); W.Williams, *Saint Bernard of Clairvaux* (Manchester, 1935). Many works concerned with Bernard could be cited; for example, see G. R. Evans, *The Mind of Bernard of Clairvaux* (Oxford, 1983); P. Dinzelbacher, *Bernhard von Clairvaux: Leben und Werk des berühmten Zisterziensers* (Darmstadt, 1998), as well as many of the writings of J. Leclercq. See the outline list in SCSC, pp. 212–14, or his *Recueil d'études sur Saint Bernard et ses écrits,* 5 vols (Rome, 1962–92).
9. M.Meschini, *San Bernardo e la seconda crociata* (Milan, 1998).

10. Horn, *Studien*; M.Hoch, *Jerusalem, Damaskus und der Zweite Kreuzzug: Konstitutionelle Krise und äußere Sicherheit des Kreuzfahrerkönigreiches Jerusalem, AD 1126–54* (Frankfurt, 1993); R. Hiestand, '"Kaiser" Konrad III., der zweite Kreuzzug und ein verlorenes Diplom für den Berg Thabor', *Deutsches Archiv für Erforschung des Mittelalters* 35 (1979), pp. 82–128; idem, 'The Papacy and the Second Crusade', in SCSC, pp. 32–53; idem, 'Reconquista, Kreuzzug und heiliges Grab: Die Eroberung von Tortosa 1148 im Lichte eines neuen Zeugnisses', *Gesammelte Aufsätze zur Kulturgeschichte Spaniens* 31 (1984), pp. 136–57; idem, 'Kingship and Crusade in Twelfth-Century Germany', in *England and Germany in the High Middle Ages*, ed. A. Haverkamp and H. Vollrath (London, 1996), pp. 235–65.

11. E.-D. Hehl, *Kirche und Kreig im 12. Jahrhundert. Studien zu kanonischem Recht und politischer Wirklichkeit*, Monographien zur Geschichte des Mittelalters, 19 (Stuttgart, 1980); H.-D. Kahl, 'Crusade Eschatology as seen by St Bernard in the years 1146 to 1148', in SCC, pp. 35–47. For Kahl's numerous articles, see the bibliographies in idem, pp. 231–2; SCSC, p. 216.

12. SCC; SCSC.

13. *QP*.

14. T. Madden, *A Concise History of the Crusades* (Lanham, ML, 1999), p. 54.

15. W. Williams, *Saint Bernard of Clairvaux* (Manchester, 1935), p. 265.

16. BCE, no. 247, p. 141; tr. BSJ, no. 323, p. 399.

17. J. S. C. Riley-Smith, *The First Crusaders, 1095–1131* (Cambridge, 1997); idem, 'Family Traditions and Participation in the Second Crusade', in SCC, pp. 101–8.

18. Constable, SC, pp. 265, 276.

19. Helmold of Bosau, *Chronica Slavorum*, ed. and tr. H. Stoob (Darmstadt, 1963), pp. 216–17; tr. F. J. Tschan, *The Chronicle of the Slavs* (New York, 1935), p. 172.

20. Forey, 'Second Crusade', p. 171 takes a similar line with regard to the issue of formal direction.

21. *EE*, cols 1203–4. Even though this was a papal letter, Eugenius gives no suggestion that it was part of a formal plan.

22. Forey, 'Second Crusade', p. 165.

23. See below, p. 137.

24. 'Annales Rodenses', *MGH* 16.718.

25. 'Annales Magdeburgenses', *MGH* 16.188–9; 'Annales Colonienses maximi', *MGH* 17.761–3; 'Annales Palidenses', *MGH* 16.82–3.

26. Robert of Torigny, 'Chronicon', *MGH* 6.497–8; 'Sigeberti Gemblacensis, Continuatio Praemonstratensis', *MGH* 6.447, 453–4.

27. Henry of Huntingdon, *Historia Anglorum*, ed. and tr. D. E. Greenway (Oxford, 1996), pp. 752–53. On the perception that Lisbon was an integral part of the crusade, see also: G. Constable, 'A Further Note on the Conquest of Lisbon', in *The Experience of Crusading 1: Western Approaches*, ed. M. G. Bull and N. Housley (Cambridge, 2003), pp. 43–4.

28. Sigebert of Gembloux, 'Continuatio Valcellensis', *MGH* 6.459–60.

29. P. Bec, *La Lyrique française au moyen âge (XIIe–XIIIe s.)*, 2 vols (Paris, 1977–8), 2.86.

30. Otto of Freising, *GF*, pp. 188–9; tr. p. 64.

31. *De oorkonden der graven van Vlaanderen*, no. 112, pp. 182–3; Otto of Freising, *GF*, pp. 200–1; tr. pp. 70–1; 'Annales Coloniensis maximi', p. 761.

Notes to Chapter 1

1. Riley-Smith, *FC*, pp. 169–88.

2. H. E. Mayer, *Mélanges sur l'histoire du royaume Latin de Jérusalem*, Mémoires de l'académie des inscriptions et belles-lettres, n.s. 5 (Paris, 1984), pp. 59–72.

3. Phillips, *Defenders*, pp. 19–43.

4. Ibid., pp. 44–72.

5. H.E.Mayer, 'The Origins of the County of Jaffa', *Israel Exploration Journal* 35 (1985), at pp. 40–5.

6. OV 6.100–105; J. P. Phillips, 'The French Overseas', in *The Oxford History of France, 900–1200*, ed. M. G. Bull (Oxford, 2002), p. 170; J. A. Green, *Henry I, King of England and Duke of Normandy* (Cambridge, 2006), p. 100.

7. P. Rogghé, 'Osto de Saint Omer, Vlaams Tempelier uit de XIIe eeuw', *Appeltjes van het Meetjesland* 20 (1969), pp. 245–69.

8. There is a hint of the Knights Templar about this description, but it is odd, given the date of writing, that Otto did not mention the order by name; on the other hand, the fact that he was describing events of *c.*1105 at this point in his text – in other words, events from a period when the Templars were not yet founded – indicates that he was not discussing the order. Otto of Freising, *Ddc*, pp. 514–15; tr. pp. 414–15.

9. Galbert of Bruges, *De multro, traditione et occisione gloriosi Karoli comitis Flandriarum*, ed. J. Rider, *CCCM* 131 (Turnhout, 1994), p. 31; translated as *The Murder of Count Charles the Good*, tr. J. B. Ross (New York, 1958), p. 113.

10. Walter of Thérouanne, *MGH*.12.540.

11. Ekkehard of Aura, 'Chronicon Universale', *MGH* 6.262. Riley-Smith, *First Crusaders*, pp. 158–60, lists some other men who probably served in the defence of the Holy Land at this time.

12. OV 6.310–13; WT, p. 633; tr. 2.50.

13. *The Rule of the Templars*, tr. J. Upton-Ward (Woodbridge, 1992), p. 31.

14. WT, pp. 681–2; tr., 2.102–4.

15. *QP*, p. 90.

16. J. P. Phillips, *The Crusades, 1095–1197* (London, 2002), pp. 56–8.

17. J. S. C. Riley-Smith, *The Knights of St John in Jerusalem and Cyprus, 1050–1310* (London, 1967), p. 58.

18. M. Barber, *The New Knighthood: A History of the Order of the Temple* (Cambridge, 1994), pp. 6–31.

19. *Papsturkunden für Kirchen im Heiligen Lande*, ed. R. Hiestand, Vorarbeiten zum Oriens Pontificius III (Göttingen, 1985); idem, 'The Papacy and the Second Crusade'; B. Hamilton, *The Latin Church in the Crusader States* (London, 1980).

20. Riley-Smith, *FC*, pp. 7–22; Housley, *Contesting the Crusades*, pp. 48–51.

21. J. S. C. Riley-Smith, *The First Crusade and the Idea of Crusading* (London, 1986), pp. 120–34; A. C. Mullinder, 'The Crusade of 1101', unpublished PhD thesis (University of Swansea, 1996). Pope Paschal II made the punishment for deserters utterly clear in his letter of early 1100, 'Epistolae et privilegia', *PL* 163.45–46.

22. J. G. Rowe, 'Paschal II, Bohemund of Antioch and the Byzantine Empire', *Bulletin of the John Rylands Library* 40 (1966), pp. 165–202; W. B. McQueen, 'Relations between the Normans and Byzantium 1071–1112', *Byzantion* 56 (1986), pp. 427–76.

23. OV 3.183–4.

24. Suger, *VLG*, p. 48; tr. p. 45.

25. *Recueil d'annales angevines et vendômoises*, ed. L. Halphen (Paris, 1903), pp. 68–9.

26. W. Holtzmann, 'Zur Geschichte des Investiturstreites', *Neues Archiv der Gesellschaft für ältere deutsche Geschichtskunde* 50 (1935), p. 280.

27. WT, p. 495; tr. 1.460–1.

28. Hamilton, *Latin Church*, p. 172; R.-J. Lilie, *Byzantium and the Crusader States, 1095–1204*, tr. 7. C. Morris and J. E. Ridings (Oxford, 1993), pp. 61–6; M.Angold, *The Byzantine Empire, 1025–1204: A Political History*, 2nd edn (London, 1997), pp. 129–31.

29. Ekkehard of Aura, 'Hierosolymitana', *RHC Oc.* 5.29–32, 37–8; Richard of Poitiers, 'Chronicon', *RHGF* 12.412.

30. 'Historia belli Sacri', *RHC. Oc.* 3.228–29; AA, pp. 702–3.

31. Ekkehard of Aura, Hierosolymitana', pp. 37–8.

32. Bartolf of Nangis, 'Gesta Francorum Iherusalem Expugnantium', *RHC Oc.* 3.538.

33. OV, 5.376–7.

34. A. C. Krey, ' A Neglected Passage in the *Gesta*', in *The Crusades and Other Historical Essays Presented to Dana C. Munro*, ed. L. Paetow (New York, 1928), pp. 66–78 may be stretching matters to suggest that this circulation of the *Gesta* was part of a planned propaganda campaign.

35. OV 6.69–70. Rowe interprets this visit in less than charitable terms: 'an ostentatious piece of pious humbug' ('Paschal II', p. 182).

36. OV 6.69–70.

37. Ibid., 6.71–2. Orderic wrote this section of his work around 1136–7; p. xviii.

38. Suger, *VLG*, pp. 44–51; tr. pp. 43–6.

39. 'Chronicon Malleacense', *RHGF* 12.405.

40. OV 6.68–71; McQueen, 'Normans and Byzantium', pp. 462–3. Robert Guiscard's alliance with the deposed Emperor Michael VII Doukas in the 1080s was a similar plan: to use a

claimant to the Byzantine throne in order to advance his own cause. Angold, *Byzantine Empire*, p. 129.

41. OV 6.68–9.
42. *Quadripartitus*, ed. F. Liebermann (Halle, 1892), p. 161.
43. *Chronique de Saint-Pierre-le-Vif de Sens, dite de Clarius*, ed. and tr. R.-H. Bautier and M. Gilles (Paris, 1979), pp. 146–7.
44. OV 6.101–2.
45. WT, p. 504; tr. 1.470–2; OV 6.101–2. See the list of crusaders in Riley-Smith, *FC*, pp. 239–42.
46. Rowe, 'Paschal II', pp. 182–95.
47. McQueen, 'Normans and Byzantium', p. 463.
48. Holtzmann, 'Zur Geschichte des Investiturstreites', p. 280.
49. OV 6.100–5; AA, pp. 754–61.
50. Anna Comnena, *The Alexiad*, tr. E. A. S. Dawes (London, 1967), p. 318.
51. OV 6.103–4.
52. Caffaro, 'De liberatione civitatum Orientis', ed. L. T. Belgrano, *Fonti per la storia d'Italia* 11, (Genoa 1890), p. 122.
53. Ibid., p. 123. En route to the Levant Bertrand plundered Byzantine lands in Thessaly. He was summoned to Constantinople where he was given rich gifts and became the emperor's vassal, which brought him into opposition with Alexius's enemies in Antioch. Lilie, *Byzantium and the Crusader States*, pp. 82–3.
54. Caffaro, 'De liberatione', p. 124.
55. For details on the Genoese holdings in the Levant, see S. A. Epstein, *Genoa and the Genoese, 958–1528* (Chapel Hill NC, 1996), pp. 28–33; E. H. Byrne, 'The Genoese Colonies in Syria', in *The Crusades and Other Historical Essays Presented to Dana C. Munro*, ed. L. J. Paetow (New York, 1928), pp. 139–82.
56. Snorri Sturlusson, *Heimskringla*, tr. L. M. Hollander (Austin TX, 1964), pp. xv–xxvi.
57. Ibid., p. 688.
58. WT, p. 517; tr. 1.486–8.
59. FC, pp. 543–4; tr. p. 199.
60. Snorri Sturlusson, pp. 689–94; FC, p. 546; tr. p. 199; WT, p. 517; tr. 1.486–8; Ibn al-Athir, *The Chronicle of Ibn al-Athir for the Crusading Period*, p. 152.
61. Snorri Sturlusson, pp. 696–9. For the relic, see also A. Frolow, *La Relique de la vraie croix*, (Paris, 1961), 1.309–10.
62. Cerbanus Cerbani, 'Translatio mirifici martyris Isidori a Chio in civitatem Venetam', RHC Oc. 5.322–3; OV 6.128–9. J. S. C. Riley-Smith, 'The Venetian Crusade of 1122–24', in *I communi italiani nel regno crociato di Gerusalemme*, ed. G. Airaldi and B. Z Kedar (Genoa, 1986), pp. 339–50.
63. Riley-Smith, *FC*, pp. 176–7.
64. Calixtus II, *Bullaire*, ed. U. Robert, 2 vols (Paris, 1891), vol. 2, no. 249, pp. 364–5.
65. *Decrees of the Ecumenical Councils*, ed. and tr. N. J. Tanner (New York, 1991), p. 191.
66. Ibid., p. 192.
67. Ibid.; see also a letter of Calixtus with similar phrasing: *Bullaire*, vol. 2, no. 454, pp. 266–7.
68. Ibid., pp. 242–4.
69. *Historia Compostellana*, ed. E. Falque Rey, CCCM 70 (Turnhout, 1988), pp. 270–2; Calixtus II, *Bullaire*, 2, no. 454, pp. 266–7; R. A. Fletcher, *Saint James's Catapult: The Life and Times of Diego Gelmírez of Santiago de Compostela* (Oxford, 1984).
70. *The Anglo-Saxon Chronicle*, ed. and tr. D. Whitelock (London, 1961), pp. 194–5.
71. *Cartulaire général de l'ordre du Temple, 1119?–1150*, ed. A. d'Albon (Paris, 1913), no. 12, pp. 8–10; Phillips, *Defenders*, p. 38.
72. Riley-Smith, *FC*, pp. 244–6 gives a list of known participants.
73. WT, pp. 621–2; tr. 2.40–3; IQ, pp. 197–200.
74. Riley-Smith, *FC*, pp. 147, 152–3.
75. Ibid., pp. 145–6; for Flanders, see also T. de Hemptinne, 'Les Épouses des croisés et pèlerins Flamands aux XIe et XIIe siècles', in *Autour de la Première Croisade*, ed. M. Balard, Byzantina Sorbonensia 14 (Paris, 1996), pp. 83–95.
76. OV 5.228–3.
77. Riley-Smith, *First Crusade and the Idea of Crusading*, pp. 130–4.
78. OV 6.102–5.
79. Ibid., pp. 103–4.

80. WM, pp. 692–4.
81. Henry of Huntingdon, *Historia Anglorum*, pp. lxviii, 485.
82. Barber, *The New Knighthood*, pp. 39–49.
83. Lilie, *Byzantium and the Crusades*, pp. 117–45; see also Phillips, *Defenders*, pp. 61–71.
84. *Papsturkunden für Kirchen im Heiligen Lande*, no. 49, p. 136.
85. OV 6.506–7.

Notes to Chapter 2

1. Riley-Smith, *First Crusade and the Idea of Crusading*; H. E. J. Cowdrey, 'Pope Urban II and the Idea of the Crusade', *Studi Medievali* 36 (1995), pp. 721–42; M. G. Bull, *Knightly Piety and the Lay Response to the First Crusade* (Oxford, 1993), esp. pp. 205–17.
2. FC, pp. 305–6; tr. p. 123.
3. Raymond of Aguilers, *Historia Francorum qui ceperunt Iherusalem*, ed. J. H. and L. L. Hill, Documents relatifs à l'histoire des croisades IX (Paris, 1969), p. 151; tr. J. H. and L. L. Hill (Philadelphia PA, 1968), p. 128.
4. Hagenmeyer, *Epistolae*, no. 20, pp. 175–6; tr. E. Peters, *The First Crusade*, 2nd edn (Philadelphia PA, 1998), p. 296.
5. Paschal II, in Hagenmeyer, *Epistolae*, no. 22, p. 178.
6. Riley-Smith, *First Crusade and the Idea of Crusading*, pp. 122–3.
7. GN, p. 83; mistranslated in R. Levine at p. 26 (Guibert of Nogent, *The Deeds of God through the Franks*, Woodbridge, 1997).
8. For example, the smutty stories concerning the behaviour of Arnulf of Chocques, later elected patriarch of Jerusalem: Raymond of Aguilers, *Historia Francorum*, p. 154; tr. p. 131.
9. P. Classen, '*Res Gestae*, Universal History, Apocalypse: Visions of Past and Future', in *Renaissance and Renewal in the Twelfth Century*, ed. R. L. Benson and G. Constable (Oxford, 1982), p. 414 notes that he omitted a discussion of the crusades in his survey of twelfth-century narratives and registers the subject's huge importance. Likewise, B. Guénee, *Historique et culture dans l'Occident medieval* (Paris, 1980), writes at p. 360: 'La croisade, aussi, joua dans le développement de l'histoire un role primordial' – but does not analyse the relevant writings in particular detail.
10. Riley-Smith, *First Crusade and the Idea of Crusading*, p. 135.
11. L. Shopkow, *History and Community: Norman Historical Writing in the Eleventh and Twelfth Centuries* (Washington DC, 1997) discusses these matters in detail. In her analysis of the historical writing in Normandy she reaches a rather pessimistic view of the size of audiences (largely because of the barrier of the Latin language) and then she transposes this downbeat assessment to the remainder of medieval Europe, pp. 243–4, 248–9. E. Van Houts, *Memory and Gender in Medieval Europe, 900–1200* (London, 1999) also considers the recording of the past and analyses the Norman Conquest at pp. 123–42.
12. J. Rubenstein, 'What is the *Gesta Francorum* and who was Peter Tudebode?' *Revue Mabillon*, n.s. 16 (2005), p. 197.
13. Ibid., pp. 187–8, 197, 202.
14. *Gesta Francorum*, ed. and tr. R. Mynors, introduction by R. M. T. Hill (London, 1962).
15. GN, pp. 24–5, 51–6; J.Rubenstein, *Guibert of Nogent: Portrait of a Medieval Mind* (New York, 2002), pp. 95–101.
16. Riley-Smith, *First Crusade and the Idea of Crusading*, p. 136.
17. R. Hiestand, 'Il cronista medievale e il suo pubblico: alcune osservazioni in margine alla storiografia delle crociate', *Annali della Facoltà di lettere e filosofia dell'Università di Napoli* 27 (1984–5), pp. 213–15, 227.
18. Robert of Rheims, p. 723; tr. p. 77.
19. WM, p. 150.
20. Peter Tudebode, *Historia de Hierosolymitano Itinere*, ed. J. H. and L. L. Hill, Documents relatifs à l'histoire des croisades XII (Paris, 1977); tr. J. H. and L. L. Hill (Philadelphia PA, 1974). For the composition of this work see pp. 1–4 of the translation and J. France, 'The Anonymous *Gesta Francorum* and the *Historia Francorum qui ceperunt Iherusalem* of Raymond of Aguilers and the *Historia de Hierosolymitano itinere* of Peter Tudebode: An Analysis of the Textual Relationship between Primary Sources for the First Crusade', in *The Crusades and their Sources: Essays Presented to Bernard Hamilton*, ed. J. France and

W. G. Zajac (Aldershot, 1998), pp. 39–70; but see more recently Rubenstein, 'What is the *Gesta Francorum*?', pp. 189–204.

21. Raymond of Aguilers, *Historia*.
22. *Canso d'Antioca*, ed. and tr. C. Sweetenham and L. M. Paterson (Aldershot, 2003), pp. 6–9.
23. Ibid., pp. 1–9, 26.
24. FC, pp. 42–8; Hiestand, 'Il cronista medievale e il suo pubblico', p. 210.
25. Bartolf of Nangis, 'Gesta Francorum expugnantium Iherusalem', pp. xxxvi-xxxvii, 489–543; H. S. Fink, introduction to the translation of FC, pp. 18–22.
26. GN, pp. 329–34; tr. pp. 155–7.
27. AA, pp. xxxiv–xxxv; S. B. Edgington, 'Reviewing the evidence', in *The First Crusade: Origins and Impact*, ed. J. P. Phillips (Manchester, 1997), at pp. 60–3.
28. Ekkehard of Aura, 'Hiersolymitana', pp. ii-xvi, 1–40; Hiestand, 'Il cronista medievale e il suo pubblico', p. 210.
29. R. D. Face, 'Secular history in twelfth-century Italy: Caffaro of Genoa', *Journal of Medieval History* 6 (1980), pp. 169–84, although Caffaro did not formally present his work to the city consuls until 1152; ibid., p.171.
30. 'Chronica monasterii Casinensis', *MGH* 34, esp. pp. 475–86; C. Cahen, *La Syrie du nord à l'époque des croisades* (Paris, 1940), pp. 8–9; J. France, 'Use of the Anonymous *Gesta Francorum* in the Early Twelfth Century: Sources for the First Crusade', in *From Clermont to Jerusalem: The Crusades and Crusader Societies, 1095–1500* ed. A. V. Murray (Turnhout, 1998), p. 37.
31. Robert of Rheims, p. 740; tr. p. 90.
32. Riley-Smith, *First Crusade and the Idea of Crusading*, p. 152.
33. Ibid.
34. Gilo of Paris, *Historia vie Hierosolimitane*, ed. and tr. C. W. Grocock and J. E. Siberry, Oxford Medieval Texts (Oxford, 1997), pp. xxiv, lvii–lxiv.
35. Ibid., pp. xiii–xxiv – the dating of the 'Charleville Poet's' contribution is difficult to ascertain, other than it was after 1118.
36. Ibid., p. 3.
37. Ralph of Caen, 'Gesta Tancredi in expeditione Hierosolymitana', *RHC Oc.* 3. 587–716; *The Gesta Tancredi of Ralph of Caen: A History of the Normans on the First Crusade*, tr. B. S. Bachrach and D. S. Bachrach (Aldershot, 2005), pp. 1–4.
38. Walter the Chancellor, *Galterii Cancellarii Bella Antiochena*, ed. H. Hagenmeyer (Innsbruck, 1896), pp. 52–5; *Walter the Chancellor's The Antiochene Wars*, tr. T. S. Asbridge and S. B. Edgington (Aldershot, 1999), pp. 8–10.
39. WM, 2.xvii-xxxv; R. M. Thomson, *William of Malmesbury* (Woodbridge, 2003), pp. 178–88.
40. WM, p. 655.
41. Henry of Huntingdon, *Historia Anglorum*, pp. lxviii, 425.
42. Ibid., p. 423.
43. OV 5.4–5.
44. OV 5.4–7; Shopkow, *History and Community*, pp. 231–5.
45. OV 1.112–15.
46. Walter of Thérouanne, 'Walteri vita karoli comitis flandriae', p. 540.
47. 'Chronicon S. Andrae Castri Cameracesii', *MGH* 7.544–5.
48. 'Historia Belli Sacri', pp. xiii-xvii, 165–229; Rubenstein, 'What is the *Gesta Francorum*?', pp. 181–3, 201–2.
49. William's dedication is to be found in *RHC Oc.* 3.317–18. See also the important article by J. Rubenstein, 'Putting History to Use: Three Crusade Chronicles in Context', *Viator* 35 (2004), pp. 131–67; note also the comments on the presentation of literary works in Shopkow, *History and Community*, pp. 219–24.
50. OV 5.343.
51. Lambert of Ardres, 'Historia comitum Ghisensium', *MGH* 24.626–7; *The History of the Counts of Guines and Lords of Ardres*, tr. L.Shopkow (Philadelphia PA, 2001), pp. 164–5.
52. Ibid., pp. 164–6.
53. *La Chanson d'Antioche*, ed. S. Duparc-Quioc, Documents relatifs à l'histoire des croisades XI, 2 vols (Paris, 1977–8), 2.144–5.
54. *Canso d'Antioca*, p. 6.
55. *La Chanson d'Antioche*, p. 19; tr. E. Peters, *The First Crusade*, 2nd edn (Philadelphia PA, 1998), p. 303.

56. *La Chanson d'Antioche*, 1.71, 208–11, 306–7, 442.
57. M.Routledge, 'Songs', in *The Oxford Illustrated History of the Crusades*, ed. J. S. C. Riley-Smith (Oxford, 1995), pp. 92–3. See also D. A. Trotter, *Medieval French Literature and the Crusades (1100–1300)* (Geneva, 1988).
58. I. Short, 'A Study in Carolingian Legend and its Persistence in Latin Historiography', *Mittellateinisches Jahrbuch* 7 (1972), pp. 127–52, at p. 129. For the 'Pilgrimage of Charlemagne', see 'Le Voyage de Charlemagne à Jérusalem et à Constantinople', ed. M. Tyssens (Ghent, 1977); for the 'Pseudo-Turpin', see *Liber Sancti Jacobi: Codex Calixtinus*, tr. A. Moraljo, C. Torres, J. Feo and X. Carro Otero (Santiago de Compostela, 1999), and the comments in W. J. Purkis, *Crusading Spirituality in the Holy Land and Iberia, c.1095–c.1187* (Woodbridge, forthcoming). Lambert of Ardres shows this interest in hearing about crusading heroes for the late twelfth century. He recounted that Lord Arnold II of Guines enjoyed hearing about the adventures of Charlemagne, Roland, Oliver and King Arthur of Britain and he listened 'to his ears' delight [about] the land of Jerusalem and the siege of Antioch and of the Arabs and Babylonians and deeds done overseas'. Lambert of Ardres, 'Historia', p. 607; tr. p. 130.
59. Geoffrey of Monmouth, *Historia Regum Brittaniae*, ed. A. Griscom and R. Ellis Jones (London, 1929), pp. 437–8; *The History of the Kings of Britain*, tr. L. Thorpe (London, 1966), p. 216.
60. R. L. Crocker, 'Early Crusade Songs', in *The Holy War*, ed. T. P. Murphy (Columbus OH, 1976), pp. 82–3; G. Spreckelmeyer, *Das Kreuzzugslied des lateinischen Mittelalters* (Munich, 1924), pp. 85–9, 184–219; J.Szövérffy, *Secular Latin Lyrics and Minor Poetic Forms of the Middle Ages: A Historical Survey and Literary Repertory from the Tenth to the Late Fifteenth Century*, Vol. 1 (Concord NH, 1992), pp. 369–73.
61. S. Schein, *Gateway to the Heavenly City: Crusader Jerusalem and the Catholic West (1099–1187)* (Aldershot, 2005), pp. 29–31.
62. OV 6.286–7.
63. Robert of Torigny, p. 482.
64. Walter of Thérouanne, 'Walteri vita Karoli comitis Flandriae', p. 540. See also OV 6.162 where Robert is described as 'bellicosi Ierosolimitae'.
65. Suger, *VLG*, p.142; tr. p. 90. Riley-Smith, *First Crusaders*, p. 149 lists others known in this way.
66. Henry of Huntingdon, *Historia Anglorum*, p. 459.
67. Suger, *VLG*, pp. 174–9; tr. pp. 106–9.
68. Guibert of Nogent, *De vita sua*, ed. E. R. Labande (Paris, 1981), pp. 410–11.
69. Riley-Smith, *FC*, pp. 156–7; for more details on Thomas's career see D.Barthélemy, *Les deux ages de la seigneurie banale. Pouvoir et société dans la terre des sires de Coucy (XIe–XIIe s.)* (Paris, 1984), pp. 69–99.
70. H. W. C. Davis, 'Henry of Blois and Brian Fitz-Count', *English Historical Review* 25 (1910), pp. 297–303.
71. OV 5.356–9; 6.68–71.
72. WM, p. 693.
73. OV 6.70–1.
74. Ibid.
75. WT, p. 495; tr. 1, 460–1.
76. OV 6. 68–73, 100–5; Suger, *VLG*, p. 48; tr. p. 45.
77. H.Tanner, 'In His Brothers' Shadow: The Crusading Career and Reputation of Count Eustace III of Boulogne', in *The Crusades: Other Experiences, Alternate Perspectives*, ed. K. I. Semaan (Binghampton NY, 2003), pp. 86, 88. N. L. Paul, 'Crusade and Family Memory before 1225', unpublished Ph.D. thesis, University of Cambridge, 2005; J. Dunbabin, 'Discovering a Past for the French Aristocracy', in *The Perception of the Past in Twelfth-Century Europe*, ed. P. Magdalino (London, 1992), pp. 1–14.
78. Suger, *VLG*, p. 38; tr., p. 41.
79. *La Chronique de Morigny (1095–1152)*, ed. L. Mirot (Paris, 1909), pp. 40–1.
80. OV 6.394–5.
81. Ibid., 6.158, 162.
82. *Bibliotheca Cluniacensis*, ed. M. Marrier and A. Quercentan (Matiscone, 1915), col. 1352; tr. by Tanner in 'In His Brothers' Shadow', pp. 89–90.
83. Henry of Huntingdon, *Historia Anglorum*, p. 715.

84. *The Gesta Tancredi of Ralph of Caen*, pp. 14–15; M. G. Bull, 'Overlapping and Competing Identities in the Frankish First Crusade' in, *Le Concile de Clermont de 1095 et l'appel à la croisade* ed. A. Vauchez (Rome, 1997), pp. 195–211.
85. A. Katzenellenbogen, 'The Central Tympanum at Vézelay: Its Encyclopedic Meaning and its Relation to the First Crusade', *Art Bulletin* 26 (1944), pp. 141–51.
86. Raymond of Aguilers, *Historia Francorum*, p. 151; tr. p. 128.
87. Katzenellenbogen, 'Central Tympanum', pp. 143–51.
88. A. Derbes, 'Crusading Ideology and the Frescoes of S. Maria in Cosmedin', *Art Bulletin* 77 (1995), pp. 460–78.
89. C. B. Bouchard, *Sword, Miter and Cloister: Nobility and the Church in Burgundy, 980–1198* (Cornell NY, 1987), pp. 155, 273–5; Riley-Smith, *First Crusaders*, pp. 176–7; idem, 'Family Traditions and Participation in the Second Crusade', in SCC, p. 102.
90. This message is conveniently summarised in P. Cole, '"O God, the heathen have come into your inheritance" (Ps. 78.1): The Theme of Religious Pollution in Crusade Documents, 1095–1188', in *Crusaders and Muslims in Twelfth-Century Syria*, ed. M.Shatzmiller (Leiden, 1993), pp. 84–112, esp. at 84–100. It should be indicated that these frescoes and their themes of cleansing and the triumph of the Church over its enemies could also be connected to the recent end of the schism with the German Empire.
91. R. Lejeune and J. Stiennon, *La légende de Roland dans l'art du Moyen Age*, 2nd edn, (Brussels, 1966), 2, plates 43–50; Derbes, 'Crusading Ideology', pp. 460–3.
92. A. Derbes, 'A Crusading Fresco Cycle at the Cathedral of Le Puy', *Art Bulletin* 73 (1991), pp. 561–76.
93. D. Denny, 'A Romanesque Fresco in Auxerre Cathedral', *Gesta* 25 (1986), pp. 197–202.
94. L. Seidel, 'Images of the Crusades in Western Art', in *The Meeting of Two Worlds: Cultural Exchange between East and West during the Period of the Crusades*, ed. V. P. Goss (Kalamazoo, 1986), at p. 385.
95. Ibid., p. 386.
96. M. Camille, *The Gothic Idol: Ideology and Image-Making in Medieval Art* (Cambridge, 1989), pp. 4–7.
97. There is good reason to link this architectural programme to the planning of the Second Crusade itself. C. F. O'Meara, *The Iconography of the Façade of St Gilles-du-Gard* (New York, 1977).
98. E. Lapina, 'The Mural Paintings of Berzé-la-Ville in the Context of the First Crusade and the Reconquista', *Journal of Medieval History* 31 (2005), pp. 309–26.
99. C. Morris, 'Picturing the Crusades: The Uses of Visual Propaganda, *c*.1095–1250', *The Crusades and their Sources: Essays Presented to Bernard Hamilton*, ed. J. France and W. G. Zajac (Aldershot, 1998), pp. 202–3; Lejeune and Stiennon, *La légende de Roland dans l'art du Moyen Age*, 2, plates 14–19.
100. Ibid., pp. 204–5; *Provence: Art, Architecture, Landscape*, ed. R. Tomar (Cologne, (1999), pp. 368–71; M.Baylé, 'Le décor sculpte de Saint-Georges-de-Boscherville: Quelques questions de style et iconographie', *Anglo-Norman Studies* 8 (1985), pp. 27–45.
101. Lejeune and Stiennon, *La légende de Roland dans l'art du Moyen Age*, 1, pp. 61–71, 72–6; 2, plates, 38–9, 43–4, 47–8.
102. C. Morris, *The Sepulchre of Christ and the Medieval West* (Oxford, 2005), pp. 230–40. For some pre-1099 examples see also his 'Memorials of the Holy Places and Blessings from the East: Devotion to Jerusalem before the Crusades', in *The Holy Land, Holy Lands, and Christian History*, ed. R. L. Swanson, Studies in Church History 36 (Woodbridge, 2000), pp. 90–109; Schein, *Gateway to the Heavenly City*, pp. 63–4.
103. C. Morris, 'Bringing the Holy Sepulchre to the West: S. Stefano, Bologna, from the Fifth to the Twelfth Century', *Studies in Church History* 33 (1997), at pp. 39, 56.
104. Lists of some of the pilgrims from this period can be found in Riley-Smith, *First Crusaders*, pp.166–7 (for the Limousin, Marseilles and Champagne); R. Röhricht, *Die Deutschen im Heiligen Lande, 650–1291* (Innsbruck, 1894), pp. 22–6.
105. For Eric of Denmark and his wife; see below, p. 234; also: K. Naß, 'Eine Hildesheimer Weltchronik des 12. Jahrhunderts in Auszügen des Dietrich Engelhus', in *Die Reichschronik des Annalista Saxo und die sächsiche Geschichtsschreibung im 12 Jahrhundert, MGH, Schriften* 41(1996), p. 418; for Henry: *Livro preto da Sé de Coimbra*, ed. A. da Costa, L. Ventura and T. Veloso, 3 vols (Coimbra, 1977–9), Vol. 1, no. 80, p. 116; for Hugh:

Cartulaires de l'abbaye de Molesme, ed. J. Laurent, 2 vols (1907–11), Vol. 2, no. 17, pp. 321–3; *Cartulaire de Montier-la-Celle*, ed. C. Lalore (Paris, 1890), nos 14–18, pp. 284–7; BCE 7.85–6; for Paris OV 6.310–11.

106. *Cartulaires des abbayes de Tulle et de Roc-Amadour*, ed. J.-B. Champeval (Brive, 1903), p. 140; *Cartulaire de l'abbaye de Saint-Père de Chartres*, ed. B. E. C. Guérard, 2 vols (Paris, 1840), Vol. 2, no. 156, pp. 368–9; no. 149, pp. 363–4. Guérard lists another 14 pilgrims making agreements with this institution between 1101 and 1145.

107. OV 3.164–7.

108. *Jerusalem Pilgrimage, 1099–1185*, ed. and tr. J. Wilkinson, Hakluyt Society, 2nd series, Vol. 167 (London, 1988).

109. Lambert of Ardres, p. 626; tr. p. 164.

110. *Chronique et cartulaire de l'abbaye de Bergues Saint-Winnoc*, ed. A. Pruvost (Bruges, 1875–8), p. 107.

111. *Chronique de Saint-Pierre-le-Vif de Sens*, pp. 184–9.

112. A. Boas, *Jerusalem in the Time of the Crusades* (London, 2001), p. 200; Schein, *Gateway to the Heavenly City*, p. 85.

Notes to Chapter 3

1. The 1145 document is in *EE*, cols 1064–6; that of 1 March 1146 has been re-edited by R. Grosse (*QP*). There is a translation based on this latter document in Appendix 1 below. For the subsequent history of the bull, see Phillips, *Defenders*, pp. 148–50, 153, 188, 256; J. G. Rowe, 'Alexander III and the Jerusalem Crusade: An Overview of Problems and Failures', in *Crusaders and Muslims in Twelfth-Century Syria*, ed. M. Shatzmiller (Leiden, 1993), at pp. 118–26. It is possible that Eugenius reissued *Quantum praedecessores* as early as 1150; see below, p. 271.

2. Alexander III, 'Epistolae et privilegia', *PL* 200.384–6; *Papsturkunden für Templer und Johanniter*, ed. R. Hiestand, Vorarbeiten zum Oriens Pontificius 1–2 (Göttingen, 1972–84), vol. 1, pp. 251–3, no. 53.

3. Alexander III, 'Epistolae', cols 599–601 (*Cor nostrum* was issued in two slightly different versions in 1181); cols 1294–7; *Papsturkunden in Sizilien*, ed. P. Kehr (Göttingen, 1899), no. 26, pp. 329–30.

4. See below, pp. 40–1.

5. *Les chansons de croisade avec leurs mélodies*, ed. J. Bédier and P. Aubry (Paris, 1909), pp. 8–11; tr. M. Routledge in J. P. Phillips, *The Crusades, 1095–1197* (London, 2002), pp. 182–3.

6. J. P. Phillips, 'Ideas of Crusade and Holy War in *De expugnatione Lyxbonensi* (The Conquest of Lisbon)', in *The Holy Land, Holy Lands, and Christian History*, ed. R. N. Swanson, Studies in Church History 36 (Woodbridge, 2000), pp. 134–5.

7. 'Annales Reicherspergenses', *MGH* 17.461; *La Chronique de Morigny*, pp. 82–3.

8. J. H. Pryor, *Geography, Technology and War: Studies in the Maritime History of the Mediterranean, 649–1571* (Cambridge, 1988), pp. 3–4, 51–3.

9. J. G. Rowe, 'The Origins of the Second Crusade: Pope Eugenius III, Bernard of Clairvaux and Louis VII of France', in SCC, p. 81.

10. 'Historia Ducum Venetorum', *MGH* 14.73; J. S. C. Riley-Smith, 'The Venetian Crusade of 1122–24', pp. 337–50.

11. Calixtus II, *Bullaire*, vol. 2, no. 249, pp. 364–5; M. Stroll, *Calixtus II (1119–1124): A Pope Born to Rule* (Leiden, 2004), pp. 441–5.

12. *QP*, p. 90.

13. For Eugenius's early career, see Horn, *Studien*, pp. 19–40.

14. *Regesta regni Hierosolymitani, 1097–1291*, ed. R. Röhricht (Innsbruck, 1893), no. 153, p. 38; H. E. Mayer, 'Angevins *versus* Normans: The New Men of King Fulk of Jerusalem', *Proceedings of the American Philosophical Society* 133 (1991), at p. 13.

15. D. F. Glass, *Portals, Pilgrimage and Crusade in Western Tuscany* (Princeton, 1997), p. 56.

16. R. Somerville, 'The Council of Pisa, 1135: A Re-examination of the Evidence for the Canons', *Speculum* 45 (1970), pp. 98–114.

17. Bernard of Pisa's letters are published in Bernard of Clairvaux's 'Epistolae', *PL* 182.547–9.

18. Ibid.

19. BCE, no. 345, pp. 286–8; tr. in BSJ, pp. 458–9.

20. There is some suggestion that Bernard had become a cardinal, but Horn, *Studien*, pp. 42–5, discounts this. For more details on the hurried election process, see Boso, *Le Liber Pontificalis*, ed. L. Duchesne, 3 vols (Paris, 1955–7), 2.386.

21. BCE, no. 237, pp. 113–15; tr. in BSJ, pp. 385–6.

22. BCE, no. 238, p. 117; tr. in BSJ, p. 278.

23. John of Salisbury, *Historia Pontificalis*, ed. and tr. M. Chibnall (London, 1956), pp. 51, 61–2.

24. Boso, *Le Liber Pontificalis*, 2.386.

25. Robert of Torigny, 'Chronicon', p. 501.

26. M. Barber, *The Two Cities: Medieval Europe 1050–1320* (London, 1992), p. 127.

27. Hiestand, 'Papacy and the Second Crusade', in SCSC, p. 37.

28. C. J. Tyerman, *God's War: A New History of the Crusades* (London, 2006), pp. 275, 278, 281.

29. For the most detailed profile of Alberic, see R. Manselli, 'Alberico, cardinale vescovo d'Ostia e la sua attività di legato pontificio', *Archivio della Società Romana di storia patria* 78 (1955), pp. 23–68; B. Zenker, *Die Mitglieder des Kardinalkollegiums von 1130 bis 1159* (Würzburg, 1964), pp. 15–18.

30. Richard of Hexham, 'De gestis regis Stephani et de bello standardi', in *Chronicles of the Reigns of Stephen, Henry II and Richard I*, 4 vols, ed. R. Howlett, Rolls Series 82 (1884–9), 3.167.

31. Ibid., pp. 167–71.

32. Peter the Venerable, *Letters*, ed. G. Constable, 2 vols (Cambridge MA, 1967), Vol. 1, no. 84, p. 221.

33. WT, pp. 688–99; tr. 2.110–11; *Regesta regni Hierosolymitani*, nos 203, 208, pp. 50, 52.

34. Alberic witnessed a charter given at the Lateran Palace on 4 March 1144; see *Acta Pontificum Romanorum inedita*, ed. J. von Pflugk-Harttung, 3 vols (Tübingen, 1881–6), Vol. 1, no. 194, pp. 171–3. For the legation, see *Chronicle of Morigny*, pp. 80–81; *Papsturkunden in Frankreich*, ed. W. Wiederhold (Göttingen, 1907), 2.87; W. Janssen, *Die päpstlichen Legaten in Frankreich vom Schisma Anaklets II. bis zum Tode Coelestins III (1130–1198)* (Cologne, Graz, 1961), pp. 41–6.

35. For Alberic at Viterbo, see *Acta Pontificum Romanorum inedita*, 1, no. 198, pp. 177–80. For his presence with Eugenius, see *EE*, cols 1068–253 (*passim*).

36. Zenker, *Die Mitglieder des Kardinalkollegiums*, pp. 146–8; I. S. Robinson, *The Papacy, 1073–1198: Continuity and Innovation* (Cambridge, 1990), p. 159.

37. Constable, SC, p. 259, n. 235.

38. For Guido's presence at the *curia*, see *EE*, cols 1051–1200; for his appearance in Germany, see Henry VI, 'Urkunden', in Conrad III, *Die Urkunden Konrads III. und seines Sohnes Heinrich*, ed. F. Hausmann, MGH DD (Vienna, 1969), no. 4, pp. 523–5.

39. Conrad III, *Urkunden*, nos 8, 52, 83; pp. 16 (1138) 88 (1140), 148 (1142); Eugenius, cols 1015–17, 1051; Robinson, *Papacy*, pp. 159, 316; Zenker, *Die Mitglieder des Kardinalkollegiums*, pp. 26–8.

40. Conrad III, *Urkunden*, no. 133, pp. 241–3.

41. *EE*, col. 1156; Conrad III, *Urkunden*, n. 184, pp. 332–3.

42. BCE, no. 362, pp. 309–10; tr. pp. 386–7; Zenker, *Die Mitglieder des Kardinalkollegiums*, pp. 89–92.

43. Horn, *Studien*, p. 391, n. 910.

44. BCE, nos 230–2, pp. 100–4; tr. pp. 299–300, 380–2; Eugenius III, cols 1068–1231 (*passim*); Zenker, *Die Mitglieder des Kardinalkollegiums*, pp. 44–6.

45. Bull, *Knightly Piety*, pp. 21–69; arguments concerning Cluny and the First Crusade are outlined in G. Constable, 'Cluny and the First Crusade', *Le Concile de Clermont de 1095 et l'appel à la croisade* (Rome, 1997), pp. 183–93.

46. B. Z. Kedar, *Crusade and Mission: European Approaches towards the Muslims* (Princeton, 1984), pp. 44–8.

47. H. E. J. Cowdrey, 'Two Studies in Cluniac History', *Studi Gregoriani* 11 (Rome, 1978), pp. 146–7;

48. Lapina, 'Mural Paintings of Berzé-la-Ville', pp. 309–26.

49. Katzenellenbogen, 'Central Tympanum', pp. 150–1.

50. Peter the Venerable, *Liber contra sectam sive haeresim Saracenorum*, edited in J. Kritzeck, *Peter the Venerable and Islam* (Princeton, 1964), p. 231.

51. Kedar, *Crusade and Mission*, pp. 99–103.

52. Peter the Venerable, *Letters*, 1, no. 131, p. 332; 2, pp. 260–3.

53. William of Tyre referred to Otto as 'a man of letters', WT p. 760; tr. 2.184.

54. See Otto, *Ddc*, pp. 554–7, tr. pp. 441–3; *EE*, col. 1066.
55. For details of these disputes see below, pp. 129–31. Eugenius himself was trying to arbitrate in a struggle between Duke Wladislas of Bohemia and Bishop Henry of Moravia: *EE*, cols 1044–5.
56. D. Girgensohn, 'Das Pisaner Konzil von 1135 in der Überlieferung des Pisaner Konzils von 1409', in *Festschrift für Hermann Heimpel*, 3 vols (Göttingen, 1971–2), 2.1099–100.
57. N. Housley, 'Crusades against Christians: Their Origins and Early Development, c. 1000–1216', in *Crusade and Settlement: Papers Read at the First Conference of the Society for the Study of the Crusades and the Latin East and Presented to R. C. Smail*, ed. P. W. Edbury (Cardiff, 1985), p. 23.
58. *Papsturkunden in Spanien: I. Katalonien*, ed. P. Kehr (Berlin, 1926), no. 54, pp. 322–4.
59. Gelasius II, 'Epistolae et privilegia', *PL* 163, cols 489–1; Lucius II in *Papsturkunden in Spanien, I: Katalonien*, no. 53, pp. 320–22.
60. *Papsturkunden in Spanien, I: Katalonien*, no. 23, pp. 287–8.
61. Gelasius II, 'Epistolae', col. 508.
62. *Papsturkunden für Templer und Johanniter*, no. 10, pp. 215–16; Barber, *The New Knighthood*, pp. 56–8.
63. *Papsturkunden in Frankreich*, no. 22, pp. 91–92; *Papsturkunden in Spanien, II: Navarra und Aragon*, ed. P. Kehr (Berlin, 1928), no. 57, pp. 360–1.
64. For an overview of Henry and his activities, see M. Lambert, *Medieval Heresy: Popular Movements from the Gregorian Reform to the Reformation*, 3rd edn (Oxford, 2002), pp. 52–7.
65. *BCE*, no. 241, pp. 125–7; tr. in *BSJ*, pp. 387–9.
66. Bernard of Clairvaux, 'Vita prima', *PL* 185, cols 313–14, 337–8; Geoffrey, Bishop of Chartres 'Epistola Gaufredi', ibid., cols 410–16. William of Puylaurens, writing several decades later, reported that the knights and people of Verfeil, east of Toulouse, drove the abbot away without ceremony. Guillaume de Puylaurens, *Chronique*, ed. J. Duvernoy (Paris, 1976), pp. 26–7.
67. *BCE*, no. 241, pp. 125–7; tr. in *BSJ*, pp. 387–9.
68. For Henry's career, see *Ottonian Germany: The Chronicon of Thietmar of Merseburg*, tr. D. A. Warner (Manchester, 2001).
69. 'Adalberti vita Heinrici II imperatoris', *MGH* 4.798.
70. J. P. Phillips, 'Armenia, Edessa and the Second Crusade', in *Knighthoods of Christ*, ed. N. Housley (Aldershot, 2007), pp. 39–50.
71. Otto of Freising, *Ddc*, pp. 554–7, tr. pp. 441–3.
72. B. Hamilton, 'The Armenian Church and the Papacy at the Time of the Crusades', *Eastern Churches Review* 10 (1978), p. 66.
73. C. MacEvitt, 'Christian Authority in the Latin East: Edessa in Crusader History', in *The Medieval Crusade*, ed. S. Ridyard (Woodbridge, 2004), pp. 71–83; J. H. Forse, 'The Armenians and the First Crusade', *Journal of Medieval History* 17 (1991), pp. 13–22.
74. C. Dowsett, 'A Twelfth-Century Armenian Inscription at Edessa', in *Iran and Islam*, ed. C. E. Bosworth (Edinburgh, 1971), pp. 200–1.
75. MacEvitt, 'Christian Authority in the Latin East', pp. 78–9; J. B. Segal, *Edessa 'The Blessed City'* (Oxford, 1970), p. 239.
76. Guiragos of Kantzag, 'Chronicle', *RHC Arm.* 1.417–18.
77. Hamilton, 'Armenian Church', pp. 61–3.
78. *WT*, p. 699; tr. 2.122.
79. Samuel of Ani, 'Extrait de la Chronographie de Samuel d'Ani', *RHC Arm.* 1.450.
80. A. B. Schmidt and P. Halfter, 'Der Brief Papst Innocenz II. an den armenischen Katholikos Gregor III.: Ein wenig beachtetes Dokument zur Geschichte der Synode von Jerusalem (Ostern 1141)', *Annuarium Historiae Conciliorum* 31 (1999), pp. 50–71.
81. Van Lint dates the text between January and September 1146, but, given that the author clearly knows of the coming of the Second Crusade and that news of that expedition could not have reached the Levant before May 1146, the date of composition should be adjusted appropriately. Nersēs Šnorhali, 'Lament on Edessa', tr. T. M. van Lint, in *East and West in the Crusader States*, ed. K. Ciggaar and H. Teule (Leuven, 1999), pp. 49–105.
82. Nersēs, 'Lament', p. 49.
83. Ibid., p. 50
84. Ibid., pp. 100–1.

85. Rowe is wrong to assert that only a few preachers were sent out: 'Origins of the Second Crusade', in SCC, p. 85.
86. Anonymous of Bologna, 'The Principles of Letter-Writing – *Rationes dictandi*', in *Three Medieval Rhetorical Arts*, ed. and tr. J. J. Murphy, 2nd edn (Berkeley CA, 1985), pp. vi–xxiii, 5–25.
87. Ibid., p. 7.
88. Otto of Freising, *GF*, p. 210, tr. p 75; Nicholas of Clairvaux, 'Epistolae', *PL* 182, cols 671–2.
89. *De expugnatione Lyxbonensi*, ed. and tr. C. W. David (New York, 2001) reveals the laborious nature of this process: see pp. 68–71. The renegade Cistercian preacher Ralph used the abbot of Lobbes as his translator, 'Gesta abbatum Lobbiensium', *MGH* 21.329.
90. Anonymous of Bologna, pp. 21–4.
91. *QP*, p. 90.
92. The Genoese chronicler Caffaro participated in campaigns in the immediate aftermath of the First Crusade and the year before the Second Crusade, which reveals that this was possible.
93. *Papsturkunden in Spanien*, 1, no. 54, p. 322.
94. *QP*, p. 90.
95. Ibid.
96. Gregory VIII's bull is in Ansbert, 'Historia de expeditione Friderici imperatoris: Quellen zur Geschichte des Kreuzzugs Kaiser Friedrichs I', ed. A. Chroust, *MGH Scriptores rerum Germanicarum, nova seria*,(1928), 5.10.
97. 'Sigeberti Continuatio Praemonstratensis', p. 452.
98. WT, pp. 234–5; tr. 1.189.
99. My thanks to Professor Bernard Hamilton for indicating these facts to me.
100. FC, pp. 209–15; tr. pp. 89–92; AA, pp. 168–81; 'Petite chronique du règne de Baudouin Ier', in GN, pp. 69–72, 363–4. Later writers such as William of Newburgh who mentioned the Second Crusade referred to the early Christian history of the city in some detail; see his 'Historia rerum Anglicarum' in *Chronicles of the Reigns of Stephen, Henry II and Richard I*, ed. R. Howlett, 4 vols, Rolls Series 82 (London, 1884–9), 2.58–9.
101. A. A. Beaumont Jr, 'Albert of Aachen and the County of Edessa', in *The Crusades and Other Historical Essays Presented to Dana C. Munro*, ed. L. J. Paetow (New York, 1928), pp. 101–38.
102. Otto of Freising, *Ddc*, p. 550, tr. pp. 439–40; 'The Pilgrimage of Etheria', in *The Crusades: A Reader*, ed. S. J. Allen and E. Amt (Peterborough, Ontario, 2003), pp. 3–4. Edessa is barely mentioned in the series of guides to the Levant assembled in *Jerusalem Pilgrimage, 1099–1185*, ed. and tr. J.Wilkinson, Hakluyt Society, 2nd series, Vol. 167 (London, 1988).
103. 'Tractatus de reliquiis S. Stephani Cluniacum delatis', *RHC Or.* 5.317–20.
104. Hugh, archbishop of Edessa, 'Epistola', *PL* 155, cols 477–80; G. Marlot, *Histoire de la ville, cité et université de Reims*, 4 vols (Rheims, 1843–46), Vol. 3, no. 19, 699. On Hugh's posthumous reputation, see R. Hiestand, 'L'archevêque Hugues d'Edesse et son destin posthume', in *Dei gesta per Francos: Crusade Studies in Honour of Jean Richard*, ed. M. Balard, B. Z. Kedar and J. S. C. Riley-Smith (Aldershot, 2001) pp. 171–7.
105. *QP*, p. 91.
106. See the examples given in J. S. C. Riley-Smith, 'King Fulk of Jerusalem and "The Sultan of Babylon"', in *Montjoie: Studies in Crusade History in Honour of Hans Eberhard Mayer*, ed. B. Z. Kedar, J. S. C. Riley-Smith and R. Hiestand (Aldershot, 1997), pp. 57–8; Frolow, *La Relique de la vraie croix*.
107. For example, Robert of Rheims, pp. 728–9, tr. pp. 79–80; FC, pp. 134–5, tr. p. 66; Baldric of Dol, 'Historia Jerosolimitana', *RHC. Or.* 4, pp. 12–14.
108. *QP*, p. 91.
109. Paul, *Crusade and Family Memory before 1225*.
110. Shopkow, *History and Community*, pp. 96–117.
111. Gilo of Paris, *Historia vie Hierosolimitanae*, p. 3.
112. Robert of Rheims, p. 728; tr. p. 80.
113. *QP*, p. 91.
114. Constable, SC, p. 249; Hehl, *Kirche und Kreig*, pp. 127–8.
115. Riley-Smith, *First Crusade and the Idea of Crusading*, pp. 27–9.
116. Urban II to Vallombrosa, *Papsturkunden in Florenz*, ed. W.Wiederhold (Göttingen, 1901), pp. 313–14; FC, pp. 133–5; tr. p. 66; Robert of Rheims, pp. 727–8; tr. pp. 79–80.
117. *QP*, p. 91.

118. Robert of Rheims, p. 741; tr. p. 92; see also the discussion in J. S. C. Riley-Smith, 'The First Crusade and St Peter', in *Outremer: Studies in the History of the Crusading Kingdom of Jerusalem presented to Joshua Prawer*, ed. B. Z. Kedar, H. E. Mayer and R. C. Smail (Jerusalem, 1982), pp. 45–7.

119. P. J. Cole, *The Preaching of the Crusades to the Holy Land, 1095–1270* (Cambridge MA, 1991), pp. 24–32.

120. William of Poitiers, *The Gesta Guillelmi of William of Poitiers*, ed. and tr. R. H. C. Davis and M. Chibnall (Oxford, 1998), pp. 90–1.

121. GN, pp. 112–13, tr. p. 42.

122. FC, pp. 116–17, 589; tr. pp. 58, 214.

123. J. Folda, *The Art of the Crusaders in the Holy Land, 1098–1187* (Cambridge, 1995), Plate 4.19, p. 74.

124. R. Hiestand, 'Gaufridus abbas Templi Domini: an underestimated figure in the early history of the kingdom of Jerusalem', in *The Experience of Crusading 2: Defining the Crusader Kingdom*, ed. P. W. Edbury and J. P. Phillips (Cambridge, 2003), p. 49.

125. QP, pp. 91–2.

126. J. A. Brundage, 'Crusaders and Jurists: The Legal Consequences of Crusader Status' in, *Le Concile de Clermont de 1095 et l'appel à la croisade* (Rome, 1997), pp. 140–8.

127. Hagenmeyer, *Epistolae*, no. 19, pp. 174–5.

128. Ivo of Chartres, 'Epistolae', *PL* 162, cols 170–4, 176–7; *Decrees of the Ecumenical Councils*, pp. 191–2; Robinson, *Papacy*, pp. 336–8.

129. Brundage, 'Crusaders and Jurists', p. 147.

130. QP, p. 91.

131. FC, pp. 432–3; tr. p. 166; Siberry, *Criticism of Crusading 1095–1274* (Oxford, 1985), pp. 75–6.

132. QP, p. 92.

133. Robinson, *Papacy*, pp. 337–40.

134. QP, p. 92.

135. Robinson, *Papacy*, pp. 13–15; Horn, *Studien*, pp. 175–7. Otto of Freising, *Ddc* gives an account of this period, pp. 552–5, 558–9; tr. pp. 440–1, 444.

136. OD, pp. 8–9.

137. Nicholas of Clairvaux, 'Epistolae', *PL* 182, col. 672; for Denmark, see BCE, no. 458, pp. 434–7, tr. in BSJ, pp. 463–4; Otto of Freising, *GF*, pp. 210–11; tr. p. 75.

138. 'Historiae Tornacenses partim ex Herimanni libris excerptae', *MGH* 14.345; *HGRL*, p. 126; Eugenius to the bishop of Salisbury, *Regesta pontificum Romanorum*, ed. P. Jaffé *et al.* 2 vols (Leipzig, 1885–8), 2, no. 8959, p. 36.

Notes to Chapter 4

1. *Chronique de Morigny*, pp. 83–3; 'Annales Reicherspergenses', *MGH* 17.461; Otto of Freising, *Ddc*, pp. 556–67; tr. p. 443.

2. G.Koziol, 'England, France, and the Problem of Sacrality in Twelfth-Century Ritual', in *Cultures of Power: Lordship, Status, and Process in Twelfth-Century Europe*, ed. T. N. Bisson (Philadelphia PA, 1995), pp. 146–8.

3. M. G. Bull, 'The Capetian Monarchy and the Early Crusade Movement: Hugh of Vermandois and Louis VII', *Nottingham Medieval Studies* 30 (1996) pp. 30, 34–46.

4. For details of events in this paragraph, see Y. Sassier, *Louis VII* (Paris, 1991); L. Grant, *Abbot Suger of St-Denis: Church and State in Early Twelfth-Century France* (London, 1998), pp. 142–55; T. Evergates, 'Louis VII and the Counts of Champagne', SCC, pp. 109–17; G. Constable, 'The Disputed Election at Langres in 1138', *Traditio* 13 (1957), pp. 119–52.

5. BCE, no. 221, pp. 85–6; tr. in BSJ, no. 297, pp. 364–6.

6. G. Ferzoco, 'The Origins of the Second Crusade', in SCC, pp. 91–9; Rowe, 'Origins of the Second Crusade', SCC, pp. 79–89.

7. OD, pp. 6–7.

8. Suger, 'Vie de Suger', in *Oeuvres complètes de Suger*, ed. A. Lecoy de la Marche (Paris, 1867), pp. 393–4.

9. E. A. R. Brown and M. W. Cotheren, 'The Twelfth-Century Crusading Window of the Abbey of Saint Denis', *Journal of the Warburg and Courtauld Institutes* 49 (1986), pp. 1–40.

10. P. Spufford, *Power and Profit: The Merchant in Medieval Europe* (London, 2002), pp. 140–73, esp. 165–9. There is a reference in Bernard of Clairvaux's *Vita* to a journey from Clairvaux to Rome taking twenty days, but this was not in midwinter. Poole calculated that a letter could get from Rome to Canterbury in twenty-nine days in the twelfth century, but, again, this presumably did not mean in winter. R. L. Poole, 'The Early Correspondence of John of Salisbury', in *Studies in Chronology and History*, ed. A. L. Poole (Oxford,1934), p. 263.

11. OD, pp. 8–9.

12. See above, pp. 41–2.

13. A. Grabois, 'The Crusade of King Louis VII: A Reconsideration', in *Crusade and Settlement*, ed. P. W. Edbury (Cardiff, 1985), pp. 94–104; Phillips, *Defenders*, pp. 78–82.

14. OD, pp. 6–7.

15. Otto of Freising, *GF*, pp. 200–1; tr. p. 70.

16. 'Sigeberti Continuatio Praemonstratensis', p. 452.

17. Grabois, 'Crusade of King Louis VII', p. 97.

18. Ibid., pp. 94–5, 98–101.

19. For the king's behaviour on the crusade, see OD pp. 118–21; for the failure to attack Edessa, see below, p. 210.

20. *Chronique de Morigny*, p. 83; 'Historia gloriosi regis Ludovici VII, filii Ludovici grossi', *RHGF* 12.126–7: '*Cuius infortunii fama postquam ad aures piissimi Regis Ludovici pervenit, zelo Sancti Spiritus imbutus, ad pietatem commotus est*'.

21. OD, pp. 6–7.

22. A similar combination of the wish for personal salvation and the desire to execute a broader military purpose has been attributed to Louis IX; C. Smith, *Crusading in the Age of Joinville* (Aldershot, 2006), pp. 116–17.

23. Bull, 'Capetian Monarchy and the Early Crusade Movement', p. 45.

24. Ibid.; BCE no. 247, pp. 140–1, tr. in BSJ, p. 398.

25. For similar events in England, see M. Biddle, 'Seasonal Festivals and Residence: Winchester, Westminster and Gloucester in the Tenth to Twelfth Centuries', *Anglo-Norman Studies* 8 (1986), pp. 51–63.

26. H. J. Wurm, *Gottfried, Bischof von Langres* (Würzburg, 1886); Constable, 'Disputed Election at Langres', p. 141.

27. OD, pp. 6–7.

28. Ibid., pp. 8–9.

29. BCE, no. 247, pp. 140–1; tr. in BSJ, pp. 398–9.

30. OD, pp. 6–7; Otto of Freising, *GF*, pp. 200–1; tr. p. 70.

31. Otto of Freising, *GF*, ibid.; also pp. 206–7; tr. p. 73.

32. 'Historia gloriosi regis Ludovici VII', pp. 125–7.

33. Evergates, 'Louis VII and the Counts of Champagne', pp. 110–12; Grant, *Abbot Suger*, pp. 152–5.

34. WT, p. 130; tr. 1.88; R. Somerville, 'The French Councils of Pope Urban II: Some Basic Considerations', *Annuarium historiae conciliorum* 2 (1970), p. 65.

35. Hugh of Poitiers, *The Vézelay Chronicle*, tr. J. Scott and J. O. Ward (Binghampton NY, 1992), pp. 80–5.

36. Ibid., pp. 16–22.

37. Katzenellenbogen, 'Central Tympanum'; see also V. R. Mouilleron, *Vézelay: The Great Romanesque Church* (New York, 1999).

38. Otto of Freising, *GF*, pp. 200–1; tr. pp. 70–1.

39. OD, pp. 8–9.

40. Ibid.

41. *Chronique de Morigny*, p. 83.

42. OD, pp. 8–9; 'Chronicon Senonense sanctae Columbae', *RHGF* 12.288.

43. Louis VII, *Études*, nos 166–8, pp. 152–3.

44. OD, pp.10–11.

45. BCE, no. 247, pp. 140–1; BSJ, p. 399.

46. Otto of Freising, *GF*, pp. 200–1; tr. p. 71; *De oorkonden der graven van Vlaanderen*, no. 90, p. 150.

47. P. Rassow, 'Die Kanzlei St. Bernhards von Clairvaux', *Studien und Mitteilungen zur Geschichte des Benediktinerordens* 34 (1913), pp. 243–79 noted the smallest differences in the texts. On

Bernard's crusading letters in general, see J. Leclercq, 'L'encyclique de Saint Bernard en faveur de la croisade', *Revue Bénédictine* 81 (1971), pp. 282–308; E. Delaruelle, 'L'idée de croisade chez Saint Bernard', *Mélanges Saint Bernard* (Dijon, 1954), pp. 53–67.

48. Otto of Freising, *GF*, p. 216; tr. p. 78.
49. For the basic text to Speyer and Eastern *Francia* and Bavaria, see BCE, no. 363, pp. 311–17. For the letter to England, see BSJ, pp. 460–3. For the letter to Cologne, see J. Groven, 'Die Kölnfahrt Bernhards von Clairvaux', *Annalen des historisches Vereins für den Niederrhein* 120 (1932), pp. 1–48, with the text at pp. 44–8. For the letter to Brescia, see A. Theiner, *Baronii Annales ecclesiastici* 18 (Bar-le-Duc, 1869), pp. 646–7. For the letter to the Hospitallers, see J. Leclercq, 'Un document sur S. Bernard et la seconde croisade', *Revue Mabillon* 43 (1953), pp. 1–4.
50. BCE, nos 265, pp. 320–2; 457, pp. 432–3; 458, pp. 434–7; tr. in BSJ, pp. 463–8; Rassow, 'Die Kanzlei St Bernhards von Clairvaux', pp. 261–79.
51. Nicholas of Clairvaux, 'Epistolae', *PL* 182.671–2. See also J. Leclercq, 'L'encyclique de Saint Bernard', pp. 306–8.
52. In his letter to the duke of Bohemia, Bernard mentioned that he was sending a copy of the missive to the pope. See his 'Epistolae', no. 458, pp. 454–7; tr. in BSJ, pp. 463–4.
53. Otto of Freising gives evidence for this: *GF*, pp. 210–11; tr. p. 75.
54. Meschini, *San Bernardo*, pp. 75–84, 100–2.
55. BCE, no. 363, p. 315; tr. in BSJ, p. 462; OD, pp. 10–13.
56. See also Meschini, *San Bernardo*, pp. 75–84.
57. BCE, no. 363, p. 311; tr. in BSJ, p. 460. Note that this is a translation of the letter to the English people, although the core text is the same down to the last two paragraphs discussed below.
58. Try reading these words aloud – you will get a real sense of passion and energy.
59. BCE, no. 363, p. 312; tr. in BSJ, p. 461.
60. Ibid.
61. Robert of Rheims, p. 730; tr. p. 82; Baldric of Bourgeuil, 'Historia Jerosolimitana', p. 16; *QP*, p. 91.
62. BCE, no. 363, p. 312; tr. in BSJ, p. 461.
63. A view expressed by historians such as Grabois, 'Crusade of King Louis VII', p. 94.
64. *Papsturkunden für Kirchen im Heiligen Lande*, no. 13, pp. 116–17.
65. C. Hillenbrand, *The Crusades: Islamic Perspectives* (Edinburgh, 1999), pp.114–15.
66. BCE, no. 363, p. 313; tr. in BSJ, p. 461.
67. Nicholas of Clairvaux, 'Epistolae', cols 671–2.
68. BCE, no. 363, p. 313; tr. in BSJ, p. 461.
69. Ibid.
70. Ibid., no. 363, p. 314; tr. in BSJ, p. 462.
71. 'Anonymous of Bologna', pp. 7–16.
72. BCE, no. 363, pp. 314–15; tr. in BSJ, p. 462.
73. 'Liber ad milites Templi de laude novae militiae', in *Sancti Bernardi Opera*, ed. J. Leclercq and H. Rochais, 8 vols (Rome, 1955–77), 3.212–39.
74. D. Nicholas, *Medieval Flanders* (London, 1992), pp. 97–123; N. J. G. Pounds, *An Economic History of Medieval Europe* (London, 1974), pp. 243–4.
75. BCE, no. 363, p. 315; tr. in BSJ, p. 462.
76. Ibid., no. 363, pp. 316–17; tr. pp. 462–3.
77. Ibid., no. 363, pp. 315–16, in notes section.
78. Ibid.; Meschini, *San Bernardo*, pp. 83–4. Meschini suggests that because this idea is found in only one of the thirty-seven manuscripts of Bernard's letters, and because its message is so out of step with the others and with *Quantum praedecessores*, this may be one of the false letters alluded to below.
79. BCE, no. 363, p. 317; See Greven, 'Die Kölnfahrt', pp. 47–8; Leclercq, 'L'encyclique', pp. 299–300.
80. BCE, no. 363, p.317.
81. BCE, no. 55, p. 147; tr. in BSJ, p. 85. There is a eulogy to Geoffrey: 'Gaufridi II episcopi Carnotensis elogium', *RHGF* 14.333.
82. W. Janssen, *Die päpstlichen Legaten in Frankreich von Schisma Anaklets II. bis zum Tode Coelestins III (1130–1198)* (Cologne and Graz, 1961), pp. 17–30.
83. *Chronique de Morigny*, pp. 66, 68.

84. Nicholas of Clairvaux, 'Epistolae', col. 672.
85. P. L. Grill, 'Der hl. Bernhard von Clairvaux und Morimond, die Mutterabei der österreichis-chen Cistercienserklöster', *Festschrift zum 800 jahrgedächtnis des todes Bernhards von Clairvaux* (Vienna, 1953), pp. 102–3.
86. E. Willems, 'Cîteaux et la seconde croisade', *Revue d'histoire ecclésiastique* 49 (1954), n. 9, p. 135.
87. Otto of Freising, *GF*, pp. 210–11; tr. p. 75.
88. The best introduction to this subject is Routledge, 'Songs' , pp. 91–111.
89. *Canso d'Antioca*, p. 6; OV, V.343.
90. *Les chansons de croisade avec leurs mélodies*, ed. J. Bédier and P. Aubry (Paris, 1909), pp. 8–11 Routledge, 'Songs', pp. 94, 97–8; P.Bec, *La Lyrique française au moyen âge (XIIe-XIIIe s.)*, 2 vols (Paris, 1977–8), 2.86.
91. GN, p. 156; tr. p. 66; Robert of Rheims, p. 727; tr., p. 80; *DeL*, pp. 70–3.
92. *Decrees of the Ecumenical Councils*, pp. 199–200; M.Keen, *Chivalry* (New Haven CT, 1984), pp. 84, 94, 96.
93. BCE, no. 376, pp. 339–40; tr. BSJ, pp. 476–7.
94. Exodus 14: 30.

Notes to Chapter 5

1. *De oorkonden der graven van Vlaanderen*, no. 90, p. 150.
2. Otto of Freising, *GF*, pp. 200–1, 208–9; tr. pp. 70, 74.
3. Alberic of Trois Fontaines, 'Chronica a monacho novi monasterii Hoiensis interpolata', *MGH* 23.839.
4. He had been complaining of ill-health as recently as during his journey to southern France in the summer of 1145.
5. B. Ward, *Miracles and the Medieval Mind*, 2nd edn (Aldershot, 1987), p. 178.
6. Ibid., pp. 180–2.
7. Phillips, *Defenders*, pp. 271–5.
8. A. V. Murray, 'The Origins of the Frankish Nobility of the Kingdom of Jerusalem, 1100–1118', *Mediterranean Historical Review* 4 (1989), pp. 281–300.
9. H. E. Mayer, 'The Crusader Principality of Galilee between Saint-Omer and Bures-sur-Yvette', in *Itinéraires d'Orient. Hommages à Claude Cahen. Res Orientales* 6 (1994), pp. 157–67; P. Rogghé, 'Oste de Saint Omer', pp. 245–59.
10. Phillips, *Defenders*, pp. 273–5; Nicholas, *Medieval Flanders*, pp. 97–123.
11. *De oorkonden der graven Vlaanderen*, no. 90, p. 150; J. Pitra, 'De itinere S. Bernardi', *PL* 185, col. 1813.
12. On Bernard's journey, see 'De itinere S. Bernardi', cols 1823–24. For Alvisus's death, see below, p. 189.
13. *De oorkonden der graven van Vlaanderen*, no. 90, p. 150.
14. Ibid., nos 91–2, pp. 151–2.
15. *DeL*, pp. 52–5; OD, pp. 52–5; J. P. Phillips, 'The Murder of Count Charles the Good and the Second Crusade', *Medieval Prosopography* 19 (1998), p. 59.
16. 'De itinere S.Bernardi', col. 1825.
17. Ibid., cols 1812, 1824.
18. Ibid., cols 1812–13.
19. Henry IV, *MGH, Diplomata Regum et Imperatorum Germaniae, Vol. 6: Heinrici IV Diplomata*, 2 vols (Weimar, 1953–9), vol. 2, no. 459, pp. 619–20.
20. 'De itinere S. Bernardi', cols 1827–8.
21. Notwithstanding the fact that the principal source for the miracles is the 'Vita' of Saint Bernard, other writers also recorded his healing powers, for example Otto of Freising, *GF*, p. 208; tr. p. 75; Helmold of Bosau, *Chronica Slavorum*, pp. 214–17; tr. p. 171.
22. Edgington, 'Albert of Aachen, St Bernard and the Second Crusade', SCSC, p. 60.
23. The literature on this subject is vast. See especially R. Chazan, *European Jewry and the First Crusade* (Berkeley CA, 1987); idem, *God, Humanity and History: The Hebrew First Crusade Narratives* (Berkeley, 2000); also, in a broader context, see the essay collections *Jews and Christians in Twelfth-Century Europe*, ed. M. A. Singer and J. Van Engen (Notre Dame IN, 2001); *Juden und Christen zur zeit der Kreuzzüge*, Vorträge und Forschungen XLVII, ed. A. Haverkamp (Sigmaringen, 1999).

24. Guibert of Nogent, *De vita sua*, pp. 246–9.
25. *Mainz Anonymous*, tr. R. Chazan, *European Jewry and the First Crusade* (Berkeley CA, 1987), p. 225.
26. Ephraim of Bonn, 'Sefer Zekhirah, or The Book of Remembrance', in *The Jews and the Crusaders*, ed. and tr. S. Eidelberg (Madison WI, 1977), p. 126.
27. R. Chazan, 'Ephraim of Bonn's Sefer Zechirah', *Revue des études juives* 132 (1973), pp. 119–26.
28. Ephraim of Bonn, p. 121, n. 6.
29. *GF*, pp. 206–7; tr. p. 74.
30. 'Annales Rodenses', p. 718.
31. Edgington, 'Albert of Aachen', p. 57.
32. 'Gesta abbatum Lobbiensium', p. 329.
33. R. Chazan, 'From the First Crusade to the Second: Evolving Perceptions of the Christian–Jewish Conflict', in *Jews and Christians in Twelfth-Century Europe*, ed. M. A. Singer and J. van Engen (Notre Dame IN, 2001), p. 47; idem, *Medieval Stereotypes and Modern Antisemitism* (Berkeley CA, 1997), pp. 41–6.
34. BCE, no. 363, p. 316; tr. in BSJ, pp. 462–3.
35. BCE, no. 365, pp. 320–2; tr. in BSJ, pp. 465–6.
36. BCE, no. 365, pp. 321–2; tr. in BSJ, p. 466.
37. Otto of Freising, *GF*, pp. 208–9; tr. p. 74.
38. Ibid. (tr. pp. 74–75).
39. Ephraim of Bonn, pp. 121–2.
40. Chazan, *European Jewry*, pp. 86–99.
41. Ephraim of Bonn, p. 125.
42. Ibid., pp.122–5. Ham is unidentified by Eidelberg; it could be Ham-en-Artois in the diocese of Thérouanne, Flanders.
43. Ibid., p. 131. For an interesting analysis of the position of the Jews in England around the time of the Second Crusade, see E. Rose, *The Monk, the Knight, the Bishop and the Jew: Law and Libel in Medieval England* (Philadelphia PA, forthcoming).
44. 'Annales Herbipolenses', *MGH* 16.3–4.
45. Ephraim of Bonn, pp.128–33.
46. J. P. Phillips, 'Papacy, Empire and the Second Crusade', in *SCSC*, pp. 15–31; Runciman, *History of the Crusades*, 2.255–7.
47. G. A. Loud, 'Some Reflections on the Failure of the Second Crusade', *Crusades* 4 (2005), pp. 1–14.
48. For example, Berry's chapter 'The Second Crusade' in Setton's *History of the Crusades* (Wisconsin, 1969–89) states that 'Louis and the other rulers implemented his [Eugenius's] plan' (1.465).
49. WT, pp. 760–1; tr. pp. 184–5; IQ, pp. 280, 282; JK, pp. 59–73.
50. 'Annales Reicherspergenses', p. 461.
51. Otto of Freising, *GF*, pp. 200–7; tr. pp. 71–3; *Ddc*, pp. 554–9; tr. pp. 441–3. Given his presence at the papal court when the bull was issued, perhaps Otto copied it at the time, hence the inclusion of the text in his *Gesta Frederici*.
52. Otto of Freising, *Ddc*, pp. 550–1; tr. pp. 438–9.
53. Otto of Freising, *Ddc*, pp. 558–89, tr. pp. 444–5; *GF*, pp. 188–9, tr. pp. 63–6. These tumultuous times were widely reported in contemporary chronicles; see, for example, 'Annales Palidenses', *MGH* 16.82; 'Annales S. Petri Erphesfurdenses', *MGH* 16.20.
54. Robert of Rheims, p. 727; tr. p. 79.
55. A. V. Murray, 'The Army of Godfrey of Bouillon: The Structure and Dynamics of a Contingent on the First Crusade', *Revue Belge de philologie et d'histoire* 70 (1992), pp. 301–29.
56. J. France, *Victory in the East: A Military History* (Cambridge, 1994), pp. 91–2, 142; Tyerman, *God's War: A New History of the Crusades*, pp. 100–6.
57. Hagenmeyer, *Epistolae*, no. 21, pp. 176–7.
58. Riley-Smith, *First Crusade and the Idea of Crusading*, pp. 124–6.
59. A. Mullinder, 'The Crusade of 1101', unpublished PhD thesis, University of Swansea, 1996.
60. I. S. Robinson, *Emperor Henry IV of Germany, 1056–1106* (Cambridge, 1999), p. 318.
61. AA, pp. 648–51.
62. Riley-Smith, 'Venetian Crusade of 1122–24', pp. 342–3.

63. G. Constable, 'The Place of the Magdeburg Charter of 1107/8 in the History of Eastern Germany and of the Crusades', *Vita Religiosa im Mittelalter: Festschrift für Kaspar Elm zum 70 Geburtstag*, ed. F. J. Felten and N. Jaspert (Berlin, 1999), pp. 283–99, translation at p. 297.

64. D. H. Green, *The Millstätter Exodus: A Crusading Epic* (Cambridge, 1966), pp. 1–29; 228–95; on the dating of the text and the circulation of crusading ideas in Germany at this time, see pp. 296–370.

65. BCE, no. 363, p. 317. Not translated in BSJ.

66. Ekkehard of Aura, 'Chronicon Universale', p. 262.

67. BCE, no. 244, pp. 134–6; tr. in BSJ, pp. 394–5.

68. M. G. Newman, *The Boundaries of Charity: Cistercian Culture and Ecclesiastical Reform, 1098–1180* (Stanford CA, 1996), pp. 178–80.

69. R. W. Southern, *Scholastic Humanism and the Unification of Europe* (Oxford, 1995), p. 211. Odo of Deuil invoked the principle of the two swords when he described the regency arrangements in France; OD, pp. 14–15.

70. H. Cosack, 'Konrads III. Entschluß zum Kreuzzug', *Mitteilungen des Instituts für Österreichische Geschichtsforschung* 35 (1914), pp. 278–96 – followed by, for example, Runciman, *Crusades*, 2.255–7.

71. Romauld of Salerno, 'Annales', *MGH* 19.424.

72. Conrad III, *Urkunden*, no. 184, p. 333.

73. Ibid., no. 133, pp. 241–3; no. 149, pp. 272–4.

74. Wibald of Stavelot, 'Epistolae', *Bibliotheca rerum Germanicarum*, ed. P. Jaffé, 6 vols (Berlin, 1864–73), Vol. 1, no. 150, p. 233.

75. R. Folz, *Les Saints rois du moyen âge en Occident (VIe–XIIIe siècles)* (Brussels, 1984), pp. 84–91.

76. *EE*, cols 1118–19.

77. Henry II, 'Die Urkunden Heinrichs II und arduins', ed. H. Bresslau (Berlin, 1957), *MGH DD*, 3.170.

78. 'Adalberti vita Heinrici II imperatoris', *MGH* 4.798.

79. T. Reuter, *Germany in the High Middle Ages 800–1056* (London, 1991), pp. 254–5.

80. E. Holthouse, 'The Emperor Henry II', *Cambridge Medieval History*, Vol. 3, *Germany and the Western Empire*, ed. H. M. Gwatkin *et al.* (Cambridge, 1922), pp. 221–8, 238–40, 246–50.

81. B. Hill Jr, *Medieval Monarchy in Action: The German Empire from Henry I to Henry IV* (London, 1972), pp. 61–9.

82. Otto of Freising, *GF*, p. 280; tr. p. 111.

83. *Papsturkunden für Kirchen im Heiligen Lande*, no. 63, pp. 193–5.

84. Caffaro, *CAT*, p. 21.

85. 'Vita Prima S. Bernardi', *PL*, 185, col. 373.

86. Ibid.

87. Ibid.

88. Ibid., cols 374–81.

89. Ward, *Miracles and the Medieval Mind*, p. 182.

90. Gerald of Wales, *The Autobiography of Giraldus Cambrensis*, ed. and tr. H. E. Butler (London, 1937), p. 101.

91. 'Vita Prima S. Bernardi', cols 377–8.

92. Ibid., col. 375.

93. The duke's letter to Louis VII of France in early 1147 suggests this; see J. Leclercq (ed.), 'Un Document sur Saint Bernard et la seconde croisade', *Revue Mabillon* 43 (1953), p. 2. Otto of Freising claimed that the duke took the cross on Christmas Eve at his estate at Peiting, c. 30 miles south-west of Münich. Perhaps this was a public ceremony designed to demonstrate Welf's commitment and to gather further support. Otto of Freising, *GF*, pp. 210–11; tr. p. 76.

94. 'Vita Prima S. Bernardi', col. 381.

95. 'Chronicon Laetiense', *MGH* 14.500.

96. Otto of Freising, *GF*, pp. 200–1; tr. p. 70.

97. 'Vita Prima S. Bernardi', col. 381.

98. Ibid., col. 382.

99. Otto of Freising, *GF*, pp. 208–9; tr. pp. 74–5.

100. 'Vita prima S. Bernardi', col. 383.

101. *EE*, cols 1175–6.

102. 'Vita Prima S. Bernardi', cols 388–99.

103. Ibid., col. 400; Leclercq, 'Document sur Saint Bernard', p. 2.
104. 'Vita Prima S. Bernardi', cols 401–2.
105. *EE*, cols 1183–1201; J. Tyler, *The Alpine Passes in the High Middle Ages* (Oxford, 1930), pp. 14–17; Spufford, *Power and Profit*, pp, 140–69. Even Horn, *Studien*, ignores this section of the journey, giving full detail, however, to the French leg of the pope's travels.
106. 'Regesta comitum Sabaudiae', ed. D. Carruti, *Bibliotheca Storica Italiana*, 5 (Turin, 1889), no. 294, pp. 105–6.
107. OD, pp. 78–9, 100–1.
108. D. Crouch, *The Reign of King Stephen, 1135–1154*, (Harlow, 2000), p. 219.
109. C. J. Tyerman, *England and the Crusades, 1095–1588* (Chicago, 1988), p. 32

Notes to Chapter 6

1. 'Historia gloriosi regis Ludovici VII', *RHGF* 12.126.
2. Willems, 'Cîteaux et la seconde croisade', p. 138. This group planned to take a relic of St George with them on the crusade.
3. 'Vita Prima S. Bernardi', col. 376; Otto of Freising, *GF*, pp. 210–11, tr. p. 75.
4. G. Constable, 'The Financing of the Crusades in the Twelfth Century', in *Outremer: Studies in the History of the Crusading Kingdom of Jerusalem presented to Joshua Prawer*, eds B. Z. Kedar, H. E. Mayer and R. C. Smail (Jerusalem, 1982), pp. 64–88; Riley-Smith, *First Crusaders*.
5. Unlike Riley-Smith, I have not chosen to include 'possibles' in my study. The relative lack of narrative sources for the Second Crusade compared to the First may also have reduced the number of individuals who could be identified.
6. J. Richard, *Le comté de Tripoli sous la dynastie Toulousaine, 1102–87* (Paris, 1945), pp. 4–6.
7. J. A. Brundage, 'An Errant Crusader: Stephen of Blois', *Traditio* 16 (1960), pp. 380–95.
8. E. Siberry, 'The Crusading Counts of Nevers', *Nottingham Medieval Studies* 34 (1990), pp. 64–6; Bouchard, *Sword, Miter and Cloister*, pp. 346–7.
9. On Simon, see C. Vleeschouwers, 'Chronologische problemen aangaande de bisschoppen van Doornik (1146–1218): episcopaatsjaren en jaarstijl', *Handelingen van het genootschap voor Geschiedenis* 117 (1980), at p. 13; and 'Sigeberti continuatio Praemonstratensis', p. 453. Waleran II's presence at Vézelay was noted by Robert of Torigny rather than by the 'Historia gloriosi regis Ludovici VII'; See Torigny's 'Chronicon', p. 497. See also *Cartulaire de l'abbaye de Saint-Martin de Pontoise* , ed. J. Depoin (Pontoise, 1885), p. 321 and D. Crouch, *The Beaumont Twins: The Roots and Branches of Power in the Twelfth Century* (Cambridge, 1986), pp. 64–9, 160. For William III of Warenne, see OD, pp. 54–5, 122–3; and E. Van Houts, 'The Warenne View of the Past, 1066–1203', *Anglo-Norman Studies* 26 (2003), pp. 103–21.
10. J. S. C. Riley-Smith, 'Family Traditions and Participation in the Second Crusade', in SCC, p. 102.
11. Riley-Smith, 'Family Traditions', p. 102; *Chartes du Bourbonnais, 918–1522*, ed. J. Monicat and B. de Fourneaux (Moulins, 1952), no. 19, p. 39; OD, pp. 28–9, 54–5, 138–9.
12. *Crusade Charters*, ed. and tr. C. K. Slack (Tempe AR, 2001), no. 1, pp. 2–3; Barthélemy, *Les deux ages de la seigneurie banale* (Paris, 1984), pp. 87, 100.
13. Riley-Smith, *FC*, pp. 46, 213.
14. For Everard III of Breteuil, see OD, pp. 51–2, 121–2; for Everard III of Le Puiset, see Riley-Smith, *FC*, p. 205.
15. Riley-Smith, *FC*, pp. 169–88.
16. Bouchard, *Sword, Miter and Cloister*, pp. 373–5.
17. For Drogo I, see OV 5.30; for Drogo II, see also Louis VII, 'Epistolae', *RHGF* 16.500.
18. D. Gurney, *Record of the House of Gournay*, 2 vols (London, 1848–58), 1.67–9; 2.748–9; OV 5.31, n. 11. See the genealogy in: D. Power, *The Norman Frontier in the Twelfth and Early Thirteenth Centuries* (Cambridge, 2004), pp. 504–5 (see also pp. 356–8).
19. Riley-Smith, *FC*, pp. 229, 249.
20. Ibid., p. 203.
21. 'Chronicon Senonense sanctae Columbae', *RHGF* 12.288.
22. Arnulf of Lisieux, *Letters*, ed. F. Barlow, Camden Third Series 61 (1939), pp. xi–xxv.
23. Geoffrey of Vigeois, 'Chronica', *RHGF* 12. 422, 436.

24. *Cartulaires du chapitre de l'église métropolitaine Sainte-Marie d'Auch*, ed. C. Lacave La Plagne Barris (Paris, 1899), no. 64, pp. 65–6.
25. Bouchard, *Sword, Miter and Cloister*, pp. 275–7; OD, pp. 110–11.
26. Phillips, 'Murder of Charles the Good and the Second Crusade', pp. 64–5.
27. Galbert of Bruges, *De multro, traditione et occisione gloriosi Karoli comitis Flandriarum*, in *CCCM* 131; J. Rider, *God's Scribe: The Historiographical Art of Galbert of Bruges* (Washington DC, 2001).
28. E. Warlop, *The Flemish Nobility before 1300*, 4 vols (Kortrijk, 1975–6), 1. 185–245.
29. Phillips, 'Murder of Charles the Good and the Second Crusade', p. 69.
30. Warlop, *Flemish Nobility*, 1.228–30.
31. Ibid., 1.224–8.
32. Riley-Smith, *FC*, pp. 93–7.
33. *Cartulaire de l'abbaye de Vigeois en Limousin (954–1167)*, ed. M. de Montégut (Limoges, 1907), no. 316, pp. 213–14; Riley-Smith, *FC*, p. 103.
34. H. Tanner, *Families, Friends and Allies: Boulogne and Politics in Northern France and England, c.879–1160* (Leiden, 2004), p. 224.
35. 'Les premiers seigneurs de Ramerupt', ed. H. d'Arbois de Jubainville, *Bibliothèque de l'école des Chartes* 22 (1861), no. 3, pp. 456–7.
36. *Recueil des chartes de l'abbaye de Cluny*, ed. A. Bernard and A. Bruel, 6 vols (Paris, 1876–1903), Vol. V, no. 4131, pp. 473–4; Bouchard, *Sword, Miter and Cloister*, pp. 301, 304–5.
37. R. Röhricht, *Die Deutschen im Heiligen Lande, 650–1291* (Innsbruck, 1894), p. 28. Adalbert junior died at the siege of Damascus: 'Annales Colonienses maximi', *MHG* 17.761–2.
38. *Crusade Charters*, no. 4, pp. 26–7.
39. Hugh of Poitiers, *Monumenta Vizeliacensia: Textes relatifs à l'histoire de l'abbaye de Vézelay*, ed. R. B. C. Huygens, 2 vols (Turnhout, 1976–80), 1.423; tr. *The Vézelay Chronicle*, tr. J. Scott and J. O. Ward (Binghampton, NY, 1992), p. 164; Siberry, 'Crusading Counts of Nevers', p. 66.
40. *Crusade Charters*, no. 4, pp. 24–9.
41. Louis VII, 'Epistolae', p. 500.
42. Riley-Smith, *FC*, p. 102.
43. Robert of Torigny, 'Chronicon', p. 497.
44. 'Historia gloriosi regis Ludovici VII', p. 126.
45. J.-L. Bazin, *Brancion, les seigneurs, la paroisse, la ville* (Mâcon, 1908), pp. 9–13.
46. *Cartulaire de la Commanderie de Richerenches de l'ordre du Temple (1136–1214)*, ed. M. de Ripert-Monclar (Avignon, 1907), no. 43, pp. 45–6.
47. *DeL*, pp. 100–3.
48. *Urkundenbuch des Herzogthums Steiermark: Band I: 798–1192*, ed. J. Zahn (Graz, 1875), no. 294, p. 302.
49. *Urkundenbuch des Landes ob der Enns*, 11 vols (Vienna, 1852–83), Vol. 2, nos 155–8, pp. 227–39, esp. at p. 236.
50. 'Annales Rodenses', p. 718.
51. *Die Traditionen des Klosters Weihenstephan*, ed. B. Uhl (Munich, 1972), no. 152, pp. 128–9.
52. J. France, 'Patronage and the First Crusade', in *The First Crusade: Origins and Impact*, ed. J. P. Phillips (Manchester, 1997), pp. 5–20.
53. *Cartulaire général de l'Yonne*, ed. M. Quantin (Auxerre, 1854–60), Vol. 1, no. 283, p. 437.
54. *Urkundenbuch des Herzogthums Steiermark*, no. 270, p. 281.
55. A. Czerny, 'Das älteste Todtenbuch des Stiftes St Florian', *Archiv für Österreichische Geschichte* 56 (1878), pp. 318, 343, n. 212.
56. Lambert of Ardres, 'Historia comitum Ghisensium', *MGH* 24.633; tr. pp. 177–8.
57. Crouch, *Beaumont Twins*, pp. 66–8, 160.
58. *Historia Vizeliacensia*, p. 423, tr. *Vézelay Chronicle*, p. 164.
59. M. G. Bull, 'The Diplomatic of the First Crusade', in *The First Crusade: Origins and Impact*, ed. J. P. Phillips (Manchester, 1997), pp. 35–56. For the growth in literacy, see M. T. Clanchy, *From Memory to Written Record: England, 1066–1307*, 2nd edn (Oxford, 1993).
60. *Urkundenbuch des Herzogthums Steiermark*, no. 267, pp. 279–80; *Die Traditionen, Urkunden und Urbare des Klosters Neustift bei Freising*, ed. H.-J. Busley (Munich, 1961), no. 3, pp. 6–8.
61. *Urkundenbuch für die Geschichte des Niederrheins, 799–1200*, ed. T. J. Lacomblet, Vol. 1 (Düsseldorf, 1840), no. 361, p. 248.
62. *Die Traditionen des Klosters Tegernsee, 1003–1242*, ed. P. Acht (Munich, 1952), no. 250, p. 189.
63. *Tiroler Urkundenbuch*, ed. F. Huter (Innsbruck, 1937), 1. no. 224, p. 98.

64. Ibid., 1. no. 223, p. 97.
65. *Die Traditionen des Klosters Wessobrunn*, ed. R.Höppl (Munich, 1984), nos 28–9, pp. 42–5.
66. *Cartulaire de la Commanderie de Richerenches*, no. 43, p. 45.
67. 'Les premiers seigneurs de Ramerupt', no. 3, pp. 456–7.
68. *Cartulaire de la Commanderie de Richerenches*, no. 60, pp. 60–3.
69. *Cartulaire de Saint Vincent de Mâçon*, ed. M.-C.Ragut (Mâçon, 1864), no. 584, pp. 350–1.
70. *De oorkonden der graven van Vlaanderen*, no. 112, p. 183.
71. Ibid., no. 91, p. 151; N. Huyghebaert, 'Une comtesse de Flandre à Béthanie', *Les cahiers de Saint-André* 21 (1964), pp. 1–13.
72. *Die Traditionen des Kollegiatstifts St Kastulus in Moosburg*, ed. K.Höflinger (Munich, 1994), no. 76, p. 78.
73. *Die Traditionen des Hochstifts des Klosters S.Emmeran*, ed. J. Widemann (Munich, 1943), no. 831, p. 398.
74. *Urkundenbuch der Stadt Strassburg*, ed. W. Wiegand (Strasbourg, 1879), no. 99, p. 81.
75. 'Petite chronique du règne de Baudouin Ier', in GN, pp. 69–72; 361–6, at 364.
76. 'Annales Mosomagenses', *MGH* 3.162.
77. For a discussion of this practice, see Riley-Smith, *FC*, pp. 158–60.
78. *De oorkonden der graven van Vlaanderen* no. 63, pp. 106–8.
79. Ibid., no. 114, pp. 185–6.
80. Adalbert went before 1136, the date of the document noted above: 'Schenkungsbuch der ehemaligen Gefürsteten Probstei Berchtesgaden', *Schenkungsbücher Bayerischer Klöster*, Vol. 1, ed. F. M. Wittman and K. A. Muffat (Munich, 1856), no. 215, pp. 363–4. See also nos 101, pp. 295–7; 145, p. 323.
81. *Recueil des chartes de l'abbaye de Cluny*, Vol. 4, nos 3896, pp. 246–8; 4106, p. 456; 4131, pp. 473–4. See also Bouchard, *Sword, Miter and Cloister*, pp. 304–5.
82. *Crusade Charters*, no. 1, p. 2.
83. *Cartulaire du prieuré de Saint-Etienne de Vignory*, ed. J. d'Arbaumont (Langres, 1882), no. 22, p. 180.
84. *Cartulaire de Saint Lambert de Liège*, ed. S. Bormans and E. Schoolmeesters, 6 vols (Brussels, 1893–1933) Vol. 1, no. 36, pp. 58–60.
85. *Recueil des chartes de l'abbaye de Saint-Benoît-sur-Loire*, ed. M. Prou and A. Vidier, Documents publiés par la Société historique et archéologique du Gatinais, 5 (Paris, 1900–1907), Vol. 1, no. 150, 340–3; Constable, 'Medieval Charters', p. 80.
86. 'Annales Herbipolenses', p. 3.
87. *DeL*, pp. 100–4, 110–13.
88. Riley-Smith, 'Early Crusaders to the East and the Cost of Crusading', pp. 237–58.
89. 'Annales Reicherspergenses', p. 461.
90. A. V. Murray, 'Money and Logistics in the Forces of the First Crusade: Coinage, bullion, service, and supply, 1096–99 in *Logistics and Warfare*, pp. 229–49.
91. Ekkehard of Aura, 'Hierosolymitana', p. 17. Orderic Vitalis is just one of several other chroniclers to mention the famine of 1095; See OV 5.11.
92. FC, p. 154; tr. p. 72.
93. 'Annales Herbipolenses', p. 3; 'Annales Rodenses', p. 719. Other writers to note the famine included the author of the 'Annales Coloniensis maximi', p. 761, and the continuator of Sigebert of Gembloux's chronicle, 'Continuatio Gemblacensis', *MGH* 6.389.
94. *Recueil des chartes de l'abbaye de Saint-Benoît-sur-Loire*, 1, no. 150, pp. 340–3; Constable, 'Medieval Charters', p. 80.
95. Murray, 'Money and Logistics', pp. 236–8.
96. Constable, 'Financing of the Crusades'; J. F. Benton, 'The Revenue of Louis VII', *Speculum* 42 (1967), pp. 84–91, which highlights the far smaller income of Louis compared to that of his son, Philip Augustus.
97. Robert of Torigny, 'Chronica', *MGH* 6.497; Ralph of Diceto, 'Ymagines Historiarum', ed. W. Stubbs, Rolls Series 68 (London, 1876), 1. 256–7; Shopkow, *History and Community*, p. 236.
98. C. DeVic and J. J. Vaisette, *Histoire générale de Languedoc*, 16 vols (Toulouse, 1872–1905), 3.736; Constable, 'Financing of the Crusades', p. 68.
99. W. C. Jordan, *Louis IX and the Challenge of the Crusade* (Princeton, 1979), pp. 94–9.
100. Fleury charter discussed by Constable, 'Financing the Crusades', pp. 64–5; for the text, see: 'Fragmentum historicum ex veteri membrana de tributo Floriacensibus imposito', *RHGF* 12.94–5.

101. Peter the Venerable, *Letters*, 1.327–330.
102. Ibid., p. 329.
103. Chazan, 'From the First to the Second Crusade', pp. 46–50.
104. Peter the Venerable, *Letters*, 1.330.
105. Y. Friedman, 'An Anantomy of Anti-Semitism: Peter the Venerable's Letter to Louis VII, King of France (1146)', *Bar-Ilan Studies in History* (1978), pp. 95–100. Berry, 'Peter the Venerable and the Crusades', pp. 148–50.
106. Ephraim of Bonn, p. 131.
107. *QP*, p. 92.
108. Louis VII, 'Epistolae', p. 487.
109. *De oorkonden der graven Vlaanderen*, no. 118, pp. 193–4.
110. *Württembergisches Urkundenbuch*, 11 vols (Stuttgart, 1849–1913), 2, no. 324, p. 40.
111. *Cartulaires du chapitre de l'église métropolitaine Sainte-Marie d'Auch*, ed. C. Lacave La Plagne Barris (Paris, Auch, 1899), no. 64, pp. 65–6.
112. *Actes des évêques de Laon des origins à 1151*, ed. A. Dufour-Malbezin (Paris, 2001), no. 283, pp. 403–4.
113. Translation from Constable, 'Financing of the Crusades', p. 65.
114. Louis VII, *Études sur les Actes de Louis VII*, ed. A. Luchaire (Paris, 1885), no. 215, p. 168.
115. *Cartulaire de l'abbaye de Noyers*, ed. C. Chevalier (Tours, 1872), no. 556, p. 584.
116. *Die Traditionen des Klosters Wessobrunn*, no. 30, pp. 45–7.
117. C. B. Bouchard, *Holy Entrepreneurs* (Cornell, NY 1991), p. 120.
118. This charter can easily be consulted in T. Evergates, *Feudal Society in Medieval France: Documents from the County of Champagne* (Philadelphia PA, 1993), no. 87, pp. 110–11.
119. Louis VII, *Études*, no. 195, pp. 381–2. For other charters by Adam see *Recueil de chartes et documents de Saint-Martin-des-Champs*, ed. J. Depoin, 5 vols (Paris, 1912–21), 2. nos 290, 290*bis*, pp. 162–3.
120. *Die Traditionen des klosters Weihenstephan*, ed. B. Uhl (Munich, 1972), no. 134, pp. 112–13.
121. Ibid., no. 131, p. 111.
122. *Cartulaire de Notre-Dame de Josaphat*, ed. C.Metais (Chartres, 1911), no. 141, pp. 177–8.
123. 'Premier cartulaire de l'abbaye d'Absie', *Archives Historiques de Poitou* 25 (1895), p. 38.
124. See *Crusade Charters*, no. 4, pp. 26–7.
125. Evergates, *Feudal Society*, no. 86, p. 109.
126. Louis VII, *Études*, no. 176, p. 378.
127. *Cartulaire de l'abbaye d'Afflighem*, ed. E. de Marneffe (Louvain, 1894–1901), no. 78, p. 121.
128. *Cartulaire de l'abbaye de Noyers*, ed. C. Chevalier (Tours, 1872), no. 553, pp. 581–2.
129. *Cartulaires inédits de la Saintonge*, ed. T. Grasilier, 2 vols (Niort, 1871), 2, no. 124, pp. 99–100.
130. *Cartulaire des Templiers de Douzens*, ed. P. Gérard and E. Magnou (Paris, 1965), no. 4, pp. 275–7. Roger made this donation on 19 July; this date – later than the departure date of the main armies in the north – together with his location at a port, suggests that some crusaders made their way to the Levant independently of the royal forces.
131. 'Les premiers seigneurs de Ramerupt', no. 3, pp. 456–7.
132. Lambert of Ardres, *Historia*, p. 633, tr. p. 177.
133. *Die Traditionen, Urkunden und Urbare des Klosters Neustift bei Freising*, no. 3, pp. 6–8.
134. 'Annales Rodenses', p. 720.
135. *Urkundenbuch des Herzogthums Steiermark*, no. 338, p. 324.
136. *Cartulaire de l'abbaye de Noyers* no. 555, p. 583.
137. Lambert of Ardres, *Historia*, p. 632, tr. p. 176.
138. *Translatio S. Mamantis*, in *Acta Sanctorum*, 17 August 3: 443D.
139. 'Fragmentum historicum ex veteri membrana de tributo Floriacensibus imposito', p. 95.
140. Adam of Bremen, *Magistri Adam Bremensis gesta Hammaburgensis ecclesiae pontificum*, ed. and tr. B. Schmeidler (Hanover, 1917), pp. 189–90, text at p. 190; translated as *History of the Archbishops of Hamburg-Bremen*, tr. F. J. Tschan, new introduction by T. Reuter (New York, 2002), p. 153.
141. 'Chronicon Senonense sanctae Columbae', *RHGF*, 12.288.
142. 'Annales Rodenses', p. 718.
143. *Crusade Charters*, no. 4, pp. 24–33. See also nos 5–6, pp. 34–47 for further examples.
144. Lambert of Ardres, *Historia*, pp. 593, 633; tr. pp. 104–5, 178.

145. *De oorkonden der graven van Vlaanderen*, nos 110–14, pp. 178–86; de Hemptinne, 'Les épouses des croisés et pèlerins Flamands aux XIe et XIIe siècles', pp. 92–5; Phillips, 'Murder of Count Charles the Good and the Second Crusade', pp. 72–3.
146. *De oorkonden der graven van Vlaandern*, nos 110–13, pp. 178–84.
147. Ibid., nos 110–14, pp. 178–86. On Thierry's household, see also pp. xxv–lx.
148. There is no explicit evidence that Gislebert took the cross, but he appeared in 42 of the 109 surviving charters for Thierry's rule between July 1128 and June 1147, when the crusade set out. He did not witness any of Sibylla's charters. He reappeared in the count's first surviving charter on his return, and was again a regular witness.
149. Hugh wrote that Pons was related to the count, a claim rejected by modern historians. See Hugh of Poitiers, *Monumenta Vizeliacensia*, p. 424; *The Vézelay Chronicle*, pp. 165–6, n. 4.
150. *Liber instrumentorum memorialium: Cartulaire des Guillems de Montpellier*, ed. A. Germain (Montpellier, 1884), pp. 177–83, no. 95.
151. *Le Cartulaire du chapitre cathedral Saint-Etienne d'Agde*, ed. R. Foreville (Paris, 1995), no. 258, pp. 307–8.

Notes to Chapter 7

1. 'Vita Prima S. Bernardi', col. 400.
2. Welf wrote: 'For we have received the cross from the most holy hands of the Abbot of Clairvaux, just as the others have, for the remission of our sins, and we have set it within the clothing of our body and of our heart.' J. Leclercq, 'Un document sur Saint Bernard et la seconde croisade', *Revue Mabillon* 43 (1953), p. 2.
3. OD, pp. 6–9.
4. J. France, *Victory in the East: A Military History* (Cambridge, 1994), pp. 102–3.
5. OD, pp. 14–15.
6. See below, p. 210 for a more detailed discussion of this.
7. Sassier, *Louis VII*, pp. 156–60.
8. OD, pp. 12–13.
9. J. P. Phillips, 'Odo of Deuil's *De profectione Ludovici VII in Orientem* as a source for the Second Crusade', in *The Experience of Crusading 1: Western Approaches*, eds. M.G.Bull and N.Housley (Cambridge, 2003), pp. 80–95. For other analyses of Odo's work, see the study devoted to his writing technique by C. A. Cioffi, 'The Epistolary Style of Odo of Deuil in his "*De profectione Ludovici VII in Orientem*"', *Mittellateinisches Jahrbuch* 23 (1988), pp. 76–81. For a more eccentric interpretation, see B. Schuste, 'The Strange Pilgrimage of Odo of Deuil', in *Medieval Concepts of the Past: Ritual, Memory and Historiography*, ed. G. Althoff, J. Fried and P. J. Geary (Cambridge, 2002), pp. 253–78.
10. OD, pp. 10–15.
11. Ibid., pp. 12–13.
12. WT, pp. 691–2; Phillips, *Defenders*, pp. 52–3, 58, 63.
13. Ibid., pp. 58–9, 130–1.
14. OD, pp. 4–5.
15. L. Grant, *Abbot Suger of St-Denis: Church and State in Early Twelfth-Century France* (London, 1998), pp. 142–57.
16. 'Vie de Suger', pp. 393–4; A. Grabois, 'Le privilège de croisade et la régence de Suger', *Revue historique de droit Français et Etranger*, 42 (1964), pp. 458–65; Hehl, *Kirche und Kreig*, pp. 121–4 discussed Suger's appointment from the perspective of the canonical acceptability of a churchman acting in wordly affairs.
17. OD, pp.14–15; Hugh of Poitiers, *Historia Vizeliacensia*, p. 423; *Vézelay Chronicle*, pp. 164–65; A. Poulet, 'Capetian Women and the Regency: The Genesis of a Vocation', in *Medieval Queenship*, ed. J. C. Parsons (Stroud, 1994), pp. 93–116.
18. Louis VII, *Études*, nos 176, 178, pp. 156–7.
19. OD, pp. 12–13.
20. Louis VII, *Études*, p. 64.
21. These figures are based on the charters in Luchaire's *Études sur les Actes de Louis VII*. The 1146 figure is vague because a large number of them (22 charters) are reckoned to have been issued between August 1146 and March or April 1147. Some of them must have fallen after 1 January 1147; that would inflate the 1147 figure even more. See nos 198–222, pp. 162–71.

22. Louis VII, *Études*, nos 198–222, pp. 162–71.
23. For Eugenius's itinerary, see Horn, *Studien*, pp. 271–3.
24. 'Annales S. Benigni Divionensis', *MGH* 5.44.
25. P. Acht, 'Die Gesandtschaft König Konrads III. an Papst Eugens III. in Dijon', *Historisches Jahrbuch* 74 (1955), pp. 668–73.
26. Horn, *Studien*, pp. 273–74.
27. Robinson, *Papacy*, p. 21.
28. *EE*, cols 1205–42; Horn, *Studien*, pp. 246–54; 274–6.
29. Leclercq, 'Un document sur Saint Bernard', pp. 1–4.
30. E. Pellegrin (ed.), '*Membra disiecta Floriacensia*', *Bibliothèque de l'école des Chartes* 117 (1959), pp. 22–3.
31. V. Grumel, 'Au seuil de la IIe croisade: Deux lettres de Manuel Comnène au pape', *Etudes Byzantines* 3 (1945), pp. 143–67.
32. Letter of Manuel to Louis, in Louis VII, 'Epistolae', *RHGF* 16.9–10, tr. J. Harris.
33. Eugenius III, 'Epistolae', *RHGF* 15.440–1.
34. W. Ohnsorge, 'Ein Beitrag zur Geschichte Manuels I von Byzanz', *Festschrift Albert Brackmann dargebracht von Freunden, Kollegen und Schülern*, ed. L. Santifaller (Weimar, 1931), pp. 391–3.
35. Lilie, *Byzantium and the Crusader States*, pp. 94–5.
36. Stroll, *Calixtus II: A Pope Born to Rule*, pp. 445–6.
37. J. T. Lees, *Anselm of Havelberg: Deeds into Words in the Twelfth Century* (Leiden, 1998), pp. 40–7; 222–81.
38. Peter the Deacon, 'Chronica monasterii Casinensis', *MGH* 7.833; J. G. Rowe, 'The Papacy and the Greeks (1122–53)', *Church History* 28 (1959), p. 120.
39. Otto of Freising, *GF*, p. 200; tr. p. 70.
40. *EE*, col. 1252. The dating of this letter to July does not tie in with other evidence indicating that the pope had already assigned Henry to the Wendish crusade.
41. OD, pp. 14–17.
42. Suger of St Denis, *Abbot Suger on the Abbey Church of St Denis and its Art Treasures*, ed. and tr. E. Panofsky, 2nd edn (Princeton, 1979), pp. 59–61.
43. J. Bouton, 'Bernard et les monastères bénédictins non clunisiens', in *Bernard de Clairvaux* (Paris, 1953), p. 222.
44. E. A. R. Brown and M. W. Cothren, 'The Twelfth-Century Crusading Window of the Abbey of Saint-Denis', *Journal of the Warburg and Courtauld Institutes* 49 (1986), pp.1–40; concerning the dating of the windows, see pp. 21–37.
45. Suger, 'Vie de Suger', p. 394.
46. Phillips, *Defenders*, pp. 104–18.
47. Brown and Cothren, 'Crusading Window', pp. 3–13.
48. R. Folz, *Le souvenir et la légende de Charlemagne dans l'empire germanique medieval* (Paris, 1950), pp. 134–42; Short, 'A Study in Carolingian Legend', pp. 127–33.
49. Robert of Rheims, pp. 728, 732; tr. 80, 84; Ralph of Caen, *Gesta Tancredi*, p. 627; tr. p. 53.
50. *The Song of Roland*, ed. F.Whitehead (Oxford, 1947), p. vi.
51. This is the *Liber Sancti Jacobi: Codex Calixtinus*, translated by A. Moraljo *et al.* in 1999.
52. Brown and Cothren, 'Crusading Window', p. 8. This statement is inaccurate if Charlemagne is depicted on the frescoes at Sta Maria of Cosmedin, Rome.
53. Ibid., pp. 16–21.
54. '*Parti*' means Parthians, in other words, Persians, a term favoured by some writers of the First Crusade to differentiate between the various Muslim groups of the region; others, for example, were identified as Turks. Ibid., p. 18.
55. Peter the Venerable, 'De laude dominici sepulchri', ed. G. Constable in 'Petri Venerabilis Sermones Tres', *Revue Bénédictine* 64 (1954), pp. 232–54. See also V. G. Berry, 'Peter the Venerable and the Crusades', in *Petrus Venerabilis, 1156–1956. Studies commemorating the Eighth Centenary of his Death*, ed. G. Constable and J. Kritzeck, Studia Anselmiana 40 (Rome, 1956), pp. 141–62. A more negative view of Peter's involvement in the Second Crusade is put forward by Iogna-Prat, who wrote that 'Peter stood back'. Given his presence at so many relevant meetings connected with the crusade, this seems a misplaced judgement. D.Iogna–Prat, *Order and Exclusion: Cluny and Christendom face Heresy, Judaism and Islam (1000–1150)* (Ithaca NY, 2003), p. 333.
56. Peter the Venerable, *Letters*, ed. G. Constable, Vol. 1, no. 144, pp. 353–60.

57. Ibid., nos 80, 82–3, pp. 214–17, 219–21.
58. Ibid., no. 44, pp. 140–1.
59. Ibid., no. 75, pp. 208–9; Berry, 'Peter the Venerable', pp. 143–4.
60. Peter the Venerable, *Letters*, Vol. 1. no. 111, p. 279.
61. Ibid., no. 130, pp. 327–30.
62. The best discussion of the sermon is in Cole, *Preaching the Crusades*, pp. 49–52, and much of the comment here follows her analysis.
63. Peter the Venerable, 'De Laude Dominici Sepulchri', p. 233.
64. Ibid., p. 246.
65. Ibid., p. 247.
66. Ibid., p. 244; Cole, *Preaching the Crusades*, p. 50.
67. Cole, *Preaching the Crusades*, p. 52.
68. Grant, *Suger of Saint-Denis*, pp. 245–50.
69. L. Levillain, 'Essai sur les origines du Lendit', *Revue Historique* 52 (1927), pp. 241–76; G. Bautier, 'L'envoi de la relique de la vraie croix à Notre-Dame de Paris en 1120', *Bibliothèque de l'école de Chartes* 129 (1971), pp. 387–97.
70. R. I. Moore, *The Formation of a Persecuting Society* (Oxford, 1987), pp. 45–65.
71. G. Koziol, 'England, France and the Problem of Sacrality', in *Cultures of Power: Lordship, Status and Process in Twelfth-Century Europe*, ed. T. N. Bisson (Philadelphia PA, 1995), pp. 128–9.
72. 'Fragment d'un cartulaire de l'ordre de Saint-Lazare en Terre Sainte', ed. C. de Marsy, *Archives d'Orient Latin* 2 (Paris, 1884), p. 132. Louis also made gifts to lepers at Etampes and Paris; Louis VII, *Études*, nos 201–3, 208, 218, pp. 164–6, 169.
73. Suger, *VLG*, 218–21; tr. p. 128; Grant, *Abbot Suger of Saint Denis*, pp. 116–17. Berry's translation of Odo of Deuil assumes that these objects were one and the same: see OD, pp. 16–17.
74. Ibid.
75. J. B. Gillingham, *Richard I* (New Haven and London, 1999), pp. 87, 128; P. Munz, *Frederick Barbarossa: A Study in Medieval Politics* (London, 1969), pp. 386–91.
76. Conrad III, *Urkunden*, no. 184, p. 333.
77. Ibid., no. 164, pp. 295–8; Otto of Freising, *GF*, p. 188; tr. p. 64.
78. 'Chronographus Corbiensis', in *Bibliotheca rerum Germanicarum* 1, *Monumenta Corbiensia*, ed. P. Jaffé (Berlin, 1864), pp. 53–4; Conrad III, *Urkunden*, nos 167–8, pp. 302–5.
79. Otto of Freising, *GF*, p. 210; tr. p. 76.
80. Robinson, *Papacy*, pp. 454–5.
81. Conrad III, *Urkunden*, no. 184, pp. 332–3; Otto of Freising, *GF*, p. 216; tr. pp. 78–9.
82. Conrad III, *Urkunden*, no. 178, p. 321.
83. J. P. Phillips, 'Papacy, Empire and the Second Crusade', in *SCSC*, pp. 15–31; G. A. Loud, 'Some Reflections on the Failure of the Second Crusade', *Crusades* 4 (2005), pp. 1–14.
84. H. Cosack, 'Konrads III. Entschluss zum Kreuzzug', *Mitteilungen des Instituts für Öster-reichische Geschichtsforschung* 35 (1914), pp. 278–96. Others who have followed Cosack's line include: Berry, 'Second Crusade', p. 475–6; Mayer, *Crusades*, p. 95; Runciman, *History of the Crusades*, 2.255.
85. Conrad III, *Urkunden*, no. 184, p. 333.
86. Constable, SC, p. 278 states that Conrad apologised for taking the cross without the pope's 'permission'; he gives a rather more negative sense to the phrase than Eugenius simply not knowing what had happened would presuppose.
87. Conrad III, *Urkunden*, no. 198, p. 358.
88. *EE*, cols 1299–1300. Robinson, *Papacy*, p. 456 also notes the positive tone of this letter as a sign of good relations between the pope and Conrad.
89. Robinson, *Papacy*, p. 458.
90. Conrad III, *Urkunden*, no. 185, p. 333; Acht, 'Die Gesandtschaft König Konrads III. an Papst Eugens III. in Dijon', pp. 668–73; Magdalino, *Empire of Manuel Komnenos*, pp. 47–9.
91. R. Hiestand, 'Kingship and Crusade in Germany', in *England and Germany in the High Middle Ages*, ed. A. Haverkamp and H. Vollrath (Oxford, 1996), pp. 248–53.
92. Alberic of Trois Fontaines, 'Chronica a monacho novi monasterii Hoiensis interpolata', *MGH* 23.839.
93. OD, pp. 22–5.
94. Conrad III, *Urkunden*, no. 176, p. 318.
95. Otto of Freising, *GF*, p. 218; tr., p.79; OD, pp. 24–5, 66–9.

96. Ibid., p. 192; tr. p. 66.
97. Otto of Freising, *GF*, pp. 190–8; tr., pp. 66–9. F. Makk, *The Árpads and the Comneni: Political Relations between Hungary and Byzantium in the Twelfth Century* (Budapest, 1989), pp. 35–41.
98. Otto of Freising, *GF*, pp. 176–80; tr. pp. 54–9.
99. Ibid., pp. 174–80; tr. pp. 56–8; Magdalino, *Empire of Manuel I*, pp. 38–43; Lilie, *Byzantium*, pp. 134, 140, 148.
100. 'Annales Herbipolenses', p. 3. The bishop died in Aquilia, in November, en route home. That may indicate that he was also in contact either with the papacy or with Roger II and that discussions concerning Conrad's involvement in the crusade were, at this stage, purely hypothetical.
101. BCE, no. 457, pp. 432–3; tr. in BSJ, pp. 467–8.
102. Otto of Freising, *GF*, pp. 210–12; tr. p. 76.
103. K. V. Jensen, 'Denmark and the Second Crusade: The Formation of a Crusader State?', in SCSC, p. 164.
104. Wibald of Stavelot, '*Epistolae*', no. 150, p. 242; Acht, 'Die Gesandtschaft König Konrads III. an Papst Eugens III. in Dijon', pp. 668–73.
105. Wibald of Stavelot, '*Epistolae*' no. 150, p. 243.
106. Constable, SC, p. 256, n. 222.
107. BCE, no. 457, p. 433; tr. in BSJ, p. 467. Note that, like Wibald, Bernard described the pagans as being those 'across the River Alba', p. 433, although this line is omitted in the translation.
108. *EE*, col. 1203.
109. Henry VI, *Urkunden*, in Conrad III, *Urkunden*, no. p. 528.
110. Conrad III, *Urkunden*, nos. 188–9, pp. 339–45; Otto of Freising, *GF*, p. 216; tr. p. 79.
111. BCE, no. 457, p. 433; tr. in BSJ, pp. 467–8.

Notes to Chapter 8

1. H. V. Livermore, 'The "Conquest of Lisbon" and its Author', *Portuguese Studies* 6 (1991), pp.1–16. See also C. W. David 'The Authorship of *De expugnatione Lyxbonensi*', *Speculum* 7 (1932), pp. 50–7 for more background on the author, although Livermore rightly overturns the main conclusion.
2. Constable, 'Second Crusade', p. 221; *DeL*, pp. 40, 45.
3. Livermore, 'The "Conquest of Lisbon"', p. 4.
4. For these episodes, see Phillips, *Defenders*, pp. 129–32; A. J. Duggan, 'Servus servorum Dei', in *Adrian IV: The English Pope (1154–1159): Studies and Texts*, ed. B. Bolton and A. J. Duggan (Aldershot, 2003), pp. 191–2.
5. R. Mortimer, 'The Family of Rannulf de Glanville', *Bulletin of the Institute of Historical Research* 54 (1981), pp. 1–16.
6. J. P. Phillips, 'Ideas of Crusade and Holy War in *De expugnatione Lyxbonensi* (The Conquest of Lisbon)', in *The Holy Land, Holy Lands and Christian History*, ed. R. N. Swanson, Studies in Church History 36 (2000), pp. 123–41.
7. S. B. Edgington, 'The Lisbon Letter of the Second Crusade', *Historical Research* 69 (1996), pp. 328–39; translated as 'Albert of Aachen, Saint Bernard and the Second Crusade' in SCSC, pp. 61–7.
8. For the charter, see Livermore, 'The Conquest of Lisbon', p. 14, and Henry of Huntingdon, *Historia Anglorum*, pp. 752–3. The 'Foundation Document' of the monastery of St Vincent can be found in *A Conquista de Lisboa aos Mouros: Relato de um Cruzado*, ed. and tr. A. A. Nascimento, introduction by M. J. V. Branco (Lisbon, 2001), pp. 177–201. See G. Constable, 'A Further Note on the Conquest of Lisbon in 1147', pp. 39–44. On the origins of the crusaders, see *DeL*, pp. 104–7; St Vincent, 'Foundation Document', pp. 180–1.
9. For Eugenius's letters, see p. 59 above; for Bernard's letters see BCE, no. 363, pp. 311–16; tr. in BSJ, pp. 460–3; *Regesta pontificum Romanorum*, 2, no. 8959, p. 36; for his letters sent to Brittany, see Nicholas of Clairvaux, 'Epistolae', col. 672.
10. Tyerman, *England and the Crusades*, pp. 15–21; *DeL*, pp. 22–6.
11. *DeL*, pp. 21–3.
12. BCE, no. 363, p. 315; tr. in BSJ, p. 462; P. Strait, *Cologne in the Twelfth Century* (Gainesville, FL, 1974).
13. William of Malmesbury, *De Gestis Pontificum Anglorum*, ed. N. E. S. A. Hamilton, Rolls Series 52 (London, 1870), p. 425.

14. H. Jenkinson, 'William Cade, a Financier of the Twelfth Century', *English Historical Review* 28 (1913), pp. 209–27. Galbert of Bruges, *De multro traditione et occisione gloriosi Karoli comitis Flandriarum*, pp. 31–2; tr. pp. 113–14.

15. R. Sherman, 'The Continental Origins of the Ghent Family of Lincolnshire', *Nottingham Medieval Studies* 22 (1978), pp. 23–5; G. Beech, 'Aquitanians and Flemings in the Refoundation of Bardney Abbey (Lincolnshire) in the Later Eleventh Century', *Haskins Society Journal* 1 (1989), pp. 73–90. A Walter of Ghent died in 1139 and was buried at Bardney Abbey: Richard of Hexham, 'De gestis Regis Stephani et de bello Standardi', p. 178. See also D. Crouch, *The Reign of King Stephen, 1135–1154* (Harlow, 2000), p. 160.

16. E. Amt, *The Accession of Henry II in England: Royal Government Restored, 1149–59* (Woodbridge, 1994), pp. 82–5.

17. Williams, *Saint Bernard of Clairvaux*, p. 80.

18. *Kölner Schreins Urkunden des zwölften Jahrhunderts. Quellen zur Rechts und Wirthschaftgeschichte der Stadt Köln*, ed. R. Hoeniger, 2 vols (Bonn, 1884–93), Vol. 2, pp. 20, 22, 25, 50, 53.

19. Forey, 'Second Crusade', pp. 168–9; Tyerman, *England and the Crusades*, p. 33.

20. J. P. Phillips, 'Saint Bernard of Clairvaux, the Low Countries and the Lisbon Letter of the Second Crusade', *Journal of Ecclesiastical History* 48 (1997), pp. 485–97; A. J. Forey, 'The Siege of Lisbon and the Second Crusade', *Portuguese Studies* 20 (2004), pp. 1–13. It will be seen below that, in light of Forey's comments on the reliability of Bernard's letter to Afonso, I have withdrawn that element of my argument from the discussion. The other ideas put forward in my article are, I suggest, sufficient for the basic principle to remain sound. Further to Forey on Bernard's letter, see also G. F. Borges, 'Saint Bernard et le Portugal: la légende et l'histoire', *Mélanges Saint Bernard* (Dijon, 1953), pp. 134–50.

21. M. Bennett, 'Military Aspects of the Conquest of Lisbon, 1147', in SCSC, p. 74.

22. 'De expugnatione Scalabis', *Portugaliae Monumenta Historica, I, Scriptores* (Lisbon, 1856), pp. 94–5.

23. Bourges, 'Saint Bernard et le Portugal', p. 138.

24. St Vincent, 'Foundation Document', pp. 178–9.

25. Riley-Smith, *First Crusaders*, pp. 204–5; Bouchard, *Sword, Miter and Cloister*, p. 258; *Livro preto da Sé de Coimbra*, Vol. 1, no. 80, p. 116.

26. *Cartulaire général de l'Ordre du Temple*, no. 10, p. 7; no. 24, p. 17.

27. Ibid., no. 439, p. 275; Barber, *New Knighthood*, p. 33.

28. Lucius II, 'Epistolae et privilegia', *PL* 179, cols 860–1; H. V. Livermore, *A New History of Portugal*, second edition (Cambridge, 1976), pp. 47–54; B. F. Reilly, *The Kingdom of León-Castilla under King Alfonso VII, 1126–1157* (Philadelphia PA, 1998), pp. 57–89.

29. Ibn al-Athir, *The Chronicle of Ibn al-Athir for the Crusading Period from al-Kamil fi'l-Ta'rikh. Part 1: 491–541 1097–1146*, p. 378.

30. *Acta Pontificum Romanorum inedita*, ed. von Pflugk-Harttung, no. 386, pp. 341–2; J. F. O'Callaghan, *Reconquest and Crusade in Medieval Spain* (Philadelphia PA, 2003), p. 42.

31. *De oorkonden der graven van Vlaanderen*, no. 92, p. 152.

32. See Introduction, pp. xxvii–xxviii. Tyerman is far too dismissive of the Lisbon campaign; see his *God's War*, p. 311.

33. Robert of Torigny, 'Chronicon', pp. 497–8.

34. 'Sigeberti Gemblacensis Continuatio Valcellensis', pp. 459–60.

35. 'Annales Palidenses', p. 83; Helmold of Bosau, *Chronica Slavorum*, pp. 216–17; 'Annales Brunwilarenses', *MGH* 16.727. Helmold of Bosau, as noted above, included the attack on Lisbon as one of the three parts of the Second Crusade, along with the expeditions to the Holy Land and the Baltic.

36. The thirteenth-century writer Abbot Albert of Stade described a pilgrimage to the Holy Land that went from Flanders, to Devon, to Brittany and then into the Bay of Biscay: 'Annales Stadenses', *MGH* 16.340.

37. *DeL*, pp. 52–3; 'Lisbon Letter', p. 336, tr. p. 63; 'Foundation Document of the Monastery of St Vincent', pp. 178–9.

38. Bennett, 'Military Aspects', p. 74, n. 22.

39. 'Sigeberti Gemblacensis continuatio Praemonstratensis', p. 453.

40. *DeL*, n. 5, pp. 53–4.

41. Saher's men included those of Bristol: *DeL*, pp. 104–5.

42. *DeL*, pp. 56–7.

43. Ralph of Caen, 'Gesta Tancredi in expeditione Hierosolymitana', *RHC Oc.* III, p. 676; tr. pp. 117–18.
44. Gratian, 'Decretum', in *Corpus Juris Canonici*, ed. A. Friedberg, 2 vols (Leipzig, 1879–81); Vol. 1, *Causa* 23, *quaestio* 1, *capitulum* 4, cols 892–3.
45. *DeL*, p. 57, n. 5.
46. Ibid., pp. 60–1.
47. Ibid., pp. 60–3.
48. Ibid., pp. 64–5.
49. 'Lisbon Letter', p. 337; tr. p. 63.
50. Ibid.; *DeL*, pp. 68–9.
51. Ibid., pp. 68–9.
52. Ibid., pp. 70–1.
53. Ibid.; BCE, no. 363, p. 314, tr. in BSJ, p. 462.
54. BCE, ibid.; Nicholas of Clairvaux, 'Epistolae', col. 671; *DeL*, pp. 70–1.
55. John 20: 29; *DeL*, pp. 70–1.
56. Ibid.
57. GN, pp. 132, 156; *Les Chansons de croisade avec leurs mélodies*, eds J. Bédier and P. Aubry (Paris, 1909), pp. 8–11; see Appendix 2, below.
58. *DeL*, pp. 70–3. Hehl has shown how this penitential element of the expedition, linked by the author to a 'new baptism', is an echo of Bernard's emphasis on the opportunity for re-birth or inner conversion offered by the Second Crusade. Hehl, *Kirche und Krieg*, pp. 130–4, 137–9; BCE, no. 458, p. 435; tr. in BSJ, pp. 463–4.
59. BCE, no. 363, p. 314; tr. in BSJ, p. 462; *DeL*, pp. 72–3.
60. OV, 3.183.
61. *DeL*, pp. 76–9.
62. BF, *World*, p. 153.
63. *DeL*, pp. 78–9.
64. S. Throop, 'Vengeance and the Crusades', *Crusades* 5 (2006), pp. 21–31.
65. Peter the Venerable, *Letters*, Vol. 1, no. 51, p. 152.
66. Riley-Smith, *First Crusade and the Idea of Crusading*, p. 147.
67. Hehl, *Kirche und Krieg*, pp. 138–40, 259–61.
68. Gratian 'Decretum', Vol. 1, *Causa* 23, *quaestiones* 1 and 2, cols 889–92; F. Russell, *The Just War in the Middle Ages* (Cambridge, 1975), pp. 60–6.
69. *DeL*, pp. 80–1.
70. Ibid., pp. 82–3.
71. Ibid., pp. 84–5.
72. Ibid.
73. 'Lisbon Letter', p. 337; tr. p. 63.
74. *DeL*, pp. 84–5.
75. Ibid., pp. 88–91.
76. Ibid., pp. 92–3.
77. Ibid., pp. 94–5. The 'Sigeberti continuatio Praemonstratensis', p. 453 indicated a population of 200,500.
78. *DeL*, pp. 96–9.
79. Ibid, pp. 98–9.
80. Ibid., pp. 100–1.
81. Ibid., pp. 102–3.
82. Ibid., pp. 104–5.
83. Ibid.
84. Ibid., pp. 104–7.
85. R. H. C. Davis, *The Normans and their Myth* (London, 1976), p. 124; Shopkow, *History and Community.*
86. *DeL*, pp. 106–9.
87. *QP*, p. 90.
88. *DeL*, pp. 108–9.
89. Ibid., pp. 108–11.
90. Ibid., pp. 110–15.
91. Borges, 'Saint Bernard', p. 138.
92. GF, p. 40.

93. Koran: *Surah* 49:13. 'O mankind! We created you from a single [pair] of a male and a female and made you into nations and tribes that you may know each other (not that you may despise each other).

94. Lay discusses the relationship between motives of crusade and reconquista and the religious and the secular expressed in this speech, arguing that there was 'no suggestion of religious antipathy as a cause for action' on the part of the locals. Given the archbishop's complaints about losing Christian lands and ruined churches – which are obvious parallels to the First Crusade – this interpretation is open to question. S. Lay, 'The Reconquest as Crusade in the Anonymous "De expugnatione Lyxbonensi"', *Al-Masaq* 14 (2002), p. 127.

95. *DeL*, pp. 114–19.
96. Ibid., pp. 118–19.
97. J. P. Phillips, 'The French Overseas', in *The Oxford History of France, 900–1200*, ed. M. G. Bull (Oxford, 2002), p. 181.
98. *DeL*, pp. 118–19.
99. For the bishop of Oporto, see ibid., pp. 72–7; for the Muslim elder, see, pp. 120–3. Hervey of Glanville used a similar phrase too, ibid., pp. 105–9.
100. Ibid., pp. 120–1.
101. Bernard of Clairvaux, 'De consideratione ad Eugenium papam', in *Sancti Bernardi Opera*, ed. J. Leclercq and H. Rochais, 8 vols (Rome, 1955–77), 3.412–13.
102. *DeL*, pp. 124–9.
103. Ibid., pp. 128–31; France, *Victory in the East*, pp. 232–43.
104. 'Lisbon Letter', p. 338; tr. p. 64.
105. B. Z. Kedar, *Crusade and Mission: European Approaches towards the Muslims* (Princeton, 1984), pp. 85–96, esp. at p. 89, n. 130.
106. *DeL*, pp. 132–3.
107. Henry of Huntingdon, *Historia Anglorum*, pp. 752–3.
108. St Vincent, 'Foundation Document', pp. 180–3.
109. G. Constable, 'A Further Note on the Conquest of Lisbon in 1147', in *The Experience of Crusading 1:Western Approaches*, ed. M. G. Bull and N. Housley, 2 vols (Cambridge, 2004), p. 42. See Livermore, 'The "Conquest of Lisbon"', p. 4 for a translation and comments on the charter given to Raol concerning the foundation of the cemetery of the English, and for his gift of it to the canons of Santa Cruz, Coimbra – a document witnessed by many of the Portuguese court.
110. 'Lisbon Letter', p. 338; tr. p. 64.
111. *DeL*, pp. 134–5.
112. 'Lisbon Letter', p. 338; tr. p. 64.
113. Ibid.; *DeL*, pp. 140–3. Kahl suggests that this brutality was a result of some of the crusade preaching campaign in northern Europe, especially by Bernard, who stressed an apoca-lyptic theme, the need to extirpate the Heathen as a precursor to the days of the Last Emperor (*Endkaisertum*); the victors at Lisbon were the only crusaders in a position of such superiority that they could implement this practice. H.-D. Kahl, 'Die weltweite Bereinigung der Heidenfrage – ein übersehenes Kriegsziel des Zweiten Kreuzzugs', *Spannungen und Widersprüche. Gedenkschrift für František Graus*, ed. S. Burghartz *et al.* (Sigmaringen, 1992), pp. 63–85.
114. Ibid., pp. 136–7.
115. *DeL*, pp. 138–9.
116. Ibid., pp. 140–3.
117. 'Lisbon Letter', pp. 338–9; tr. p. 65.
118. Ibid.
119. *DeL*, pp. 146–7.
120. *QP*, p. 92.
121. *DeL*, pp. 152–3.
122. Ibid., pp. 152–5.
123. Ibid., pp. 152–3.
124. Ibid., pp. 154–5. An earlier reference to the True Cross is hidden by the translation; see pp. 146–7 where '*sacrosanctam ligni dominici*' is translated 'a bit of sacred wood of the cross' rather than 'the sacred wood of the Lord', i.e. the True Cross.
125. Livermore. 'The "Conquest of Lisbon"', p. 7.
126. *DeL*, pp. 156–7; BCE, no. 363, p. 315; tr. in BSJ, no. 391, p. 462.

127. *DeL*, pp. 158–9.
128. France, *Victory in the East*, pp. 348–9.
129. *DeL*, pp. 158–65.
130. 'Lisbon Letter', p. 339; tr. p. 65.
131. *DeL*, pp. 164–7.
132. Ibid., pp. 168–9.
133. Ibid., pp. 172–5.
134. Ibid., pp. 174–7.
135. St Vincent, 'Foundation Document', pp. 188–91; Constable, 'Further Note on the Conquest of Lisbon', p. 43.
136. John of Hexham wrote the continuation of Simeon of Durham's *Historia*; see his *Opera Omnia*, ed. T. Arnold, 2 vols, Rolls Series 75 (London, 1882–5), 2.324.
137. 'Annales Sancti Disibodi', *MGH* 17.27–8; tr. 'Lisbon Letter', p. 67.
138. *DeL*, pp. 180–3.
139. J. S. C. Riley-Smith, 'Crusading as an Act of Love', *History* 65 (1980), pp. 177–92.
140. *DeL*, pp. 182–3.
141. Ibid., pp. 184–5, citing John 17:3.
142. Riley-Smith, 'Crusading as an Act of Love', pp. 185–90.
143. OD, pp. 70–1.
144. For the Baltic, see pp. 236–9 below; for Iberia, see, 266–8.
145. *DeL*, pp. 118–19; Hillenbrand writes of 'a prevailing mood of pragmatism at local level between Christians and Muslims' in Portugal. See C. Hillenbrand, 'A Neglected Episode of the Reconquista: A Christian Success in the Second Crusade', *Revue des Etudes Islamiques* 54 (1986), p. 169.
146. Duodechin's letter, 'Annales Sancti Disibodi', p. 28; tr. in the 'Lisbon Letter', p. 67.

Notes to Chapter 9

1. OD, pp. 48–51.
2. Conrad III, *Urkunden*, no. 195, p. 355.
3. John of Salisbury, *Historia Pontificalis*, ed. and tr. M. Chibnall (Oxford, 1956), p. 54; 'Annales Herbipolenses', p. 5.
4. OD, pp. 88–9.
5. WT, pp. 754–5; tr. 2.179.
6. OD, pp. 50–1.
7. John Kinnamos, *The Deeds of John and Manuel Comnenus*, tr. C. M. Brand (New York, 1976), p. 60; Niketas Choniates, *O City of Byzantium – The Annals of Niketas Choniates*, tr. H. J. Magoulias (Detroit, 1984), p. 38; Helmold of Bosau, p. 218; tr. p. 174.
8. Kugler, *Studien*, pp. 130–1, n. 50, proposed amending these figures to 90,000. See Bernhardi, *Konrad III*, p. 598.
9. 'Annales Palidenses', pp. 82, 84; 'Casus monasterii Petrishusensis', *MGH* 20.674.
10. 'Annales Egmundani', *MGH* 16.456.
11. Henry of Huntingdon, *Historia Anglorum*, p. 754; France, *Victory in the East*, pp. 122–42.
12. Otto of Freising, *GF*, pp. 216–19; tr. p. 79.
13. OD, pp. 32–35.
14. Poole, 'Germany, 1125–52', *Cambridge Medieval History* 5.352.
15. Otto of Freising, *GF*, p. 218; tr. 79–80; OD, pp. 34–5, 40–1; Z. Hunyadi, 'King and crusaders: Hungary in the Second Crusade', in *The Second Crusade in Perspective*, ed. J. T. Roche and J. M. Jensen (Turnhout, 2007, forthcoming).
16. Niketas Choniates, p. 36.
17. Ibid., pp. 59–60, p. 36.
18. Ibid., pp. 43–5; Otto of Freising, *GF*, pp. 198–201; tr. pp. 69–70; John Kinnamos, p. 76. F. Chalandon, *Histoire de la domination Normande en Italie et en Sicile*, 2 vols (Paris, 1907), 2.135–9.
19. Niketas Choniates, p. 45.
20. John Kinnamos, p. 58.
21. Niketas Choniates, p. 36.
22. Ibid, pp. 35–6.

23. John Kinnamos., p. 61.
24. Ibid.; Niketas Choniates, p. 36.
25. OD, pp. 42–3; Niketas Choniates, p. 37.
26. John Kinnamos, p. 61; Niketas Choniates, p. 37.
27. OD, pp. 46–7.
28. Magdalino, *Empire*, pp. 44–46.
29. Harris, *Byzantium and the Crusades* (London, 2003), pp. 22–4, 95–6; see also comments in the encomium written by 'Manganeios Prodromos' in 1147, cited in E. Jeffreys and M. Jeffreys, 'The "Wild Beast from the West": Immediate Literary Reactions in Byzantium to the Second Crusade', in *The Crusades from the Perspective of Byzantium and the Muslim World*, ed. A. E. Laiou and R. P. Mottahedeh (Washington DC, 2001), pp. 105–6.
30. Otto of Freising, *GF*, pp. 218–21; tr. pp. 80–1.
31. John Kinnamos, p. 63.
32. 'Annales Herbipolenses', p. 4.
33. John Kinnamos, p. 63; Otto of Freising, *GF*, p. 220; tr. p. 81.
34. Niketas Choniates, pp. 36–7.
35. Conrad III, *Urkunden*, no. 195, p. 394.
36. J. P. Phillips, *The Fourth Crusade and the Sack of Constantinople* (London, 2004), pp. 147–8.
37. John Kinnamos, p. 36.
38. Ibid., pp. 64–5.
39. Niketas Choniates, pp. 36–7.
40. 'Annales Herbipoleneses', p. 4.
41. John Kinnamos, p. 67.
42. Niketas Choniates, p. 38.
43. Jeffreys and Jeffreys, 'The "Wild Beast from the West"', pp. 101–16.
44. R. D. Thomas, 'Anna Comnena's Account of the First Crusade. History and Politics in the Reigns of the Emperors Alexius I and Manuel I Comnenus', *Byzantine and Modern Greek Studies* 15 (1991), pp. 269–312; P. Stephenson, 'Anna Comnena's *Alexiad* as a Source for the Second Crusade?', *Journal of Medieval History* 29 (2003), pp. 41–54; P. Magdalino, 'The Pen of the Aunt: Echoes of the Mid-Twelfth Century in the Alexiad', *Anna Komnene and Her Times*, ed. T. Gouma-Peterson (New York, 2000), pp. 19–24.
45. Jeffreys and Jeffreys, 'The "Wild Beast from the West"', p. 109.
46. Niketas Choniates, p. 38.
47. Conrad III, *Urkunden*, no. 194, p. 353. Conrad was careful not to describe Manuel as an emperor but rather as a royal ruler.
48. John Kinnamos, p. 68.
49. OD, pp. 88–9; M. Hendy, *Studies in the Byzantine Monetary Economy, c.300–1450* (Cambridge, 1985), describes the physical environment in this district, pp. 41–4.
50. John of Salisbury, *Historia Pontificalis*, pp. 53–4.
51. Conrad III, *Urkunden*, no. 195, p. 354.
52. WT, p. 744; tr. 2.168.
53. *Gesta Francorum*, p. 23.
54. OD, pp. 88–9.
55. Ibid, pp. 98–101.
56. 'Annales Palidenses', p. 83.
57. J. Roche, 'Conrad III and the Second Crusade: Retreat from Dorylaion?', *Crusades* 5 (2006), pp. 87–8.
58. B. S. Bachrach, 'Crusader Logistics: From Victory at Nicaea to Resupply at Dorylaion', *Logistics of Warfare*, pp. 43–5.
59. J. W. Nesbitt, 'Rate of March of Crusading Armies in Europe: a Study in Computation', *Traditio* 19 (1963), pp. 167–82.
60. Journey time for Conrad is discussed in J. France, 'Logistics and the Second Crusade', *Logistics of Warfare*, p. 81. Peter the Hermit managed to travel from Cologne to Constantinople in 104 days, an average of *c.* 14–15 miles a day: C. R. Glasheen, 'Provisioning Peter the Hermit: from Cologne to Constantinople', *Logistics of Warfare*, p. 119.
61. M. Hendy, *Studies in the Byzantine Monetary Economy c. 300–1450* (Cambridge, 1985), p. 43.
62. OD, pp. 88–9.
63. John Kinnamos, pp. 53, 68.
64. Niketas Choniates, pp. 31–2; John Kinnamos, pp. 37–56.

65. Conrad III, *Urkunden*, no. 195, p. 354. The 'Anonymous Syriac Chronicle' stated that Conrad marched for 10 days from Constantinople on a bad road with treacherous guides and no water or food. *Anonymi auctoris Chronicon ad AC 1234 pertinens*, ed. I. B. Chabot, tr. A. Abouna, introduction J. M. Fiey, 2 vols (Louvain, 1952–74), 2.111; also tr. by A. S. Tritton and H. A. R. Gibb, 'The First and Second Crusades from an Anonymous Syriac Chronicle', *Journal of the Royal Asiatic Society* (1933), p. 298.

66. OD, pp. 90–1.

67. J. H. Pryor, 'Digest', *Logistics of Warfare*, pp. 281–3; see also, Bachrach 'Crusader Logistics', pp. 50–62.

68. 'Annales Herbipolenses', p. 4; 'Annales Palidenses', p. 83.

69. 'Annales Herbipolenses', p. 6.

70. Roche, 'Conrad III and the Second Crusade', pp. 94–7.

71. Conrad III, *Urkunden*, no. 195, p. 355.

72. OD, pp. 92–3.

73. Ibid., pp. 92–5. Bernard's death was widely reported, for example in the 'Annales Pegaviensis', *MGH* 16.258, 'Annales Magdeburgenses', p. 188, 'Annales Palidenses', p. 83.

74. WT, p. 746, tr. 2.171.

75. 'Annales Reicherspergenses', p. 462.

76. John Kinnamos, p. 68.

77. OD, pp. 92–7.

78. 'Annales Herbipolenses', pp. 6–7.

79. WT, p. 748, tr. 2.173

80. Conrad III, *Urkunden*, no. 195, p. 355.

81. Bachrach, 'Crusader Logistics' p. 61.

82. OD, pp. 94–5.

83. Hiestand, 'Kingship and Crusade', p. 258.

84. OD, pp. 90–1; WT, pp. 745–6; tr. 2.170; 'Anonymous Syriac Chronicle', 2.111; tr. p. 298.

85. WT, pp. 743–4; tr., 2.168.

86. Ibid., p. 744; tr. 2.169.

87. Lilie, *Byzantium*, pp. 150–2.

88. WT, p. 747; tr. 2.171–2, followed by Runciman, *History of the Crusades*, 2.268.

89. OD, pp. 94–5.

90. Loud, 'Some Reflections', pp. 6–9.

91. A detailed list of these individuals will be published in the future.

92. 'Annales Reicherspergenses', p. 462.

93. Adolf of Berge, for example, died at Damascus: 'Annales Coloniensis maximi', p. 761.

94. J. S. C. Riley-Smith, 'Casualties and Knights on the First Crusade', *Crusades* 1 (2002), pp. 17–18; J. M. Powell, *Anatomy of a Crusade, 1213–1221* (Philadelphia PA, 1986), pp. 166–72. If, however, you simply double my figures to cover the 49% of 'unknowns' then you arrive intriguingly close to Riley-Smith and Powell's percentages.

95. WT, p. 745; tr., 2.169.

96. C. Cahen, *The Formation of Turkey: The Seljukid Sultanate of Rūm: Eleventh to Fourteenth Century*, tr. P. M. Holt (Harlow, 2001), pp. 21–2.

97. WT, p. 742; tr. 2.166–7. The Würzburg Annalist makes a similar point: 'Annales Herbipolenses', p. 4.

98. IQ, p. 281.

99. Ibid.

100. 'Annales Reicherspergenses', p. 462.

101. WT, p. 748; tr. 2.174; Conrad III, *Urkunden*, no. 195, p. 334; John of Salisbury, *Historia Pontificalis*, p. 54.

102. John Kinnamos (pp. 70–1) suggests that Conrad petitioned the emperor in order to be able to return to Constantinople and Manuel, seeing the king's present weakness, acceded. See also WT, pp. 748–9, tr. 2.174.

103. Conrad III, *Urkunden*, no. 195, p. 355.

104. OD, pp. 50–1, 112–13; 'Annales Reicherspergenses', p. 462; 'Annales Herbipolenses', p. 5.

105. P. Grierson, 'A Crusader's Hoard of 1147 from Side (Turkey)', in *Lagom: Festschrift für Peter Berghaus zum 60. Geburtstag*, ed. T. Fischer and P. Ilisch (Münster, 1981), pp. 195–203. Grierson also notes other hoards connected with the progress of the Second Crusade through the Byzantine Empire.

Notes to Chapter 10

1. J. P. Phillips, 'Odo of Deuil's *De profectione Ludovici VII in Orientem* as a source for the Second Crusade', in *The Experience of Crusading 2: Defining the Crusader Kingdom*, ed. P. W. Edbury and J. P. Phillips (Cambridge, 2003), pp. 80–95.
2. H. Mayr-Harting, 'Odo of Deuil, the Second Crusade and the Monastery of Saint Denis', in *The Culture of Christendom: Essays in Memory of Denis L. T. Bethell*, ed. M. A. Meyer (London, 1993), p. 227.
3. Ibid., pp. 232–3, 237–8.
4. M. Angold, *The Byzantine Empire, 1025–1204: A Political History*, 2nd edn (London, 1997), p. 11. Runciman regarded Odo as 'hysterically anti-Greek', *Crusades*, 2.274, n. 2 – a dramatic overstatement.
5. Phillips, 'Odo of Deuil', pp. 85–90.
6. OD, pp. 20–1.
7. Ibid., pp. 22–3.
8. France, *Victory in the East*, pp. 107–21.
9. OD, pp. 24–9.
10. Ibid., pp. 30–9; Hunyadi, 'King and crusaders: Hungary in the Second Crusade' (forthcoming).
11. Suger, 'Epistolae', *RHGF* 15.487.
12. OD, pp. 30–3; Phillips, 'Odo of Deuil', pp. 81–2.
13. OD, pp. 24–5.
14. Ralph of Caen, *Gesta Tancredi*, p. 676; tr. pp. 117–18.
15. OD, pp. 42–3.
16. Ibid., pp. 44–5.
17. John Kinnamos, pp. 68–9.
18. France, 'Logistics and the Second Crusade', p. 81.
19. OD, pp. 44–7.
20. For Alvisus's epitaph, see 'Historia monasterii Aquicinctini', *MGH* 14.588. His death was also reported in Louis VII, 'Epistolae', *RHGF*, 15.488.
21. OD, pp. 52–5.
22. Suger, 'Epistolae', *RHGF* 15.496.
23. OD, pp. 54–5.
24. Letter of Manuel to Louis, in Louis VII, 'Epistolae', pp. 9–10.
25. OD, pp. 54–5.
26. Ibid., pp. 56–7.
27. *EE*, col. 1252.
28. OD, pp. 56–7.
29. Harris, *Byzantium and the Crusades*, pp. 98–101.
30. OD, pp. 66–9.
31. Ibid., pp. 58–9. Robert of Rheims was one writer who reported that the First Crusaders followed in Charlemagne's footsteps: p. 732, tr. p. 84.
32. John Kinnamos, p. 69.
33. OD, pp. 58–61.
34. Suger, 'Epistolae', p. 496. William of Tyre also wrote that Louis and his nobles were well received by the emperor and given fine gifts: WT, p. 747; tr. 2.172.
35. John Kinnamos, p. 69; OD, pp. 66–7.
36. I am grateful to Dr Jonathan Harris for this point. For the relic's fate, see also Niketas Choniates, p. 191.
37. OD, pp. 66–7.
38. M. Huglo, 'Les chants de la *missa Greca* de Saint-Denis', in *Essays Presented to Egon Wellesz*, ed. J. Westrup (Oxford, 1966), pp. 74–83.
39. Suger of Saint-Denis, 'Epistolae', p. 488.
40. OD, pp. 68–71. On the possibility of a Greek patriarch in Antioch, see Lilie, *Byzantium and the Crusader States*, p. 155, n. 52; V. Grumel, 'Notes pour *l'Oriens Christianus*: 1: Deux patriarches d'Antioche au XIIe siècle', *Echos d'Orient* 33 (1934), pp. 53–8.
41. OV 6.506–7.
42. OD, pp. 70–1.
43. Suger, 'Epsitolae', p. 488.
44. OD, pp. 72–5.

45. Murray, 'Money and Logistics', pp. 232–43.
46. OD, pp. 72–7.
47. Ibid., pp. 76–9.
48. Ibid., pp. 78–9.
49. Ibid., pp.14–15; 80–1.
50. Ibid., pp. 80–1.
51. Ibid.
52. The location was not named explicitly, but given that the French seemed to have moved inland and considering Odo's statement that the emperor provided for his safety by a fleet on the nearby sea, Nicaea, with its location on a large lake, seems to be indicated.
53. OD, pp. 80–5. See also: 'Annales Egmundani', p. 456; 'Annales Pegavienses', p. 258; 'Annales Palidenses', p. 83.
54. OD, pp. 90–1.
55. Ibid., pp. 96–9.
56. Ibid., pp. 100–1.
57. Ibid., pp. 104–7.
58. WT, p. 749; tr. 2.174 .
59. OD, pp. 106–9.
60. WT, p. 750, tr. 2.175; OD, pp. 108–11.
61. Niketas Choniates, pp. 39–42.
62. Ibid., pp. 41–2.
63. OD, pp. 108–113; Gesta Francorum, pp. 68–9.
64. H. Barnes and M. Whittow, 'Medieval Castles: Antioch-on-the-Maender', Anatolian Archaeology 4 (1998), pp. 17–18.
65. OD, pp. 112–13.
66. Ibid.
67. Berry translates 'invenientes' as 'find'; 'devise' seems more appropriate and conveys a sense of the immediacy of the discussion. OD, pp. 114–15.
68. Ibid., pp. 108–9.
69. Ibid., pp. 114–15.
70. Ibid., pp. 114–17.
71. WT, p.750; tr. 2.175.
72. Ibid., p. 751; tr. 2.176.
73. Bachrach, 'Crusader Logistics', p. 56, gives detailed figures for the First Crusade. Bearing these findings in mind, the problems experienced by its successor become more comprehensible, if no less predictable.
74. OD, pp. 118–21.
75. Ibid.
76. Ibid.
77. WT, p. 752, tr. 2.177.
78. OD, pp. 118–19.
79. Ibid., pp. 122–3; WT, pp. 751–3; tr. 2.176–8; Suger, 'Epistolae', p. 496.
80. Ibid.
81. OD, pp. 122–3.
82. WT, pp. 751–2, tr. 2.177.
83. Cartulaire général de l'ordre du Temple, no. 448, p. 279.
84. OD, pp. 124–7.
85. John of Salisbury, Historia Pontificalis, p. 54.
86. John of Joinville, Vie de Saint Louis, ed. and tr. J. Monfrin (Paris, 1995), pp. 104–9.
87. WT, pp. 753–4; tr. 2.178.
88. OD, pp. 128–31.
89. France, Victory in the East, pp. 369–73.
90. Suger, Epistolae, RHGF 15.496.
91. OD, pp. 134–5.
92. Ibid., pp. 136–7.
93. Ibid., pp. 140–3.
94. Ibid., pp. xxii–xxv.
95. Ibid., p. xxiii. A piece of knowledge only (realistically) available from May 1148, when the French were poised to leave Antioch for Jerusalem.

96. Some of this discussion derives from Phillips, *Defenders*, pp. 85–96. See also the views of Magdalino, *Empire of Manuel I Komnenos*, pp. 49–52, who stresses Manuel's limited control over the border regions; and Lilie, *Byzantium*, pp. 154–63, whose view is closer to that expressed here.

97. OD, pp. 88–9.

98. Niketas Choniates, p. 39.

99. Michael the Syrian, *Chronique de Michel le Syrien, patriarche jacobite d'Antioche (1166–99)* ed. and tr. J.-B. Chabot, 4 vols (Paris, 1899–1910), Vol. 3, p. 275.

100. John Kinnamos, pp. 32–3.

Notes to Chapter 11

1. The poem survives in a later Old French form – given Raymond's background, the original may have been in Occitan. L. M. Paterson, 'Occitan Literature and the Holy Land', in *The World of Eleanor of Aquitaine: Literature and Society in Southern France between the Eleventh and Thirteenth Centuries*, ed. M. G. Bull and C. Léglu (Woodbridge, 2005), pp. 85–9.

2. WT, p. 754; tr. 2.180.

3. IQ, pp. 282–3.

4. WT, p. 671; tr. 2.93.

5. WT, pp. 674–6; tr. 2.94–7; IQ, pp. 248–52; Usama Ibn Munqidh, *An Arab-Syrian Gentleman and Warrior in the Period of the Crusades*, tr. P. K. Hitti (New York, 1929), pp. 25–7.

6. WT, pp. 718–20; tr., pp. 2.140–2.

7. This dating is based upon the dispatch of a letter by Louis from Antioch at the time (a letter which made no mention of this trouble), combined with the sense that, once he had rejected Raymond's plans, the French departed from the principality fairly swiftly. Suger, *Epistolae, RHGF* 15.496.

8. WT, p. 755; tr. 2.180.

9. Grabois, 'Crusade of Louis VII', p. 99; Runciman, *History of the Crusades*, 2.278–9.

10. Suger, 'Epistolae', pp. 496, 501.

11. Benton, 'Revenue of Louis VII', p. 91.

12. IQ, pp. 274–5; 'Anonymous Syriac Chronicle', pp. 104–11, tr. pp. 292–8; Segal, *Edessa*, pp. 251–4. Michael the Syrian, p. 270, estimated that 30,000 people died.

13. Michael the Syrian, p. 272. It was in this campaign that Baldwin of Marash, the subject of a lengthy elegy by Gregory the Priest, died. See Matthew of Edessa, *Armenia and the Crusades: 10th to 12th Centuries*, tr. A. E. Dostaurian (Lanham ML, 1993), pp. 243–57.

14. Hoch, *Jerusalem, Damaskus und der Zweite Kreuzzug*, pp. 116–21.

15. OD, pp. 70–1.

16. Suger, 'Epistolae', p. 496.

17. Ohnsorge, 'Ein Beitrag zur Geschichte Manuels I von Byzanz', p. 392.

18. Further reading on this is considerable. See, particularly, J. Martindale, *Eleanor of Aquitaine* (forthcoming); P. McCracken, 'Scandalizing Desire: Eleanor of Aquitaine and the Chroniclers', in *Eleanor of Aquitaine: Lord and Lady*, ed. B. Wheeler and J. C. Parsons (Basingstoke, 2002), pp. 247–64; R. Barber, 'Eleanor of Aquitaine and the Media', in *The World of Eleanor of Aquitaine: Literature and Society in Southern France between the Eleventh and Thirteenth Centuries*, ed. M. G. Bull and C. Léglu (Woodbridge, 2005), pp. 13–28; G. Duby, *The Knight, the Lady and the Priest: The Making of Modern Marriage in Medieval France*, tr. B. Bray (London, 1983), pp. 192–6. Runciman's comments in *Crusades* 2.278–9 create a splendidly imaginative picture of Eleanor and her ladies enjoying the glamorous Antiochene court after their hardships in Asia Minor.

19. WT, p. 768; tr. 2.193–5.

20. John of Salisbury, *Historia Pontificalis*, pp. xix–xxx; 52–3.

21. WT, p. 755; tr. 2.180–1.

22. John of Salisbury, *Historia Pontificalis*, p. 52.

23. C. B. Bouchard, 'Eleanor's Divorce from Louis: The Uses of Consanguinity', *Eleanor of Aquitaine: Lord and Lady*, pp. 223–35.

24. John of Salisbury, *Historia Pontificalis*, p. 53.

25. WT, p. 755; tr. 2.180–1.
26. Suger, 'Epistolae', *PL* 186, col. 1378.
27. WT, p. 755; tr. 2.181.
28. 'Annales Herbipolenses', p. 7.
29. Magdalino, *Empire of Manuel I Komnenos*, p. 52, n. 93.
30. Conrad III, *Urkunden*, no. 195, pp. 354–5.
31. John Kinnamos, p. 71; WT, p. 755; tr., 2.181.
32. 'Annales Herbipolenses', p. 7.
33. Otto of Freising, *GF*, pp. 262–5, tr., p. 102; WT, pp. 755–6; tr. 2.181.
34. This point may be reinforced by the burial of one of the king's leading *advocates*, Frederick of Bogen, in the Templars' cemetery. Otto of Freising, *GF*, pp. 262–5; tr. p. 102.
35. R. Hiestand, '"Kaiser" Konrad III., der zweite Kreuzzug und ein verlorenes Diplom für den Berg Thabor', *Deutsches Archiv für Erforschung des Mittelalters* 35 (1979), pp. 82–126.
36. WT, p. 746; tr., 2.170
37. Otto of Freising, *GF*, pp. 264–5; tr. p. 102.
38. 'Annales Herbipolenses', p. 6.
39. IQ, p. 280.
40. WT, p. 756; tr. 2.182; 'Sigeberti Gemblacensis Continuatio Praemonstratensis', p. 454. These rumours also reached the writer of the 'Anonymous Syriac Chronicle', pp. 87, 111; tr., p. 298.
41. WT, pp. 756–7; tr. 2.182.
42. Ibid.
43. D. Pringle, *The Churches of the Crusader Kingdom of Jerusalem. A Corpus*, 3 vols (Cambridge, 1993–2007), 2.153–6.
44. Hoch, *Jerusalem, Damaskus und der Zweite Kreuzzug*, pp. 43–75, 141–5; B. Hamilton, 'Women in the Crusader States: The Queens of Jerusalem (1100–1190)', *Medieval Women: Studies in Church History, Subsidia I*, ed. D. Baker (Oxford, 1978), pp. 151–3.
45. WT, pp. 760–1; tr. pp. 184–5.
46. H. E. Mayer, *The Crusades*, 2nd edn, tr. J. B. Gillingham (Oxford, 1990), p. 103; Runciman, *Crusades*, 2.281.
47. Hoch, *Jerusalem, Damaskus und der Zweite Kreuzzug*, pp. 115–21; summarized in English as 'The Choice of Damascus as the Objective of the Second Crusade: A Re-Evaluation', in *Autour de la Première Croisade*, ed. M. Balard, Byzantina Sorboniensia 14 (Paris, 1996), pp. 359–69.
48. M. Hoch, 'The Crusaders' Strategy against Fatimid Ascalon and the "Ascalon Project" of the Second Crusade', in *SCC*, pp. 120–3.
49. Phillips, *Defenders*, pp. 23–43; J. Richard, 'Le siège de Damas dans l'histoire et dans la légende', in *Cross-Cultural Convergences in the Crusader Period: Essays Presented to Aryeh Grabois on his Sixty-fifth Birthday*, ed. M. Goodich, S. Menache and S. Schein (New York, 1995), pp. 225–8.
50. R. C. Smail, 'The Crusaders and the Conquest of Damascus', unpublished paper read at Izhak Ben-Zvi Institute, Jerusalem 1984 (later published in Hebrew).
51. Hoch, 'Choice of Damascus', p. 363. He does comment in note 21, however, that it is possible that the 1140 treaty was never formally rescinded. See also WT, pp. 724–5; tr. 2.147–8.
52. Hoch, *Jerusalem, Damaskus und der zweite Kreuzzug*, pp. 90–113; idem, 'Choice of Damascus', p. 365.
53. WT, pp. 762–3, tr. 2.187. It would be hard for the orchards to spread that far north because of Mount Kaisoun overlooking the city; the distance west is possible.
54. Ibn Jubayr, *The Travels of Ibn Jubayr*, tr. R. J. C. Broadhurst (London 1952), pp. 271–2.
55. WT, pp. 763–4; tr. 2.188.
56. John Kinnamos, p. 70.
57. Such mighty deeds were often ascribed to crusader leaders. Godfrey of Bouillon performed a similar feat at the siege of Antioch (GN, pp. 284–5; tr. p. 133), as did Richard the Lionheart at the battle of Jaffa: Ambroise, *Estoire de la Guerre Sainte*, ed. and tr. M. Ailes and M. Barber, 2 vols (Woodbridge, 2003), 1.187, tr. 2.185. Conrad's bravery was also reported by, amongst others, John of Salisbury, *Historia Pontificalis*, p. 57.
58. Ibn al-Athir, 'Extrait du Kamel-Althevaykh', *RHC Or.* 1.468.
59. Kugler, *Studien*, pp. 194–201; Berry, 'Second Crusade', pp. 507–11; Runciman, *Crusades*, 2.281–5; J. P. Niederkorn, 'Traditio, a quibus minime cavimus. Ermittlungen gegen König

Balduin III. von Jerusalem, den Patriarchen Fulcher und den Templerorden wegen Verrats bei der Belagerung von Damaskus (1148)', *Mitteilungen des Instituts für Österreichische Geschichtsforschung* 95 (1987), pp. 53–68.

60. Ibn Jubayr, *Travels*, p. 20.

61. WT, pp. 879–1; not in the translation.

62. Ibid., p. 768; tr. 2.193.

63. Ibid., p. 768; tr. 2.193–4. William may have confused this incident with Thierry's bid to take control of Shaizar in 1157; see Phillips, *Defenders*, pp. 271–81.

64. Hoch, *Jerusalem, Damaskus und der zweite Kreuzzug*, pp. 130–1.

65. WT, pp. 768–9, tr. 2.194.

66. Conrad III, *Urkunden*, no. 197, p. 357.

67. 'Annales Palidenses', p. 83; 'Annales Rodenses', p. 719.

68. John of Salisbury, *Historia Pontificalis*, p. 57.

69. 'Annales Herbipolenses', p. 7.

70. John of Salisbury, *Historia Pontificalis*, pp. 56–8.

71. Michael the Syrian, *Chronicle*, p. 276; Anonymous Syriac Chronicle, pp. 87–8, 112; tr. pp. 298–9; 'A New Syriac Fragment Dealing with the Second Crusade', ed. and tr. W. R. Taylor, *Annual of the American School of Oriental Research* 11 (1929–30), p. 123 mentioned that the 'kings became divided amongst themselves'.

72. WT, pp. 675–6; tr. 2.96–7; IQ, pp. 248–52.

73. Forey, 'Failure of the Siege of Damascus', p. 20.

74. IQ, p. 284.

75. Sibt al-Jauzi, 'Mirror of the Times', tr. in F. Gabrieli, *Arab Historians of the Crusades* (London, 1969), p. 62.

76. J. W. Meri, *The Cult of Saints among Muslims and Jews in Medieval Syria* (Oxford, 2002), pp. 29–56, 195–8.

77. Ibn Jubayr, *Travels*, pp. 271, 287, 295.

78. Translation from Meri, *Cult of Saints among Muslims and Jews*, pp. 50–1. On Ibn 'Asakir see also: S. A. Mourad and J. E. Lindsay, 'Rescuing Syria from the Infidels: The Contribution of Ibn 'Asakir of Damascus to the *jihad* campaign of Sultan Nur al-Din', *Crusades* 6 (2007), pp. 37–55.

79. Ibid., pp. 171, 290; Meri, *Cult of Saints among Muslims and Jews*, pp. 43–52.

80. IQ, pp. 284–6.

81. John of Salisbury, *Historia Pontificalis*, p. 57.

82. Ibn al-Athir, 'Extrait du Kamel Altevarykh', pp. 468–70.

83. Forey, 'Failure of the Siege of Damascus', pp. 17–18.

84. WT, p. 767; tr. 2.192.

85. John of Salisbury, *Historia Pontificalis*, pp. 57–8.

86. Conrad III, *Urkunden*, no. 197, p. 357; WT, p. 769; tr. 2.195; see also the analysis of Hoch, 'Crusaders' Strategy against Fatimid Ascalon', pp. 123–4.

87. Hoch, *Jerusalem, Damaskus und der Zweite Kreuzzug*, p. 134.

88. Magdalino, *Empire of Manuel I Komnenos*, pp. 52–3.

89. 'Fragment d'un cartulaire de l'ordre de Saint-Lazare en Terre Sainte', p. 132.

90. 'Annales Casinenses', *MGH* 19.310.

91. John of Salisbury, *Historia Pontificalis*, pp. 60–2; Louis VII, 'Epistolae', pp. 513–14, 518–19; Louis VII, *Études*, p. 64.

Notes to Chapter 12

1. Helmold of Bosau, pp. 216–17, tr. p.172. For a discussion of Helmold's career and writings, see F. J. Tschan, 'Helmold: Chronicler of the North Saxon Missions', *Catholic Historical Review* 16 (1930–1), pp. 379–412.

2. For a general introduction, see E. Christiansen, *The Northern Crusades*, 2nd edn (Harmondsworth, 1997), pp. 1–49; or, in closer detail, K. Lotter, 'The Crusading Idea and the Conquest of the Region East of the Elbe', in *Medieval Frontier Societies*, ed. R. Bartlett and A. Mackay (Oxford, 1989),pp. 267–85.

3. Helmold of Bosau, pp. 86–9, 108–9, 198–9; tr. pp. 84, 98, 164.

4. Adam of Bremen, *Magistri Adam Bremensis gesta Hammaburgensis ecclesiae pontificum*, ed. and tr. B. Schmeidler (Hannover, 1917); translated as *History of the Archbishops of Hamburg-Bremen*, tr. F. J. Tschan, new introduction by T. Reuter (Columbia, 2002).
5. Adam of Bremen, pp. 101–3; tr. p. 83.
6. Ibid., pp. 132–3; tr. p. 105.
7. Ibid., pp. 132–3, tr. pp. 105–6.
8. Ibid., pp. 193–6; tr. pp. 156–8. This was a phrase also used by Gregory VIII in *Audita Tremendi* after the fall of Jerusalem in 1187: Ansbert, 'Historia de expeditione Friderici imperatoris: Quellen zur Geschichte des Kreuzzugs Kaiser Friedrichs I', ed. A. Chroust, *MGH Scriptores rerum Germanicarum, nova seria* (1928), 5.5–10.
9. Text in *Urkundenbuch des Erzstifts Magdeburg (937–1192)*, ed. F. Israel and W. Möllenberg (Magdeburg, 1937), no.193, pp. 249–52; G. Constable, 'The Place of the Magdeburg Charter of 1107/08 in the History of Eastern Germany and of the Crusades', *Vita Religiosa im Mittelalter: Festschrift für Kaspar Elm zum 70 Geburtstag*, ed. F. J. Felten and N. Jaspert (Berlin, 1999), pp. 283–99, translation of the letter at pp. 296–9; Lotter, 'Conquest', pp. 274–8.
10. *Urkundenbuch der Erzstifts Magdeburg*, no. 193, p. 251.
11. Ibid., p. 250.
12. Ibid., pp. 250–1.
13. Hagenmeyer, *Kreuzzugsbriefe*, no. 21, pp. 176–7.
14. I. S. Robinson, *Emperor Henry IV of Germany, 1056–1106* (Cambridge, 1999), p. 318.
15. Riley-Smith, *Crusades: Idea and Reality*, p. 75.
16. Robinson, *Papacy*, p. 424.
17. P. Knoch, 'Kreuzzug und Siedlung. Studien zum Aufruf der Magdeburger Kirche von 1108', *Jahrbücher für die Geschichte Mittel- und Ostdeutschlands* 23 (1974), pp. 9–16.
18. R.Bartlett, *The Making of Europe: Conquest, Colonisation and Cultural Change, 950–1350* (London, 1993), pp. 133–96.
19. Constable, 'Magdeburg Charter', p. 299.
20. Lotter, 'Conquest', p. 277.
21. K. Guth, 'The Pomeranian Missionary Journeys of Otto I of Bamburg and the Crusade Movement of the Eleventh to Twelfth Centuries', in SCC, pp. 13–23; Lotter, 'Conquest', pp. 278–80.
22. Guth, 'Pomeranian Missionary Journeys', p. 18.
23. Ibid., p. 19.
24. P. Taylor, 'Moral Agency in Crusade and Colonization: Anselm of Havelberg and the Wendish Crusade of 1147', *International Historical Review* 22 (2000), pp. 757–84; J. T. Lees, *Anselm of Havelberg: Deeds into Words in the Twelfth Century* (Leiden, 1998), pp. 62–72.
25. *Hamburgisches Urkundenbuch*, 1, ed. J. M. Lappenberg *et al.*, 4 vols (Hamburg, 1907–67), Vol. 1, no. 180, p. 170.
26. Helmold of Bosau, pp. 196–7; tr. p. 158.
27. Ibid., pp. 198–9; tr. p. 160.
28. Ibid., pp. 186–9 ; tr. pp. 152–4.
29. Robert of Ely, 'Vita Kanuti ducis altera', *MGH* 29.11.
30. Helmold of Bosau, pp. 372–5; tr. p. 276.
31. Lotter, 'Conquest', p. 283.
32. Helmold of Bosau, pp. 206–9; tr., pp. 166–7.
33. K. V. Jensen, 'The Blue Baltic Border of Denmark in the High Middle Ages: Danes, Wends and Saxo Grammaticus', in *Medieval Frontiers: Concepts and Practices*, ed. D. Abulafia and N. Berend (Aldershot, 2002), pp. 186–91.
34. Lotter, 'Conquest', p. 273.
35. Helmold of Bosau, pp. 222–3; tr. p. 176.
36. J. M. Jensen, 'Denmark and the Holy War: A Redefinition of a Traditional Pattern of Conflict, 1147–1169', in *Scandinavia and Europe 800–1350: Contact, Conflict and Coexistence*, ed. J. Adams and K. Holman (Turnhout, 2003), p. 224; building upon W. Ohnsorge, *Päpstliche und gegenpäpstliche Legaten in Deutschland und Skandinavien, 1159–1181*, Historische Studien, 188 (Berlin, 1929), p. 104, n. 1.
37. Tyerman, *The Invention of the Crusades*, p. 31 is therefore somewhat wide of the mark to suggest that it was not until 1188 that the Danish court was 'introduced to crusading for the first time'.

38. Hagenmeyer, *Epistolae et chartae*, pp. 61, 141–2, no. 6; Robert of Ely, 'Vita Kanuti ducis altera', p. 10.
39. J. M. Jensen, 'Sclavorum expugnator: Conquest, Crusade and Danish Royal Ideology in the Twelfth Century', *Crusades* 2 (2003), p. 69.
40. K. V. Jensen, 'Denmark and the Second Crusade', p. 165.
41. Ibid., pp. 167–8.
42. Otto of Freising, *GF*, pp. 210–13; tr. p. 76.
43. BCE, no. 457, p. 433; tr. in BSJ, no. 394, p. 467.
44. J. A. Brundage, 'St Bernard and the Jurists', in SCC, pp. 27–8; I. Fonnesberg-Schmidt, *The Popes and the Baltic Crusades, 1147–1254* (Leiden, 2006), pp. 30–1.
45. BCE, no. 457, p. 433; tr. BSJ, no. 394, p. 467.
46. J. S. C. Riley-Smith, *The Crusades: A Short History* (London, 1987), p. 96.
47. Ivo of Chartres, 'Decretum', *PL* 161, no. 182, col. 106; Gratian, 'Decretum', Vol. 1, *Distinctio* 45, *capitulum* 3–5, cols 160–2; Bernard of Clairvaux, *Opera*, Vol. 2, Sermon 66, pp. 186–7; Fonnesberg-Schmidt, *Popes and the Baltic Crusades*, p. 10.
48. Burchard of Worms, 'Decretum', *PL* 140, col. 742.
49. A. P. Vlasto, *The Entry of the Slavs into Christendom* (Cambridge, 1970), pp. 148–51; Taylor, 'Moral Agency in Crusade and Colonization', p. 773; Lotter, 'Conquest', p. 289.
50. Lotter, 'Conquest', pp. 288–92; Hehl, *Kirche und Krieg*, pp. 134–5 is less convinced.
51. H.-D. Kahl, 'Crusade Eschatology as Seen by St Bernard in the Years 1146 to 1148', in SCC pp. 35–47. For a broader study of the Sibylline texts in a prophetic rather than a political tradition, see A. Holdenreid, *The Sibyl and Her Scribes: Manuscripts and Interpretation of the Latin Sibylla Tiburtina, c.1050–1500* (Aldershot, 2006); pp. 72, 76 for points concerning the crusade.
52. Kahl, 'Die weltweite Bereinigung der Heidenfrage', pp. 66–79.
53. Lotter, 'Conquest', pp. 286–90.
54. 'Casus monasterii Petrishusensis', p. 674.
55. Acht, 'Die Gesandtschaft König Konrads III', pp. 672–3.
56. *EE*, cols 1203–4.
57. Fonnesberg-Schmidt indicates that there is no record of temporal privileges similar to those granted to the crusaders going to the Holy Land being awarded to the Wendish crusaders: *The Popes and the Baltic Crusades, 1147–1254* (Leiden, 2006), pp. 33–4.
58. Ibid., col. 1203. See also a letter of Eugenius to the bishop of Moravia, ibid., col. 1262.
59. 'Annales Magdeburgenses', p. 188.
60. Vincent of Prague, 'Annales', *MGH* 17, 663.
61. Helmold of Bosau, pp. 220–1; tr. p. 175.
62. Ibid., pp. 222–7; tr. pp. 176–80.
63. Saxo Grammaticus, *Saxonis Gesta Danorum*, ed. J. Olrik and H. Raeder, 2 vols (Copenhagen, 1931–57), 1.376; tr. E. Christiansen, *Saxo Grammaticus: Danorum Regum Heroumque Historia, Books X–XVI*, 3 vols (Oxford, 1981), 1.364.
64. Saxo Grammaticus, n. 57, 2.726–7, Christiansen translation.
65. 'Annales Magdeburgenses', 188.
66. Saxo Grammaticus, p. 376; tr. p. 364.
67. K.V. Jensen, 'Formation of a Crusader State?', p. 168.
68. Helmold of Bosau, pp. 228–9; tr. p. 180. Just to balance out the mutual disdain between the Germans and the Danes, it should be recorded that Saxo stated that from the former came 'only self-indulgence and sausages'. 'Blue Baltic Border', p. 185.
69. Saxo Grammaticus, pp. 376–7; tr. pp. 364–5.
70. Helmold of Bosau, pp. 228–9; tr. p. 180.
71. N. Blomqvist, *The Discovery of the Baltic, 1075–1225* (Leiden, 2005), p. 220.
72. Helmold of Bosau, pp. 228–9; tr. pp. 180–1.
73. Ibid.
74. Vincent of Prague, p. 663; 'Annales Magdeburgenses', p. 188; T. Manteuffel, *The Formation of the Polish State*, tr. A. Gorski (Detroit, 1982), pp. 126–7, 131.
75. 'Annales Magdeburgenses', p. 188.
76. Vincent of Prague, 'Annales', p. 663.
77. Ibid.
78. 'Annales Magdeburgenses', p. 190.
79. Taylor, 'Anselm and the Wendish Crusade', p. 777.

80. Wibald, 'Epistolae', no.150, pp. 244–5.
81. Kahl, 'Die weltweite Bereinigung der Heidenfrage', pp. 86–9.
82. Adam of Bremen, p. 166; tr. p. 133.
83. Helmold of Bosau, pp. 208–9; tr. p. 167.
84. Lees, *Anselm of Havelberg*, p. 76, n. 20 regards Lotter's idea as too subtle.

Notes to Chapter 13

1. J. F. O'Callaghan, *Reconquest and Crusade in Medieval Spain* (Philadelphia PA, 2003), pp. 15–17; R. A. Fletcher, 'Reconquest and Crusade in Spain, c.1050–1150', *Transactions of the Royal Historical Society*, 5th series, 37 (1987), p. 34.
2. Fletcher, 'Reconquest', pp. 35–6. For examples of good relations between Christians and Muslims, see F. L. Cheyette, *Ermengard of Narbonne and the World of the Troubadours* (Ithaca NY, 2001), pp. 83–5.
3. *Documentos correspondientes al reinado de Sancho Ramírez*, ed. J. Sarrullana and E. Ibarra, 2 vols (Zaragoza, 1904–13), Vol. 1, no. 48, pp. 187–9; trans. O'Callaghan, *Reconquest and Crusade*, p. 8.
4. O'Callaghan, *Reconquest and Crusade*, pp. 24–7.
5. See Housley, *Contesting the Crusades*, pp. 100–5 for an excellent summary.
6. H. E. J. Cowdrey, *The Cluniacs and Gregorian Reform* (Oxford, 1970), pp. 214–25; Fletcher, 'Reconquest', pp. 38–42; Bull, *Knightly Piety*, pp. 70–114 (although Bull disagrees with Fletcher concerning the impact of outside influences in the peninsula), N. Jaspert, 'Capta est Dertosa, clavis Christianorum. Tortosa and the Crusades', in SCSC, p. 91.
7. Urban II, 'Epistolae et privilegia', PL 151, 302–3; in 1091 Urban appointed Bishop Berenguer of Vic as archbishop of Tarragona and also confirmed the rights associated with the seat: ibid., col. 332–3.
8. *Papsturkunden in Spanien. I: Katalonien*, no. 23, pp. 287–8; translated from Riley-Smith, *Crusades: Idea and Reality*, p. 40.
9. Urban II, 'Epistolae et privilegia', cols 504–6.
10. *Historia Compostellana*, ed. E. Falque Rey, CCCM 70 (Turnhout, 1988), pp. 24–6, 77–8; Sigebert of Gembloux, 'Chronica', p. 367; Paschal II, 'Epistolae et privilegia', cols 25–6, 64–5; A. Ubieto Arteta, 'La participación navarro-aragonesa en la primera cruzada', *Príncipe de Viana* 8 (1947), pp. 357–84; O'Callaghan, *Reconquest and Crusade*, pp. 33–34.
11. O'Callaghan, *Reconquest and Crusade*, pp. 33, 181.
12. Ibid, p. 34.
13. Housley, *Contesting the Crusades*, pp. 102–4.
14. S. Barton, 'From Tyrants to Soldiers of Christ: the Nobility of Twelfth-Century León-Castile and the Struggle against Islam', *Nottingham Medieval Studies* 44 (2000), p. 34.
15. *Liber maiolichinus de gestis Pisanorum illustribus*, ed. C. Calisse, *Fonti per la Storia d'Italia* 29 (Rome, 1904), no. 1, pp. 137–40; B. F. Reilly, *The Contest of Christian and Muslim Spain, 1031–1157* (Oxford, 1992), pp. 174–7.
16. Gelasius II, 'Epistolae et privilegia', PL 163. 508; OV 6.396–403; Housley, 'Jerusalem and the Crusade Idea', p. 34; O'Callaghan, *Reconquest and Crusade*, pp. 36–8.
17. *Decrees of the Ecumenical Councils*, pp. 190–3.
18. Calixtus II, *Bullaire*, Vol. 2, no. 454, pp. 266–7.
19. Stroll, *Calixtus II: A Pope Born to Rule*, p. 446; L.McCrank, 'The Foundation of the Confraternity of Tarragona by Archbishop Oleguer Bonestruga, 1126–9', *Viator* 9 (1978), pp. 162–4.
20. *Historia Compostellana*, p. 379.
21. C. Stalls, *Possessing the Land: Aragon's Expansion into Islam's Ebro Frontier under Alfonso the Battler, 1104–1134* (Leiden, 1995) provides a clear overview of Alfonso's career.
22. P. Rassow, 'La confradía de Belchite', *Annuario de historia del derecho espanol* 3 (1926), pp. 200–26; the document setting out the rationale of the order is at pp. 224–5.
23. *Documentos para el estudio de la reconquista y repoblación del valle del Ebro*, ed. J. M. Lacarra, 2 vols (Zaragoza, 1982–5), 1.182–4.
24. CAI, p. 174; BF, *World*, p. 186.
25. OV 6.410–11; O'Callaghan, *Reconquest and Crusade* is wrong to translate this as 'crusaders of Christ', p. 40.

26. Barber, *New Knighthood*, pp. 28–31.
27. Reilly, *Alfonso VII*, pp. 15–89.
28. *CAI*, p. 172; BF, *World* p. 184; Reilly, *Alfonso VII*, p. 57; D. Pringle, *Secular Buildings in the Crusader Kingdom of Jerusalem* (Cambridge, 1997), pp. 64–5.
29. For the troubles in the Islamic world at the time of the First Crusade, see C. Hillenbrand, 'The First Crusade: The Muslim Perspective', in *The First Crusade: Origins and Impact*, ed. J. P. Phillips (Manchester, 1997), pp. 130–41.
30. As Kennedy explains, the Almohads' emphasis on the unity of God gave them the name *Muwahhidūn*, which became Hispanicised as *Almohade*; H. Kennedy, *Muslim Spain and Portugal. A Political History of al-Andalus* (Harlow, 1996), p. 198. For an excellent explanation of the rise of the Almohads, see idem, pp. 196–200.
31. The remainder of this paragraph is a very simple summary of Kennedy, *Muslim Spain and Portugal*, pp. 179–203.
32. Al-Makkari, *A History of the Mohammedan Dynasties in Spain*, tr. P. de Gayangos, 2 vols (London, 1840–1), 2.309.
33. Reilly, *Alfonso VII*, p. 94.
34. Von Pflugk-Harttung, *Acta Pontificum Romanorum inedita*, Vol. 2, no. 386, pp. 341–2.
35. *Papsturkunden in Spanien, I Katalonien*, no. 54, pp. 322–4.
36. For the bull of Lucius II, see ibid., no. 53, pp. 320–2; for Gelasius, see 'Epistolae et Privilegia', *PL* 163.508.
37. Reilly, *Alfonso VII*, pp. 90–1.
38. BF, *World*, pp.148–50, 155–61. See also the comments by R. McCluskey, 'Malleable Accounts: Views of the Past in Twelfth-Century Iberia', in *The Perception of the Past in Twelfth-Century Europe*, ed. P. Magdalino (London, 1992), pp. 217–19.
39. *PA*, p. 255; BF, *World*, p. 250.
40. See Purkis, *Crusading Spirituality in the Holy Land and Iberia*, forthcoming.
41. *PA*, p. 255; BF, *World*, p. 250.
42. Caffaro, *CAT*; tr. J. B. Williams, 'The Making of a Crusade: The Genoese anti-Muslim Attacks in Spain, 1146–1148', *Journal of Medieval History* 23 (1997), pp. 48–53; Classen, 'Res Gestae, Universal History, Apocalypse: Visions of Past and Future', in *Renaissance and Renewal in the Twelfth Century*, ed. R. L. Benson and G. Constable (Oxford, 1982), pp. 396–8.
43. A summary of his career and writings can be found in R. D. Face, 'Secular History in Twelfth-Century Italy: Caffaro of Genoa', *Journal of Medieval History* 6 (1980), pp. 169–84.
44. Caffaro, 'Annales Ianuenses', ed. L. T. Belgrano, *Fonti per la Storia d'Italia* 11 (Genoa, 1890), pp. 3–75; Caffaro, 'De liberatione civitatum Orientis', ed. L. T. Belgrano, *Fonti per la Storia d'Italia* 11 (Genoa, 1890), pp. 97–124.
45. S. A. Epstein, *Genoa and the Genoese, 958–1528* (Chapel Hill NC, 1996), pp. 28–33; E. H. Byrne, 'The Genoese Colonies in Syria', in *The Crusades and Other Historical Essays Presented to D. C. Munro*, ed. L. J. Paetow (New York, 1928), pp. 139–82.
46. Epstein, *Genoa*, p. 31; WT, p. 471, tr. 1.437.
47. B. Z. Kedar, 'Genoa's Golden Inscription in the Church of the Holy Sepulchre: A Case for the Defence', *I communi italiani nel regno crociato di Gerusalemme*, ed. G. Airaldi and B. Z. Kedar (Genoa, 1986), pp. 317–35.
48. H. E. J. Cowdrey, 'The Mahdia Campaign of 1087', *English Historical Review* 92 (1977), pp. 1–29.
49. *CAI*, p. 246; BF, *World*, p. 248; B. Garí, 'Why Almería? An Islamic Port in the Compass of Genoa', *Journal of Medieval History* 18 (1992), pp. 211–31.
50. Caffaro, 'Annales Ianuenses', pp. 33–5.
51. *CDDRG*, nos 166–7, pp. 204–9.
52. R. Rogers, *Latin Siege Warfare in the Twelfth Century* (Oxford, 1992), pp. 172–6.
53. *CDDRG*, nos 167–8, pp. 206–14, esp. 208, 211.
54. Reilly, *Alfonso VII*, p. 94.
55. *CAI*, p. 247; BF, *World*, p. 249.
56. Caffaro, *CAT*, p. 21.
57. *Papsturkunden für Kirchen im Heiligen Lande*, no. 63, pp. 193–5.
58. J. L. Rodríguez de Diego, *El tumbo del monasterio cisterciense de la Espina* (Valladolid, 1982), no. 2, pp. 185–7.
59. *CDDRG*, nos 168–9, pp. 210–17.

60. Jaspert, 'Capta est Dertosa: clavis Christianorum. Tortosa and the Crusades', pp. 92–3; Cheyette, *Ermengard of Narbonne*, pp. 83–5.
61. Jaspert, 'Capta est Dertosa: clavis Christianorum. Tortosa and the Crusades', p. 92; Hiestand, 'Reconquista, Kreuzzug und heiliges Grab', p. 140.
62. *CDDRG*, no. 46, pp. 54–7.
63. L. T. Belgrano, 'Frammento di poemetto sincrono per la conquista di Almería nel MCXVII', *Atti della Società Ligure di Storia Patria* 19 (1888), pp. 401–2; Reilly, *Contest of Christian and Muslim Spain*, pp. 176–80.
64. *Cartulaire général de l'ordre du Temple*, no. 314, pp. 204–5.
65. N. Jaspert, *Stift und Stadt. Das Heiliggrabpriorat von Santa Anna und das Regularkanonikerstift Santa Eulalia del Camp im mittelalterlichen Barcelona (1145–1423)* (Berlin, 1996), pp. 61–3, 118–23.
66. *Liber instrumentorum memorialium: Cartulaire des Guillelms de Montpellier*, no. 152, pp. 284–5.
67. A. L. Lewis, 'The Guillems of Montpellier, a Sociological Appraisal', *Viator* 2 (1971), pp. 159–69; A. Germain, *Histoire de la commune de Montpellier*, 3 vols (Montpellier, 1851), pp. 11–21; Cheyette, *Ermengard of Narbonne*, p. 90. See also the highly detailed will left by William VI, dated 11 December 1146; *Liber instrumentorum memorialium Cartulaire des Guillems de Montpellier*, no. 95, pp. 177–83.
68. Reilly, *Alfonso VII*, p. 94; Kennedy, *Muslim Spain and Portugal*, pp. 200–3.
69. Ibid.
70. *EE*, cols 1203–4.
71. Caffaro, *CAT*, p. 22.
72. Williams, 'The Making of a Crusade', p. 48, n. 79.
73. Caffaro, *CAT*, p. 22.
74. See above, pp. 119–20.
75. Caffaro, *CAT*, p. 22. The estimate of late June is based on our knowledge that Alfonso was at Baeza on 1 August 1147 (BF, *World*, p. 262). The Genoese had waited a month before contacting him there and had sailed from Genoa to Minorca, then to Cabo de Gata, pausing there before contacting the emperor. This date also fits in with the election of the consuls in late January.
76. Williams, 'The Making of a Crusade', p. 34.
77. Phillips, *The Fourth Crusade and the Sack of Constantinople*, pp. 105–6.
78. *PA*, p. 266; BF, *World*, p. 262; Caffaro, *CAT*, pp. 23–4.
79. *PA*, p. 256; BF, *World*, p. 251.
80. Ibid.
81. *QP*, p. 90.
82. *Les chansons de croisade avec leurs mélodies*, p. 8; translated by Routledge in Phillips, *Crusades*, pp. 182–3. See Appendix 2, pp. 283–4 below.
83. *PA*, pp. 255–66; BF, *World*, pp. 251–61.
84. *PA*, p. 257; BF, *World*, p. 251.
85. *PA*, pp. 255–6; BF, *World*, pp. 250–1.
86. Throop, 'Vengeance and the Crusades', pp. 25–31.
87. See Chapter 8 above for a discussion of this topic.
88. Reilly, *Alfonso VII*, pp. 97–8.
89. *PA*, p. 266; BF, *World*, p. 261.
90. Caffaro, *CAT*, pp. 23–4.
91. Reilly, *Alfonso VII*, pp. 98–9.
92. Caffaro, *CAT*, pp. 24–5.
93. Ibid., pp. 25–6.
94. Ibid., pp. 26–7.
95. Ibid., pp. 27–8.
96. *DeL*, pp.164–5.
97. Caffaro, *CAT*, p. 28.
98. There was an undisciplined rush to grab property in Lisbon in which the Mozarabic bishop was murdered, but this unfortunate episode aside, there seems to have been no mass slaughter. *DeL*, pp. 176–7.
99. *CDDRG*, nos 182–3; pp. 228–30.
100. Caffaro, *CAT*, p. 30.

101. S. Barton, 'A Forgotten Crusade: Alfonso VII of León-Castile's Campaign for Jaen (1148)', *Historical Research* 73 (2000), pp. 312–20.
102. Reilly, *Alfonso VII*, p. 102.
103. Jaspert, 'Capta est Dertosa: clavis Christianorum. Tortosa and the Crusades', p. 92; D. J. Smith, 'The Abbot–Crusader: Nicholas Brakespear in Catalonia', in *Adrian IV: The English Pope (1154–1159): Studies and Texts*, ed. B. Bolton and A. J. Duggan (Aldershot, 2003), p. 33.
104. *EE*, col.1346.
105. Barton, 'A Forgotten Crusade', p. 319.
106. For details of the dispute, see Horn, *Eugenius III*, pp. 157–66.
107. Robinson, *Papacy*, pp. 22, 270.
108. *EE*, cols 1345–47.
109. A papal bull of 22 June is, by some historians, dated to 1148 and thus connected to this episode. The content of the bull seems applicable – Eugenius promised that all who fought for the defence of the Christian faith and against 'the infidel and the enemies of the cross of Christ' would receive the same remission of sins as 'Pope Urban established for all those going abroad for the liberation of the Oriental Church'. Count Ramon was heartily praised, and the crusaders' wives and children were, for the first time in a crusading bull in Spain, explicitly brought under papal protection. Amongst those who follow this line are: O'Callaghan, *Reconquest and Crusade*, p. 46; Reilly, *Alfonso VII*, p. 102; J. Goñi Gaztambide, *Historia de la Bula de la Cruzada en España* (Vitoria, 1958), p. 86. But, as Forey, 'Second Crusade', p. 175, n. 70 indicates, the bull was issued at Segni, thus it belongs in 1152 (when the crusading context could fit too) – the date assigned by Migne, *EE*, col. 1539. Given this ambiguity, the bull has not been included in the main text here.
110. Caffaro, *CAT*, p. 31.
111. G. Constable, 'A Note on the Route of the Anglo-Flemish Crusaders of 1147', *Speculum* 28 (1953), pp. 525–6; Hiestand, 'Reconquista', pp. 149–54.
112. Cheyette, *Ermengarde of Narbonne*, esp. pp. 85–7, 91–5; J. Caille, 'Les seigneurs de Narbonne dans le confit Toulouse–Barcelone au xiie s.', *Annales de Midi* 97 (1985), p. 232. Ermengard had been a widow since 1134; later she married Count Manrique of Lara, who had been at the siege of Almería; ibid., p. 233. See also the comments by M. Bennett, 'Virile Latins, Effeminate Greeks and Strong Women: Gender Definitions on Crusade', *Gendering the Crusades*, ed. S. B. Edgington and S. Lambert (Cardiff, 2001), pp. 26–7.
113. *CDDRG*, 1, no. 190, pp. 236–8; Smith, 'The Abbot-Crusader', p. 35. The abbot's presence is attested in a letter of 1156 from Ramon Berenguer to (by then) Pope Adrian IV, in which the count recalled how the churchman had witnessed the capture of Tortosa and Lerida; ibid., p. 31.
114. Rogers, *Latin Siege Warfare*, pp. 179–82.
115. Caffaro, *CAT*, p. 32.
116. Ibid., pp. 33–5.
117. For the subsequent financial problems suffered by the Genoese after the crusade, see Epstein, *Genoa*, pp. 49–53; Williams, 'The Making of a Crusade', pp. 36–7; H.Kreuger, 'Post-War Collapse and Rehabilitation in Genoa (1149–62)', in *Studi in onore di Gino Luzzatto*, 2 vols (Milan, 1949–50), 1. 119–28.
118. Caffaro, *CAT*, p. 21; translation based upon Williams, 'The Making of a Crusade', pp. 39–40.
119. *GN*, pp. 101–3; tr. p. 37.
120. Caffaro, *CAT*, p. 21.
121. *Liber iurium reipublicae Genuensis*, ed. E. Ricotti, Historiae patriae monumenta, vol. 7, part 1 (Turin, 1854), no. 94, p. 150, tr. Williams, 'The Making of a Crusade', pp. 38–9.
122. Epstein, *Genoa*, 9–53; Williams, 'The Making of a Crusade', *passim*.
123. Gratian, 'Decretum', Vol. 1 Causa 23, quaestio 1, *capitula* 2, 4–6, cols 891–4; F. Russell, *Just War in the Middle Ages*, p. 61.
124. C. Di Fabio, *La cattedrale di Genova nel medioevo, secoli vi-xiv* (Genoa, 1998), pp. 88–91.
125. Williams, 'The Making of a Crusade', p. 40.
126. *Corpus inscriptionorum medii aevi Liguriae III. Genova, centro storico*, ed. A. Silva, Collana storica di fonti e studi, Vol. 52 (Genoa, 1987), pp. 130–1, tr. in Williams, 'The Making of a Crusade', pp. 41–2.
127. Williams, 'The Making of a Crusade', pp. 43–4.
128. DeVic and Vaissete, *Histoire générale de Languedoc*, 3.739.

129. The document itself is in Hiestand, 'Reconquista', pp. 156–7; see also, N. Jaspert, 'Bonds and Tensions on the Frontier: the Templars in Twelfth-Century Western Catalonia', in *Mendicants, Military Orders and Regionalism in Europe*, ed. J. Sarnowsky (Aldershot, 1999), p. 25.

130. Hiestand, 'Reconquista', pp. 148–50; Jaspert, 'Capta est Dertosa: clavis Christianorum. Tortosa and the Crusades', pp. 97–100.

131. Constable, SC, p. 233, n. 80. Constable also indicates that the new abbot of Grandeselve was Alexander of Cologne, who became a monk during Bernard's preaching of the crusade in the Rhineland, Groven, 'Die Kölnfahrt Bernhards von Clairvaux', pp. 10–12.

132. Jaspert, 'Capta est Dertosa: clavis Christianorum. Tortosa and the Crusades', writes that this campaign 'generally lacked the crusading lustre of the Tortosa expedition', p. 96.

133. L. M. Paterson, 'Syria, Poitou and the *reconquista* (or Tales of the Undead). Who was the Count in Marcabru's *Vers del lavador*?', in SCSC, p. 133.

134. *Marcabru: A Critical Edition*, ed. S. Gaunt, R. Harvey and L. M. Paterson (Cambridge, 2000), pp. 434–53, text at pp. 438–41; Paterson, 'Syria, Poitou and the *reconquista*', pp. 133–49.

135. For the subsequent history of Lerida, see J. Bolòs, 'Changes and Survival: The Territory of Lleida (Catalonia) after the Twelfth-Century Conquest', *Journal of Medieval History* 27 (2001), pp. 313–29.

136. Reilly, *Alfonso VII*, p. 108.

137. Cited in Constable, SC, p. 232.

138. *Papsturkunden in Spanien I: Katalonien*, 1, no. 57, pp. 327–8.

139. Reilly, *Alfonso VII*, pp. 108–10.

Notes to Chapter 14

1. WT, pp. 768–9; tr. 2.196.

2. Ibid., p. 769; tr. 2.196.

3. IQ, pp. 281–2, 285, 287.

4. Gregory the Priest, *Armenia and the Crusades* pp. 257–9; 'Epistola A. Dapiferi Militiae Templi', RHGF 15.540.

5. Y. Tabaa, 'Monuments with a Message: Propagation of *jihad* under Nur ad-Din (1146–74)', in *The Meeting of Two Worlds: Cultural Exchange between East and West during the Period of the Crusades*, ed. V. P. Goss (Kalamazoo, 1986), pp. 224–5.

6. WT, p. 774; tr. 2.200–1; H. E. Mayer, 'Studies in the History of Queen Melisende of Jerusalem', *Dumbarton Oaks Papers* 26 (1972), pp. 129, 181.

7. 'Epistola A. Dapiferi Militiae Templi', pp. 540–1.

8. Principal discussions of this subject are: Phillips, *Defenders*, pp. 100–118; G. Constable, 'The Crusading Project of 1150', in *Montjoie: Studies in Crusade History in Honour of Hans Eberhard Mayer*, ed. B. Z. Kedar, J. S. C. Riley-Smith and R. Hiestand (Aldershot, 1997), pp. 67–75; T. Reuter, 'The "non-crusade" of 1149–50', in SCSC, pp. 150–63.

9. BCE, no. 380, p. 344; tr. in BSJ, no. 408, p. 478; on Bernard and the crusade plans, see also Bolton, 'The Cistercians and the Aftermath of the Second Crusade', pp. 131–40.

10. 'Vie de Suger', p. 399.

11. Peter the Venerable, *Letters*, 1, no. 166, pp. 399–400; tr. Berry, 'Peter the Venerable and the Crusades', p. 160.

12. BCE, no., 364, p. 319; tr. in BSJ, no. 398, pp. 469–70.

13. Suger, 'Vie de Suger', p. 399.

14. EE, cols 1414–15.

15. 'Sigeberti continuatio Praemonstratensis', p. 455; 'Chronicon S. Martini Turonensis', RHGF 12.474.

16. Constable, 'Crusading Project of 1150', p. 74.

17. BCE, no. 521, p. 483; tr. in BSJ, no. 400, p. 473.

18. Peter the Venerable, *Letters*, 1, no. 130, p. 327.

19. OD, pp. 10–11; BCE, no. 363, p. 314; tr. in BSJ, no. 391, p. 462.

20. Suger, 'Vie de Suger', p. 399.

21. John of Salisbury, *Historia Pontificalis*, pp. 11–12.

22. *Chronique de Morigny*, p. 85; 'Life of Suger', p. 398.

23. *Marcabru: A Critical Edition*, pp. 440–1; the poet may also have made a reference to the controversy concerning Queen Eleanor and Raymond of Antioch, ibid., pp. 204–5.
24. As we saw in Chapter 1, there was some criticism of the crusades of 1101, 1107–8 and 1129. For some later views on the failure of the Second Crusade, see P. W. Edbury, 'Looking back on the Second Crusade: Some Late Twelfth-Century English Perspectives', in SCC, pp. 163–9.
25. John of Salisbury, *Historia Pontificalis*, p. 55.
26. Constable, SC, pp. 266–76.
27. 'Vita Prima S. Bernardi', cols 308–9, 516; 'Annales Brunwilarenses', p. 727.
28. G. Constable, 'A Report of a Lost Sermon by St Bernard on the Failure of the Second Crusade', in *Studies in Medieval Cistercian History Presented to J. F. O'Sullivan*, ed. J. F. O'Callaghan, Cistercian Studies Series No.13 (Spencer, MA, 1971), pp. 49–54; idem, 'Crusading Project of 1150', p. 73.
29. Bernard of Clairvaux, 'De consideratione ad Eugenium papam', pp. 410–13; Siberry, *Criticism of Crusading*, pp. 79–80.
30. Hiestand, 'Papacy and the Second Crusade', pp. 46–7.
31. Adrian IV, 'Epistolae et privilegia', PL 188, col. 1616.
32. BCE, no. 256, p. 164; tr. in BSJ, no. 399, pp. 471–2.
33. Suger himself planned to channel money from his monastic estates to the East through the Templars. 'Vie de Suger', pp. 399–400.
34. 'Sigeberti continuatio Praemonstratensis', p. 455; 'Chronicon S. Martini Turonensis', p. 474; Siberry, *Criticism of Crusading*, p. 191; Bolton, 'Cistercians and the Aftermath of the Second Crusade', pp. 131–40.
35. R. H. C. Davis, *King Stephen*, 3rd edn (Harlow, 1990), pp. 104–112; Crouch, *The Reign of King Stephen*, pp. 239–49.
36. John of Salisbury, *Historia Pontificalis*, pp. 62–67; R. I. Moore, *The Origins of European Dissent* (Oxford, 1978), pp. 115–36.
37. Runciman, *Crusades*, 2.286; Berry, 'Second Crusade', p. 511; Lilie, *Byzantium and the Crusader States*, p. 162.
38. Phillips, *Defenders*, p. 118; Constable, 'Crusading Project of 1150', pp. 67–8; Reuter, 'The "non-crusade" of 1150', pp. 151, 159; Rowe, 'Papacy and the Greeks', pp. 311–20.
39. BCE, no. 244, pp. 134–6; tr. BSJ, no. 320, pp. 394–5.
40. Romauld of Salerno, 'Annales', p. 425; Horn, *Studien*, p. 72.
41. Wibald of Stavelot, 'Epistolae', no. 198 pp. 316–17.
42. Ibid., no. 252, p. 377.
43. Peter the Venerable, *Letters*, Vol. 1, no. 163, p. 394.
44. Ibid., no. 163, p. 395.
45. Conrad III, *Urkunden*, no. 229, p. 406.
46. Gregory the Priest, pp. 258–9; on Gregory see also G. Beech, 'A Little-Known Armenian Historian of the Crusading Period: Gregory the Priest (1136–62)', in *Truth as Gift: Studies in Honor of John R. Sommerfeldt*, ed. M. Dutton, D. M. LaCorte and P. Lockey (Kalamazoo, MI, 2004), pp. 119–43.
47. The following section represents a concise summary of Phillips, *Defenders*, pp. 118–281.
48. M. Gervers, 'Donations to the Hospitallers in England in the Wake of the Second Crusade', in SCC, pp. 155–61.
49. Alexander III, 'Epistolae', cols 1296–7; M. Pegg, 'Le Corps et l'authorité: La lèpre de Baudouin IV', *Annales* 45 (1990), pp. 265–87; B. Hamilton, *The Leper-King and his Heirs: Baldwin IV and the Crusader Kingdom of Jerusalem* (Cambridge, 2000).
50. P. W. Edbury and J. G. Rowe, *William of Tyre: Historian of the Latin East* (Cambridge, 1988), pp. 24–31.
51. J. Leclercq, 'Gratien, Pierre de Troyes et la seconde croisade', *Studia Gratiana* 2 (1954), pp. 585–93.
52. Reilly, *Contest of Christian and Muslim Spain*, pp. 223–30; idem, *Alfonso VII*, p. 134.
53. Christiansen, *Northern Crusades*, pp. 65–72; I. Fonnesberg-Schmidt, *Popes and the Baltic Crusades*, pp. 43–65.

BIBLIOGRAPHY

PRIMARY SOURCES

Note: For those wishing to read further, and in an effort to make this subject more accessible, some readers may prefer to consult translations into English rather than the original language of some of the texts. I have therefore cited and provided a reference to translations whenever this was possible. At times I disagree with the translators and indicate so in the appropriate note.

Acta Pontificum Romanorum inedita, ed. J. Pflugk-Harttung, 3 vols (Stuttgart, 1881–6).
Actes des évêques de Laon des origins à 1151, ed. A. Dufour-Malbezin (Paris, 2001).
'Adalberti vita Heinrici II imperatoris', *MGH* 4. 792–811.
Adam of Bremen, *Magistri Adam Bremensis gesta Hammaburgensis ecclesiae pontificum*, ed. and tr. B. Schmeidler (Hanover, 1917); translated as *History of the Archbishops of Hamburg–Bremen*, tr. F. J. Tschan, new introduction by T. Reuter (New York, 2002).
Adrian IV, 'Epistolae et privilegia', *PL* 188, cols 1361–1640.
Alberic of Trois Fontaines, 'Chronica a monacho novi monasterii Hoiensis interpolata', *MGH* 23.631–950.
Albert of Aachen, *Historia Ierosolimitana: History of the Journey to Jerusalem*, ed. and tr. S. B. Edgington (Oxford, 2007).
Albert of Stade, 'Annales Stadenses', *MGH* 16.271–379.
Alexander III, 'Epistolae et privilegia', *PL* 200, cols 69–1466.
Al-Makkari, *A History of the Mohammedan Dynasties in Spain*, tr. P. de Gayangos, 2 vols (London, 1840–1).
Ambroise, *Estoire de la Guerre Sainte*, ed. and tr. M. Ailes and M. Barber, 2 vols (Woodbridge, 2003).
The Anglo-Saxon Chronicle, ed. and tr. D. Whitelock (London, 1961).
Anna Comnena, *The Alexiad*, tr. E. A. S. Dawes (London, 1967).
'Annales Brunwilarenses', *MGH* 16.724–8.
'Annales Casinenses', *MGH* 19.303–20.
'Annales Colonienses maximi', *MGH* 17.723–847.
'Annales Egmundani', *MGH* 16.442–79.
Annales Herbipolenses', *MGH* 16.1–12.
'Annales Magdeburgenses', *MGH* 16.105–96.
'Annales Mosomagenses', *MGH* 3.160–6.
'Annales Palidenses', *MGH* 16.48–98.
'Annales Pegavienses', *MGH* 16.232–70.
'Annales Reicherspergenses', *MGH* 17.439–76.
'Annales Rodenses', *MGH* 16.688–723.
'Annales S. Benigni Divionensis', *MGH* 5.37–50.
'Annales S. Petri Erphesfurdenses', *MGH* 16.15–25.

'Annales Sancti Disibodi', *MGH* 17.4–30.

Anonymi auctoris Chronicon ad AC 1234 pertinens, ed. I. B. Chabot, tr. A. Abouna, introduction by J. M. Fiey, 2 vols (Louvain, 1952–74); tr. A. S. Tritton and H. A. R. Gibb, 'The First and Second Crusades from an Anonymous Syriac Chronicle', *Journal of the Royal Asiatic Society* (1933), pp. 69–101; 273–305.

Anonymous, 'A New Syriac Fragment Dealing with Incidents in the Second Crusade', ed. and tr. W. R. Taylor, *Annual of the American School of Oriental Research* 11 (1929–30), pp. 120–31.

Anonymous, 'Petite chronique du règne de Baudouin Ier', in GN, pp. 69–72; 361–6.

Anonymous of Bologna, 'The Principles of Letter-Writing – *Rationes dictandi*', in *Three Medieval Rhetorical Arts*, ed. and tr. J. J. Murphy, 2nd edn (Berkeley CA, 1985), pp. 5–25.

d'Arbois de Jubainville, H. (ed.), 'Les premiers seigneurs de Ramerupt', *Bibliothèque de l'école des Chartes* 22 (1856), pp. 440–58.

Arnulf of Lisieux, *Letters*, ed. F. Barlow, Camden Society, Third Series 61 (1939).

Baldric of Dol, 'Historia Jerosolimitana', *RHC Or.*4.3–111.

Bartolf of Nangis, 'Gesta Francorum expugnantium Iherusalem', *RHC Oc.* 3.xxxvi–xxxvii, 489–543.

Bec, P., *La Lyrique française au moyen âge (XIIe-XIIIe s.)* 2 vols (Paris, 1977–8).

Belgrano, L. T., 'Frammento di poemetto sincrono per la conquista di Almeria nel MCXVII', *Atti della Società Ligure di Storia Patria* 19 (1888), pp. 401–2.

Bernard of Clairvaux: for editions of individual crusade letters by Bernard, see: to Brescia, A. Theiner, *Baronii Annales ecclesiastici* 18 (Bar-le-Duc, 1869), pp. 646–7; to Cologne, J. Greven, 'Die Kölnfahrt Bernhards von Clairvaux', *Annalen des historisches Vereins für den Niederrhein* 120 (1932), pp. 1–48, with the text at pp. 44–8; to the Hospitallers, J. Leclercq, 'Un document sur S. Bernard et la seconde croisade', *Revue Mabillon* 43 (1953), pp. 1–4.

Bernard of Clairvaux, 'De consideratione ad Eugenium papam', in *Sancti Bernardi Opera*, ed. J. Leclercq and H. Rochais, 8 vols (Rome, 1955–77), 3.379–473.

Bernard of Clairvaux, 'Epistolae', in *Sancti Bernardi Opera*, ed. J. Leclercq and H. Rochais, 8 vols (Rome, 1955–77), vols 7–8; many translated in *The Letters of Saint Bernard of Clairvaux*, new edn, tr. B. S. James, introduction by B. M. Kienzle (Stroud, 1998).

Bernard of Clairvaux, 'Liber ad milites Templi de laude novae militiae', in *Sancti Bernardi Opera*, ed. J. Leclercq and H. Rochais, 8 vols (Rome, 1955–77), 3.212–39.

Bernard of Pisa, 'Epistolae' in *PL* 182.547–9.

Bibliotheca Cluniacensis, ed. M. Marrier and A. Quercetan (Matiscone, 1915), col. 1352; tr. H. J. Tanner, 'In His Brothers' Shadow: The Crusading Career and Reputation of Count Eustace III of Boulogne', in *The Crusades: Other Experiences, Alternate Perspectives*, ed. K. I. Semaan (Binghampton NY, 2003), pp. 89–90.

Boso, *Le Liber Pontificalis*, ed. L. Duchesne, 3 vols (Paris, 1955–7).

Burchard of Worms, 'Decretum', *PL* 140, cols 537–1057.

Caffaro, 'Annales Ianuenses', ed. L. T. Belgrano, in *Fonti per la Storia d'Italia* 11 (Genoa, 1890), pp. 3–75.

Caffaro, 'De liberatione civitatum orientis', ed. L. T. Belgrano, in *Fonti per la Storia d'Italia* 11 (Genoa, 1890), pp. 97–124.

Caffaro, 'Cafari ystoria captionis Almarie et Turtuose ann. 1147 et 1148', ed. L. T. Belgrano, in *Fonti per la Storia d'Italia* 11 (Genoa, 1890), pp. 77–91; tr. J. B. Williams, 'The Making of a Crusade: The Genoese anti-Muslim Attacks in Spain, 1146–1148', *Journal of Medieval History* 23 (1997), pp. 48–53.

Calixtus II, *Bullaire*, ed. U. Robert, 2 vols (Paris, 1891).

Canso d'Antioca, ed. and tr. C. Sweetenham and L. M. Paterson (Aldershot, 2003).

Cartulaire de l'abbaye d'Afflighem, ed. E. de Marneffe (Louvain, 1894–1901).

Cartulaire de l'abbaye de Noyers, ed. C. Chevalier (Tours, 1872).

Cartulaire de l'abbaye de Saint-Martin de Pontoise, ed. J. Depoin (Pontoise, 1885).

Cartulaire de l'abbaye de Saint-Père de Chartres, ed. B. E. C. Guerard, 2 vols (Paris, 1840).

Cartulaire de l'abbaye de Vigeois en Limousin (954–1167), ed. M. de Montégut (Limoges, 1907).

Cartulaire de la Commanderie de Richerenches de l'ordre du Temple (1136–1214), ed. M. de Ripert-Monclar (Avignon, 1907).

Cartulaire de Montier-la-Celle, ed. C. Lalore (Paris, 1890).

Cartulaire de Notre-Dame de Josaphat, ed. C. Metais (Chartres, 1911).

Cartulaire de Saint Lambert de Liège, ed. S. Bormans and E. Schoolmeesters, 6 vols (Brussels, 1893–1933).

Cartulaire de Saint Vincent de Mâcon, ed. M.-C. Ragut (Mâcon, 1864).

Cartulaire des Templiers de Douzens, ed. P. Gérard and E. Magnou (Paris, 1965).

Cartulaire du chapitre cathédral Saint-Étienne d'Agde, ed. R. Foreville (Paris, 1995).

Cartulaire du prieuré de Saint-Étienne de Vignory, ed. J. d'Arbaumont (Langres, 1882).

Cartulaire généralé de l'Yonne, ed. M.Quantin (Auxerre, 1854–60).

Cartulaire général de l'ordre du Temple 1119?-1150, ed. A. d'Albon (Paris, 1913).

Cartulaires de l'abbaye de Molesme, ed. J. Laurent, 2 vols (1907–11).

Cartulaires des abbayes de Tulle et de Roc-Amadour, ed. J.-B. Champeval (Brive, 1903).

Cartulaires du chapitre de l'église métropolitaine Sainte-Marie d'Auch, ed. C. Lacave La Plagne Barris (Paris, Auch, 1899).

Cartulaires inédits de la Saintonge, ed. T. Grasilier, 2 vols (Niort, 1871).

'Casus monasterii Petrishusensis', *MGH* 20.621–83.

Cerbanus Cerbani, 'Translatio mirifici martyris Isidori a Chio in civitatem Venetam', *RHC Oc.* 5.321–34.

Chanson d'Antioche, ed. S. Duparc-Quioc, Documents relatifs à l'histoire des croisades XI, 2 vols (Paris, 1977–8).

Chartes du Bourbonnais, 918–1522, ed. J. Monicat and B. de Fourneaux (Moulins, 1952).

'Chronica monasterii Casinensis', *MGH* 34.458–607.

'Chronicon Laetiense', *MGH* 14.487–582.

'Chronicon Malleacense', *RHGF* 12.400–8.

'Chronicon S. Andreae Castri Cameracesii', *MGH* 7.526–50.

'Chronicon S. Martini Turonensis', *RHGF* 12.461–78.

'Chronicon Senonense sanctae Columbae', *RHGF* 12.287–9.

Chronique de Morigny (1095–1152), ed. L. Mirot (Paris, 1909).

Chronique de Saint-Pierre-le-Vif de Sens, dite de Clarius, ed. and tr. R.-H. Bautier and M. Gilles (Paris, 1979).

Chronique et cartulaire de l'abbaye de Bergues Saint-Winnoc, ed. A. Pruvost (Bruges, 1875–8).

'Chronographus Corbiensis', ed. P. Jaffé in *Bibliotheca rerum Germanicarum 1, Monumenta Corbiensia* (Berlin, 1864), pp. 43–65.

Conrad III, *Die Urkunden Konrads III. und seines Sohnes Heinrich*, ed. F. Hausmann, *MGH DD* 9 (Vienna, 1969).

Corpus inscriptionorum medii aevi Liguriae III. Genova, centro storico, ed. A. Silva, Collana storica di fonti e studi, vol. 52 (Genoa, 1987), pp. 130–1; tr. J. B. Williams, 'The Making of a Crusade: The Genoese anti-Muslim Attacks in Spain, 1146–1148', *Journal of Medieval History* 23 (1997), pp. 41–2.

Crusade Charters, 1138–1270, ed. and tr. C. K. Slack (Tempe AR, 2001).

Czerny, A. (ed.), 'Das älteste Todtenbuch des Stiftes St Florian', *Archiv für Österreichische Geschichte* 56 (1878), pp. 257–368.

Decrees of the Ecumenical Councils, ed. and tr. N. J. Tanner, 2 vols (New York, 1991). All references are to Volume 1.

De expugnatione Lyxbonensi, ed. and tr. C. W. David, with new foreword and bibliography by J. P. Phillips (New York, 2001).

'De expugnatione Scalabis', *Portugaliae Monumenta Historica, I, Scriptores* (Lisbon, 1856), pp. 94–5.

De oorkonden der graven van Vlaanderen (Juli 1128–17 Januari 1168) II. Uitgave Band I, ed. T. de Hemptinne and A. Verhulst, with L. De Mey (Brussels, 1988).

Die Traditionen des Hochstifts des Klosters S. Emmeran, ed. J. Widemann (Munich, 1943).

Die Traditionen des Klosters Tegernsee, 1003–1242, ed. P. Acht (Munich, 1952).

Die Traditionen des Klosters Weihenstephan, ed. B. Uhl (Munich, 1972).

Die Traditionen des Klosters Wessobrunn, ed. R. Höppl (Munich, 1984).

Die Traditionen des Kollegiatstifts St Kastulus in Moosburg, ed. K. Höflinger (Munich, 1994).

Die Traditionen, Urkunden und Urbare des Klosters Neustift bei Freising, ed. H.-J. Busley (Munich, 1961).

Documentos correspondientes al reinado de Sancho Ramírez, ed. J. Sarrullana and E. Ibarra, 2 vols (Zaragoza, 1904–13).

Documentos para el studio de la reconquista y repoblación del valle del Ebro, ed. J. M. Lacarra, 2 vols (Zaragoza, 1982–5).

Ekkehard of Aura, 'Chronicon Universale', *MGH* 6.33–265.

Ekkehard of Aura, 'Hiersolymitana', *RHC Oc.* 5.ii–xvi, 1–40.

Ephraim of Bonn, 'Sefer Zekhirah, or The Book of Remembrance', in *The Jews and the Crusaders: The Hebrew Chronicles of the First and Second Crusades*, ed. and tr. S. Eidelberg (Madison WI, 1977), pp. 117–33.

'Epistola A. dapiferi militiae Templi', *RHGF* 15.540–1.

Eugenius III, 'Epistolae et privilegia', *PL* 180. 1013–1614.

Eugenius III, 'Epistolae', *RHGF* 15.426–83.

Eugenius III, 'Quantum Praedecessores', in R. Grosse, 'Überlegungen zum Kreuzzugsaufruf Eugens III. von 1145/46. Mit einer Neuedition von JL 8876', *Francia* 18 (1991), pp. 85–92.

'Fragment d'un cartulaire de l'ordre de Saint-Lazare en Terre Sainte', ed. C. de Marsy, *Archives de l'Orient Latin* 2 (Paris, 1884), pp. 121–57.

'Fragmentum historicum ex veteri membrana de tributo Floriacensibus imposito', *RHGF* 12.94–5.

Fulcher of Chartres, *Historia Hierosolymitana (1095–1127)*, ed. H. Hagenmeyer (Heidelberg, 1913); translated as *A History of the Expedition to Jerusalem, 1095–1127*, tr. F. R. Ryan, introduction by H. S. Fink (Knoxville TN, 1969).

Galbert of Bruges, *De multro, traditione et occisione gloriosi Karoli comitis Flandriarum*, ed. J. Rider, *CCCM* 131 (Turnhout, 1994); translated as *The Murder of Count Charles the Good*, tr. J. B. Ross (New York, 1958).

Gelasius II, 'Epistolae et privilegia', *PL* 163. 487–513.

Geoffrey, bishop of Chartres, elegy: 'Gaufridi II episcopi Carnotensis elogium', *RHGF* 14.333.

Geoffrey, bishop of Chartres, 'Epistola Gaufredi', *PL* 185. 410–16.

Geoffrey of Monmouth, *Historia Regum Brittaniae*, ed. A. Griscom and R. Ellis Jones (London, 1929); tr. L. Thorpe, *The History of the Kings of Britain* (London, 1966).

Geoffrey of Vigeois, 'Chronica', *RHGF* 12.421–51.

Gerald of Wales, *The Autobiography of Giraldus Cambrensis*, ed. and tr. H. E. Butler (London, 1937).

'Gesta abbatum Lobbiensium', *MGH* 21.307–33.

Gesta Francorum et aliorum Hierosolimitanorum, ed. and tr. R. Mynors, introduction by R. M. T. Hill (London, 1962).

Gilo of Paris, *Historia vie Hierosolimitane*, ed. and tr. C. W. Grocock and J. E. Siberry (Oxford, 1997).

Gratian, 'Decretum', in *Corpus Iuris Canonici*, ed. A. Friedberg, 2 vols (Leipzig, 1879–81).

Gregory VIII, 'Audita Tremendi', in Ansbert, 'Historia de expeditione Friderici imperatoris: Quellen zur Geschichte des Kreuzzugs Kaiser Friedrichs I', ed. A. Chroust, *MGH Scriptores rerum Germanicarum, nova seria*, 5 (1928), pp. 6–10.

Gregory the Priest, *Armenia and the Crusades: 10th to 12th Centuries*, tr. A. E. Dostaurian (Lanham ML, 1993), pp. 241–80.

Guibert of Nogent, *Dei gesta per Francos*, ed. R. B. C. Huygens, *CCCM* 127A (Turnhout, 1996); translated as *The Deeds of God through the Franks*, tr. R. Levine (Woodbridge, 1997).

Guibert of Nogent, *De vita sua*, ed. and tr. E.-R. Labande (Paris, 1981).

Guiragos of Kantzag, 'Chronicle', *RHC Arm.* 1.413–30.

Hagenmeyer, H. (ed.), *Epistolae et chartae ad primi belli sacri spectantes: Die Kreuzzugsbriefe aus den Jahren 1088–1100* (Innsbruck, 1901).

Hamburgisches Urkundenbuch, ed. J. M. Lappenberg *et al.*, 4 vols (Hamburg, 1907–67).

Helmold of Bosau, *Chronica Slavorum*, ed. and tr. H. Stoob (Darmstadt, 1963); tr. F. J. Tschan, *The Chronicle of the Slavs* (New York, 1935).

Henry II, 'Die Urkunden Heinrichs II und Arduins', ed. H. Bresslau (Berlin, 1957), *MGH DD* 3.

Henry IV, 'Die Urkunden Heinrichs IV', ed D. von Gladiss and A. Gawlik, *MGH DD* 6: *Heinrici IV Diplomata*, 2 vols (Berlin, Weimar, Hanover, 1941–78).

Henry VI, *Urkunden*, in *Die Urkunden Konrads III. und seines Sohnes Heinrich*, ed. F. Hausmann, *MGH DD* 9 (Vienna, 1969), pp. 519–32.

Henry of Huntingdon, *Historia Anglorum*, ed. and tr. D. E. Greenway (Oxford, 1996).

'Historia Belli Sacri', *RHC Oc.* 3.xiii–xvii, 165–229.

Historia Compostellana, ed. E. Falque Rey, *CCCM* 70 (Turnhout, 1988).

'Historia Ducum Venetorum', *MGH* 14.72–89.

'Historia gloriosi regis Ludovici VII, filii Ludovici grossi', *RHGF* 12.124–33.

'Historia Monasterii Aquicinctini', *MGH* 14.588.

'Historiae Tornacenses partim ex Herimanni libris excerptae', *MGH* 14.327–52.

Hugh, archbishop of Edessa, 'Epistola', *PL* 155. 477–80.

Hugh of Poitiers, *Monumenta Vizeliacensia: Textes relatifs à l'histoire de l'abbaye de Vézelay*, ed. R. B. C. Huygens, 2 vols, *CCCM* 42 (Turnhout, 1976–80); translated as *The Vézelay Chronicle*, tr. J. Scott and J. O. Ward (Binghampton NY, 1992).

Ibn al-Athir, 'Extrait du Kamel-Althevaykh', *RHC Or.* 1.189–744.

Ibn al-Athir, *The Chronicle of Ibn al-Athir for the Crusading Period from al-Kamil fi'l-Ta'rikh. Part 1: 491–541 1097–1146*, tr. D. S. Richards (Aldershot, 2006).

Ibn Jubayr, *The Travels of Ibn Jubayr*, tr. R. J. C. Broadhurst (London, 1952).

Ibn al-Qalanisi, *The Damascus Chronicles of the Crusades*, ed. and tr. H. A. R. Gibb (London, 1932).

Innocent II, 'Epistolae et privilegia', *PL* 179.21–686.

Ivo of Chartres, 'Decretum', *PL* 161.47–1022.

Ivo of Chartres, 'Epistolae', *PL* 162.11–288.

Jerusalem Pilgrimage, 1099–1185, ed. and tr. J. Wilkinson, Hakluyt Society, Second Series, Vol. 167 (London, 1988).

John Kinnamos, *The Deeds of John and Manuel Comnenus*, tr. C. M. Brand (New York, 1976).

John of Hexham, *Historia*, in *Opera Omnia*, ed. T. Arnold, 2 vols, Rolls Series 75 (London, 1882–5), 2.284–332.

John of Joinville, *Vie de Saint Louis*, ed. and tr. J. Monfrin (Paris, 1995).

John of Salisbury, *Historia Pontificalis*, ed. and tr. M. Chibnall (London, 1956).

Kölner Schreinsurkunden des zwölften Jahrhunderts. Quellen zur Rechts und Wirthschaftsgeschichte der Stadt Köln, ed. R. Hoeniger, 2 vols (Bonn, 1884–94).

Lambert of Ardres, 'Historia comitum Ghisensium', *MGH* 24.550–642; tr. L. Shopkow, *The History of the Counts of Guines and Lords of Ardres* (Philadelphia PA, 2001).

Leclercq, J. (ed.), 'Un Document sur saint Bernard et la seconde croisade', *Revue Mabillon* 43 (1953), pp. 1–4.

Les chansons de croisade avec leurs mélodies, ed. J. Bédier and P. Aubry (Paris, 1909).

Liber instrumentorum memorialium: Cartulaire des Guillems de Montpellier, ed. A. Germain (Montpellier, 1884).

Liber iurium reipublicae Genuensis, ed. E. Ricotti, *Historiae patriae monumenta*, vol. 7, part 1 (Turin, 1854).

Liber maiolichinus de gestis Pisanorum illustribus, ed. C. Calisse, *Fonti per la Storia d'Italia* 29 (Rome, 1904).

Libro preto da Sé de Coimbra, ed. A. da Costa, L. Ventura and M. Teresa Veloso, 3 vols (Coimbra, 1977–9).

'Lisbon Letter', text edited by S. B. Edgington in 'The Lisbon Letter of the Second Crusade', *Historical Research* 69 (1996) pp. 336–9; translated in 'Albert of Aachen, Saint Bernard and the Second Crusade', SCSC, pp. 61–7.

Louis VII, 'Epistolae', *RHGF* 16.1–170.

Louis VII, *Études sur les Actes de Louis VII*, ed. A. Luchaire (Paris, 1885).

Lucius III, 'Epistolae et privilegia', *PL* 179, cols 823–936.

Lucius III, 'Epistolae et privilegia', *PL* 201, cols 1069–379.

Mainz Anonymous, tr. R. Chazan, *European Jewry and the First Crusade* (Berkeley CA, 1987), pp. 225–42.

Manuel Comnenus, Letter to Louis, in Louis VII, '*Epistolae*', *RHGF* 16.9–10.

Manuel Comnenus, Letter to Eugenius III, ed. W. Ohnsorge, 'Ein Beitrag zur Geschichte Manuels I von Byzanz', in *Festschrift für Albert Brackmann dargebracht von Freunden, Kollegen und Schülern*, ed. L. Santifaller (Weimar, 1931), pp. 391–3.

Marcabru: A Critical Edition, ed. S. Gaunt, R. Harvey and L. M. Paterson (Cambridge, 2000).

Matthew of Edessa, *Armenia and the Crusades: 10th to 12th Centuries*, tr. A. E. Dostaurian (Lanham ML, 1993), pp. 1–239.

Michael the Syrian, *Chronique de Michel le Syrien, patriarche jacobite d'Antioche (1166–99)*, ed. and tr. J.-B. Chabot, 4 vols (Paris, 1899–1910). All references to volume 3.

Nersēs Šnorhali, 'Lament on Edessa', tr. T. M. van Lint, in *East and West in the Crusader States II: Context, Contacts, Confrontations*, ed. K. Ciggaar and H. Teule, Orientalia Lovaniensia Analecta 92 (Leuven, 1999), pp. 49–105.

Nicholas of Clairvaux, 'Epistolae', *PL* 182.671–74.

Niketas Choniates, *O City of Byzantium – The Annals of Niketas Choniates*, tr. H. J. Magoulias (Detroit, 1984).

Odo of Deuil, *De profectione Ludovici VII in Orientem*, ed. and tr. V. G. Berry (New York, 1948).

Orderic Vitalis, *The Ecclesiastical History*, ed. and tr. M. Chibnall, 6 vols (Oxford, 1969–80).

Otto of Freising, *Chronica sive historia de duabus civitatibus*, ed. A. Hofmeister and W. Lammers, tr. A. Schmidt (Darmstadt, 1961); translated as *The Two Cities*, tr. C. C. Mierow (New York, 1928).

Otto of Freising, *Gesta Frederici seu rectius Chronica*, ed. G. Waitz, B. Simson and F.-J. Schmale, tr. A. Schmidt (Darmstadt, 1965); translated as *The Deeds of Frederick Barbarossa*, tr. C. C. Mierow (New York, 1953).

Ottonian Germany: The Chronicon of Thietmar of Merseburg, tr. D. A. Warner (Manchester, 2001).

Papsturkunden für Kirchen im Heiligen Lande, ed. R. Hiestand, Vorarbeiten zum Oriens Pontificius III (Göttingen, 1985).

Papsturkunden für Templer und Johanniter, ed. R. Hiestand, Vorarbeiten zum Oriens Pontificius I–II (Göttingen, 1972–84).

Papsturkunden in Florenz, ed. W. Wiederhold (Göttingen, 1901).

Papsturkunden in Frankreich, ed. W. Wiederhold (Göttingen, 1907).

Papsturkunden in Sizilien, ed. P. Kehr (Göttingen, 1899).

Papsturkunden in Spanien, I: Katalonien, ed. P. Kehr (Berlin, 1926).

Papsturkunden in Spanien, II: Navarra und Aragon, ed. P. Kehr (Berlin, 1928).

Paschal II, 'Epistolae et privilegia', *PL* 163, cols 31–448.

Peter the Deacon, 'Chronica monasterii Casinensis', *MGH* 7.727–844.

Peter the Venerable, 'De laude dominici sepulchri', in G. Constable, 'Petri Venerabilis Sermones Tres', *Revue Bénédictine* 64 (1954), pp. 232–54.

Peter the Venerable, *Liber contra sectam sive haeresim Saracenorum*, ed. J. Kritzeck, *Peter the Venerable and Islam* (Princeton NJ, 1964), pp. 220–91.

Peter the Venerable, *Letters*, ed. G. Constable, 2 vols (Cambridge MA, 1967).

Peter Tudebode, *Historia de Hierosolymitano Itinere*, ed. J. H. and L. L. Hill, Documents relatifs à l'histoire des croisades XII (Paris, 1977); tr. J. H. and L. L. Hill (Philadelphia PA, 1974).

Peters, E. (ed and tr.), *The First Crusade: The Chronicle of Fulcher of Chartres and Other Source Materials*, 2nd edn (Philadelphia PA, 1998).

'Pilgrimage of Etheria', in *The Crusades: A Reader*, ed. S. J. Allen and E. Amt (Peterborough, Ontario, 2003), pp. 3–4.

Pitra, J., 'De itinere S.Bernardi', *PL* 185.1797–832.

'Premier cartulaire de l'abbaye d'Absie', *Archives Historiques de Poitou* 25 (1895).

'Pseudo-Turpin', in *Liber Sancti Jacobi: Codex Calixtinus*, tr. A. Moraljo, C. Torres, J. Feo and X. Carro Otero (Santiago de Compostela, 1999).

Quadripartitus, ed. F. Liebermann (Halle, 1892).

Ralph of Caen, 'Gesta Tancredi in expeditione Hierosolymitana', *RHC Oc.* 3.587–716; translated as *The Gesta Tancredi of Ralph of Caen: A History of the Normans on the First Crusade*, tr. B. S. and D. S. Bachrach (Aldershot, 2005).

Ralph of Diceto, 'Ymagines Historiarum', in *Opera*, ed. W. Stubbs, 2 vols, Rolls Series 68 (London, 1876).

Raymond of Aguilers, *Historia Francorum qui ceperunt Iherusalem*, ed. J. H. and L. L. Hill, Documents relatifs à l'histoire des croisades IX (Paris, 1969); tr. J. H. and L. L. Hill (Philadelphia PA, 1968).

Recueil d'annales angevines et vendômoises, ed. L. Halphen (Paris, 1903).

Recueil de chartes et documents de Saint-Martin-des-Champs, ed. J. Depoin, 5 vols (Paris, 1912–21).

Recueil des chartes de l'abbaye de Cluny, ed. A. Bernard and A. Bruel, 6 vols (Paris, 1876–1903).

Recueil des chartes de l'abbaye de Saint-Benoît-sur-Loire, ed. M. Prou and A. Vidier, Documents publiés par la Société historique et archéologique du Gatinais, 5 (Paris, 1900–7).

'Regesta comitum Sabaudiae', ed. D. Carruti, *Biblioteca Storica Italiana*, 5 (Turin, 1889).

Regesta pontificum Romanorum, ed. P. Jaffé *et al.* 2 vols (Leipzig, 1885–8).

Regesta regni Hierosolymitani, 1097–1291, ed. R. Röhricht (Innsbruck, 1893).

Richard of Hexham, 'De gestis regis Stephani et de bello Standardi', in *Chronicles of the Reigns of Stephen, Henry II and Richard I*, ed. R. Howlett, Rolls Series 82 (1884–9), 3.139–78.

Richard of Poitiers, 'Chronicon', *RHGF* 12.411–21.

Robert of Ely, 'Vita Kanuti ducis altera', *MGH* 29.11–20.

Robert of Rheims, 'Historia Hierosolymitana', *RHC Oc.* 3.717–882; translated as *Robert the Monk's History of the First Crusade*, tr. C. Sweetenham (Aldershot, 2005).

Robert of Torigny, 'Chronicon', *MGH* 6.475–535.

Rodríguez de Diego, J. L., *El tumbo del monasterio cisterciense de la Espina* (Valladolid, 1982).

Romauld of Salerno, 'Annales', *MGH* 19.387–461.

The Rule of the Templars, tr. J. Upton-Ward (Woodbridge, 1992).

St Vincent, 'Foundation Document of the Monastery of St Vincent', ed. and tr. A. A. Nascimento, in *A Conquista de Lisboa aos Mouros: Relato de um Cruzado*, introduction by M. J. V. Branco (Lisbon, 2001), pp. 177–201.

Samuel of Ani, 'Extrait de la Chronographie de Samuel d'Ani', *RHC Arm.* 1.447–68.

Saxo Grammaticus, *Saxonis Gesta Danorum*, ed. J. Olrik and H. Raeder, 2 vols (Copenhagen, 1931–57).

'Schenkungsbuch der ehemaligen Gefürsteten Probstei Berchtesgaden', *Schenkungsbücher Bayerischer Klöster*, Vol. 1, ed. F. M. Wittman and K. A. Muffat (Munich, 1856).

Sibt al-Jauzi, 'Mirror of the Times', tr. F. Gabrieli, in *Arab Historians of the Crusades* (London, 1969).

Sigebert of Gembloux, 'Chronica', *MGH* 6.268–374.

Sigebert of Gembloux, 'continuatio Praemonstratensis', *MGH* 6.447–56.

Sigebert of Gembloux, 'continuatio Valcellensis', *MGH* 6.458–60.

Snorri Sturlusson, *Heimskringla*, tr. L. M. Hollander (Austin TX, 1964).

Song of Roland, ed. F. Whitehead (Oxford, 1947).

Spreckelmeyer, G. (ed.), *Das Kreuzzugsleid des lateinischen Mittelalters* (Munich, 1924).

Suger, *Abbot Suger on the Abbey Church of St Denis and its Art Treasures*, ed. and tr. E. Panofsky, 2nd edn (Princeton, 1979).

Suger, 'Epistolae', *RHGF* 15.483–532.

Suger, *Vie de Louis VI le Gros*, ed. and tr. H. Waquet (Paris, 1964); translated as *The Deeds of Louis the Fat*, tr. R. C. Cusimano and J. Moorhead (Washington DC, 1992).

Suger, 'Vie de Suger', in *Oeuvres complètes de Suger*, ed. A. Lecoy de la Marche (Paris, 1867), pp. 239–317.

Tiroler Urkundenbuch, ed. F. Huter (Innsbruck, 1937).

'Tractatus de reliquiis S. Stephani Cluniacum delatis', *RHC Or.* 5.317–20.

Translatio S. Mamantis, in *Acta Sanctorum quotquot toto orbe coluntur*, ed. Société des Bollandistes 70 vols so far (Antwerp, Brussels and Tonglerloe, 1643ff). Augusti III pp. 440–6.

Urban II, 'Epistolae et privilegia', *PL* 151.283–558.

Urkundenbuch der Stadt Strassburg, ed. W. Wiegand (Strasbourg, 1879).

Urkundenbuch des Erzstifts Magdeburg (937–1192), ed. F. Israel and W. Möllenberg (Magdeburg, 1937).

Urkundenbuch des Herzogthums Steiermark; Band I: 798–1192, ed. J. Zahn (Graz, 1875).

Urkundenbuch des Landes ob der Enns, 11 vols (Vienna, 1852–83).

Urkundenbuch für die Geschichte des Niederrheins, 799–1200, ed. T. J. Lacomblet, Vol. 1 (Düsseldorf, 1840).

Usama Ibn Munqidh, *An Arab–Syrian Gentleman and Warrior in the Period of the Crusades*, tr. P. K. Hitti (New York, 1929).

Vincent of Prague, 'Annales', *MGH* 17.654–83.

'Vita Prima S. Bernardi', *PL* 185, cols 225–466.

Le Voyage de Charlemagne à Jérusalem et à Constantinople, ed. M. Tyssens (Ghent, 1977).

Walter of Thérouanne, 'Walteri vita karoli comitis flandriae', *MGH* 12.537–61.

Walter the Chancellor, *Galterii cancellarii, Bella Antiochena*, ed. H. Hagenmeyer (Innsbruck, 1896); tr. T. S. Asbridge and S. B. Edgington, *Walter the Chancellor's The Antiochene Wars* (Aldershot, 1999).

Wibald of Stavelot, 'Epistolae', *Bibliotheca rerum Germanicarum*, ed. P. Jaffé, 6 vols (Berlin, 1864–73), Vol. 1.

William of Grassegals: Dedication to Louis VII: *RHC Oc.* 3.317–18.

William of Malmesbury, *Gesta Regum Anglorum*, ed. and tr. R. A. B. Mynors, R. M. Thomson and M. Winterbottom, 2 vols (Oxford, 1998–99).

William of Malmesbury, *De Gestis Pontificum Anglorum*, ed. N. E. S. A. Hamilton, Rolls Series 52 (London, 1870).

William of Newburgh, 'Historia rerum Anglicarum', in *Chronicles of the Reigns of Stephen, Henry II and Richard I*, ed. R. Howlett, 4 vols, Rolls Series 82 (London, 1884–9), 1.1–408; 2.409–53.

William of Poitiers, *The Gesta Guillelmi of William of Poitiers*, ed. and tr. R. H. C. Davis and M. Chibnall (Oxford, 1998).

William of Puylaurens, *Chronique*, ed. J. Duvernoy (Paris, 1976).
William of Tyre, *Chronicon*, ed. R. B. C. Huygens, 2 vols (continuous pagination), *CCCM* 63, 63A (Turnhout, 1986); translated as *A History of Deeds Done beyond the Sea*, tr. E. A. Babcock and A. C. Krey, 2 vols (New York, 1948).
Württembergisches Urkundenbuch, 11 vols (Stuttgart, 1849–1913).

SECONDARY WORKS

Acht, P., 'Die Gesandtschaft König Konrads III. an Papst Eugens III. in Dijon', *Historisches Jahrbuch* 74 (1955), pp. 668–73.
Amt, E., *The Accession of Henry II in England: Royal Government Restored, 1149–59* (Woodbridge, 1994).
Angold, M., *The Byzantine Empire, 1025–1204: A Political History*, 2nd edn (London, 1997).
Bachrach, B. S., 'Crusader Logistics: From Victory at Nicaea to Resupply at Dorylaion', *Logistics of Warfare*, pp. 43–62.
Barber, M., *The Two Cities: Medieval Europe 1050–1320* (London, 1992).
Barber, M., *The New Knighthood: A History of the Order of the Temple* (Cambridge, 1994).
Barber, R., 'Eleanor of Aquitaine and the Media', in *The World of Eleanor of Aquitaine: Literature and Society in Southern France between the Eleventh and Thirteenth Centuries*, ed. M. G. Bull and C. Léglu (Woodbridge, 2005), pp. 13–28.
Barnes, H., and M. Whittow, 'Medieval Castles: Antioch-on-the-Maender', *Anatolian Archaeology* 4 (1998), pp. 17–18.
Barthélemy, D., *Les deux ages de la seigneurie banale. Pouvoir et société dans la terre des sires de Coucy (xie–xiie s.)* (Paris, 1984).
Bartlett, R., *The Making of Europe: Conquest, Colonisation and Cultural Change, 950–1350* (London, 1993).
Barton, S., 'A Forgotten Crusade: Alfonso VII of León-Castile's Campaign for Jaen (1148)', *Historical Research* 73 (2000), pp. 312–20.
Barton, S., 'From Tyrants to Soldiers of Christ: the Nobility of Twelfth-Century León-Castile and the Struggle against Islam', *Nottingham Medieval Studies* 44 (2000), pp. 28–48.
Bautier, G., 'L'envoi de la relique de la vraie croix à Notre-Dame de Paris en 1120', *Bibliothèque de l'école de Chartes* 129 (1971), pp. 387–97.
Baylé, M, 'Le décor sculpté de Saint-Georges-de-Boscherville: Quelques questions de style et iconographie', *Anglo-Norman Studies* 8 (1985), pp. 27–45.
Bazin, J.-L., *Brancion, les seigneurs, la paroisse, la ville* (Maçon, 1908).
Beaumont Jr, A. A., 'Albert of Aachen and the County of Edessa', in *The Crusades and Other Historical Essays Presented to Dana C. Munro*, ed. L. J. Paetow (New York, 1928), pp. 101–38.
Beech, G., 'Aquitanians and Flemings in the Refoundation of Bardney Abbey (Lincolnshire) in the Later Eleventh Century', *Haskins Society Journal* 1 (1989), pp. 73–90.
Beech, G., 'A Little-Known Armenian Historian of the Crusading Period: Gregory the Priest (1136–62)', in *Truth as Gift: Studies in Honor of John R. Sommerfeldt*, ed. M. Dutton, D. M. LaCorte and P. Lockey (Kalamazoo MI, 2004), pp. 119–43.
Bennett, M., 'Military Aspects of the Conquest of Lisbon, 1147', in SCSC, pp. 71–89.
Bennett, M., 'Virile Latins, Effeminate Greeks and Strong Women: Gender Definitions on Crusade', in *Gendering the Crusades*, ed. S. B. Edgington and S. Lambert (Cardiff, 2001), pp. 16–30.
Benton, J. F., 'The Revenue of Louis VII', *Speculum* 42 (1967), pp. 84–91.
Bernhardi, W., *Konrad III* (Leipzig, 1883).
Berry, V. G., 'Peter the Venerable and the Crusades', in *Petrus Venerablilis, 1156–1956. Studies Commemorating the Eighth Centenary of his Death*, ed. G. Constable and J. Kritzeck, Studia Anselmiana 40 (Rome, 1956), pp. 141–62.
Berry, V. G., 'The Second Crusade', in *A History of the Crusades*, 6 vols, ed. K. M. Setton (Wisconsin, 1969–89), 1.463–511.
Biddle, M., 'Seasonal Festivals and Residence: Winchester, Westminster and Gloucester in the Tenth to Twelfth Centuries', *Anglo-Norman Studies* 8 (1986), pp. 51–63.
Blomqvist, N., *The Discovery of the Baltic, 1075–1225* (Leiden, 2005).
Boas, A. J., *Jerusalem in the Time of the Crusades* (London, 2001).

Bolòs, J., 'Changes and Survival: The Territory of Lleida (Catalonia) after the Twelfth-Century Conquest', *Journal of Medieval History* 27 (2001), pp. 313–29.

Bolton, B., 'The Cistercians and the Aftermath of the Second Crusade', in SCC, pp. 131–40.

Borges, G. F., 'Saint Bernard et le Portugal: la legénde et l'histoire', *Mélanges Saint Bernard* (Dijon, 1953), pp. 134–50.

Bouchard, C. B., *Sword, Miter and Cloister: Nobility and the Church in Burgundy, 980–1198* (Cornell NY, 1987).

Bouchard, C. B., *Holy Entrepreneurs* (Ithaca NY 1991).

Bouchard, C. B., 'Eleanor's Divorce from Louis: The Uses of Consanguinity', in *Eleanor of Aquitaine: Lord and Lady*, ed. B. Wheeler and J. C. Parsons (London, 2002), pp. 223–35.

Bouton, J., 'Bernard et les monastères bénédictins non clunisiens', in *Bernard de Clairvaux* (Paris, 1953), pp. 219–49.

Brown, E. A. R. and M. W. Cothren, 'The Twelfth-Century Crusading Window of the Abbey of Saint Denis', *Journal of the Warburg and Courtauld Institutes* 49 (1986), pp. 1–40.

Brundage, J. A., 'An Errant Crusader: Stephen of Blois', *Traditio* 16 (1960), pp. 380–95.

Brundage, J. A., 'St Bernard and the Jurists', in SCC, pp. 25–33.

Brundage, J. A., 'Crusaders and Jurists: The Legal Consequences of Crusader Status', in *Le Concile de Clermont de 1095 et l'appel à la croisade*, ed. A Vauchez (Rome, 1997), pp. 140–48.

Bull, M. G., *Knightly Piety and the Lay Response to the First Crusade: The Limousin and Gascony, c.970–c.1130* (Oxford, 1993).

Bull, M. G., 'The Capetian Monarchy and the Early Crusade Movement: Hugh of Vermandois and Louis VII', *Nottingham Medieval Studies* 40 (1996), pp. 25–45.

Bull, M. G., 'Overlapping and Competing Identities in the Frankish First Crusade', in *Le Concile de Clermont de 1095 et l'appel à la croisade*, ed. A. Vauchez (Rome, 1997), pp. 195–211.

Bull, M. G., 'The Diplomatic of the First Crusade', in *The First Crusade: Origins and Impact*, ed. J. P. Phillips (Manchester, 1997), pp. 35–56.

Byrne, E. H., 'The Genoese Colonies in Syria', in *The Crusades and Other Historical Essays Presented to D. C. Munro*, ed. L. J. Paetow (New York, 1928), pp. 139–82.

Cahen, C., *La Syrie du nord à l'époque des croisades* (Paris, 1940).

Cahen, C., *The Formation of Turkey: The Seljukid Sultanate of Rūm: Eleventh to Fourteenth Century*, tr. P. M. Holt (Harlow, 2001).

Caille, J., 'Les seigneurs de Narbonne dans le conflit Toulouse-Barcelone au xiie s.', *Annales de Midi* 97 (1985), pp. 227–44.

Camille, M., *The Gothic Idol: Ideology and Image-Making in Medieval Art* (Cambridge, 1989).

Chalandon, F., *Histoire de la domination Normande en Italie et en Sicile*, 2 vols (Paris, 1907).

Chazan, R., 'Ephraim of Bonn's Sefer Zechirah', *Revue des études juives* 132 (1973), pp. 119–26.

Chazan, R., *European Jewry and the First Crusade* (Berkeley CA, 1987).

Chazan, R., *Medieval Stereotypes and Modern Antisemitism* (Berkeley CA, 1997).

Chazan, R., *God, Humanity and History: The Hebrew First Crusade Narratives* (Berkeley, 2000).

Chazan, R., 'From the First Crusade to the Second: Evolving Perceptions of the Christian–Jewish Conflict', in *Jews and Christians in Twelfth-Century Europe*, ed. M. A. Singer and J. Van Engen (Notre Dame IN, 2001), pp. 46–62.

Cheyette, F. L., *Ermengard of Narbonne and the World of the Troubadours* (Ithaca NY, 2001).

Christiansen, E., *The Northern Crusades*, 2nd edn (Harmondsworth, 1997).

Cioffi, C. A., 'The Epistolary Style of Odo of Deuil in his "*De profectione Ludovici VII in Orientem*"', *Mittellateinisches Jahrbuch* 23 (1988), pp. 76–81.

Clanchy, M. T., *From Memory to Written Record: England, 1066–1307*, 2nd edn (Oxford, 1993).

Classen, P., '*Res Gestae*, Universal History, Apocalypse: Visions of Past and Future', *Renaissance and Renewal in the Twelfth Century*, ed. R. L. Benson and G. Constable (Oxford, 1982), pp. 387–417.

Cole, P. J., *The Preaching of the Crusades to the Holy Land, 1095–1270* (Cambridge MA, 1991).

Cole, P. J., '"O God, the heathen have come into your inheritance" (Ps. 78.1): The Theme of Religious Pollution in Crusade Documents, 1095–1188', in *Crusaders and Muslims in Twelfth-Century Syria*, ed. M. Shatzmiller (Leiden, 1993), pp. 84–112.

Constable, G., 'The Second Crusade as Seen by Contemporaries', *Traditio* 9 (1953), pp. 213–79.

Constable, G., 'A Note on the Route of the Anglo-Flemish Crusaders of 1147', *Speculum* 28 (1953), pp. 525–26.

Constable, G., 'The Disputed Election at Langres in 1138', *Traditio* 13 (1957), pp. 119–52.

Constable, G., 'A Report of a Lost Sermon by St Bernard on the Failure of the Second Crusade', *Studies in Medieval Cistercian History Presented to J. F. O'Sullivan*, ed. J. F. O'Callaghan, Cistercian Studies Series No. 13 (Spencer MA, 1971), pp. 49–54.

Constable, G., 'The Financing of the Crusades in the Twelfth Century', in *Outremer: Studies in the History of the Crusading Kingdom of Jerusalem Presented to Joshua Prawer*, ed. B. Z. Kedar, H. E. Mayer and R. C. Smail (Jerusalem, 1982), pp. 64–88.

Constable, G., 'Medieval Charters as a Source for the History of the Crusades', in *Crusade and Settlement: Papers Read at the First Conference of the Society for the Study of the Crusades and the Latin East and Presented to R. C. Smail*, ed. P. W. Edbury (Cardiff, 1985), pp. 73–89.

Constable, G., 'Cluny and the First Crusade', in *Le Concile de Clermont de 1095 et l'appel à la croisade*, ed. A. Vauchez (Rome, 1997), pp. 183–93.

Constable, G., 'The Crusading Project of 1150', in *Montjoie: Studies in Crusade History in Honour of Hans Eberhard Mayer*, ed. B. Z. Kedar, J. S. C. Riley-Smith and R. Hiestand (Aldershot, 1997), pp. 67–75.

Constable, G., 'The Place of the Magdeburg Charter of 1107/08 in the History of Eastern Germany and of the Crusades', in *Vita Religiosa im Mittelalter: Festschrift für Kaspar Elm zum 70 Geburtstag*, ed. F. J. Felten and N. Jaspert (Berlin, 1999), pp. 283–99; translation of the charter at pp. 296–9.

Constable, G., 'A Further Note on the Conquest of Lisbon in 1147', in *The Experience of Crusading 1: Western Approaches*, ed. M. G. Bull and N. Housley, 2 vols (Cambridge, 2003), pp. 39–44.

Cosack, H., 'Konrads III. Entschluss zum Kreuzzug', *Mitteilungen des Instituts für Österreichische Geschichtsforschung* 35 (1914), pp. 278–96.

Cowdrey, H. E. J, *The Cluniacs and Gregorian Reform* (Oxford, 1970).

Cowdrey, H. E. J., 'The Mahdia Campaign of 1087', *English Historical Review* 92 (1977), pp. 1–29.

Cowdrey, H. E. J., 'Two Studies in Cluniac History', *Studi Gregoriani* 11 (Rome, 1978), pp. 1–298.

Cowdrey, H. E. J., 'Pope Urban II and the Idea of the Crusade', *Studi Medievali* 36 (1995), pp. 721–42.

Crocker, R. L., 'Early Crusade Songs', in *The Holy War*, ed. T. P. Murphy (Columbus OH, 1976), pp. 78–98.

Crouch, D., *The Beaumont Twins: The Roots and Branches of Power in the Twelfth Century* (Cambridge, 1986).

Crouch, D., *The Reign of King Stephen, 1135–1154* (Harlow, 2000).

David, C. W., 'The Authorship of *De expugnatione Lyxbonensi*', *Speculum* 7 (1932), pp. 50–7.

Davis, H. W. C., 'Henry of Blois and Brian Fitz-Count', *English Historical Review* 25 (1910), pp. 297–303.

Davis, R. H. C., *The Normans and their Myth* (London, 1976).

Davis, R. H. C., *King Stephen*, 3rd edn (Harlow, 1990).

De Hemptinne, T., 'Les épouses des croisés et pèlerins Flamands aux XIe et XIIe siècles', in *Autour de la première croisade*, ed. M. Balard (Paris, 1996), pp. 83–95.

Delaruelle, E., 'L'idée de croisade chez Saint Bernard', *Mélanges Saint Bernard* (Dijon, 1954), pp. 53–67.

Denny, D., 'A Romanesque Fresco in Auxerre Cathedral', *Gesta* 25 (1986), pp. 197–202.

Derbes, A., 'A Crusading Fresco Cycle at the Cathedral of Le Puy', *Art Bulletin* 73 (1991), pp. 561–76.

Derbes, A., 'Crusading Ideology and the Frescoes of S. Maria in Cosmedin', *Art Bulletin* 77 (1995), pp. 460–78.

DeVic, C., and J. J. Vaisette, *Histoire générale de Languedoc*, 16 vols (Toulouse, 1872–1905).

Di Fabio, C., *La cattedrale di Genova nel medioevo, secoli vi–xiv* (Genoa, 1998).

Dinzelbacher, P., *Bernhard von Clairvaux: Leben und Werk des berühmten Zisterziensers* (Darmstadt, 1998).

Dowsett, C., 'A Twelfth-Century Armenian Inscription at Edessa', *Iran and Islam*, ed. C. E. Bosworth (Edinburgh, 1971), pp. 197–227.

Duby, G., *The Knight, the Lady and the Priest: The Making of Modern Marriage in Medieval France*, tr. B. Bray (London, 1983).

Duggan, A. J., 'Servus servorum Dei', *Adrian IV: The English Pope (1154–1159): Studies and Texts*, ed. B. Bolton and A. J. Duggan (Aldershot, 2003), pp. 181–210.

Dunbabin, J., 'Discovering a Past for the French Aristocracy', in *The Perception of the Past in Twelfth-Century Europe*, ed. P. Magdalino (London, 1992), pp. 1–14.

Edbury, P. W., 'Looking Back on the Second Crusade: Some Late Twelfth-Century English Perspectives', in SCC, pp. 163–9.

Edbury, P. W. and J. G. Rowe, *William of Tyre: Historian of the Latin East* (Cambridge, 1988).

Edgington, S. B., 'The Lisbon Letter of the Second Crusade', *Historical Research* 69 (1996), pp. 328–39.

Edgington, S. B., 'Reviewing the evidence', in *The First Crusade: Origins and Impact*, ed. J. P. Phillips (Manchester, 1997), pp. 57–77.

Edgington, S. B., 'Albert of Aachen, St Bernard and the Second Crusade', in SCSC, pp. 54–70.

Epstein, S. A., *Genoa and the Genoese, 958–1528* (Chapel Hill NC, 1996).

Evans, G. R., *The Mind of Bernard of Clairvaux* (Oxford, 1983).

Evergates, T., 'Louis VII and the Counts of Champagne', in SCC, pp. 109–17.

Evergates, T., *Feudal Society in Medieval France: Documents from the County of Champagne* (Philadelphia PA, 1993).

Face, R. D., 'Secular History in Twelfth-Century Italy: Caffaro of Genoa', *Journal of Medieval History* 6 (1980), pp. 169–84.

Ferzoco, G., 'The Origins of the Second Crusade', SCC, pp. 91–99.

Fletcher, R. A., *Saint James's Catapult: The Life and Times of Diego Gelmírez of Santiago de Compostela* (Oxford, 1984).

Fletcher, R. A., 'Reconquest and Crusade in Spain, c.1050–1150', *Transactions of the Royal Historical Society*, 5th series, 37 (1987), pp. 31–47.

Folda, J., *The Art of the Crusaders in the Holy Land, 1098–1187* (Cambridge, 1995).

Folz, R., *Le souvenir et la légende de Charlemagne dans l'empire germanique médiéval* (Paris, 1950).

Folz, R., *Les saints rois du moyen âge en Occident (VIe–XIIIe siècles)* (Brussels, 1984).

Fonnesberg-Schmidt, I., *The Popes and the Baltic Crusades, 1147–1254* (Leiden, 2006).

Forey, A. J., 'The Failure of the Siege of Damascus in 1148', *Journal of Medieval History* 10 (1984), pp. 13–23.

Forey, A. J., 'The Second Crusade: Scope and Objectives', *Durham University Journal* 86 (1994), pp.165–75.

Forey, A. J., 'The Siege of Lisbon and the Second Crusade', *Portuguese Studies* 20 (2004), pp. 1–13.

Forse, J. H., 'The Armenians and the First Crusade', *Journal of Medieval History* 17 (1991), pp. 13–22.

France, J., *Victory in the East: A Military History* (Cambridge, 1994).

France, J., 'Patronage and the First Crusade', in *The First Crusade: Origins and Impact*, ed. J. P. Phillips (Manchester, 1997), pp. 5–20.

France, J., 'The Anonymous *Gesta Francorum* and the *Historia Francorum qui ceperunt Iherusalem* of Raymond of Aguilers and the *Historia de Hierosolymitano itinere* of Peter Tudebode: An Analysis of the Textual Relationship between Primary Sources for the First Crusade', in *The Crusades and their Sources: Essays Presented to Bernard Hamilton*, ed. J. France and W. G. Zajac (Aldershot, 1998), pp. 39–70.

France, J., 'Use of the Anonymous *Gesta Francorum* in the Early Twelfth Century: Sources for the First Crusade', in *From Clermont to Jerusalem: The Crusades and Crusader Societies, 1095–1500* (Turnhout, 1998), pp. 29–42.

France, J., 'Logistics and the Second Crusade', in *Logistics of Warfare*, pp. 77–93.

Friedman, Y., 'An Anatomy of Anti-Semitism: Peter the Venerable's Letter to Louis VII, King of France (1146)', *Bar-Ilan Studies in History* (1978), pp. 87–102.

Frolow, A., *La relique de la vraie croix*, 2 vols (Paris, 1961–65).

Garí, B., 'Why Almería? An Islamic Port in the Compass of Genoa', *Journal of Medieval History* 18 (1992), pp. 211–31.

Germain, A., *Histoire de la commune de Montpellier*, 3 vols (Montpellier, 1851).

Gervers, M., 'Donations to the Hospitallers in England in the Wake of the Second Crusade', in SCC, pp. 155–61.

Gillingham, J. B., *Richard I* (New Haven and London, 1999).

Girgensohn, D., 'Das Pisaner Konzil von 1135 in der Überlieferung des Pisaner Konzils von 1409', in *Festschrift für Hermann Heimpel*, 3 vols (Göttingen, 1971–72), 2.1098–1122.

Glasheen, C. R., 'Provisioning Peter the Hermit: From Cologne to Constantinople', *Logistics of Warfare*, pp. 119–29.

Glass, D. F., *Portals, Pilgrimage and Crusade in Western Tuscany* (Princeton, 1997).

Goñi Gaztambide, J., *Historia de la Bula de la Cruzada en España* (Vitoria, 1958).

Grabois, A., 'Le privilège de croisade et la régence de Suger', *Revue historique de droit Français et Étranger*, 42 (1964), pp. 458–65.

Grabois, A., 'The Crusade of King Louis VII: A Reconsideration', in *Crusade and Settlement: Papers Read at the First Conference of the Society for the Study of the Crusades and the Latin East and Presented to R. C. Smail*, ed. P. W. Edbury (Cardiff, 1985), pp. 94–104.

Grant, L., *Abbot Suger of St-Denis: Church and State in Early Twelfth-Century France* (London, 1998).

Green, D. H., *The Millstätter Exodus: A Crusading Epic* (Cambridge, 1966).

Green, J. A., *Henry I, King of England and Duke of Normandy* (Cambridge, 2006).

Grierson, P., 'A Crusader's Hoard of 1147 from Side (Turkey)', *Lagom: Festschrift für Peter Berghaus zum 60. Geburtstag*, ed. T. Fischer and P. Ilisch (Münster, 1981), pp. 195–203.

Grill, L., 'Der hl. Bernhard von Clairvaux und Morimond, die Mutterabei der österreichischen Cistercienserklöster', in *Festschrift zum 800 jahrgedächtnis des todes Bernhards von Clairvaux* (Vienna, 1953), pp. 31–118.

Grumel, V., 'Notes pour l'*Oriens Christianus*: 1: Deux patriarches d'Antioche au XIIe siècle', *Echos d'Orient* 33 (1934), pp. 53–58.

Grumel, V., 'Au seuil de la IIe croisade: Deux lettres de Manuel Comnène au pape', *Etudes Byzantines* 3 (1945), pp. 143–67.

Guénée, B., *Historique et culture dans l'Occident médieval* (Paris, 1980).

Gurney, D., *Record of the House of Gournay*, 2 vols (London, 1848–58).

Guth, K., 'The Pomeranian Missionary Journeys of Otto I of Bamburg and the Crusade Movement of the Eleventh to Twelfth Centuries', in SCC, pp. 13–23.

Hamilton, B., 'The Armenian Church and the Papacy at the Time of the Crusades', *Eastern Churches Review* 10 (1978), pp. 61–87.

Hamilton, B., 'Women in the Crusader States: The Queens of Jerusalem (1100–1190), in *Medieval Women. Studies in Church History Subsidia 1*, ed. D. Baker (Oxford, 1978), pp. 143–74.

Hamilton, B., *The Latin Church in the Crusader States* (London, 1980).

Hamilton, B., *The Leper-King and his Heirs: Baldwin IV and the Crusader Kingdom of Jerusalem* (Cambridge, 2000).

Harris, J., *Byzantium and the Crusades* (London, 2003).

Haverkamp, A. (ed.), *Juden und Christen zur Zeit der Kreuzzüge*, Vorträge und Forschungen XLVII (Sigmaringen, 1999).

Hehl, E-D., *Kirche und Kreig im 12. Jahrhundert. Studien zu kanonischem Recht und politischer Wirklichkeit*, Monographien zur Geschichte des Mittelalters, 19 (Stuttgart, 1980).

Hendy, M., *Studies in the Byzantine Monetary Economy, c.300–1450* (Cambridge, 1985).

Hiestand, R., '"Kaiser" Konrad III., der zweite Kreuzzug und ein verlorenes Diplom für den Berg Thabor', *Deutsches Archiv für Erforschung des Mittelalters* 35 (1979), pp. 82–128.

Hiestand, R., 'Reconquista, Kreuzzug und heiliges Grab: Die Eroberung von Tortosa 1148 im Lichte eines neuen Zeugnisses', *Gesammelte Aufsätze zur Kulturgeschichte Spaniens* 31 (1984), pp. 136–57.

Hiestand, R., 'Il cronista medievale e il suo pubblico: alcune osservazioni in margine alla storiografia delle crociate', *Annali della Facoltà di lettere e filosofia dell'Università di Napoli* 27 (1984–5), pp. 207–27.

Hiestand, R., 'Kingship and Crusade in Twelfth-Century Germany', in *England and Germany in the High Middle Ages*, ed. A. Haverkamp and H. Vollrath (London, 1996), pp. 235–65.

Hiestand, R., 'The Papacy and the Second Crusade', in SCSC, pp. 32–53.

Hiestand, R., 'L'archêveque Hugues d'Edesse et son destin postume', in *Dei gesta per Francos: Crusade Studies in Honour of Jean Richard*, ed. M. Balard, B. Z. Kedar and J. S. C. Riley-Smith (Aldershot, 2001), pp. 171–7.

Hiestand., R., 'Gaufridus abbas Templi Domini: An underestimated figure in the early history of the kingdom of Jerusalem', in *The Experience of Crusading 2: Defining the Crusader Kingdom*, ed. P. W. Edbury and J. P. Phillips (Cambridge, 2003), pp. 48–59.

Hill Jr, B., *Medieval Monarchy in Action: The German Empire from Henry I to Henry IV* (London, 1972).

Hillenbrand, C., 'A Neglected Episode of the Reconquista: A Christian Success in the Second Crusade', *Revue des Etudes Islamiques* 54 (1986), pp. 163–70.

Hillenbrand, C., 'The First Crusade: The Muslim Perspective', in *The First Crusade: Origins and Impact*, ed. J. P. Phillips (Manchester, 1997), pp. 130–41.

Hillenbrand, C., '"Abominable Acts", The Career of Zengi', in SCSC, pp. 111–32.

Hillenbrand, C., *The Crusades: Islamic Perspectives* (Edinburgh, 1999).

Hoch, M. 'The Crusaders' Strategy against Fatimid Ascalon and the "Ascalon Project" of the Second Crusade', in SCC, pp. 120–3.

Hoch, M., *Jerusalem, Damaskus und der Zweite Kreuzzug: Konstitutionelle Krise und äußere Sicherheit des Kreuzfahrerkönigreiches Jerusalem, AD 1126–54* (Frankfurt, 1993).

Hoch, M., 'The Choice of Damascus as the Objective of the Second Crusade: A Re-evaluation', *Autour de la Première Croisade*, ed. M.Balard, Byzantina Sorboniensia 14 (Paris, 1996), pp. 359–69.

Holdenreid, A., *The Sibyl and Her Scribes: Manuscripts and Interpretation of the Latin Sibylla Tiburtina, c.1050–1500* (Aldershot, 2006).

Holthouse, E., 'The Emperor Henry II', *Cambridge Medieval History*, Vol. 3, *Germany and the Western Empire*, ed. H. M. Gwatkin, J. P. Whitney, J. R. Tanner and C. W. Previté-Orton (Cambridge, 1922), pp. 215–52.

Holtzmann, W., 'Zur Geschichte des Investiturstreits', *Neues Archiv der Gesellschaft für ältere deutsche Geschichtskunde* 50 (1933–5), pp. 246–319.

Horn, M., *Studien zur Geschichte Papst Eugens III. (1145–53)* (Frankfurt, 1992).

Housley, N., 'Jerusalem and the Development of the Crusade Idea, 1099–1128', in *The Horns of Hattin*, ed. B. Z. Kedar (Jerusalem, 1982), pp. 27–40.

Housley, N., 'Crusades against Christians: Their Origins and Early Development, c. 1000–1216', in *Crusade and Settlement: Papers Read at the First Conference of the Society for the Study of the Crusades and the Latin East and Presented to R. C. Smail*, ed. P. W. Edbury (Cardiff, 1985), pp. 17–36.

Housley, N., *Contesting the Crusades* (Oxford, 2006).

Huglo, M., 'Les chants de la *missa Greca* de Saint-Denis', in *Essays Presented to Egon Wellesz*, ed. J.Westrup (Oxford, 1966), pp. 74–83.

Hunyadi, Z., 'King and crusaders: Hungary in the Second Crusade', in *The Second Crusade in Perspective*, ed. J. T. Roche and J. M. Jensen (Turnhout, 2007, forthcoming).

Huyghebaert, N., 'Une comtesse de Flandre à Béthanie', *Les Cahiers de Saint-André* 21 (1964), pp. 3–15.

Iogna-Prat, D., *Order and Exclusion: Cluny and Christendom Face Heresy, Judaism and Islam (1000–1150)* (Ithaca NY, 2003).

Janssen, W., *Die päpstlichen Legaten in Frankreich vom Schisma Anaklets II. bis zum Tode Coelestins III. (1130–1198)* (Cologne, Graz, 1961).

Jaspert, N., *Stift und Stadt. Das Heiliggrabpriorat von Santa Anna und das Regularkanonikerstift Santa Eulalia del Camp im mittelalterlichen Barcelona (1145–1423)* (Berlin, 1996).

Jaspert, N., 'Bonds and Tensions on the Frontier: The Templars in Twelfth-Century Western Catalonia', in *Mendicants, Military Orders and Regionalism in Europe*, ed. J. Sarnowsky (Aldershot, 1999), pp. 19–45.

Jaspert, N., '*Capta est Dertosa: clavis Christianorum*. Tortosa and the Crusades', SCSC, pp. 90–110.

Jeffreys E. and M. Jeffreys, 'The "Wild Beast from the West": Immediate Literary Reactions in Byzantium to the Second Crusade', in *The Crusades from the Perspective of Byzantium and the Muslim World*, ed. A. E. Laiou and R. P. Mottahedeh (Washington DC, 2001), pp. 101–16.

Jenkinson, H., 'William Cade, a Financier of the Twelfth Century', *English Historical Review* 28 (1913), pp. 209–27.

Jensen, J. M., 'Denmark and the Holy War: A Redefinition of a Traditional Pattern of Conflict, 1147–1169', in *Scandinavia and Europe 800–1350: Contact, Conflict and Coexistence*, ed. J. Adams and K. Holman (Turnhout, 2003), pp. 219–36.

Jensen, J. M., 'Sclavorum expugnator: Conquest, Crusade and Danish Royal Ideology in the Twelfth Century', *Crusades* 2 (2003), pp. 55–81.

Jensen, K. V., 'Denmark and the Second Crusade: the Formation of a Crusader State?', in SCSC, pp. 164–79.

Jensen, K. V., 'The Blue Baltic Border of Denmark in the High Middle Ages: Danes, Wends and Saxo Grammaticus', in *Medieval Frontiers: Concepts and Practices*, ed. D. Abulafia and N. Berend (Aldershot, 2002), pp. 173–93.

Jordan, W. C., *Louis IX and the Challenge of the Crusade* (Princeton, 1979).

Kahl, H.-D., 'Crusade Eschatology as Seen by St Bernard in the Years 1146 to 1148', in SCC pp. 35–47.

Kahl, H.-D., 'Die weltweite Bereinigung der Heidenfrage – ein übersehenes Kriegsziel des Zweiten Kreuzzugs', in *Spannungen und Widersprüche. Gedenkschrift für František Graus*, ed. S. Burghartz *et al.* (Sigmaringen, 1992), pp. 63–85.

Katzenellenbogen, A., 'The Central Tympanum at Vézelay: Its Encyclopedic Meaning and its Relation to the First Crusade', *Art Bulletin* 26 (1944), pp. 141–51.

Kedar, B. Z., *Crusade and Mission: European Approaches towards the Muslims* (Princeton, 1984).

Kedar, B. Z., 'Genoa's Golden Inscription in the Church of the Holy Sepulchre: A Case for the Defence', in *I comuni italiani nel regno crociato di Gerusalemme*, ed. G. Airaldi and B. Z. Kedar (Genoa, 1986), pp. 317–35.

Keen, M., *Chivalry* (New Haven CT, 1984).

Kennedy, H., *Muslim Spain and Portugal. A Political History of al-Andalus* (Harlow, 1996).

Knoch, P., 'Kreuzzug und Siedlung. Studien zum Aufruf der Magdeburger Kirche von 1108', *Jahrbücher für die Geschichte Mittel- und Ostdeutschlands* 23 (1974), pp. 1–33.

Koziol, G., 'England, France, and the Problem of Sacrality in Twelfth-Century Ritual', in *Cultures of Power: Lordship, Status, and Process in Twelfth-Century Europe*, ed. T. N. Bisson, (Philadelphia PA, 1995), pp. 124–48.

Kreuger, H., 'Post-war Collapse and Rehabilitation in Genoa (1149–62)', in *Studi in onore di Gino Luzzatto*, 2 vols (Milan, 1949–50), 1. 119–28.

Krey, A. C., 'A Neglected Passage in the *Gesta*', in *The Crusades and Other Historical Essays Presented to Dana C. Munro*, ed. L. Paetow (New York, 1928), pp. 66–78.

Kugler, B., *Studien zur Geschichte des zweiten Kreuzzugs* (Stuttgart, 1866).

Lambert, M., *Medieval Heresy: Popular Movements from the Gregorian Reform to the Reformation*, 3rd edn (Oxford, 2002).

Lapina, E., 'The Mural Paintings of Berzé-la-Ville in the Context of the First Crusade and the Reconquista', *Journal of Medieval History* 31 (2005), pp. 309–26.

Lay, S., 'The Reconquest as Crusade in the Anonymous "De expugnatione Lyxbonensi"', *Al-Masaq* 14 (2002), pp. 123–30.

Leclercq, J., 'Gratien, Pierre de Troyes et la seconde croisade', *Studia Gratiana* 2 (1954), pp. 585–93.

Leclercq, J., 'L'Encyclique de Saint Bernard en faveur de la croisade', *Revue Bénédictine* 81 (1971), pp. 282–308.

Leclercq, J., *Recueil d'études sur Saint Bernard et ses écrits*, 5 vols (Rome, 1962–92).

Lees, J. T., *Anselm of Havelberg: Deeds into Words in the Twelfth Century* (Leiden, 1998).

Lejeune, R., and J. Stiennon, *La légende de Roland dans l'art du moyen âge*, 2nd edn, 2 vols (Brussels, 1968).

Levillain, L., 'Essai sur les origins du Lendit', *Revue Historique* 52 (1927), pp. 241–76.

Lewis, A. L., 'The Guillems of Montpellier, a Sociological Appraisal', *Viator* 2 (1971), pp. 159–69.

Lilie, R.-J., *Byzantium and the Crusader States, 1095–1204*, tr. J. C. Morris and J. E. Ridings (Oxford, 1993).

Livermore, H. V., *A New History of Portugal*, 2nd edn (Cambridge, 1976).

Livermore, H. V., 'The "Conquest of Lisbon" and its Author', *Portuguese Studies* 6 (1991), pp. 1–16.

Lotter, K., 'The Crusading Idea and the Conquest of the Region East of the Elbe', in *Medieval Frontier Societies*, ed. R. Bartlett and A. Mackay (Oxford, 1989), pp. 267–85.

Loud, G.A., 'Some Reflections on the Failure of the Second Crusade', *Crusades* 4 (2005), pp. 1–14.

McCluskey, R., 'Malleable Accounts: Views of the Past in Twelfth-Century Iberia', *The Perception of the Past in Twelfth-Century Europe*, ed. P. Magdalino (London, 1992), pp. 211–25.

McCracken, P., 'Scandalizing Desire: Eleanor of Aquitaine and the Chroniclers', in *Eleanor of Aquitaine: Lord and Lady*, ed. B. Wheeler and J. C. Parsons (Basingstoke, 2002), pp. 247–64.

McCrank, L., 'The Foundation of the Confraternity of Tarragona by Archbishop Oleguer Bonestruga, 1126–29', *Viator* 9 (1978), pp. 157–77.

MacEvitt, C., 'Christian Authority in the Latin East: Edessa in Crusader History', *The Medieval Crusade*, ed. S.Ridyard (Woodbridge, 2004), pp. 71–83.

McQueen, W. B., 'Relations between the Normans and Byzantium 1071–1112', *Byzantion* 56 (1986), pp. 427–76.

Madden, T., *A Concise History of the Crusades* (Lanham ML, 1999).

Magdalino, P., *The Empire of Manuel I Komnenos, 1143–1180* (Cambridge, 1993).

Magdalino, P., 'The Pen of the Aunt: Echoes of the Mid-Twelfth Century in the Alexiad', *Anna Komnene and Her Times*, ed. T. Gouma-Peterson (New York, 2000), pp. 19–24.

Makk, F., *The Árpads and the Comneni: Political Relations between Hungary and Byzantium in the Twelfth Century* (Budapest, 1989).

Manselli, F., 'Alberico, cardinale vescovo d'Ostia e la sua attività di legato pontificio', *Archivio della Società Romana di storia patria* 78 (1955), pp. 23–68.

Manteuffel, T., *The Formation of the Polish State*, tr. A. Gorski (Detroit, 1982).

Marlot, *Histoire de la ville, cité et université de Reims*, 4 vols (Rheims, 1843–6).

Martindale, J., *Eleanor of Aquitaine* (forthcoming).

Mayer, H.E., 'Studies in the History of Queen Melisende of Jerusalem', *Dumbarton Oaks Papers* 26 (1972), pp. 95–182.

Mayer, H. E., *Mélanges sur l'histoire du royaume Latin de Jérusalem*, Mémoires de l'académie des inscriptions et belles-lettres, n.s. 5 (Paris, 1984), pp. 59–72.

Mayer, H. E, 'The Origins of the County of Jaffa', *Israel Exploration Journal* 35 (1985), pp. 35–45.

Mayer, H. E., *The Crusades*, 2nd edn, tr. J. B. Gillingham (Oxford, 1990).

Mayer, H. E., 'Angevins *versus* Normans: The New Men of King Fulk of Jerusalem', *Proceedings of the American Philosophical Society* 133 (1991), pp. 1–25.

Mayer, H. E., 'The Crusader Principality of Galilee between Saint-Omer and Bures-sur-Yvette', *Itinéraires d'Orient. Hommages à Claude Cahen*, Res Orientales 6 (1994), pp. 157–67.

Mayr-Harting, H., 'Odo of Deuil, the Second Crusade and the Monastery of Saint Denis', in *The Culture of Christendom: Essays in Memory of Denis L. T. Bethell*, ed. M. A. Meyer (London, 1993), pp. 225–41.

Meri, J. W., *The Cult of Saints among Muslims and Jews in Medieval Syria* (Oxford, 2002).

Meschini, M., *San Bernardo e la seconda crociata* (Milan, 1998).

Moore, R. I. *The Origins of European Dissent* (Oxford, 1978).

Moore, R. I., *The Formation of a Persecuting Society* (Oxford, 1987).

Morris, C., 'Bringing the Holy Sepulchre to the West: S. Stefano, Bologna, from the Fifth to the Twelfth Century', *Studies in Church History* 33 (1997), pp. 31–59.

Morris, C., 'Picturing the Crusades: The Uses of Visual Propaganda, *c.*1095–1250', in *The Crusades and their Sources: Essays Presented to Bernard Hamilton*, ed. J. France and W. G. Zajac (Aldershot, 1998), pp. 195–216.

Morris, C., 'Memorials of the Holy Places and Blessings from the East: Devotion to Jerusalem before the Crusades', in *The Holy Land, Holy Lands, and Christian History*, ed. R. L. Swanson, Studies in Church History 36 (Woodbridge, 2000), pp. 90–109.

Morris, C., *The Sepulchre of Christ and the Medieval West* (Oxford, 2005).

Mortimer, R., 'The Family of Rannulf de Glanville', *Bulletin of the Institute of Historical Research* 54 (1981), pp. 1–16.

Mouilleron, V.R., *Vézelay: The Great Romanesque Church* (New York, 1999).

Mourad, S. A. and J. E. Lindsay, 'Rescuing Syria from the Infidels: The Contribution of Ibn 'Asakir of Damascus to the *jihad* campaign of Sultan Nur al-Din', *Crusades* 6 (2007), pp. 37–55.

Mullinder, A., 'The Crusade of 1101', unpublished PhD thesis, University of Swansea, 1996.

Munz, P., *Frederick Barbarossa: A Study in Medieval Politics* (London, 1969).

Murray, A. V., 'The Origins of the Frankish Nobility of the Kingdom of Jerusalem, 1100–1118', *Mediterranean Historical Review* 4 (1989), pp. 281–300.

Murray, A. V., 'The Army of Godfrey of Bouillon: The Structure and Dynamics of a Contingent on the First Crusade', *Revue Belge de philologie et d'histoire* 70 (1992), pp. 301–29.

Murray, A. V., 'Money and Logistics in the Forces of the First Crusade: Coinage, Bullion, Service and Supply, 1096–99', in *Logistics of Warfare*, pp. 229–250.

Naß, K., 'Eine Hildesheimer Weltchronik des 12. Jahrhunderts in Auszügen des Dietrich Engelhaus', *Die Reichschronik des Annalista Saxo und die sächsische Geschichtsschreibung im 12 Jahrhundert*, MGH Schriften 41(1996), pp. 400–19.

Nesbitt, J. W., 'Rates of March of Crusading Armies in Europe: A Study in Computation', *Traditio* 19 (1963), pp. 167–82.

Newman, M. G., *The Boundaries of Charity: Cistercian Culture and Ecclesiastical Reform, 1098–1180* (Stanford CA, 1996).

Nicholas, D., *Medieval Flanders* (London, 1992).

Niederkorn, J. P., 'Traditio, a quibus minime cavimus. Ermittlungen gegen König Balduin III. von Jerusalem, den Patriarchen Fulcher und den Templerorden wegen Verrats bei der Belagerung von Damaskus (1148)', *Mitteilungen des Instituts für Österreichische Geschichtsforschung* 95 (1987), pp. 53–68.

O'Callaghan, J. F., *Reconquest and Crusade in Medieval Spain* (Philadelphia PA, 2003).

O'Meara, C.F., *The Iconography of the Façade of St Gilles-du-Gard* (New York, 1977).

Ohnsorge, W., *Päpstliche und gegenpäpstliche Legaten in Deutschland und Skandinavien, 1159–1181*, Historische Studien, 188 (Berlin, 1929).

Paterson, L. M., 'Syria, Poitou and the *reconquista* (or Tales of the Undead). Who was the count in Marcabru's *Vers del lavador*?', in SCSC, pp. 133–49.

Paterson, L.M., 'Occitan Literature and the Holy Land', in *The World of Eleanor of Aquitaine: Literature and Society in Southern France between the Eleventh and Thirteenth Centuries*, ed. M. G. Bull and C. Léglu (Woodbridge, 2005), pp. 83–99.

Paul, N., 'Crusade and Family Memory before 1225', unpublished Ph.D. thesis, University of Cambridge, 2005.

Pegg, M, 'Le corps et l'authorité: la lépre de Baudouin IV', *Annales* 45 (1990), pp. 265–87.

Pellegrin, E. (ed.), 'Membra disiecta Floriacensia', *Bibliothèque de l'école des Chartes* 117 (1959), pp. 5–56.

Phillips, J. P., *Defenders of the Holy Land: Relations between the Latin East and the West, 1119–1187* (Oxford, 1996).

Phillips, J. P., 'Saint Bernard of Clairvaux, the Low Countries and the Lisbon Letter of the Second Crusade', *Journal of Ecclesiastical History* 48 (1997), pp. 485–97.

Phillips, J. P., 'The Murder of Count Charles the Good and the Second Crusade: Household, Nobility, and Traditions of Crusading in Medieval Flanders', *Medieval Prosopography* 19 (1998), pp. 55–75.

Phillips, J. P., 'Ideas of Crusade and Holy War in *De expugnatione Lyxbonensi* (The Conquest of Lisbon)', in *The Holy Land, Holy Lands and Christian History*, ed. R. N. Swanson, Studies in Church History 36 (2000), pp. 123–41.

Phillips, J. P., 'Papacy, Empire and the Second Crusade', in SCSC, pp. 15–31.

Phillips, J. P., *The Crusades, 1095–1197* (London, 2002).

Phillips, J. P., 'The French Overseas', in *The Oxford History of France, 900–1200*, ed. M. G. Bull (Oxford, 2002), pp. 167–96.

Phillips, J. P., 'Odo of Deuil's *De profectione Ludovici VII in Orientem* as a source for the Second Crusade', in *The Experience of Crusading 1: Western Approaches*, eds M.G.Bull and N.Housley (Cambridge, 2003), pp. 80–95.

Phillips, J. P., *The Fourth Crusade and the Sack of Constantinople* (London, 2004)

Phillips, J. P., 'Armenia, Edessa and The Second Crusade', in *Knighthoods of Christ*, ed. N. Housley (Aldershot, 2007), pp. 39–50.

Poole, R. L., 'Germany, 1125–52', in *Cambridge Medieval History*, vol. 5, *The Contest of Empire and Papacy*, ed. J. R. Tanner, C. W. Previté-Orton and Z. N. Brooke (Cambridge, 1926), pp. 334–59.

Poole, R. L., 'The Early Correspondence of John of Salisbury', in *Studies in Chronology and History*, ed. A. L. Poole (Oxford, 1934), pp. 259–86.

Poulet, A., 'Capetian Women and the Regency: Genesis of a Vocation', in *Medieval Queenship*, ed. J. C. Parsons (Stroud, 1994), pp. 93–116.

Pounds, N. J. G., *An Economic History of Medieval Europe* (London, 1974).

Powell, J. M., *Anatomy of a Crusade, 1213–1221* (Philadelphia PA, 1986).

Power, D., *The Norman Frontier in the Twelfth and Early Thirteenth Centuries* (Cambridge, 2004).

Pringle, D., *Secular Buildings in the Crusader Kingdom of Jerusalem* (Cambridge, 1997).

Pringle, D., *The Churches of the Crusader Kingdom of Jerusalem. A Corpus*, 3 vols (Cambridge, 1993–2007).

Pryor, J. H., *Geography, Technology and War: Studies in the Maritime History of the Mediterranean, 649–1571* (Cambridge, 1988).

Pryor, J. H., 'Digest', *Logistics of Warfare*, pp. 275–92.

Purkis, W. J., *Crusading Spirituality in the Holy Land and Iberia, c.1095–c.1187* (Woodbridge, forthcoming).

Rassow, P., 'Die Kanzlei St. Bernhards von Clairvaux', *Studien und Mitteilungen zur Geschichte des Benediktinerordens* 34 (1913), pp. 243–79.

Rassow, P., 'La confradía de Belchite', *Annuario de historia del derecho espanol* 3 (1926), pp. 200–26.

Reilly, B. F., *The Contest of Christian and Muslim Spain, 1031–1157* (Oxford, 1992).

Reilly, B. F., *The Kingdom of León-Castilla under King Alfonso VII, 1126–1157* (Philadelphia PA, 1998).

Reuter, T., *Germany in the High Middle Ages 800–1056* (London, 1991).

Reuter, T., 'The non-crusade of 1149–50', in SCSC, pp. 150–63.

Richard, J., *Le comté de Tripoli sous la dynastie Toulousaine, 1102–87* (Paris, 1945).

Richard, J., 'Le siege de Damas dans l'histoire et dans la légende', in *Cross-Cultural Convergences in the Crusader Period: Essays Presented to Aryeh Grabois on his Sixty-Fifth Birthday*, ed. M. Goodich, S. Menache and S. Schein (New York, 1995), pp. 225–35.

Rider, J., *God's Scribe: The Historiographical Art of Galbert of Bruges* (Washington DC, 2001).

Riley-Smith, J. S. C., *The Knights of St John in Jerusalem and Cyprus, 1050–1310* (London, 1967).

Riley-Smith, J. S. C., 'Crusading as an Act of Love', *History* 65 (1980), pp. 177–92.

Riley-Smith, J. S. C., 'The First Crusade and St Peter', in *Outremer: Studies in the History of the Crusading Kingdom of Jerusalem Presented to Joshua Prawer*, ed. B. Z. Kedar, H. E. Mayer and R. C. Smail (Jerusalem, 1982), pp. 41–63.

Riley-Smith, J. S. C., 'The Venetian Crusade of 1122–24', in *I comuni italiani nel regno crociato di Gerusalemme*, ed. G. Airaldi and B. Z. Kedar (Genoa, 1986), pp. 337–50.

Riley-Smith, J. S. C., *The First Crusade and the Idea of Crusading* (London, 1986).

Riley-Smith, J. S. C., *The Crusades: A Short History* (London, 1987).

Riley-Smith, J. S. C., 'Family Traditions and Participation in the Second Crusade', in SCC, pp. 101–8.

Riley-Smith, J. S. C., 'Early Crusaders to the East and the Costs of Crusading, 1095–1130', in *Cross-Cultural Convergences in the Crusader Period: Essays Presented to Aryeh Grabois on his Sixty-Fifth Birthday*, ed. M. Goodich, S. Menache and S. Schein (New York, 1995), pp. 237–58.

Riley-Smith, J. S. C., 'King Fulk of Jerusalem and "The Sultan of Babylon"', in *Montjoie: Studies in Crusade History in Honour of Hans Eberhard Mayer*, ed. B.Z.Kedar, J.S.C.Riley-Smith and R. Hiestand (Aldershot, 1997), pp. 55–66.

Riley-Smith, J. S. C., *The First Crusaders, 1095–1131* (Cambridge, 1997).

Riley-Smith, J. S. C., 'Casualties and Knights on the First Crusade', *Crusades* 1 (2002), pp. 13–28.

Riley-Smith, L. and J. S. C., *The Crusades: Idea and Reality, 1095–1274* (London, 1981).

Robinson, I. S., *The Papacy, 1073–1198: Continuity and Innovation* (Cambridge, 1990).

Robinson, I. S., *Emperor Henry IV of Germany, 1056–1106* (Cambridge, 1999)

Roche, J., 'Conrad III and the Second Crusade: Retreat from Dorylaion?', *Crusades* 5 (2006), pp. 85–94.

Rogers, R., *Latin Siege Warfare in the Twelfth Century* (Oxford, 1992).

Rogghé, P., 'Osto de Saint Omer, Vlaams Tempelier uit de XIIe eeuw', *Appeltjes van het Meetjesland* 20 (1969), pp. 245–69.

Röhricht, R., *Die Deutschen im Heiligen Lande, 650–1291* (Innsbruck, 1894), pp. 22–6.

Rose, E., *The Monk, the Knight, the Bishop and the Jew: Law and Libel in Medieval England* (Philadelphia PA, forthcoming).

Routledge, M., 'Songs', *The Oxford Illustrated History of the Crusades*, ed. J. S. C. Riley-Smith (Oxford, 1995), pp. 91–111.

Rowe, J. G., 'The Papacy and the Greeks (1122–53)', *Church History* 28 (1959), pp. 115–30, 310–27.

Rowe, J. G., 'Paschal II, Bohemund of Antioch and the Byzantine Empire', *Bulletin of the John Rylands Library* 40 (1966), pp. 165–202.

Rowe, J. G., 'The Origins of the Second Crusade: Pope Eugenius III, Bernard of Clairvaux and Louis VII of France', in SCC, pp. 78–89.

Rowe, J. G., 'Alexander III and the Jerusalem Crusade: An Overview of Problems and Failures', in *Crusaders and Muslims in Twelfth Century Syria*, ed. M. Shatzmiller (Leiden, 1993), pp. 112–32.

Rubenstein, J., *Guibert of Nogent: Portrait of a Medieval Mind* (New York, 2002).

Rubenstein, J., 'Putting History to Use: Three Crusade Chronicles in Context', *Viator* 35 (2004), pp. 131–67.

Rubenstein, J., 'What is the *Gesta Francorum* and who was Peter Tudebode?' *Revue Mabillon*, n.s. 16 (2005), pp. 179–204.

Runciman, S., *A History of the Crusades*, 3 vols (Cambridge, 1951–4).

Russell, F., *The Just War in the Middle Ages* (Cambridge, 1975).

Sassier, Y., *Louis VII* (Paris, 1991).

Schein, S., *Gateway to the Heavenly City: Crusader Jerusalem and the Catholic West (1099–1187)* (Aldershot, 2005).

Schmidt, A. B., and Halfter, P., 'Der Brief Papst Innozenz' II. an den armenischen Katholikos Gregor III.: Ein wenig beachtetes Dokument zur Geschichte der Synode von Jerusalem (Ostern 1141)', *Annuarium Historiae Conciliorum* 31 (1999), pp. 50–71.

Schuste, B., 'The Strange Pilgrimage of Odo of Deuil', *Medieval Concepts of the Past: Ritual, Memory and Historiography*, ed. G. Althoff, J. Fried and P. J. Geary (Cambridge, 2002), pp. 253–78.

Segal, J. B., *Edessa, 'The Blessed City'* (Oxford, 1970).

Seidel, L., 'Images of the Crusades in Western Art: Models as Metaphors', in *The Meeting of Two Worlds: Cultural Exchange between East and West during the Period of the Crusades*, ed. V. P. Goss, (Kalamazoo, 1986), pp. 377–91.

Sherman, R., 'The Continental Origins of the Ghent Family of Lincolnshire', *Nottingham Medieval Studies* 22 (1978), pp. 23–35.

Shopkow, L., *History and Community: Norman Historical Writing in the Eleventh and Twelfth Centuries* (Washington DC, 1997).

Short, I., 'A Study in Carolingian Legend and its Persistence in Latin Historiography', *Mittellateinisches Jahrbuch* 7 (1972), pp. 127–52.

Siberry, E., *Criticism of Crusading, 1095–1274* (Oxford, 1985).

Siberry, E., 'The Crusading Counts of Nevers', *Nottingham Medieval Studies* 34 (1990), pp. 64–70.

Singer, M. A. and J. Van Eugen (eds), *Jews and Christians in Twelfth-Century Europe* (Notre Dame IN, 2001).

Smail, R. C., 'The Crusaders and the Conquest of Damascus', unpublished paper read at Izhak Ben-Zvi Institute, Jerusalem 1984 (later published in Hebrew).

Smith, C., *Crusading in the Age of Joinville* (Aldershot, 2006).

Smith, D. J., 'The Abbot–Crusader: Nicholas Brakespear in Catalonia', *Adrian IV: The English Pope (1154–1159): Studies and Texts*, ed. B. Bolton and A. J. Duggan (Aldershot, 2003), pp. 29–40.

Somerville, R., 'The French Councils of Pope Urban II: Some Basic Considerations', *Annuarium historiae conciliorum* 2 (1970), pp. 56–65.

Somerville, R., 'The Council of Pisa, 1135: A Re-examination of the Evidence for the Canons', *Speculum* 45 (1970), pp. 98–114.

Southern, R. W., *Scholastic Humanism and the Unification of Europe* (Oxford, 1995).

Spreckelmeyer, G., *Das Kreuzzugslied des lateinischen Mittelalters* (Munich, 1924).

Spufford, P., *Power and Profit: The Merchant in Medieval Europe* (London, 2002).

Stalls, C., *Possessing the Land: Aragon's Expansion into Islam's Ebro Frontier under Alfonso the Battler, 1104–1134* (Leiden, 1995).

Stephenson, P., 'Anna Comnena's *Alexiad* as a Source for the Second Crusade?', *Journal of Medieval History* 29 (2003), pp. 41–54.

Strait, P., *Cologne in the Twelfth Century* (Gainesville FL, 1974).

Stroll, M., *Calixtus II (1119–1124): A Pope Born to Rule* (Leiden, 2004).

Szövérffy, J., *Secular Latin Lyrics and Minor Poetic Forms of the Middle Ages: A Historical Survey and Literary Repertory from the Tenth to the Late Fifteenth Century*, Vol. 1 (Concord NH, 1992), pp. 369–73.

Tabaa, Y., 'Monuments with a Message: Propagation of *jihad* under Nur ad-Din (1146–74)', in *The Meeting of Two Worlds: Cultural Exchange between East and West during the Period of the Crusades*, ed. V. P. Goss (Kalamazoo, 1986), pp. 223–40.

Tanner, H., 'In His Brothers' Shadow: The Crusading Career and Reputation of Count Eustace III of Boulogne', *The Crusades: Other Experiences, Alternate Perspectives*, ed. K. I. Semaan (Binghampton NY, 2003), pp. 83–99.

Tanner, H., *Families, Friends and Allies: Boulogne and Politics in Northern France and England, c.879–1160* (Leiden, 2004).

Taylor, P., 'Moral Agency in Crusade and Colonization: Anselm of Havelberg and the Wendish Crusade of 1147', *International Historical Review* 22 (2000), pp. 757–84.

Thomas, R. D., 'Anna Comnena's account of the First Crusade. History and Politics in the Reigns of the Emperors Alexius I and Manuel I Comnenus', *Byzantine and Modern Greek Studies* 15 (1991), pp. 269–312.

Thomson, R., *William of Malmesbury* (Woodbridge, 2003).

Throop, S., 'Vengeance and the Crusades', *Crusades* 5 (2006), pp. 21–38.

Toman, R. (ed.), *Provence: Art, Architecture, Landscape* (Cologne, 1999).

Trotter, D., *Medieval French Literature and the Crusades (1100–1300)* (Geneva, 1988).

Tschan, F. J., 'Helmold: Chronicler of the North Saxon Missions', *Catholic Historical Review* 16 (1930–1), pp. 379–412.

Tyerman, C. J., *England and the Crusades, 1095–1588* (Chicago, 1988).

Tyerman, C. J.,*God's War: A New History of the Crusades* (London, 2006).

Tyler, J., *The Alpine Passes in the High Middle Ages* (Oxford, 1930).

Ubieto Arteta, A., 'La participación navarro-aragonesa en la primera cruzada', *Príncipe de Viana* 8 (1947), pp. 357–84.

Vacandard, E., *Vie de Saint Bernard , abbé de Clairvaux*, 2 vols (Paris, 1927).

Van Houts, E., *Memory and Gender in Medieval Europe, 900–1200* (London, 1999).

Van Houts, E., 'The Warenne View of the Past, 1066–1203', *Anglo-Norman Studies* 26 (2003), pp. 103–21.

Vlasto, A. P., *The Entry of the Slavs into Christendom* (Cambridge, 1970).

Vleeschouwers, C., 'Chronologische problemen aangaande de bisschoppen van Doornik (1146–1218): episcopaatsjaren en jaarstijl', *Handelingen van het genootschap voor Geschiedenis* 117 (1980), pp. 5–55.

Ward, B., *Miracles and the Medieval Mind*, 2nd edn (Aldershot, 1987).

Warlop, E., *The Flemish Nobility before 1300*, 4 vols (Kortrijk, 1975–6).

Willems, E., 'Cîteaux et la seconde croisade', *Revue d'histoire ecclésiastique* 49 (1954), pp. 116–51.

Williams, J. B., 'The Making of a Crusade: The Genoese anti-Muslim Attacks in Spain, 1146–1148', *Journal of Medieval History* 23 (1997), pp. 29–53.

Williams, W., *Saint Bernard of Clairvaux* (Manchester, 1935).

Wurm, H. J., *Gottfried, Bischof von Langres* (Würzburg, 1886).

Zenker, B., *Die Mitglieder des Kardinalkollegiums von 1130 bis 1159* (Würzburg, 1964).

INDEX

Note: Page references in bold type indicate maps and plans